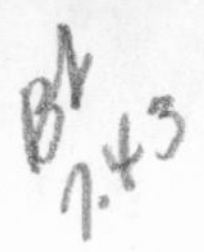

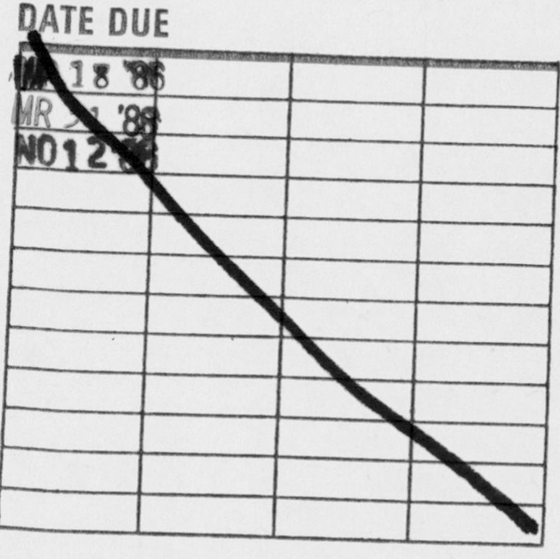
DATE DUE

THE COSTS OF DEMOCRACY

THE COSTS OF DEMOCRACY

BY

ALEXANDER HEARD

CHAPEL HILL
THE UNIVERSITY OF NORTH CAROLINA PRESS

Manufactured in the United States of America

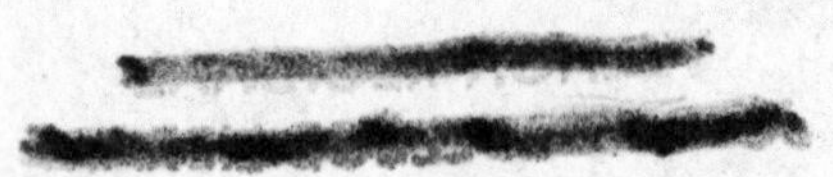

PRINTED BY THE SEEMAN PRINTERY, DURHAM, N. C.
REPRINTED BY THE NORTH CAROLINA STATE UNIVERSITY PRINT SHOP, RALEIGH, 1966

THIS BOOK IS DEDICATED WITH RESPECT AND AFFECTION TO THE MEMORY OF

WILL WINTON ALEXANDER

PREFACE

IF THE DEMOGRAPHER had to take his own census and the election analyst had to tally the ballots, they would be in the same predicament as the student of campaign finance. There are no convenient, dependable data on the sources and uses of political money; a student must forage far and wide to find materials with which to work. In consequence, any broad study of money in elections is necessarily a cooperative venture. The studies initiated in 1953 at the University of North Carolina in Chapel Hill, which are concluded in this book, have received aid of some sort from over 1,000 persons. My acknowledgments are inevitably incomplete, yet they indicate the many kinds of people whose good will and help have been essential. I can burden none of them with the results, but I feel a sense of personal debt to each that is difficult to express and impossible to repay.

Politicians know what politicians do better than anyone else. More than 600 of them have contributed fact and opinion to this study in off-the-record conversations. I myself conferred with over 100 of these from coast to coast; associates making intensive studies within single states interviewed the others. Many of the interviews lasted several hours and at least one consumed an entire day. The persons consulted, with remarkably few exceptions, spoke freely and instructively. They were assured anonymity if they desired it and most did. For that reason no source is cited for much information that is offered. For that reason, also, I regretfully cannot name the persons who assisted in this way.

For some decades committees of the United States Congress have compiled various types of campaign-finance information. They have on several occasions opened their files to students pursuing private inquiries. The Senate Subcommittee on Privileges and Elections continued this practice and gave me access to information accumulated by it about the 1952 and 1956 elections. Moreover, I served as a consultant to the Subcommittee in the latter year, when it was known as the Gore Committee, and was privileged to participate in planning the work undertaken and in the subsequent collection and analysis of data. I appreciate deeply these opportunities and in particular wish to thank the successive chairmen of the Subcommittee, Senators Thomas C. Hennings, Jr., Albert Gore, Mike Mansfield, and Theodore Francis Green. James H. Duffy, chief counsel, Sadi J. Mase, associate chief counsel, and Alice Clark, then clerk of the Subcommittee, kept me continuously in their debt. My obligations are unusually deep to the members of the special staff assembled during the chairmanship of Senator Gore, especially John P. Moore, special counsel; Andrew D. Mapes, minority counsel; E. Wayles Browne, Jr., chief statistician; Arthur John Keeffe, legal consultant; Irvin Lechliter, Robert Greenburg, Joseph A. Roney, Emmett C. Yokley, Walter J. Bristow, Jr., Stephen Pace, Jr., and Richard P. Donovan, assistant counsels; Fred S. Peabody, chief accountant; Sam Akelson, assistant chief accountant; Florence T. Hincks, assistant statistician; Edward Corneaby, investigator; Irene Burton, secretarial assistant; and John I. Meehan of the Library of Congress. Several other persons were helpful in important ways: William G. Allen, administrative assistant to Senator Gore; William M. Cochrane, secretary to the late Senator W. Kerr Scott and later administrative assistant to Senator B. Everett Jordan; Langdon C. West, administrative assistant to Senator Hennings; and Jack Spain, administrative assistant to Senator Sam J. Ervin, Jr. After the dissolution of the special staff of the Gore Committee, E. Wayles Browne, Jr., with the assistance of Shirley A. Preston, spent several months tabulating and analyzing data, especially those appearing in Chapter 11. Much of this information had been gathered but not used by the Gore Committee.

Over the years I have testified several times before Senate committees. In October, 1956, Senator Gore requested that I present to his committee a number of compilations and analyses of 1952 information that had previously been prepared in Chapel Hill. These materials, running to 98 printed pages, were published in Part 2 of the Gore Committee *Hearings*. Some of the information is not available elsewhere, and at several places I have cited these *Hearings*. More elaborate information sometimes appears in them than could be included in the present text. For the most part, sources of 1952 information that came from campaign reports filed pursuant to federal and state laws are not cited.

American elections are essentially state and local affairs. A large number of persons throughout the country furnished information and opinion of several types about campaign finance in their states. Others aided in arranging this help. Assistance of special value was rendered in abstracting data from campaign reports and in evaluating state reporting systems. Many of these collaborators worked intimately in reports submitted by candidates and committees and discussed them critically with depository officials, candidates, campaign managers, and others. They provided a legion of illustrative practices that have made it possible to read the provisions of state statutes with an increased sense of reality. Many of those who helped were old personal friends; many are still strangers. All made voluntary contributions of great utility to our work. Whatever merit the book may have stems in large measure from their help. Among those who aided in this way were: Spencer D. Albright, Ethan P. Allen, Paul H. Appleby, Robert S. Babcock, Stephen K. Bailey, Edwin P. Banks, William M. Benson, Clarence Berdahl, Charles A. Bloomfield, Hugh A. Bone, A. C. Breckenridge, R. Wallace Brewster, Franklin M. Bridge, L. K. Caldwell, Douglas Carlisle, Wesley Chumlea, Robert A. Dahl, Royden Dangerfield, Manning J. Dauer, I. Ridgway Davis, Robert B. Dishman, Paul Dolan, Cortez A. M. Ewing, Elliott Falk, Barbara Ferkiss, James W. Fesler, Thomas A. Flinn, Milton Folds, Phillip Foss, Betty Ann Garter, T. C. Geary, Inez B. Gill, Lee S. Greene, Marvin A. Harder, Harry L. Hobson, Victor Hoffman, John T. Holden, Lynwood M. Holland, Freeman Holmer, John M. Howell, Hoyt M. Jackson, Donald Bruce Johnson, Charles B. Judah, Wally Kaempfer, Gladys M. Kammerer, Francine Kapner, V. O. Key, Jr., Robert E. Lane, Avery Leiserson, Victor A. Maccini, Harvey C. Mansfield, Boyd A. Martin, James W. Martin, Roscoe C. Martin, Raymond L. McIlvenna, Dayton D. McKean, Robert McKnelly, Joseph E. McLean, James W. Miller, J. Erroll Miller, Malcolm Moos, Pat Moynihan, Frank Munger, Arthur Naftalin, Peter H. Odegard, Vincent Ostrom, Thomas Payne, Roy V. Peel, Lawrence L. Pelletier, Clara Penniman, Walter B. Pentz, Keith S. Petersen, O. C. Press, H. S. Pressler, Hugh Douglas Price, Coleman B. Ransome, Jr., Emmette S. Redford, Ross R. Rice, Allan R. Richards, Elston Roady, William R. Ross, E. E. Schattschneider, Joseph A. Schlesinger, John W. Schwada, Lloyd M. Short, Ruth C. Silva, Robert Sink, Leslie J. Spencer, Kathryn M. Staton, Donald S. Strong, Bert E. Swanson, Carl B. Swisher, John C. Wahlke, O. Douglas Weeks, Edward W. Weidner, Norman Wengert, York Y. Willbern, Paul G. Willis, and William H. Young.

Many of the state correspondents prepared written reports, often of considerable length. I am happy that several of these persons were able to use information thus accumulated in publications of their own. Often faculty members invited students to meet academic requirements by writing papers that would assist our study. Especially useful, as the citations in the text indicate, were theses and dissertations written to fulfill degree requirements. Those at the University of North Carolina were written under my direction. In all cases, students and their mentors cooperated with unparalleled personal generosity. They were receptive to suggestions for the subject, design, and procedures of the research. Often the topics were extraordinarily difficult to develop. The scarcity of reliable data inevitably produced difficulties and frustrations. None of these students was deterred, however, all completing their research and their degrees satisfactorily. The theses and dissertations completed in connection with the preparation of this book were:

Herbert E. Alexander. "The Role of the Volunteer Political Fund Raiser: A Case Study in New York in 1952." Ph.D. dissertation, Yale University, 1958. Pp. 307.

Harrison R. Bryan, Jr. "The Role of Money in [Utah] Politics." Master's thesis, University of Utah, 1954. Pp. 130.

Joan Sacknitz Carver. "A Study of Campaign Expenditures by Selected Committees in 1952." Master's thesis, University of North Carolina, 1957. Pp. 257.

Truman S. Casner. "Money in Politics: New Jersey." Senior thesis, Princeton University, 1955. Pp. 140.

Gloria Resch Cook. "The Relationship between Political Parties and Pressure Groups." Master's thesis, University of North Carolina, 1956. Pp. 266.

Richard Fellenberg. "Regulation of Campaign Funds at the Federal and State Levels." Senior thesis, University of New Hampshire, 1955. Pp. 139.

Joan Combs Grace. "The Impact of Campaign Funds on Party and Factional Structures." Master's thesis, University of North Carolina, 1958. Pp. 219.

Ernest Eugene Harrill. "The Structure of Organization and Power in Canadian Political Parties: A Study in Party Financing." Ph.D. dissertation, University of North Carolina, 1958. Pp. 304.

Margaret A. Hunt. "Certain Social and Economic Characteristics of Campaign Contributors in a National Election Year." Master's thesis, University of North Carolina, 1958. Pp. 183.

Lester W. Milbrath. "The Motivations and Characteristics of Political Contributors: North Carolina General Election 1952." Ph.D. dissertation, University of North Carolina, 1956. Pp. 364.

John Robert Owens. "Party Campaign Funds in Connecticut, 1950-1954." Ph.D. dissertation, Syracuse University, 1956. Pp. 334.

Dwynal B. Pettengill. "Campaign Finance in Maryland." Ph.D. dissertation, The Johns Hopkins University, 1959. Pp. 281.

Leonard Carl Rowe. "Political Campaign Funds in California." Ph.D. dissertation, University of California, 1957. Pp. 246.

Bradbury Seasholes. "Labor Union Financial Participation in the 1952 Election." Master's thesis, University of North Carolina, 1958. Pp. 157.

A number of additional persons supplied valued professional research assistance. At the University of North Carolina these included Peggy L. P. Cook, John Crittenden, Owen R. Easley, Jr., Janet D. Head, Fred L. McGee, Stanley Pearl, Roger Peele, and John Rendleman. At Harvard University they included Avard W. Brinton, Michael A. Heuer, and Roberta Selleck. Roy W. Holsten volunteered substantial aid in connection with one phase of the work in North Carolina. Mary Alice Jamison Griffin spent several months in precise and diligent work in the Office of the File Clerk of the United States House of Representatives. John T. Dempsey graciously helped with a number of assignments in Washington, D.C. Federal, state, and local government employees in dozens of offices and depositories made official reports available and provided other information. The cooperation of the Office of the File Clerk was essential, and I am happy to record my special appreciation to Doris P. Shaw, Julia Virginia Whitamore, Robert M. Miller, and Jesse C. Hughes. Officers of both major parties in every state helped in one way or another, as did officials of the two national committees. Especially cooperative were Edward L. Bacher, executive secretary of the Republican national finance committee, and Mary C. Salisbury, comptroller of the Democratic national committee.

From the outset I felt that a desirable perspective would be facilitated if some familiarity could be gained with practices in other nations. Aside from James K. Pollock's *Money and Politics Abroad* (New York: Alfred A. Knopf, 1932), and an occasional subsequent article, little has been written about this subject. Consequently, I sought the aid of scholars who had recently lived abroad and who might know something of foreign politics firsthand. The Institute of International Education, the International Educational Exchange Service of the Department of State, and the Ford Foundation supplied lists of Americans with recent foreign residence. Many persons to whom we wrote kindly referred us to others. Written reports on money in the politics of over 30 nations were received, and several visitors to the United States gave information concerning their own countries. Among the many people who helped in these ways were: Jon Aase, Gabriel A. Almond, Morley Ayearst, Samuel H. Beer, George I. Blanksten, Arnold Brecht, R. V. Burks, Charles W. Churchill, Sven Claussen, Taylor Cole, David S. Collier, E. M. Coulter, Alfred de Grazia, Sebastian de Grazia, Alfred Diamant, Paul S. Dull, Murray Edelman, Rupert Emerson, Victor Feather, Burton R. Fisher, Russell H. Fitzgibbon, Meredith P. Gilpatrick, Eric F. Goldman, Bertram Gross, Henry C. Hart, Lashley G. Harvey, Ferrel Heady, Gunnar Heckscher, Gunnar Helén, F. A. Hermens, Robert Kelson, Louis G. Kesselman, Lionel H. Laing, Joseph G. LaPalombara, Carl Leiden, George Lenczowski, Daniel S. McHargue, Dean E. McHenry, Lennox A. Mills, Rodney L. Mott, Clement C. Motten, Edward E. Palmer, Norman D. Palmer, Richard L. Park, Galo Plaza, Henry Reiff, Stein Rokkan, Dankwart A. Rustow, Theodore Saloutos, James W. Spain, Murray S. Stedman, Jr., Philip B. Taylor, Jr., John Seabury Thomson, Herbert Tingsten, George O. Totten, Thomas Truman, Amry Vandenbosch, John A. Vieg, Robert A. Walker, and Robert E. Ward.

Aid in obtaining special sets of information was given by Leo Troy of the National Bureau of Economic Research; Richard J. Shepherd, director of the Information Center of the Public Relations Society of America, and several members of the Society; George E. Pelletier of the Aerojet-General Corporation; W. R. Atkinson of the Psychological

Service Center, Memphis, Tennessee; Angus Campbell and Warren E. Miller of the Survey Research Center, University of Michigan; Marvin A. Harder of the University of Wichita; Newton N. Minow, Archibald S. Alexander, Arthur M. Schlesinger, Jr., and Roger L. Stevens, associated with Adlai E. Stevenson's 1956 presidential nomination campaign; three officials of the Commonwealth of Puerto Rico, A. Fernos-Isern, resident commissioner in the United States House of Representatives, Samuel H. Quiñones, president of the Senate, and Elías Rivera, assistant secretary of the Treasury; and three officials of the state of Minnesota, Byron G. Allen, commissioner of agriculture, Joseph M. Robertson, commissioner of taxation, and Arthur Naftalin, commissioner of administration. Robert E. Agger kindly supervised the analysis of certain data supplied by the Survey Research Center. Special assistance came from David B. Truman who, among other things, provided the story about Little Orphan Annie at the beginning of Chapter 4, and from Samuel J. Eldersveld, who put at my disposal much sound counsel as well as unpublished data from his studies of the Detroit Metropolitan Area. Lester W. Milbrath lent valuable aid at several points, especially in developing the first two sections of Chapter 4 and the first section of Chapter 5. Frank C. Newman and John Van Doren, in the course of their own work, cooperated in many ways. It was a privilege to reciprocate where possible, especially to participate in the publication of Mr. Van Doren's *Big Money in Little Sums* (Chapel Hill: Institute for Research in Social Science, University of North Carolina, 1956), a study undertaken for the Louis H. Harris Memorial Fund. Help of many kinds was supplied by scores of colleagues and friends in addition to those already mentioned, including: Harry S. Ashmore, Sidney Baldwin, Joseph L. Bernd, Francis F. Bradshaw, David Butler, Richard S. Childs, Charles L. Clapp, Benjamin V. Cohen, Jane Dicks Connolly, Paul T. David, Lambert Davis, Lewis A. Dexter, Dale E. Doty, Alex N. Dragnich, Thomas H. Eliot, Hugh L. Elsbree, Robert Engler, Merle Fainsod, Jason Finkle, John Lieper Freeman, Carl J. Friedrich, Oliver Garceau, William C. Gibbons, Ralph M. Goldman, Frederick H. Harris, John Harris, Kenneth Hechler, Pendleton Herring, Arthur N. Holcombe, Floyd Hunter, Harry Kantor, Milton Katz, Harold D. Lasswell, John Lederle, Donald R. Matthews, Frank McCallister, Richard H. McCleery, Daniel H. Pollitt, Ithiel de Sola Pool, Henrietta Poynter, Nelson Poynter, Edwin H. Rhyne, John P. Roche, Jasper B. Shannon, Edward A. Shils, George L. Simpson, Jr., M. Brewster Smith, Georgia Smart Spalding, Harold Stein, Claude Teague, William H. Vanderbilt, Ridley Whitaker, Arthur N. Whitehill, Jr., and H. H. Wilson.

James K. Pollock made the first systematic study of election finances, published in 1926, and he gave valued encouragement to the present venture. Louise Overacker, the most recent and prolific writer on the subject, not only aided with her counsel but supplied data from her own studies for further analysis. All who seek to understand American politics owe much to these pioneers, and I especially am in their debt.

The first draft of the manuscript was typed largely by Ruth Carpenter. The second draft was typed by Karen Elder. Natalie Dean typed a portion of the first draft, assisted in numerous matters with the second, handled much correspondence, helped in the preparation of the index, and in an abundance of other ways aided in bringing the book to completion. Others who over a period of years helped with typing, correspondence, filing, library work, statistical computations, and in similar ways included Greta H. Coffey, Brunhilde Ferguson, Joan N. Gilbert, Keota Holroyd, Kathryn G. Myers, Eliot Chace Nolen, June W. Plott, and Dorothy B. Templeton. Marion Gleason, secretary of the Department of Government at Harvard University, Ina Freeman, secretary of the Department of Political Science at the University of North Carolina, and Frances Schnibben, administrative assistant and office manager of the Institute for Research in Social Science at the University of North Carolina, were invariably helpful.

V. O. Key, Jr., read the first draft of the manuscript and portions of the second draft. Herbert E. Alexander and E. Wayles Browne, Jr., read the second draft. All made innumerable constructive criticisms. A number of persons with special knowledge commented on portions of the manuscript, much to my benefit: Samuel H. Beer, Marver Bernstein, Kenneth M. Birkhead, Jonathan Daniels, Paul T. David, Herbert Kaufman, Stanley Kelley, Jr., Carlton G. Ketchum, Dayton D. McKean, Lester W. Milbrath, Warren E. Miller, Frank C. Newman, Joseph L. Rauh, Jr., C. B. Robson, W. B. Sanders, Wallace S. Sayre, Bradbury Seasholes, Lloyd Strickland, John W. Thibaut, Gus Tyler, and Henry Zon.

The University of North Carolina provided the setting and opportunity for the work, which was carried out as an activity of the Political Behavior Committee of its Institute for Research in Social Science. Continuous support and understanding were afforded by C. B. Robson, chairman of the Department of Political Science, and Gordon W. Blackwell, director of the Institute. They were succeeded in those positions by Frederic N. Cleaveland and Daniel O. Price. I owe special gratitude to Professor Cleaveland and my other colleagues in the Department of Political Science for their forebearance and assistance over the years. Katharine Jocher, associate director of the Institute, was always helpful. In more recent times, my associates in the Graduate School, especially Professor James R. Gaskin and Mrs. Sally Denton Coe, have with understanding and without request relieved me of many burdens. The administrative officers of the University have at all junctures lent support and encouragement, for which I thank them, especially Chancellor William B. Aycock and President William C. Friday.

During 1957-58 I held an appointment at Harvard University as Ford Research Professor of Government. Without this interval, the manuscript could not have been completed in its present form. I am deeply grateful to Harvard University for this opportunity, and in particular to Dean McGeorge Bundy and to Professor Samuel H. Beer, then chairman of the Department of Government.

My interest in campaign finance originated some years ago while engaged in studies of southern politics. The research for the present study was begun with a grant from the Edgar Stern Family Fund. It was hoped from the beginning that the activities financed by the grant would produce a number of by-products in addition to the present publication. Many of these have been mentioned. Wherever an opportunity appeared, encouragement was given to the responsible study of campaign finance by others. From time to time information was put at the disposal of journalists and other writers. One of the products was a brief interim report of my own published in 1956, *Money and Politics* (New York: Public Affairs Pamphlet No. 242). I am profoundly grateful to the directors of the Fund, and to its executive secretary, Helen Hill Miller, for their support. The late Will W. Alexander was formerly administrative officer of the Fund. My sense of obligation to him, as well as my admiration and friendship for him, are evidenced by the dedication of the book to his memory. Without the initiative and assistance of the Stern Fund this book and the enterprises associated with it would not have been undertaken. The University of North Carolina and Harvard University gave additional financial aid to the research. At both institutions, funds originating in grants of more general purpose from the Ford Foundation afforded necessary support. I also wish to acknowledge a grant from the Ford Foundation under its program for assisting American university presses in the publication of works in the humanities and the social sciences. Neither the foundations nor the universities, however, are responsible for the lines of inquiry that were followed, the way the work was conducted, nor the conclusions reached. I have been free throughout to carry on the research as I chose, and did not consult the foundations nor the universities in so doing. Despite all the help from others, mine alone is the responsibility for the statements made and the conclusions reached.

For seven years my wife and children have encouraged this undertaking in the ways that are the most important. The book is as much theirs as mine. I must say something, also, of three persons already mentioned who have given unusual help at several stages. Professor Key's personal and professional aid extended far beyond his critical reading of the original research design and of the manuscript. His tolerant encouragement of the person linked with his judicious skepticism of subject matter make an unmatched combination from which many political scientists have benefited. It is a special grace to have enjoyed his and Mrs. Key's favor for so many years. Herbert E. Alexander did field work in New York State, wrote one of the most useful of the dissertations, and while associated with me as an administrative assistant and research fellow during the academic year 1954-55 carried a heavy burden of research administration. More recently, as director of the Citizens' Research Foundation, an organization devoted to the study of money in politics, he has rendered valuable help. I first met E. Wayles Browne, Jr., on the staff of the Gore Committee. He helped me greatly in the preparation of exhibits presented to that committee. Subsequently, he spent uncountable hours over a period of many months making special tabulations of Gore Committee data. On numerous occasions since he has given generously of his time.

A word concerning the organization of *The Costs of Democracy* may prove helpful to the reader. After an introductory chapter, the book takes up five major phases of campaign finance. The effect of expenditures on the outcome of elections is discussed in Chapter 2. The significance of contributing as a form of political action and as an avenue to preferment is considered in Chapters 3 and 4. Sources of campaign funds are treated in Chapters 5, 6, and 7. Here, several sorts of financial constituencies are examined, including interest groups, businesses, public employees, the underworld, and organized labor. Chapters 8 through 12 describe the ways funds are raised and their effects on the internal management of the parties and on the nominating process. The remaining chapters are concerned with the revision and regulation of existing practices. Chapter 13 examines legal controls not previously dealt with. Chapters 14 and 15 examine the uses to which money is put—the need for campaign expenditures—including the changing character and function of expenditures. Chapter 16 inspects proposals for altering the present system and suggests modifications that might prove feasible.

Alexander Heard
Chapel Hill, North Carolina

CONTENTS

FIGURE

TABLES

THE COSTS OF DEMOCRACY

1

MONEY IN POLITICS

IN ONE OF HIS stories of Continental intrigue, Eric Ambler has a character say that the thing to know about an assassination is not who fired the shot, but who paid for the bullet. Happily, American politics does not normally include assassination; it embraces more complicated and intricate relationships among people. These people are sometimes connected with each other by financial linkages, however, and one way to study American politics is to analyze these connections.

Studying politics through political finance has advantages and limitations like those of studying the human body through X-rays. Much invisible to the naked eye can be seen, but the penetration is still partial. Financial transactions can reveal important relationships, but they comprise only one of a vast variety of ways individuals and groups are significantly associated in politics. What the physician sees by X-rays, moreover, is essentially an external condition, albeit on the inside of the body. The cause and cure of the lung spot or the bone chip are determined by other means. Like the medical symptom, money by itself is neutral. It gains political meaning only from the ways it is used and the purposes sought through its use. The study of political finance has validity and greatest utility as part of the larger study of politics.

The giving, receiving, and handling of political money is a unique and especially important form of political action. In the United States it ranks next to voting itself in deserving study. Any type of individual or organized activity that affects the choice of public officials, and the decisions they make, is a meaningful act of political participation. Although giving money to politics is but one of these types, the money itself can be converted—through its power to buy goods and services—into other kinds of political activity. Money is thus a sort of interchangeable political part.

A contemporary political theorist, A. D. Lindsay, has observed, "Democracy is a theory of society as well as a theory of government."[1]

1. *The Modern Democratic State* (New York: Oxford University Press, 1947), vol. 1, p. 249.

The United States is both a democracy and a pecuniary society that permits large concentrations of economic power. The interconnection of government with the rest of American society can be especially illuminated by the flow of funds from the rest of society into the channels of politics. The study of money in politics necessarily probes the organization of society in its relationship to the functions and actions of government.

When reflecting on them separately, Americans revere both their economic wealth and their political democracy. In contrast, the two juxtaposed in government inspire something less than reverence. The explanation may lie partly in the distrust that Charles Dickens, after a tour of the United States, concluded must be native to Americans. If so, the natural skepticism was nurtured by appalling spectacles of civic corruption in nineteenth-century America. Deep-set suspicions have for decades attended any kind of money in politics. Abuses real and abuses assumed have prompted an immense corpus of legislation seeking to purify the country's politics by regulating the money in it. Scarcely ever, in the past hundred years, has there been a time when legal controls were not being advocated or condemned somewhere in the United States. Such a subject pricks the curiosity.

The subject is not limited to the government of the United States, although most that is known about it is. Money finds widespread, significant, and frequently illegal use in the politics of most nations. Not only is it a weapon of political rivalry in domestic politics, but citizens of one nation, with interests in another, cross national boundaries to use their money in foreign politics. Political money at times becomes an instrument of foreign policy for nations seeking the establishment of friendly governments in other nations. Even in dictatorships, finance plays a part in the propaganda and coercion by which regimes are supported. Wherever there is government, there is money in politics.

1. IN DEFENSE OF INQUIRY

The late Victor Hunt Harding used to say it was impossible to write a satisfactory book about political finance. "Cap" Harding was a political scientist who for years practiced his politics as executive director of the Democratic Congressional campaign committees. You can write a superficial story with lots of flashy incidents, he said. It will sell, but will be no good. Or you can try to understand and interpret what goes on. In that event you cannot document what you say, and—hapless fate—"the historians will blast you out of the water."

The data.—Others have hardly been more sanguine, and with probable cause. The ramifications of the subject are formidable enough, leading as they do throughout the whole political system and the rest of society. But the bête noire of all students of political finance is the dearth of hard, comprehensive, readily available information. What does exist is immediately confounded by the folklore of conjecture and gossip that underlies much public comment on the subject. Even the gentlest of compatriots has shown misgivings. What can be built with so few bricks, and most of them uneven, made with little straw?

The difficulties are well advertised. Widely held hostile assumptions concerning money in politics discourage politicians from publicizing their financial operations. One hardly knows which they fear most, that the public would not, or would, understand. Success in extracting information by statute has been uneven. In some localities, for limited periods, official information on the sources and uses of election funds has been useful for analysis. Official reports always lack uniformity, and never can be read literally like election returns. Yet, when supplemented by data from other sources, and used discriminatingly, such information can deepen understanding of political finance and of the broader processes of politics.

Deficiencies of data beset students of many phases of American life. Those who work with statistics on the cause of death, or the incidence of crime, know the reservations that must attend their interpretation. Like much data used in social analysis, limitations surround the data of political finance. But help can be found. Not all of the answers, but help. More than 600 persons who know something firsthand about political finance contributed information and ideas to the present inquiry through personal interviews. These ranged from presidential candidates and national finance chairmen, through large and small donors, to the raisers and spenders of funds at state, county, and precinct levels. The chances for accuracy seem better than those of the paleontologist who deduces from dead data the evolution of life through 500 million years. The challenges are less appalling that those faced by the scholar who would learn why birds migrate or how to curb the rise of mental illness. The subject is like the Carlsbad Cavern. It can be explored chamber by chamber, some portions with gratifying throughness while others remain remote.

The skeptics.—Two types of skeptics view with special reserve the exertions required by this quest. One declares it impossible to learn the truly significant facts of political finance. The other holds that for practical purposes of legislative action enough is known already. Not more study, but ways to generate a public opinion that will effectively demand legislative remedies are what is needed. A degree of plausibility attaches to both types of skepticism. Yet detailed probing of the subject makes it appear, like W. S. Gilbert's cream, that things are seldom what they seem. Many assumptions taken for granted in popular discussion do not hold up when examined realistically:

1. For example, the real costs of political campaigning have *not* soared steadily upward. Despite recent spurts caused by the use of television in some types of elections, the long-run dollar increase appears no greater than rises in the price level and the national income.

2. The costs of campaigning in the United States, moreover, are *no* extraordinarily high compared to corresponding costs in some othe nations. The cost per vote per office seems, in fact, to be lower than i some other places.

3. The old notion that the side with more money will for that reaso win, or will usually do so, is *not* correct.

4. And it has been repeatedly demonstrated that he who pays th piper does *not* always call the tune, at least not in politics. Politicians prize votes more than dollars.

5. Contrary to frequent assertion, American campaign monies are *not* supplied solely by a small handful of fat cats. Many millions of people now give to politics. Even those who give several hundred dollars each number in the tens of thousands.

6. And the traditional fat cats are *not* all of one species, allied against common adversaries. Big givers show up importantly in both parties and on behalf of many opposing candidates.

7. The labor movement is *not* a bottomless source of campaign money to be funnelled wherever labor's foes run for office. Of crucial importance in some localities, it is of minor importance in most.

8. It is *not* correct to conclude, as is the fashion, that by American standards satisfactory legal regulation has been achieved in Great Britain or elsewhere. American ambitions far exceed anything attempted in Great Britain and in most of the world. In foreign eyes, American legislative regulation falls short because it attempts the impossible.

9. At any rate, all attempts at legal control in the United States have *not* been futile. Much has been accomplished that was intended by those who passed the laws, as well as much that was not.

10. Furthermore, politicians who handle money are *not* infallibly shrewd, invariably self-seeking, ingeniously efficient cynics. The incidence of confusion, error, and administrative inefficiency in party and campaign affairs is appalling and costly.

To point out that the entire subject of political finance has been over-dramatized is not to minimize its importance. The notions that have generally prevailed have greatly oversimplified the facts and the functions of money in politics. Further probing is by no means futile. No single inquiry like the present one can overcome all the difficulties of understanding, and resolve all the questions of public policy, that have so long plagued the subject. Yet it may contribute modestly to the comprehension with which this dimension of political affairs is viewed.

2. FUNCTIONAL NEEDS AND PUBLIC REGULATION

Defining "money" and "politics."—This could itself occupy a treatise. Both concepts seem simple enough, but when put to analytical use the haziness of their boundaries quickly becomes apparent.

For the most part, the money of concern will be cash contributions and expenditures made in political campaigns, but contributions of goods and services, made in lieu of cash, are in many instances significant. And less direct types of monetary aid, such as the extension of credit or promises of future financial favors, may also at times be important. A broad conception of money as any type of direct or indirect financial resource will provide the perspective within which money, more narrowly defined as cash dollars, will be treated.

What is political will be approached in a similar fashion. This inquiry chiefly concerns the financing of campaigns for the nomination and election of public officials. From this starting point, the concept of politics extends along two different planes. First, there are other important phases of political activity, such as referenda and lobbying, that involve legislative, executive, and judicial agencies of government. Second, a wide range of factors, remote from particular elections, influences the selection of elected officials and the decisions they make in office. For example, the occupational eligibility of persons for political careers, and broad trends in public moods, have enormous significance in the processes by which public officials are chosen. To focus on the financial aspects of nominations and elections will not blind us to the larger perimeters of the political process nor to the wide variety of nonfinancial as well as financial factors that may be significant.

Total costs.—Will Rogers complained in 1931 that politics had become so expensive it took lots of money to get beat with. Bartlett picked up the quotation and it now appears several times a year in discussions of political finance. It reflects a popular view that is no less disapproving because it is hard to know how much money *is* needed to get beat with.

Total financial outlays for political campaigning in 1952 probably came to around $140,000,000. At least this is the conclusion of a conscientious estimate made by the staff of the University of North Carolina project. The estimate covered out-of-pocket cash expenditures made by parties, committees, and individuals in connection with nomination and general election campaigning for all offices at all levels during the calendar year.[2] The market value of goods and services given in kind for campaign purposes—and not counting the enormous but indeterminable amounts of part-time voluntary work that were contributed—amounted to at least 5 per cent of the cash total. It may have come to a great deal more. Of the estimated total of $140,000,000, roughly 14 per cent (over $19,000,000), was spent at the national level—that is, through organizations and activities operating in two or more states. Another 48 per cent (over $67,000,000) was spent in statewide political activities within individual states, and the remaining 38 per cent (over $53,000,000) was spent through district and local-level activities. Presidential election expenditures were made at all levels, and expenditures

2. The way the estimate was made is explained on page 372, below.

on behalf of candidates for governor and other statewide offices were normally made at both state and local levels. So many political organizations make expenditures on behalf of more than one candidate that it is usually impossible to pinpoint the total outlays that benefit any particular candidate.

Each election has its own personality and distinctive combination of characteristics. Generalizations concerning one year which are based on experience in another consequently need to be cautious. Estimates corresponding to that for 1952 do not exist for later years, but expenditures probably rose in 1956. The freeze on new television stations in effect until 1952 was abandoned, and by 1956 the number of commercial stations had increased fourfold to around 500. In part because of increased use of this form of broadcasting, total campaign costs after 1952 doubtless rose. There is no hard evidence, however, to suggest that the increase of total expenditures in 1956 over 1952 was really very great. An increase of 10 per cent seems to be a generous guess, making it possible that 1956 expenditures at the outside were around $155,000,000.[3]

Whether these estimates are accurate, or off 10, 20, or 50 per cent, the sums are not capricious, resulting merely from the whims or ambitions of politicians. Acknowledging all of the financial waste that characterizes partisan politics, these sums result basically from the functional necessities of a democratic system of government. That Americans elect so many of their public officials, well over half a million at all levels of government, accounts in important measure for the size of the election bill. The expenses of nominating and electing public officials are among the inevitable financial costs of democracy. These financial costs are as inevitable as are other costs of democratic government—an omnipresent degree of demagogy in public debate, for example. The latter is introduced by the foibles of human nature in a political system that depends for its operation on the feelings, judgment, mutual respect, and self-interest of large numbers of people. The need to expose an electorate to the views and personalities of those who through its favor seek to govern automatically creates financial necessities.

Dissatisfactions.—The dependence of the political process in the United States on money for its proper functioning long ago created dissatisfactions. As expressed, these have been essentially two in number. The need for money from private contributions opened opportunities to swap party and public favors for the cash. Moreover, contestants have seldom enjoyed equal financial resources. The accusation was

3. On September 10, 1956, the U.S. Senate Subcommittee on Privileges and Elections (under the chairmanship of Senator Albert Gore, cited hereafter as the Gore Committee) asked the author to estimate what the total of 1956 expenditures would probably come to. The guess of $175,000,000 made at that time seemed, after the election, to have been too high.—*Hearings* (Washington: Government Printing Office, 1956), part 1, p. 77.

easy that those with more than others enjoyed an advantage unfair to their opponents and unhealthy for the democracy.

These, at least, have been the surface symptoms of discontent. One suspects that beneath unhappiness with special aspects of money in politics often lies fear or misunderstanding of party government itself. In all politics, as in all life, the task is to convert the energies of private ambition into the performance of public function. Ideally, personal gratification and social utility will be harmonized and maximized in government and in society. Unquestionably, wealth in many forms enjoys privileges in democratic politics. To hold these privileges within bounds acceptable to the prevailing democratic ethic becomes a proper and necessary goal of public regulation. Yet one must guard against forgetting that money at work in politics is not, per se, deplorable. It may simply reflect a citizen's political goals and his preferences among candidates, which are, after all, legitimate end products of a democratically organized politics and society.

Old remedies.—All the states and the federal government have in one way or another attempted to regulate campaign finance. The controls imposed have stemmed from two kinds of motivation, often intermingled but nevertheless different. Desire to protect the integrity of government and the conditions necessary for its proper working has been one kind of impulse. Desire to create rules of the game favorable to certain political interests and unfavorable to others has been a second kind of impulse. The attempts to reform American campaign finance have consequently been controversial. These attempts have often been elaborate, have seldom acknowledged adequately the inherent financial needs of the electoral system, and have generally been declared failures. The failures have been neither so universal nor so complete as conventionally supposed, but where success has been met the objectives have been limited and the conditions favorable. A widespread disparagement of this exercise of the sovereign power has understandably developed.

Public cynicism toward the legal regulation of money in elections has in fact become a cardinal feature of the whole subject. In the attempts made to remedy the abuses and overcome the dissatisfactions associated with campaign finance, the functional necessity and ethical propriety of financing campaigns by some means have frequently become obscured. The ineffectiveness of statutes has resulted basically from legislative intent out of harmony with the needs of the electoral system. The country has experienced a minor sort of American dilemma. Its political behavior has not conformed to the norms expressed in statutory goals. This kind of conflict is not unknown in the land of the Volstead and Sherman Acts. The ethical absolutism frequently remarked upon by foreign observers has led to all sorts of impossible demands on the conduct of those whose lot it is to make self-government in the United

States succeed. The failures of the legislation have been misinterpreted as iniquities of the politicians whom the legislation sought to regulate. In a phrase used by Vernon L. Parrington, "a snarl of inconsequential criticism" has resulted, but little analysis of causes and alternatives. One is driven to conclude that the self-excoriation must be a consequence of guilt feelings in the national conscience. Certainly some of the legislation could only have as its function the symbolic expiation of sin.

The chief feature of existing regulatory legislation is its negative character. Attempts are made, for example, to limit the amounts that candidates, committees, or parties may spend in an election. The limits fixed have usually fallen below the inescapable costs of campaigning. Much legislation also prohibits individuals from giving more than a specified sum to a political cause. This limitation has customarily been imposed without concern for alternative sources of revenue. Candidates and campaign organizations in most places are required to file public reports of their receipts and expenditures. The statutes characteristically make no attempt to insure the accuracy of the reports nor to make the information effectively available to the public.

New departures.—A shift in approach has occurred in recent years. The trend first became conspicuous in testimony before Congressional committees about 1955. Its chief characteristic is a positive quality. What must be done, the newer proposals ask, to insure effective elections under present conditions in the United States? Doing this, it is argued, is the swiftest way to eliminate many of the old abuses and is a prerequisite for eliminating others.

What may prove wise or efficacious can be judged only in the light of objectives desired. The goals of regulation command broad consensus only when stated broadly. Most commentators, and probably most citizens, would agree upon three general aspirations: (1) all candidates who enjoy important popular support should be able to compete on reasonably equitable financial terms; (2) candidates and parties should be able to get the needed financial backing without mortgaging their political souls; and (3) these things should be accomplished in ways that create confidence in the electoral system and respect for the statutes that regulate it.

The public and private measures that appear best designed to accomplish these purposes will be examined in detail. Various proposals are dependent for effectiveness upon the adoption of others. It is proposed here that several principles, if followed, offer hope for feasible action:

1. Campaign expenditures must be recognized as vital to the American way of choosing public officials. The expenditures are inherently neither good nor bad, neither high nor low. They are simply necessary. And in the United States they can easily be met. Corruption of the

ballot, after all, is met by outlawing specific offenses and not by abolishing voting.

2. Since political campaigns are essential to the operation of American government, it is appropriate to give them every form of government support that is necessary and feasible. This suggestion calls for piecemeal action wherever the practical conditions of politics permit. Action can take the form of direct subsidies, as in the Commonwealth of Puerto Rico, or of indirect subsidies, as in the states of California and Minnesota which have made certain political contributions deductible for income tax purposes. Tax deductions, or tax credits, not only shift some of the financial burden to government, but improve the respectability and ease of fund-raising. Government can encourage equal access to the electorate by subsidizing and regulating channels of communication, especially radio and television broadcasting.

3. Other forms of public subsidy should be encouraged, too, by means of neutral or bipartisan campaign funds raised from public donations. The United States has a long history of generous support of worthy causes through public fund-raising campaigns.

4. Simplified reports of receipts and expenditures in nomination and election campaigns should be called for from all significant political groups—by law where possible and by request where not.

5. Special law enforcement units especially insulated from partisan pressures should be created to enforce all regulations adopted.

6. Finally, steady efforts should be made to improve public understanding of campaign finance and the efforts to control it. Then the cynicism that scars American politics will be dissipated and the constructive purposes of campaign expenditures recognized.

3. POLITICAL REPRESENTATION AND SOCIAL CHANGE

Most regulation of campaign finance is intended ostensibly to curtail the "influence" of money in politics. Like all participants in politics, those who supply and use campaign monies may, and often do, exercise political influence. Influence in its broadest sense is integral to representative government. The sensitivity of politicians to factors that affect the outcome of elections is the springhead of responsive and responsible government. Politicians are as alert to the financial contributions to their success as to other types of help. Deeper understanding of political money means deeper understanding of representative government.

Distortions in representation.—Political parties function as connecting organs joining government to the rest of society. They are the principal type of intermediate organization that links the citizen and his specialized groups with the forums of government decision-making. As such, political parties provide complex and sensitive channels through which varied interests express themselves and seek representation in government. These channels are frequently subtle and indirect transmitters of the demands, viewpoints, and ideals of affected citizens. But they serve not solely as relay pipes for political pressures; they act also as sieves separating consequential issues from those which are dispensable and arbitrating among conflicting claims.

The processes of political finance constitute one set of mechanisms through which political representation is achieved. As true of other instruments of representative government, a greater or lesser degree of distortion is inherent in their operation. Almost any system of legislative districts, for example, contains intentional or unintentional elements of malapportionment and gerrymander. The degree of each shifts with changes in population and partisan sentiment. Similarly, some instruments of representation are more accessible to certain citizens than to others. Travelling salesmen in states without absentee voting are handicapped politically, as are persons who cannot meet age or literacy requirements. Owners of successful newspapers, on the contrary, are assured of wide audiences for their political opinions. The opportunities for self-assertion will alter with changes in the voting laws and with changes in the capital needed to start a newspaper. In like ways, distortions in the representative processes of political finance change from time to time.

Changing mechanisms.—The operations of campaign finance are affected by shifts in the interests that assert claims through them. The appearance of oil, of the automobile, and of atomic warfare account for political pressures that have direct impact, not simply on government policies, but also on the processes, both internal and external to government, by which public policies are made. Whether a potential political interest becomes and remains an active one depends on many things, including changes in the scope of governmental regulation. The stake of small businessmen in government expands with the expanding concept of interstate commerce as interpreted by the Supreme Court of the United States. Pressures on government increase as the decisions of government become more important to more people, and what sort of people want a part in financing political activities affects the ease of raising money, the procedures for doing so, and the rewards expected.

Modifications are reflected in the style of politics. President John Adams once declined to speak in German at the opening of the Pennsylvania Canal. To do so, he said disapprovingly, would be outright electioneering aimed at German-speaking citizens (which is what his supporters had in mind).[4] The tempo of politics was, however, to change. Simon Cameron, known as "the Great Winnebago" to commemorate a handsome theft from the Winnebago Indians early in his career, has been named among the first in American politics to purchase personal political power by the lavish use of cash.[5] But this was late in

4. Florence Weston, "The Presidential Election of 1828" (Ph.D. dissertation, Catholic University of America, 1938), p. 161.

5. Samuel P. Orth, *The Boss and the Machine—A Chronicle of the Politicians and Party Organization* (New Haven: Yale University Press, 1919), pp. 128-29.

the Republic's youth, the middle of the nineteenth century. And politics has so changed that a counterpart of this political buccaneer, who became a senator of the United States and Lincoln's secretary of war, cannot be found in the middle of the twentieth century.

Changes in the style and substance of politics originate from many sources. Among them, the impact of technological change has been great. The refinement of the fund-raising dinner as a major source of party income, for example, is in important part a product of technological change. Improved transportation makes attendance at the dinners possible, and closed-circuit broadcasting adds dollar-catching attractions. The effects of technological developments on party organization and procedure have never been analyzed systematically. Many will be evident, along with the results of other types of change, in the operations of campaign finance.

Functional representation.—The chapters ahead examine one set of evolving mechanisms by which representation of interests in American politics is achieved. The role of money is not confined to the selection of public officials, but this crucially important phase of the political system will occupy most attention. The anatomy and physiology of campaign finance are the focus. The fortunes of particular individuals and of interest groups which may have stakes in government are incidental.[6] As late as the 1930's in the United States, a rising demand for formal institutions of functional representation seemed likely. Economic councils and senates where special interests as such would be represented appeared a natural consequence of the increasing diversity and importance of organized economic interests.[7] There are numerous legislative, administrative, and quasi-judicial agencies that partially serve this purpose. Yet the lack of demand for formal functional representation, especially in the formulation of state and federal legislation, suggests that the political needs of functional interests are met in other ways.[8]

6. Those exercised over blatant instances of purchased governmental privilege may be impatient with concern for the social utility of the broader processes in which individual acts occur. This problem is encountered whenever a functional interpretation is attempted of behavior that runs against public norms or private values. A sociological explanation of the rise of Huey Long, for example, may outrage individuals whose personal liberties were trampled by the tyrant.

7. Charles E. Merriam, "Government and Society," in President's Committee on Social Trends, *Recent Social Trends in the United States* (one-volume ed.; New York: McGraw-Hill Book Company, Inc., 1934), p. 1515. It is sometimes forgotten that M. Ostrogorski in his study of *Democracy and the Organization of Political Parties* (New York: The Macmillan Company, 1902) envisioned the deterioration of American political parties because of the incongruous elements they contained. He advocated alliances around individual issues and single-purpose associations.—vol. 2, pp. 658-63.

8. A sociologist has observed that "wherever strong interests are organized, they will be represented in government in one form or another—officially or unofficially, openly or covertly."—Robin M. Williams, Jr. *American Society—A Sociological Interpretation* (New York: Alfred A. Knopf, 1952), p. 259.

Among these other ways are the channels of influence created by the private financing of political campaigns.

Cash is far more significant in the nominating process than in determining the outcome of elections. Many factors unrelated to finance affect whether and how people vote. Few individuals can seriously seek a nomination, however, without assurance of the essential funds necessary to get a campaign under way. Those who can guarantee or withhold these assurances occupy an important strategic position in American politics. The fund-raiser as a distinct political type has mounted in significance as ability to finance campaigns by large donations from a few contributors has declined. Tax legislation, especially the gift tax, has reduced the free funds that in former days wealthy persons shoveled to their political agents. A few persons still place upwards of $100,000 into campaign activities in a single year. Nonetheless, the solicitation of funds in both parties has become a complex affair dependent on solicitors who possess access to political money.

The trend is toward larger numbers of small and large contributors. The means by which their gifts are funnelled to the support of candidates are of singular importance in understanding the representation of interests in American politics. There has been a fractionalization of political interests. The complexity of decision-making processes in government has increased. A corresponding multiplication in the points of access through which influence can be brought to bear on governmental decisions has occurred. Those who give, solicit, receive, and use campaign funds comprise one important segment of the vast network of interconnecting personal, official, and political relationships that is government.

The motivations underlying political giving are diverse. It is demonstrable that the admitted goals and the inferable incentives of campaign contributors are diverse and of differing social worth. Yet throughout life individuals do the same things for different "reasons" and do different things out of the same impulses. These simple facts are part of the working knowledge of political financiers and become increasingly important as appeals are made to larger numbers of givers. It is important to remember them when analyzing the functions of campaign finance in representative government.

The trail of money through factions and parties reveals curious patterns of communication and organizational structure. The decentralization of American parties is etched vividly in financial terms by the dependence of national-level activities upon fund-raising at state and local levels. The dependence for essential campaign functions on groups auxiliary to the parties becomes equally apparent. Many and varied financial transactions are found among units of parties and auxiliary groups at all levels. This passage of funds to and fro suggests mutual endeavor rather than hierarchy and authority. The importance of nonparty groups emphasizes the great significance of amateurism in American politics, as do the facts of political solicitation and the staffing of campaign organizations.

Sometimes the United States is viewed abroad and at home as a sham democracy. The power of wealth, it is charged, runs roughshod over the people's interests and over their political will. To illuminate even slightly the role of money in politics helps to expose the basis for this judgment. It helps also to demonstrate that, at bottom, it is wrong. Improved understanding of these matters contributes to what Aldous Huxley calls our education for freedom. Only a partial exploration is possible. At the end, one feels like Sir James George Frazer on completing *The Golden Bough*: ". . . as often happens in the search after truth, if we have answered one question, we have raised many more; if we have followed one track home, we have had to pass by others that opened off it and led, or seemed to lead, to far other goals. . . ."

2

DOES MONEY WIN ELECTIONS?

THE REAL QUESTION, of course, is what *does* win elections?

Politicians campaign for the most part by instinct and shrewd guessing. Neither they nor laborious scholars can lay out a set of infallible rules for controlling the outcome of elections. Yet the notion is common that the side with more money has a better chance of winning. The belief is not discouraged by practical politicians who must pry campaign gifts out of their followers, but it springs initially from uncertainty as to what constitutes effective campaigning. Afraid to leave any stone unturned, campaigners usually expand the volume of electioneering until time and money run out. The calendar heeds no man, but somebody else always has more money, and may part with some of it.

No neat correlation is found between campaign expenditures and campaign results. Even if superiority in expenditures and success at the polls always ran together, the flow of funds to a candidate might simply reflect his prior popular appeal rather than create it. Our understanding of voting behavior is not so precise that all the financial and nonfinancial factors that contribute to success can be sorted out with confidence. Yet it is clear that under some conditions the use of funds can be decisive. And under others no amount of money spent by the loser could alter the outcome. The kinds of information available limit the analyses that can be made, but they do show clearly that financial outlays cannot guarantee victory in elections. By a process of negative findings, it is possible to box off the question and examine it in perspective.

1. THE EXCEPTIONS AND THE RULE

It was once held a general rule that "expenditures are a reliable index of the outcome of the election."[1] The generalization seems to have rested chiefly on experience in American presidential elections from about 1896 through the Hoover victory of 1928. It was manifest to contemporaries during the McKinley elections of 1896 and 1900 that Re-

1. Noted in Louise Overacker, "Campaign Funds in a Depression Year," *American Political Science Review,* 27 (1933), 770.

publicans spent more than Democrats, and imbalances were claimed for prior elections as well. Partisans explained defeat by their lack of funds. In the days of tightly controlled and highly vendible state and local political machines, with ballot integrity only slightly protected by statutes and effective public opinion, the claims were often plausible.[2]

The rule develops.—The great dust up over campaign funds after 1900 led both parties from 1904 onward to reveal information about the cost of their national campaign efforts. The results made it look as though money were the thing. The winners' percentages of the combined direct expenditures made by the Republican and Democratic national committees were as follows:[3]

Year	*%*	*Party*	*Year*	*%*	*Party*	*Year*	*%*	*Party*
1904	75	Rep.	1912	51	Dem.	1920	75	Rep.
1908	72	Rep.	1916	53	Dem.	1924	75	Rep.
						1928	56	Rep.

Every time, the winning side had seemingly spent the most. No account was taken of expenditures for third candidates or at state and local levels, nor of bandwagon gifts coming to the winner after the election, nor of other influences. Yet victory and superior money appeared to run together. The view was bolstered among professional students of government by an article published in 1928 by George A. Lundberg. Professor Lundberg demonstrated that in 156 cases drawn from state and local politics, the side that reported spending the most money won in all but 11.[4] It was clear to all who thought about the matter that many factors

2. Eugene H. Roseboom considers Tilden's failure in 1876 to "supply funds which might have made safe the three doubtful southern states" to have been a fatal error. "As it was, the national headquarters centered its efforts and funds on New York and Indiana, and did a good job."—*A History of Presidential Elections* (New York: The Macmillan Company, 1957), p. 242. Concludes another historian, Harry S. Truman: "In Grant's second election to the presidency, the chief factor was money."—*Memoirs by Harry S. Truman—Years of Trial and Hope* (New York: Doubleday and Company, 1956), vol. 2, p. 198. And Harold L. Ickes, who worked for McKinley in 1896: "I have never doubted that if the Democrats had been able to raise enough money, even for legitimate purposes, Bryan would have been elected."—*Autobiography of a Curmudgeon* (New York: Reynal & Hitchcock, 1943), p. 80.

3. Louise Overacker, *Money in Elections* (New York: The Macmillan Company, 1932), p. 73. During this period most national-level expenditures were made through the national committees. "Direct expenditures" include only money actually spent, excluding funds transferred to another organization. If spent by the latter, the transferred money would be counted among *its* direct expenditures.

4. "Campaign Expenditures and Election Results," *Social Forces,* 6 (1928), 452-57. The combined expenses of state and local committees were available for 1920 and 1922 in Ohio, Nevada, and Oregon. In five of these six cases, the party reporting the highest spending won. Voting and spending on eight initiative and referendum measures showed that in each case the winning side reported spending the most. The remaining 142 cases were New York counties in 1922, 1924, or 1926. In 132 of them the party committee reporting the largest outlay carried the county.

affect election results, but the money spent might still serve as a good index to electoral strength.

The rule collapses.—The victories of Franklin Roosevelt and Harry Truman destroyed this notion. The Democratic share of total direct expenditures reported by national campaign groups on behalf of both parties was as follows:[5]

Year	*% Party*	*Year*	*% Party*	*Year*	*% Party*
1932	49 Dem.	1940	35 Dem.	1948	39 Dem.
1936	41 Dem.	1944	42 Dem.		

Again, total campaign outlays at all levels are not represented in the figures. The evidence at hand indicated, however, that if they were, the Republican margin would have been greater still.

In retrospect, the difficulty seems clear. It was like the old slogan, "As Maine goes, so goes the country." At a time when Maine was invariably Republican, this rule held up as long as the country also went Republican. Republicans generally have more money available for the presidential race, and as long as they won, a correlation between expenses and success was maintained, with deviations explainable.[6]

5. Derived from articles by Louise Overacker in the *American Political Science Review*: "Campaign Funds in a Depression Year," 27 (1933), 770; "Campaign Funds in the Presidential Election of 1936," 31 (1937), 476, 478; "Campaign Finance in the Presidential Election of 1940," 35 (1941), 713; and "Presidential Campaign Funds, 1944," 39 (1945), 900, 906. The 1948 data come from reports in the National Archives. The 1932 figures are for the regular national committee of each party, but those for subsequent years include known expenditures by other national-level groups active in the presidential race.

6. In 42 Pennsylvania counties, information on 1952 expenditures by the county committee of both parties was available. In 36 of these, the party reporting the highest disbursements carried the county for its presidential candidate. Eisenhower, however, carried all but 10 of Pennsylvania's 67 counties that year, including most of the 42 mentioned above, and in virtually all cases Republican expenditures were reported as greatest. One suspects that a different picture would have been found in 1936, when FDR carried 41 counties. (Professor Lundberg's study, previously cited, does not report which New York counties are included in his analysis. Nor does it say in how many of his cases was the largest campaign fund attributed to the Republican and in how many to the Democratic party. If his counties included a large number of upstate Republican bailiwicks, the findings may be less significant than at first appeared.)

The chairman of the Republican executive committee in Allegheny County (Pittsburgh), Sheriff Thomas E. Whitten, had this to say in 1952 about money and electoral success: "Consistently over the years the Republican expenditures in Allegheny County have been substantially greater than those of the Democrats, but to show you that money has had little effect, although we have for 20 years spent more than they, we lost the county in 1932 by about 37,000; we lost in 1936 by 190,000; we lost in 1940 by 110,000; we lost in 1944 by about 105,000; and we lost in 1948 by slightly under 80,000. This year we sort of bailed ourselves out and got down to the 11,000 level. Actually the amount of money spent in the past did not influence it."—U.S. House of Representatives Special Committee to Investigate Campaign Expenditures, 1952, *Hearings* (Washington: Government Printing Office, 1952), p. 144.

Other illustrations of candidates' defeating their better financed opponents can be marshalled. In the British general elections of 1950 and 1951, for example, the candidate who reported the highest expenditures was defeated in 42 and 36 per cent, respectively, of the constituencies.[7] The socialist parties in Europe often reached the peak of their power while relatively poor, and the rise of proletarian parties elsewhere has generally had the effect of minimizing the influence of cash on election results. The case of Maine is well to remember, nevertheless. A shift of votes toward one candidate or another, even though not a decisive one in what was then an overwhelmingly Republican Maine, might foretell a shift in the rest of the country that *would* be decisive. So, too, if nonfinancial variables affecting election behavior could be held constant, might it not be shown that the use of funds has, in fact, a direct effect, if not always a decisive one?

2. UNEQUAL WAR CHESTS[8]

In some nations, political parties are often found that enjoy several times the financial resources of one or more of their opponents. In comparison, the gap separating Republican and Democratic expenditures in the United States is usually moderate.[9]

7. Full information on votes polled and expenses reported appears in "Election Expenses" published by Her Majesty's Stationery Office after each election. Were it not for the ceilings on expenditures by candidates, which result sometimes in both candidates spending near the maximum, the relatively uncomplicated British parliamentary elections would make useful objects of study for those interested in campaign finance. There are also expenditures by central party organizations, however, and broad drifts of opinion across the nation, as well as other factors, that presumably affect the outcome of British elections and would have to be taken into account.

J. F. S. Ross pointed out that in the 1950 elections, "After making full allowance for every local variation in the legal maximum, the *average* successful Conservative spent 4 per cent more than the *average* unsuccessful, while the *average* successful Labour candidate spent 10 per cent more than the *average* unsuccessful."— *Elections and Electors* (London: Eyre & Spottiswoode, 1955), p. 275. (Italics added.)

8. Generally, information about national-level committees is taken from federal reports filed pursuant to law with the Clerk of the U.S. House of Representatives. Information about state activities in 1952 comes from reports filed pursuant to state laws. Gore Committee data are often used for 1956. For comments on the extent of the Gore Committee's coverage, see pages 388-89, below.

9. The Republican advantage has often been exaggerated. Much money is transferred among political committees. The same sum may consequently show up on the books of several different groups. The total receipts or disbursements of a set of committees cannot therefore simply be added together to give a meaningful result. This has often been done, however, and because Republicans shuttle their money about more than Democrats, more of it gets counted two or three times and any comparison between the parties becomes distorted. See pages 283-317, below.

The best index for comparison is direct expenditures, that is, money spent for goods and services used in the campaign. Democratic committees are more likely to carry large deficits from an election year into an off-year, however, so that their direct expenditures may not in fact fully reflect the dollar value of

Political-committee expenditures.—In 1952, with a Democratic administration in power and a national hero as the Republican presidential candidate, all the Republican national-level campaign groups as a whole outspent the corresponding Democratic groups (with national labor expenditures included) in a ratio of about 55 to 45. The direct expenditures for the full calendar year were as follows:

		Percentage
18 national Republican committees:	$6,608,623	55
15 national Democratic committees:	*$4,532,926*	*38*
15 national labor groups:	*797,544*	*7*
Total on behalf of Democrats:	$5,330,470	45
Grand Total:	$11,939,093	100

In 1956, with the chances for an Eisenhower victory dimmed only by the uncertainties of his health, the Republican margin among national-level direct expenditures[10] increased to about 62-38, as follows:

		Percentage
11 national Republican committees:	$7,778,702	62
11 national Democratic committees:	*$4,306,651*	*34*
17 national labor groups:	*540,735*	*4*
Total on behalf of Democrats:	$4,847,386	38
Grand Total:	$12,626,088	100

These ratios tell an important part of the story, but expenditures at state, district, and local levels comprise around six-sevenths of total costs for all types of campaigns in the country. At these lower levels, each party normally spends more than its rival in states it traditionally dominates. But in the competitive party states, the Republicans customarily spend the most.

Official reports do not cover all cash outlays made during a campaign. In a few states, the available data can be used with some degree of faith as reflecting reasonably well the proportionate division of expenditures between the parties. A tabulation was made for a number of states of

their campaign activities. In 1956, for example, a debt of $800,000 was run up by the Democratic national committee in the form of unpaid bills for telephone, telegraph, newspaper advertising, air transportation, printing, hotel accommodations, etc. These are reported as expenditures when eventually paid.

Direct expenditures are made by campaign groups not affiliated with the parties but obviously sympathetic to one or the other. In 1952 four such groups favorable to Democrats reported spending $205,400 and two such groups favorable to Republicans reported spending $190,100. The Gore Committee *Report* (Washington: Government Printing Office, 1957) lists 10 groups of this kind spending some $187,000 during the 1956 campaign period, substantially more than half of which could reasonably be assigned as beneficial to Republicans.—Ex. 29, p. 17.

10. For the full calendar year, like the 1952 data, with the exception of information for one minor Democratic group and the labor groups, which is for the period January 1–November 30, 1956.

1952 general election data from several hundred committees operating at all political levels. Notions of the relative completeness of the data were obtained from interviews with practical politicians. It was concluded that in some instances the total direct expenditures reported probably serve as a roughly reliable index to the relative expenditures of the two parties.[11] The results for four states can be summarized as follows:[12]

State	*Total Disbursements*	*Total Direct Expenditures*	*Party Percentages of Dir. Exps.*		*Party Percentages of Pres. Vote*	
			Rep.	*Dem.*	*Rep.*	*Dem.*
Connecticut	$2,160,000	$1,290,000	61	39	56	44
Maryland	870,000	570,000	57	43	56	44
Massachusetts	3,470,000	3,030,000	51	49	54	46
Pennsylvania	5,640,000	3,280,000	69	31	53	47

The funds included above were spent for many candidates in addition to those for president, but the division of the presidential vote tells something of the balance of party strength in each state in 1952.

No comparable tabulations are available for other years. Certain information was compiled for 1956 by the United States Senate Subcommittee on Privileges and Elections under the chairmanship of Senator Gore. Full information on no single state was obtained, but information from several types of campaign committees in all states was collected. These data suggest a slightly larger Republican financial advantage at state and local levels generally during the period of the active campaign (September 1–November 30, 1956) than was noted at the national level for the full year. They also suggest that Republicans enjoyed a somewhat larger advantage in 1956 than in 1952:[13]

Campaign Committees	*Total Disbursements*	*Total Direct Expenditures*	*Party Percentage of Direct Expenses*	
			Rep.	*Dem.*
351 statewide	$22,480,000	$12,570,000	64	36
350 local (from 100 largest counties)	9,650,000	6,510,000	59	41

11. Noteworthy consistencies were found between the two parties in the proportions of total expenditures reported as being made for specific purposes. They would be unlikely in reports made of whole cloth. See pages 391-93, below.

12. Where available, known labor expenditures have been included with those of the Democrats. The data for Pennsylvania are least satisfactory.

13. Labor-committee expenditures are included with those of Democrats in computing the percentages.—Gore Committee *Report,* pp. 39-40. The chief omissions from the 1956 data are some committees active on behalf of candidates for state offices, all local committees in counties other than the 100 largest, and a large share of committees on behalf of candidates for the U.S. House of Representatives. There is no reason to think, however, that the division of funds between the parties in these instances would veer so sharply, or involve such large sums of money, as to affect significantly the ratios arrived at.

It is safe to conclude that in the United States as a whole in 1956 Republican candidates benefited by at least 60 per cent of all campaign expenditures made during the general election. The actual proportion was probably a bit higher, and it was no doubt higher than in 1952.

Television and radio payments.—These conclusions rest on information supplied by political organizations themselves. There is one independent check. In both 1952 and 1956 television and radio stations and networks supplied a Senate subcommittee with information on expenditures made for political broadcasts. Television and radio costs constitute the most significant single expenditure in the minds of many campaign managers.[14] Here is how the broadcasting expenditures were divided:[15]

	Radio			*Television*		
	Total For Both Parties	*Percentage Rep.*	*Percentage Dem.*	*Total For Both Parties*	*Percentage Rep.*	*Percentage Dem.*
1952	$3,070,000	59	41	$2,950,000	56	44
1956	3,060,000	54	46	6,530,000	58	42

The Republican share of costs for radio and television combined was thus around 57 per cent in both years. This is slightly lower than the estimated Republican proportion of the combined expenditures made by both parties for all purposes mentioned earlier. The difference is plausible. Democratic campaign managers would be expected to concentrate their inferior resources where they feel the greatest need, which is often for radio and television time. Thus Democrats would be expected to spend a relatively larger percentage of their available money for broadcasting than the Republicans.

14. See pages 388-91, below.

15. The figures are not exactly comparable for the two years. The 1952 data are the amounts paid stations and networks on behalf of presidential, vice presidential, Senatorial, and Congressional general election candidates (*only*) for the period August 1–November 4, 1952. They "do not include production costs paid to agencies or others not directly connected with the radio and television stations nor preprogram advertising costs both of which are substantial. Preemption costs or reservation, however, are included. Nearly 100-per cent cooperation was obtained from both radio and television stations."—U.S. Senate Subcommittee on Privileges and Elections, *Proposed Amendments to Federal Corrupt Practices Act* (Washington: Government Printing Office, 1953), p. 2.

An independent study of *network* broadcasting time purchased on behalf of both parties in 1952 was made using information provided by the networks and the A. C. Nielsen Company. It reported Republican radio network time purchased as 23 hours, Democratic time as 23 hours and 15 minutes. Republican TV network time purchased totalled 15 hours, Democratic time 19 hours and 50 minutes.—Herbert R. Craig, "Distinctive Features of Radio-TV in the 1952 Presidential Campaign" (Master's thesis, State University of Iowa, 1954), pp. 129-32.

The 1956 data are the amounts paid for radio and television broadcasts over stations and networks on behalf of Democratic and Republican general election candidates for *all* offices during the period September 1–November 6, 1956. Included are costs of spots, programs, and other charges, such as production, connection, and preemption costs. The information is complete for all national networks, for about 97 per cent of television stations, and about 90 per cent of radio stations. —Gore Committee *Report,* Ex. 24, pp. 1-2.

On the average across the country Republican candidates in 1952 and 1956 had at least half again as much money spent on their behalf as did their Democratic opponents.[16] This is a nationwide average and tells nothing of the balance of funds between opponents in particular races. Even if full information on political expenditures were known, this would be difficult to learn. It is virtually impossible to know how much of the money spent on a party ticket as a whole ought to be allocated as benefiting a particular candidate. A clear impression of the balance between the parties within individual states is gained, nevertheless, by judiciously scrutinizing information obtained by the Gore Committee. Data on expenditures were obtained especially from statewide party campaign committees and from special committees supporting candidates for the United States Senate. This information makes it seem likely that total Republican direct expenditures exceeded Democratic direct expenditures in four-fifths of the states in 1956.

Expenditures made for radio and television time within each state during the 1956 general elections reveal something of the variations in Republican financial superiority. In 33 states (69 per cent), Republicans spent more for these purposes. The margin enjoyed by each party within individual states varied considerably. The following figures show the number of states in which the Republican percentage fell at various levels:

Republican Percentage of Radio-TV Campaign Expenditures in State	*Number of States*
0-19	2[17]
20-29	2[18]
30-39	3
40-49	8
50-59	17
60-69	12
70-79	3[19]
80-100	1[20]
Total	48

16. Even considerably larger outlays by labor organizations on behalf of Democratic candidates than accounted for in the above computations would not bring the Republican share below 60 per cent and the Democratic share above 40 per cent in 1956. The greater advantage seemingly enjoyed by Republicans in 1956 than in 1952 may plausibly be explained by Mr. Eisenhower's control of the White House and probable reelection. It may well be asked whether the division of funds between the two parties does not vary markedly from one presidential election to another. (As 1960 approached, Republicans complained loudly that their receipts had fallen off badly after the 1958 defeats.) Given the division of state capitols and seats in the Congress between the two parties, and the verity that hope springs eternal in the political breast, the answer is probably not. No compelling reasons appear, either, for supposing that the division of funds would be greatly changed in mid-term years.

17. Alabama and South Carolina.

18. Arkansas and Georgia.

19. Ohio, Utah, and Wisconsin.

20. New Hampshire.

In one-third of the states Republicans commanded 60 per cent or more of the radio-television money, and Democrats did so in about one-seventh. This tabulation includes the so-called one-party states of both parties. More significant is the division of radio and television costs in 24 states where Senate races were held in 1956 outside of the South (excluding New Hampshire and Vermont). Total Republican expenditures for air time were greater in 19, and, for air time specifically on behalf of Senatorial candidates, in 17:

Republican Percentage of Radio-TV Campaign Expenditures in State	*Number of States with Indicated Percentage of—*	
	Total Radio-TV Expenditures in State	*Radio-TV Expenditures for Senatorial Candidates*
0-19	0	1[21]
20-29	0	0
30-39	1	2
40-49	4	4
50-59	13	8
60-69	3	2
70-79	3[22]	4[23]
80-100	0	3[24]
Total	24	24

In six of these states, the Republican share of total radio and television costs exceeded 60 per cent, and the Democratic share did so in only one. Of radio-television funds devoted specifically to Senatorial contests, in nine of the states Republicans spent 60 per cent or more of the total for both parties, and Democrats did so in only three.

An over-all Republican advantage runs through these figures. It is evident, however, that the margins separating the parties varied considerably from state to state and in some states favored Democratic candidates. But, to return to our original question, what difference does it all make?

3. MONEY AND VOTING BEHAVIOR

Many years ago A. W. Dunn asked William Barnes, Jr., how a forthcoming election would turn out. Barnes, a Republican politician in New York, declared he would know definitely only about Albany County, and then only after dough day. Dough day was the day county chairmen and state leaders assembled in Manhattan to receive their apportionment of money. After the distribution, Barnes announced

21. Arizona.
22. Ohio, Utah, and Wisconsin.
23. Colorado, Kansas, North Dakota, and Wisconsin.
24. Ohio, Oklahoma, and Utah.

Albany would give a Republican majority of 6,000, which it then did, with 200 votes to spare.[25]

The attic of history is overflowing with recollections of the decisive importance of cash in ancient successes at the polls. If all election expenditures had immediate and predictable effects, analyzing the relationship between campaign funds and voting behavior would be simple. Clear, also, would be the consequences of unequal war chests. Unhappily for the student—though happily for the free debate of American politics—the effects of most campaign spending are neither so visible nor so certain as those of Mr. Barnes's dough-day handouts. Even the importance of election-day expenses, which still account for approximately one-eighth of campaign costs, has diminished. In the days of the old bosses money could buy a sure number of votes. Money could buy the support of leaders and could pay the costs of getting dependable followers to the polls to vote, some more than once. But bosses and machines have changed.[26] In a day of radically strengthened legal safeguards and altered public attitudes, the effectiveness of election-day expenditures is no longer so predictable.

The effectiveness of expenditures.—Relatively more money is now spent for organizational activities and communications during the campaign before election day. The effects of these outlays usually remain matters of conjecture. Sometimes pinpoint cases demonstrate the utility of specific campaign exertions. In the summer of 1954, United States Representative Pat Sutton of Tennessee opposed Senator Estes Kefauver for their state's Democratic Senatorial nomination. Mr. Sutton made extensive use of a device called the talkathon—a continuous personal television-radio appearance lasting more than a day. By this means he sought unsuccessfully to defeat his more widely and favorably known opponent. In July, one of the talkathons was held in Memphis. On the day before, 300 adults chosen at random were asked by phone whether they had ever heard of Pat Sutton and to say who he was. The questions were asked of 300 others similarly chosen the day after. The percentage who said they had heard of Sutton increased from 35 before the talkathon to 68 after it, and the percentage who identified him as a candidate for the Senate rose from 9 to 45.[27] Similarly, television seems

25. Arthur Wallace Dunn, *From Harrison to Harding—A Personal Narrative, Covering a Third of a Century, 1888-1921* (New York: G. P. Putnam's Sons, 1922), vol. 1, pp. 401-2.

26. Empirical evidence on the state of modern bossism is found in Paul T. David, Malcolm Moos, and Ralph M. Goldman, *Presidential Nomination Politics, 1952* (Baltimore: The Johns Hopkins University Press, 1954), where the bossed and unbossed character of state delegations to the national conventions is reviewed.

27. Awareness of Senator Kefauver also increased. Three questions were asked of each respondent, the final one as follows: "Can you tell me who are the candidates for the next election to the U.S. Senate from Tennessee?" Before the Sutton talkathon, 26 per cent mentioned Kefauver, and 41 per cent did so after it. The study was made by the Psychological Service Center, Memphis, and the results were made available by its director, W. R. Atkinson, with the permission of Robert Snowden, a Sutton backer, at whose request the study was made.

unmistakably to have aided in transforming Adlai Stevenson in 1952 from a little known state governor to a widely recognized national figure.[28] Although specific consequences of the use of television can sometimes be isolated in instances like these, the impact on the outcome of elections generally remains cloudy.[29] That other types of campaign activity have demonstrable effects in specific situations has also been shown. Samuel J. Eldersveld demonstrated the effectiveness of mail and personal contact in activating voters and changing attitudes in certain municipal elections in Ann Arbor, Michigan.[30] Canvassing by party workers in 1952 and 1956 appears to have activated a goodly number of persons who otherwise might not have voted.[31] Yet campaign

28. The Survey Research Center of the University of Michigan asked respondents in a national sample which medium of communications had given them the most information about the campaign. Television led the responses with 31 per cent, radio following with 27 per cent, and newspapers next with 22 per cent.—Angus Campbell, Gerald Gurin, and Warren E. Miller, "Television and the Election," *Scientific American,* 188 (May, 1953), 46-48. Using a panel of respondents in Ohio, Kentucky, and Indiana, members of the department of marketing of Miami University, Oxford, Ohio, concluded (in part) that "with respect to the influence of television in projecting the personal traits of Stevenson, it seems clear that Stevenson gained more than did Eisenhower from this medium."—*The Influence of Television on the Election of 1952* (Oxford Research Associates, Inc., December, 1954), p. 47. See the report of a California study in Ithiel de Sola Pool, "TV: A New Dimension in Politics," in Eugene Burdick and Arthur J. Brodbeck, *American Voting Behavior* (Glencoe, Illinois: The Free Press, 1959), pp. 236-61.

Following the 1958 elections, voters in a sample drawn from four metropolitan areas of New York State were asked what sources of information they used during the election to help them form opinions about gubernatorial candidates Nelson A. Rockefeller and W. Averell Harriman. Eighty-five per cent cited newspapers and 77 per cent television. The next most frequent source referred to was family, friends, and associates, mentioned by 45 per cent. When asked which they considered the most important source, 40 per cent of the respondents stated newspapers and 38 per cent television.—*Television and the Political Candidate* (New York: Research Department, Cunningham & Walsh, Inc., March, 1959), p. 7.

29. See Charles A. H. Thomson, *Television and Presidential Politics* (Washington: The Brookings Institution, 1956), pp. 61-72; Herbert A. Simon and Frederick Stern, "The Effect of Television Upon Voting Behavior in Iowa in the 1952 Presidential Election," *American Political Science Review,* 49 (1955), 470-77; and Campbell *et al., op. cit.* Those interested in "Evaluating Mass Media Campaigns" will find an article so titled by C. R. Wright in the *International Social Science Bulletin,* 7 (1955), 417-30. The self-selection of media audiences always creates the possibility that differences in them existed before the decision of individuals to join the audience, rather than as a consequence of their doing so. This basic problem handicaps any attempt to draw conclusions concerning the effectiveness of money spent on television rather than for other purposes.

30. "Experimental Propaganda Techniques and Voting Behavior," *American Political Science Review,* 50 (1956), 154-65. An earlier study showed that it is possible to evaluate devices used to interest people in elections. It also demonstrated the effectiveness of doing so by a mail canvass.—Harold Foote Gosnell, *Getting Out the Vote—An Experiment in the Stimulation of Voting* (Chicago: University of Chicago Press, 1927).

31. Morris Janowitz and Dwaine Marvick, *Competitive Pressure and Democratic*

efforts, including the various ways money may be employed, are intricately intermingled with each other and with other factors of presumptive effect on election results. Discerning the precise effect of particular campaign activities usually becomes extremely difficult.[32] Students of the subject agree that campaign exertions influence voting behavior to some degree, but they do not agree on the detailed character of their impact nor on their relative importance to other factors affecting voting behavior.

The uncertainties also pervade the thinking of practical politicians, as anyone who has listened to their shop talk can testify.[33] Campaign managers, lacking certain knowledge, take no chances. They assume it is best to spend the most money and to seem to spend the least.[34]

Consent (Ann Arbor: Institute of Public Administration, University of Michigan, 1956), pp. 76-83; Phillips Cutright and Peter H. Rossi, "Grass Roots Politicians and the Vote," *American Sociological Review,* 23 (1958), 171-79.

32. Statistical tools for solving problems involving multiple variables are used successfully in many fields. Their use in analyzing voting behavior is impeded by the difficulty of isolating and quantifying the factors influencing elections that are to be studied. For a "first approach" to a method of "gauging the influences on the election result and of resolving a winning combination of forces into its component parts," see Donald E. Stokes, Angus Campbell, and Warren E. Miller, "Components of Electoral Decision," *American Political Science Review,* 52 (1958), 367-87.

Norman John Powell has concluded: "The major propaganda implications of this case example appear to be these: *First,* the basic reasons impelling most people to vote as they do are determined by factors other than the verbal materials disseminated by the politician. *Second,* verbal material is useful in shifting the opinions of a slight percentage of the electorate. But such material is imperative, particularly where the election may be close, to persuade the critical few and hold the already favorably persuaded many. And elections, of course, may turn out to be close indeed. *Third,* verbal material whose content strikes effectively at the individual's fundamental concerns may result in pronounced voting shifts. *Fourth,* political organization and personal communication are likely to be most effective in influencing the individual's political behavior. *Fifth,* nondemocratic devices for achieving political victory exist because many persons are neither interested nor knowledgeable about politics. *Sixth,* the interested and competent citizen who believes in the democratic process can become significant politically—if he chooses."—*Anatomy of Public Opinion* (New York: Prentice-Hall, Inc., 1951), p. 522. See the discussion in Avery Leiserson, *Parties and Politics—An Institutional and Behavioral Approach* (New York: Alfred A. Knopf, 1958), pp. 254-69.

33. Austin Ranney and Willmoore Kendall have summarized existing beliefs among politicians on why voters do what they do and how parties can make the most of it.—*Democracy and The American Party System* (New York: Harcourt, Brace and Co., 1956), pp. 340-44. Much relevant literature is cited. Of British Parliamentary elections it was said, "it is probable that many agents have a stereotyped picture of what their pattern of expenditures ought to be and strive to conform to it, irrespective of the effectiveness of spending the money in different ways. It is possible to argue, for example, that meetings and expensively produced election addresses cost more than they are worth."—R. S. Milne and H. C. Mackenzie, *Straight Fight* (London: The Chiswick Press, 1954), p. 68.

34. Democrats have seldom lost an opportunity to try to convert their financial disadvantage into a propaganda advantage by emphasizing (and usually exag-

Charles Michelson's assessment of the 1936 presidential campaign epitomizes the practical viewpoint. He served as publicity director for the Democratic national committee in the days of Franklin Roosevelt. He concluded, "Probably the result of the election would have been just the same had neither the Democratic nor the Republican national committee functioned at all." But, nevertheless, "It was up to us to take nothing for granted."[35]

A scheme for analysis.—Not feeling confident of the effects on campaign success of activities that money buys, we are handicapped in estimating the significance of different amounts of money spent on behalf of different candidates. It is possible, nevertheless, to identify factors that bear on the outcome of elections and to note which of them are significantly related to expenditures. Figure 1 sets forth two broad categories of factors. Most of the *given conditions* of a campaign are fixed at the outset; *controllable campaign activities* require decisions during the campaign. It seems as certain as such things can be that the given conditions of the 1952 and 1956 presidential races were such that no amount or kind of campaigning by Governor Stevenson could have brought him victory. The same is true of candidates nominated by minority parties in many jurisdictions across the United States. The given conditions of campaigns include (1) the predispositions of voters, (2) the context of issues, (3) the personalities and records of the candidates, and (4) the character of the formal and informal political organizations initially at the disposal of the opponents. The controllable activities of the campaign itself include (1) organizational, (2) communications, and (3) election-day exertions. Ideally, the latter are designed to maximize the opportunities available to a candidate in his given circumstances.

The given conditions of a campaign.—On the left-hand of Figure 1 are listed the given conditions of a campaign. There are other ways to classify and subdivide the context in which a political campaign occurs, but this four-way division is sufficient for our purposes. These conditions are produced by many factors external and internal to the community holding the election. Some of the most important are ***not*** related to the direct use of funds. Thus the tenacity of diehard partisan voters finds its roots deep in historical circumstances, represented by

gerating) the disparity of funds between the two parties. In April, 1956, Speaker Rayburn whammed the tocsin in claiming for the GOP a "fifty-to-one financial advantage over our party."—*New York Times,* April 21, 1956. Senator Paul Douglas "defied the Texas oil barons to come into Illinois and spend their worst" when running for reelection in 1954, a time when not all observers were sure that the good Senator really had the light part of the purse.—Joseph Alsop in *The Asheville Citizen* (N.C.), October 9, 1954, and the *Chicago Sun-Times,* October 11, 1954.

35. Ranney and Kendall, *op. cit.*, p. 355. For an appreciation of the importance of campaign skills, see Harold F. Gosnell, *Champion Campaigner—Franklin D. Roosevelt* (New York: The Macmillan Company, 1952).

Figure 1

A PERSPECTIVE ON THE SIGNIFICANCE OF CAMPAIGN EXPENDITURES TO THE OUTCOME OF ELECTIONS

Given Conditions of a Campaign					
	Which Are Affected by				
			Non-Monetary Factors		
Type	The Volume of Expenditures by		Decisions on the Use of Money, Made by		Other Non-Monetary Factors
	Pol. Orgs.	Others	Pol. Orgs.	Others	
1. Predispositions of voters	**1**	**2**	**3**	**4**	**5**
2. Context of issues	**6**	**7**	**8**	**9**	**10**
3. Candidates—personal qualities and records	**11**	**12**	**13**	**14**	**15**
4. Political organization—formal and informal	**16**	**17**	**18**	**19**	**20**

Controllable Campaign Activities					
	Which Are Affected by				
			Non-Monetary Factors		
Type	The Volume of Expenditures by		Decisions on the Use of Money, Made by		Other Non-Monetary Factors
	Pol. Orgs.	Others	Pol. Orgs.	Others	
1. Organizational	**21**	**22**	**23**	**24**	**25**
2. Communications	**26**	**27**	**28**	**29**	**30**
3. Election Day	**31**	**32**	**33**	**34**	**35**

cell **5**. The issues facing candidates and electorate may be thrust up by war, depression, or clashes of values beyond the control of a current generation (**10**). A candidate magnificently endowed with the personal equipment of a politician cannot be manufactured at will, regardless of the funds employed (**15**). Political structures are partly reflections of other dimensions of social organization (**20**).

Other factors, however, that help to mold the given conditions of a campaign *can* be directly affected by the use of cash and other economic resources of a community. It is not necessary to specify precisely the causal relationships between expenditures and these given conditions to recognize that money spent between political campaigns has an impact on them.[36] The utility of funds in building organizational structures (**16, 17**) and grooming candidates (**11, 12**) is manifest. The predispositions of voters, the norms of social groups to which they belong, are affected in the long run by the general *climate of opinion* that prevails. Vast amounts of cash are spent each year through nonpolitical channels that condition this climate (**2**). Every communication that reaches an individual contributes to it. Motion pictures, radio, television, newspapers, magazines, books, speeches, schools, circular mailings, and ten billion dollars in advertising each year have significant bearing on the information people have, the political images they receive, the attitudes they form, and the actions they take. The American community is knit together by a host of public and private communications systems and by an even more complex mesh of interpersonal contacts. Recognized centers of opinion leadership exist through which attitudes and actions may be influenced. The information and attitudes emanating from these leadership centers help to form a climate of opinion in a community. The climate may be homogeneous or splintered, fixed or changing, but it is one of the materials with which campaigners are forced to work.

Everything that goes on in a community, be it a village or a nation, may ultimately affect the setting in which political campaigns occur. The political battlefield extends far beyond any immediate campaign—as the budgets and behavior of parties, factions, candidates, and interest groups testify. The participants are far more diverse than the candidates and their organized supporters, and the political battlefield has been broadening, doubtless in consequence of the "growing realization of the similarity of social power, regardless of its manifestations."[37] With the growth of business and government, increasing numbers of economic issues become political issues. Labor unions, public utilities, farm organizations, and multitudes of other interest groups take their cases

36. The given conditions will not usually change *during* a campaign. A candidate may die, of course, or Hungarians may rise in revolt to affect the basic issues in debate, both developments beyond the control of the partisans.

37. Alfred McClung Lee, "Power-Seekers," in Alvin W. Gouldner (ed.), *Studies in Leadership—Leadership and Democratic Action* (New York: Harper & Brothers, 1950), p. 672.

directly to the people in a variety of ways. The cases they take affect the climate in which men run for office. The United States is really in a continuous political campaign. Candidates and parties show this in every move they make. Organized social and economic interests manifest it too. The agencies of communications and community power are brought into action by whatever groups can command them.

The channels to opinion formation are so various and so numerous that appraisal of the net advantage to political contestants—parties, candidates, points of view—can only be impressionistic. Generally, the view emerges that any net partisan benefits lie with those broad and heterogeneous groups called conservatives and Republicans.[38] If this is correct, such benefits nevertheless do not guarantee election victories.[39]

Activities that shape the climate of opinion customarily lie outside the usual concept of political campaigning and the monies involved are beyond the customary definition of campaign finance. However, all the energies that seek to mold this climate affect the outcome of campaigns as certainly—which is not to say how certainly—as campaign activities themselves, and the sums of money engaged are infinitely larger.

The controllable conditions of a campaign.—Campaign activities on the right side of Figure 1 are divided into three classes: organizational, communications, and election-day operations. That the sheer volume of campaign expenditures is not necessarily decisive in the outcome of elections has already been shown. After all, men must use judgment in spending money (as represented by cells **23, 24, 28, 29, 33, 34**—and also by **3, 4, 8, 9, 13, 14, 18, 19**). They must decide what to use it for: for a larger office staff or more field agents; for a registration drive by mail or by personal contact; for more newspaper or more handbill advertising;

38. Studies of the ownership and control of mass communications and of the transmission and enforcement of community values usually lead to this conclusion. There is, however, opinion in a different vein. The attacks on philanthropic foundations during the 1950's partly stemmed from persons in disagreement with what they felt to be a consistently "leftist" drift in educational and research activities financed by the foundations. Bias has been charged in what historians teach about business. "The American historian has not done right by the American businessman" is a quotation opening a *Fortune* article on the subject by Edward N. Saveth. —"What Historians Teach about Business," 45 (April, 1952), 118ff.

In any society, it would seem that the climate of opinion will tend to reflect values that are widely shared in the community, not all of which will be compatible. Without doubt, attitudes can be and are changed by mass communication. The task of determining empirically the impact of all mass communication in the United States on attitudes relevant to political controversy and relevant to the success of parties or factions in elections would be something of an undertaking. A convenient and stimulating collection of materials on modifying attitudes and opinions will be found in Wilbur Schramm (ed.), *The Process and Effects of Mass Communication* (Urbana: University of Illinois Press, 1954), especially pp. 207-356.

39. Even if they did, some would argue that this hardly matters, because elections are a subsidiary level of controversy, at times irrelevant to the capture and exercise of real power. See C. Wright Mills, *The Power Elite* (New York: Oxford University Press, 1956), pp. 242-68.

for sending funds to this locality or to that; for a broadcast by this senator or that representative. In addition to decisions about the ***medium*** of expenditure are decisions about the *content* of the actions financed. The decision of Harry Truman in 1948 to ride his campaign on the record of the Eightieth Congress and the social and economic issues he generated from it apparently won him the election. The tables might have been turned had Governor Dewey chosen different tactics of debate.[40] The significant use of campaign cash embraces not only its volume but also how it is spent.[41]

In recent years much has been said about the increasing ability of experts in advertising and public relations to influence popular tastes and opinions.[42] It has even been contended that through what is called motivational research and the techniques of hidden persuasion the outcome of elections can be decisively influenced through skillful use of the mass media, especially television. Since the skill and the media cost money, a possibility is seen that a party or candidate could translate a financial advantage more or less directly into an electoral advantage—as once could be done in many places through election-day expenditures. No evidence is yet at hand, however, to confirm the fear that men so well understand themselves that in the context of a political campaign they can predictably control the opinions and actions of other men.[43] Moreover, as Figure 1 indicates, the judgment necessary in the use of money is only one of the "nonmonetary" elements—that is, something other than the volume of money—affecting both the given conditions of a campaign and the character and effectiveness of campaign activities. Many factors wholly unrelated to money influence the outcome of a campaign. Shrewdness in dealing with crucial state and local leaders (25), shrewdness in choice of campaign routes, and skill in campaigning (30) and in energizing voluntary workers to get out the vote (35) have

40. Angus Campbell and Robert L. Kahn, *The People Elect a President* (Ann Arbor: Survey Research Center, University of Michigan, 1952), pp. 40-53 and *passim.* The significance of another nonfinancial influence in the election is discussed by O. P. Williams in "The Commodity Credit Corporation and the 1948 Presidential Election," *Midwest Journal of Political Science,* 1 (1957), 111-24.

41. James A. Farley had this to say about the affluent Liberty League set up in the 1930's to oppose Franklin Roosevelt: "The individuals who financed it might just as well have given their very generous donations directly to further the campaign of President Roosevelt because the result would have been the same. The American people resented the idea of a league formed by organized wealth to further its own political interests. . . . The League . . . caused a reaction in his favor, and above all else its directors made a major error in assuming that volume alone is a prime factor in political publicity as it is in commercial advertising."—*Behind the Ballots—The Personal History of a Politician* (New York: Harcourt, Brace and Company, 1938), p. 295.

42. For example, see Vance Packard, *The Hidden Persuaders* (New York: David McKay Company, 1957).

43. A series of instructive essays on the state of our knowledge of mass media in political campaigning appears in Burdick and Brodbeck, *op. cit.*

effects along with other types of campaign resources, like a long patronage roll.[44]

The variable significance of money.—Figure 1 can be viewed as representing all the factors that affect the outcome of an election. The elements represented can be viewed as operating in dynamic interaction with each other to produce the results of the balloting.[45] Each of the 35 numbered cells embraces a relevant element. One of Senator Bilbo's old campaign managers in Mississippi used to say that if all other things were equal, money could win an election. But in Mississippi, as elsewhere, all other things are seldom equal, and Senator Bilbo himself was known for his reliance on personal campaign qualities. A colorful, magnetic, spellbinding, unscrupulous orator, the Senator had welded to himself over the years followers who voted and worked for him regardless of the formal paraphernalia of campaign organization. His screams from the stump would be printed throughout his state without benefit of paid advertisements. Senator Bilbo depended on nonmonetary factors for success, more so than most of his contemporaries. The pull on the voters he exerted through the influences symbolized in cells **5**, **10**, **15** and **30** reduced greatly the importance of exertions symbolized, for example, by cells **21**, **26**, and **31**.

Another type of election will illustrate a different combination of factors that can prove decisive. In some states referenda are held. The issues are often novel to the voters and do not divide them along party or factional lines. The parties, in fact, may not become engaged at all. A referendum may become a contest between *ad hoc* combinations of fervent amateurs and miscellaneous oldsters. Under such circumstances the given conditions of a campaign probably exert less control on the outcome than in elections between party candidates for public office. Expenditures for organizational and communications purposes (22, 27) may thus more clearly determine the success of the campaign.[46] Even in these circumstances volume of expenditures is not enough. Money can

44. Any political campaign provides illustrations of the significance of nonmonetary factors to election results. Jack Redding supplies a volume of them from *Inside the Democratic Party* (New York: The Bobbs-Merrill Company, Inc., 1958). See especially pp. 46, 84, 115, 182, 227, 246-50, 258-59, 262.

45. No effort is made here to spell out every relevant factor, though it is thought all can be brought within the categories presented. For example, suffrage regulations and practices obviously bear on the outcome of elections. They can be viewed as falling under "predispositions of voters," for the predispositions depend on who the voters are.

46. Apparently in the numerous referenda held in California the side reporting the highest expenditures usually wins.—Winston W. Crouch, *The Initiative and Referendum in California* (Los Angeles: The Haynes Foundation, 1950), p. 32. When an issue is repeatedly submitted to the electorate over a period of years, opinion might be expected to crystallize, thus reducing its malleability by well financed propaganda campaigns. Relevant here is Joseph T. Klapper's discussion of "What We Know About the Effects of Mass Communication: The Brink of Hope," *Public Opinion Quarterly,* 21 (1957), 453-74.

be used efficaciously or it can be wasted. What goes on in our cells 23-24 and 28-29 may become decisive.

Every election is different. The significance of money will differ in each. In closely balanced contests—for example, the presidential elections between 1876 and 1896—a tiny shift in *any* factor of campaign effectiveness can affect the outcome.[47] The keen comment on a critical issue, the muddiness of roads to the polls, the absence of money in a key ward can prove decisive. But the situation is like a legislative vote carried by a margin of one. Sooner or later everybody on the winning side claims that *his* was the decisive vote. Actually, all of the individual voters acting together were decisive, and all campaign exertions that help victory constitute in combination the winning margin.

4. ESSENTIAL COSTS AND THE CHOICE OF CANDIDATES

Seldom will nonfinancial elements of campaigning free a candidate from financial needs to the extent enjoyed by Senator Bilbo. This is especially unlikely when organized parties are opposing each other. Regardless of the fluctuating significance of financial and nonfinancial elements from one campaign to another, in virtually all campaigns a basic amount of organizational work, communication through commercial media, and getting-out-the-vote must be accomplished if the candidate expects to compete seriously. These things require money. Unless money to meet these minimum, essential expenses is available—regardless of how large or small the amount—contestants lacking it will be decisively handicapped. Many factors determine the sums required for conducting competitive elections under the diverse conditions prevailing in the United States, and we shall later be concerned with what they are.[48]

Despite a general financial inferiority, it cannot be argued convincingly that the Democratic party has lost a single presidential election in the twentieth century for want of funds.[49] If the facts could be known, the

47. Samuel Lubell notes that the election returns during this general period "reveal an almost unbelievable rigidity in party allegiances. Who won the Presidency was settled from one election to the next by the shifting of a finger count of states, chiefly Indiana, New York and Connecticut." Within states, he found counties unwaveringly loyal.—*Revolt of the Moderates* (New York: Harper and Brothers, 1956), p. 225. Party managers were acutely aware that for the want of a nail the kingdom might be lost. They shovelled money into doubtful areas in a mood of panic exceeding anything seen in the later days of a more nationalized, mass communications politics.

48. See pages 380-87, below.

49. Every Democratic chairman, treasurer, and finance chairman has his tales of dead-heat races against financial deadlines. In October, 1956, a Democratic closed-circuit television program, planned to hook up dinners in thirty cities, was nearly cancelled because the party could not make full payment in advance ($150,000 to $175,000) to Theatre Network Television, Inc., which had been retained to handle arrangements. At the last second, Sheraton Closed Circuit Television, Inc., granted the credit and took over.—*New York Times,* October 21, 1956. Some days later the Columbia Broadcasting System announced that it had

number of candidates at lower political levels whose defeat could be ascribed simply to a shortage of funds would probably be comparatively few. There are other consequences, however, of the need to meet minimum essential campaign costs. The need to do so, for example, takes heavy toll of the energies of party leadership, doubtless with an adverse effect on other campaign operations. Democratic leadership especially during a national election moves from one financial crisis to another, crises that divert the attention of even the top managers—especially of the top managers—from the serious business of debate, tactics, and action.

The necessity for obtaining essential election funds has its most profound importance in the choosing of candidates. The monies can usually be assured, and often can be withheld, by the relatively small corps of political specialists whose job it is to raise money. If a prospective candidate cannot get assurances of the support necessary to meet the basic costs of a campaign, he may as well abandon hope of winning. If the assurances are not forthcoming, his party or faction will take note. As a consequence, money probably has its greatest impact on the choice of public officials in the shadow land of our politics where it is decided who will be a candidate for a party's nomination and who will not. There are many things that make an effective candidate, but here is a choke point in our politics where vital fiscal encouragement can be extended or withheld. This influence of important fund-raisers and of large contributors is more persuasive with newcomers than with demonstrated vote-getters, more controlling with challengers than with champions. But the incumbent of even such an important office as United States senator has bowed before the prospects of a lean campaign chest. The effect of money in politics is probably more certain in determining who the candidates will be than in determining the outcome of elections.[50]

---

dropped a five-minute TV election plug because the Democrats failed to pay in advance.—*Ibid.*, October 27, 1956.

50. Money in the nominating process is treated in Chapter 12, pages 318-43, below. Steps to assist contestants to meet basic campaign needs probably offer the most feasible ways of improving campaign financing. What might be done is discussed in Chapter 16, pages 429-71, below.

3

A FORM OF POLITICAL ACTION

NO LESS AN AUTHORITY than George E. Allen has concluded that the whole subject of influence in government "has largely escaped the understanding of journalists and scholars alike." Mr. Allen, a wag who has been around enough to write a book called *Presidents Who Have Known Me,* says the trouble is they don't know what Washington juice is made of. Juice, out west where the term is used, is what you have when you get a traffic ticket fixed. In Washington, most men in the federal government want power, and that comes in the last analysis from votes. People who think that many of them are corruptible for lesser stakes do not know what it is all about. "They will sometimes go along with policies they don't believe in personally for votes but almost never for any other kind of gain. Some consider this corruption; others call it response to the will of the people and therefore democracy in action."[1]

Political influence, or pressure, is not better understood in the United States for reasons that run deep in the nation's history. The chief of the difficulties is not the empirical task of learning what goes on. To be sure, on such matters men are reticent, but a substantial documentation exists of attempts to influence the legislative, executive, and judicial branches of American government at all levels. The greater difficulties lie in recognizing distinctions among different kinds of pressure operating in government and in evaluating these pressures in the light of what we want politicians in a democracy to do.

The job of evaluation and interpretation is especially perplexing because our expectations of elected representatives are in conflict. The classic debate between the advocates of virtual and direct representation has never been resolved. Some Americans hold with Sir Edmund Burke that a legislator's first responsibility is to represent the whole nation. He should give second place to his constituents' special claims. Another viewpoint imposes on an elected official the explicit duty of

1. (New York: Simon and Schuster, 1950), p. 217-19. The book begins: "Mine has been the kind of life that attracts autobiographers, but not biographers."

representing the views of those who choose him. Americans generally handle the conflict by professing allegiance to Sir Edmund's goal but expecting an official to ignore it when their personal parochial interests are involved. Any elected officeholder is hard put to satisfy these contradictory images of how he should behave.

Differing attitudes toward the propriety of campaign contributions is another cause of confusion. The impossibility of conducting popular elections without money can hardly be denied. There is, nevertheless, a robust skepticism of the motives behind any donation to a political cause. Many lurid episodes stud the political history of the United States in which campaign monies have served as bribes by which special interests bought special privileges from politicians. Corruption in municipal politics in the last half of the nineteenth century especially cast a pall of suspicion over campaign donations and expenses. In time, circumstances changed. Gross forms of corruption subsided. Measures such as the secret ballot and legal prohibitions against bribery became reasonably effective, but the cynicism lingered.

Moreover, Americans often cherish false illusions concerning the nature of popular election campaigns. These illusions originate partly in an oversimplified view of man as a rational animal. They also stem to some extent from an understandable omission by the men who wrote and first put into practice the American Constitution. The forefathers did not prepare for the conditions that resulted as the nation and the suffrage grew. Ever-increasing numbers of voters, scattered in diverse groups across a vast geography, called for tactics of campaign organization and persuasion for which neither electoral institutions nor public attitudes were prepared. The cacophonous turmoil of modern political campaigning does not conform to the concept of rational political debate we have inherited as ideal for democratic government (although it has its own rationale and functional utility, as we shall later discuss). Much of the turmoil involves the use of money, giving the impression that money is a cause, whereas it is really a symptom, of the condition.

The American system of elections is a remarkably successful instrument of self-government. The naïve cynicism toward it and democratic government in general that often prevails obstructs full appreciation of its achievements. This naïve cynicism also colors the popular view of campaign finance, rendering it universally and automatically suspect. The understanding of campaign gifts will be improved if they are conceived as only one of several forms of political action in which people may engage, any of which may become a source of influence in government. To understand this form of political behavior we must ask what kinds of people give, how many give, what they give, to whom they give, and under what circumstances they give. We must also examine the impact of their gifts on the functioning of government—their part in the juice of politics.

1. THE POLITICAL INVOLVEMENT OF CONTRIBUTORS

Political contributing is but one form of participation in politics. It is but one type of political activity that may affect the outcome of elections and thereby open to the person undertaking it a special possibility for influence in government. Yet campaign giving has usually in the past been excluded from the forms of political action extolled as civic virtues. Public officials may listen attentively to large financial contributors. They also listen attentively to ward leaders, to campaign managers, to confidential advisers, and to those who contribute in other ways to their political success, a fact likely to be ignored.

Persons who contribute money, in fact, are often otherwise involved also in the political process. The campaign donor is frequently stereotyped as a moneybags who sits on the sidelines giving nothing of himself but his money. The picture is accurate for limited types of contributors. Compared with persons who do not give, however, contributors are often highly active politically. Their contributing is added to other forms of political involvement. It becomes difficult to attribute whatever political stature they enjoy solely to their role as contributor.

A case study of one state.—These observations rest on limited foundations of systematic evidence. Campaign contributors have seldom been studied, and until recently perhaps not at all, to learn the extent of their total involvement in politics. The efforts before us are acknowledgedly limited, but they afford some plausible inferences.

Lester W. Milbrath interviewed 98 persons who made contributions to certain state campaign committees in North Carolina during the 1952 general election. These persons made up four samples whose names were drawn at random from contributors listed on official reports: 25 from those reported as giving $100 or more to the Democratic party; 25 from those reported as giving less than $100 to that party; 23 from those reported as giving $100 or more to the Republican party; and 25 from those reported as giving less than $100 to that party. In addition, Milbrath interviewed 52 noncontributors, four groups of 13 each. These were chosen at random from the residential neighborhood of every alternate contributor interviewed. Extensive questionnaires were answered by each of the 150 persons.[2]

The general conclusion was clear: for the samples in question, contributors were significantly more active in their party in all ways studied

2. "The Motivations and Characteristics of Political Contributors: North Carolina General Election 1952" (Ph.D. dissertation, University of North Carolina, 1956). Milbrath drew his Democratic samples from the official report of the Democratic state executive committee. The comparable Republican campaign in North Carolina was carried on through two groups, the Republican state executive committee and the state Citizens for Eisenhower-Nixon. The Republican samples were drawn from their reports.

By choosing the noncontributors from the residential neighborhoods of contributors, it was hoped to minimize variations in social and economic status when comparing other characteristics of contributors and noncontributors.

than were noncontributors.[3] This was true for particular items of behavior like voting, working in a campaign, holding party office. It was evident also in the way the groups of contributors and noncontributors were distributed along a composite political participation scale.[4] A rating of 10 on the scale would represent maximum involvement in the political activities studied by all persons in the group; a rating of zero would indicate no activity at all of the types studied by any person in the group. Here is the average score for the persons in each group:

25 High Democratic Contributors	8.20
23 High Republican Contributors	5.20
25 Low Republican Contributors	5.20
26 High Noncontributors[5]	2.65
25 Low Democratic Contributors	2.24
26 Low Noncontributors[5]	1.70

Both groups of High Contributors rank substantially higher than the High Noncontributors. Both groups of Low Contributors were more active than the Low Noncontributors. The state government of North Carolina lies securely in the hands of the Democratic party. This fact gives tangible purpose to Democratic political activity. High Democratic Contributors tended especially to be deeply involved in political

3. *Ibid.*, p. 222.

4. Ten kinds of political participation made up the PPS scale: (1) voting in at least three of the last five elections; (2) deliberately contacting a politician, usually by writing to him; (3) attending one or more party meetings; (4) giving five or more hours to a political campaign; (5) identifying oneself as an active party member, in contrast to only voting with a party and never actively supporting its cause; (6) attending a political caucus; (7) being consulted on policy by public officials and political leaders at least once a year; (8) soliciting political funds from others; (9) holding some public office, appointive or elective; and (10) holding some party office. These items "scaled" readily, the notion being that generally a person who displayed one type of behavior (attending a party caucus, for example) is pretty likely to have engaged also in the other behaviors ranking lower on the list, items (1) through (5) in this case.—*Ibid.*, p. 229.

The procedure rests on the assumption that there was in operation a single participation variable, active in different persons to different degrees. One score could consequently be used to indicate the depth of the involvement in political activity of a respondent in comparison with others in the sample. The 10 items of behavior scaled by Guttman's technique, showing a coefficient of reproducibility of .942 and a Jackson plus percentage ratio of .7359, both well above the suggested minimum for the acceptance of the hypothesis of scalability.—*Ibid.*, pp. 67, 228, citing Louis Guttman, "The Basis for Scalogram Analysis," in Samuel Stouffer, *et. al., Measurement and Prediction* (Princeton: Princeton University Press, 1950), vol. 4 of *Studies in Social Psychology in World War II*, pp. 60-90; and Angus Campbell, Gerald Gurin, and Warren Miller, *The Voter Decides* (Evanston: Row, Peterson and Company, 1954), p. 189. Milbrath threw together behaviors 4 and 5, 6 through 8, and 9 and 10, leaving him with seven fairly clearcut ranks (including 0), by one of which each of the 150 respondents was classified.—*Op. cit.*, p. 230.

5. Referring to Noncontributors living in the residential neighborhoods of High Contributors and Low Contributors, respectively.

life: for example, seven of the 25 gave more than 200 hours each to a single political campaign.[6]

The data underlying the rankings point to two types of contributors whose political involvement tends to be circumscribed. Both High and Low Republican Contributors were on the average quite active. The Highs ranked no higher, however, because nine of the 23 had done no more than contribute, vote, and express their views to a politician. They fit the stereotype of the sidelines contributor. They reside in great numbers in other states, like New York, where there is a thick layer of wealthy prospects, solicited by both parties, many of whom find it easier to give money than time to politics.[7] The Low Democratic Contributors ranked low because 24 of the 25 in the sample were state employees who gave in response to gentle hint and long custom but were for the most part otherwise politically inert. They were, nevertheless, more active than their counterparts among the Noncontributors.[8]

The nation.—Answers to questions asked by the Survey Research Center of the University of Michigan in its 1952 and 1956 presidential-election studies support the principal North Carolina finding: those who make political gifts are significantly more active politically than those who do not.

Four per cent in 1952 and 10 per cent in 1956 of the nationwide sample interviewed responded affirmatively when asked: "Did you give any money or buy tickets or anything to help the campaign for one of the parties or candidates?"[9] The incidence of contributing rose markedly with regularity in voting. The following percentages of the persons in each category said they had given:

Persons Who Vote	*Percentage* 1952	1956
Never	1.0	2.3
Some of time	2.0	4.2
Most of time	3.7	10.1
Regularly	6.4	14.8

6. Here and subsequently it will prove desirable to refer separately to Milbrath's samples with the following symbols: HDC for High Democratic Contributors; HRC for High Republican Contributors; LDC for Low Democratic Contributors; LRC for Low Republican Contributors; HNC for Noncontributors selected from residential neighborhoods of High Contributors; and LNC for Noncontributors selected from residential neighborhoods of Low Contributors. The percentage of each sample that had never been active in a political campaign was: HDC, 16; HRC, 48; LDC, 76; LRC, 40.

7. Herbert E. Alexander presents evidence on the political activities of large contributors in "The Role of the Volunteer Political Fund Raiser: A Case Study in New York in 1952" (Ph.D. dissertation, Yale University, 1958), pp. 80-107.

8. For Milbrath's general discussion of these matters, see *op. cit.*, pp. 201-44. Milbrath's respondents were contributors to the regular Democratic organization. Many Democrats gave small amounts through other channels, e.g., the Ruml $5.00 certificates.

9. Campbell, *et. al.*, *op. cit.*, p. 30, for 1952. Mr. Campbell and the Center made available unpublished data for both 1952 and 1956.

Similarly, persons who had taken part in other types of political activity included a larger proportion of givers than did the whole sample:

Persons Who	*Percentage Making Contributions*	
	1952	*1956*
Attended political meetings	25.4	45.2
Worked in campaign	31.0	50.0
Belonged to a political organization	31.0	50.0

These scraps of evidence suggest that political giving should be viewed as one component of a general dimension of political involvement and should be conceived as such in assessing its significance as a source of political influence.

2. 8,000,000 GIVERS

The proportion of the population making campaign contributions has been rising sharply. The available evidence points both to a recent upward spurt and to a long-term trend.

The national surveys.—It has never been possible in the United States to trace detailed fluctuations from year to year and place to place in the level of contributing. The data of the subject are too crude. They do, however, permit gross estimates of the number of contributors and sometimes of the relative importance of gifts of various sizes.

The Survey Research Center's studies provide the best basis for estimating the total number of political givers in the country. Probably over eight million different persons gave money or bought something of value in aid of a party or candidate in the general elections of 1956, an increase from over three million in 1952.[10] In both years the num-

10. Only the report on the Center's 1952 study is in print at the time this is being written. See Campbell, *et. al., op. cit.* The same principles were used in both years to infer from the Center's data the number of contributors. In 1952, 4 per cent of the total sample (1,614 cases) said they had made a financial contribution as indicated.—p. 30. (In 1956 the percentage was 10.) The number of people of voting age in 1952 was given as 98.5 million. The survey was designed to represent a universe that was probably five to 10 million less than this. Four per cent of the sample would then represent between 3.5 and 3.7 million persons. The cautious estimate of 3.0 million is used, however, because of a discrepancy between the percentage of persons in the sample who said they voted and the percentage of people of voting age who actually voted. This suggests that a few persons may have said they voted (and may also have said they contributed) when actually they did not. If 91 million is taken as the size of the survey universe (98.5 minus 7.5), and 74 per cent of them voted, as they claimed, the total vote would have been 67.3 million, compared with 61.6 million who actually voted for president (there may have been others who voted, but not for president). The larger of these figures is about 9 per cent greater than the smaller. If an error of this size appeared in the responses to the question about contributions, the number actually contributing in 1952 would still have been around 3.3 million. It is not suggested here that an error of these proportions actually occurred in the survey's data on voter turnout. (See *ibid.*, pp. 47.) The difficulty may stem from an overestimate in census figures of the size of the eligible voting population.

ber of separate contributions would have been greater because some persons give more than once. The number of persons giving during the full calendar year would also have run higher. The Center's question pertained to the general-election campaign, and some persons doubtless gave only in connection with nominations and other campaigns earlier in the year.

The upward jump in 1956 at first appears puzzling. The startling increase in contributing was not matched by increases in other types of political activity. Here are the percentages of respondents who said they did certain things in each of the years:

Activity	*1952*	*1956*
Voted	74	73
Attended political meetings	7	7
Worked in campaign	3	3
Belonged to a political organization	2	3
Conversed on behalf of a party or candidate	27	28
Contributed	4	10

No reason is apparent why the responses to the Center's question about political giving should be less reliable than responses about other forms of political action. The explanation for this evident change in political behavior between 1952 and 1956 must be sought elsewhere.

Two developments have taken place that may well have bearing. Public discussion of the subject mounted noticeably both before and after 1952.[11] In speeches, legislative hearings, and other public forums persons desiring to change existing conditions advocated measures to increase popular participation in campaign finance. Contributing was frequently urged as a virtuous political act, the responsibility of all citizens desiring a healthy politics. In 1955 Minnesota adopted a statute permitting taxpayers to deduct certain political contributions and expenditures in computing state income taxes. This official approbation of the propriety of small and modest campaign gifts symbolized an increasing respectability of political giving across the whole country. By 1956 attitudes were such that the Advertising Council of America stood ready to undertake a nationwide public service advertising campaign to encourage bipartisan fund-raising. Nothing came of it that year because of difficulties between the two parties. Two years later, however, the American Heritage Foundation expanded its customary registration and voting drives to include contributing. In collaboration with the Advertising Council and the national committees of both parties the call went out for all good citizens to give to the party of their choice.

11. Only eight references appeared under "Campaign funds" in the *Readers' Guide to Periodical Literature* during the four years between December, 1944, and November, 1948. The number rose to 42 in the next four-year period, 1948-1952, and to 73 between December, 1952, and November, 1956.

The impact of all this on the receptivity of citizens to political solicitations is hard to demonstrate. The Gallup Polls revealed only a slight rise in the expressed willingness of people to make $5.00 contributions.[12] Campaign leaders in both parties, however, stated that concerted efforts had been made to broaden the base of givers in 1956.[13] These were no novel assertions, but the Survey Research Center's data supported both claims.

Three per cent of Stevenson's supporters made contributions in 1952 and 12 per cent did so in 1956. The rise among Eisenhower supporters was from 5 to 9 per cent. Among those who claimed they had given, about 64 per cent favored Eisenhower in 1952, compared with about 55 per cent in 1956. By these calculations, 1,900,000 of the 3,000,000 givers in the former year voted for Ike (or, if they did not vote, preferred him to Stevenson),[14] whereas around 4,400,000 of the 8,000,000 in the latter year did so.

Personal solicitation is the most effective way to raise money. Respondents were not asked whether they had been solicited for money, but they were asked whether a party representative had called them up or come around to see them during the campaign. The percentage saying one or both parties had been in touch with them in this way jumped from 12 to 18 between the two elections. In the two years, respectively, about 11 and 19 per cent of those contacted contributed, in contrast to about 3 and 8 per cent of those not contacted. In 1952, 55 per cent of those contacted were approached by someone from the Democratic party and

12. In 1948, 1952, and 1956 this question was put in nationwide polls: "If you were asked, would you contribute $5 to the campaign fund of the political party you prefer?" The percentage of affirmative answers rose from 29 to 34 and then to 35. Between 1952 and 1956 the percentage of negative responses fell from 54 to 50, while those having no opinion went from 12 to 15.—Releases of July 27, 1952, and September 12, 1956.

13. Gore Committee *Hearings,* part 2, pp. 395-400; U.S. House of Representatives Special Committee to Investigate Campaign Expenditures, 1956, *Hearings* (Washington: Government Printing Office, 1957), pp. 79-80, 83.

14. Derived from Campbell, *et. al., op. cit.,* p. 30. Of all persons who contributed in 1952, about 64 per cent preferred Eisenhower and 36 per cent Stevenson. This does not necessarily mean, however, that 64 per cent of the contributors gave to Republican recipients and 36 per cent to Democrats. More than 27 per cent of people who called themselves Democrats preferred Ike for president, and they may well have given to state and local Democratic causes as well as, or instead of, giving in aid of Eisenhower. On the other hand, less than 6 per cent of those who called themselves Republicans preferred Stevenson, and the number of them making Republican donations would presumably be much less.—Derived from *ibid.,* pp. 93, 109. In predominantly Democratic North Carolina, Milbrath found that among his 48 Republican contributors, there were 12 who identified themselves as Democrats, and 14 others who thought of themselves as Democrats locally and Republicans nationally. Among 50 Democratic contributors, there was only one person who identified himself as a Republican.—*Op. cit.,* p. 212. In other parts of the nation this situation may have been reversed.

in 1956 the figure rose to 63 per cent.[15] On the other hand, the percentage approached by Republicans fell from 63 to 61.[16] These hints of evidence support the hypotheses that a rise in the rate of contributing has actually occurred, that increased party contact with the mass of citizens is one explanation (the increased contacts presumably including increased solicitations), and that these things took place in a climate increasingly receptive to the idea of political contributing.[17]

Other evidence.—We have assumed for so long that campaign giving is confined to the few that estimates numbering contributors in the millions arouse suspicion. Data pieced together from other sources, nevertheless, lend credibility to them.

In 1950, 7 per cent of 8,000 respondents in a national cross-section sample recalled having made one or more contributions to a candidate or party during the previous four years.[18] There is no inconsistency between this result and the 4 per cent of respondents who reported making a gift during one campaign two years later. A Gallup Poll estimated that 2,700,000 families made campaign gifts during the mid-term election year 1954,[19] not far from the cautious 3,000,000 estimate for the presidential year 1952. Carlton G. Ketchum, long-time finance director of the Republican national finance committee, is probably the technically best informed person on Republican fund-raising. He judged that close to 2,300,000 persons gave to the Republican party in 1952.[20] Given the

15. Contributions among members of labor unions rose slightly more than among others between the two years, presumably accounting in part for the Democratic improvement.

16. The Gallup Polls reported that the percentage of "Democrats" saying they were willing to give $5.00 to their party if asked went from 28 to 34 between 1952 and 1956, while the corresponding "Republican" percentage fell from 44 to 38.—Releases of July 27, 1952, and September 12, 1956.

17. Perhaps relevant is the fact that among female respondents the percentage who reported making contributions rose from around 3 to 9 per cent between 1952 and 1956; the increase among males was from 6 to 11. The increases were roughly equal among the geographic regions except for the Far West where the proportion of people in the sample who contributed declined. The percentage of the people in each of the following income groups who said they gave something to politics was:

Annual Family Income	*1952*	*1956*
Less than $3,000	2	2
$3,000-$4,999	3	6
$5,000-$7,499	7	12
$7,500-$9,999	14	17
$10,000 and over	17	31

The number of cases in the income categories was often small.

18. Julian L. Woodward and Elmo Roper, "Political Activity of American Citizens," *American Political Science Review,* 44 (1950), 874.

19. Release of March 4, 1955. This was 6 per cent of the nation's 48,000,000 families.

20. Letter to author dated July 29, 1959. See also Gore Committee *Hearings,* part 2, pp. 446-47.

possibility that Mr. Ketchum's partially impressionistic estimate may have been high,[21] this does not seem far from the 1,900,000 givers who were calculated from the Survey Research Center's data to have favored Eisenhower that year.[22]

Political committees sometimes submit reports showing the number of contributions of all sizes they claim to have received. In 1952, for example, the Republican national committee reported more than 17,500 gifts of all sizes and the national Citizens for Eisenhower-Nixon listed more than 20,000. The chairman of the Democratic national committee

Table 1

THE NUMBER OF REPORTED GIFTS TO SELECTED POLITICAL COMMITTEES, 1952

Type of Committee	No. of Committees for which Data Were Available	No. of Contributions Reported—All Sizes
Statewide—Republican		
Regular	20	96,561
Finance	5	50,204
Volunteer, for president	12	4,051
Volunteer, for senator	12	4,439
Volunteer, for governor	4	927
Nomination, for senator	7	1,662
Nomination, for governor	4	1,164
Statewide—Democratic		
Regular	19	38,277
Volunteer, for president	16	32,964
Volunteer, for senator	20	6,107
Volunteer, for governor	2	1,336
Nomination, for senator	7	1,667
Nomination, for governor	5	17,249
Countywide—Republican		
Regular	32	12,651
Finance	5	27,844
Volunteer, for president	51	5,078
Countywide—Democratic		
Regular	20	13,687
Finance	2	1,078
Volunteer, for president	20	13,301
Sub-county—Republican		
Miscellaneous	24	5,039
Sub-county—Democratic		
Miscellaneous	15	412
Totals	302	335,698

21. It would seem especially easy to overlook a distinction between contributors and contributions, the latter of course outnumbering the former.

22. Although not all who favored Ike necessarily gave to Republican causes. See footnote 14 on page 43, above.

claimed 126,000 contributions.[23] The number of individual contributors is not as great as the number of contributions listed on reports of this kind, because some persons give more than once, but other characteristics of the reports often result in their reflecting fewer contributions than were actually received. Contributions often show up under the name of a single individual or organization that collected them, rather than in the names of the persons who gave. Campaign reports submitted by some 3,500 political committees at all levels of government during 1952 were studied. Most of the committees were not required to indicate the total number of contributions received.[24] Some did, however, and the results for 302 of them accounting for more than a third of a million contributions made at state and local levels are shown in Table 1. The reports studied were chosen for their apparent completeness. They are not a sample in any sense, and comparisons between the parties and types of committees cannot be made. Yet the data in the table are not manifestly out of line with a total of 3,000,000 contributors estimated as giving to the many thousands of committees and candidates active across the country in 1952.

Some support can also be found for the 1956 estimate. Nine per cent of the respondents in a Gallup Poll said they gave money in 1956, and 9 per cent of a sample interviewed in the Detroit area said they made a campaign gift in 1956.[25] These percentages are close to the 10 per cent of the Survey Research Center's 1956 national sample that reported doing so. As discussed in a later chapter, the number of contributors associated with labor unions according to the Center's 1956 survey conforms to an estimate derived from other sources.[26] A private poll conducted after the 1958 elections found 6 per cent of those interviewed saying they had given in that mid-term year.

The upward trend.—Over the last century as well as more recently the share of the population that gives to politics has been growing. Trends in the number of contributions cannot be traced satisfactorily through political committee reports.[27] Reflections on the sources of

23. Presumably including his estimate of the sale of the Ruml $5.00 certificates. —U.S. House of Representatives Special Committee to Investigate Campaign Expenditures, 1952, *Hearings,* p. 157.

24. Statutes generally require that only contributions above a certain size be itemized. For various reasons committees sometimes list all their contributors, which opens the opportunity for a tedious chore of counting by those so inclined.

25. Unpublished data from Gallup Poll Survey #575, available in the Roper Public Opinion Research Center, Williams College, Williamstown, Massachusetts, and from the Detroit Area Study, 1956, conducted by Samuel J. Eldersveld and Daniel Katz, University of Michigan.

26. See pages 191-94, below.

27. Reporting practices vary importantly. One of the largest Republican finance committees used to accompany its transfers of funds to the national committee with voluminous lists of individuals in whose names the contributions were to be reported. The practice was subsequently abandoned, the money thereafter being reported simply as a single committee transfer. The state of political accounting

campaign money, however, lead to the inference that the proportion of the population that gives money to politics increased substantially between the nineteenth century and the middle of the twentieth. One gathers from the history books that insofar as mass giving was concerned it was to be found chiefly in political assessments levied on public employees. Legions of officeholders under various degrees of duress gave for the enrichment of party coffers.[28] Even, however, if all government employees had been solicited, which they were not, and all those solicited had given something, which they did not, the number would have constituted a substantially smaller part of the population than did contributors in 1952 and 1956. Knowledge of the number of persons employed in government during most of the nineteenth century is scanty. The best guess at the total number of government employees at all levels in 1900 seems to be not much over 1,000,000.[29] About 235,000 were in the federal executive service.[30] The population in 1900 was 75,000,000, less than half what it was in the 1950's. Contributions by all public employees would not have amounted to as large a segment of the population as gave in the latter period.

---

generally does not encourage comparative analysis. There is a flavor of change, however, in bits of information that pop up. In 1904 there appear to have been around 590 contributions to the Republican national committee while by 1928 the number was reported as 143,749. The Democratic figure in 1904 seems to have been of the same order as the Republican, and by 1928 it rested at 90,546.—Louise Overacker, *Money in Elections* (New York: The Macmillan Company, 1932), pp. 132-35. A contemporary, however, reports 105,000 contributors to the Democratic national committee in 1908.—Perry Belmont, *An American Democrat—The Recollections of Perry Belmont* (New York: Columbia University Press, 1940), p. 475. The reported totals fell off sharply after 1928. For 1932-44, see Professor Overacker's quadrennial articles in the *American Political Science Review*, appearing the year after each presidential election. The Democratic national committee received 9,470 contributions in 1948 and 26,202 in 1952 (presumably excluding the Ruml $5.00 certificates), according to Chairman Paul M. Butler.—Gore Committee *Hearings*, part 2, p. 396. (See footnote 23 on page 46, above.) The Republican national committee received around 14,000 in 1948. In 1952 the figure was 17,517 and in 1956, 12,113, neither truly meaningful, however, because of the extensive solicitation programs at state and local levels by which money for the national level is raised and then transmitted in lump sums. Adequate data are not available for comparisons of contributions to state and local committees over the years.

28. See, for example, Harry J. Carman and Reinhard H. Luthin, *Lincoln and the Patronage* (New York: Columbia University Press, 1943), pp. 288-95; Frank H. Heck, *The Civil War Veteran in Minnesota Life and Politics* (Oxford, Ohio: The Mississippi Valley Press, 1941), p. 128; and Matthew Josephson, *The Politicos 1865-1896* (New York: Harcourt, Brace and Company, 1938), pp. 35, 61, 221-22; also the references cited on pages 145-46, below.

29. 1,100,000 including public education.—Solomon Fabricant, *The Trend of Government Activity in the United States since 1900* (New York: National Bureau of Economic Research, Inc., 1952), pp. 168-70.

30. Leonard D. White, *Trends in Public Administration* (New York: McGraw-Hill Book Co., Inc., 1933), p. 243. The figure is for 1901. Fabricant, *op. cit.*, p. 176, shows 215,000 different individuals (89,000 full-time equivalents) working for the Post Office Department in 1900.

3. MULTIPLE VOTING

A deeply cherished slogan of American democracy is "one man—one vote." It rallied defenders of a pure ballot in days when gangs of repeaters were herded on election day from polling place to polling place to vote more than once. It still symbolizes the egalitarian spirit of political democracy.

By their talents and energies, some men have always taken greater part in government than others and thus, in a way, cast more than one vote. Concern over the private financing of political campaigns stems in significant measure from the belief that a gift is an especially important kind of vote. It is grounded in the thought that persons who give in

Table 2

THE RELATIVE IMPORTANCE OF SMALL AND LARGE POLITICAL GIFTS TO NATIONAL-LEVEL COMMITTEES OF THE MAJOR PARTIES, 1948, 1952, AND 1956

Committees	Percentage of Receipts from Individuals Given in these Sums								
	1948			1952			1956		
	Under $100	$100-$499	$500 and over	Under $100	$100-$499	$500 and over	Under $100	$100-$499	$500 and over
Republican									
National	12	21	67	13	27	60	13	18	69
Senatorial	1	3	96	1	7	92	1	6	93
Congressional	1	7	92	2	10	88	2	11	87
Citizens for Eisenhower	—	—	—	12	18	70	12	18	70
Miscellaneous[a]	16	51	33	29	24	47	22	15	63
All	9	17	74	12	20	68	10	16	74
Receipts from Individuals	$2,074,942			$4,328,536			$3,837,337		
Total Receipts	3,508,607			7,994,294			9,258,771		
Democratic									
National	10	21	69	18	24	58	43	23	34
Senatorial	2	9	89	2	9	89	3	16	81
Congressional[b]	23	17	60	1	2	97	1	6	93
Headquarters[c]	—	—	—	18	14	68	42	11	47
Volunteers for Stevenson	—	—	—	24	14	62	48	14	38
Stevenson-Sparkman Forum	—	—	—	21	4	75	—	—	—
Miscellaneous[d]	9	34	57	9	21	70	5	41	54
All	10	21	69	19	18	63	38	18	44
Receipts from Individuals	$1,565,989			$3,466,174			$2,507,629		
Total Receipts	2,136,298			4,436,844			5,030,431		

[a] 3 committees in 1948, 14 in 1952, 7 in 1956.
[b] Democratic Congressional Campaign Committee and Democratic National Congressional Committee combined.
[c] For 1952, the 1952 Campaign Headquarters and Travel Committee, Springfield, Illinois; for 1956, the Stevenson-Kefauver Campaign Committee.
[d] 4 committees in 1948, 8 in 1952, 5 in 1956.

larger sums or to more candidates than their fellow citizens are in effect voting more than once.

Large gifts—how significant?—Estimates for 1952 indicate that at least one-quarter of the total cash election bill for the United States—$140,000,000 for all offices at all levels—was met by contributions of $500 or more, and that at least another one-fourth was met by gifts between $100 and $499. No less than one-half of the total value of political contributions in that year consequently came in amounts of over $100.

It has long been realized that the bulk of the income received by formally organized *national-level* campaign groups from individual contributors has arrived in sums of $500 or more. For some years before 1956, the proportion generally ran around two-thirds for both parties, while about one-fifth additional came in sums of $100 up to $499. The details for regular and volunteer campaign groups active at the national level in 1948, 1952, and 1956 are laid out in Table 2.[31]

At lower political levels, however, the significance of $500-and-over gifts compared to those of $100-499 falls abruptly. Information corresponding to that for the national level has not previously been available for state and local political activities, where around six-sevenths of political expenditures are made. The data offered in Table 3 show that for formal groups at the state level the proportion of income from gifts of $500 and over in 1952 ranged between one-third and one-half, and

31. The relative importance of gifts of less than $100 appears to have been essentially uniform in all years before 1956. Here is the percentage of the funds reported received from individuals by the regular, national-level committees of each party in amounts of less than $100:

Year	*Democratic*			*Republican*		
	Presi-dential years	*Mid-term years*	*Off-years*	*Presi-dential years*	*Mid-term years*	*Off-years*
1945			7			20
1946		15			17	
1947			6			15
1948	10			9		
1949			5			23
1950		12			7	
1951			19			10
1952	17			9		
1953			8			21
1954		14			8	
1955			5			21
1956	36			9		

The above percentages apply to the Republican national committee, Senatorial campaign committee and Congressional campaign committee—as a group, and to the Democratic national committee, Senatorial campaign committee, Congressional campaign committee, and national Congressional committee—as a group. The percentage for the Republican national committee alone in the presidential years 1916-1944 varied between 8 and 15, and for the Democratic national committee alone in the presidential years 1912-1944, between 13 and 29.

from gifts of $100-499, between one-fourth and one-third.[32] In the relatively small number of local-level groups for which information was available, the importance of the larger gifts fell again,[33] while those between $100 and $499 remained about the same as at the state level.[34]

32. John Robert Owens has collected information demonstrating that the relative importance of contributions of different size may vary with the type of elections being held, e.g., between the year of a presidential election and of mid-term elections. Here are the percentags of income by size of contribution to the Democratic and Republican state central committees of Connecticut in three years:

Amount	*1950*		*1952*		*1954*	
	Dem.	*Rep.*	*Dem.*	*Rep.*	*Dem.*	*Rep.*
Less than $100	5.8	25.2	15.7	9.3	11.4	30.7
$100-499	12.3	34.9	29.5	43.6	15.2	37.4
$500 and over	81.9	39.9	54.8	47.1	73.4	31.9
Total	100.0	100.0	100.0	100.0	100.0	100.0

The Democratic committee apparently depended less on large gifts in presidential years and the Republican committee more so. But these are only one committee in each party. The percentages for all Democratic and Republican committees computed by Owens for 1952 were:

	Dem.	*Rep.*
Less than $100	24.3	30.5
$100-499	31.8	49.2
$500 and over	23.9	20.3
Labor and other	20.0	0.0
Total	100.0	100.0

—"Party Campaign Funds in Connecticut, 1950-1954" (Ph.D. dissertation, Syracuse University, 1956), pp. 151-52. In Elmira, New York, in 1948, gifts of $100 and over amounted to about half of total contributions to the two party *county* committees.—Bernard R. Berelson, Paul F. Lazarsfeld, and William N. McPhee, *Voting—A Study of Opinion Formation in a Presidential Campaign* (Chicago: University of Chicago Press, 1954), p. 154.

33. As discussed later in this section, the significance of a contribution of any specified size depends partially on the total size of the campaign fund to which it is given.

34. The estimates previously mentioned of the over-all importance in the nation of contributions of $100-499 and of $500 or more are not straight-line projections from the percentages in Table 3. The local-level groups included in the table are not representative of all local political activities. There are vast numbers of candidacies for town, city, county, and other offices to which no contribution of $500, or even of $100, is made. Neither do the formal groups at the state level reflect the whole of campaign finance there.

It has been estimated that the percentage of total campaign *expenditures* made in 1952 through activities at each of the three levels was as follows: national, 14; state, 48; district and local, 38. The volume of *receipts* from *individuals,* which is being discussed in the text, is not found at each of these levels in the same proportion. A large portion of the money spent at the national level is raised at lower levels, and there is in addition considerable swapping of funds between the lower levels.

Several million dollars is raised each election year, moreover, from personal contributions to labor political committees, and a few other committees, not covered by Table 3. Most of these gifts are in sums of less than $100. Also, many lump

Table 3

THE RELATIVE IMPORTANCE OF SMALL AND LARGE POLITICAL GIFTS TO MAJOR-PARTY COMMITTEES AT ALL LEVELS, 1952 AND 1956

Political Committees		Percentage of Receipts from Individuals Given in these Sums				
		1952[a]				1956[b]
Level	Party and Type	No. of Committees for which Information Available	Under $100	$100-$499	$500 and over	$500 and over
National	*Republican*	18	12	20	68	74
	Democratic	15	19	18	63	44
State	*Republican*					
	Regular	29	41	28	31	43
	Finance	7	22	38	40	41
	Volunteer	32	36	28	36	41
	Candidate—election	16	18	33	49	59
	Candidate—nomination	11	17	36	47	(c)
	Democratic					
	Regular	24	30	26	44	34
	Volunteer	24	46	20	34	41
	Candidate—election	22	16	35	49	49
	Candidate—nomination	12	20	42	38	(c)
Local	*Republican*					
	Regular, county	35	38	30	32	20
	Regular, sub-county	25	51	33	16	(c)
	Finance, county	5	28	32	40	39
	Volunteer, various	59	37	36	27	23
	Democratic					
	Regular, county	24	32	45	23	24
	Regular, sub-county	18	28	33	39	(c)
	Finance, county	2	21	42	37	(c)
	Volunteer, various	28	39	25	36	9

[a] Based on reports generally covering full calendar year. All national-level committees are included. All state-level committees were included for which data were available. The percentage received in a specified amount varies somewhat from committee to committee and from state to state. The candidate committees were all for U.S. senator or governor. The number of states in which the candidate committees used are located is as follows: *Republican*, election 9; nomination, 8; *Democratic*, election, 10; nomination, 6. Some local-level committees which handled sums of money deemed small in the setting were excluded even though data were available. The number of states in which the local committees that were used are located is as follows: *local, Republican*, regular county, 7; regular sub-county, 4; finance county, 4; volunteer, 12; *local, Democratic*, regular county, 5; regular sub-county, 4; finance county, 1; volunteer, 10.

[b] All national-level committees are included (11 Republican, 11 Democratic), using information for full calendar year. All other data used pertain to September 1-November 30. The state-level regular, finance, and volunteer committees include about 98 per cent of those active on behalf of the presidential candidates, a total of 268. The candidate committees, 77 in all, were active in elections for U.S. senator. The county committees included number 350, all located in the 100 largest counties.

[c] No data available.

sums recorded as made by an individual actually constitute collections made from others.

With allowances for these factors, it was estimated that in 1952 about $35-000,000 was raised in sums of $500 and over, and about the same amount in sums of $100-499. A file was assembled of more than 13,000 of the 1952 political gifts

The Democratic national committee did not reach as many sizeable givers in 1956 as usual.[35] The percentage of receipts from individuals given in sums of $500 and over to the national-level Democratic committees, taken together, was consequently depressed below that of previous years. The dependence of both major parties in the past on medium and large gifts has been shared by most minor parties and other groups that engage in campaign activities. Three committees behind the Wallace Progressive candidacy in 1948, for example, could garner only a third of their gifts in sums of less than $100, as shown in Table 4. There is wide variation among the organizations treated in the table, which were chosen on the basis of available data. But none was without any contributions of $500 or more, and most could count on at least a third of their income from gifts of $100 or more.

Large givers—how many?—From facts like these it is usually argued that the intent of popular suffrage is subverted. Only people of means can make even a $100 contribution. Consequently, the forces of wealth dominate the political life of the nation. Whether political gifts have the cumulative effect thus claimed needs to be examined. Certainly the bulk of political money is supplied by a relatively small number of people.

The best data on the question pertain to 1952. In that year somewhere around 150,000 different persons appear to have made at least one gift of at least $100—to some committee or candidate, at some level

---

of $500 or more. The contributions it contained totalled about $14,000,000, made by about 9,500 different persons. Examination of the coverage of the campaign reports from which these contributions were taken led to the conclusion that probably in 1952 there were more than 20,000 different persons who gave in this sum or higher. Before making the estimates here described, it was inferred from the contributions file that the total from $500-and-over gifts probably therefore came to about $28,000,000, or 20 per cent of total expenditures. The $35,000,000 estimate reported in the text (one-fourth of $140,000,000) is probably more dependable.

Given the crudeness of the data, and the necessity for exercising judgment at various points in arriving at these estimates, the difference between the two results indicates something of the range of error that must be expectd. The least systematic information is available for the local level. In computing the estimates reported in the text, it was judged, on the basis of impressions gained from interviews and observation, that if all types of local-level political activities were included, probably no more than 10 per cent of individual receipts were in sums of $500 and over, and no more than 25 per cent in the sums between $100 and $499. If these estimates err, they are probably low. One of the special sources of uncertainty at the local level is the covert manner in which underworld money is handled. The local-level data for 1956 in Table 3 all came from the 100 largest counties in the country, and the data for 1952 came for the most part from very large counties.

35. The increase in the percentage coming in sums of less than $100 (see footnote 31, page 49) was due partly to a drop in the total income of the committee *from individuals* and partly to an increase in the volume of small gifts. The latter added to $344,000 in 1952 and to $557,000 in 1956. The total income of the committee was about the same in both years. Democratic national committee officials attributed the boost in small gifts simply to the efforts made to attract such contributions.

of government, for either a nomination or an election campaign.[36] Probably about 20,000 of the 150,000 persons—husband and wife counted as one—made at least one gift of $500 or over, and persons giving an aggregate of $10,000 or more may have numbered around 200.[37] While 1952 is not representative of all presidential election years, much less other years, it provides the best estimates at hand of the number of persons who made political gifts of specified sizes during one year:

Givers in 1952 of	*Estimated Number of Persons*	*Gifts Met This Estimated Percentage of Total U.S. Election Bill*
Any sum	3,000,000	100
At least 1 $100 gift	150,000	50
At least 1 $500 gift	20,000	25
At least $10,000 total	200	3

Size is relative.—Some candidates and campaign committees receive so many large contributions that no one of them can be deemed truly crucial to the financial health of the recipient. The importance of any gift to its recipient, moreover, will vary enormously from one setting and one occasion to another. What donors get in return for what they give will be discussed in the next chapter, but it will be prudent to bear in mind that a large donation may be of little importance under some conditions and a small donation may be of great importance under others. In some locales, a day's work at the polls can be had for the price of a taxi ride in New York.

36. There were additional persons whose total gifts added to more than $100 but who gave no single sum so large. The estimate was arrived at using the information presented in Table 5 on page 56. It was assumed that 20,000 or so *persons* gave in sums of $500 and over. Allowance was made for the differing proportions of total receipts probably collected at the three political levels referred to in the table and for differences between the parties. In the 1952 file of $500-and-over gifts, the number of different contributors came to 73 per cent of the number of gifts. (In the 1956 list of $500-and-over gifts, the number of contributors came to 75 per cent of the number of gifts.) It was assumed that the same relationship would exist between the number of gifts of $100-499 and the number of persons making them.

37. Among the 9,500 individuals in the 1952 file of $500-and-over gifts there were 110 people whose contributions as recorded in that file came to $10,000 or more. (Husband and wife always treated as one person. There were five persons in the group who were themselves candidates.) They totalled slightly under $2,000,000. If the file were about half complete, as judged, and the other half did not differ markedly from the half present, the number of these giant contributors was probably around 200 and their contributions of $500 and more came to around $4,000,000, which is close to 3 per cent of $140,000,000. The data available for 1956 are in line with those of 1952. Of 8,100 persons whose gifts of $500 were known, 111 reported they had made total contributions of $10,000 and over (in sums of $100 up) for an aggregate of $2,300,000.

Table 4

THE RELATIVE IMPORTANCE OF SMALL AND LARGE POLITICAL GIFTS TO SELECTED MINOR PARTIES AND OTHER GROUPS, 1948, 1952, AND 1956[a]

Year	Organization	Total Receipts[b]	Percentage of Receipts from Individuals Given in these Sums		
			Under $100	$100-$499	$500 and over
1948	3 Wallace Committees[c]	$1,133,863	36	44	20
1948	National States' Rights Democratic Campaign Committee	163,442	11	18	71
1952	Socialist Labor Party of America	88,018	70	27	3
1956	Socialist Labor Party of America	22,727	(d)	(d)	26
1952	Americans for Democratic Action	162,120	62	19	19
1956	Americans for Democratic Action	183,279	68	8	24
1952	Christian Nationalist Crusade	202,360	42	47	11
1956	Christian Nationalist Crusade	160,716	85	14	1
1952	National Committee for an Effective Congress	31,068	18	45	37
1956	National Committee for an Effective Congress[e]	75,403	26	21	53
1952	1952 Civil Liberties Appeal	15,107	70	20	10
1956	A Clean Politics Appeal	71,707	85	13	2
1952	Americans for America	42,491	49	11	40
1956	For America	80,534	41	11	48
1956	National Committee for T. Coleman Andrews and Thomas H. Werdel	37,828	13	12	75

[a] Data for full calendar years except: 1952, Socialist Labor Party, to October 31; 1952, National Committee for an Effective Congress, May 1-November 7; all 1956 data are generally through November 30; 1956, Socialist Labor Party, September 1-November 30.

[b] Given to indicate scale of committee operations. In all cases except one, receipts from individuals constituted more than half of total receipts, and usually a larger share. About 16 per cent of the States' Rights committee income was reported as contributions direct from individuals, the rest as transfers of funds from subsidiary or cooperating political groups.

[c] Progressive Party; National Wallace for President Committee; Young Progressives of America.

[d] Not ascertainable.

[e] In 1956 this organization collected on behalf of itself and cooperating groups about $212,000. Of that amount $157,990 was distributed to the campaigns of various candidates. Of the latter sum, 26 per cent was reported as collected in sums of over $500, 18 per cent in sums of $100-$500, and 56 per cent in sums under $100.—U.S. Senate Special Committee to Investigate Political Activities, Lobbying, and Campaign Contributions, *Hearings* (Washington: Government Printing Office, 1957), pp. 1026, 1038.

Any campaign contributor can cite his gifts to support whatever personal plea he wants to make. The political visibility of individual contributors is necessarily affected, nevertheless, by the number of them with whom candidates and their handlers deal and on whom they depend. A contributor, one of six or seven giving $100 to a local campaign, will command greater attention from those who use his money than one whose $500 gift gets lost among 850 others like it to the

Republican national committee, or among 900 others like it to the Democratic national committee, as it would have been in 1952. In addition, those two committees received more than 2700 and 3400 donations, respectively, in sums of $100 to $499 in that year. Each becomes a fairly small fish in a fairly large pond.[38]

Even at lower levels contributions in the hundreds of dollars may be numerous, though their frequency generally decreases. The number of gifts of between $100 and $499 and of $500 and over that were made to some 400 political committees at national, state, and local levels in 1952 is shown in Table 5.[39] Each of the 95 Republican committees at the state level received, on the average, 200 donations of $100-$499 and 34 of $500 and over. The state-level Democratic averages for 82 committees were 103 and 26, respectively. The Republican averages for 124 local committees were 32 and six, and the Democratic figures for 72 local committees were 54 and seven. These variations should induce caution in assessing the importance of political giving as a channel to preferment in government. Sweeping generalizations are likely to prove inaccurate.

The long ballot.—Americans are accustomed to a long ballot. In almost every election they vote simultaneously for candidates for several offices. Some of them also make campaign contributions to several committees or candidates active in the same election. Multiple giving is another feature of campaign finance that affects the potential influence contributors may acquire.

How many contributors give to more than one recipient cannot be precisely estimated. There are bits of evidence, however, that provide some rough indications. It would appear that a substantial segment of campaign givers do so. A file that was compiled of all known contributions of $500 or more made in 1952 contained about 9,500 different names. About 19 per cent of them gave to two or more different candidates or committees. Among the 8,100 contributors similarly compiled in 1956, some 15 per cent showed up on the reports as doing likewise. These are minimum percentages, for in neither year was the file of contributions complete. The difference between the 1952 and 1956 percentages, for example, is accounted for partly by the inclusion in the 1952 file of many gifts to nomination campaigns. The 1956 file was

38. The number of 1952 gifts of $100-499 and $500 and over received from individuals by committees at the national level were, respectively, as follows: *Republican committees*: national, 2753, 863; Senatorial, 110, 207; Congressional, 309, 373; Citizens for Eisenhower, 1763, 921; 14 others, 782, 207; *Democratic committees*: national, 3421, 919; Senatorial, 42, 69; Congressional (2 combined), 3, 15; headquarters, 212, 104; Stevenson-Sparkman Forum Committee, 135, 210; Volunteers for Stevenson, 654, 299; 8 others, 73, 32.

39. The ratios of the number of gifts of $100-499 to the number of gifts of $500 and over are fairly consistent within each party at the state level. They are generally consistent between the two parties at all levels. These similarities one would expect, and they add confidence in the reliability of the data. The information in this table was used in estimating the number of givers in amounts of $100 and more in 1952. See footnote 36, page 53, above.

Table 5

THE RATIO OF THE NUMBER OF GIFTS OF $100-$499 TO THE NUMBER OF GIFTS OF $500 AND OVER, 1952[a]

Political Committees		No. of Committees for which Information Available	No. of Gifts of		Ratio: (A) divided by (B)
Level	Party and Type		$100-$499 (A)	$500 and over (B)	
National	*Republican*	18	5,717	2,571	2.2
	Democratic	15	4,540	1,648	2.8
State	*Republican*				
	Regular	29	4,539	822	5.5
	Finance	7	10,734	1,765	6.1
	Volunteer	32	1,838	301	6.1
	Candidate—election	16	1,245	248	5.0
	Candidate—nomination	11	637	132	4.8
	Democratic				
	Regular	24	3,109	934	3.3
	Volunteer	24	1,255	286	4.4
	Candidate—election	22	1,692	469	3.6
	Candidate—nomination	12	2,349	455	5.2
Local	*Republican*				
	Regular, county	35	1,322	210	6.3
	Regular, sub-county	25	262	24	10.9
	Finance, county	5	1,893	415	4.6
	Volunteer, various	59	431	62	7.0
	Democratic				
	Regular, county	24	2,409	211	11.4
	Regular, sub-county	18	349	64	5.4
	Finance, county	2	190	25	7.6
	Volunteer, various	28	935	200	4.7

[a] Based on reports generally covering the full calendar year. All national-level committees are included. All state-level committees are included for which data were available. The candidate committees were all for U.S. senator or governor. The number of states in which the candidate committees used are located is as follows: *Republican*, election, 9; nomination, 8; *Democratic*, election, 10; nomination, 6. Some local-level committees which handled sums deemed small in the setting were excluded even though data were available. These had few gifts of over $100. The number of states in which the local committees that were used are located is as follows: *local, Republican*, regular county, 7; regular sub-county, 4; finance county, 4; volunteer, 12; *local, Democratic*, regular county, 5; regular sub-county, 4; finance county, 1; volunteer, 10.

made up almost exclusively of reports pertaining solely to the general elections.

Among some categories of contributors the percentage who are multiple givers is higher. In North Carolina, 87.5 per cent of a 1952 sample of Democratic donors of $100 or more said that they had made more than one political gift during that year. Over 78 per cent of the similar Republican sample said the same. Among Democratic givers of less than $100, the percentage fell to 20, and among Republicans who gave in these smaller amounts, to 40. North Carolina is a one-party state, yet it has a vigorous opposition party. Contributors to the main campaign committees of each party are more likely than in certain other settings to be tapped for both primary and general election contributions.

The North Carolina data suggest two conclusions that seem justified from impressions gained by other means. Persons who give relatively large sums are more likely to send financial support to two or more political causes than are those who give smaller amounts. And it seems evident that certain large givers are highly oriented toward politics, like persons who engage vigorously in other forms of political action.

An analysis of the contributing record of 259 persons who gave at least $5,000 to political causes in 1956 tells something of the multiple giving of the giant political contributors.[40] This group of 259 unquestionably includes a large share of all giant contributors, and the practices of multiple giving found within it should be fairly representative.[41] The 259 people reported they gave to an average of eight different recipients. Ninety-four per cent gave to more than one. Of the total group:

6	per cent gave to 1 recipient only
27	per cent gave to 2 or 3 recipients
23	per cent gave to 4 or 5 recipients
30	per cent gave to between 6 and 10 recipients
12	per cent gave to between 11 and 30 recipients
2	per cent gave to between 55 and 65 recipients
100	

These gifts were strewn across the country and through all levels of politics. If American politics is divided for this purpose into four levels —national, state, Congressional district, and local—82 per cent of the 259 contributors gave at more than one level, 44 per cent gave at more than two levels, and 9 per cent gave at more than three, i.e., at all four levels. Some 25 per cent gave in more than one state to candidates for office (not counting the presidency).[42] Nine per cent of the total gave to candidates in two states, 7 per cent in three, and 9 per cent in four or more, the top being four persons who gave in 14 different states.[43]

40. On the basis of reports of contributions submitted by political committees and candidates, the Gore Committee identified 365 persons who, alone or with their spouses, it thought might have given $5,000 or more in the aggregate during 1956. (Most of the reports available to the committee pertained only to federal elections, and, with the notable exception of national-level committees, covered only the period of the active campaign, September 1–November 30, 1956.) These 365 persons were asked, in effect, to submit the full record of their political gifts of $100 or more for the calendar year 1956. Some 259 reports showing total gifts of $5,000 or more were returned, along with 33 showing a total of less than $5,000 each.

41. Comparisons between the major parties with respect to these and some of the other data discussed in this section will be found on pages 120-29, below.

42. There were some persons who did not give in more than one state but who gave to more than one jurisdiction in the same state.

43. This is an analysis of contributions to state and local *candidates*. An analysis of all contributions made by the 259 persons showed that 51 per cent of them made some sort of political gift in more than one state (to the Citizens for Eisenhower, for example, in several different states). Those giving in two or three states amounted to 34 per cent of the total, and those in four or more to 17 per cent. Four persons gave in 21 states.

An element of order.—It would be a mistake to assume that candidates and party managers are automatically attentive to the thousands of persons who give moderate sums to political causes. It would be equally fallacious to assume that politicians disregard this band of their constituents. They are, naturally enough, sensitive and often responsive to the interests of their financial constitutents as they understand them. Politicians may even cater explicitly to the masses of small givers through the periodic attempts that are made to solicit funds from them. Among candidates dependent for funds on a small coterie of supporters, often candidates for local offices, the relationship between benefactors and beneficiaries is not obscure. It is more difficult to discern the patterns of communications and organization that relate political leaders to their financial supporters when the latter number in the thousands and the millions.

One element of order is introduced by the systems through which political money is solicited and transmitted, matters to be taken up at some length in later chapters. Fund-raisers, operating individually or as part of a systematic money-raising campaign, become connecting links between givers and receivers. As such they not only help to fuel the engines of politics, they also comprise an important segment of the political structure of the country.

4. SPLIT-TICKET GIVING

A village editor once wrote that those who give simultaneously to both political parties "are doing more to undermine and destroy the U.S. government than all the conspiring Communists in the world."[44] An extreme judgment, no doubt, but not a unique one. Indignant censure or cynical grins greet almost every mention of the subject.

Giving across party lines takes many forms which together constitute an important type of political participation. Our concern here is with two-party giving by *individuals*. Different members of social, economic, and family groups frequently give to different parties, but those practices will be examined later.[45]

Types of two-party giving.—Among the approximately 9,500 persons whose recorded campaign contributions of $500 or more made in 1952 have been analyzed, a shade under 1 per cent—86 persons and three husband-wife combinations—were found giving to recipients in both the Democratic and Republican parties. About the same proportion did so among the 8,100 persons whose 1956 contributions could be studied—65 individuals and three husband-wife combinations.[46]

44. *Chapel Hill News Leader* (N.C.), August 22, 1956.

45. The present discussion is based largely on general-elections data. Much that will be said applies also to the practice of giving to more than one candidate in direct primaries.

46. The 1952 and 1956 materials differed in certain respects. The contributions were drawn from reports made by political committees numbering about 3,500 in 1952 and about 900 in 1956. The 1952 reports generally covered the entire

These 157 cases[47] of two-party giving found in two presidential election years obviously do not indicate the extent of the practice in the United States.[48] The instances identified are sufficiently numerous,

calendar year, and the dates of the contributions were usually available. The 1956 reports, most of them collected by the Gore Committee, were largely confined to the campaign period, September 1–November 30, and the dates of the contributions were generally not available. Although every effort was made to get uniform geographic coverage in assembling the 1952 data, more complete information was obtained from some states than others. The 1956 coverage was geographically more complete for the period treated.

Moreover, for 1956, personal reports prepared by 259 of the largest aggregate contributors were studied. These contributors were asked to list all political gifts of $100 and over made during the calendar year. Of the 20 persons in this group found to have given to both parties, three would not have been identified had gifts of lower than $500, the usual cutoff point, been excluded. Some of the differences between the two sets of data make it more likely to locate cross-party contributors for 1952, others of the differences make it more likely to do so for 1956.

Of 110 persons whose known gifts of $500 and over in 1952 totalled $10,000 or more, eight (7 per cent) were on record as giving to both parties. Of 259 persons who reported that they had given $5,000 or more in 1956 in amounts of $100 or more, 20 (8 per cent) listed recipients in both parties.

47. Involved are 138 different individuals and six husband-wife combinations; 13 persons gave both ways in both years. In each of the two years there were 21 additional persons who were found to have given to political committees or candidates of one party and also to nonparty political committees, such as the Americans for Democratic Action, Americans for America, and the National Committee for an Effective Congress.

Some nonparty groups spend funds in ways more beneficial to one party than the other, and some make transfers of funds to candidates in both parties. There was in 1956, for example, a special nonparty committee formed explicitly to raise money for two Democratic Senatorial candidates (Stengel in Illinois and Marland in West Virginia) and two Republican candidates (Wiley in Wisconsin and Cooper in Kentucky). Among the thousands of persons in the United States who give to such nonparty groups are therefore many whose gifts actually, though indirectly, aid more than one party. The manager of one of the nonparty groups stated, in fact, that some people give through his committee primarily to avoid being labeled publicly as a partisan contributor.

48. Many primary and general election activities escape the campaign reports. The variety of initials, spellings, and addresses used by different committees (or even the same one) in reporting an individual's contributions make the compilations of a person's contributing record a formidable task. It is further complicated by the presence in large cities of many persons of the same name. Undoubtedly some cases that were excluded from the present analysis could have been included had clear identification been possible.

Many people, moreover, dislike identification as a contributor, especially if they would show up giving to both parties, and consequently make some or all of their contributions through intermediaries. Said one lawyer, who covers up contributions for certain of his clients: "They are often, or usually, Republicans and want to avoid any embarrassment by having it known that they have given to Democrats." Elsewhere in the country it is equally awkward to be tabbed a Republican. There is no way to spot cases of this type from the record. The people who handle such money give the impression that considerably less of it shows up on the books than goes unreported, or than is covered up through the use of dummy names.

nevertheless, to tell something of the variety of cases in which cross-party giving occurs. Four broad types are encountered.

1. There are individuals who give to opposing sides in the same contest, to the Democratic national committee and to the Citizens for Eisenhower-Nixon, for example.

2. Closely related are contributors who take part in the nominating contests of one party, while backing the other party in the subsequent general election, or who take part in the nominating contests of both parties for the same office.

3. The gifts of a large proportion of cross-party givers do not, however, meet themselves in head-on collision. These donors give on behalf of one party's candidates in some jurisdictions and at some levels, and on behalf of the opposing party in others.

4. Finally, there are persons who shift their partisan allegiance during the campaign year, favoring one party or candidate early in the year and another later. Within these broad classes all of the cases to be discussed fit, as follows:

	Number of cases[49]	
Contributions go to the opposing party	*1952*	*1956*
In the same contest	40	43
In a nomination campaign	7	2
In different jurisdictions	37	23
After a switch in allegiance	5	0
Total	89	68

Because of the nature of the data, the number of cases falling by each of the headings does not necessarily reflect—at least not precisely—the incidence of the different kinds of two-party giving.

Switches in allegiance.—Critics who sit in judgment on such matters may question the propriety of giving to one party early in an election year and to a different one later on. Givers, like voters, however, change their preferences, contributing thereby to the gaiety of elections.

Shifts between election years can be more easily detected than shifts within the same year. They can be part of the same process of opinion formation, and the major proportions they often assume are indicative of what may go on within a single year as the election approaches. One veteran Democratic fund-raiser reported he and friends had added up one and three-quarters million dollars which they estimated had been given on behalf of Eisenhower in 1952 by persons of their knowledge who had formerly made Democratic contributions. A comparison of donors of $500 and over to the Democratic and Republican national committees during 1933-1945 turned up 60 people who had shifted party at least

49. In a few instances persons who made multiple gifts to both parties could have been classified in several ways. Each of these cases was assigned to the first of the categories listed here for which it could qualify.

once, including one who alternated four times in seven years. At least 16 persons who had given to one of the top-level regular committees of one party in 1948 changed over and gave to one such committee of the other party in 1952.[50] In years like 1952 and 1956, the nominees of one or both parties remain in doubt until convention time. Contributors may therefore fall victim early in the year to what one who did so called "impetuous judgments." Early donations are often stimulated by fund-raising dinners that are intentionally timed in advance of the campaign.

Head-on collisions.—Contributions on behalf of opposing candidates in the same contest especially intrigue students of political influence. Thirty-seven such contributors were located among 1952 givers, and 40 among those of 1956.[51] In the bulk of the cases, the contributions went to committees in direct opposition to each other in the same jurisdiction and at the same level. In the rest, the gifts went to groups in opposition but at different levels—for example, the Republican national committee and the New York Democratic state committee.[52]

Most of the 1952 contributors who could be identified held important positions in important businesses: 21 of 22, the other being a lawyer. Of the 21, four were brewers and three were in aviation.[53] The practice

50. In both of these comparisons, the number of switches detected would have been greater had contributors to a wider range of committees been examined. Of the 60 who changed between 1933 and 1945, 40 went from Democratic to Republican (13 in 1936, 2 in 1938, 13 in 1940, 1 in 1942, and 11 in 1944); 12 went from Republican to Democratic (2 in 1937, 2 in 1941, 1 in 1943, 6 in 1944, and 1 in 1945); and 8 shifted more than once, 3 ending up Democratic and 5 Republican.

In making the 1948-1952 comparison, contributors in those two years were compared who had given to the national, Senatorial, and Congressional campaign committees of each party. Of the 16 who shifted, 11 moved to the Republicans and 5 to the Democrats. Persons who showed up giving to both parties in the same year were not included in the tally. A similar comparison of 1944 and 1948 contributors showed 6 moving to the Republican side in 1948 and 1 to the Democratic side.

51. There were three husband-wife combinations, in addition, in each year. Man and wife often participate in politics independently of each other; in other cases the two people appear to act as one.

52. The combinations of opposing recipients were as follows:

	1952	*1956*
Both at national level	22	10
Both at state level, same state	3	13
Both at local level, same locality	3	1
1 at national, 1 at state level	6	12
1 at state, 1 at local level, same state	3	2
1 at national, 1 at local level	0	2
	37	40

53. The list of the 22 follows, showing one 1952 business identification for each (most had many), and the known record of their 1952 contributions of $500 and over. This is an *illustrative* list of persons who gave to both parties *openly*. Many others did so covertly. Individuals who gave after the election (November

4) are marked with an asterisk. (A list for 1956 can be derived from the Gore Committee *Report,* especially Exs. 21 and 28.)

*John D. Allen, Chicago, president, Brink's Inc.: Democratic national committee, 10/24, $500; Republican Congressional campaign committee, 11/12, $500.

L. D. Bell, Buffalo, founder, Bell Aircraft Corporation: New York Democratic state committee, 10/11, $500; Republican finance committee, Erie County, New York, 9/26, $500.

R. A. L. Bogan, Chicago, executive vice president and director, the Greyhound Corporation: Stevenson-Sparkman Forum Committee, 11/3, $1,000; Republican national committee, 9/30, $1,000; national Citizens for Eisenhower-Nixon, 10/30, $1,000.

Camille Dreyfus, New York, chairman, Celanese Corporation of America: Democratic national committee, 3/8, $500, 9/29, $1,000; Republican national committee, 10/14, $1,000.

W. F. Fippinger, New York, secretary and director, F. & M. Schaefer Brewing Co.: Democratic Senatorial campaign committee, 6/6, $1,000; Republican Senatorial campaign committee, 8/22, $1,000.

Frances W. Freed, Washington, president and director, Paramount Motors Corporation: Democratic national committee, 10/31, $500; Republican national committee, 10/28, $1,000.

George Friedland, Philadelphia, president, Food Fair Stores, Inc.: Democratic national committee, 3/31, $1,000, 11/3, $4,000; Democratic campaign committee of Philadelphia, 10/31, $1,000; Republican central campaign committee, Philadelphia County, 10/31, $1,000.

Clayton Gengras, West Hartford, Connecticut, president and treasurer, Gengras Motors, Inc.: Ribicoff, Democratic candidate for U.S. senator, $1,000; Connecticut Republican finance committee, $1,000.

*Benjamin Lazrus, New York, chairman of board, Benrus Watch Co.: Democratic national committee, 10/3, $1,000; Celler, Democratic nomination for U.S. representative, New York, 6/26, $500; New York United Republican Finance Committee, 11/10, $750.

*Oscar M. Lazrus, New York, president, Benrus Watch Co.: Democratic national committee, 10/3, $1,000; New York United Republican Finance Committee, 11/10, $750.

*S. Ralph Lazrus, New York, director, Benrus Watch Co.: Democratic national committee, 10/3, $1,000; New York United Republican Finance Committee, 11/10, $750.

Adolph Levitt, New York, chairman, Doughnut Corporation of America: Democratic Senatorial campaign committee, 9/9, $500; national Citizens for Eisenhower-Nixon, 10/31, $500.

Alfred Liebmann, New York, chairman of executive committee and vice president, Liebmann Breweries Co.: Democratic Senatorial campaign committee, 9/9, $1,000; Republican Senatorial campaign committee, 9/12, $1,000; New York United Republican Finance Committee, 10/1, $2,000, 10/30, $500.

Morris Miller, Silver Spring, Maryland, lawyer: Democratic campaign committee, Maryland, $500; Beall, Republican candidate for U.S. senator, Maryland, $500.

*Raymond A. Norden, New York, president and director, Seaboard and Western Airlines, Inc.: Kennedy, Democratic candidate for U.S. senator, Massachusetts, 11/5, $500; Heselton, Republican candidate for U.S. representative, Massachusetts, 11/12, $500.

*W. O'Neil, Akron, president, General Tire Co.: Democratic national committee, 10/22, $1,000; Republican Congressional campaign committee, 11/12, $1,000.

R. J. Schaefer, Brooklyn, president, F. & M. Schaefer Brewing Co.: New York Democratic state committee, 9/30, $1,000; Cashmore, Democratic candidate

was obviously settled policy for several who engaged in it. Three persons named Lazrus of the Benrus Watch Company gave to both parties, in each case sending the same amount on the same date to the same committee. R. J. Schaefer, president of the F. & M. Schaefer Brewing Company in Brooklyn, has on several occasions sent contributions to both sides, the official reports recording that he did this in 1940 and 1956 as well as 1952.[54] Emil G. Sick, Seattle brewer, turned up on both sides in 1944, 1948, and 1952. It was a similar case with several New Yorkers: Irving Geist in 1944, 1952, and 1956; E. B. Lewis, Jr., in 1948, 1952, and 1956; Camille Dreyfus in 1944 and 1952; and Manuel Kulukundis in 1952 and 1956. The circumstances in ten 1952 cases were of the type that raise eyebrows. In nine of them, persons gave to Democratic committees before the election and to Republicans afterwards, including the Messrs. Lazrus. Both contributions of the tenth person were reported as received after the election. One went to a victorious Democrat, United States Senator John F. Kennedy, and the other to a victorious Republican, United States Representative J. W. Heselton, both of Massachusetts.[55]

The curmudgeon Ickes once wrote scornfully that this practice of giving to both sides "shows how deep are the convictions of this type

---

for U.S. senator, New York, 10/28, $1,000; Democratic campaign committee, Kings County, New York, 10/3, $1,000; New York United Republican Finance Committee, 9/26, $1,500; Republican county committee, Westchester County, New York, 9/26, $1,000.

Emil G. Sick, Seattle, chairman of board, Sicks' Breweries, Ltd.: Democratic national committee, 10/24, $500; Democratic Senatorial campaign committee, 9/9, $500; Republican Senatorial campaign committee, 10/13, $500.

Robert F. Six, Denver, president and director, Continental Airlines: Democratic national committee, 9/2, $1,000; Stevenson-Sparkman Forum Committee, 11/3, $1,000; Colorado Democratic state central committee, $500; Republican Congressional campaign committee, 9/30, $1,000.

Stephen D. Stephanidis, New York, chairman of board, Prudential Steamship Corporation: Democratic national committee, 11/3, $1,500; New York United Republican Finance Committee, 10/30, $1,000.

Edgar B. Stern, New Orleans, director, Sears, Roebuck and Co.: Democratic 1952 Campaign Headquarters Travel Committee, 10/2, $2,500; national Volunteers for Stevenson, 10/8, $2,500 (wife), 10/23, $1,000, 10/27, $1,000; New York Volunteers for Stevenson, 11/3, $500; Miller, Democratic nomination for U.S. senator, Virginia, 6/28, $500 (wife); Benton, Democratic candidate for U.S. senator, Connecticut, $500 (wife); national Citizens for Eisenhower-Nixon, 9/16, $1,000; Schmitt, Republican nomination for U.S. senator, Wisconsin, $500.

*J. Gordon Turnbull, Los Angeles and Cleveland, consulting engineer: Democratic national committee, 9/25, $1,500; Republican Congressional campaign committee, 11/28, $1,500.

54. In 1952 Mr. Schaefer's Republican gifts were listed from his residence in Westchester County, his Democratic ones from his business address in Brooklyn.

55. One southern senator noted after his successful nomination campaign that people he was sure had supported his opponent came by to give him money. Having been opposed by a "business candidate" in the primary, he confessed he found it easier in many ways to raise money after his victory than before it.

of citizen."[56] In the eyes of an old Progressive, this type of citizen had no political convictions. But it is well to remember there are *other* kinds of conviction. The first concern of most businessmen is necessarily a profit-and-loss operation. The degree of profit and of loss frequently depends on the decisions of public officials. Double-giving is to many businessmen nothing but insurance, the name customarily given to it by them. If the precaution proves to be ineffective or excessive, they observe that fire insurance costs even when the house does not burn.

It is probably true, as one company official contended, that most persons give to opposing parties to preserve whatever friendships they have with politicians who do or may control governmental power. Yet there are other explanations, too. Some contributors argue earnestly that they give to both parties out of belief in the two-party system. Both sides must have money for the system to function effectively.[57] One corporation vice president complains that he feels compelled to follow company practice and make a Republican contribution each election. A conscientious Democrat, he then matches it with a Democratic gift to keep peace with himself.

Solicitors prey upon victims who are obligated to them without regard to party preference. Thereby are explained some of the more curious aberrations. One west Texas oil producer gave $5,000 to the Stevenson-Sparkman campaign. Along with 40 or 50 others he was later summoned to Houston by officials of the company that customarily bought his oil. They wanted funds for Ike. He was down for $2,500, which he forthwith gave over, thereafter apologizing to the Democratic treasurer, explaining he had no choice. People give according to who solicits them, a Democratic fund-raiser was told in Massachusetts. He was handed a list of prospects, many of them obviously Republicans. Get the right man to ask them, was the philosophy, and they will come through.

Politicians themselves exact tribute from the opposition through various types of shakedown, a few of which were said to have been used in the Democratic extremity of 1948. American legislators are errand boys for their constituents. Entrenched officeholders develop skills in representation invaluable to their constituents regardless of party. All hands develop a vested interest in a perennial incumbent and support him in consequence. Moreover, in many localities candidates and not parties provide the crucial points of access to government decision-

56. *The Secret Diary of Harold L. Ickes: The First Thousand Days, 1933-1936* (New York: Simon and Schuster, 1954), p. 695.

57. Republican George Eccles, president of the First Security Corporation of Utah, says he gives to both parties because "I believe in the two-party system. . . . I believe it is important to maintain the financial strength of *both* major parties." Democrat Joseph Barr, owner of theatres in Indianapolis, says the same: "You find some forward-looking men who contribute to both parties. Some of these men feel it is the best way to keep the two-party system going."—Quoted by Duncan Norton-Taylor, "How to Give Money to Politicians," *Fortune,* 53 (May, 1956), 240-41.

making. Those with something at stake maintain liaison with the significant individuals involved whether in one party or the other.

Giving to nomination campaigns.—The financial requirements of nominating contests lead to another type of cross-party financial activity. Leonard F. Schmitt was a candidate in Wisconsin's Republican Senatorial primary of 1952. His contributors included many people usually found in the Democratic camp. They were out to fight Senator Joseph R. McCarthy, Schmitt's opponent, wherever they could find him. In a similar mood, persons gave to the Eisenhower nomination campaign but opposed him in the later election. The desire to improve the quality of candidates will hardly be condemned. Those will be viewed askance, however, who take their civic obligation as seriously as one Marylander. In 1952 he gave to a candidate in both the Republican and Democratic Senatorial primaries in his state.

Giving in different jurisdictions.—The remaining type of two-party givers split their gifts much as voters split their ticket. They give to candidates of different parties, but not candidates opposing each other. More than a third of the illustrations of cross-party donations sighted in 1952 and 1956 were of this kind. Most of them fall into two categories. First, there are presidential Republicans in one-party Democratic states, persons who give to candidates in the Democratic primaries for state office but send their money to aid the Republican national ticket in the general election.[58] (Some presidential Democrats show up elsewhere, too.) Second, there are candidates for the United States Senate or House of Representatives who appeal to affluent members of the opposing party. Senator William Benton is a prime illustration, as he himself noted of his successful 1950 Senatorial effort:[59] "I fortunately had friends all over the United States and some of them put every possible kind of friendly pressure on everybody they knew in order to try to raise money for me. A very considerable percentage of the contributions . . . was from Republicans." Democrat Stuart Symington showed up in the reports as a special favorite of Republicans in his successful race for the Senate in Missouri in 1952. To a lesser extent so did John F. Kennedy in Massachusetts and Harry F. Byrd in Virginia. All of these men enjoy good standing in sectors of the national business community. They attract what Senator Benton called "emotional money."[60] A Republican like Senator Jack Javits of New York

58. Lester W. Milbrath was told by 12 of 23 randomly chosen North Carolina Republican contributors of $100 or more that they had made contributions in the Democratic primaries of their state.—*Op. cit.*, p. 90. There have been occasions of *sub rosa* transfers between parties within the same state, but these are unlikely to appear on public reports. In 1952, in one southern state, Republican forces diverted funds to a leading Democrat to shore up his enthusiasm for Ike. The money was used in a different, though simultaneous, contest.

59. U.S. Senate Subcommittee on Privileges and Elections, *Hearings* (Washington: Government Printing Office, 1952), p. 58.

60. *Ibid.*, pp. 58-59.

will pull money across the lines in the other direction. Cross-party givers often aver they give to candidates and not to parties, being interested in the personal qualities of public officials and the policies they support, rather than in party organization.[61] This is the argument for independent, split-ticket voting that has traditionally enjoyed wide endorsement in the United States.[62]

The influence of institutions.—It seems a safe guess that in a presidential year not over 5 per cent of the people who give in sums of $500 and up do so to opposing sides in the ways that have been described. If at least 20,000 persons contributed in such amounts in 1952, probably around 1,000 of them thus gave "against themselves." The practice prevails among contributors of smaller sums, too, and if the total could be known it would run to many thousands.[63]

Few Americans dispose of their cash this way merely for a frolic. The public has been shown that cross-party giving is normal procedure for highly suspicious political manipulators like Henry Grunewald, Bernard Goldfine, and Arthur Samish.[64] It has certainly characterized the political machinations of figures in the underworld, as made clear by Abner ("Longie") Zwillman in describing the "nonsectarian" activi-

61. The money often gets spread around on the advice of intermediaries (see pages 269-74, below), as was apparently the case with Mr. Harry Boyd Earhart of Michigan. Mr. Earhart's name turned up on a list of contributors to U.S. Senator Alton Lennon, candidate in the 1954 Democratic Senatorial primary in North Carolina. A Republican, a former president of the White Star Refining Company, and at that time eighty-four years old, Mr. Earhart told reporters who queried him about the gift that he gave money to a lot of candidates after looking over the field and deciding which he liked best, but he could not remember hearing of an Alton Lennon.—*The News and Observer* (Raleigh, N.C.), May 27, 1954.

62. The cases of two-party contributions in different jurisdictions that were identified fell into the following types:

Gifts	*1952*	*1956*
By presidential Republicans, or Democrats	11	0
To U.S. Senatorial candidate of other party	19	12
To U.S. Congressional candidate of other party	0	4
In different jurisdictions within the same state	3	1
Others	4	6
	37	23

63. Assessment of state employees has been a well-established procedure for political fund-raising in Indiana. During a heated Republican factional fight in 1954, "some state employees, playing both sides of the fence, made contributions of two per cent to both factions."—Frank James Munger, "Two-Party Politics in the State of Indiana" (Ph.D. dissertation, Harvard University, 1955), p. 96.

64. Drew Pearson has reported his interviews on this subject with Grunewald—*The News and Observer* (Raleigh, N.C.), September 27, 1954; Goldfine testified before a special committee of the U.S. House of Representatives that he had contributed heavily to both party funds, probably $100,000 over the years—AP dispatch of July 17, 1958; an early instance of Samish's simultaneous support of opposing candidates in California was told in the famous, suppressed *Legislative Investigative Report,* submitted by H. R. Philbrick, December 28, 1938, p. IV-4.

ties of his Third Ward Political Club in Newark, New Jersey, during the 1930's.[65] Yet this particular type of political behavior, like much political behavior, is more a product of political institutions than of the motives and morals of individual men. Where control of government is divided among elected officials and political parties, and is likely in time to pass from one group of partisans to another, those with continuous, politically-vulnerable stakes in the society seek to hedge against political vicissitudes. This is true everywhere.

The Liberal and Conservative parties in Canada have drawn their support, not only from the same types of business and financial interests, but on occasion from the same firms and individuals.[66] Chinese businessmen in the Philippines give not to a single party but to opposing political groups.[67] Some Japanese business firms contribute to both the conservative and socialist parties, and some, with an eye on future trade with Communist China, have made donations to the Japanese Communist party.[68] In Denmark, the Danish Employers' Association is occasionally revealed to have made cash contributions to more than one party. In Uruguay, industrialists are said to have provided funds to both the Colorado and Herrera parties. And so it goes around the globe wherever governments are chosen through popular elections. Contributors seek to advance their interests. Indeed, they may do so through all other forms of political participation as well. As one old hand remarked, he never gives money to both sides. He has found other ways to persuade both parties that he is their friend.

65. U.S. Senate Special Committee to Investigate Organized Crime in Interstate Commerce (hereafter cited as the Kefauver Crime Committee), *Hearings* (Washington: Government Printing Office, 1951), part 12, p. 615.

66. Ernest Eugene Harrill, "The Structure of Organization and Power in Canadian Political Parties: A Study in Party Financing" (Ph.D. dissertation, University of North Carolina, 1953), pp. 232-54.

67. Avelino B. Lim, "Money and Philippine Politics" (typescript), p. 5.

68. Nobutaka Ike, *Japanese Politics* (New York: Alfred A. Knopf, 1957), p. 201.

4

WHY PEOPLE GIVE

SOME YEARS AGO a turn of fate left Little Orphan Annie with no prospect of toys for Christmas. Readers immediately sent a flood of gifts to her at the Chicago newspaper that ran the comic strip. If any of the sentimentalists who feared for Annie's Christmas grew up to become political contributors, they have doubtless confounded the rules of self-interest that supposedly govern such people. The human being is a complicated animal, and human actions are colored by many hues of motive. The driving designs of monied men for an early gain are but one type of incentive to political action. They mingle with other spurs of human conduct to stimulate millions of Americans to make political gifts. To understand the full role of money in politics, we must seek the many reasons people give.

1. THE GOALS OF GIVING

There have been many studies striving to learn "why" some people vote and others do not, and why those who vote choose the candidates they do. The general procedure centers on identifying the characteristics of individuals and their environment that are associated with various types of voting behavior. Under most conditions, for example, it appears that persons of high economic status and educational achievement are likely to vote in greater proportion than others. This type of analysis has been extended in recent years beyond identification of the social and economic characteristics of voters and nonvoters. Attempts have been made to learn how voters and nonvoters perceive the efficacy of political action, how they view parties and candidates, how their behavior may be affected by membership in various groups, what inducements to vote they have been presented with, and so on. Attempts have also been made to classify individuals by characteristics of personality to learn what personality types seem to be associated with what types of political behavior.

Why people contribute, like why they vote, is a complicated matter. Some contributors, in truth, rush to the victor's bandwagon after an election.[1] Yet what even this small sector of contributors gain by doing so is not always apparent. Victory does not lessen a politician's skepticism of fair-weather friends. In the main, there is no simple and predictable connection between contributions and the desire for political privilege. Many factors other than the hope for special favor prompt donations.[2] It has already been pointed out, for example, that persons who are *generally* active in politics are more likely to give than persons who are not. Whatever moves them to other types of political participation seems also to move them toward financial participation. What contributors want in return for their gifts, moreover, has a bearing on what they get. A political gift does not automatically carry influence in proportion to its size. It does not necessarily carry influence at all. There are also other kinds of gratification that givers seek and receive as a consequence of their giving.

Motivations are complex.—Psychologists are concerned with concepts of motivation, but an outlander to their discipline quickly appreciates the extreme difficulty of defining and utilizing such concepts. The situation seems to have been put accurately by Sigmund Koch: "Behavior is never motivated by a single need; it is always a complex function of a plurality of coacting needs. In this immensely complex area we have virtually no soundly established knowledge."[3] What is true of behavior in general applies also to politics. Gardner Murphy has concluded that "Politics is thus a typical example of a very complex blend of many motives."[4] Despite these common-sense conclusions of the specialists, political observers have usually attributed political donations to highly simplified incentives. In the Western world, and particularly in the United States, these attributed incentives have often been economic in character. A profit-motive theory has frequently been advanced to explain gifts made in politics: a man gives as best suits his immediate personal interests, particularly his pocketbook. Even the

1. An analysis was made of contributions of $500 and over reported by the regular national-level committees of the major parties in 1948 and 1952. (The committees were the national, Senatorial, and Congressional campaign committees.) In 1948, 23 Republican gifts and 237 Democratic gifts from persons who had not previously given were made after the results of the election were known. In 1952, in accord with the outcome of the election, there were 245 Republican and 26 Democratic post-election donations of this type.—The details, including dollar values, are presented in the Gore Committee *Hearings,* part 2, p. 532.

2. A contrary view, vigorously set forth, may be found in Ferdinand Lundberg, *The Treason of the People* (New York: Harper & Brothers, 1954), especially pp. 179-81, which contain a six-part classification of campaign contributors, all motivated by immediate and generally anti-social self-interest.

3. "The Current Status of Motivational Psychology," *Psychological Review,* 58 (1951), 151.

4. "Social Motivation," in Gardner Lindzey (ed.), *Handbook of Social Psychology* (Cambridge: Addison-Wesley, 1954), vol. 2, p. 610.

facts of economic life are somewhat more complex, however, as students of economic behavior point out: "Every person on the contemporary economic scene—the owner manager, the corporation executive, the farmer, the worker, the union officer, the consumer, the saver, the investor—now emerges as an extremely complex figure whose attitudes, motives, and behavior vary from culture to culture, from society to society, from period to period, and from individual to individual."[5] Comparable diversity characterizes the wellsprings of political giving. This basic fact has been recognized by careful students of politics.[6] And it has been pointed to by professional politicians.[7] But the difficulties of identifying and classifying the kinds of gratification sought through political gifts are formidable. They are so formidable, in fact, that discussion of the subject has not proceeded much beyond acknowledging the complexity and deploring the difficulty.

Six categories.—A limited attack on the subject was made through lengthy, intensive interviews with four samples of North Carolinians who made campaign contributions to the presidential race in 1952.[8]

Table 6

DISTRIBUTION OF RESPONDENTS BY DOMINANT "GOALS" OF THEIR GIFTS: FOUR SAMPLES OF NORTH CAROLINA CONTRIBUTORS, GENERAL ELECTION, 1952

Goal	Contributors Who Gave to Specified Committees			
	$100 or More		Less than $100	
	Dem.	Rep.	Dem.	Rep.
Government policy	13	18	3	13
Personal identification	3	3	18	12
Duty and responsibility	0	0	1	0
Government privilege	4	0	3	0
Private privilege	0	2	0	0
Entree	5	0	0	0
Total samples	25	23	25	25

5. Albert Lauterbach, *Man, Motives, and Money—Psychological Frontiers of Economics* (Ithaca: Cornell University Press, 1954), p. 238.

6. James K. Pollock, *Party Campaign Funds* (New York: Alfred A. Knopf, 1926), pp. 130-40; Louise Overacker, *Money in Elections* (New York: The Macmillan Company, 1932), pp. 199-200.

7. Often in interviews, and by Edward J. Flynn in *You're the Boss* (New York: The Viking Press, 1947), pp. 123-24; by James A. Farley in *Behind the Ballots—The Personal History of a Politician* (New York: Harcourt, Brace and Co., 1938), p. 237; by Richard L. Neuberger in *Adventures in Politics—We Go to the Legislature* (New York: Oxford University Press, 1954), p. 141.

8. Many of the results of this research, which has already been cited, are reported by Lester W. Milbrath in "The Motivations and Characteristics of Political Contributors: North Carolina General Election 1952" (Ph.D. dissertation, University of North Carolina, 1956).

Each contributor was asked questions intended to reveal his social and economic circumstances, his patterns of political activity, various personality characteristics, the conditions under which he contributed, the expectations he held when contributing, and the consequences that may have followed as a result of his contributing. Each respondent was also asked to say why he thought he had given and why he thought other people give to politics. Each respondent was then classified according to a dominant goal, as well as subsidiary goals, that were judged to have prompted his act of contributing.

The classification of goals developed in this process will be laid out briefly. The technical and theoretical dangers in the procedures followed were abundant. Nevertheless, the resulting classification of types of gratification sought through contributing will introduce a framework for consideration of the subject that has not previously been present.[9] Many persons possessing the political objectives and interests to be mentioned do not make contributions. An attempt was therefore made to learn why some people give and others do not. After the categories of goals are presented, personal characteristics that distinguish givers from nongivers, and situational characteristics that appear to encourage giving, will be discussed. Some of the factors that account for the recent upsurge in the number of political contributors will become apparent.

Six broad categories of goals were constructed on the basis of the North Carolina interviews.[10] The number of cases from each of the four samples that fell into each category varied as shown in Table 6. The categories arrived at were as follows:

1. Concern for government policy. Some contributors were interested in policies identified with a political party, some in policies identified with a particular candidate. Others were moved by concern for individual policies or general trends without especially associating them with a party or candidate.

2. Personal identification with a group or an individual. Some contributors identified themselves blindly with one party, without regard to contemporary issues. Some felt deep identification, even emotional

9. It would seem that similar problems beset all who are imprudent enough to try to discern why people do things. Speaking of businessmen, an author in *Fortune* observes that "... recently a lot of businessmen and advertising men, too, have [become] ... convinced that the consumer's apparent reasons for buying (or not buying) are seldom his 'real' reasons, and that the consumer himself (or herself) seldom knows those 'real' reasons."—Perrin Stryker, "Motivation Research," *Fortune*, 53 (June 1956), 144.

10. In addition to other questions, respondents were asked in open-ended questions why they gave and why they thought other people give; they were subsequently asked to answer a multiple-choice question concerning their own incentives in giving. The 19 options offered in the latter question were formulated to cover all the supposed "reasons" persons give in politics, as reflected in the written and spoken lore of the subject.

involvement, with a candidate. Others found it desirable to conform to the expectations of groups to which they belonged.

3. Feelings of duty and responsibility to be politically active, and to support the political process with money, that were not hinged to more immediate or tangible incentives.

4. Desire for governmental privileges, including political patronage, government purchases, franchises, protection from or by means of law enforcement, and special statutes.

5. Desire for private privileges from nongovernmental sources, affecting such things as jobs, credit facilities, purchase orders, and avoidance of many types of sanctions. Campaign solicitors, employers, and others outside government may exercise their private power for political ends.

6. Desire for entree. Persons aspiring to leadership in party, community, or state, or who foresee the possible need for help with a political problem, normally seek to establish general good will by any means available to them.

Selfishness: a false concept.—All of these categories embrace the satisfaction of psychological needs or material aspirations of one kind or another. There is no dichotomy between selfish and unselfish incentives. The social value and political consequences of contributions stemming from different types of motives may differ radically from each other, but they are all made in pursuit of some kind of personal satisfaction. The first three headings in the classification can be viewed as involving community-oriented motivations, although they may also involve personal satisfactions. In contrast, the fourth and fifth headings are concerned with special privileges. The final category may involve both types of incentive.[11] The volume and impact of campaign gifts are not to be explained by any narrow concept of self-interest. The variety of impulses that lead to contributing is critically important to any efforts that are made to alter the sources of campaign funds.

The proportion of the contributors in the North Carolina samples who were classified under each of the six headings is evident from Table 6. They do not, however, necessarily reflect the distribution of these goals among all contributors, either in North Carolina or in the United States.[12] It must be remembered also that each individual was classified

11. Elaborated in Milbrath, *op. cit.*, pp. 26-33.

12. There are many reasons for this. The random samples were drawn from official reports as described above, page 38. Not all contributors to a political organization necessarily show up on the official reports. The incentives of contributors may vary from one type of recipient organization to another. It has already been noted that receipts from the sale of the Ruml $5.00 certificates to aid Governor Stevenson were not reported through the Democratic state committee, thus an important type of small Democratic contributor did not appear in the universe from which the sample of small Democratic contributors was drawn. All but one of the low Democratic givers in the sample was a state employee.

by what was *judged* to be his *dominant* goal. Most individuals clearly had subsidiary goals in addition.[13] Despite these limitations, the interview data used in constructing the table buttress observations made in conversation by persons of long and varied experience with political finance.

Concern for "government policy" motivates contributing just as it motivates voting. This concern looms as more important than the desire for some sort of special personal privilege. Of the 18 High Republican Contributors, for example, who were judged to have been concerned chiefly about policy matters, 13 were clearly aroused by opposition to the policies of the Democratic administration then in office and four by confidence in what they conceived to be policies identified with General Eisenhower personally. Of the 13 High Democratic Contributors classified as primarily interested in government policies, 11 perceived the broad programs of the Democratic party as in the long run best for the nation and the state. The latter was not surprising since Democrats were firmly in control of the state government. This local domination also explains why nine High Democrats and no High Republicans showed up opposite "government privilege" and "entree" in Table 6. The samples of contributors were chosen on the basis of gifts to state rather than national political committees. Republicans had less incentive to seek either of these goals through contributions at the state level than the Democrats. Gifts to one of the national-level Republican campaign organizations would be another matter. Among the Low Contributors, 13 of the Republicans displayed anxiety over government policies. Ten of the 13, like most of the corresponding High Republican Contributors, professed alarm over the policies of the existing Democratic administration.

Thirty of the Low Contributors—18 Democrats and 12 Republicans —were deemed to have been stimulated chiefly by "personal identification." Their presence emphasizes a consideration frequently advanced by political solicitors: the utility of getting prospective donors into situations where they are carried along with the crowd. Fourteen of the Democrats and five of the Republicans in question were apparently swayed by desire to conform to a social reference group. The 14 Democrats are particularly instructive. Of the 25 Low Democrats in the sample, 24 worked for the state of North Carolina and 21 for the highway department. Most of the 24 state employees were motivated by more subtle influences than fear for their jobs, although fear was judged to have dominated in three cases. The context in which the appeal for funds was generally made—the average contribution for all 25 was

---

Although containing approximately the same number of persons, the samples were drawn from universes that differed widely in size, as follows: HDC, 62; HRC, 123; LDC, approximately 12,500; LRC, 413.

13. Individual contributors offered from one to seven motives for their own giving, averaging more than three each.

$2.50—did not seem to generate conscious fear of reprisals from higher-ups. Officials were usually meticulous in giving assurances that contributing was optional, and there was no evidence of penalties against those who exercised the option not to give. The decisive influence seemed to be the pressure to conform to the prevailing behavior of the employee group, solicitations often being made as the men assembled for work assignments at the beginning of the day. Kicking in small sums at campaign time to the Democratic state committee is a deeply imbedded custom. Not to do so would violate group expectations in a conspicuous and uncomfortable way. Solicitors, as we shall see, find in the urge to conform a powerful weapon in appealing for large contributions as well.

2. THE CAUSES OF GIVING

Incentives like those outlined above were held by many persons who did not contribute in 1952. If some of these persons gave, why not others?

Stimulus and predisposition.—The factors that affect whether persons make contributions can be grouped in two broad categories. One of these embraces the numerous kinds of environmental stimuli that reach prospective donors, including the immediate circumstances of their decision to give or not to give. The other embraces a variety of factors that are personal and internal to the individual. These include not only social and economic characteristics, like income and occupation, but less measurable qualities of personality. An individual's general level of political involvement also falls in this category. The term predisposition is used here to designate this set of factors.[14]

The act of giving, in this conception, depends on the dynamic interaction of environmental stimuli and predispositional factors. Exploration within this framework reveals several factors of environment and of predisposition that are positively related to contributing. The factors for study were chosen largely from the beliefs of solicitors as to the types of people who constitute good prospects and the effective ways of appealing to them.

Our concern at the moment is with contributors. In later chapters the elaborate fund-raising campaigns carried on by parties and candidates will be studied in detail, as will the conditions and practices that create the need for funds. Throughout, the considerable exertions required to fill political war chests will be evident. Citizens who must be dragooned into giving far outnumber those who cheerfully proffer donations without being asked. It is well to remember that there are differences among contributors in the goals and circumstances of their giving. Loose

14. In the professional literature the term is not used uniformly. Note Murray S. Stedman, Jr., "Pressure Groups and the American Tradition," *The Annals*, 319 (1958), 124-29.

generalizations that imply all donors are alike obstruct understanding of the roles they actually play and of the demands they actually make in the processes of politics.

The context of giving.—Many transitory influences affect contributing behavior. Our focus will be on a small number of environmental and predispositional characteristics that seem to be related to campaign giving. There are numerous other environmental and predispositional factors, many of which change from election to election, that may influence decisively individual actions. These transitory features comprise an important part of the context within which fund-raising at any particular time must proceed.

The intensity of competition, for example, has a noticeable effect on the proportion of a population that contributes. Differences are visible from one campaign to another and more generally between jurisdictions of differing party rivalry.[15] One consequence of this condition is the likelihood that contributing to general-election campaigns will mount if party competition continues to invade the old one-party hegemonies (e.g., Maine and Florida). The issues and personalities of a campaign stimulate contributors. A speech in Omaha in 1948 by Senator Taft advocating sliding parities prompted immediate Democratic contributions from several farm groups.[16] The appeal of the Eisenhower personality seems clearly to have pulled many young businessmen into contributing and soliciting who had barely shown an interest in politics before. The level of economic prosperity in a community also helps to determine the level of political contributing. We shall see that the proportions of persons contributing rises as income rises. Since 1940 the volume of free money available to Americans above basic living needs has mounted sharply.[17] The increase in the number of contributors in recent years

15. In both its 1952 and 1956 general-election studies, the Survey Research Center found that a smaller percentage of southern respondents said they made contributions than did residents of other sections. Political competition and voting participation were lower in the South in both elections. The percentage of respondents saying they had given in each section was as follows:

	U.S.	*Northeast*	*Midwest*	*Far West*	*South*
1952	*4*	5	4	9	2
1956	*10*	13	11	10	6

16. Jack Redding, *Inside the Democratic Party* (New York: The Bobbs-Merrill Company, Inc., 1958), p. 151. Writing "Reflections on Money and Party Politics in Britain," Frank C. Newman observes, "On the big issues it is the [party] programme that attracts the money; the money does not structure the programme." —*Parliamentary Affairs,* 10 (1956-57), 316.

17. Per capita disposable personal income, with adjustments for changes in the price level, rose 53 per cent between 1940 and 1956. This is income after personal taxes and other government revenues have been deducted. —Derived from U.S. Bureau of the Census, *Statistical Abstract of the United States: 1958* (Washington: Government Printing Office, 1958), p. 304.

probably would not have occurred without this affluence. The specific stakes individuals have in government action lead them to contribute. A former Governor of Illinois has testified that he and other bankers traded political donations for deposits of state and county monies.[18] Many industries in addition to the oil industry enjoy depletion allowances for federal tax purposes, privileges their members seek to preserve through various types of political activity, including contributing.

Illustrations abound of varied types of stimuli that trigger predisposed persons to give to politics to achieve the goals outlined earlier. Some persons are more predisposed than others, however, and under some conditions are more vulnerable to appeals for funds than under others.

Habitual contributors.—It is prudent to ask at the outset whether many contributors make their donations regularly and voluntarily without prodding. Clearly some do, but the extent of habitual contributing in the United States—which is not necessarily the same as voluntary contributing—has not hitherto been studied. We do not know precisely what funds at various levels come from a durable core of supporters nor whether this core changes in importance. From the evidence at hand, nevertheless, several reasonable judgments can be drawn.

The number of repeat contributors to national-level committees who show up year after year with sizeable gifts is relatively small. This is the oral testimony of national fund-raisers and is confirmed by the experience of the Democratic and Republican national committees. The number of repeaters is indicated by the following data on the individuals reported as giving $500 or more to these committees during each of the years between 1933 and 1945, inclusive:

	Number of Individuals Making a Contribution of $500 or more during 1933-45 to the:	
	Republican National Committee	*Democratic National Committee*
In at least 1 year	3821	1966
In 2 or more years	880	309
In 3 or more years	329	137
In 4 or more years	135	40
In 5 or more years	72	17

The percentage of the total value of individual contributions that came in certain years to these committees from persons who gave in four different years, and in five or more different years, were as follows:[19]

18. *New York Times*, October 12, 1956.

19. Margaret A. Hunt, "Certain Social and Economic Characteristics of Campaign Contributors in a National Election Year" (Master's thesis, University of North Carolina, 1958), p. 91. Miss Hunt lists the individuals involved on pp. 153-56.

	Gave in Four Years to		Gave in Five or More Years to	
	Republican National Committee	*Democratic National Committee*	*Republican National Committee*	*Democratic National Committee*
1936	3.0	3.4	6.0	4.7
1940	4.1	3.5	6.8	5.3
1944	4.0	2.0	7.3	2.9
1952	1.3	0.6	3.9	0.9

Among those recorded as giving directly to the two national committees during 1933-45, more than 75 per cent of the Republicans and almost 85 per cent of the Democrats gave in only one year.[20] At lower levels, the situation appears to be somewhat different. A larger share of the costs of campaigning is probably borne by a coterie of party faithful. State finance directors among Republicans speak of persons who give as routinely as they pay their club dues and church donations. The importance of repeaters seems to vary from state to state, partly because of the differing effectiveness of solicitation procedures. Most persons in the four samples of North Carolina contributors could be classed as regular donors to the party. The respondents, who had given to the state committees of both parties in 1952, were asked in 1954 how many different contributions they had made during the previous six years (1948-54). The period included three general and four primary elections. The average numbers of different contributions reported were:[21]

20. The proportion of the funds received from one-time contributors might be different, though in all probability not greatly. A limitation prevailed during part of this period on the size of contribution that could be made to a single committee in any one year. Man and wife were treated as one "individual" in the analysis. Even though some repeat contributors may have been disguised behind dummy names, and practices varied throughout the period with regard to the reporting of individuals whose gifts were transferred from state and local groups, and some donors gave to other national-level committees, the evidence is clear that neither party at this level could have depended for its support on a band of dues-paying devotees. For the proportion of funds coming from contributions of $500 and over, see pages 48-54, above. Louise Overacker provided the files of contributions used in making this analysis.

21. Milbrath, *op. cit.*, p. 187. Of the persons making up the four samples, 80 per cent gave at least once each two years. If a projection is made to the entire state, as though the four universes from which the samples were drawn comprised all contributors, 95 per cent would be regulars.—*Ibid.*, p. 297. As with other aspects of political finance, intensive study of reports submitted by selected state and local political groups over a period of years would elaborate our knowledge of this point. Among 22 donors of $500 or more to state-level committees in New York in 1952, Herbert E. Alexander found on interviewing them that seven had given with regularity since 1946 and 13 had given off and on for about 20 years.—"The Role of the Volunteer Political Fund Raiser: A Case Study in New York in 1952" (Ph.D. dissertation, Yale University, 1958), p. 81.

Democratic contributors of $100 or more in 1952	9.6
Republican contributors of $100 or more in 1952	8.4
Democratic contributors of less than $100 in 1952	4.0
Republican contributors of less than $100 in 1952	5.1

Democrats predominate in North Carolina, but not enough to render party activity unnecessary. This steady balance between the parties may produce a faithful band who put up a larger share of the comparatively modest party budget than corresponding groups provide in other states where different conditions prevail.[22]

Habitual contributing and voluntary contributing, however, are not synonymous. Many of the faithful have to be reminded. Both the frequency and volume of voluntary giving are clearly lower.[23] Political financiers report almost unanimously that personal solicitation is essential to raise money in what, under prevailing conditions, would be thought of as meaningful sums, let us say in amounts of $100 or more. Personal solicitation is infinitely more effective than appeals over mass media in raising sums of any size. And between mail solicitation and direct personal contact over the telephone or face-to-face, direct personal contact is always declared more effective.

Solicit down, not up.—Careful steps are taken in all types of fund-raising to put prospective donors under pressure. The goal is to make it significantly more comfortable to give than to refuse to give. Two broad tactics are employed. Prospective contributors are assigned to solicitors whom they view as equal or superior in status,[24] persons whom they wish to please. And the human urge to conform is played upon. Situations are utilized in which members of groups valued by the prospect set the style of giving. The appeal of a wisely chosen solicitor

22. At least so it would seem in Connecticut from the analyses made by John Robert Owens of "core" Democratic and Republican contributors.—"Party Campaign Fund in Connecticut, 1950-1954" (Ph.D. dissertation, Syracuse University, 1956), pp. 207-11.

23. Among the total of 98 persons in the four North Carolina samples, only 21 said they could recall receiving no appeal for funds and consequently claimed to have given on their own initiative. Of these, however, 11 were high Democratic givers, largely political practitioners so deeply involved in party affairs that giving was a matter of routine. The others were: HRC, 4; LDC, 1; LRC, 5. Voluntary contributions have special significance because of privilege and influence often sought through them.

24. Among the 98 persons in the four North Carolina samples, 43 of those solicited responded to a question about the status of the solicitor who approached them. Twenty rated the solicitor more important than themselves, 21 as peers, and two persons said they were solicited by persons they considered of a status beneath their own. The last two were Low Democratic Contributors; otherwise the differences between the samples were not important. Only three persons were solicited by individuals of lesser occupational status.—Milbrath, *op. cit.*, p. 176. Alexander found virtually the same situation among solicitors and givers of large sums in New York.—*Op. cit.*, pp. 60-79.

may, in fact, constitute an enticement to conform to the behavior of the solicitor and all he represents.

Reciprocity is at the heart of effective solicitation. As the director of the united fund in one of America's largest cities observed, "We send a guy's best customer after him." In political soliciting the reciprocities need not be political. A titan of New York campaign finance argued that business reasons and friendship compel contributions if "you get the right people to contact the right people." "I give a man a tip on a good stock and he wants to show his appreciation when I ask him for a check for Eisenhower." "A person hates to turn down someone he knows and respects, just for his personal ego."[25] Personal ego gets mightily entangled in the whole strategy. Prestige may be gained by complying with the pleas of persons of prestige, and political contributing through the right channels may thereby aid in the struggle for status. The desire for status is one of the fulcrum points for leverage in political soliciting.[26] The desire for prestige and appreciation in fact undergirds much political ambition, often transcending in importance more tangible favors.[27]

Leading Democratic fund-raisers during the Roosevelt and Truman administrations saw that large contributors (who cared about such things) were invited to White House social events and presented to the President when he was on tour in their states.[28] Republican fund-raisers also acknowledge that some of their contributors appreciate this kind of recognition. Almost one-third of the guests (other than governmental officials) at the 38 White House stag dinners during the first two years

25. Relevant is the experience of a national civic organization. The organization depends for part of its support on contributions raised by local affiliates across the nation. The New York office has learned from long experience that the size of contributions coming from a city depends on the level at which the local solicitor operates in his community's affairs. It has nothing to do with the nature of the organization or its program. The "right man" attracts checks of $50.00 to $100. In another city a less affluent and prominent person pulls in checks for $5.00 and $10.00, indicating the reciprocity he enjoys with his friends and associates. Impressed by the achievements of its fund-raiser in a western city, this organization thought the man's methods might be useful to its representatives elsewhere. Asked how he did it, the man said he ran a large department store and simply asked his suppliers to help the worthy cause.

26. A report from California in 1957 had Republican ladies dangling parties in fashionable homes as bait to attract their political-club dues of $50.00.

27. A gentleman of some experience in these matters once explained politicians to his Secretary of Labor: "They'd rather have a nice jolly understanding of their problems than lots of patronage. A little patronage, a lot of pleasure, and public signs of friendship and prestige—that's what makes a political leader secure with his people and that is what he wants anyhow."—Frances Perkins, *The Roosevelt I Knew* (New York: The Viking Press, 1946), p. 20.

28. After a turn on the presidential yacht *Williamsburg* during the Truman administration, J. Howard McGrath, then chairman of the Democratic national committee, mused soulfully, ". . . think what we could do if he'd only let us invite a few contributors along for a trip like this one. We'd have no finance problem at all."—Redding, *op. cit.*, p. 167.

of the Eisenhower administration were known to have made Republican campaign gifts of $500 or more in 1952.[29] Solicitors consciously and unconsciously play on the susceptibilities of their friends and associates.[30] They even achieve what in some circles is called the soft shakedown, a genteel indication that "if you don't scratch my back I won't scratch yours." They give to each other's pet causes[31] and open social, economic, and political doors to each other—not so much as negotiated favors, but as the natural behavior of companions in a valued circle. "We're all in it together," explained one contributor, when asked whether the contributing of several of his friends accounted for his own gifts. "I guess they wouldn't influence me more than I would influence them." Solicitors who can inspire confidence and apply the squeeze without being offensive are a prized type of politician.[32]

Climate of conformity.—The tightest squeeze is the drive to conformity. "It's like you back in North Carolina," said a Texan, eye-deep in his state's politics. "Somebody comes around and asks you for two dollars for charity and you may not want to give it but you don't want to be thought a heel, so you reach down in your pocket and get the two dollars. They do the same thing here. They can't turn you down when you lay it on the line." Especially when you lay it on the line at a luncheon for twenty, none of whom wants to be thought a heel by the other nineteen, even when asked for $10,000 each. ("You then tell them that if they can go out and raise that money among their friends,

29. The number of guests totalled 555. Of these, 81 were administration officials. Among the 474 others, known contributors of $500 or more during 1952 numbered 149, 131 of whom gave solely to Republicans, 8 solely to Democrats, and 10 to recipients in both parties. The guests included 294 persons classified as businessmen, of whom 111 were known to have contributed. The list of guests appeared in *U.S. News and World Report,* February 4, 1955, pp. 34-41. Shortly thereafter the White House announced that the guest lists would no longer be released to the press. "Some old friends of the President were reported hurt at not being included, and some business men had protested after seeing names of rivals."—*New York Times,* March 5, 1955. There seems to be a hierarchy in such things. In one state, the finance chairman was invited to a stag dinner, and the finance committee's paid secretary was included in an afternoon tea.

30. Among the North Carolina contributors who had been solicited, all but one was approached by a person well known to him personally. Lumping the four samples together, the respondents classified the solicitors as business acquaintances (45 per cent), friends (34 per cent), relatives (11 per cent), and in other relationships (10 per cent). The classifications were about the same for all four samples, except that all but one of the Low Democrats were classed as business acquaintances, meaning fellow workers in the state government.

31. One Chicagoan reported that each year he makes a small contribution to "the seeing eye, or something like that," because a friend asks him to, a friend who responds to the Chicagoan's plea for funds for Hull House.

32. The necessity for confidence in individual solicitors is presumably least with highly institutionalized fund-raising systems that have earned the respect of their clienteles. But confidence that the money will wind up at the right destination is important, the most important element in soliciting in the opinion of one former Democratic national treasurer.

okay, do so, but give us the dough now and let's not get fooling around . . .")[33] This drive to conformity is mercilessly exploited in all types of fund-raising, not the least for worthy causes of church, charity, and school.[34] Operative in all social settings, it may prove more vital to Republican than to Democratic solicitations because of the clique and class consciousness of the social and economic constituencies of the Republican party.[35]

Political fund-raisers set up group situations for trapping contributions. The cocktail parties and teas that are given to raise money are usually carefully engineered.[36] After the pitch, selected guests quickly move forward to break the ice and set the pace. It is important for early contributions to fall at the optimum level. The rest of the crowd almost invariably follows the standard set by the beginners.[37]

Candidates on tour provide favorable opportunities for these events. Ordinarily a presidential candidate is "advanced." One or more men go to the localities he will visit to check on local preparations. The advance men are concerned among other things with the individuals to be invited to meet the candidate. A crucial event of the candidate's visit is usually a social event where he says a few words (perhaps alluding to the scarcity of campaign funds). Afterward his "financial henchmen" (as one advance man called them) move in to capitalize on the euphoria. For at least one presidential candidate, the carefully selected

33. The honor roll of contributors is familiar in nonpolitical fund-raising. Michigan Democrats have at times issued "The Michigan Green Book of Democratic Party Contributions" which lists donors to the party by county and by frequency of giving, though not by amount.

34. "Well, here's your pledge all filled out and ready for you to sign," said Jack Purcell to H. M. Pulham, Esquire, raising funds for their twenty-fifth Harvard reunion.

"Attaboy," Bo-jo said. "Shake it out of him."

"Now, wait a minute, Jack . . ."

"It's what you're down for, Harry. Out of the fifteen I've seen already fourteen of them have signed in full."

—Thus in the language of John P. Marquand, unerring literary photographer of American upper-class compulsions to conformity, in *H. M. Pulham, Esquire* (Boston: Little, Brown and Co., 1941), p. 390. Contemporary fund-raising practices that exploit human frailties for supposedly worthy causes are discussed and deplored by Vance Packard in *The Hidden Persuaders* (New York: David McKay Company, 1957), pp. 222-24.

35. Negative effects are felt, too. Stories abound of businessmen who help Democratic candidates on the side but will not do so publicly because they fear being "out of step" with the groups in which they circulate.

36. See pages 245-47, below.

37. Undoubtedly characteristic of behavior in many situations. A controlled experiment among 50 graduate students contributing to a gift for a retiring departmental secretary demonstrated that the amounts volunteered were markedly affected by what the donors thought were the sizes of the gifts that had already been made.—Robert R. Blake, Milton Rosenbaum, and Richard A. Duryea, "Gift-Giving as a Function of Group Standards," *Human Relations*, 8 (1955), 61-73.

"fat cats" were split up and crowded into rooms intentionally small to create an aura of intimacy with the great man.[38]

Social and economic variables.—Environmental and institutional factors account only partially for the contributing behavior of Americans. Persons react in different ways to the appeals they receive. Some display a higher predisposition toward contributing than others. It is hypothesized that some minimum predisposition and some minimum environmental stimulus must both be present for contributing to occur. Several factors will be examined as evidences of predisposition toward contributing. Even a brief exploration of predispositional variables will further demonstrate the complexity of motivational factors that explain political giving.

To give, one must have. The proportion of persons in various income brackets who make political contributions rises with income. The Survey Research Center's study of the 1956 election found that none of its respondents with family incomes under $1,000 per year said they had given money or bought something to aid a candidate or party. Thirty-one per cent of those with annual family incomes of $10,000 or more said they had done so. The rise in contributing between these extremes of income was relatively even.[39] A larger share of persons in professional, business, and managerial groups said they had contributed (18 to 19 per cent) than was so of persons in other occupational groups (6 to 8 per cent).[40] Persons in middle life were more likely to contribute than persons in their twenties or over 65.[41] All of this simply

38. "Teas for the sisterhood" are also arranged. Candidates vary in their effectiveness on fund-raising occasions. A local manager usually goes over the guest list with the candidate, briefing him on the people to be present. An old hand who specialized in businessmen recalled that Franklin Roosevelt and Harry Truman were quick to catch a clue of identification when these people were presented and would "run away with it, butter it up beautifully." Adlai Stevenson appears to appeal more to "intellectual" and "emotional" people than businessmen. Stevenson was severely criticized by the sponsor of one cocktail party that flopped because after his talk he did not move into the crowd shaking hands around the room.

39. See footnote 17, page 44, above. The same trend is found in charitable fund-raising campaigns.—David L. Sills, *The Volunteers—Means and Ends in a National Organization* (Glencoe, Illinois: The Free Press, 1957), p. 178. It is "broadly true that families with after-tax incomes under $4,000 are obliged to spend just about everything on the necessities of food, clothing, shelter, transportation, and medical care. As they move over the $4,000 line, they have extra income with which they can exercise a number of options. . . . By the time that families move over the $7,500 line, about half their income is discretionary . . ." —Sanford S. Parker and Lawrence A. Mayer, "The Decade of the 'Discretionary' Dollar," *Fortune,* 59 (June, 1959), 136.

40. The percentages of affirmative responses, by occupation, were as follows: housewife, 6 per cent; retired, 6 per cent; farm operator, 6 per cent; nonskilled, 7 per cent; white collar, 7 per cent; skilled, 8 per cent; business and managerial, 18 per cent; professional, 19 per cent. The 1952 data are consistent with these.

41. Those who said they gave in 1956 were, by age brackets, as follows: 21-24, 6 per cent; 25-34, 7 per cent; 35-44, 13 per cent; 45-54, 12 per cent; 55-64, 11 per cent; 65 and over, 6 per cent.

means that persons who are better situated in life than others to make campaign contributions are more likely to do so.

Personality.—If almost one-third of the people with annual family incomes of $10,000 or more made political donations in 1956, why not the other two-thirds? Since contributing is closely related to other types of political participation, this is really to ask why some persons are generally more active in politics than others who have many of the same external characteristics.

Solicitors in and out of politics develop their sucker lists, the soft touches. These practical politicians talk about temperament. One of them, who for years has tapped Texas millionaires for political funds, concludes that some of his friends simply are tight and others are not. Another has worked the same clientele from a different angle. He points to the late Hugh Roy Cullen as proof that "some guys just have to get rid of the stuff (while others just can't)." In 1953 Cullen was carried away after the University of Houston defeated Baylor at football, and forthwith announced at a student rally that the "great spirit and determination shown by the Cougars" moved him to present the University with $2,250,000 in oil payments.[42] A member of the Republican national committee reflected on Mr. John Hay Whitney's appearances before national conclaves of the party some years before he became Ambassador to London. The national committeeman, not a jolly type, noted with incredulity that Mr. Whitney was "enjoying" himself if any man ever did. The "thrill" they get out of it, the sport of the thing,[43] the socializing that goes with politicking, playing the big dog, indulging a hobby—these are the rewards many get from politics, including contributing to politics, say the fellows who are in it themselves.

Men and women are stirred in their use of money by deep-seated characteristics that defy easy analysis. "The psychological meaning of money to various cultures, societies, groups, and individuals is an extensive subject in itself."[44] Lord Duveen and the Mizner brothers could create a craze for art forms and institutionalize them as badges of standing in American life, with the price as the gauge. A little girl found happiness as the mascot of a San Francisco fire department. Decades later she willed money to erect a firemen's memorial atop Telegraph Hill. The land is fertile with generous and curious and

42. *New York Times,* November 11, 1953. Long an enormous benefactor of the university, Mr. Cullen may well have given the money in one way or another anyway, but that is not the point. The features of personality that produce this kind of conduct are what intrigued our Texas solicitor.

43. "Politics is the national sport of the American people—not baseball, or football, or any other athletic game," says James A. Farley, *op. cit.,* p. 237. John Dos Passos has one of his characters commending a candidate for giving up a good business to devote himself to the public service, to which a friend replies, "Congratulatin' a racehorse for givin' up the plow eh."—*Number One* (New York: Lion Books, Inc., 1954), p. 56.

44. Lauterbach, *op. cit.,* p. 46.

sentimental spenders. The logic of superficial self-interest no more abounds among contributors to politics than among other people.

A few students of politics have of late directed their attention to characteristics of personality as necessary for explaining political behavior. For present purposes it is sufficient to acknowledge the manifest validity of this concern. Qualities of personality, no matter how elusive in research and analysis, join other factors of predisposition in helping to determine whether and how persons give money to political causes.[45] As such, they aid in revealing political contributing as human behavior that is produced by a complex interaction of external stimuli with the internal set, or receptivity, of particular individuals.[46]

3. CHANNELS TO PREFERMENT

Lincoln Steffens spent a long life exposing the frailties of government. Corruption, he concluded, is not the special province of particular classes or groups. It is those who seek privileges of any kind who corrupt government, and at the end he reached the lugubrious judgment that wherever pressure is brought to bear, society and government cave in. Campaign contributions, because of their regularity, were especially bad sources of pressure and, therefore, of corruption.[47]

Society and government, of course, do not always cave in, and because of the variety of motivations that prompt them, not every campaign gift becomes a source of pressure. To know in every instance which does and which does not—and if it does, how much pressure it generates —is an impossible empirical task. Yet illustrations abound both of privileges bought and of the failure of money to buy what it sought.[48]

45. Daniel J. Levinson has proposed that "the ways in which the ego carries out its internal functions will heavily influence, though not entirely determine, the individual's selection, creation, and synthesis of modes of political participation."—"The Relevance of Personality for Political Participation," *Public Opinion Quarterly,* 22 (1958), 7.

46. In his studies of North Carolina contributors, Milbrath experimented with several personality scales and ratings. Particularly interesting was his use of a "sociability" scale. He hypothesized that a predisposition toward social interaction is an important personality prerequisite for active participation in politics. He concluded that sociability, as defined, was highly correlated with political participation, but more highly so with certain types than others, e.g., more so with soliciting than contributing funds.—*Op. cit.,* pp. 245-77, and subsequent analysis, as yet unpublished.

47. *The Autobiography of Lincoln Steffens* (New York: Harcourt, Brace and Company, 1931), pp. 416, 469, 479.

48. Episodic material of both kinds is not hard to come by. Mr. James S. Kemper, Chicago insurance executive named ambassador to Brazil in 1953, forthrightly told friends his appointment was a reward for Republican campaign contributions and fund-raising.—*Fortune,* 50 (November 1954), 123. Mr. James Bruce has been no less frank in attributing his ambassadorship to Argentina to his financial role in the Democratic party. Later he was irate enough to call Harry Truman a double-crosser for withholding an assignment he thought had been promised, presumably to the Court of St. James, or so it is widely believed in the trade. The failure of Franklin Roosevelt to accord what John L. Lewis thought justly

One can discern typical features that help to define the general impact of campaign gifts on government.

Guilt by association.—One of the basic problems in interpretation has been put cleanly by Senator Richard L. Neuberger:

> If Maurine or I ever would take $100 in cash behind the locked door of a hotel room to cast our vote for or against a specific legislative bill, we would be guilty of receiving a bribe. If apprehended, we would go to jail in disgrace—as we should.
>
> But if, at the next election, we accept not $100 in cash but $1000 in a check from the same donor, it is all perfectly legal, providing the check is made out to the Neuberger-for-election committee.[49]

Bribery can occur in any activity, with anything of value as the bait. But we usually think of money as the bait, and usually associate bribery with public officials, so that payment of money to a public official, regardless of the circumstances, immediately becomes suspect. Direct bribes and legitimate campaign contributions can be distinguished from each other only by the intentions motivating them, the use made of the money, and the nature of the *quid pro quo,* if any.

In the years surrounding World War II, a great deal was said about guilt by association. Motives were inferred and conclusions reached concerning national loyalty on the basis of circumstancial evidence. In many cases the inferences were absurd, and in some they proved correct. The same type of reasoning is often employed in evaluating political gifts. Journals of opinion that denounce guilt by association in the usual context are among the first to conclude, from no better evidence, that a political contribution equals a bribe.[50]

The amusing possibilities were illustrated in 1956. It became known that a contribution had been offered to a supporter of Senator Francis Case by a representative of Howard B. Keck, president of the Superior Oil Company. The Harris-Fulbright natural gas bill was before the Senate and the action was widely interpreted as an attempted bribe. A special investigating committee was appointed, and Senator Barry Goldwater of Arizona was named to it. The press then quoted Senator Goldwater as saying he himself had received a campaign contribution

---

due him in return for contributions to the Democratic campaign of 1936 led to Lewis' dramatic split with Roosevelt and the Democratic party.—Perkins, *op. cit.,* pp. 156-61. Memoirs and off-the-record interviews of politicians are replete with tales of influence and unrequited financial favors.

49. *Op. cit.,* p. 132.

50. Officials of firms that do business with government are forever being charged with seeking preference in the award of government contracts through their campaign gifts. The record does not invariably support such a simple hypothesis. Officials of the largest prime military contractors with federal agencies seem to lean overwhelmingly Republican regardless of which party is in office. See Gore Committee *Hearings,* part 2, pp. 519-24, and *Report,* 78-82.

from Mr. Keck. He could not remember the amount, but a report of the contribution was on file in Arizona. The Senator's contention that he saw no reason to resign from the committee provoked a brief clamour.[51] It soon appeared, however, that Senator Goldwater was not sure that *his* was the same Mr. Keck. On checking, it seemed that a committee supporting the Senator four years before had received a gift of $250 from one Matthew Keck of Chicago, apparently no kin.[52]

The incident illustrates the tenuous nexus frequently existing between contributors and those to whose campaign they give. Politicians attract financial support, like votes, because of views they hold. That their contributors agree with them ought to surprise no one.[53] A Maryland inquiry suggests that many candidates for high office actually know, or even know about, a small proportion of those who support their campaigns with sizeable gifts.[54] In the study of North Carolina contributors, those who gave $100 and over said they were consulted by government officials substantially more often than did small contribu-

51. *New York Times,* March 5, 1956.

52. UP dispatch, March 5, 1956.

53. In 1948, for example, both Wallace and Thurmond attracted contributions away from Truman in significant numbers.—Redding, *op. cit.,* pp. 132, 146.

54. While there are many kinds of relationships between candidates and contributors, it seems probable that candidates and party officials are more remote from contributors, as a class, than is generally assumed. Dwynal B. Pettengill experimented with a procedure to spot the gross outlines of these relationships. He asked several types of Maryland politicians to examine a pack of cards. On each card was written a name. The pack contained every recorded contributor of $500 or more to statewide and county campaign committees of both parties in 1952, and to campaigns for the U.S. Congress, plus the names of candidates for the Congress and their campaign treasurers. Each person interviewed was asked to indicate (1) those persons he knew personally, and (2) those he did not know but could identify.

Among those interviewed were six candidates for U.S. Representative. Of the 92 Republican contributors in the pack, the candidates said they knew personally an average of 15 and could identify 15 others. Of 64 Democratic contributors, they said they knew an average of 12 and could identify nine others. Candidates seemed only moderately more familiar with contributors to their own party than to the other party. Among the contributors were 21 who had given to the campaign of one of the six candidates. Of those, six were declared to be personal friends, and two others were identified, by the candidate on whose behalf the gift was made.

Three persons formally designated as campaign treasurers were interviewed. On the average, they knew considerably fewer of the contributors personally but could identify considerably more of them. Applied to a larger number of respondents of different political roles, this investigative procedure might reveal distinctive patterns of acquaintanceship and interaction. It seems reasonable to suppose that, in general, in larger constituencies candidates will be intimately acquainted with a lesser proportion of their financial supporters than in smaller ones. There are legal reasons, of course, for keeping candidates uninformed about the financial aspects of their campaigns. Mr. Pettengill's studies are reported in "Campaign Finance in Maryland" (Ph.D. dissertation, The Johns Hopkins University, 1959).

tors, but some of the larger contributors asserted they had not been consulted at all.[55]

Perceptions of monetary power.—The North Carolina interviews also revealed that persons differently related to politics expressed significantly different attitudes toward the power of money in politics. In the four samples interviewed, the data show in general that the more involved the respondent was in politics the less importance he placed on the power of money.[56] Marked differences in attitude are also observable among persons who have played an intimate part in the linkages between political finance and government decision-making. Some individuals near the point of decision are likely to see only those donors who are after something. They may assert, as a presidential aide did, that "no guy gives a large sum without expecting something in return." The national treasurer of the same party, referring to approximately the same period in time, gave his impression that "more than one-half" the large givers had something they wanted in mind. Fatigued solicitors may put the proportion lower still.[57]

55. The respondents said they were consulted by government officials on matters of policy as follows:

	HDC	*HRC*	*LDC*	*LRC*
Not at all	2	7	21	13
Occasionally	8	11	4	8
3 or more times a year	15	5	0	4
Total for each sample	25	23	25	25

It was a rare event, toward the end of 1931, when John J. Raskob, chairman of the Democratic national committee, announced he was polling 90,000 givers to the 1928 Democratic campaign as to what the party platform on prohibition should be. —Frank Friedel, *Franklin D. Roosevelt—The Triumph* (Boston: Little, Brown and Company, 1956), pp. 238-39.

56. Milbrath, *op. cit.*, pp. 70-71, 252. Milbrath employed a "power of money" scale based on respondents' agreement or disagreement with six statements. Scaling criteria were met. A person perceiving that money commands considerable influence ranked high on the scale. The contributors and noncontributors who responded to the test were ranked on the scale as follows:

	Low	*High*		*Low*	*High*		*Low*	*High*
HDC	14	6	LDC	9	9	HNC	9	17
HRC	20	1	LRC	10	11	LNC	5	19

This phenomenon is probably related to the "feelings of powerlessness" in public affairs that are more widespread among Americans in lower-income and lower-educational strata than among attentive publics.—Gabriel A. Almond, *The American People and Foreign Policy* (New York: Harcourt, Brace and Company, 1950), pp. 227-28.

57. Differences of opinion on this matter often stem from differences in definition of terms like "wanting something specific," "having something in mind," "wanting something in return," "access," and "entree." To try to distinguish between "selfish" and "unselfish" behavior misses the point. The problem is to discern the *kinds* of gratification achieved through, in this case, contributing. Officeholders differ in their own perceptions and awareness of pressures upon them. —See Lewis Anthony Dexter, "The Representative and His District," *Human Organization*, 16 (1957-58), 11-12.

From politicians it is easy over a period of years to assemble an anthology of special tales and broad summaries of the influence of money in politics. The resulting body of varied material is not entirely consistent within itself, but from it emerge several broad conclusions that are more significant for understanding the subject than an array of individual events.

Access.—Access is the concept most frequently used by practical politicians to describe the objectives of large contributors. Sometimes they call it entree, or the chance to get a hearing, or the right to get on the inside when necessary, or as one person not a politician put it, a "sense of camaraderie."[58] The concept is a familiar one.[59] Access may be an end in itself, a source of ego-satisfaction, for access often carries with it prestige and a sense of intimacy with power.[60] Access may be a way to other ends. It does not equate to decisive influence, but it means the opportunity to make one's case at crucial times and places. In the pluralistic struggle of American politics, the degree of access commanded by an individual or group affects directly the advantage or disadvantage he enjoys. Politicians argue that regardless of the motive behind a large political gift, the donor can later, if he insists, command access to at least some phase of the decision-making process of interest to him. This is the justification for the efforts made in subsequent chapters to identify the characteristics of large political givers. The concept of access makes no imputations of motive, nor does it assume that all who can will use it. But the "real money" will.[61] At the least,

58. Blair Bolles, *How to Get Rich in Washington—Rich Man's Division of the Welfare State* (New York: W. W. Norton and Co., 1952), p. 29.

59. It is discussed at length in David B. Truman, *The Governmental Process* (New York: Alfred A. Knopf, 1951).

60. See Muzafer Sherif and Hadley Cantril, *The Psychology of Ego-Involvements* (New York: John Wiley & Sons, 1947), pp. 96-101. One governor's secretary, curious as to why an unknown person with no apparent political interests should suddenly kick $5,000 into the campaign, found out shortly after inauguration. The donor came to the state capital and asked for an appointment. The appointment was arranged and the governor was carefully briefed on the man's first name—which he used heartily in greeting the stranger. The donor's face glowed, he passed the time of day, departed within five minutes, and neither then nor later asked for anything, expect the right to say he had dropped in on the governor, who called him by his first name.

This incentive to contributing is found everywhere. One of Canada's severest critics of influence attaching to campaign contributions in that nation was, nevertheless, "able to give examples from his experience of contributions which appeared to be motivated entirely by desire to be recognizd by prominent people since the donors stood to gain nothing."—Ernest Eugene Harrill, "The Structure of Organization and Power in Canadian Political Parties: A Study in Party Financing" (Ph.D. dissertation, University of North Carolina, 1958), p. 244.

61. Politicians are sometimes inclined to think only in terms of the "real money," the contributors who press for access, they being the ones who require most attention. Any experienced fund-raiser, however, can divide his contributors between those who never ask for anything and others who are frequent callers. They sometimes make more refined differentiations based on their evaluation of the

effective access "speeds things up." As the governor of a large state observed, "Really any person who wants this access in government as we have it can get it. The influence may come in that a contributor may get it faster and at a higher level than another person." Access is in fact generally taken as an indirect evidence of influence by both the impressionable public and serious students.

The competition for access, however, is stiff. It is sometimes stiffer than it need be, as Jonathan Daniels has observed: "A nickel phone call may be more effective in making an engagement with an official than a fee to a lawyer who pretends he carries influence."[62] But personal initiative alone does not guarantee attentiveness nor access to the most sensitive points in the decision-making process, and competitors for a public decision will also employ claims resulting from other kinds of political participation in seeking effective access. Potential points of access abound in American government. All persons who participate in the activities surrounding a governmental decision constitute potential points of access. If the matter is legislation, they include the originator of the idea, the officials of a political convention if the idea was suitable for a party platform, the draftsman, the introducer of the bill, the legislative officer who refers the bill, the members and staff of the committee receiving the bill, the legislators who debate the bill, the staff of the chief executive who will sign or veto the bill, and abundant others—including all persons consulted at any point by those more directly responsible. The influence that may be exerted through different points of access is not uniform, but there are many of them and many ways to reach them.

Politicians and contributors themselves do not agree that contributing is more effective in yielding access than other types of service rendered to candidates and parties.[63] Money is but one contribution that can be

degree of immediate self-interest involved in the requests made by contributors. Access finds its greatest importance in sporadic use on restricted issues and specific occasions, seemingly a characteristic of middle-class political parties wherever they may be.—See Maurice Duverger, *Political Parties: Their Organization and Activity in the Modern State* (translated by Barbara and Robert North) (New York: John Wiley & Sons, 1954), pp. 148, 185-86.

62. *Frontier on the Potomac* (New York: The Macmillan Co., 1946), p. 137.

63. Milbrath asked his contributors whether working in a campaign or contributing money gives the most influence. The responses were as follows:

	Working	*Contributing*	*Ambiguous or No Answer*	*Total*
HDC	18	1	6	25
HRC	11	6	6	23
LDC	15	5	5	25
LRC	15	4	6	25

Among 30 important fund-raisers and 22 important contributors in New York interviewed by Alexander, over three-fourths of both groups seemed to think that the act of contributing alone gives great access.—*Op. cit.*, p. 109. It seems reason-

made to electoral success and contributing to electoral success is but one factor affecting access. The weight of political contributions in affairs of government may be exceeded by other sources of influence. An old regimental comrade may spend hours with a chief executive that are, literally, priceless. And in any event, in the long run Mr. George Allen is right: few American politicians will be corrupted for a lesser consideration than the favor of the voters.

The many powers of wealth.—The special character of money complicates its significance as a channel to political preferment. Money is a unique medium of exchange. It is a universal, transferable unit infinitely more flexible in its uses than the time, or ideas, or talent, or influence, or controlled votes that also constitute contributions to politics.

Money can be accumulated in a bank account and as economic resources—as factories, trained personnel, customer good will, and in all the forms of economic power familiar to a semi-capitalist society. The inherent power of wealth exists without regard to how political campaigns are paid for. People with money will spend it to get what they want. If the system of campaign finance offers a way of doing this, they will spend money on political campaigns. If different arrangements obtained, the power of wealth would still manifest itself in other ways, as it does at present. It becomes incredibly difficult to distinguish between the impact of political gifts that emanate from pools of wealth and the impact of other kinds of influence that emanate from the same concentrations of economic power. In the United States, many economic activities are intricately intertwined with government. The economic units affected—business, farm, and labor groups, to start with—will inevitably seek to protect and advance their interests in all their relationships with government. They will do this regardless of the characteristics of the political system, including the ways elections are financed.

During the nineteenth century, government played a lesser role in equalizing the power of competing groups in society than it undertook later on. As government increasingly became a regulator and arbiter, the presumption grew that government would protect the economically weak from the strong. This especially became a charge of the federal government in the years following the Great Depression. The extent of the regulatory power that gravitated to the federal government inexorably led—one could truthfully say required—the economic and social units involved to seek representation at every relevant point within government and in many forums of public opinion outside it.[64]

---

able to suppose that if the number of small and large contributors increases, financial participation will increasingly resemble other types of political activity in the access and influence accorded to it.

64. A dilemma necessarily results and puts the reformer in quite a crush. The forms of political action employed by regulated groups inevitably tend to become more numerous and subtle and difficult to evaluate. At the same time, the ex-

It is unnecessary to elaborate on the varied sources of political power that inhere in different forms of economic concentration and social organization. The potential votes in mass-membership farm organizations and the campaign utility of labor organizations are two illustrations. The use of skilled and articulate spokesmen in arenas of discussion and decision is another, as is the employment of private sanctions and rewards to enlist support for political ends. And there is the press, uncertain though its influence may be. Officials move from business to government and back, learning names and folkways and the crucial points of access. Gigantic, interdependent industrial and financial complexes, embracing vast credit, employment, and service facilities on which literally millions of persons depend, possess within themselves sources of influence over the nation's life that far exceed in significance a few thousand dollars in campaign gifts.[65] As will appear later, most large contributions originate in some sector of the business community. They comprise but one politically significant activity of businessmen.

The illusion of power.—Another limitation on the significance of campaign gifts occasionally gets forgotten. Many governmental decisions are made within close confines, so close sometimes that in fact there is only an illusion of discretion. Antoine De Saint-Exupéry wrote accurately of the nature of power in the instruction his king gave to the Little Prince:

"If I ordered a general to fly from one flower to another like a butterfly, or to write a tragic drama, or to change himself into a sea bird, and if the general did not carry out the order that he had received, which one of us would be wrong?" the king demanded. "The general, or myself?"

"You," said the little prince firmly.

"Exactly. One must require from each one the duty which each one can perform." The king went on. "Accepted authority rests first of all on reason. If you ordered your people to go and throw themselves into the sea, they would rise up in revolution. I have the right to require obedience because my orders are reasonable."

---

pectation increases that government will maintain a general balance among competing elements in society. Government especially is expected in its own activities to maintain a posture of impartiality. This is hard to do, since the impartiality of decisions is likely to be judged by their effects on those doing the judging. These expectations lead to the demand that the forms of political action that have grown up—or at least the visible ones of which the attentive public is conscious—be limited or rendered innocuous. The answer lies at least partly in orderly and effective official channels for the representation of interests.

65. S. E. Finer has outlined what he feels to be all the conceivable advantages private businessmen might possess in influencing political action. See "The Political Power of Private Capital," *The Sociological Review,* 3 (1955), 279-94, and 4 (1956), 5-30. On the power of industrial organizations, and "the reciprocal relations between state power and economic power" within the structure of capitalist nationalism, see R. A. Brady, *Business as a System of Power* (New York: Columbia University Press, 1943).

After this the Little Prince inquired when he could have his promised sunset, and the king assured him he would command it. "But, according to my science of government, I shall wait until conditions are favorable," which the almanac revealed to be that evening at twenty minutes before eight, "And you will see how well I am obeyed."[66]

This is what politicians mean when they say most of the actions that contributors and solicitors seek from government would be taken anyway, though perhaps not so quickly. (Many donors compete against each other for contrary goals, hence some necessarily lose while others win.) There is a vast range in the character of governmental decisions in which contributors may be interested. Those making them obviously enjoy greater discretion at certain times than at others. Yet a multitude of influences streams through the life of government, molding its potentialities and actions. An observer long experienced in the upper reaches of government cites "the actually structured *mores* built up under and in association with political democracy" as providing the principal, pervasive restraint on decision-makers, public or private. Writes Paul H. Appleby: "It is the pluralistic pool of ideas and attitudes, their actual form and their potentiality for crystallizing significantly, that much more narrowly defines for decision-makers the positively and generally feasible and acceptable. In all organizations vested with any substantial power in our society, the area of discretion available to the decision-makers is very much narrower, and the complicated process of decision-making much more limiting of discretion, than most people are inclined to believe."[67]

66. *The Little Prince* (translated by Katherine Woods) (New York: Reynal & Hitchcock, 1943), p. 38. In more professional language: "One of the first practical axioms of command is never to give an order that cannot or will not be obeyed, and even the most dictatorial authority discovers points beyond which it cannot go."—Robin M. Williams, Jr., *American Society—A Sociological Interpretation* (New York: Alfred A. Knopf, 1952), p. 206. See also pp. 213-14 on the rule of law. On the significance of a "cultural context that limits and guides what politicians will offer in their bids for votes and what demands groups will assert with expectation of finding support," see Samuel H. Beer, "Pressure Groups and Parties in Britain," *American Political Science Review,* 50 (1956), 1-23.

67. "Managing Complexity," *Ethics: An International Journal of Social, Political, and Legal Philosophy,* 64 (no. 2, part 1, 1954), 97-98. As to legislative behavior, Professor Truman comments: "Although the legislator's role is in part defined by limited expectations and norms prevailing in his constituency and in the interest groups with which he identifies himself, it is also the creation of the norms more widely recognized in the society. . . . The norms of official behavior inevitably partake of the quality of myth, of professed values. On the other hand, they are also operating values that affect all legislative behavior in some measure and that place limits upon both the methods and the content of group demands upon the legislature. *In a stable political system the competing demands of organized groups are meaningless unless they are viewed in the context of these limiting and defining norms."—Op. cit.,* pp. 350-51. (Italics added.) Compare restraints on corporate behavior as analyzed by Adolf A. Berle, Jr., *The 20th Century Capitalist Revolution* (New York: Harcourt, Brace and Company, 1954): ". . . the political effects of community judgments are apt, in the long run, to be decisive."—p. 115.

The vigor of advocacy.—Within the general context of government decision-making, the success of particular contributors in converting access into influence may depend on local and transitory circumstances. A candidate in financial distress may fall prey more easily to the demands of an insistent contributor than one with adequate resources. Democratic leaders have generally advocated revisions in the system of campaign finance more vocally than Republicans. Part of the stimulus is the relatively parlous condition of Democratic treasuries. Their concern stems also, however, from acquaintance with the results of immediate dependence on financial backers. The relative affluence of Republican finances seems to grant Republican leaders greater opportunity to flout the claims of individual supporters, if they want to.

The degree to which fund-raising is administratively institutionalized affects the relationship between givers and receivers. Some gifts are made through a professionalized program, using solicitors drafted into party service on a relatively impersonal basis. These contributions may be viewed quite differently inside a party from gifts solicited in highly personal ways by fund-raisers operating independently. Many a candidate has had to swallow commitments made without his knowledge but in his name by a free-wheeling solicitor.

The initiative contributors take in pressing claims for preferment in return for financial support may well be affected by the alternative channels of access open to them. A contributor to a party may, for example, have a better chance of getting what he wants by virtue of access, separately established, to a regulatory commission.

The character of the office and the constituency, moreover, partly determine whether contributors seek commitments and get delivery on them. A plausible impression prevails that despite conspicuous improvements state legislators are still more accessible to influence by money than most elected officials. The size of constituency, type of decisions made by the official, and degree of effective exposure to public view may all affect the frequency and specificity of commitments.

Something has been said earlier about the number of contributions of various sizes made to different recipients, both within the same and different parties. The data suggested the patterns of potential access set up by a segment of the political contributions made in the United States. The characteristics of persons who make these contributions and thereby gain potential access to government are next to be examined.

It would be a mistake, however, to envision the political function of their donations as confined solely to a narrow concept of access. Contributors need not always assert themselves to have their views respected. Candidates and party managers seek to anticipate the reaction of contributors as well as of voters, thereby according them important indirect influence. Contributors, like voters, derive a sense of participation in government. They are consequently readier to accept the outcome of elections and other political processes. A chief utility of the existing system of election finance is the opportunity it affords persons of means to take a meaningful, but generally nondecisive, part in politics. Throughout it all, the private financing of elections, with all its imperfections and distortions, becomes one of the many instruments by which "the organized power which is government [is made] subservient and sensitive to the whole complex common life of society."[68]

68. A. D. Lindsay observes further that "the expression of general approval or disapproval conveyed in votes will be sure to be only one among several ways of ensuring this control."—*The Modern Democratic State* (New York: Oxford University Press, 1947), vol. 1, p. 283. We have refrained from discussing the variety of specific objectives contributors may seek through access. They are no different from the objectives that may be sought through access established by other means. The stakes in government are numerous, and they differ with the level and functions of a government as well as with more transitory matters of policy. Whenever government touches an individual or a group interest, it creates an objective for access.

5

GROUP INVOLVEMENT THROUGH GIVING

EACH OF THE blind men was correct in thinking the elephant was like the part he touched. Yet all contradicted each other when describing the animal. Nominations and elections are the principal concern of this book, but money is also significant in other phases of political life. Throughout the four-year election cycle, larger sums in the aggregate are probably spent in these other phases: in initiative and referenda campaigns; in the representation of political interests before legislative, executive, and judicial agencies; and in activities designed to influence the general climate of political opinion.[1]

1. As good a guess as any is that annual cash expenditures on nominations and elections have not in recent years exceeded an *average* of $100,000,000. Compare other costs.

Initiative and referenda campaigns appear infrequently in most states, but in California where they occur on the grandest scale costs run into the millions. Indicative, if not typical, was the $4,874,500 spent for and against Proposition Four in 1956. Expenditures for and against measures frequently exceed $100,000. Leonard Carl Rowe brought together data on this point in "Political Campaign Funds in California" (Ph.D. dissertation, University of California, 1957), pp. 52-57, 85-92.

The costs of direct legislative and administrative lobbying run into tens of millions of dollars a year. Amounts reported by lobbyists registered under the Federal Lobbying Act of 1946 exceeded $6,000,000 a year during 1947-56, and all hands acknowledged much more was actually spent.—George B. Galloway, "A Report on the Operation of Title III of the Legislative Reorganization Act of 1946," in U.S. Senate Special Committee to Investigate Political Activities, Lobbying, and Campaign Contributions (hereafter cited as McClellan Lobby Committee), *Report* (Washington: Government Printing Office, 1957) (Senate Report No. 395, 85th Congress, 1st Session), pp. 193-94. In four states alone, containing about one-sixteenth of the population, around $750,000 was officially reported as spent for lobbying in 1951, and no one thought the figure complete.—Belle Zeller (ed.), *American State Legislatures* (New York: Thomas Y. Crowell Company, 1954), pp. 226-27. In a fifth state, some 400 accredited lobbyists reported expenses of about $800,000 in 1953.—Earl C. Behrens, "Sacramento Story," *San Francisco Chronicle,* August 17, 1953. In 1957, 283 registered lobbyists in Ohio

The next three chapters are addressed to selected groups and categories of people who donate to nomination and election campaigns. Group participation in these campaigns may take several forms, however, and consequently a variety of relationships is found between political parties and nonparty groups. Some individuals are active in both types of organization, providing a basis for parallel or cooperative action. Some nonparty organizations undertake active campaigning in the manner of parties themselves. Some operate as factions within a party, even across state lines. Campaign contributing by members of nonparty groups is an important type of connecting link and seemingly one of increasing significance.[2] Each of the groups and categories of individuals selected

reported spending about $70,000; 176 in South Dakota, $80,000; 302 in Massachusetts, $242,000; and 384 in Wisconsin, $320,000.—Belle Zeller, "Regulation of Pressure Groups and Lobbyists," *The Annals,* 319 (1959), 95.

The immense range of activities known as indirect lobbying require many millions of dollars per year. In 1947, the National Association of Manufacturers spent over $4,600,000, of which two-thirds appears to have gone for public relations activities connected with NAM's interest in labor legislation.—Richard W. Gable, "NAM: Influential Lobby or Kiss of Death?" *Journal of Politics,* 15 (1953), 263, citing NAM sources. The American Medical Association's campaign against compulsory health insurance, costing $4,678,000 over three and one-half years, stimulated $2,000,000 worth of voluntary advertising by others.—McClellan Lobby Committee *Report,* p. 48. The Natural Gas and Oil Resources Committee spent $1,753,000 between October, 1954, and March, 1956, in a "long range public information program . . . to inform the public concerning . . . the harmful effects of Federal regulation" and other matters.—*Ibid.,* p. 11.

Beyond these activities is a less tangible realm. The climate of opinion in which people vote and public officials work is created by the multitude of communications they receive on limitless numbers of subjects. Institutional advertising by groups with a stake in public policy seeks to encourage general points of view relevant to specific political controversies by exploiting highly valued symbols, e.g., liberty, security. How much of the ten billion dollars spent annually in the United States for advertising goes for institutional advertising cannot be said, but it runs into the millions. Apparently there are no estimates.—Letter from H. C. Barksdale, Advertising Research Foundation, Inc., New York, dated July 14, 1958. *Printer's Ink,* July 11, 1958, has a breakdown of the 1957 advertising volume of $10,300,000,000. The estimated 1959 figure was $10,600,000.—*Ibid.,* January 9, 1959.

2. The composite activities of a political group define its relationship to political parties and whether or not it, in fact, may become or cease to be a party itself. Henry W. Ehrmann has pointed to the significance of studying these operating relationships between parties and other groups.—(Ed.), *Interest Groups on Four Continents* (Pittsburgh: University of Pittsburgh Press, 1958), p. 5. Gloria Resch Cook did this for several groups about which testimony was offered before the U.S. House of Representatives Select Committee on Lobbying Activities (the Buchanan Committee), the voluminous hearings of which were published in 1950. She concluded that the testimony indicated increasing interest and belief by pressure groups in campaigning for the nomination and election of candidates, that "lobbies are growing more and more concerned with staffing government and this involves an interesting duplication of the political party's function."—"The Relationship between Political Parties and Pressure Groups" (Master's thesis, University of North Carolina, 1956), pp. 248-49. The nature and function of interest groups, vis-à-vis political parties, can serve as a basis for categorizing political systems. See Gabriel A. Almond, "A Comparative Study of Interest Groups and

for study has a presumptive stake in government policy and administration. Others might have been chosen, but these are sufficient to illustrate the variety that prevails in this kind of political action and to demonstrate existing minimum levels of financial participation.

Individuals give for many varied reasons. Whatever incentives prompt the gift, however, access to government can result. The contributing behavior of members of a group is one index to that group's actual or potential involvement in politics. Membership in more than one politically relevant group does not limit the opportunities for access possessed by a person; it merely indicates the extent of the interests on behalf of which he might use his access. For a group's involvement to be significant, it is not necessary to attribute collusion to the persons within a group who make political contributions. On many occasions, action is taken collaboratively, but the degree varies from group to group and from time to time. Within some categories of contributors who share common characteristics, like government employees in different jurisdictions, personal interaction may in fact be low or nonexistent. But alert politicians are automatically sensitive to the interests of their political supporters, including those who give them money. Whether contributors seek it or not, by their giving they become part of the many-sided context of pressures in which governments function.

In general, the groups chosen for examination were selected on two assumptions: that the welfare of economic interests in American society is usually bound up with the formulation and administration of public policies; and that, in consequence, individuals and groups with economic stakes engage in political activity. The first assumption needs no defense, and if one wishes, the second can be viewed as an hypothesis to be tested. Political philosophers across the centuries have regarded property, "in its various forms and distribution, and the social groups which arise out of economic processes, as the fundamental materials for the science of government."[3] The addition of other materials of politics in modern popular governments has not made property less fundamental. In a vast regulatory government like the United States, where the lives and livelihoods of persons are touched constantly and directly by government, the relationships between economic and political life are inescapably intimate. The analysis of political givers throws into relief broad configurations of political life that are important in understanding the workings of the party system.

---

the Political Process," *American Political Science Review,* 52 (1958), 270-82. It must be remembered that the Tammany Society at its inception was not connected with party politics—John S. Jenkins, *History of Political Parties in the State of New York* (Auburn, New York: Alden & Markham, 1846), pp. 155-56.

3. Charles A. Beard, *The Economic Basis of Politics* (New York: Alfred A. Knopf, Inc., 1934), p. 67.

1. ORGANIZED INTERESTS

In all nations organized interests play politics according to their resources and the prevailing political ethic. The nineteenth century saw much lobbying by bribery in the United States, and the bribes often took the form of campaign gifts. Grossly illegal activities have declined conspicuously, but campaign giving continues to be an important form of political action by organized interests with the wherewithal. This is true in other democratic nations as well as in the United States.[4] An association of the indigent reminds politicians of the voting strength of its adherents. Men of means find it easier to make political donations. Those so disposed may read blackmail or bribery into either transaction, but both forms of participation are currently characteristic of the American electoral system.

An index to giving.—Campaign gifts by members and officials of interest groups indicate one aspect of their personal involvement and also something of the involvement of the interest groups to which they belong. Known campaign gifts of $500 and over afford the best available index. This index does not reveal the full financial activity of those concerned, but it constitutes a dependable indicator of the *minimum* level of involvement, and as such is useful. Gifts of $500 and over expose only the slender peak of a mountain of smaller contributions. Moreover, not all gifts of $500 and larger are known. Yet the data are adequate as rough indicators of minimum levels of contributing and to reveal gross comparisons between different types of groups.[5]

4. Americans residing in numerous foreign lands were good enough to answer queries on this and related points. Testimony by local observers appears in Ehrmann, *op. cit.*, on Australia, pp. 21, 24-25; Finland, p. 58; France, p. 69; Germany, pp. 108-09; Great Britain, pp. 134, 261; and Sweden, p. 163. See also Philip Williams, *Politics in Post-War France: Parties and the Constitution in the Fourth Republic* (London: Longmans Green & Co., 1954), p. 356; and J. D. Stewart, *British Pressure Groups—Their Role in Relation to the House of Commons* (Oxford: The Clarendon Press, 1958), pp. 223-37.

Practices in Great Britain are especially noteworthy. Some have stated that pressure groups in America secure more influence by contributing to party funds than in Great Britain.—G. R. Strauss, "Pressure Groups I Have Known," *Political Quarterly,* 29 (1958), 40-46. But Samuel H. Beer has concluded, "British custom has always been far more tolerant than American of the legislator who is intimately connected with outside interests. One may doubt that the subsidy for political expenses which Richard Nixon received from his well-to-do supporters would cause much excitement in Britain where not only the M.P.'s sponsored by trade unions but also quite a few others receive help from interested organizations in the form of contributions to election expenses and even to personal income."—"Pressure Groups and Parties in Britain," *American Political Science Review,* 50 (1956), 5.

5. Data for two election years were used: for 1952, a file was accumulated of around 9,500 individuals who made a reported gift of $500 or more to nomination and election campaigns at all levels of government throughout the country.

For 1956, some 8,100 different contributors of $500 and more were listed by the Gore Committee *Report.* This compilation included few gifts to nomination

Each to his own.—A high level of known campaign giving does not characterize equally all lobbyists and members of all interest groups. Contributing does not, in fact, appear to distinguish registered lobbyists as a class from other categories of citizens with the resources to give to politics. Of some 918 persons who filed as lobbyists under the Federal Lobbying Act in the first three quarters of 1950, only about 4.5 per cent were known to have given $500 or more during 1952. The comparable percentage for the 1,250 members of the New York Stock Exchange and the 400 members of the Midwest Stock Exchange was in each case four, and for the 500 members of the American Stock Exchange it was five. Any category of persons possessing a degree of financial means will normally include some campaign contributors.[6]

The variations are considerable among officials of organizations with clearly identifiable political interests. Very few leaders of the various kinds of organizations listed in Table 7 showed up making donations of as much as $500 during 1952 or 1956. An examination of the several types of selected organizations,[7] in fact, indicates that only among business interests were high proportions of the officials studied found to have made contributions. Even among them, however, the proportion giving varies sharply from one organization to another. Organization policy toward this type of political action by its officials, the current intimacy of the group's concern with governmental decisions, differences in personal affluence and predisposition, and similar factors account for these differences. It is abundantly clear, nevertheless, that political contributing in large sums is an important form of participation by some classes of businessmen. The officials of organizations whose members have a visible and continuing stake in government policy and action—like members of the American Petroleum Institute and the National Association of Manufacturers—habitually engage in this form of political

campaigns, and for state and local committees generally covered only the period September 1–November 30, rather than the full year.

In all times and places, contributions to nomination campaigns, and to general elections for state and local officers in some states, are especially likely to go unreported, or, if reported, to remain hidden in inaccessible depositories. Some individuals have their gifts reported in other names, a practice accounting for the impecunious hangers-on who occasionally show up giving sums equal to a goodly share of their annual income. Underworld sources, in particular, are likely to avoid the public record.

6. The details of these and other analyses of 1952 contributions were submitted to the Gore Committee and appear in its *Hearings,* part 2, especially pp. 529-32. The 1956 analyses to follow are based on adjusted data in the Gore Committee *Report,* especially pp. 86-89.

7. Many additional organized interests are active financially and otherwise in politics. For comments on certain segments of the Jewish community in America, for example, see pages 262-63 and 267-68, below. A highly informed Negro leader observed that in politics, as in charities, Negroes are accustomed to being on the receiving end where money is concerned. They give, as they vote, more enthusiastically for qualified Negro candidates than for others.

Table 7

KNOWN CAMPAIGN CONTRIBUTORS OF $500 AND OVER BELONGING TO SELECTED ORGANIZED GROUPS, 1952 AND 1956[a]

Type of Interest	Organizational Group	Year	No. of Names Checked	% Found to Have Given	No. Giving to Rep.	No. Giving to Dem.	No. Giving to Both
Farm	American Farm Bureau Federation: officers and directors	1952	23	0	0	0	0
	National Farmers Union: officers and directors	1952	18	0	0	0	0
	National Grange: officers and members	1952	118	0	0	0	0
Veterans	American Legion:						
	past national commanders	1952	27	7	0	2	0
	officers, national executive committee and alternates	1952	137	3	0	4	0
	AMVETS:						
	officers	1952	15	0	0	0	0
	committee chairmen	1952	17	6	0	1	0
	Veterans of Foreign Wars: officers and directors	1952	27	4	0	1	0
Miscellaneous	American Tariff League, Inc.:						
	officers	1952	5	0	0	0	0
	board of managers	1952	31	13	4	0	0
	General Federation of Women's Clubs: officers, committee members, staff	1952	87	1	1	0	0
	League of Women Voters:						
	officers	1952	5	0	0	0	0
	directors	1952	8	0	0	0	0
	National Housing Conference, Inc.:						
	directors	1952	64	11	2	5	0
	committee members	1952	25	16	2	2	0
	National Tax Equality Association: officers	1952	6	0	0	0	0
Professional	American Bar Association:						
	House of Delegates	1952	227	4	5	4	0
		1956	232	3	5	1	0

(*Table 7 Continued*)

Type of Interest	Organizational Group	Year	No. of Names Checked	% Found to Have Given	No. Giving to Rep.	Dem.	Both
Professional (con't)	American Medical Association:						
	officers	1952	7	0	0	0	0
		1956	6	0	0	0	0
	trustees and committee members	1952	125	2	2	0	0
		1956	150	0	0	0	0
Business	American Iron and Steel Institute:						
	officers	1952	7	14	1	0	0
		1956	9	22	2	0	0
	directors	1952	30	43	13	0	0
		1956	30	47	14	0	0
	American Petroleum Institute:						
	officers	1952	8	37	3	0	0
		1956	8	37	3	0	0
	directors	1952	132	27	32	1	2
		1956	131	21	27	0	0
	honorary directors	1952	11	64	7	0	0
		1956	18	39	7	0	0
	Association of American Railroads:						
	officers	1952	9	0	0	0	0
		1956	10	0	0	0	0
	directors	1952	22	5	1	0	0
		1956	20	20	4	0	0
	Chamber of Commerce of the United States:						
	officers and directors	1952	14	36	4	0	1
		1956	18	22	4	0	0
	Manufacturing Chemists Association:						
	officers	1952	7	0	0	0	0
		1956	7	0	0	0	0
	directors	1952	23	17	4	0	0
		1956	27	11	3	0	0

(*Table 7 Continued*)

Type of Interest	Organizational Group	Year	No. of Names Checked	% Found to Have Given	No. Giving to		
					Rep.	Dem.	Both
Business (con't)	three committees	1952	16	50	8	0	0
	National Association of Electric Companies:						
	officers	1952	10	20	2	0	0
		1956	7	0	0	0	0
	directors	1952	27	11	3	0	0
		1956	27	4	1	0	0
	National Association of Manufacturers:						
	officers	1952	13	24	3	0	0
	regional vice presidents	1952	14	21	3	0	0
	honorary vice presidents	1952	14	43	5	1	0
	directors	1952	130	15	18	2	0
		1956	130	14	17	0	0
	National Association of Real Estate Boards:						
	officers	1952	18	0	0	0	0
		1956	5	0	0	0	0
	directors	1952	162	1	1	0	0
		1956	218	1	1	1	0
	National Coal Association:						
	officers	1952	8	0	0	0	0
	directors	1952	47	23	11	0	0
		1956	47	28	13	0	0

[a] Details for 1952 were submitted to the Gore Committee and appear in its *Hearings*, part 2, pp. 530-32. The 1956 data, adjusted, came from the Gore Committee *Report*, pp. 86-89.

action. The incomplete data indicate that in two successive presidential election years upwards of one-fourth of the individuals in leadership positions in certain trade associations made at least one campaign gift of at least $500. This is a *characteristic* form of political expression for such individuals and the groups of which they are a part. For that reason a closer look will be taken later in this chapter at the contributing behavior of businessmen.

Two professional societies are included in Table 7, the American Bar Association and the American Medical Assocation. By the index here used, few of their officials were financially active in politics in 1952 and 1956. This need not mean, however, that the members of these professions were financially inactive not that association officials were inactive in organizing this financial participation. As the examination of organized labor's political activities will demonstrate, there are other types of financial participation in politics than large individual gifts.

The opposition of the American Medical Association to compulsory health-insurance legislation has been open and vigorous. The Association financed its efforts by collections of $25.00 each from members, a process by which several million dollars were amassed for political action. Moreover, the medical profession has often proved a lucrative source of campaign gifts of medium and small size for Republican committees all across the country. Healing arts committees have frequently been organized as a way to mobilize political opinion and campaign contributions. Close reading of the 1952 receipts of local-level committees, for example, showed large numbers of physicians making gifts in Black Hawk County, Iowa; Tippecanoe County, Indiana; Hancock County, Ohio; Dade County, Florida; and elsewhere.

Few officials of the American Bar Association showed up as givers in Table 7, but many lawyers throughout the country were active as politi-

Table 8

KNOWN CAMPAIGN GIVING IN SUMS OF $500 AND OVER BY MEMBERS OF LAW FIRMS IN SELECTED CITIES, 1952[a]

City	No. of firms	No. of firms with members who contributed to			
		Total	Rep. only	Dem. only	Both parties
Boston	83	18	8	9	1
Philadelphia	68	7	5	2	0
Pittsburgh	51	12	9	2	1
Baltimore	55	8	5	2	1
Washington	278	54	16	34	4
New York	406	87	41	35	11
Total	941	186	84	84	18

[a] Data submitted to the Gore Committee and appearing in its *Hearings*, part 2, pp. 529-30.

cal contributors. Members of all the law firms listed in Martindale-Hubbell, the legal directory, for six important cities were checked against the file of 1952 contributors. In one-fifth of these firms at least one member—and often more than one—had made a gift. See Table 8. Lawyers are likely to differ in their political persuasions. In this they are like their clients, whom they often represent in politics as in other matters.[8] The number of firms with members who gave only to Republicans was the same as those with members giving only to Democrats, and there were a number of firms with at least one member who gave to one party while another member gave to the other. Firms with members favoring Republicans outnumbered those favoring Democrats in four of the six cities studied, and the balance was about equal in a fifth city. In Washington, D.C., however, with a Democratic national administration in power in 1952, the firms with members showing a Democratic leaning were more than twice as numerous as those with members who gave to Republican recipients.[9]

Standard procedure.—Lobbying methods change as the partisans and the operating conditions of politics change. In the twentieth century, individuals and groups assert themselves in many complicated, indirect ways designed to shape public attitudes. They also follow more direct, time-honored routes intended to secure the sympathy of legislatures and executives. Campaign contributions are still a standard and important link between the political process and many interest groups.

These links are more numerous than the analysis of relatively large donations ($500 and over) suggests. Extensive verbal inquiries make it clear that gifts of smaller sums by lobbyists are a pervasive feature of politics at all levels.[10] The influence that may result from small campaign gifts is understandably more significant at lower than at higher levels. There is none of the "goofy stuff" in Congress, concluded one interest-group official in Washington, that goes on around state

8. C. Wright Mills concludes that "the higher cliques of lawyers and investment bankers are the active political heads of the corporate rich and the members of the power elite."—*The Power Elite* (New York: Oxford University Press, 1956), p. 291.

9. For mention of the lawyer's role in fund-raising, see pages 270-74, below.

10. Four per cent of a sample of 100 registered lobbyists in Washington, D.C., apparently made campaign gifts averaging $500 or more during the five years previous to 1957. But 68 per cent had given in smaller sums.—Lester W. Milbrath, "The Political Party Activity of Washington Lobbyists," *Journal of Politics,* 20 (1958), 345. Suggestive, though not typical, are the activities of Arthur H. Samish, California lobbyist. For one of many examples, in 1936 Mr. Samish had a hand in distributing gifts of from $100 to $700 to 57 candidates for the legislature.—H. R. Philbrick, *Legislative Investigative Report,* submitted December 28, 1938, pp. V-6, V-7. Mr. Samish was given quite a boost to national recognition, and to his troubles with the law, by Lester Velie's article in *Collier's,* August 13, 1949, "The Secret Boss of California," reprinted in David Farrelly and Ivan Hinderaker, *The Politics of California—A Book of Readings* (New York: The Ronald Press Company, 1951), pp. 171-97.

legislatures. (He had been a state legislator, and in that capacity claimed he was in fact a "lobbyist" for his group.) Some groups with limited resources direct their gifts to races for the United States House of Representatives, where they assume greater importance than if given to better-financed candidates for the Senate or the presidency.[11] Lobbyists serve as transmitting agents on occasion, one Washington lobbyist observing that "we make contributions for some of our people who don't want to be recorded as contributing." The climate is revealed by the practices of some lawyers and public relations people. Though not registering formally as lobbyists, they habitually equip themselves to serve their clients better by making modest gifts to friendly candidates.

2. CORPORATION OFFICIALS AND POLITICAL ACTION

Americans constantly extoll wide popular participation in politics as a prerequisite for sound self-government. When any group converts a civil liberty into effective political action, however, political opponents tend to cry foul. Union members, Negroes, Catholics, tenant farmers, corporation officials, whoever marshals telling political power is likely to be charged with coercion or corruption.

Classic anomaly: oil and Ike.—The illogic of American attitudes toward campaign giving was highlighted by the reaction to Senator Francis Case's disclosure in 1956. Two special Senate committees investigated the $2,500 contribution offered by an oil company attorney for the Senator's re-election campaign later that year. Senator Case favored the pending Harris-Fulbright natural gas bill, as did the officials of the oil company. Most of the press and a share of the public writhed in outrage for several months, and eventually the President of the United States vetoed the natural gas legislation, charging that "acceptable standards of propriety" had been violated.[12]

11. The files of large 1952 and 1956 contributors used in these analyses are notably deficient with respect to supporters of candidates for the U.S. House of Representatives. The official reports pertaining to House races that are filed with the Clerk of the House are generally of little value. Contributions are often so handled that the candidate cannot or need not report them. The same is usually true of reports filed by Congressional candidates in the states. The number of such candidates is so large, in any event, that the volume of work in tabulating what little information might be gleaned from them is formidable. Moreover, and especially, the Senate Subcommittee on Privileges and Elections has customarily refrained as a matter of parliamentary courtesy from including elections to the House within the scope of its special inquiries. The Gore Committee did, in 1956, tabulate all gifts of $500 and over that appeared on the public reports made to the Clerk.

12. Eventually it was decided through the courts that John M. Neff and Elmer Patman had violated the law by not registering under the Federal Lobbying Act. They were fined $2,500 each and given suspended one-year sentences. The Superior Oil Company was fined $10,000 for "aiding and abetting" the failure of the men to register. The men and the company pleaded guilty and in return the government dropped more serious charges, as one way out of a situation created by selective law enforcement that should have been as embarrassing to the enforcers as to the transgressors.—*New York Times,* December 15, 1956.

Officials of corporations and their representatives had for decades routinely made campaign contributions, often in sums larger than $2,500 and regardless of whether legislation of immediate interest to them was pending. The President himself occupied a questionable position, although it went unnoticed. During the 1952 campaign he advocated tidelands oil legislation favored by most of the oil industry and opposed by his Democratic opponent. In that year officers and directors of the 22 largest oil companies alone gave more than $300,000 in reported sums of $500 or more to Republican candidates and committees, including a goodly number of Senate and House candidates and some committees supporting Eisenhower personally.[13] The tidelands bill subsequently passed the Congress and the President signed it. Neither Democrats nor Republicans suggested that he veto it because proprieties had been violated, and Republicans welcomed donations from oil company officials during the ensuing presidential campaign. In 1956, officers and directors of the 29 largest oil companies gave more than $350,000 in recorded amounts of $500 and larger to a variety of candidates and committees of the President's party.[14]

If it were assumed that a bribe had been attempted of Senator Case, it must be assumed that bribery of President Eisenhower had been accomplished—hardly an admissible assumption. Bribery is usually difficult to define. If one chooses, the whole process of representative government can be interpreted as a process of bribery in which political support is swapped for political responsiveness. Whether a campaign gift constitutes financial bribery of the person or one of the forms of political bribery by which representative government is made sensitive to the will of the governed is customarily hard to determine.[15]

13. For details, see Gore Committee *Hearings,* part 2, pp. 505-12. Comparable Democratic gifts were around $6,000.

14. Derived from the Gore Committee *Report,* pp. 77-78 and Exs. 26 and 28.

15. Politicians exploit the ambiguity. Texas Republicans threw a $100-a-plate "appreciation dinner" early in 1958 for Joe Martin, their party's leader in the lower house of Congress. In sending out letters of invitation, national committeeman Jack Porter, not known for his finesse, emphasized that the former Speaker had always been a friend of Texas, "especially the oil and gas producing industries." The letter gave Mr. Martin generous credit for mustering two-thirds of the Republicans in the House behind industry-favored legislation and said he would be called on to do so again. Wherewith Democrats chortled and charged a pay-off and the Republican national committee announced with the President's approval that it would have none of the $100,000 profits from the dinner. After some wishy-washy wavering by their chairmen, the Republican Senate and House campaign committees also decided not to accept any of the tainted dollars, and they were "kept" in Texas. One consequence of the incident was to kill, as the Case episode had done two years before, any chance that the natural gas bill, heavily favored by Texas oil men, would pass that year.—*New York Times,* February 12, 1958, *et. seq.*

Democrats have on occasion been more alert. Harold Ickes wrote that in 1935 he was shown a list of Texas oil contributors to the Democratic national committee who had been induced to give on the "representation" that certain legislation would

The dependent economy.—Like labor unions, business corporations have an enormous stake in politics. Always true, the larger and more apparent the stakes, the more vigorous has been their political activity. The big businessman is very busy indeed, wrote Lincoln Steffens at the beginning of the twentieth century. He is busy and businesslike with politics.[16] He had been busy then for some time and would continue so with the nominating and electing of public officials on whose decisions the welfare of his enterprises rested. "The strain of universal suffrage on the virtue of the country is tremendous," observed Whitelaw Reid as he dug deep for Mark Hanna.[17] No single class or interest ever won complete control of American government; all had to work through politicians for what they wanted or thought they needed. As the twentieth century advanced, the interdependence of economic and political life increased. "The great development of our day," concludes a student of American society, "is the centralization of structure, both of business and labor organization and of the state, and this increasingly means that economic problems become political problems."[18] Government acts on business, not solely through explicit limiting legislation, but through its fiscal policies, its contractual programs, its regulatory agencies, its own production of goods and services, its subsidies, its taxes, its loans, its investigations, and in a myriad of other ways, often technical in character and opaque to the public, including the loopholes it leaves in its statutes and their enforcement. And corporations do not confine themselves to defensive actions to protect against a hostile or misguided government. Wherever advantages can be gained through regulation and control, they are happy to be along.[19]

The stockholders' money.—It must be assumed that corporations play politics as their officials think their interests dictate. To assume less would be a vote of no-confidence in the American businessman, and

be defeated. He reports that he immediately called the matter to the attention of the President and others in the administration to forestall the "nice scandal" he foresaw if it should appear that the party had acted in return for these gifts.—Harold L. Ickes, *The Secret Diary of Harold L. Ickes—The First Thousand Days, 1933-1936* (New York: Simon and Schuster, 1954), pp. 414-15. Ickes stated that oilman Walter Jones at one time gave over $100,000 to the Democratic campaign fund. —*The Secret Diary of Harold L. Ickes—The Inside Struggle, 1936-1939* (New York: Simon and Schuster, 1954), p. 27.

16. *The Shame of the Cities* (New York: McClure, Phillips & Co., 1904), p. 5.

17. Paxton Hibben, *The Peerless Leader* (New York: Farrar and Rinehart, Inc., 1929), p. 194. Virtue was strained without universal suffrage, too. Nineteenth-century American businesses overseas often sought and occasionally achieved control of foreign governments by various means including financing local political parties.—Adolf A. Berle, Jr., *The 20th Century Capitalist Revolution* (New York: Harcourt, Brace and Company, 1954), p. 136.

18. Robin M. Williams, Jr., *American Society—A Sociological Interpretation* (New York: Alfred A Knopf, 1952), pp. 505-06.

19. Adolf A. Berle, Jr., cites illustrations in the aluminum, oil, and sugar industries.—*Op. cit.*, pp. 49-50.

one not justified by the record.[20] Before laws to the contrary, corporation officials gave corporation funds to parties and candidates with a generous hand. Dramatic attempts were made to coerce the votes of employees and otherwise to contribute to electoral victory. Where laws still permit, business organizations give and spend money in elections. The National Democratic Club of New Jersey reported contributions between mid-August and mid-October of 1952 from some 60 business organizations, most of which seemed to be corporations. In the same campaign the Democratic state central committee of Indiana listed more than 20 companies as donors to its treasury. Senator Joseph R. McCarthy's opponent in the 1952 Wisconsin Republican Senatorial primary was the recipient of company gifts. The Republican finance director in a large state indicated that his industry division had openly solicited corporate gifts for state candidates.[21] Company names often show up in finance reports, the significance here not being whether a statute has been violated but in the evidence of corporate disposition toward political action.[22]

20. Some corporations plan their political relations with the same care used in planning their employee and community relations. Corporations with immediate political interests usually designate one or more persons to manage their political affairs, often keeping a foot in all important political camps. (Sam Pryor, Republican, and Carroll Cone, Democrat, have often been referred to by politicians as Pan American Airways' "vice presidents for political affairs.") Corporations may even shift these assignments to accommodate to changes in governmental personnel. In trying to calculate the value of goods and services contributed in kind to political activities, it is not hard to reach several hundred thousand dollars fast for a single company. Great variety marks the political activities of corporaions and their officials, a matter discussed by Robert A. Dahl in "Business and Politics: A Critical Appraisal of Political Science," *American Political Science Review,* 53 (1959), 1-34.

21. Corporations pour tens of thousands of dollars of their stockholders' money into referenda and lobbying campaigns when they deem the issues important. In 1956, California oil companies divided over a ballot measure. The Union Oil Company spent more than $200,000 in opposition to it and the Richfield Oil Corporation over $650,000 in favor of it.—*Wall Street Journal,* December 11, 1956.

Corporations often undertake politically oriented advertising. Ads, obviously pitched to the Senatorial campaign then going on in Ohio, were placed in Sunday newspapers between September 3 and November 5 (two days before the election), 1950. These were largely paid for by 269 corporations, giving a total of $77,042. Twelve companies gave $1,000 each and the others smaller sums.—U.S. Senate Subcommittee of Privileges and Elections, *Hearings* (Washington: Government Printing Office, 1952), pp. 188-92.

Corporate political activity in Britain was conspicuous during the years the Labor Government sought to nationalize key industries. Certain of the public appeals are described by H. H. Wilson in "Techniques of Pressure—Anti-Nationalization Propaganda in Britain," *Public Opinion Quarterly,* 15 (1951-52), 225-42.

22. There is a whole catalogue of instances of corporate checks illegally sent to campaign treasurers and of corporate contributions inadvertently reported in states where they are illegal. Usually the error is courteously called to the attention of the offenders with the suggestion that adjustments be made.

Typical is the testimony of John Paulding Brown, counsel for the Volunteers for Stevenson in 1952: "We had a system of screening contributions. We had

In all nations, business concerns with interests directly affected by governmental action are highly sensitive politically. The question is not whether they will be politically active, but to what extent and in what ways. Everywhere, given the opportunity, they make cash gifts to campaigns.[23] A lot of corporation presidents, said one board chairman quoted in the big corporations' magazine, *Fortune,* "just reach in the till and get $25,000 to contribute to political campaigns—just as labor unions do."[24]

The power of hierarchy.—Cash from the till is but one form of corporate political action. The hierarchical administrative structure of a corporation can be turned to many uses. The network of communications, friendships, and relationships of dependence that make up a business bureaucracy can be highly useful in soliciting both votes and money. The secret ballot has largely eliminated gross attempts to coerce votes, though more subtle forms of persuasion may be attempted. There is as yet no secret banking booth in which a man may make a campaign gift (or decline to do so) without his preference becoming known. Employees receive the kind of letter reportedly sent in 1956 by Jack Warner, head of Warner Brothers motion pictures, soliciting funds. The letter

---

three or four people engaged in examining checks as they came in. We would look for these prohibited contributions. We did get checks that were obviously drawn on corporate accounts. We would simply send them back with a polite letter pointing out the statutory reference, saying that we hoped that they would come back under some individual name. . . . Sometimes they did not come back."—U.S. House of Representatives Special Committee to Investigate Campaign Expenditures, 1952, *Hearings* (Washington: Government Printing Office, 1952), pp. 35-36.

The spirit of events is indicated by a Democrat who reported to the Senate Subcommittee on Privileges and Elections that he made five gifts in 1956 totalling $6,200, but he was not sure in whose name they had been made. The West Virginia ones may have been in the name of his engineering firm, which he gave; the Pennsylvania ones in the name of another such firm, or its manager, also named. Some solicitors point out, however, that a corporate check may be charged to the personal account (within the corporation) of a corporate official, hence in reality be a personal gift.—Herbert E. Alexander, "The Role of the Volunteer Political Fund Raiser: A Case Study in New York in 1952" (Ph.D. dissertation, Yale University, 1958), p. 166.

23. In Japan, for one illustration, business concerns have regularly given to several parties simultaneously. In Australia, for another, powerful industrial, commercial, and financial companies have set up machinery for raising and supplying campaign funds.—Chitoshi Yanaga, *Japanese People and Politics* (New York: John Wiley & Sons, 1956), pp. 258-60; Louise Overacker, *The Australian Party System* (New Haven; Yale University Press, 1952), pp. 216-18 and *passim.* The practice is not confined to nations like these (and Canada, the Philippines, Sweden, Germany, Great Britain—where it is evident), but may exist also in economically quite different areas, such as the West Indies.—Morley Ayearst, "A Note on Some Characteristics of West Indian Political Parties," *Social and Economic Studies,* 3 (1954), 192.

24. Duncan Norton-Taylor, "How to Give Money to Politicians," *Fortune,* 53 (May, 1956), 238. On techniques of evasion of legal prohibitions against corporate giving, see pages 132-35, below.

read in part: "Please make your check payable to the United Republican Finance Committee and send same to my office. Many thanks for your early attention."[25] Or the kind of letter dated August 6, 1956, that went from an official of Fiberboard Products, Inc., after a luncheon with a member of the Republican finance committee. It began:

> Dear Employee:
>
> For those who believe in freedom, there is only one place to go, namely to the Republican Party. . . .
>
> I have personally sent my check for $1,000 which is in excess of 1 per cent of my salary. I tell you this for whatever guide it may be to you in making your decision. I know you will realize on thinking that this is not a pressure letter. . . .
>
> Many organizations throughout the United States are presenting this story to their people at this time. . . . If you believe in the importance of this campaign as I do, and make a contribution, will you tear off the section below and send a memorandum of your action. Your signature is not required.[26]

The president of a large engineering firm in New York with branches in several cities candidly confided that sometimes his executives definitely prefer one side in an election. In such cases they give attention to contributions and to a campaign for votes. In a neighboring state, the Citizens for Eisenhower in 1952 mailed campaign materials to lists of employees provided by company executives, the operation being financed personally, it was said, by the officials. During every campaign stories sprout alleging company coercion of officers and employees to give to the party of the company's choice.

The important point is no longer, if it once was, that screws are turned to compel an employee to give contrary to his predilection. This may happen but usually not.[27] The point is that a large administrative complex like General Motors—or the United Automobile Workers—provides ready-made channels for mobilizing by persuasion and propaganda the political sentiment and energy of vast numbers of people. The word can be passed and a vogue created quickly. Latent inclinations to give or to vote or to favor a candidate are triggered. Inducement to conformity is created by the climate of talk and activity. And it is easiest to influence this climate from a spot high in an organization.

25. Drew Pearson, "The Washington Merry-Go-Round," *The News and Observer* (Raleigh, N.C.), October 28, 1956.

26. Gore Committee *Hearings,* part 2, pp. 558-59.

27. William F. Hufstader, vice president of General Motors in charge of distribution, was long active in the Republican party in Michigan. In 1952 he telephoned six dealers in Detroit (one for each line of GM cars) asking them to solicit contributions from automobile dealers in the Detroit area. They were told to send the gifts straight to the Wayne County Republican finance committee. Five of the six agreed to help and one declined. No evidence was offered that the one declining suffered in any way.—U.S. Senate Subcommittee of the Committee on Interstate and Foreign Commerce (hereafter cited as the Monroney Committee), *Hearings* (Washington: Government Printing Office, 1956), part 1, pp. 761-62.

A North Carolina study has already been mentioned in which a random sample of certain classes of 1952 contributors to statewide political committees was interviewed. Of 23 persons who gave $100 or more to Eisenhower's state campaign, four turned out to be dealers in cars made by the Ford Motor Company. Three of them had given because solicited by other automobile dealers, and the fourth had been active himself as a solicitor. Three of the four had not previously been active in politics, and this included the solicitor. The solicitor, who collected something over $2,000, had travelled for Ford, acquired many friends on the east coast, and become well known in dealers' associations at state, regional, and national levels. He said his single excursion into politics was prompted by resentment at the way the federal government was going. He had friends active at the top level of the Citizens for Eisenhower. He got caught up in the fever for Ike and went all out.

How many Ford company dealers got caught up in the fever for Ike in 1952 is hard to say, but apparently there were a lot of them, scattered all the way from Florida to California. The contagion may well have started with Henry Ford II's personal assistant, Allen W. Merrell, long an active Republican in Michigan and in 1952 a member of the Republican national finance committee. Mr. Merrell asked for and received Mr. Ford's permission to "call together a selected group of Ford dealers . . . to ask the members of the group—all strong Eisenhower supporters—to solicit automobile dealers." Mr. Ford specified that no pressure was to be exerted, none of the sales force or other company personnel was to take part in the solicitation, and no company money was to be spent. He later stated that Mr. Merrell held two meetings with dealers ("as a private citizen and as a member of the Republican national finance committee") and that he, Mr. Ford, had never known who had made contributions and who had not. Some of the dealers in Chicago, California, and elsewhere felt under some pressure, nevertheless, and one who had called a meeting on the west coast told a Senate investigator: "Of course, we weren't partisan; if they had asked us to raise funds for the Democrats, we would have done that, too." The reaction was perhaps understandable in 1952 when the lives of many dealers depended on an adequate supply of automobiles, and when Mr. Merrell's close relationship to Mr. Ford was widely known throughout the industry.[28]

To imply that an individual's private political role cannot easily be separated from his corporate position is not to argue that all corporate

28. *Ibid.*, pp. 960-71. A Democrat has stated that the Republican Attorney General of Michigan was denied renomination by his party in 1948 because he specified charges against Republicans for their money-raising tactics in auto-manufacturing circles. The scarcity of cars allegedly provided leverage by which Republican campaign gifts were pried out of auto-hungry dealers. The Attorney General even claimed the Republican administration permitted cooperative dealers to avoid state sales taxes on the turnover of their used cars.—Jack Redding, *Inside the Democratic Party* (New York: The Bobbs-Merrill Company, 1958), p. 264.

officials should become political eunuchs, but it is important to recognize that no conscious pressure need be used by an organizational leader to influence his subordinates, as many commentators were to observe apropos inquiries by Mr. Sherman Adams to federal agencies concerning the affairs of his friend Bernard Goldfine. A corporation, a trade association, a labor union, a government bureau, any organization is a potential campaign structure. It is a potential money-raising structure. The extent to which it will be activated and turned one direction or another depends on many variables internal and external to the organization. But the processes of politics include the latent capacity of all types of human organization to influence political behavior.

Gifts by corporate officials.—One important link between corporate life and political life is found in the campaign donations of corporation officials. These constitute an important source of income for candidates and campaign committees in both political parties. They may not constitute corporate political activity in a technical sense, for the gifts take the form of voluntary personal contributions. Yet they are, in their impact, a form of political participation that increases the importance of the corporate community and of individual companies in the financial constituencies of officeholders. The same principle applies to other groups in society, including organized labor. The activities of other groups have, in fact, spurred elements of the business community to encourage business officials as a class to take part in politics. The talk gained impetus during the Eisenhower years.[29] Numerous business organizations urged their personnel to take a constructive part in politics.[30] Several of the nation's largest corporations participated in programs conducted by the Effective Citizens Organization to introduce uninitiated businessmen to the realities of effective political action.[31]

29. See J. J. Wuerthner, Jr., *The Businessman's Guide to Practical Politics* (Chicago: Henry Regnery Company, 1959), and Horace E. Sheldon, "Businessmen Must Get Into Politics," *Harvard Business Review,* 37 (March-April, 1959), 37-47. A warning flag was thrown up by Charles P. Taft in "Should Business Go in for Politics?" *New York Times Magazine,* August 30, 1959, pp. 10ff.

30. Among those with active programs were General Electric, Johnson & Johnson, General Dynamics, Chrysler, U.S. Steel.—*Wall Street Journal,* July 23, 1958. In 1958 the Chamber of Commerce of the United States announced plans to establish a training program to get businessmen into politics at the precinct level.—*New York Times,* October 3, 1958. Henry R. Luce had taken the message overseas. In Paris, in 1957, before 1,800 businessmen from 35 countries he labeled as "not good" the modern political record of businessmen. Too many had supported Hitler, Italian Fascism, Japanese militarism, American isolationism; too few had opposed communism. Mr. Luce did not say so, but the support he decried often took the form of financial succor to political leaders, parties, and movements. He urged upon his international audience "a little greater wisdom about politics." —"The Character of the Businessman," *Fortune,* 56 (August, 1957), 109.

31. Toward this end ECO sponsored a series of workshops in academic settings at which politicians and others spoke. By 1959 over 500 companies had been represented at the workshops.—*Fortune,* 60 (December, 1959), 101.

As Senator Barry Goldwater, chairman of the Republican Senatorial campaign committee, has implied, campaign giving in certain segments of the business community is already heavy. In a plea for "warm bodies to ring doorbells," the Senator has observed that "it's still hard to convince businessmen that the least of our problems is money."[32] A large share of all the campaign money spent in the United States originates with persons engaged in some form of legitimate or illegitimate business activity. In some jurisdictions the guts of the politics is the competition of rival economic enterprises, the political forum replacing the market place as the arena of the free enterprise system. The task for the analyst is to get some notion about the extent of this type of political action among persons in various sorts of enterprise.[33]

The available data point to a high level of financial activity in politics by certain officials of certain corporations. They also show that with several types of corporations a large proportion of firms have officials who give. The heavy known involvement of oil company officers and directors has already been alluded to.[34] Other groups of corporations with manifest stakes in the political system are found to be similarly connected to the political process, e.g. the leading airline companies, defense contractors, and firms participating in the atomic energy program.[35] Given the financial resources of officials of large corporations

32. *Congressional Quarterly,* 16 (1959), 58.

33. The limitations of the data mentioned in footnote 5 on page 98 above, need to be remembered. The geographic coverage for the two years was not uniform, a fact especially relevant in comparing the contributing record of persons connected with firms located in different parts of the country. Husband and wife are treated as one. Comparisons between different types of organizations are necessarily rough and tentative.

34. Probably the most significant single figure in American political finance is 27.5 That is the oil depletion allowance, the percentage of gross sales oil and gas producers may apply as a tax credit against their net taxable income. Although the allowance may not exceed 50 per cent of net revenue, it—together with credits for foreign taxes paid—seems to cost the federal treasury around $750,000,000 annually. The companies benefitting have over-all paid income taxes at about half the prevailing general corporate tax rate in the 1950's. Small wonder that oil interests give willingly in both parties to protect this happy state of affairs, which has existed since 1926.—Walter Adams and Horace M. Gray, *Monopoly in America—The Government as Promoter* (New York: The Macmillan Company, 1955), pp. 79-80, 194. This book discusses the effect on profit levels, and on the concentration of economic power, of federal legislative action, e.g., accelerated amortization and rapid depreciation provisions of tax bills, defense procurement and surplus property disposal policies, atomic energy legislation—all creating potent political interests.

On the wide range of political interests of the numerous and diverse segments of the oil industry, and the many ways oil interests seek to influence government and public opinion, see the six articles by Robert Engler under the general title, "Oil and Politics," *New Republic* 133 (August 29–October 3, 1955).

35. Gore Committee *Report,* pp. 72-73, 78-85.

and the stakes their corporations have in politics,[36] these findings ought to surprise no one. Nor should they cast a stigma on either the individuals or their companies.

The largest corporations.—The political behavior of officials of the nation's largest business enterprises presumably is not representative of all corporate officials. As a group, they probably give more on the average to politics than their lower-paid counterparts, although great unevenness is found among small and medium-sized corporations in the political activities of their personnel.[37] There is special significance, however, in the behavior displayed by the leaders of the largest enterprises in America's highly integrated and concentrated corporate community. They not only exercise vast economic and social power by virtue of their positions or their wealth; they set a style for others to follow.

In 1952, 92 of the 100 largest corporations were found to have officers or directors who made a known political contribution of $500 or larger to some nomination or election campaign somewhere in the country. It is probable that a complete file of contributions would have included most of the remaining eight. (Five of them were located in parts of the country from which the data on contributors were notably deficient.) In 1956, 199 of 225 of the nation's largest firms had officials whose names turned up in the file of contributors for that year. Table 9 summarizes the 1952 information and Table 10 does so for 1956.

The dollar figures in each table are net totals. Some persons served with more than one company, and in such cases their gifts were counted only once. The importance of this source of campaign funds is great. In 1956 the donations from officials of the 225 companies accounted for over 18 per cent of the total value of known gifts of $500 or more.[38]

Campaign giving is not confined to one or two persons in each of these organizations who happen to be interested in politics. Table 11

36. The stake is a continuing one, in war and peace. "Between 1940 and 1944, some $175 billion worth of prime supply contracts—the key to control of the nation's means of production—were given to private corporations. A full two-thirds of this went to the top one hundred corporations—in fact, almost one-third went to ten private corporations. . . . It had cost some $40 billion to build all the manufacturing facilities existing in the United States in 1939. By 1945, an additional $26 billion worth of high-quality new plant and equipment had been added—two-thirds of it paid for directly from government funds."—Mills, *op, cit.*, pp. 100-1.

37. To the contrary, however, one writer made a survey of corporate public relations activities before 1950. "Of replies received from every section of America, and from leaders in nearly every major business classification, one pattern seems to run consistently throughout: 'We never take part in legislative activities.'" They have not gone into local politics, was the conclusion, either for the election of candidates or the influencing of legislation.—Louis B. Lundberg, *Public Relations in the Local Community* (New York: Harper & Brothers, 1950), p. 31.

38. Computed from the Gore Committee *Report,* Exs. 25 and 26.

Table 9[a]

MINIMUM INVOLVEMENT OF CORPORATION OFFICIALS[b] IN CAMPAIGN FINANCE, 1952: KNOWN GIFTS OF $500 AND OVER BY OFFICERS AND DIRECTORS OF THE 100 LARGEST U.S. CORPORATIONS[c]

Type of Corporation	No. of Firms	Number with Known Contributors[d]	Net Totals of Known Contributions[d]		
			Total	To Rep.	To Dem.
Manufacturing	27	26	$ 384,360	374,260	10,100
Commercial banks	28	24	298,948	253,948	45,000
Transportation	12	12	143,416	127,916	15,500
Life insurance	16	15	86,065	85,065	1,000
Trade	1	1	22,500	13,000	9,500
Public utilities	7	7	20,100	20,100	0
Savings banks	3	1	4,020	4,020	0
Finance and investment	6	6	55,500	54,000	1,500
Total	100	92	$1,014,909	932,309	82,600

[a] The detailed data from which this table was constructed, including the names of individuals, their firms, and the amounts of their gifts, were presented to the Gore Committee and printed in its *Hearings*, part 2, pp. 461-504.
[b] Man and wife are counted as one.
[c] As measured by 1953 total assets. Taken from a list compiled and classified by the National City Bank, New York.
[d] Some individuals served as an officer or director of more than one corporation. The amount of each such person's contribution has been allocated to the corporation with which he is primarily identified. Without the elimination of such duplicate money the Republican total would have been higher by $599,495, and the Democratic total by $11,500.

Table 10[a]

MINIMUM INVOLVEMENT OF CORPORATION OFFICIALS[b] IN CAMPAIGN FINANCE, 1956: KNOWN GIFTS OF $500 AND OVER BY OFFICERS AND DIRECTORS OF THE LARGEST U.S. CORPORATIONS[c]

Type of Corporation	No. of Firms	No. with Known Contributors[d]	Net Totals of Known Contributions[d]			
			Total	To Rep.	To Dem.	To Other[e]
Manufacturing	100	96	$1,136,247	1,050,197	73,750	12,300
Commerical banks	25	25	259,275	253,775	5,500	0
Transportation	25	24	321,375	315,900	5,475	0
Life insurance	25	20	107,625	102,125	4,000	1,500
Trade	25	17	86,525	69,300	14,500	2,725
Public utilities	25	17	25,800	25,300	500	0
Total	225	199	$1,936,847	1,816,597	103,725	16,525

[a] The detailed data from which this table was constructed, including the names of individuals, their firms, and the amounts of their gifts appear in the Gore Committee *Report*, Exhibit 25, pp. 1-39. The *Report* points out that the Gore Committee received some additional data after this exhibit was prepared. Inclusion of the new data might have produced minor changes in the totals, but the substance of the analysis here would not be affected.
[b] Man and wife are counted as one.
[c] Taken from the directory of largest corporations issued as a supplement to *Fortune* for July 1956. Criteria of size were in each case dollar measures for 1955, as follows: for the 100 manufacturing (industrial) firms and the 25 trade (merchandising) firms, sales; for the public utilities, commercial banks, and life insurance companies, assets; for the transportation companies, operating revenues.
[d] Some individuals serve as an officer or director of more than one corporation. The amount of each such person's contribution has been allocated to the corporation with which he is primarily identified. Without the elimination of such duplicate money the Republican total would have been higher by $1,213,359, the Democratic total by $7,125, and the total for others by $18,250.
[e] Miscellaneous political groups not affiliated with either major party.

shows that in 1956 around one-twelfth of the positions of officer in the corporations studied were held by persons who had made a known gift of $500 or more, and about one-fourth of the directorships were held by such campaign contributors. The 1952 analysis showed about the same results. Some contributors (and noncontributors) held more than one corporate position, but the 1956 analysis showed 742 different contributors holding these corporate positions, donating an average of more than $2,600 each. If all gifts of all sizes actually made were included in the analysis, the results would reveal materially greater coporate political involvement.

Table 11

PERCENTAGE OF POSITIONS OF OFFICER AND DIRECTOR OF LARGEST U.S. CORPORATIONS HELD BY KNOWN CAMPAIGN GIVERS OF $500 OR MORE: BY TYPE OF CORPORATION, 1952 AND 1956[a]

Type of Corporation	1952			1956		
	No. of Firms	% of Positions Held by Known Contributors[b]		No. of Firms	% of Positions Held by Known Contributors[b]	
		Officer	Director		Officer	Director
Manufacturing	27	14	34	100	17	25
Commercial banks	28	5	35	25	2	33
Transportation	12	4	29	25	5	29
Life insurance	16	6	24	25	2	14
Trade	1	4	32	25	9	13
Public utilities	7	0	18	25	3	13
Savings banks	3	4	20	0	0	0
Finance and investment	6	6	17	0	0	0
Total	100	7	29	225	8	23

[a] Computed from Gore Committee *Hearings*, part 2, pp. 461-504 (1952), and *Report*, Exhibit 25 (1956). Lists of officials taken from *Poor's Register of Directors and Executives*. The *Report* points out that the Gore Committee received some additional data after Exhibit 25 was prepared. Inclusion of the new data might have produced minor changes in the percentages, but the substance of the analysis here would not have been affected. For criteria of size used in ranking firms, see footnote (c) in Tables 9 and 10.

[b] Individuals who served as both an officer and a director in the same firm are classified as both. Some contributors and some noncontributors served more than one firm. The percentages were figured by dividing the total number of positions into the number held by a person who made a contribution. See comments in text. Man and wife were counted as one.

To illustrate the contributing behavior of officials of particular corporations, information concerning a number of them is presented in Table 12. These firms fall at the top and bottom of the rankings for each of the categories treated in Table 11.[39] As evident from the previous tables, the proportion of corporation officials who give to politics as disclosed by this analysis differs from one firm to another.

39. An exception is made in the case of transportation companies to include the two largest airlines. The transportation firms ranked 1, 2, 24, and 25 were all railroads.

Table 12

PERCENTAGE OF OFFICERS AND DIRECTORS OF SELECTED LARGE U.S. CORPORATIONS KNOWN TO HAVE MADE A CAMPAIGN GIFT OF $500 OR MORE, 1956[a]

Rank by Size[b]	Corporation	Officers: Total No.	Officers: No. Known to Have Contributed	Officers: % Contributing	Directors[c]: Total No.	Directors[c]: No. Known to Have Contributed	Directors[c]: % Contributing
	Manufacturing						
1	General Motors	35	23	66	19	14	74
2	Standard Oil (N.J.)	11	4	36	6	3	50
3	Ford Motor	33	8	24	2	0	0
4	U.S. Steel	27	9	33	13	7	54
5	Chrysler	21	1	5	10	4	40
96	United Merchants & Manufacturers	17	0	0	10	1	10
97	Pillsbury Mills	23	0	0	6	2	33
98	Standard Oil (Ohio)	15	0	0	5	2	40
99	American Radiator & Standard Sanitary	12	1	9	10	2	20
100	Deere	16	2	13	7	0	0
	Commercial Banks						
1	Bank of America (S.F.)	23	1	4	23	3	13
2	Chase Manhattan	107	0	0	22	13	59
24	New York Trust	28	0	0	15	4	27
25	Republic National Bank of Dallas	73	0	0	22	2	9
	Transportation						
1	Pennsylvania RR	20	0	0	14	6	43
2	New York Central	35	1	3	13	4	31
12	American Airlines	25	6	24	12	2	17
15	Pan American World Airways	23	3	13	13	3	23
	Life Insurance						
1	Metropolitan	17	4	24	20	9	45
2	Prudential	52	0	0	22	2	9
24	American National	10	0	0	8	0	0
25	Equitable of Iowa	10	0	0	13	2	15
	Trade						
1	Great A. & P Tea	4	0	0	9	0	0
2	Sears Roebuck	18	0	0	10	4	40
24	Jewel Tea	13	0	0	6	0	0
25	The Grand Union	14	0	0	6	1	17
	Public Utilities						
1	American Tel. & Tel.	17	0	0	16	3	19
2	Pacific Gas & Electric	20	0	0	12	5	42
24	Texas Eastern Transmission	17	0	0	6	2	33
25	Pacific Lighting	7	1	14	7	1	14

[a] Computed from Gore Committee *Report*, Exhibit 25. Lists of officials taken from *Poor's Register of Directors and Executives—1956*. The *Report* points out that the Gore Committee received some additional data after Exhibit 25 was prepared. Inclusion of the new data might have produced minor changes, but the substance of the analysis here would not have been affected.

[b] For criteria of size used in ranking firms, see footnote (c) in Tables 9 and 10.

[c] Individuals who served as both an officer and a director in the same firm are classified as an officer. Man and wife were counted as one in identifying contributions. The definition of officer is sometimes open to ambiguity, especially in firms with large numbers of them. Decisions were made in each case as to what group would be treated as officers, and the determination was adhered to in all analyses. The total number of directors given for each company does not include those directors who were also officers, hence the seemingly few directors in some cases.

Tables 10 and 11 suggest, for example, that officials of manufacturing concerns, transportation companies, and commercial banks engaged more in this type of political action during 1956 than officials of life insurance, public utility, and trade firms. The 1952 data are not wholly comparable because the number of firms in each category is generally less. Again, however, the percentages for life insurance and utility executives fell below those for the other types of firms.[40] In general, the proportion of officials making gifts declined with the size of the firm, as indicated by Table 12.[41]

The data for 1952 and 1956 show another similarity. A spot check of the contributions of officials of individual companies disclosed frequent parallels between 1952 and 1956. Compare, for example, the number of officers and directors in the top two firms in each of the six categories in Table 12 who made a known gift in 1952 and 1956.[42]

	Officers		*Directors*	
	1952	*1956*	*1952*	*1956*
General Motors	6	23	8	14
Standard Oil (N.J.)	2	4	0	3
Bank of America (S.F.)	1	1	0	3
Chase Manhattan	3	0	14	13
Pennsylvania	0	0	6	6
New York Central	1	1	4	4
Metropolitan Life	4	4	5	9
Prudential Life	0	0	2	2
Great A & P Tea	0	0	0	0
Sears Roebuck	1	0	5	4
American Tel. & Tel.	0	0	6	3
Pacific Gas & Electric	0	0	4	5

In many of the cases, the number of officials involved in both years was identical, or varied by only one. The recurring patterns suggest that a degree of stability characterizes the contributing habits of corporate

40. Only one trading firm—Sears Roebuck—was covered in the 1952 analysis, hence that category in Table 11 cannot be compared for the two years. A separate analysis that included the 15 largest trade firms in 1952, however, found 10 per cent of the persons holding officerships and 16 per cent of those holding directorships to have made a known gift of $500 or more. For details, see the Gore Committee *Hearings,* part 2, pp. 513-18. These percentages compare closely with those for 1956, 9 and 13 respectively.

41. This feature increases the consistency between the 1952 and 1956 results in Tables 9 and 10 and in Table 11, because more firms were included in all categories save one in 1956 than in 1952.

42. The 1952 data may be found in the Gore Committee *Hearings,* part 2, pp. 482-504. The 1952 figures opposite the Chase Manhattan Bank are for the Chase National Bank.

officials. It may be pure coincidence that despite the turnover of leadership in the New York Central Railroad between 1952 and 1956, the number of officers and directors who were known givers remained the same. Yet even with changes in personnel, more than half of the 72 individuals with the 12 companies who were listed as giving in 1952 also turned up among the officials who were listed in 1956.

A general feature.—Officials of large-scale economic enterprises necessarily have an intimate interest in public policy. That they become involved in politics ought to occasion no wonder. Differences in the contributing behavior of officials of different types of corporations doubtless stem in some measure from the immediacy of their political concerns. The interlocking character of large-scale American economic organization, however, tends to induce harmony of interest and action on general policy matters. The patterns of political giving observed among officials of the corporate giants are found also in other sectors of the business community.

An analysis of the 76 largest banks in six eastern cities found 48 with at least one official making a known gift of $500 or more in 1952. This was true of 27 of the 35 New York banks on the list.[43] Spot checks around the nation for 1952 showed officials of eight of nine airlines chosen at random among the known givers. Of four American firms involved in the controversy over an import levy on Swiss watches, all had officials who made recorded contributions. It was the same with 11 of 12 dairy and food products companies, five of five entertainments companies, five of five textile corporations. Among the 10 leading radio and television licensees, eight had officials who gave reported contributions of $500 or more in 1956. The same was true of 39 out of the 47 leading underwriters of investment bonds and 20 of the 37 top advertising agencies.[44]

Not all of the gifts made by officials of these and similar economic organizations go equally to the parties or to competing candidates. Yet, over-all, the bulk of American campaign activities is financed by businessmen. The way they distribute their support between the two parties is a crucial aspect of their political behavior.[45]

43. Details are reported in the Gore Committee *Hearings,* part 2, p. 529.

44. Gore Committee *Report,* pp. 71-76. The radio-television licensees were ranked by 1955 revenues; the 47 underwriters were those whose capital worth exceeded $5,000,000 at the beginning of 1956; the 37 advertising agencies were those that had billings of $20,000,000 or over in 1955.

45. This chapter has barely touched on differences in company policies toward campaign giving by their officials. Some corporations appear to discourage this form of political activity while others, as already indicated, actively encourage it. Interesting material on the perceptions large campaign contributors and solicitors, including corporation officials, have of their political roles appears in Alexander, *op. cit.*

3. THE PARTIES COMPARED

The Republicanism of large corporate contributors ought not, in the abstract logic of the political system, taint either givers or receivers of campaign gifts, but the tactics of stereotypes have decreed differently. Democratic tacticians not only parlay the evidence into a black and white picture of GOP plutocracy versus the people's Democracy, they also capitalize on old suspicions to imply that evil has been done, or soon will be. For their part, most Republican spokesmen compound the confusion. Instead of publicly cherishing the preference shown by the nation's most important economic leadership, they breed further suspicion by denying that they have it.

Republican hegemony, limited.—Officials of most of the nation's largest economic enterprises overwhelmingly preferred the Republican cause in 1956. The evidence from reported contributions in Table 13 is so preponderant that even a radically disproportionate volume of covert gifts to Democrats (e.g., in southern primaries) could not upset the balance.[46] Despite diversities of interest, officials of America's *biggest businesses* display remarkable homogeneity in their political giving.[47]

Table 13

DIVISION BETWEEN THE PARTIES IN THE VALUE OF REPORTED GIFTS OF $500 AND OVER MADE BY OFFICIALS OF THE LARGEST U.S. BUSINESS ENTERPRISES, 1956[a]

Type	Percentage to	
	Rep.	Dem.
225 largest corporations	95	5
29 largest oil companies[b]	97	3
10 leading radio and TV licensees	93	7
47 leading underwriters of investment bonds	99	1
37 leading advertising agencies	99	1

[a] Derived from Gore Committee *Report*, pp. 71-78 and Exhibits 25 and 26.
[b] Includes 17 firms that are also included in the 225 largest corporations.
Note: Republican receipts from officials of the 225 largest corporations amounted to 23 per cent of total reported Republican receipts in sums of $500 and over. The corresponding Democratic percentage was 4.

46. Recipients at all levels, and committees and candidates of all types, are lumped together for each party. Particular businessmen, of course, have special favorites. See Charles J. V. Murphy in *Fortune,* "McCarthy and the Businessman," 49 (April, 1954), 156ff., and "Texas Business and McCarthy," 49 (May, 1954), 100ff.

47. One study of large corporations disclosed eight more or less clearly defined interest groupings that included 106 of the 250 larger corporations and nearly two-thirds of their combined assets.—National Resources Committee, "The Structure of Controls," in Reinhard Bendix and Seymour Martin Lipset (eds.), *Class, Status and Power—A Reader in Social Stratification* (Glencoe, Illinois: The Free Press, 1953), pp. 140-41. No significant distinctions among these groups were apparent, however, when the known contributions of their officials were tabulated.

This is one reason the Republican party is widely perceived as the party of the rich, as the party of big business.[48]

Republicans are correct, however, in insisting that this is only part of the story. Democratic money must come from somewhere, and as the economy is constructed, most of it must originate with persons engaged in business.[49] Democratic backing may be slight at the top of the nation's corporate structure, but lower down support for the parties divides more evenly. To make the kind of analysis of smaller enterprises that was made of the largest ones is, at least for those who have tried so far, impracticable. The names of officials are too difficult to identify and too numerous to check against known contributors. By examining contributors to particular political committees, however, indications are found. Persons engaged in manufacturing provide significant sums to the national committees of both parties. Among Republicans in 1952, 60 per cent of money given by manufacturers came from persons associated with the nation's 400 largest industrial firms. The comparable Democratic percentage was 38.

Multi-interest politics.—The politics of the United States is not a politics of rich versus poor, of shirtless ones against oligarchies of landowners, financiers, and industrialists.[50] Given the dispersion of wealth,

48. Even shortly after General Eisenhower's first inauguration, the Gallup Poll, in December, 1953, found one-fourth of a cross-section of voters of all parties indicating that the Republican party stands for the "rich, privileged few; big business." The next most frequent answer as to what the party stood for was given by only 7 per cent of the respondents, and only 3 per cent cited "betterment of people, low cost of living." Five per cent found no difference between the parties. —*The Washington Post,* December 16, 1953. Political advantages as well as disadvantages attach to this image of the Republican party. The Republican national finance committee has fortified its solicitors in recent years with much documentation of the benefits received by business from the Eisenhower administration. One item charted the estimated reductions in corporate income tax collections made possible by the depreciation provisions of a bill enacted by the Eighty-third Congress. "This chart will be an invaluable aid," read the accompanying memo, "to the members of Republican Finance Committees everywhere who are contacting executives of corporations for contributions to the Party."

49. Governor G. Mennen Williams has pointed out that even in Michigan's labor-strong Democratic party "people associated with business outnumbered those identified with labor in the roster of delegates and alternates to the 1956 Democratic National Convention. Nor is this an isolated phenomenon; business and professional men and women make up the majority of our county chairmen."—"Can Businessmen Be Democrats?" *Harvard Business Review,* 36 (March-April, 1958), 102.

50. Occasionally in the United States the political challenger of an entrenched social and economic oligarchy finds himself effectively blackballed with all segments of the business community. The consequences are more likely to be crippling in party primaries and in a state with a cohesive socio-politico system like Virginia.

A principal Democratic fund-raiser of 1956 claimed, without offering evidence, that his party attracted more $100,000 donors that year than its opponent. Generally, Republicans receive a larger share of the larger campaign gifts. The money reported in the 1952 file of known gifts of $500 and over was divided 60 per cent to Republicans, 38 per cent to Democrats, and 2 per cent to others. The corresponding 1956 percentages were 73, 25, and 2. Money given in 1956 by 259

it would be surprising indeed if financial supporters could not be marshalled on most sides of most issues and elections. It is well remembered that William McKinley enjoyed the generous backing of great American businesses in his successful defense of the gold standard in 1896. It is sometimes forgotten that his opponent, William Jennings Bryan, for silver at 16 to 1, was aided to the tune of $300,000 by Marcus Daly of the Anaconda Copper Company, a firm that might mine something other than copper.[51] Before and since 1896 economic interests have used their financial resources to protect or advance specific stakes in politics. Minority parties, like the Dixiecrats of 1948, have benefitted from the opportune financial support of individuals with immediate and tangible interests, like tidelands oil.[52] And as prospects changed, the activity of affected interests changed. Bankers' support of the Republicans slacked off after 1896[53] and the relative importance of certain business gifts for the Democrats shifted after 1932.[54]

These ready reactions to timely issues ought not to obscure other important characteristics of campaign giving. Maurice Duverger has observed in another connection that strictly economic criteria would not suffice to delineate divisions between parties, even class parties.[55] A wide variety of considerations affects the preferences of American voters. A wide variety of factors also affects the preferences of campaign givers. Both help account for the omnibus composition of the parties and reflect the pluralism of political interests.[56] Moreover, the rainbow of viewpoints among candidates leads contributors with ap-

persons whose gifts aggregated $5,000 or more each was divided 78, 21, and 1. The percentages for known party donors of $10,000 or more in 1952 (110 persons) were 64 Republican and 36 Democratic, in 1956 (111 persons), 76 and 24.

51. So said Daly's son-in-law, James W. Gerard, himself a munificent Democratic supporter in a later day, in *My First Eighty-Three Years in America* (Garden City, New York: Doubleday & Company, Inc., 1951), p. 92.

52. Emile B. Ader, "Why the Dixiecrats Failed," *The Journal of Politics,* 15 (1953), 365-66. Other evidence supports the author's suggestion that oilmen gave heavily to the Thurmond-Wright campaign.

53. Republican finance officers reported that in 1896 "every bank and trust company in New York City but one, and most of the insurance companies," made contributions to the national committee. In 1900 very few did and in 1904 still less.—James K. Pollock, Jr., *Party Campaign Funds* (New York: Alfred A. Knopf, 1926), p. 111.

54. Presumably a return to normalcy. See Table 14, page 124.

55. *Political Parties—Their Organization and Activity in the Modern State* (Translated by Barbara and Robert North) (New York: John Wiley & Sons, 1954), p. xv.

56. For example, the prime political concern of many businessmen who are Zionists is the welfare of Israel.

Philip S. Wilder, Jr., reported that some Republican fund-raisers told him they rely in their soliciting on a combination of traditional party loyalty, interest in particular issues, and popularity of individual candidates, factors found by the studies of the Survey Research Center to be related to voter choices.—"The National Committee of the Party in Power, 1953-1958," (a paper read at the 1958 meeting of the American Political Science Association, mimeographed), p. 17.

parently common economic interests to give to different parties in different electoral areas. Even within the same jurisdiction the financial constituencies of candidates and committees of the same party differ.[57] The purposes, records, and professed philosophies of Democratic and Republican candidates are sufficiently diverse at all levels to keep businessmen's money flowing to both parties.[58]

Bankers and brewers.—Louise Overacker pioneered in analyzing the economic and occupational characteristics of large campaign contributors. Her work demonstrated that for the two national committees, in the presidential election years 1932-1944, (a) clear differences existed between the parties in the sources of their large contributions, and (b) most types of economic interest were represented, though not equally, in both parties. These conclusions were found true also for 1952 and 1956, and for committees in addition to the two national committees.[59]

As shown by Table 14, a hefty share of $1,000-and-over gifts to the Republican national committee from 1932 through 1952 has come from bankers, brokers, industrialists, and persons in oil, mining, utilities, and related endeavors. Contributors connected with a different combination of enterprises—merchandising, hard and soft drinks, construction and building materials, publishing, advertising, amusements, radio, the professions, and public officeholding—provided a large share of comparable Democratic income. Both committees enjoyed support from both sets of contributors, but not in equal degrees. Professor Overacker's analyses revealed that within these broad groupings the most important Republican givers were manufacturers and bankers-and-brokers. The distinctively important Democratic givers were public officeholders and persons in the professions. Table 15 demonstrates that

57. Candidates for offices whose duties affect different segments of the citizenry attract different kinds of contributors. Party committees active for the same candidate may also, however, appeal to quite different classes of givers. Volunteer candidate committees are especially likely to attract an entirely different type of contributor than the regular state committee.

58. Among members of the New York, Midwest, and American Stock Exchanges who made known campaign contributions of $500 or more in 1952, between one-fifth and two-fifths in each case favored the Democratic cause.

59. The data are something short of perfect. For all years the analysis was confined to officially reported gifts of $500, or $1,000, and more. Some contributors could not be identified. Others had a number of economic interests and designation of the primary one was a matter of discretion. Moreover, as mentioned elsewhere, the reporting practices of committees affect the number of individual contributors who are listed in official reports in any given year. Certain Republican state committees once accompanied their state quota with lists of persons to whom the gifts were to be attributed. In later years similar transactions were treated as transfers of funds from committee to committee, with no individuals mentioned.

Some reported names are dummies that cloak the real donors. Many dummies doubtless fall into the "unidentifiable" category. Where the economic interest of dummies have been identified, their inclusion in the analysis may or may not be distorting. A cloak may well be associated with the same type of economic activity as the principal who put up the money.

in 1952 the party orientation of these contributors was similar as reflected in their gifts, not only to the regular national committees, but to others at the national and lower political levels. Other spot checks revealed the same tendencies,[60] suggesting that in areas of party competition a consistency in alignment between the parties and certain types of interests is to be found. Campaign donors, at least, seem to think the parties stand for something.

Table 14

GIFTS OF $1,000 AND OVER TO THE TWO NATIONAL PARTY COMMITTEES: PERCENTAGE OF TOTAL COMING FROM INDIVIDUALS IDENTIFIED WITH CERTAIN ECONOMIC INTERESTS, SELECTED PRESIDENTIAL ELECTION YEARS[a]

Groups	1932		1936		1940		1944[b]		1952	
	Rep.	Dem.	Rep.	Dem.	Rep.	Dem.	Rep.	Dem.	Rep.	Dem.
Bankers, brokers, manufacturers, oil, mining, utilities, transportation, real estate, insurance....	61	45	55	28	57	21	59	24	40	21
Brewers, distillers, merchants, soft drinks, contractors, builders, building materials, publishers, radio, advertising, amusements, professions, officeholders..................	11	22	11	50	9	47	16	46	12	30
Others and unidentifiable...	28	33	34	22	34	32	25	30	48	49
Total[c].............	100	100	100	100	100	100	100	100	100	100

[a] The group categories and percentages for 1932, 1940, and 1944 are taken from V. O. Key, Jr., *Politics, Parties and Pressure Groups* (4th ed.; New York: Thomas Y. Crowell Company, 1958) p. 544. The percentages for all years except 1952 were derived from Louise Overacker's articles in the *American Political Science Review:* "Campaign Funds in a Depression Year," 27 (1933), 776; "Campaign Funds in the Presidential Election of 1936," 31 (1937), 485; "Campaign Finance in the Presidential Election of 1940," 35 (1941), 723; "Presidential Campaign Funds, 1944," 39 (1945), 916. The details of the 1952 data may be found in Margaret A. Hunt, "Certain Social and Economic Characteristics of Campaign Contributors in a National Election Year," (Master's thesis, University of North Carolina, 1958), pp. 81-82.

[b] Percentages are based on contributions to the two national committees in all years except 1944, when a few allied organizations were also included in the analysis.

[c] The total value of $1,000-and-over gifts in each case was: *1932*: R, $1,638,942; D, $1,242,996; *1936*: R, $3, 923,958; D, $1, 275,033; *1940*: R, $1,234,127; D, $520,377; *1944*: R, $1,648,622; D, $1,224,283; *1952*: R, $757,636; D, $974,785.

The occupational categories in Table 15 are broad and suggest only general tendencies. Specialized interests within the broad groups doubtless produce political differences, and officials of competing firms jockey

60. For the Pennsylvania Republican finance committee, the percentages were: for the bankers-brokers, 7.9; manufacturers, 23.8; professions, 4.8; officeholders, 0.6. For the Democratic city committee of Philadelphia, the percentages were: bankers-brokers, 7.4; manufacturers, 1.6 (contracting and building materials were 9.2); professions, 6.4; officeholders, 1.0. John Robert Owens found in Connecticut that Democrats depended much more heavily than Republicans on "internal sources" for contributions of $500 and over, e.g., officeholders, civil servants, candidates, contractors. As in other areas, bankers, brokers, and manufacturers were more significant among Republican supporters, persons in the professions more so among Democrats.—"Party Campaign Funds in Connecticut, 1950-1954" (Ph.D. dissertation, Syracuse University, 1956), pp. 186-87, 305-6.

for favor with whatever party is in power, whether it is their party or not, especially if the party is in power twenty years. Even among bankers and brokers, whose common political bonds would seem considerable, supporters of both parties are found. Table 16 shows which party benefited from the gifts of bank officials in six eastern cities (as indicated by known campaign contributions of $500 or more in 1952).

Table 15

GIFTS OF $500 AND OVER TO SELECTED POLITICAL COMMITTEES: AMOUNT, AND PERCENTAGE OF TOTAL, COMING FROM INDIVIDUALS IDENTIFIED WITH CERTAIN ECONOMIC INTERESTS, 1952[a]

Committee	Bankers and Brokers		Manufacturers		Professions		Officeholders	
	$	%	$	%	$	%	$	%
Republican National Committee	113,230	11.7	162,603	16.8	42,600	4.4	14,500	1.4
Democratic National Committee	42,800	3.7	96,500	8.4	114,000	9.9	74,200	6.5
1952 Campaign Headquarters and Travel Committee	7,000	5.3	2,500	1.9	17,650	13.4	8,500	6.5
National Citizens for Eisenhower-Nixon	118,975	11.9	192,705	19.3	53,500	5.4	7,500	0.8
National Volunteers for Stevenson	17,500	4.2	43,000	10.2	51,550	12.3	7,000	1.7
United Republican Finance Committee of New York	218,587	25.0	122,075	14.0	107,100	12.2	2,000	0.2
New York State Democratic Committee	17,400	8.7	22,100	11.1	21,900	11.0	16,750	8.4

[a] It was not possible to learn the primary economic identification of all contributors. The percentages are based on total value of gifts in this amount to each committee.

There were many Democratic beneficiaries, though most who gave to Democratic recipients—and the recipients may have been at state or local levels as well as at the national level—were associated with banks that also had Republican contributors among their officials. When manufacturers are divided into specialized types, the Republican preference runs through most of the sub-categories, but Democrats are represented in many of them.[61]

The faithful and the opportunists.—Similar features characterize the large contributors who faithfully support the national committees of their parties over a period of years. Table 17 indicates the financial

61. Occasionally clean distinctions appear. Persons identified with iron and steel failed to show up among givers in sums of $500 and over to several important Democratic committees in 1952: the Democratic national committee, 1952 Campaign Headquarters and Travel Committee, National Volunteers for Stevenson, New York Democratic state committee, Pennsylvania Democratic state committee, Democratic Campaign Committee of Philadelphia. They had been present in previous years, however, and may well have given to committees not included in the 1952 analysis. See Louise Overacker, "Presidential Campaign Funds, 1944," *American Political Science Review,* 39 (1945), 916.

Table 16

KNOWN CAMPAIGN GIVING IN SUMS OF $500 AND OVER BY BANK OFFICIALS IN SELECTED CITIES, 1952[a]

City	No. of banks checked[b]	No. of banks with officials who contributed: Total	Banks with officers and directors who gave to: Rep. only	Dem. only	Both parties	Banks with directors (only) who gave to: Rep. only	Dem. only	Both parties
Boston..........	8	4	3	0	1	0	0	0
Philadelphia.....	12	6	1	0	0	5	0	0
Pittsburgh.......	7	5	3	0	2	0	0	0
Baltimore.......	7	4	2	0	1	1	0	0
Washington......	7	2	1	0	1	0	0	0
New York.......	35	27	9	3	10	4	0	1
Total.....	76	48	19	3	15	10	0	1

[a] This table appears in the Gore Committee *Hearings*, part 2, p. 529.
[b] Every bank located in the listed cities that appeared among the largest 400 banks in the nation was included in the analysis.

Table 17

THE IMPORTANCE OF REPEAT CONTRIBUTORS: THE PERCENTAGE OF TOTAL RECEIPTS OF THE TWO NATIONAL COMMITTEES GIVEN BY SPECIFIED REPEAT CONTRIBUTORS, SELECTED YEARS, 1936-1952[a]

Year	Percentage of Total Receipts Coming from the Persons who Gave $500 or over in *at least* five different years during 1933-45: Rep.	Dem.	Percentage of Total Receipts Coming from the Persons who Gave $500 or over in *four* different years during 1933-45: Rep.	Dem.	Total of Percentages for both Categories[b]: Rep.	Dem.
1936.............	6.0	2.2	3.0	1.6	9.0	3.8
1937.............	16.3	2.7	3.9	1.4	20.2	4.1
1938.............	9.3	2.1	3.3	1.6	12.6	3.7
1939.............	13.1	0.0	5.9	0.0	19.0	0.0
1940.............	6.3	2.9	3.8	1.9	10.1	4.8
1941.............	6.8	1.2	1.6	1.9	8.4	3.1
1942.............	13.3	2.9	.6	4.0	13.9	6.9
1943.............	11.1	0.0	2.7	1.6	13.8	1.6
1944.............	4.1	2.2	2.3	1.5	6.4	3.7
1948.............	3.4	1.8	.9	1.2	4.3	3.0
1952.............	2.1	.7	.7	.5	2.8	1.2
No. of Persons....	72	17	63	23	135	40

[a] Computed from data provided by Louise Overacker, and from data presented in her quadrennial articles in the *American Political Science Review*, *loc. cit.* See Hunt, *op. cit.* pp. 88, 91.
[b] The percentages of receipts from *individual contributions* (excluding transfers from other committees) usually run higher. For example, *1940*: R, 10.9; D 8.8; *1944*: R, 11.3; D, 4.9.

importance to each committee of persons who gave to it in four or more different years during the period 1933-1945.[62] Table 18 shows that these supporters in both parties were distributed among the economic and occupational categories in much the same manner as contributors in a single year. A corresponding analysis of persons who gave successively in 1944, 1948, and 1952 yielded the same general results.[63]

A different group altogether from the party faithful are those political opportunists who appear to give to the victorious party only after the election. Among those who gave to the national-level, regular committees in 1948 and 1952 and could be identified, the usual range of activities was represented. See Table 19. Manufacturers comprised a somewhat higher percentage in both parties than customary in analyses of full-year donations, officeholders and members of professions somewhat less. A

Table 18

THE PRIMARY ECONOMIC INTERESTS OF REPEAT CONTRIBUTORS: PERSONS WHO GAVE $500 AND OVER IN AT LEAST FOUR DIFFERENT YEARS DURING 1933-1945 TO THE TWO NATIONAL PARTY COMMITTEES[a]

Classification	No. of Persons		Total Value of Gifts by Such Persons During 1933-1945			
			Rep.		Dem.	
	Rep.	Dem.	$	%	$	%
Manufacturers						
Basic industries[b]	35	5	576,281	26.8	44,500	6.5
Consumer industries[c]	22	8	337,849	15.7	89,849	13.1
Oil, Mining	18	3	251,100	11.7	41,000	6.0
Bankers, Brokers	22	4	314,200	14.6	53,500	7.8
Mass communications, Entertainment	3	2	42,000	2.0	38,500	5.6
Merchants	7	0	106,350	4.9	0	.0
Professions	10	10	127,600	5.9	200,337	29.3
Officeholders	6	7	98,377	4.6	206,717	30.3
Other classificantions	8	0	269,000	12.4	0	.0
Unidentified	4	1	30,100	1.4	9,250	1.4
Total	135	40	2,152,857	100.0	683,653	100.0
Average			$15,947		$17,091	

[a] Computed from published and unpublished data provided by Louise Overacker.
[b] Iron and steel, machine tools, chemicals, etc.
[c] Food and drink processing, automobiles, textiles and clothing, etc.

62. The differences between the parties in the number of repeat contributors, and in the volume of their gifts, as revealed by this and succeeding tables, point to differences in their fund-raising problems and practices. See pages 212-32, below.

63. The detailed data appear in Margaret A. Hunt, "Certain Social and Economic Characteristics of Campaign Contributors in a National Election Year" (Master's thesis, University of North Carolina, 1958), pp. 163, 166.

party's post-election givers tended strongly to be associated with the same types of economic enterprise as its large givers at other times over the years.[64]

Table 19

POST-ELECTION GIFTS OF $500 AND OVER CLASSIFIED BY PRIMARY ECONOMIC INTEREST OF CONTRIBUTOR, 1948 AND 1952[a]

Classification	Per Cent of Total Value of $500-and-over Contributions That Were Made after the Election to the National-Level Regular Committees of Each Party			
	Dem. 1948[b]		Rep. 1952[c]	
Bankers and brokers		4.3		8.3
Manufacturers		16.4		32.9
Iron and Steel	.8		4.6	
Food and Beverage	8.0		3.4	
Paper, Printing	.7		2.4	
Equipment, Machine tools	.0		7.3	
Rubber	.0		3.0	
Electric products	.0		2.2	
Aviation	4.3		.0	
Textile, Clothing	.0		3.2	
Miscellaneous	2.6		6.8	
Merchants		7.0		.4
Oil, Mining		1.0		10.9
Mass communications		3.6		3.4
Politics, Officeholder		2.6		3.0
Professional		4.3		4.3
Other		5.6		3.9
Unidentified		55.2		32.9
Percentage Total		100.0		100.0
Dollar Total		$291,380		$247,663
Average Contribution		$ 1,318		$ 1,016

[a] Derived from Hunt, *op. cit.*, pp. 168-69. Financial summaries of pre- and post-election contributions (in amounts of $500 and over) for both parties in both years, by committee, appear in Gore Committee *Hearings*, part 2, p. 532. The data in this table pertain to individuals who were reported as giving only after the election, excluding those who gave both before and after. Receipts dated through election week were deemed as having been made before the election. Only slight post-election contributions were received by these Republican committees in 1948 and by the Democratic ones in 1952.

[b] The Democratic national committee, senatorial campaign committee, and two Congressional campaign committees.

[c] The Republican national committee, Senatorial campaign committee, and Congressional campaign committee.

64. Some corporations were more strongly represented than others by officials who were post-election contributors. Among the identified Democrats in 1948 were three officials of the Sperry Corporation ($12,000), three of the United Fruit Company ($15,000), and five of Universal Pictures ($5,500). Among Republicans in 1952 were three officials of Timken Roller Bearing ($3,000), three of Sylvania Electric ($3,000), four of Olin Industries ($9,000), and five each of Bridgeport Brass ($5,000) and Firestone Tire and Rubber ($5,000). Other persons in these companies may have made earlier or other political gifts in the years in question, and the post-election contributors themselves, it must be noted, may have given to other committees before the election.

The analysis of large campaign contributors demonstrates the political segmentation of the American business community. Economic diversities and the differential impact of government policies and activities on different units of the economy insure variety in the political loyalties of businessmen. Within this general context, nevertheless, a net preference for Republican candidates and policies is manifest, especially pronounced among persons associated with the nation's largest business interests. Herein, incidentally, should lie a reservoir of political energy and leadership for a party that in many parts of the United States sorely needs both.

4. COMPANY MONEY IN POLITICS

The political activities of corporation officials inevitably produce suspicion that company money is used for partisan purposes. As is true with labor unions, noted later, many legal ambiguities characterize the prohibitions that exist against corporate political giving. The practices followed constitute a type of corporate political involvement requiring special mention.

The law.—The ban against corporate contributions is a peculiarly American effort.[65] It resulted from a reaction to the political activities of banks and businesses during the nineteenth century, much as the restrictions on labor were enacted in response to union political action in the 1930's. The New York insurance investigation, reporting in 1906, provided concrete details and a compact statement from one executive of the spirit in which the gifts were made: "I don't justify the use of money for campaign purposes. I justify the use of these funds in the protection of the policyholder's interests. I don't care about the Republican side of it, or the Democratic side of it. . . . What is best for the New York Life is what moves and actuates me."[66] Spurred by the reformist spirit of the times, the Congress in 1907 adopted a measure, and several states acted both before and after this date.

In 1959, federal legislation, embodied in section 610 of Title 18 of the *U.S. Code,* stood as follows:

(1) It was unlawful for any national bank or any corporation organized by authority of any law of Congress to make a contribution or expenditure in connection with any election to any political office.

65. As a matter of policy, some political parties abroad seek to do without corporate gifts. Canada had a provision before 1930 that made it illegal for business corporations and trade unions to contribute to the support of a candidate or party. The secrecy of corporate accounts made it difficult to enforce the law against business corporations; the semi-public character of trade-union accounts made inspection and enforcement easier. The statute was repealed on the initiative of labor groups on the grounds it was unfair to the unions.—Robert M. Dawson, *The Government of Canada* (Toronto: University of Toronto Press, 1952), pp. 574-75.

66. Earl R. Sikes, *State and Federal Corrupt-Practices Legislation* (Durham: Duke University Press, 1928), p. 109.

(2) This prohibition applied to general elections and also to any primary election or political convention or caucus held to select candidates for any political office.

(3) It was also illegal for any corporation whatever to make a contribution or expenditure in connection with any election at which presidential or vice presidential electors or a Senator or Representative (or Delegate or Resident Commissioner) in Congress were to be voted for.

(4) This applied likewise to any primary election or political convention or caucus held to select candidates for any of these offices.

(5) Candidates, political committees, and other persons were forbidden to receive any of the proscribed gifts.

(6) Penalties for violation were: upon a corporation, a fine of not more than $5,000; upon an officer or director of a corporation who consents to an illegal contribution or expenditure by the corporation, a fine of not more than $1,000 and imprisonment for not more than one year, or both; upon such an officer or director where the violation was willful, a fine of not more than $10,000 and imprisonment for not more than two years, or both; upon any person who accepts a prohibited corporate contribution, the same penalties as upon an officer or director of the corporation.[67]

About thirty states by 1959 also limited the right of corporations to give money to candidates or their supporters. The provisions varied, some extending only to certain classes of corporations, such as insurance companies and public utilities.

Charges are made repeatedly in partisan debate that corporate funds flood into election campaigns. There is no doubt that corporations and their officials take active part in politics when their interests are at stake. In the nature of the case, however, activities that might be construed as illegal are discussed only with reticence by corporate officials and politicians. Several things are clear, nevertheless, about the extent of these activities as learned from people who have engaged in them. Practices vary greatly from firm to firm. Democrats as well as Republicans receive corporate favor. It is not unusual for corporate funds to make up 10 per cent of the campaign fund of a candidate for state or local office, and the percentage has gone higher. In all, in a presidential election year, several million dollars of corporate money finds its way by one process or another into political campaigning.

67. See *U.S. Code,* Title 18, sec. 610. Items (1) and (3) applying to money contributions were adopted in 1907. An amendment of 1911 extended the coverage to primaries and conventions for nomination. The decision of the Supreme Court in 1921 in Newberry *v.* United States, 256 U.S. 232, cast doubt on the right of Congress to regulate nominations. The Corrupt Practices Act of 1925 therefore specifically excluded nominations from the coverage of the federal law. By 1947, however, the trend of Supreme Court decisions led to extension of the law, in the Labor-Management Relations Act, to cover primaries, conventions, and caucuses. This act also extended the prohibition to include expenditures as well as contributions.

The Public Utility Holding Company Act of 1935 forbids utility holding companies and their subsidiaries to contribute to political campaigns.

What is legal or illegal under section 610 is badly muddled by problems of interpretation. The Gore Committee observed in 1957 that: ". . . there appears to be a wide area of permissible activity in light of judicial interpretations of the term 'expenditure' contained in that section and the constitutional questions that would arise under a statute that would prohibit all forms of participation by such organizations in the elective process."[68] The Justice Department received 54 complaints during the years 1950-56 alleging that section 610 had been violated. Of these, 39 involved labor organizations, 11 involved national banks and corporations organized under federal law, and 4 involved private corporations. The complaints were such that in 49 instances investigations were made, and of these 14 were presented to grand juries. Two indictments were obtained, both against labor organizations, and both resulted in acquittals.[69] There has never been an indictment of a corporation under section 610.[70] The Supreme Court has refrained from passing on constitutional questions when raised before it,[71] so that doubts about the constitutionality of restrictions in section 610 have not been laid.[72]

The definition of "expenditure," mentioned by the Gore Committee, has not been clarified either, although working rules are advocated by both business and labor groups. The Ohio Chamber of Commerce obtained legal advice, later widely circulated by the United States Chamber of Commerce, about what a corporation could safely spend its funds for.[73] Counsel concluded, after reviewing decisions involving expenditures

68. *Report,* p. 4.

69. Memorandum of Warren Olney, III, Assistant Attorney General, Gore Committee *Hearings,* pp. 562-65. The second acquittal, of a case against the United Automobile Workers, was by a federal court jury in November 1957.—*Washington Star,* November 14, 1957.

70. Gore Committee *Report,* p. 24. The Union Electric Company was prosecuted under the Public Utility Holding Company Act and found guilty in 1942 of contributing to candidates and party committees in three states.—Egan *v.* United States, 137 F. (2d) 369 (1943).

71. See the opinion of Mr. Justice Frankfurter, rendered for the Court, March 11, 1957, reversing an appeal from the U.S. District Court for the Eastern District of Michigan, in United States of America, Appellant, *v.* International Union United Automobile, Aircraft and Agricultural Implement Workers of America (UAW-CIO): "Matter now buried under abstract constitutional issues may, by elucidation of a trial, be brought to the surface, and in the outcome constitutional questions may disappear. Allegations of the indictment hypothetically framed to elicit a ruling from this Court . . . may not survive the test of proof . . . Because the District Court's erroneous interpretation of the statute led it to stop the prosecution prematurely, its judgment must be reversed and the case must be remanded to it for further proceedings not inconsistent with this opinion." Subsequently, the defendant was acquitted.

72. See the discussion in Robert A. Bicks and Howard I. Friedman, "Regulation of Federal Election Finance: A Case of Misguided Morality," *New York University Law Review,* 28 (1953), 975-1000.

73. Gore Committee *Report,* p. 24, and *Hearings,* pp. 556-58; "Business in politics: how far you can go," *Nation's Business,* July, 1956, pp. 25ff.

from union funds, that probably, in so far as section 610 was concerned, a corporation could make expenditures for:

1. Salaries and wages of its officers and regular employees while engaged in political activities, in the interest of the corporation, including support of a candidate for nomination or election to a Federal office.

2. Publication in any house organ or other printed document circulated at the expense of the corporation of opinion and arguments of a political nature, expressed as those of the corporation.

3. Purchase of radio or television time or newspaper space for the presentation of political views, as those of the corporation.

4. In short, any means of publicly or privately expressing the political views of the corporate management.

5. In furtherance of any nonpartisan effort to persuade voters to register and vote, or to disseminate information and opinions concerning public issues, without regard to political parties or candidates.

The practice.—Two broad types of corporate expenditures can be distinguished: money spent openly by corporations for purposes they usually claim are not or cannot constitutionally be prohibited by statute; and political costs borne indirectly by corporate funds, more likely to be thought contrary to the plain language of section 610.

In the first category, institutional advertising looms large. The McGraw-Hill Publishing Company, Inc., provided a neat illustration by publishing in the *New York Times* on October 31, 1956 (and in 15 other principal newspapers at a cost of $36,934),[74] a full-page advertisement under the heading: "How Prosperous is the U.S.A.?—An Election Year Appraisal." A summary of the information in the advertisement appeared in a box that began: "This report presents a comparison of the economic development of the U.S.A. during the four years of the current Republican Administration (1953-1956) and the four years of the Democratic Administration (1949-52)." The advertisement seemed undeniably directed at the election to take place within a few days and intended to attract support to Republican candidates. But McGraw-Hill had been advised by counsel that the advertisement was not an expenditure in connection with an election, but part of a continuing educational advertising program.[75] Closely allied are the publication and dissemination of political views in corporate publications or by other means paid for by corporate funds. In the climate of uncertainty that

74. Gore Committee *Report,* p. 17.

75. *Ibid.,* p. 17. On the vigorous political advertising of the Timken Roller Bearing Company in Ohio, see the testimony of its advertising manager.—U.S. Senate Subcommittee on Privileges and Elections, *Hearings* (Washington: Government Printing Office, 1952), pp. 435-40. One advertisement, appearing immediately after the 1950 election, read: "As the results of Tuesday's election show people cannot be coerced by CIO-PAC carpetbaggers in Ohio, Communist international organizations, or any other organization that makes great claims of controlling votes."—*Ibid.,* p. 437.

has prevailed, expenditures for these purposes are also thought to possess good prospects for constitutional protection should they be challenged.

In all campaigns, and between them, corporate personnel spend time during business hours on politics. No clean line separates political activities as a citizen from those as a corporate employee, and efforts to define one might prove futile, if not undesirable on other grounds. Some corporate personnel, however, devote full time to the nomination and election of candidates, and this aid can only be interpreted as direct financial participation in politics by their employers.

Indirect types of corporate campaign activity are numerous—and practices vary widely. Incorporated organizations may be nationwide in their operations or confined to a single town, and their political activities fluctuate with issues and candidates. The techniques of indirect corporate political participation here listed do not characterize all business enterprise in the United States but illustrate the kinds of activities that take place under present statutes.

1. *Expense accounts* permit reimbursement for outlays that individuals normally make from personal funds. Used by many officials to meet the costs of private entertainment and community giving, expense accounts also can be used to cover travel expenses, tickets to fund-raising dinners, and many miscellaneous costs connected with political action. The whole spirit of the expense-account economy in which American business found itself after World War II encouraged this.[76]

2. *Contributions in kind* are made. Bill boards, furniture, office equipment, mailing lists, and other facilities[77] can be lent for the period of a campaign. Often stamps are contributed, or a firm permits campaign mailings to be run through its stampmeter machine. In 1955 there were 12,000 company airplanes in the country, owned by 7,000 businesses. It is not surprising that some of them carry candidates and their friends.

76. One vice president was given a sum of $20,000 per year for entertainment, his contract providing that he need not account for the money. A survey of 164 corporations in 1952 showed that only 8 per cent of them paid their executives by salaries alone.—Mills, *op. cit.*, pp. 160, 390, citing Richard A. Girard, "They Escape Income Taxes—But *You* Can't!" *American Magazine,* December, 1952, pp. 16, 89. A federal Internal Revenue agent, who spent much time checking candidate tax returns, concluded that they conceal many political expenditures under claims of legitimate business expenses.

77. In 1956 a number of business firms in Portland, Oregon, including several corporations, mailed envelopes at their own expense to lists of registered Democratic voters. They were asked to do this by the Republican county committee which desired to check on the proper registration of Democrats. The envelopes (those sent in one case were empty, but they usually contained routine advertising material) bore the return address of the sender, and those returned were usually turned over to the Republican committee for use by poll watchers on election day. Some firms participating in the plan said they had not realized at the outset that only Democratic registrations were being checked.—Gore Committee *Report,* pp. 17-18.

Many companies maintain hotel suites on a year-around basis. These and other facilities can conveniently be put to political use.[78]

3. *Advertisements in political journals* paid for from corporate funds constitute indirect contributing. In New York, especially, it is the custom of parties to publish yearbooks, dinner programs, etc., made up mostly of advertisements.[79] One public relations counsel told of placing such advertising on behalf of his client. It was a public service ad, having to do with the problem of crowded school rooms, and bore the name of the public relations firm. Many of the ads appear anonymously.

4. *Payments to persons in public relations* easily find their way into electoral channels. Counsel on retainer often gives to politics on behalf of his principal. Moreover, he may lump the costs of political advertising with the costs of company advertising in billing his client.

5. *Fees to lawyers* and others whose services are retained by a corporation are said to be passed on as campaign contributions. Generally an inefficient way to contribute, because of the tax burden on the middleman, the practice is frequently mentioned, seldom illustrated.

6. *Salaries and bonuses* to corporate personnel may carry the expectation that the recipients will do their political share. Executives are expected to maintain a style of living, to give to approved charities, and to do other things appropriate to their and their company's station. Their high incomes help them meet the off-job requirements of the job. Bonuses explicitly to reimburse corporate personnel for political gifts appear to be rarer.

7. *Payments to other organizations,* such as trade associations, may wind up in political channels. One association of brewers purchased tickets to party fund-raising dinners, distributed them to its member corporations, and collected the cost in assessments on the members, which assessments, incidentally, could be charged as a business expense for tax purposes.

8. *Funds straight from the corporate treasury* are spent under some circumstances, not always in small enough amounts to be called petty cash, but presumably with some means of cover up.[80]

None of this means that limitations on corporate political gifts and expenditures have been without effect. The statutes have made corpo-

78. A group of North Carolina politicos was ferried to a meeting in 1956 with Adlai Stevenson in two "private planes which have been loaned for the occasion," one by Burlington Industries and the other by Piedmont Aviation.—*The News and Observer* (Raleigh, N.C.), August 28, 1956.

79. See pages 239, 248-49, below.

80. See footnote 24, page 109, above. A Utah corporation tax lawyer volunteered a hypothetical illustration: Corporation A normally buys ball bearings at the rate of $500 per month from corporation B. The heads of the two organizations would like to support their party with corporate funds. A then pays $1,000 a month for the same quantity of ball bearings, B using $250 of the surplus to pay increased taxes and secretly donating $250 to the party. A charges the full $1,000 as a business cost.

rate financial activity in politics considerably more awkward and inefficient than it would otherwise have been. The amount of corporate money that shows up in nomination and election campaigns is without doubt greatly reduced because of them.[81] Respect for law is not enhanced by the evasions that occur, but, given the ambition of the effort, the results are probably no worse than could reasonably be expected. By the standards of other nations, an attempt to prevent corporate contributing is incredibly bold.

5. SOCIAL POWER AND POLITICAL MONEY

Even in absolute monarchies people ask who are the powers behind the throne. Priests, jesters, royal ministers, and royal mistresses have turned the fate of nations, acting through their sovereign. Beyond types like these, the power of monarchies, even absolute ones, has always rested on supports additional to the moral authority of divine right. Groups vested with economic, occupational, or honorific privileges in the status quo characteristically undergird and stabilize regimes, thereby becoming components in the prevailing system of power.

All political systems rest on some organization of social power. It is classic in the study of government to ask what this social power is and how it is related to the form and substance of government. To answer such questions for most democratic systems is extraordinarily difficult. Legal authority is split among many governmental agents, and those who exercise it generally possess only temporary right to do so. Modern industrial societies are minutely diversified and intricately interdependent. The dominant elements of social organization are difficult to identify with certainty. The relationships between social power and political power involve networks of influence and communications that are not only complex but also changing. They evolve with the growth and decay of elements in the society; they change with personalities who emerge and recede as surrogates; and they fluctuate with the problems to be solved and the issues to be settled.

Most political observers hypothesize that the requirements of money in politics provide opportunities for those who wield social power to translate this power into political control. The testing of the hypothesis in the United States is obstructed by lack of agreement on the nature

81. Not a view universally shared. The Republican finance chairman of an important Ohio county argued that the statutes are so easy to avoid that he could see no need for having any prohibition on corporate contributions. There are so many ways corporate funds can get into politics, he continued, that there is not much incentive even to make contributions in goods and services. A Democratic manager in a nearby state reported a different experience. He had finished a campaign in which he said a fourth of the costs ($75,000 worth) had been met by contributed services: secretaries, cars, stamps, gasoline credit cards, some advertising costs including professional personnel. He would never do it again: "too damn dangerous."

of the "power structure" of the nation. American elite groups bear no titles and wear no uniforms for easy identification.[82]

The wealthy.—Economic power is one kind of social power, often the most important.[83] Even so, the manifestations of economic power can be so varied and its organization so complex that few agree fully on its character and extent. Persons of great personal wealth, nevertheless, always must be reckoned with by students of elites. The social controls and status accompanying wealth automatically give them consequence. As a result, the political behavior of the wealthy always attracts attention. Their contributing practices especially merit notice. They are more likely to be asked and are more able to give than other citizens.

Fortune magazine interviewed 50 of America's 250 or so persons who possess a capital accumulation of at least $50,000,000. Of the people in this sample, thought to be representative, it appeared from their own testimony that about two-thirds were campaign givers.[84] *Fortune* also listed 76 persons with an estimated wealth of $75,000,000 and over. Two-thirds of them gave a known gift of at least $500 in 1956 (averaging about $10,000 each, virtually all of it to Republicans). At least half of those not listed as giving in 1956 were known, however, through other sources, to have given in that or recent years, some of them in enormous sums. Well over 80 per cent of the seventy-five-millionaires were contributors to recent political campaigns, and perhaps all were. Clearly, as a class, America's very rich are regular campaign donors.

82. Willie Moretti, the late New Jersey mobster, gave his concept of an elite group while being questioned before the Kefauver Crime Committee. When asked who introduced him to Al Capone, he blurted: "Listen, well-charactered people, you don't need introductions; you just meet automatically."—*Hearings,* part 7, p. 341. For a discussion of "The Concept of Social Elites," see S. F. Nadel in the *International Social Science Bulletin,* 8 (1956), 413-24. See also Harold D. Lasswell, Daniel Lerner, and C. Easton Rothwell, *The Comparative Study of Elites* (Palo Alto: Stanford University Press, 1952), Hoover Institute Studies, Series B: Elites, #1.

83. R. M. MacIver discusses the nature of social power in terms that to this observer accurately describe the United States. He notes that social power inheres in all social relations and in all social organizations, and that the power of government is one aspect of power among many. "In this melee economic power is always prominent. But we cannot simplify the issue and claim with the Marxists that economic power is both its offspring and its servant. For in the first place economic power is multi-centered and is the scene of internecine warfare. . . . The second reason . . . is that economic power cannot be segregated from other forms of social power as though it operated by itself and sought objectives inherent in its own nature."—*The Web of Government* (New York: The Macmillan Company, 1951), pp. 90-92.

84. Less than one-third said they take a personal part in local, state, or federal politics. (This proportion is higher than for many other types in the population.) Of the remainder, they were split between those who were satisfied to make contributions and those who did no more than vote. It was assumed that those who were "active" also gave money.—Richard Austin Smith, "The Fifty-Million-Dollar Man," *Fortune,* 56 (November, 1957), esp. 176-77, 236.

More than half of *Fortune's* fortunes in this category were founded on inherited wealth. The corollary follows that many of the rich are kinsmen and share family interests of great economic importance. This circumstance has led some observers to conclude that the nation's basic power structure is in fact a network of plutocratic families.[85]

Families.—What is known about the political donations of wealthy families casts doubt on the significance of campaign gifts as tools of oligarchic, family control. The Gore Committee offered information on campaign gifts made in 1956 by persons in 12 family groups.[86] All of the families were prominent, and each was chosen for analysis because of the large aggregate volume of its members' donations.[87] The totals for some of the families, however, fell below the amounts reported for several individual contributors. The totals for the Fields, Fords, Harrimans, Lehmans, Olins, Reynolds, and Vanderbilts were all lower, for example, than the $70,000-odd given the Democrats by L. K. Christie and the $60,000-odd given mostly to Republican causes by E. L. Cord.

Members of the five other families listed by the Gore Committee gave in each instance an aggregate of $100,000 or more, which included the Du Ponts, Mellons, Pews, Rockefellers, and Whitneys. As was true in previous years, the Du Ponts led the list. Their reported gifts aggregated around $250,000; the Pews followed with slightly over $200,000, the Rockefellers around $150,000, the Whitneys around $120,000, and the Mellons just over $100,000.

85. In a book completed in 1937, Ferdinand Lundberg argued on the opening page: "The United States is owned and dominated today by a hierarchy of its sixty richest families, buttressed by no more than ninety families of lesser wealth. . . . These families are the living center of the modern oligarchy which dominates the United States, functioning discreetly under a *de jure* democratic form of government behind which a *de facto* government, absolutist and plutocratic in its lineaments, has gradually taken form since the Civil War. . . . It is the government of money in a dollar democracy." Campaign gifts are later cited as one link between the *de jure* and *de facto* governments.—*America's 60 Families* (New York: The Citadel Press, 1946), pp. 128-33.

86. *Report,* pp. 65-67. 1952 data on 11 family groups, submitted at the request of the Gore Committee, appear in the *Hearings,* part 2, pp. 525-26. Similar information on persons in 64 family groups was compiled for 1944.—U.S. Senate Special Committee to Investigate Presidential, Vice Presidential, and Senatorial Campaign Expenditures in 1944 (cited hereafter as the Green Committee), *Report* (Washington: Government Printing Office, 1945) (Senate Report No. 101, 79th Congress, 1st Session), pp. 140-51. The tabulation was made on the same basis as one for 1940.—U.S. Senate Special Committee to Investigate Presidential, Vice Presidential, and Senatorial Campaign Expenditures, 1940 (cited hereafter as the Gillette Committee), *Report* (Washington: Government Printing Office, 1941) (Senate Report No. 47, 77th Congress, 1st Session), pp. 143-47.

87. The individuals treated as members of a family were usually only those bearing the surname. In many such analyses persons have been included who were only remotely related to each other, if at all, and close relatives have been excluded because their surnames were different. A group of married sisters is less likely to attract attention than a less active combination of brothers bearing a common name.

The full meaning of these combinations of gifts is not easily apparent. The public play given family contributing results from the newsworthiness of the rich and, on occasion, from the desire of those who did not get their money to embarrass those who did. The data often seem intended to suggest that members of a selected family acted in concert or shared common political interests. The implication appears undeniable for four members of Pennsylvania's Pew family who repeatedly over the years have shown up giving identical sums to a large number of widely dispersed committees and candidates. In other cases, the evidence is not so persuasive. The dates, amounts, and destinations of political gifts by members of the same family often suggest lack of family cohesion. For example, six Vanderbilts were listed by the Gore Committee as making up one group. Three gave to Republicans, three to Democrats. Among seven Lehmans, four favored Democrats, three favored Republicans. Among five members of the Field Family, two gave to each party and one to both. Even the Rockefeller brothers, who take common counsel on matters affecting the family's public relations, including gifts to political and other causes, showed varied political preferences—a variety that is ascribed to their personal interests and judgments.[88]

The Du Pont "family" always stands out in discussions of political giving.[89] It does so not solely because of its wealth, nor because its members are especially active in politics, but because of its size. The descendants of Du Pont founder Irénée and his brother Victor numbered 1200 in 1957 and were increasing at the rate of about 30 each year. Only about 300 of these lived in or near Wilmington, Delaware, albeit they included most of the key members of the family.[90] A list of approximately 1,000 members of the family, compiled in 1951 by the family itself, was checked against the contributors of $500 or more known to the Gore Committee in 1956. The list included slightly over 600 adults (born before 1935) and slightly under 400 minors (born in 1935

88. The Rockefellers have set up ground rules for themselves, generally limiting their political contributions to party committees in localities where the propriety of the gift will be difficult to question. They are concerned, too, to hold their political donations to a small percentage of their charitable giving. Their names, at least in recent years, have always shown up on Republican finance statements. It appears, however, that occasionally some of their money has found its way indirectly to the other side. Their public relations man, Frank Jamieson, has advised on political contributions as well as other gifts. Many articles have appeared, among them one describing the interests, activities, and personalities of each brother, by Richard Austin Smith, "The Rockefeller Brothers," *Fortune,* 51 (February and March), 1955.

89. Apparently it always has. Writing in 1851, a United States senator from Delaware recorded that "these Duponts have spent a fortune for the Whig party, . . . they have been the chief prop and support of our party since its origin. . . ." Quoted in Jasper B. Shannon, *Money and Politics* (New York: Random House, 1959), pp. 20-21.

90. *Life,* August 19, 1957, p. 107.

or later). None of the latter was listed as a contributor. Eighty adults were reported as giving $255,395, of which $239,395 went to Republican recipients, $12,500 to Democrats, and $3,500 to other political causes. While these sums do not reflect all contributions and expenditures by the Du Ponts, it is significant that only 13 per cent of the adults were listed as giving in sums of $500 or more, and they for only around $3,200 each. The average for all the adults was $420 and for the whole family was $255.[91]

Compared with the apparent potential, even twice this yield would have been meager. It remains to be shown that the financial participation in politics of the Du Ponts as a family is greater than that of other collections of people of comparable wealth and station. Most families, in truth, appear to constitute less significant categories for political analysis than members of groups whose adherents share manifest, direct stakes in politics, like officials of the largest corporations.

Ruling classes.—Most contemporary students of social power do not use such simple explanatory concepts as the wealthy and their families. They correctly perceive a more intricate organization of social power, one resting on the occupancy of crucial decision points and influence roles as well as on control over the raw materials of economic power. Some of these students view political activity, especially electoral activity, as a sort of second-level procedure that serves chiefly to ratify and implement the conclusions of more remote processes of social control.[92] They are still inclined, nevertheless, to view the use of money in politics as one means by which economic and social power are extended over government.[93] The composition of ruling elites is seldom specified in sufficient detail to permit a check on their behavior as campaign contributors. When they are, inquiry leads to the not implausible finding that those defined as ruling elites who have the resources to make sizeable campaign contributions are likely to do so; and those whose importance is not related to financial position, e.g., military leaders, are

91. Spouses included; no allowance for deaths between 1951 and 1956.

92. Note particularly Mills, *op. cit.,* and Floyd Hunter's earlier work, *Community Power Structure* (Chapel Hill: University of North Carolina Press, 1953). Professor Mills is vigorously critical of notions of "romantic pluralism." —pp. 242-68, 270-71, 336-38. There are many dissents. Robert A. Dahl notes the failure to examine key decisions to see how, in fact, they are made and where the dominant initiative and veto power lie.—"A Critique of the Ruling Elite Model," *American Political Science Review,* 52 (1958), 463-69. Tallcott Parsons finds Mills in error on several scores and states there is no single well-integrated power elite but a complex and fluid set of upper groups.—"The Distribution of Power in American Society," *World Politics,* 10 (1957), 123-43. Many commentators note the absence, or the passing, of a "ruling class." See David Riesman with Nathan Glazer and Reuel Denny, *The Lonely Crowd* (Garden City, New York: Doubleday & Company, Inc., 1953), pp. 251-58.

93. In discussing the corporate rich, one of several elites, Mills opens a discussion of campaign donations by observing: "Money allows the economic power of its possessor to be translated directly into political party causes."—*Op. cit.* p. 166.

not.[94] Campaign giving appears again as only one of the links between government and society.

That large campaign gifts are likely to be found where men of money are found confuses the analysis of political contributions. One senator demonstrated that on the governing boards of six of the nation's prominent universities were some 58 men who made around $300,000 in political contributions in 1956. The finding rendered meaningless, it was argued, the identification of campaign givers among officials of other organizations, such as the American Petroleum Institute and large corporations.[95] The political behavior of a member of a group, however, becomes significant to that group to the extent that the group has political interests. The political gift of a corporate official who is also a university trustee is less relevant to his university than to his corporation only to the extent that his university has fewer, less important, or less immediate political interests than his corporation. The presence of individuals who are campaign contributors in many important political and nonpolitical groups merely emphasizes the presence of an active national-community leadership.[96]

The analysis of sources of campaign funds produces no total blueprint of social or political power nor of the connections between the two. It does reveal, however, that aggregates of social power are related to political power through the processes of political finance. Especially is this apparent among the officers and directors of the nation's largest corporations, a collection of persons who control a greater concentration

94. Professor Hunter's studies have been designed in part to identify the persons deemed by their peers in the business community to exercise greatest influence in the nation's affairs. A resulting list of 112 persons (in 1956) represented an elite corps of American businessmen. Among these, 69 were designated as more important than others. Of the top group, 57 per cent were known to have made officially reported campaign gifts of $500 or more in 1952, as were 44 per cent of the other 43. A later and more diversified national-leadership list of 100 was derived by Hunter (1958). A little less than half the list was composed of present or former government officials, military leaders, scientists, labor and religious leaders, of whom 17 per cent were known to have given $500 or more in 1956. The rest listed were largely prominent business executives, for whom the percentage was 59. See his *Top Leadership, U.S.A.* (Chapel Hill: University of North Carolina Press, 1959), pp. 177, 195-216.

95. Senator Andrew F. Schoeppel of Kansas, chairman of the Republican senatorial campaign committee, *Congressional Record,* 85th Congress, 1st Session, March 29, 1957, vol. 103, no. 55, pp. 4283-84, and *passim.*

96. Senator Schoeppel asked two rhetorical questions about his university findings. First: "Are we to assume that big business dominates these institutions, too?" Each institution would have to speak for itself, but no one would suggest that the attitudes of big businessmen go unrepresented on the governing boards where these men sit. Second: "Does this indicate that our colleges are subject to political influence?" No one has ever suggested that the gifts of corporate officials to politicians gave the politicians influence over the corporation executives.—*Ibid.,* p. 4284.

of economic power than any other.[97] Yet it is true also of other components in the structure of national power, legitimate and illegitimate, strong and weak.

97. See A. A. Berle, Jr., *Economic Power and the Free Society—A Preliminary Discussion of the Corporation* (New York: The Fund for the Republic, 1957), 20 pp. Mr. Berle has written elsewhere: "The Corporation is now, essentially, a nonstatist political institution, and its directors are in the same boat with public office-holders."—*The 20th Century Capitalist Revolution,* p. 60.

The 225 largest corporations included in the analyses earlier in this chapter embraced the 100 largest industrials, accounting for 40 per cent of total corporate industrial assets in the United States; the 25 largest utilities, accounting for 55 per cent of the total assets of privately owned United States utility systems; the 25 largest life insurance companies, accounting for 81 per cent of all United States life insurance company assets; the 25 largest banks, holding 31 per cent of total commercial-bank resources and deposits in the United States; the 25 largest transportation companies, which received 39 per cent of all revenues of private transportation companies in the United States; and the 25 largest merchandising firms, handling 7 per cent of total combined retail and wholesale sales.—Derived from *Fortune,* 54 (July, 1956), 88-89 and supplement.

6

SPECIAL SOURCES

THREE SOURCES of campaign money have special importance because of the amounts that emanate from each and the strategic position each occupies in the political process. Organized labor will be treated in the next chapter. In this chapter, something will be said about the beneficiaries of political patronage, and of political protection, as suppliers of political cash.

1. BENEFICIARIES OF PATRONAGE

Parties and candidates in need of campaign money have long imposed excises upon those who reap benefits from government. Traditionally, in the United States and abroad, such levies have been viewed as exchanges for political patronage. Tough finance chairmen have viewed as special prey anybody receiving income, honor, or desired decisions from government—whether a product of favoritism or not. They have looked to contractors, to officeholders, to persons with a stake in the enforcement of laws and the administration of regulations of any kind—persons with a stake in fire, health, and building inspections, in the award of franchises and licenses, in tax assessments, in the treatment accorded inmates of public institutions, in decisions on visa applications, in the naming of court-appointed receivers and guardians, and on and on.[1]

Trends and diversity.—Historically, two classes of patronage beneficiaries have been especially significant as sources of political money: government contractors and government officeholders, both diverse lots. They embrace the manufacturers of nuclear submarines and the builders of local sewer systems. They run from skilled diplomats to the county highway gang. Their importance as sources of campaign funds has declined in recent decades, but each remains significant in many areas.

The government contract has declined as an item of barter as purchasing procedures have improved and as superior opportunities for

1. Charles Harris Garrigues lists 28 departments of municipal government and discusses the opportunities each affords for favoritism and graft.—*You're Paying For It!—A Guide to Graft* (New York: Funk & Wagnalls, 1936), pp. 46-51.

profit have increased. Nineteenth-century practices by which every state government agency bought its own supplies on its own terms opened the doors to corruption. Central purchasing systems have eliminated much of the old waste and peculation, and contributions resulting from the compound of bribery and extortion that prevailed have diminished correspondingly. Nevertheless, important exceptions are still found in what central purchasing agents buy—common exclusions include highway materials, educational supplies, perishable goods—and only about half the states have anything like complete, centralized systems.[2]

The number of public offices filled by patronage appointees has steadily shrunk at all levels of government. Merit systems are not always free from pressures for contributions, yet as merit systems have spread, the proportion of positions occupied by appointees exposed to the coercive solicitation of campaign funds has diminished sharply.[3] Even though the trend has been a steady one, only slightly over half the states have relatively complete merit systems operated by a central personnel agency and applying to most employees. Many cities have systems covering certain employees, but in only a few are substantially all covered. Few counties have developed effective merit programs.

The unevenness of purchasing and personnel practices across the country is accompanied by unevenness in the role of contractors and officeholders in political giving. Even in similar legal settings wide variations in political customs exist. Standard procedures for raising money in one county are viewed with horror by neighbors next door. To learn why the political common law of one area diverges from that of another would lead deep into the sociology and history of communities.

Within the same political community, moreover, diverse incentives characterize contractors and employees, like other contributors, who give to campaigns. The extent to which expectation of reward is explicit shades out along a continuum. Some contributors forthrightly demand their *quid pro quo*. Others, enveloped in a protective cushion of custom, hardly ask themselves why they give.

Contractors.—Officials of corporations holding huge federal contracts frequently turn up among reported campaign contributors of $500 or more.[4] The circumstances under which many of these contracts are

2. Robert S. Babcock, *State and Local Government and Politics* (New York: Random House, 1957), p. 308.

3. Harvey C. Mansfield, "Political Parties, Patronage, and the Federal Government Service," in Wallace S. Sayre (ed.), *The Federal Government Service: It's Character, Prestige, and Problems* (New York: The American Assembly, Graduate School of Business, Columbia University, 1954), p. 94.

4. Data on 1952 reported gifts by officials of the 10 largest defense prime contractors appear in the Gore Committee *Hearings,* part 2, pp. 519-24; on 1956 reported gifts, in the Gore Committee *Report,* pp. 78-82.

Federal statute makes it illegal for "whoever" enters a contract with the

negotiated, however, put the crucial decisions distant from persons primarily concerned with party finances.[5] A causal connection between the gift and the contract can seldom be realistically inferred. Moreover, the political interests of such firms extend far beyond the award of federal contracts, providing abundant other incentives for political activity by their officials.

In state and local politics, more direct connections are observable between contributors and the business they seek. Schoolbook salesmen report utter impartiality in the textbook commission of one state; nearby, commission members must be approached individually with personal inducements long hallowed by local custom. Liquor wholesalers, road builders, and equipment dealers have stocked the campaign chest of many a candidate for governor in southern primaries.[6] Party organizations in some states and municipalities have depended heavily on the kick-backs of insurance agents, bond salesmen, architects, engineers, holders of public franchises of all kinds, including those invested with horse- and dog-racing licenses.[7] For years in Indiana after the repeal of federal and state prohibition, wholesale liquor licenses issued by the state were traded for campaign contributions, and "beer politics" in one form or another outlasted several modifications of the law. Political favoritism in business contracts extended beyond the liquor industry, e.g., to the designation of bonding company agents through whom contractors employed on a toll road had to purchase performance bonds. Elsewhere, levels of probity have differed, or at least alternative sources of political funds have been available. Even within a state like Indiana, where in some counties local contractors have been favored in return for financial support, a close observer reports it would be difficult to introduce the system into other counties not already having it.[8]

United States government to make a political contribution.—*U.S. Code,* Title 18, sec. 611. Officials of corporations with federal contracts have not been deterred by this provision, nor have there been prosecutions of them.

5. Though apparently not always, if the well publicized charges are believed that the Republican national chairman, Len Hall, in 1954 demanded, and got, contributions from officials of the Frederick H. Snare Co. before the company was awarded a multi-million dollar contract by the U.S. Government to expand its Nicaro Nickel plant in Cuba. With most defense contracts placed without competitive bidding, large corporations have taken to putting retired officers of the services on their payrolls.

6. "Figures on receipts by major candidates in recent years (1946-54) indicate that at least fifty percent of the money, handled by central headquarters and auxiliary groups, came from highway contractors and liquor dealers."—Joseph L. Bernd, *The Role of Campaign Funds in Georgia Primary Elections, 1936-1958* (Macon: The Georgia Journal, Inc., 1958), p. 3.

7. Of Pennsylvania, one report notes: "Competition for state contracts is keen, and individual representatives of business firms vie with one another in the financial support of the political parties."—Edward F. Cooke and G. Edward Janosik, *Guide to Pennsylvania Politics* (New York: Henry Holt and Company, 1957), pp. 89-90.

8. Frank James Munger, "Two-Party Politics in the State of Indiana" (Ph.D. dissertation, Harvard University, 1955), pp. 169-70, 174.

A legion of case materials from jurisdictions across the land make two points abundantly clear. First, practices vary greatly. Second, regardless of legal protections, honorable and prudent businessmen competing for government ventures make campaign contributions. Many of the gifts by company officials discussed in the previous chapter stemmed from a desire to do what was thought necessary to remain eligible. Even in the best run states, honorable and prudent public officials deem it appropriate for those who profit from public work to support the party with their cash. The word went down in one recent year in New York that no firm bidding on any state contract was to be solicited until after the awards were made. Even where the expectation is not explicit, where those who do not give are regularly awarded public business, the climate encourages giving. Many contractors routinely do so to both parties.

The remarkable thing is not how much of this goes on. The remarkable thing is how little of it goes on.[9] The root of American business doctrine and of much American business practice is virile, single-minded competition. Businessmen solicit business from each other by every known personal and organizational blandishment—all tax deductible. It would be extraordinary if they did not exert themselves with comparable vigor in pursuit of business from government.

Public employees.—Political assessments have long characterized the spoils system by which governments at all levels in the United States have been partly staffed. Officeholders dependent on their patron's election have often been asked to help fuel the campaign engines.[10] Assessments have uniformly been damned by persons intent on developing a competent, competitive, economical career civil service. Legal steps to eliminate them have been advocated as guarantees of personal political liberty (and also condemned as infringements thereof). The decline of enforceable assessments was necessarily accompanied, however, by a relative increase of political funds from other origins. Some practical politicians claim the change was for the worse. They argue it was better for politicians to depend on small sums from public employees than on large sums from persons seeking privilege—although clearly in the heyday of assessments economic buccaneers made lucrative raids on the common wealth. Civil service reform spread, nevertheless, and in doing so deprived political parties of another campaign resource at times of even greater importance: manpower on and before election day. Public agencies had on occasion served chiefly as adjuncts to party organizations, providing vocational housing for their legions of workers. The administrative waste was horrendous.

9. On the contrary, Garrigues contended that the developing skills of "professional graft" make it one of the safest of occupations, hence one far more extensively practised than usually supposed.—*Op. cit.*, p. 110 ff.

10. For the income of selected political committees coming from large contributions by officeholders, see pages 123-28, above.

The history of political assessments among federal, state, and local government employees is well known. With the growth in competition for presidential nominations and the development of national party organizations, assessments of federal employees rocketed in the second quarter of the nineteenth century. It was said that many federal field personnel gave a greater portion of their time to partisan than to administrative pursuits.[11] Assessments reached a peak in the years following the Civil War, leading to a series of federal and state reform measures in the last third of the century.[12] In 1878, at least 75 per cent of the money raised by the Republican Congressional Committee came from federal officeholders. Perhaps that is a sufficient index.[13] In 1913 some 94 per cent of city employees in Philadelphia paid assessments. In 1933 a substantial proportion of Republican funds in that city still came from levies on public employees.[14] By the middle of the twentieth century, however, important long-term changes had taken place across the country, both in the relative importance of contributions from public employees and in the circumstances under which they were made.

The federal service.—Federal officeholders as a class are no longer subject to systematic, blanket solicitation. Even before the passage of the Hatch Acts, with their prohibitions against solicitation on the job and solicitation by fellow employees,[15] the practice had largely dis-

11. Leonard D. White, *The Jacksonians* (New York: The Macmillan Company, 1954), pp. 332-37; Paul P. Van Riper, *History of the United States Civil Service* (Evanston: Row, Peterson and Company, 1958), pp. 46-47.

12. The first restrictions of any kind on campaign giving were intended to protect government employees. Federal legislation appeared as early as 1867, and the Civil Service Reform Act of 1883 prohibited officers and employees of the United States from seeking or receiving political contributions from each other and banned the collection of political funds in federal buildings. In the same year, New York and Pennsylvania passed legislation similar in purpose, and other states gradually followed.

The new statutes grew out of the movement toward merit systems for public employees and did not stem primarily from concern for the electoral system. A series of enforcement actions, court decisions, and rulings by the Attorney General slowly led to a curbing of federal assessments and removals by the beginning of the twentieth century.—*Ibid.*, pp. 75, 90-91, 99, 142, 186; Dorothy Canfield Fowler, *The Cabinet Politician—The Postmasters General, 1829-1909* (New York: Columbia University Press, 1943), p. 157.

13. See Louise Overacker, *Money in Elections* (New York: The Macmillan Company, 1932), pp. 103-5; V. O. Key, Jr., *The Techniques of Political Graft in the United States* (Chicago: The University of Chicago Libraries, 1936), pp. 68-75.

14. David Harold Kurtzman, *Methods of Controlling Votes in Philadelphia* (Philadelphia, 1935), pp. 74, 81.

15. The Hatch Act, passed originally in 1939 and later amended, extended to virtually all employees in the executive branch of the federal government restrictions on political activities that already applied to persons in the classified civil service. The exceptions: "(a) the President and Vice President of the United States; (b) persons whose compensation is paid from the appropriation for the office of the President; (c) heads and assistant heads of executive departments; and (d) officers who are appointed by the President by and with the advice and

appeared. "Voluntary contributions" among government workers at all levels is a recurring source of campaign funds, however, and one which at some times and places is still combed systematically.

Even when only known gifts of $500 and more are considered, a large proportion of political appointees to diplomatic posts show up as donors to campaigns. On July 1, 1952, there were 27 chiefs of diplomatic mission abroad who were not career Foreign Service officers (about one-third of the total). Of these, 13 were found to have given in 1952, all to Democratic recipients. Of 30 such ambassadors and ministers on October 1, 1953, after the installation of the Eisenhower administration, 11 were known to have made gifts, all but one to Republicans. The exception, Ambassador Jefferson Caffery, was a long-time diplomat who had served in many posts and was soon to retire. Many other political appointees to high federal office are found among lists of givers, although some apparently refuse to pay up, even when asked.[16]

Top federal officers reach their posts by many different routes. Some make no gifts. With others, the contribution is but one item in a composite of political activities. Occasionally an individual becomes politically conspicuous solely for his donations. So it was with Maxwell H. Gluck. Mr. Gluck, owner of a dress-shop chain who gave at least $26,500 in Republican campaign contributions before the 1956 election, was named United States Ambassador to Ceylon by President Eisenhower in the summer of 1957. When in public hearings Mr. Gluck did not know the names of the Prime Ministers of India and Ceylon, it was

consent of the Senate, and who determine policies to be pursued by the United States in its relations with foreign powers or in the Nation-wide administration of Federal laws."—U.S. Civil Service Commission, *Political Activity of Federal Officers and Employees* (Washington: Government Printing Office, January, 1956) (Pamphlet 20), p. 8.

The new legislation was stimulated in part by Republicans and Democrats seeking to hobble any political use that the Roosevelt Administration might make of the hundreds of thousands of New Deal employees in noncompetitive positions. Insofar as contributions were concerned, it became illegal for officers and employees to solicit each other, but they might make contributions to a regularly constituted political organization for its general expenditures. They might not, however, collect or handle contributions made for political purposes, nor be concerned directly or indirectly in the sale of dinner tickets for a political party organization. Administrative officials were barred from making lists of personnel available for purposes of solicitation.—*Ibid.*, pp. 12-13.

These and other provisions of the Hatch Acts apply to state and local government employees "whose principal employment is in connection with any activity which is financed in whole or in part by Federal loans or grants."—*Ibid.*, p. 19.

16. About 3 per cent of the persons listed in the *U.S. Organization Manual* for 1951-52 (120 of 3800) and in that for 1955-56 (124 of 4200) were found to have given at least one sum of $500 or more in 1952. Many of these, however, were in the legislative branch. James A. Farley relates that Harold Ickes, a Bull Moose Republican serving as Franklin Roosevelt's Secretary of the Interior, rejected a request for a $100 donation to the Democratic national committee on the grounds he could not afford it.—*Jim Farley's Story—The Roosevelt Years* (New York: McGraw-Hill Book Company, 1948), p. 188.

widely charged his appointment was a reward for his generosity.[17] Such appointments have declined as the conduct of foreign affairs has become more critical and the demand for diplomatic skill more urgent. Persons active in the finance of both parties concede, however, that with certain federal appointments in recent administrations, financial participation in politics has been part of the basis for selection. For many federal assignments, partisan political service is suitable training. The skills needed to amass or husband large sums of money, however, are considerably less like those required to run a democratic government, including its diplomacy, than are the proficiencies developed in some other types of political activity.

Lower in the federal service, three things happen. Probably the bulk of employees are never asked to give and never do. Others give voluntarily, either entirely on their own initiative or in response to general appeals directed to all citizens. Still others are solicited for voluntary contributions primarily because they are government employees. The same conditions exist in state and local governments, but the frequency of solicitation and of compulsory giving are both greater.

The experience in 1952 of the Democratic national committee in the sale of $5.00 certificates is instructive. The Ruml Plan foundered in most areas,[18] but in Washington, D.C., and in the state of Kentucky, unusual success was achieved. In Washington the mass of federal workers and their families provided a great pool of politically oriented individuals. When provided a convenient opportunity to give, and a psychological shove, many did so. In Kentucky, the achievements of the Ruml Plan resulted largely from a canvass of state employees blessed by the Governor. State employees in Kentucky by honored custom expect and are expected to pay campaign assessments.

Many persons employed by government for that very reason have special interest in public policies. A higher proportion of them than of the general population might therefore be expected to make political contributions. With federal employees especially, who are barred from many other types of political activity, it is reasonable to expect some to seize this opportunity to assert themselves politically.

To keep within the law, solicitations among federal workers are conducted off the job and by persons outside the federal service.[19]

17. Administration spokesmen denied it, and the Secretary of State emphasized that diplomatic appointments had been made among Democratic campaign contributors. One such was identified, Ambassador to Germany David K. Bruce, who was down for $1,000 in 1956, but 19 other Ike-appointees had made over $218,000 in Republican gifts in 1956 alone. The Secretary argued that an able citizen should not be barred from high service because he gave to the party of his choice, plausible enough provided such citizens were not admitted to positions for which they lacked qualifications.—*New York Times,* August 7, 1957. Mr. Gluck served about one year.

18. See below, pages 250-53.

19. The Civil Service Commission is charged with enforcing the prohibitions

Texas' china-breaking Republican national committeeman, Jack Porter, provided a sharply etched, though not typical illustration in 1954. He wrote to 500 persons who had received federal appointments in Texas under the Eisenhower administration. On the stationery of the Republican party of Texas, he requested a specified sum from each individual. The party needed the money, he said, to pay the costs of "processing" federal appointments in Texas and to help support Congressional and legislative candidates.[20] Some postmistresses asserted they were dunned for $125,[21] and other requests were said to run as high as $500. Considerably less than the total sum requested came in, and the publicity attending the episode was not relished by Mr. Porter's Republican colleagues.

Postmasters and rural mail carriers have lasted longer as patronage appointees than any other large class of federal employees. Despite legislation increasing the tenure and merit characteristics of the postal service, appointments to these posts carry special political flavor. Fund-raising in rural areas has always been a slow business. Many a party wheelhorse has found his best response in the families of persons holding, or hoping to hold, jobs as mail carriers, as postmasters, or as census workers.

In 1952, Democratic leaders in Kansas solicited postmasters and rural mail carriers in letters mailed to their homes. Follow-up calls were made at home and it was general practice to accept gifts only away from the site of employment and outside of working hours. In all, 422 postmasters, 47 per cent of the total number, made contributions. The salaries of the contributors ranged from slightly under $1,000 to slightly under $6,000. The amounts requested were scaled accordingly: those getting less than $2,000 were asked to give $25; those earning from $2,000 up to $3,000, $50; $3,000-$4,000, $75; $4,000-$5,000, $100; and

against political activity, and the statute prescribes the Commission's responsibilities to receive and act on complaints of violations at all levels of government. Its annual reports reveal that in the fiscal years 1951 through 1958, 18 federal employees were removed and 80 suspended from their jobs for activities involving political money.

In this narrow phase of campaign finance, the relatively successful enforcement of federal legislation has resulted from several conditions. Special, explicit responsibility for enforcement is focused in an agency of government where the task is congenial to the other things it must do. The remoteness of the Civil Service Commission from local affairs gives it greater freedom in acting on complaints than enjoyed by state and local officials who may next week have to make political medicine with the accused, or his cousin, or his sponsor. Moreover, many employees affected by the restrictions welcome the protections they give. Some do not, and they are sometimes vocal. But their unhappiness is directed chiefly at the broader phases of the restraints, and they have not found effective support throughout the country for their discontent. These conditions contributing to effective statutory controls do not characterize most regulation of campaign finance.

20. Drew Pearson published the text of the letter.—*The News and Observer* (Raleigh, N.C.), November 1, 1954.

21. AP dispatch, October 9, 1956.

$5,000 or more, $150. The total requested from those who gave came to $32,150, of which $18,779.50 or 58 per cent was actually received, for an average gift of $44.82. At the same time, 154 rural mail carriers, 13 per cent of those in the state, gave an average of $29.76, for a total of $4,583.

Kansas Republicans in 1952 held the governorship, dominated the state legislature, and made up the entire delegation to Congress. Democratic leaders did not ignore other sources of revenue, but effective solicitation of federal employees seemed more important to Democrats in Kansas than in other states where their party was stronger. Appeals like these create pressures that amount, for some individuals, to not very subtle coercion. In this illustration, nevertheless, the failure of many to contribute, and of others to give less than asked for, reflected a significant degree of independence.

Patronage managers know well that an applicant's party loyalty may intensify at appointment time, fade later. In areas of one-party dominance, the party label is often assumed by individuals who previously were thought to belong to the other crowd. The campaign gifts of federal workers in Kansas in 1952 demonstrated that no irrevocable loyalties are created merely by the award of jobs under a party's aegis. The variations from one Congressional District to another in the response of Kansas postmasters and rural mail carriers seemed to reflect general political sentiments. The districts displaying greatest Democratic strength in the vote for United States Representative tended to have the highest percentage of employees who gave:

Congressional District No.	*% of Total Vote for U.S. Rep. that Was Democratic, 1952*[22]	*% Who Gave*	
		Postmasters	*Rural Mail Carriers*
1	51.5	57.7	19.0
2	42.7	68.2	22.3
4	40.6	68.6	16.5
3	40.5	41.9	8.8
6	37.5	33.2	10.6
5	29.1	28.7	8.7

State and local practices.—Methodical political solicitation occurs more often in state and local governments than among federal employees. Some states are famed for their assessment practices, like Indiana, Oklahoma, Kentucky. In these and in others, however, practices vary with the character of limiting statutes, with the needs of candidates and parties, with the tactics of intraparty factional maneuvering, and with the personal attitudes and energies of political leaders.

22. Taken from Richard M. Scammon (ed.), *America Votes—A Handbook of Contemporary American Election Statistics* (New York: The Macmillan Company, 1958), p. 130.

Legal prohibitions are often effective.[23] Patronage plays a limited role in Wisconsin because of the well-developed civil service system.[24] The application of the Hatch Act to certain local government employees creates an entirely different atmosphere around their offices in county courthouses than that found next door where employees are paid entirely from local funds. H. O. Waldby reported in 1950 that in patronage-ridden Oklahoma legal provisions effectively prevented solicitation among employees of the highway patrol division and the examiners division of the Department of Public Safety. His report also illustrated variations in practices as governors with different needs and resources took office.[25]

Personal on-the-spot inquiries reveal that, in all sections of the United States, state and local government personnel are to varying extents called upon for campaign donations.[26] Moreover, persons familiar

23. About one-third of the states have restrictions against the *solicitation* of significant groups of state employees, or otherwise try to limit the freedom with which they can make political donations. Very few try to prevent voluntary contributions for political purposes. These prohibitions usually apply to partisan elections; there are fewer pertaining to nonpartisan elections.

Under most conditions, public employees can legally be solicited by persons outside of government; campaigns for voluntary contributions may be conducted in state agencies where regulations merely proscribe coercion. The *Model State Civil Service Law* (1953) of the National Civil Service League and the National Municipal League advocates prohibiting political contributions by persons in the classified service as the most effective means of preventing political activity by civil service employees (pp. 22-23).

Among 88 cities 100,000 and over in population that were surveyed, over 70 per cent prohibited solicitation among some city employees and 45 per cent banned the distribution of tickets or the making of voluntary donations. The proportion of cities possessing these prohibitions goes up with the size of the city. Among 16 cities of 500,000 and over, in partisan contests 13 banned solicitation, 9 the sale of tickets, and 8 voluntary gifts; among 21 cities of 250,000-499,999 population, the corresponding numbers were 17, 10, and 10; among 51 cities of 100,000-249,999 they were 33, 21, and 22.—Richard Christopherson, *Regulating Political Activities of Public Employees* (Civil Service Assembly, Personnel Report No. 543, 1954), p. 8.

24. Leon D. Epstein, *Politics in Wisconsin* (Madison: University of Wisconsin Press, 1958), p. 29.

25. *The Patronage System in Oklahoma* (Norman: The Transcript Company, 1950), pp. 78-82.

26. Published sources are few, and not always recent, but lead to the same conclusion. It has been said that control of the executive branch of Pennsylvania's state government is worth about $500,000 annually in contributions. More than 35,000 state jobs are dispensed as patronage, and a majority of the recipients are said to give.—Cooke and Janosik, *op. cit.*, p. 90. See the reports in Thomas C. Donnelly (ed.), *Rocky Mountain Politics* (Albuquerque: University of New Mexico Press, 1940); V. O. Key, Jr., *Southern Politics in State and Nation* (New York: Alfred A. Knopf, 1949), p. 479; Harold F. Gosnell, *Machine Politics: Chicago Model* (Chicago: University of Chicago Press, 1937), pp. 74-75; Kefauver Crime Committee, *Third Interim Report* (Washington: Government Printing Office, 1951) (Senate Report No. 307, 82nd Congress, 1st Session), pp. 140-41, on alleged gifts of $30,000 by Local 94, International Association of Fire Fighters, to the 1949 New York mayoralty campaign of William O'Dwyer, and of $3,500

with the localities can often spot public employees on campaign finance reports. Sometimes they are labeled as such, as on an Indiana report that listed a sum as coming from the Lake County Highway Department employees. At least seven other Lake County officials, including two judges, were down for varying sums, usually with "and employees" after their names. In North Carolina, some 12,500 persons were reported in 1952 as giving sums of less than $100 to the Democratic state executive committee. In a random sample of 25 of these, 24 were found to be state employees and 21 were employed in some part of the highway establishment. The inference that virtually all of these contributors worked for the state was supported by the testimony of persons experienced in collecting Democratic money. They estimated independently that about 90 per cent of highway department personnel contribute in a given election, an estimate that would put the number of highway contributors at between 10,000 and 11,000.

The state Democratic chairman customarily writes the heads of state agencies asking them to solicit their employees. He often issues a statement urging that no coercion be employed, but the nature and insistence of the appeals vary with supervisors at lower levels. One supervisor posted in red letters the names of a group of recalcitrants. They were ridiculed by the others and quickly capitulated. In North Carolina and in other localities, however,[27] it is difficult to find persons who have actually been penalized for failing to give. Admonitions are sufficient. "I gave 'cause I thought I had to," confided one license examiner with the highway patrol, although he wanted it clear he didn't trust the bossman who got the money further than he would "a new 'coon dog with a rabbit."

In addition to voluntary assessments levied by party organizations are contributions made to individual candidates. Elective state officials, especially in areas of lopsided party competition, frequently expect donations to their personal campaigns from employees in their own departments. What goes on consequently may differ from one agency to another, and from one election to the next.

---

to the 1948 presidential primary campaign of Thomas E. Dewey in Oregon; Kefauver Crime Committee, *Hearings,* part 4, pp. 160-63, and part 4-A, p. 452, on a "flower fund" in Missouri—a pool to which employees in a state office gave regularly to cover flowers, picnics, entertainments, etc., and which was easily convertible to the political needs of the head of the office.

27. A valuable study of patronage in Centre County, Pennsylvania, examined systematically the political participation of 123 political appointees holding highway jobs. Their contributing record exceeded other types of political effort, although 15 per cent claimed never to have contributed and only 79 per cent declared that they had done so at least once while holding the highway job. Although the solicitations were made systematically, "there is no reason to think that the Republicans dismissed highway employees for failure to contribute or to contribute with suitable generosity."—Frank J. Sorauf, "State Patronage in a Rural County," *American Political Science Review,* 50 (1956), 1049.

The current importance of contributions from public employees in financing the political system ought not to be minimized. In a presidential election year, somewhere between $5,000,000 and $15,000,000 in campaign gifts are probably made by officeholders at all levels in the United States.[28] In specific areas this source of money can be of great significance. A veteran of Kentucky political finance estimated that about two-thirds of the campaign money raised by an administration in his state usually came from state employees.[29] If true, political assessments in Kentucky doubtless exceed in importance those in any other state. Nevertheless, the amounts raised elsewhere have at times been important. The famous Two Per Cent Club developed during Paul V. McNutt's administration as governor of Indiana brought at least $110,000 to the Democratic state central committee in 1938, and 2 per cent schemes were in force in other states such as Illinois and Missouri.[30] County and municipal party organizations took up the practice and some Indiana county chairmen in the 1950's believed that 2 per cent of annual salary from local employees would cover all the expenses of their county organizations.[31] In most areas the sums given fall below 2 per cent of annual salaries. Even though averaging only a few dollars apiece, 1952 state-employee contributions in North Carolina supplied around one-half the $90,000 income of the Democratic state executive committee.[32]

Internal party management.—Any fund-raising dependent on special solicitors is likely to produce divided authority within a political party.

28. In 1958 there were in the United States around 1,469,000 state employees and 4,423,000 local government employees. Among employees at these levels, the largest numbers were in education (2,589,000) and health and hospitals (628,000). Politically potent highway employees numbered 525,000. Civilian employees in the federal government ran around 2,405,000.—U.S. Bureau of the Census, *Statistical Abstract of the United States: 1959* (Washington: Government Printing Office, 1959), p. 420.

29. This informant put the usual cost of an attempt to win the governorship or a seat in the United States Senate at $1,000,000. In 1958, Kentucky state employees numbered around 23,000, and those in local government another 57,000.—*Ibid.*, p. 421. Local employees contribute, but if two-thirds of a million were to be raised from state workers alone, the average assessment would come to less than $30.

30. The 2 per cent rule prevailed among political job-holders in Chicago during the 1930's.—Gosnell, *loc. cit.* In one Missouri state office in the late 1940's, 2 per cent of annual salary seems to have been collected, half of it being turned over to the state committee. Some employees gave in addition to the primary nomination campaign.—Kefauver Crime Committee, *Hearings,* part 4, p. 160.

31. Munger, *op. cit.*, p. 169.

32. It was claimed that the New Jersey State Motor Vehicle Agents Association had given $5,278 to the Republican state finance committee in 1952 and $34,757 to the "Troast for Governor Club" the next year. The money came from dues of $10.00 per year plus an assessment of 3 per cent of each agent's annual commission from the state. The by-laws of the Association required payment, and it appeared that all members had complied.—*New York Times,* September 10, 1954.

When assessments constitute an important source of funds, agency chiefs are usually important links in the chain of solicitation. Although political appointees themselves, they may acquire leverage within the party as a result. The increasing dependence of parties on voluntary contributions, however, has created other independently based sources of influence within their own structures. Civil service reform, moreover, imposed additional burdens of campaign management. Campaign work formerly performed by public employees (as in some places it still is) must be paid for. Along with other factors accounting for the decline in the old machines, these changes in party finance have conduced to a diversification and dispersion of influence within party organizations. They tend simultaneously to popularize the processes by which public officials are nominated and elected, and to complicate the maintenance of cohesive party leadership.[33]

2. UNDERWORLD MONEY AND POLITICS

A theory.—A theory, shared by many, places the underworld at the base of the American political system. It holds that in most communities illicit activities take place, and to be profitable they must depend on the tolerance of law enforcement officers and the elected officials who stand behind them. Purveyors of illegal goods and services have two prime resources, aside from their lawlessness. One is the public's demand for their products; the other is money. With the money, underworld interests buy their way into political campaigns and gain strategic posts in party organizations.

Although interested most immediately in politicians who make and enforce the law, their political significance extends far beyond. Candidates succored early move on to higher levels, filling the most important posts in federal and state governments; moreover, campaign machinery organized and financed by underworld interests out of concern for particular races becomes the machinery that campaigns for all a party's candidates. In the end, public officials at all levels wind up known by

33. It has sometimes been argued that patronage at the disposal of party managers increases their capacity for leadership and hence improves party cohesion. Frank J. Sorauf has pointed out that, in practice, much patronage is awarded on personal rather than party grounds and may create divisive personal loyalties rather than a sense of obligation to the party. He suggests, also, that the tendency for a party newly come to power to dismiss highly partisan employees encourages those holding patronage positions to be politically moderate, even to become apolitical or bipartisan.—"Patronage and Party," *Midwest Journal of Politics*, 3 (1959), 115-26. Duane Lockard has taken note of the "double machine," in which situation politicians of a weak party, desirous of an appointment from their stronger opponents, put patronage before party, thereby hindering the development of their own party.—*New England State Politics* (Princeton: Princeton University Press, 1959), p. 68.

and beholden to the underworld.[34] So runs the theory, called by some the A B C of the party system.

The theory is spasmodically fortified by revelations so startling they are often discounted as atypically melodramatic. For a time in the 1940's the New York County Democratic organization, Tammany Hall, lay under the influence of a leading underworld figure, Frank Costello.[35] In neighboring Kings County (Brooklyn), another underworld figure, Joe Adonis, exercised great influence within the Democratic organization.[36] In Missouri, the role of mobster elements in that state's politics was dramatized by the murder in 1950 of Charles Binaggio. Mr. Binaggio was a central figure in Kansas City gambling circles, the leader of the First Ward Democratic Club in that city, and acknowledged to be one of the state's important political figures. Allegedly he was murdered because he failed to deliver the political influence his underworld associates thought they were buying by financing his political activities.[37] Recurringly in other communities, large and small, evidence has erupted demonstrating linkages between politics and crime—in Phoenix City, Alabama; in Hot Springs, Arkansas; in Erie, Pennsylvania; in the Commonwealth of Massachusetts; and elsewhere, including the world symbol of urban lawlessness, Chicago.[38] At least one underworld character has been known to say privately: "Show me a punk who wants to run for office, and I'll show you a man who can be had."

The sinister picture of a country governed from the underworld does not jibe with the view most citizens have of their government. The Truman and Eisenhower Doctrines for the Middle East, the status of West Berlin, farm price supports, state's rights and civil liberties, Hell's Canyon and natural gas, the naming of cabinet officers—these and other

34. Despair has run deep, to wit: "Politics is the business of the party organization; party organization is the business of the mercenary criminal, the racketeer. . . . To entertain hope of any improvement, *power must be taken from party organizations to control public office*. And this requires almost a political revolution. . . . Political organizations should be restricted to formulating and promoting platforms and principles; and they should be deprived of the power to name candidates for office." Thus wrote a Chicago lawyer, Jacob G. Grossberg, "Mercenary Crime and Politics," in Ernest D. MacDougal (ed.), *Crime for Profit—A Symposium on Mercenary Crime* (Boston: The Stratford Company, 1933), pp. 156, 157, 161. (Italics in original.)

35. The Kefauver Crime Committee, *Third Interim Report*, p. 122. Some of the Committee's conclusions are debatable, but the evidence on this one is persuasive.

36. *Ibid.*, p. 185.

37. *Ibid.*, pp. 37-41.

38. No new phenomena in the United States. Writing of the years 1877-99, Richard P. McCormick, like other students of the period, concluded that ". . . the liquor and gambling interests were served by the Democratic party in the same manner that the emergent corporations and certain railroads looked to the Republicans for special consideration. Privileges of every sort and public offices from aldermanic posts to Senatorships were obtainable for a price."—*The History of Voting in New Jersey—A Study of the Development of Election Machinery, 1664-1911* (New Jersey: Rutgers University Press, 1953), p. 160.

daily concerns of the federal government seem remote from gangland, as do the public officials who debate them. The issues of state and local government that occupy most of the headlines do not create images of mobster politicians in the minds of reasonable men. Where lies the connection, then, between government and the underworld? How true is the theory that campaign finance links law-breakers with law-makers? Not all of the answers are clear, but some of the outlines help to keep the subject in perspective.

Kinds of crime.—Not all types of crime have actual or potential political significance, and the location and extent of those that do are not known with exactness. If the volume and kinds of illicit activities in United States communities were known, the knowledge could serve as a starting point for analyzing the political conditions in which such activities flourish and in which they are curbed. Campaign finance, however, is not the only subject about which knowledge is inexact. The United States, says a leading criminologist, "undoubtedly has the poorest [criminal] statistics of any of the nations of the free world."[39]

In the aggregate, however, the sums involved in organized crime seem to run in the neighborhood of 10 per cent of the national income, and many of the criminal activities may require political protection.[40]

39. Professor Thorsten Sellin of the University of Pennsylvania, quoted by Daniel Bell in "What Crime Wave?" *Fortune,* 51 (January, 1955), 99. Faking of police reports and the absence of inter-census population estimates for use in reporting crime rates are two of the statistical pitfalls. A popular discussion of the deficiencies of criminal statistics in the United States is given by Robert Wallace in the first installment of "Crime in the United States," *Life,* September 19, 1957, pp. 47-50. Professor Sellin discusses "The Need for Uniformity in Criminal Statistics" in Clyde B. Vedder, Samuel Koenig, and Robert E. Clark (eds.), *Criminology—A Book of Readings* (New York: The Dryden Press, 1953), pp. 121-29. In the eyes of a former assistant district attorney for the County of New York, "The statistics put out by most district attorneys are no measure of anything save the D. A.'s ability to do arithmetic. . . . But if the prosecutor's statistics are meaningless, the statistics of most police departments are even more so."—William J. Keating with Richard Carter, *The Man Who Rocked the Boat* (New York: Harper & Brothers, 1956), p. 30.

40. The categories by which criminal activities are classified vary with those who do the classifying. The relative financial importance of three main types is suggested by Harry Elmer Barnes and Negley K. Teeters. They compare conventional crime (robbery, forgery, assault, etc.), "organized crime" and racketeering (by which they mean chiefly the extortion rackets), and gambling (many types of which are illegal in most jurisdictions). On the basis of a "financial cost" of $28,000,000,000, they place the cost of conventional crime at 2 per cent of this total ($500,000,000), of organized crime and racketeering, as the terms are used here, at 27 per cent ($7,500,000,000), and of gambling at 71 per cent ($20,000,000,000). —*New Horizons in Criminology* (2nd ed.; New York: Prentice-Hall, Inc., 1952), p. 5. At times, annual income from these activities has doubtless been larger.—Walter C. Reckless, *The Crime Problem* (2nd ed.; New York: Appleton-Century-Crofts, Inc., 1955), p. 49. One 1959 estimate put the total business of organized crime at close to 10 per cent of the national income.—*Life,* February 23, 1959, p. 19.

Gambling is of supreme importance. For a brief review of types of gambling,

There are many types of organized criminal groups. Those engaged in hijacking, jewel thievery, auto thefts, warehouse robbery, kidnapping, murder, etc., can be considered one type. Racketeers are another—those who extort from legitimate or illegitimate businesses through intimidation or force. The biggest criminal business is supplying illegal goods (e.g. narcotics) and services (e.g. gambling) which large segments of the public want and buy—syndicated crime.[41] It is in the operation of syndicated crime that relationships between crime and politics gain greatest significance.[42]

Protection.—Mobsters play politics primarily for personal profit. Conventional political ambitions doubtless on occasion motivate their political activity, but generally neither party loyalties nor political ideologies dilute their singleness of purpose. What they chiefly seek is protection, the right to proceed unhampered by the law. For protection they give, first and foremost, money, known among the cognoscente of Brooklyn gamblers as ice.[43] With their money they sometimes control

---

and of the phenomenon in general, see Reckless, *op. cit.*, pp. 382-404. Here is one estimate of annual expenditures on gambling (in billions of dollars): illegal bookmaking, 8; numbers (policies, lotteries), 6; slot machines, 3; pari-mutuel bets (at the tracks), 1.6; football and basketball pools, 1; and legally bet in Nevada, 1; for a total of 20.6. These figures do not include such things as bingo, car raffles, carnival gambling, local betting on the fights. Estimated by Murray Teigh Bloom in "Gambling: America's Ugly Child," *Pageant,* April, 1950, pp. 12 ff., cited in *ibid.*, p. 45.

41. Robert G. Caldwell, *Criminology* (New York: The Ronald Press Company, 1956), pp. 74-82. The term "rackets" has two common uses: to refer narrowly to extortion and to refer more broadly to any type of organized crime.—*Ibid.*, p. 78. One author labels "political graft and corruption" as one of four types of organized crime because of the importance of the "corrupt political organization" to the other types: organized criminal gangs, criminal syndicates, and racketeers.—Ruth Shonle Cavan, *Criminology* (2nd ed.; New York: Thomas Y. Crowell Company, 1955), p. 166.

42. A fair bit has become known about organized crime and politics, although what is known does not usually have the qualities of legal evidence—as many a district attorney has been aware. It nevertheless adds up to a body of information, albeit uneven, concerning the general verity of which most people who follow such things agree. The Kefauver Crime Committee published four reports plus 13,196 pages of testimony and exhibits taken in open and executive sessions. (Additional exhibits were not published.) The hearings appear in 19 "parts" comprising 21 volumes, all printed by the Government Printing Office, Washington, D.C. in 1950 and 1951. The Library of Congress prepared a 370-page index of proper names appearing in the first 14 volumes, which constitute about four-fifths of the testimony. A number of works for popular consumption have been written from the Kefauver Crime Committee materials, the best being that appearing under the Senator's own name—Estes Kefauver (ed. by Sidney Shalett), *Crime in America* (Garden City, New York: Doubleday & Company, Inc., 1951), 174 pp. See also Robert H. Prall and Norton Mockridge, *This Is Costello on the Spot* (3rd. ed.; Greenwich, Connecticut: Fawcett Publications, Inc., 1957), 189 pp.

43. The iceman hath come often in Brooklyn. The most notorious one, Harry Gross, paid $1,000,000 annually to police officers during 1947, 1948, and 1949.—Walter Arm, *Pay Off—The Inside Story of Big City Corruption* (New York: Appleton-Century-Crofts, Inc., 1951), pp. 31, 209, and *passim.*

campaign machinery and influence votes, and this becomes another means by which they compensate officials for their cooperation, or even elect to office one of their own number. But the source of it all is money. From the tax-free enterprises of the underworld criminals are likely to acquire large quantities of just that. They look upon payments for protection as a business expense that must be met like any other operating cost.[44] Willie Moretti explained a friend's residence behind bars: "He claims he has been running without protection here and there, and a man [who] pays protection can't get arrested, I don't think."[45]

The kinds of illegal activities for which organized criminals desire protection change from time to time.[46] During prohibition, bootlegging held the great opportunities for profit. Sub-governments grew up around this rich enterprise. Al Capone headed the most prominent, having in his employ not only large numbers of private enforcers of gang law, but a sizeable proportion of the legally constituted government of Chicago as well. With the repeal of prohibition, gambling in many forms rose in prominence, especially during the prosperity of the 1940's. Illegal sales of narcotics appeared to be of rising importance in the 1950's. The free funds of the underworld bought or muscled their way into legitimate enterprises, giving them a new kind of stake in the administration of government. (Mr. Moretti was in the linen-supply business.) Hookups between underworld figures and certain labor unions became publicized, particularly in the teamsters' union and on the docks.[47]

The investigative and enforcement powers of the federal government are limited by constitutional restraints. As a consequence, law enforcement in the United States is basically a state and local matter. Almost every jurisdiction has its own police force. This decentraliza-

44. Collusion between criminals and those supposed to enforce the law is no novelty in American life. Virgil W. Peterson reminds us of the iniquities of Chicago's early days, and of New York City's Mayor Fernando Wood who in the 1850's built a powerful machine in alliance with criminal elements.—*Barbarians in Our Midst—A History of Chicago Crime and Politics* (Boston: Little, Brown and Company, 1952), p. 324.

45. The Kefauver Crime Committee, *Hearings,* part 7, p. 345.

46. Concepts of crime vary from nation to nation as well as over time, with differing social conditions, technology, cultural values, and other factors that affect the enactment of criminal statutes.—See Albert Morris, "The Concept of Crime," in Vedder, Koenig, and Clark (eds.), *op. cit.,* pp. 20-29. See also Barnes and Teeters, *op. cit.,* Chapter 1, "The Revolution in the Nature of Crime," pp. 3-57.

47. See U.S. Senate Select Committee on Improper Activities in the Labor or Management Field (cited hereafter as the McClellan Labor-Managment Committee), *Interim Report* (Washington: Government Printing Office, 1958) (Senate Report No. 1417, 85th Congress, 2nd Session), e.g., pp. 37-40, 253-54, and the Committee's published *Hearings;* William J. Keating, *op. cit.;* and Allen Raymond, *Waterfront Priest* (New York: Henry Holt and Company, 1955), 269 pp. Other types of crime have fluctuated with the years. Prostitution, for example, is reported to have gone into eclipse, and white-collar crime has become a familiar concept.

tion has social and democratic values of great importance, yet it obstructs efforts to mobilize sustained, systematic, nationwide enforcement activity; more important, it enables criminal elements to bite off piecemeal the chunks of protection they need for specific operations. These operations vary with the market for them from community to community. Confusion is often found among local authorities, and each operates from a more or less narrow political base, both conditions that increase the ease with which protection can be bought. Patterns of politico-criminal relationships consequently vary from locality to locality, and from state to state.[48]

The structure of organized crime.—No one has been able to map in detail the structure of organized crime in the United States. Samuel S. Leibowitz, who became a judge of the County Court of Kings County, New York, after a career as a famous criminal lawyer, concluded that organized crime "covers the country like a blanket."[49] Virgil W. Peterson, long an FBI agent and known for his work as operating director of the Chicago Crime Commission, agrees: "In virtually every section of the country the underworld has become part and parcel of political organizations that rule over cities and sometimes states."[50] Mr. Peterson argues that "our ruling political class"—the ward committeemen and other politicians who make slates and pull strings—are opportunists who depend on the money and campaign workers obtainable from the underworld. Honest as well as dishonest officials come to office with their support.[51] The voluble Willie Moretti of New Jersey may have agreed with the continental sweep of these appraisals, for he exclaimed before the Senate Committee, "Jeez, everything is a racket today."[52]

The contention that organized crime diminished in the early 1950's[53] is at least debatable. The *kinds* of crime change, but knowledge of the volume of organized crime is at best uncertain. Anyone who reads the newspapers, however, knows it is spread through political jurisdictions across the land.[54] The Kefauver hearings dramatized underworld opera-

48. There are about 40,000 separate public law enforcement agencies on five levels of government.—Virgil W. Peterson, "Issues and Problems in Metropolitan Area Police Services," *Journal of Criminal Law, Criminology and Police Science,* 48 (1957), 127.

49. Kefauver Crime Committee, *Hearings,* part 12, p. 548.

50. Peterson, *Barbarians in Our Midst,* p. 322.

51. *Ibid.,* pp. 333, 327-28.

52. Kefauver Crime Committee, *Hearings,* part 7, p. 334.

53. Bell, *op. cit.*

54. Citizens' crime commissions were found in many cities in the late 1950's: Baltimore, Boston, Chicago, Dallas, Ft. Worth, Gary, Houston, Kansas City, Miami, New Orleans, Pueblo, Philadelphia, St. Louis, Tampa, Utica, Washington, D.C., Wichita, and Wilmington, Delaware. Reports and correspondence from several of these crime commissions proved informative about local crime conditions. There is even a National Association of Citizens' Crime Commissions. Citizens' crime commissions come and go. There was a substantial number in the

tions in small towns[55] and medium-sized cities[56] as well as in the great metropolitan centers. Other inquiries, like those of the New York State Crime Commission[57] and the Massachusetts Crime Commission,[58] have exposed relationships between law-breakers and enforcement officers, in small communities as well as large. The prevalence of these connections is not uniform in large urban centers, much less small ones, but they constitute a generally prevailing feature of American government.

How well underworld activities are integrated from one community to another has been the subject of much speculation and disagreement. The Kefauver Crime Committee clearly confirmed the existence of criminal syndicates in big cities, some of which operated over large areas of states and sections of the country. Lesser rings operate less conspicuously in many local areas. As to linkages among them, the Committee concluded that two major crime syndicates were in operation. One was headquartered in Chicago and identified with Tony Accardo, Jacob Guzik, and the brothers Fischetti. The other was based in New York and identified with Frank Costello, Joe Adonis, and the brothers Lansky. Evidence linked both of these groups to criminal activities in numerous localities across the nation, and some outside it.

The Committee concluded that the two major syndicates, plus other criminal groups, were bound together loosely in the Mafia organization. It was believed that the Mafia (deriving its name, code of conduct, and some of its members from an ancient Sicilian society of the same name) provided a mechanism of self-government for large sectors of the underworld,[59] including a way to divide up territories. Secrecy is a cardinal canon of the Mafia,[60] and much about the organization is

1920's but soon many ceased to operate. The Kefauver Crime Committee inspired another wave.—Caldwell, *op. cit.*, pp. 702-4.

55. For example, part 5, pp. 735-43, 1302-10.

56. *Final Report* (Washington: Government Printing Office, 1951) (Senate Report No. 725, 82nd Congress, 1st Session), p. 37.

57. There were four reports of modest length published in 1953 as Legislative Documents 23, 40, 68, and 70, and one in 1954 as Legislative Document 52. See especially the first and final reports.

58. *Report* (Massachusetts Senate, No. 700, April 1957), 402 pp. At one point, when the Commission was seeking a further legislative appropriation of between $50,000 and $100,000, the debate was heightened by the charge that the underworld had $200,000,000 in a Boston bank with which to battle the probe.—Edgar M. Mills, "Crime Issue Stirs Public," *The Christian Science Monitor*, September 14, 1955.

59. *Third Interim Report*, pp. 1-2, 144-50.

60. The underworld figures brought before the Kefauver Crime Committee generally clammed up. Willie Moretti was an exception who at one point brought laughter to the hearings by protesting, "I think I told you enough."—Part 7, p. 340. Mr. Moretti apparently understated the case. Less than a year later he was gunned to death in a New Jersey tavern, the reason assigned by crime reporters being his violation on this and other occasions of the Mafia's *Omerta*, or code of silence.—Ed Reid, *Mafia* (2nd ed.; New York: The New American Library of World Literature, 1958), pp. 30-35.

surmise. Evidence that organized criminal activities widely separated in geography are related to each other has nevertheless been found, often and over a period of many years.[61] The existence of a comprehensive communications network and some type of decision-making authority seems the only explanation.[62] The Mafia, in addition to what is verifiably known about it, has become a sort of grand hypothesis necessary for explaining a major phase of the nation's organized crime.[63]

The impact of organized crime on politics.—Ruthlessness, money, and capacity for some degree of coordinated action make underworld elements formidable adversaries of the nation's decentralized, highly various law-enforcement agencies. Given the penetration of underworld money into legitimate business[64] and the demonstrated ability of many criminals to defy the law successfully, some observers have proclaimed

61. The Massachusetts Crime Commission's 1957 *Report* denies the existence of a single, controlling syndicate, and discusses the "brotherhood" of organized crime. —pp. 42-46. It offers two maps showing intercity, intercounty, and interstate bookmaking connections.—p. 346. The annual report of operating director Daniel P. Sullivan to the Crime Commission of Greater Miami, May 21, 1953 (typescript), tells something of interstate activities emanating from Florida.

62. In November of 1957 police flushed some five dozen men who were gathered in a remote hilltop mansion at Apalachin, New York. Many of them turned out to be well known criminals, laden with cash but not guns, including Vito Genovese, alleged Mafia chief. Dope peddlers, bookies, racketeers of various descriptions, as well as some seemingly legitimate businessmen were included. The visitors came from many states of the Union, Puerto Rico, and Cuba, and police officials speculated that their purpose was to divide up the underworld empire of the late Albert Anastasia, crime syndicate leader murdered the month before.—*The Boston Daily Globe,* November 14, 15, 1957. The McClellan Labor-Management Committee heard testimony early in 1957 indicating the cohesiveness of the Apalachin group. Eric Sevareid stated over television on October 26, 1958, that one of four items on the Apalachin agenda was political contributions.

63. Reid, *op. cit.,* pp. 45-46 and *passim.* Like many paperbound books made for mass sales, this one rests on use of official documents. Mr. Reid, a journalist of considerable experience in reporting on the underworld, cites a number of episodes that illustrate the long reach of the Mafia, including some involving Vito Genovese, thought by Mr. Reid to be the leading Mafia figure in the United States. Most authorities doubt that the Mafia is as pervasive and powerful as pictured by Mr. Reid. The subject is one, however, on which the authorities are not likely to have conclusive data.—Reckless, *op. cit.,* pp. 200-2. Probably the best popular treatment of the Mafia is that by Frederic Sondern, Jr., *Brotherhood of Evil: The Mafia* (New York: Farrar, Straus and Cudahy, 1959), 243 pp. The tale of Lucky Luciano's cooperation with Naval Intelligence during World War II—a factor in his subsequent, much debated parole and deportation—indicates the hierarchical character of underworld relationships.—Sid Feder and Joachim Joesten, *The Luciano Story* (New York: David McKay Company, Inc., 1954), pp. 176-229. For the story told by a former district attorney in Brooklyn of the "ring of killers and extortionists that *is* organized crime in the United States . . . proved by data and record, of how this ring controls and operates, as big business, every racket, extortion and illegitimacy across the nation," see Burton B. Turkus and Sid Feder, *Murder, Inc.—The Story of "the Syndicate"* (New York: Farrar, Straus and Young, 1951), 498 pp.

64. The Kefauver Crime Committee's conclusions on this point appear in the *Third Interim Report,* pp. 170-81.

the danger to the nation's internal security greater from the underworld than from Communism. In restricted areas public officials have indeed labored under the general domination of underworld leaders, although governments are manned by many officials, and seldom are they all simultaneously and equally corruptible. Yet, in some areas, for a while, underworld leaders have achieved total protection. On occasion, the quality of persons elected to local, state, and federal offices has been seriously conditioned by the participation of criminals in politics. If underworld interests extended to a broad range of public policies, underworld politics would unquestionably be of continuing vital significance to the very existence of the form of government. Financial gain from illegal business operations, however, is the central goal of all organized crime. The political ambitions of the underworld focus on obtaining the administrative and legislative[65] protection necessary to pursue this goal and thereby limit their potential for wider public support and broader governmental power.

Underworld campaign funds.—The bonds between the underworld and politics are found in the wards and precincts. Important among these are campaign funds, the "most important" said the Massachusetts Crime Commission.[66] The volume of money supplied by underworld sources is a subject of universal curiosity. As usual, not the least of the difficulties lies in distinguishing between campaign gifts and other kinds of gifts.[67]

Bribery and graft paid to public officials should not be confused with campaign contributions. Many millions of dollars a year have been paid direct to law enforcement officials in return for protection, none of it cloaked as a political gift.[68] Campaign gifts to candidates,

65. "Despite the colossal crime problem facing the police and the public, not a single bill was passed by the 1957 Illinois State Legislature to remove any one of numerous obstacles confronting law enforcement agencies. . . . On the other hand, a bill was introduced and passed which specified that *all* police vehicles shall bear lettering at least three inches in height in a place easily seen. . . ."—Virgil W. Peterson, *A Report on Chicago Crime for 1957* (Chicago: Chicago Crime Commission, 1958), p. 34.

66. *Report,* p. 187.

67. John English of East St. Louis, Illinois, elected police commissioner, provided the Kefauver Crime Committee a clean illustration of the confusing ambiguity between bribes and campaign contributions. Mr. English stated that from 1943 to 1949 he had received $131,425 in "political contributions." These he had reported as personal income, however, and paid federal income tax thereon, a precaution taken on the advice of his auditor. He insisted he had used the funds for continuing campaign purposes, but the Committee noted that on a salary of $4,500 to $6,000 Mr. English had been able to acquire substantial business and real-estate assets and that simultaneously for many years the Police Commissioner's city had been wide open for gambling.—Kefauver, *op. cit.,* p. 95. The Sheriff of Dade County, Florida, in which Miami is located, was similarly found to have assumed possession of some $10,600 given him as contributions but "left over" after the campaign.—*Ibid.,* p. 62.

68. Judge Leibowitz guessed that in the city of New York alone $25,000,000 had been paid to venal members of the police department to protect the gambling

campaign committees, and party organizations—separate from personal bribery—also assume significant dimensions.[69] But how significant? Virgil W. Peterson was asked whether the Chicago Crime Commission possessed evidence of political contributions by the underworld. "You can't get evidence on that," was his response.[70] An investigator for the Kefauver Crime Committee searched lists of contributors to the 1948 Missouri gubernatorial campaign, in which underworld money was widely believed to have been important, and reported none "known to be that of a criminal or hoodlum or gangster or gambler or underworld character."[71] By its own estimate, nevertheless, the Kefauver Crime Committee accumulated "considerable evidence" concerning contributions to political campaigns by gamblers and gangsters.[72]

Some sense of the sums involved can be gained from scattered scraps of evidence, though no meaningful tabulations of contributions from underworld sources are possible. After immersion in the literature of the subject, a guess—and that is what it is—of 15 per cent of expenditures at state and local levels seems as good as any. Some underworld money is channelled through regular campaign machinery and in some areas may even be reported, cloaked or not as to source. Other sums are spent directly by underworld figures themselves. By the estimate

---

rackets. Kefauver Crime Committee, *Hearings,* part 12, p. 548. As for Chicago, see Aaron Kohn (ed.), *The Kohn Report—Crime and Politics in Chicago* (Chicago: The Independent Voters of Illinois, 1953), 122 pp.

69. To which type of recipient an underworld contribution is likely to be made would appear to depend on several factors. Where the party organization is a significant political force and has strong leadership willing to cooperate with underworld elements, donations to the party may be found. Gifts direct to candidates who, if elected, will be in a position to provide the desired protection would seem under most circumstances to be a better risk. The characteristics of the persons involved all along the line affect the channels chosen for contributions, many of which it must be assumed fail in their purposes.

70. Kefauver Crime Committee, *Hearings,* part 2, p. 200.

71. *Hearings,* part 4, p. 171. A sample of the names in the 370-page Index to the Kefauver *Hearings* was checked against the master file of 1952 contributions of $500 and over compiled from campaign reports. Between 2 and 3 per cent of the names in the index showed up in the file, many of them well known persons who happened to be mentioned in the testimony. Some contributors who appeared to be underworld characters were spotted, but the predilection of the underworld for aliases, monikers, and abbreviations made identification unsure.

72. *Third Interim Report,* p. 186. Specific instances, in addition to testimony about general practices, were identified. For example, one William Molasky gave $2,500 to the gubernatorial campaign in Missouri in hopes he could name a member of the St. Louis Police Board.—*Ibid.,* p. 186. Abe Allenberg told of "contributing" $2,500 to the Democratic national committee on March 31, 1947, for which he was given a receipt and letter of appreciation by George L. Killion, treasurer of the committee. The money came from the sale by Mr. Allenberg of ten tickets for a Democratic fund-raising dinner in Miami to Frank Erickson, opulent bookmaker's bookmaker who long showed a fondness for public appearances with public officials. —*Hearings,* part 1, pp. 119, 487, 734. Mr. Erickson's habit of turning up at political gatherings proved embarrassing to the personages with whom he liked to be seen. See Prall and Mockridge, *op. cit.,* pp. 100-16.

made, the sum in 1952 would have come to around $16,000,000.[73] Persons familiar with urban crime conditions may find the figure low. The difficulty of separating bribes from contributions necessarily lays any estimate open to argument.

It is well to remember, nevertheless, that the cumulative impact of the evidence concerning underworld campaign contributions may distort the conclusions reached by students of the subject. In community after community illustrations come to light of links between crime and politics. The observer, intent on not appearing naïve, projects from these situations to the whole nation. Although, occasionally, political pressures may be used to steer investigators away from troublespots, investigations customarily cast their searchlight where they believe something is wrong, not on a random sample of communities.

Underworld contributions are often large by any standard.[74] Yet the testimony concerning them often alleges campaign gifts that in the context may not be as significant as they initially seem. One or two well-known cases are worth comment. In the mid-1940's an organization known as the Continental Press Service enjoyed a virtual monopoly of the racing news industry in the United States. Through it was sold information essential for the operation of illegal bookmaking, gambling on horse races. The operations were so extensive, and so important as a source of bankroll for other criminal activities, that Senator Kefauver labeled Continental Press as America's Public Enemy Number One. James M. Ragen headed Continental when Capone interests sought to muscle in to gain control of the wire service. Ragen resisted and correctly predicted his own murder. Before he was killed, however, he gave information to FBI agents and filed a lengthy affidavit with the state's attorney.[75] He told the state's attorney that over a three-year period the wire service had paid $600,000 in political contributions,[76] presumably in the circumstances a reliable statement. How much territory was covered by this figure is not clear. Given the far reach of Continental's activities, however, if the average of $200,000 a year is anywhere near accurate it may in fact have been small compared with total campaign costs in the numerous localities among which it presumably would have been divided.

73. The guess embraces funds given in small towns and rural areas by individuals operating on the borders of the law who want a sympathetic sheriff and prosecutor, but who are not linked to crime syndicates. The estimate applies chiefly to persons engaged in illegal gambling and racketeering. It does not extend, for example, to otherwise reputable businessmen who hope for understanding treatment from buildings inspectors and tax assessors.

74. The Republican candidate for mayor of Chicago in 1954 reported an offer of $50,000, not accepted, from a racketeer who wanted protection—not from the law but from the syndicate that was invading his racket.—Robert E. Merriam and Rachel M. Goetz, *Going Into Politics* (New York: Harper and Brothers, 1957), pp. 39-40.

75. Kefauver, *op. cit.*, p. 31.

76. *Third Interim Report,* p. 184.

Forrest Smith's campaign for governor of Missouri in 1948 is usually cited to indicate underworld penetration into politics. It was rumored that Charles Binaggio gave as much as $150,000 to the Smith campaign. But the Kefauver Crime Committee, never reluctant to reach affirmative conclusions, reported that "the most diligent efforts of the committee's investigators failed to disclose any large-scale contributions by Binaggio or his associates."[77] Manifestly, through smaller gifts, direct expenditures, and organizational work, Binaggio and associates had a hand in Smith's success.[78] Yet no evidence was offered that the sums involved constituted a large share of total campaign costs.

Even when they do, other kinds of contributors may outrank the underworld. In the same year that Smith was elected in Missouri, Fuller Warren won the Democratic nomination for governor of Florida. William H. Johnston, a Chicago and Miami operator of dog-tracks and horse-tracks "with a long career of close association with Chicago racketeers of the Capone gang," provided the Warren campaign with $100,000. Of this sum, $40,000 came from Mr. Johnston's personal funds, $35,000 from his brother, and the rest from others. This money might be classified as from the underworld. It was a smaller sum, however, than made available through each of two other persons active for Mr. Warren. Both C. V. Griffin, a large citrus grower, and Louis Wolfson, organizer of a financial and industrial empire, testified they had been responsible for even larger amounts that reached the Warren campaign chest.[79]

Episodes similar to those in Missouri and Florida are well-publicized. They involve eye-catching sums. They do not seem to be representative of general practice, however, and are doubtless less significant than inconspicuous but more persistent patterns of contributing behavior that have existed elsewhere. Fragmentary information on many local situations indicates that underworld giving to politics indeed occurs in all parts of the country—in New Orleans[80] and Tampa,[81] in California[82] and Illinois,[83] in the city of New York, and elsewhere.[84] Yet contributions vary in their political importance. In one town in New York State, the numbers people regularly give money to officials of both parties. The leader of one of the parties claims to take nothing for himself, but he provides a list of charities to which the money is paid, which

77. *Third Interim Report*, p. 40. The Committee also concluded that "there is no substantial evidence that Governor Smith made any kind of commitment to Binaggio, or that Binaggio was successful in opening up the town."—*Ibid.*, p. 40.

78. See the summary in Kefauver, *op. cit.*, pp. 84-87.

79. *Ibid.*, pp. 64-65.

80. Kefauver, *op. cit.*, p. 100.

81. *Ibid.*, pp. 71-72.

82. Prall and Mockridge, *op. cit.*, pp. 167-68.

83. Kefauver, *op. cit.*, p. 56.

84. It was even said that in 1948 numbers operators in Washington, D.C., raised $100,000 to be spent against two senators who wanted to investigate local gambling.

includes his party organization. In contrast, Joe Adonis of Brooklyn built himself into a formidable criminal and political power in substantial part by investments in the careers of aspiring politicians.[85] "He staked many little politicians who later became big politicians."[86]

In New York City especially the penetration of underworld influence into party organization has been exposed. Not only did Adonis wield great power in Brooklyn, it has been clearly demonstrated that at one time during the 1940's Frank Costello had great influence—"complete domination," said the Kefauver Crime Committee—in the operations of Tammany Hall. He knew personally the Democratic leaders or co-leaders in 10 of the 16 Manhattan districts, some for 30 years or more. He knew Carmine DeSapio well. He seemingly directed the choice of Michael J. Kennedy as Tammany leader in 1942 and demonstrated his ability to control Democratic nominations in the famous case of Thomas Aurelio, nominated and elected to the state Supreme Court. Mr. Costello denied that he made campaign contributions,[87] but nobody believed him and there was evidence that he had.[88] He was a familiar figure around political circles and was referred to by some election district captains as "the boss."[89] An open enemy of Mr. Costello was William O'Dwyer, district attorney of King's County (Brooklyn) from 1940 to 1942 and mayor of New York from 1946 to 1950. Before the Kefauver Crime Committee, Mr. O'Dwyer protested certain accusations made against him. Nevertheless, the Committee concluded that many of his intimate friends were close friends of both Costello and Adonis. The Committee also concluded that during his tenure in both the posts mentioned, neither Mr. O'Dywer nor any of his appointees "took any effective action against the top echelons of the gambling, narcotics, water-front, murder, or bookmaking rackets. In fact, his actions impeded promising investigations of such rackets."[90]

85. Kefauver Crime Committee, *Third Interim Report,* p. 140.

86. Reid, *op. cit.,* p. 42.

87. For a summary of the Kefauver Crime Committee's views of Costello's political affairs, see *Third Interim Report,* pp. 121-24.

88. New York State Crime Commission, *Second Report,* p. 11. On Costello more generally, and the context of his operations, see pp. 9-22.

89. *Ibid.,* p. 9.

90. *Third Interim Report,* p. 144. Other New York mayors have been charged with underworld connections, including in recent times Vincent Impellitteri.—Reid, *op. cit.,* p. 41; Keating, *op. cit.,* p. 220. For an earlier picture, see Craig Thompson and Allen Raymond, *Gang Rule in New York—The Story of a Lawless Era* (New York: Dial Press, 1940).

One interpretation has it that reforms in the LaGuardia administration, and the aloof attitudes of the national and state administrations, cut off some of the patronage and financial support customarily depended upon by Tammany Hall. The resulting vacuum was eagerly filled by underworld funds.

Campaign money must come from somewhere, and if the good people will not supply it the bad ones will. Before World War II, Japanese parties depended heavily on the *zaibatsu.* When the *zaibatsu* underwent liquidation after the surrender as part of the Occupation policy to deconcentrate economic power, the

In Chicago, as in New York, there has been no haziness about the existence of connections between the underworld and political party officers. The Emergency Crime Committee of the Chicago City Council in the early 1950's received sure evidence of established patterns of payments to ward committeemen by operators of gambling joints, taverns, and other activities requiring protection. Not only the policeman on the beat and his superiors, but the party organization behind the aldermen on the City Council received pay-offs.[91] And outspoken representatives of the underworld—notably Republican James J. Adducci—were elected to the legislature of Illinois where they watched over the interests of their constituents, and successfully opposed anti-crime legislation. Representative Adducci, who had been arrested a number of times in company with members of the Capone gang, acknowledged receiving campaign gifts from a well-known member of that gang. He explained that in his district it was necessary to accept finances "from any kind of business."[92]

A component of power structure.—Students of power structures and power elites in the United States have not normally embraced the underworld in their analytical models nor in their empirical descriptions. Yet the lives and economic welfare of millions of Americans are directly affected by the actions of organized criminals. Goods and services and people are ordered about on a large scale. And like other power groups in the society, underworld elements seek to influence government when and where their interests require it. As elsewhere in society, in the underworld money is only one tool of social force. Violence, the power of intimidation, conventional economic power, and conventional political activities are other sources of influence and control. Like other interest groups in society, organized criminals use the weapons of social action most available to them and most effective. Organized criminal groups can be conceived of as a special type—or set of types—of economic interest groups. Like other groups, they are limited by many restraints in achieving their goals, including a mass of statutes and the people who try to enforce them. Like other groups, they sometimes succeed in their purpose and often they fail.

Although illegal activities needing protection are found in most parts of the nation, individuals and groups getting protection do not necessarily dominate the party organizations, much less the general political life, of their areas. Their aims are generally narrow, the officials of concern to them are few, and the factors affecting electoral success are many. The occasions when organized criminal elements control the general politics of an area are rare. For every Louisiana parish run by

parties were forced to look for new sources of political money. They naturally turned to the post-war rich, including black-marketeers.—Chitoshi Yanaga, *Japanese People and Politics* (New York: John Wiley & Sons, Inc., 1956), pp. 258-60.

91. Kohn (ed.), *op. cit.*, pp. 9-10, 32-33, 46, 53, 84, 117-18.

92. Kefauver Crime Committee, *Third Interim Report*, p. 59.

a gambling czar in public office, there are scores of counties where political competition is genuine. New York City embraces the Bronx as well as Manhattan and Brooklyn, and no one can properly accuse Boss Edward J. Flynn of having been a tool of the underworld.[93] It was still possible for a political party in New York to nominate and for the voters of New York to elect Robert F. Wagner, Herbert H. Lehman, and Irving M. Ives to the United States Senate during the period of underworld political penetration publicized by the Kefauver Crime Committee. Thomas E. Dewey did not climb to fame as a champion of racketeers, and he was chosen governor of New York repeatedly in the same period. From Illinois, upstate and downstate the site of illegal underworld activity, Paul H. Douglas could be sent to the United States Senate and Adlai E. Stevenson to the governor's mansion. At menial political levels underworld influence may be great. But the underworld is like the world of legitimate business, made up of many competing parts, all of which, separately or together, comprise but one set of forces playing in the nominating and election processes. For a while in some places they may dominate, as do other interests, but their control is neither all encompassing nor permanent.

93. Mr. Flynn states that when he became chairman of the Bronx County Democratic executive committee various party leaders suggested to him that "there were many gangsters who would be able to help illegally in elections." He reports that he decided the "payoff" would be too great and that he did not want gangsters in the Bronx anyway. Although some of its people were implicated, the Bronx organization came off relatively well in the Seabury investigation of the early 1930's.—Edward J. Flynn, *You're the Boss* (New York: The Viking Press, 1947), pp. 61-62. Doubtless Mr. Flynn's tasks of leadership were simplified by the support he received from Roosevelt as president and Lehman as governor.

7

LABOR MONEY IN CAMPAIGNS

THE CONSTITUTION of the United Steelworkers of America lists as one of three chief purposes of that organization: "To secure legislation safeguarding the economic and social welfare of the workers in the industry, to protect and extend our democratic institutions and civil rights and liberties and thus to perpetuate the cherished traditions of our democracy." The Steelworkers long ago learned, in the words of its secretary-treasurer, that "the achievement of the legislative goals and enforcement of the democratic rights" envisioned by their constitution "is inextricably intertwined with the election of liberal legislators and executives."[1]

Like organized business interests before them, large sectors of organized labor have found themselves thrust into election campaigning. The 1936 elections saw an eruption of financial activity by organized labor. Reported political expenditures by interstate labor organizations ran to over $750,000. This exceeded by eight times the sum raised by the American Federation of Labor for political purposes during the previous 30 years.[2] Labor dove into active campaigning and into campaign contributing on behalf of Democratic candidates. The move provoked a fierce howl that clearly marked 1936 as a watershed year in the political alignment of social and economic interests.

Like the political rivals of corporations, the political rivals of labor have sought to shackle their opponent's ability to campaign effectively. As always, what constitutes campaigning is difficult to define. Civic action is ultimately indivisible; anything done ultimately points in some partisan direction, intended or not. It is an arbitrary decision to choose the point along the continuum of partisanship where what is done is no longer called campaigning, the rest being termed civic education

1. McClellan Lobby Committee, *Hearings,* p. 987. Other unions, and the constitution of the AFL-CIO, proclaim similar objectives.

2. Louise Overacker, "Labor's Political Contributions," *Political Science Quarterly,* 54 (1939), 56-57.

or merely the exercise of good citizenship. Where one man places the divider stems inevitably from his view of politics, and that in turn from his circumstances and interests. Nowhere else is the inherent partisan character of *all* politically related action made more evident than in the controversies surrounding labor in politics and the efforts to regulate it.

The discussion is further confounded by constitutional ambiguities. The United States Constitution and its amendments guarantee the right of individuals to engage in a wide range of activities through which partisanship is expressed and political campaigns are waged. When legislators and others seek to limit partisan campaigning, they proceed under a shade of doubt. At the beginning of 1960, the Supreme Court had not yet found it necessary to rule on the constitutionality of existing prohibitions against labor political action.[3] The most articulate union leader on matters of politics, Walter Reuther of the United Automobile Workers, claims for unions and for corporations the right to spend money to express their *own* points of view without restriction. The right would not embrace paying for a candidate's or party's opportunity to express *its* point of view, but Mr. Reuther would place virtually no restraint on the right of organized labor to campaign so long as it campaigned in its own name.[4]

Labor in politics is a hot stereotype, like Texas oil money. Conclusions are circulated without regard for differences among labor organizations and in the nature and extent of their political activities. Refined distinctions do not make good polemics. To grasp the impact and potential of labor in politics, however, the structure of the labor movement and the distribution of its members throughout the country must be understood. The types of politically relevant activities of labor organizations need also to be delineated, and the channels through which disbursements are made. Then some assessment of labor's full financial role in politics may be attempted.

1. THE ORGANIZATION OF UNION LABOR: DIVIDED, DISPERSED, DIVERSE

At the end of 1955, the American Federation of Labor and the Congress of Industrial Organizations formally merged. The action was greeted by dire warnings against the political power of the new monster. It has long been a tactic of politicians lacking labor support to paint its political potential in exaggerated colors, an undertaking joined in gladly by many labor leaders themselves. The organizational structure, political activities, and partisan preferences of American unionism, however, are highly diverse and disunited phenomena.

While labor leadership generally leaned Democratic in the quarter century following Franklin Roosevelt's first election as president, rank-

3. See Eugene H. Ruark, Jr., "Labor's Political Spending and Free Speech," *Northwestern University Law Review*, 53 (1958-59), 61-77.

4. See the *Proposal of United Automobile Workers for a Five-Dollar Ceiling on Political Contributions* (July, 1956), pp. 17-18.

and-file union members were sharply divided during the 1950's in their presidential politics. The nationwide studies of the University of Michigan's Survey Research Center showed that in union families the percentage voting for the Democratic presidential candidate fell from 81 in 1948 to 56 in 1952 and to 52 in 1956.[5] Even among members of the United Automobile Workers in Detroit, whose union has traditionally fostered a vigorous pro-Democratic political action program, about one-fourth of those voting in 1952 chose Eisenhower.[6] Political attitudes and energies vary greatly among union members. There are also sharp differences among union organizations in their size and in their politically relevant activities.

The architecture of union organization.—In 1956, there were some 189 American national and international unions comprised of about 77,000 locals and 18,477,000 members, of whom approximately 17,385,000 were living in the continental United States.[7] The latter constituted 25 per cent of the total United States labor force and 34 per cent of employment in nonagricultural establishments. Although union membership in the 1950's grew only slightly compared with the total working force, in 1933 these percentages had been 5 and 11.5, respectively, and the total membership of all unions then was only 2,857,000. Some 3,191,000 of the 1956 members were in unions then or later not affiliated with the AFL-CIO, the largest of these being the Teamsters, expelled from the CIO-AFL in 1957. From their members in 1958, unions collected upwards of $600,000,000 in dues.[8]

The numerical strength of organized labor is concentrated in about a dozen unions, the largest of which in 1956 (with their pre-merger affiliation) were:

	Number of	
	Members	*Locals*
Brotherhood of Teamsters—(AFL) Independent	1,368,082	893
United Automobile Workers—CIO	1,320,513	1,255
United Steelworkers—CIO	1,250,000	2,800
International Association of Machinists—AFL	949,683	2,076
Brotherhood of Carpenters—AFL	850,000	3,000
Brotherhood of Electrical Workers—AFL	675,000	1,720
United Mine Workers—Independent	600,000	(9)

5. These percentages are based on responses by individuals living in a family the head of which is a union member.

6. Arthur Kornhauser, Harold L. Sheppard, and Albert J. Mayer, *When Labor Votes—A Study of Auto Workers* (New York: University Books, 1956), pp. 31-32. This study was also based on a sample survey and enjoyed the cooperation of the Survey Research Center.

7. Most information for 1956 comes from U.S. Bureau of Labor Statistics, *Directory of National and International Labor Unions in the United States, 1957* (Washington: Government Printing Office, 1957). Small numbers of persons in noninterstate, independent, or unaffiliated unions are not included in most tabulations.

8. A sum somewhat smaller than the annual profits-after-taxes of General Motors.

International Hod Carriers—AFL	465,923	956
International Ladies' Garment Workers—AFL	450,802	533
Hotel and Restaurant Employees—AFL	441,000	602
Electrical, Radio and Machine Workers—CIO	397,412	457
Amalgamated Clothing Workers—CIO	385,000	639
	9,153,415	14,931[9]

Roughly half of all union membership is found in these 12 unions. A dozen others with 200,000 or more members accounted for over 3,000,000 additional adherents.

The political vitality of organized labor is rooted in the attitudes and actions of individual unions. Although in 1956 the Committee on Political Education of the combined AFL-CIO became the major political arm of the labor movement, COPE itself is dependent on the support and cooperation of member unions. These and other unions vary considerably from one to another in political activity. While the greatest financial and political *potential* lies with the largest unions, there are unions not in the list of 12 that swing far more weight than some that are, such as the Textile Workers Union of America (CIO) (202,700 members, 711 locals) and the Communications Workers of America (CIO) (259,000 members, 737 locals). In addition, the buildings trades unions often act in concert, as do the railroad unions (through the Railway Labor Political League), a fact that has often given them greater cohesion and made them politically more important than some of the larger individual unions. The Auto Workers, the Steelworkers, and the Amalgamated Clothing Workers—all affiliated with the AFL-CIO—have a long heritage of political action stemming from the early days of the CIO. Each in fact has a political action organization of its own which, although it works through COPE, may also at times make expenditures and contributions in its own name. The Machinists, the Electrical, Radio and Machine Workers, and the International Ladies' Garment Workers' Union, the latter one of the most highly involved of all unions in politics, have their own organizations that do not work through COPE.[10] Comparatively, the Hotel and Restaurant Employees are inconspicuous in political campaigns, although, like all major unions, they show concern in legislative matters touching their interests. The Carpenters, the Hod Carriers, the Brotherhood of Electrical Workers, and the Teamsters have not had formal political action organizations

9. Number of United Mine Workers locals not reported and not included in this total. Membership of the Mine Workers is taken from *The World Almanac, 1957* (New York: The New York World-Telegram and the Sun, 1957), p. 90.

10. True also of the Glass Bottle Blowers Association (AFL) (51,650 members, 239 locals) and the Retail Clerks International Association (AFL) (300,000 members, 400 locals). Henry Zon, Director of Research, COPE, provided information on several of these points.—Letter to author dated August 5, 1959.

established at the top,[11] but these may appear at lower levels, and some locals and members may be extremely active politically. All of these unions have at one time been allied in the AFL-CIO, and generally the CIO organizations among them have been the most active in political campaigning.[12] The independent United Mine Workers, once the backbone of the CIO and once the largest political contributor among unions, operates through an organization of its own, Labor's Non-Partisan League. The League makes campaign expenditures, but unlike the other separate political action groups denies that it makes contributions to candidates or their committees.

The geography of union membership.—Just as union membership is unevenly distributed among unions, it is unevenly distributed among the states.[13] Table 20 sets forth basic information on the numerical strength of union membership in each state. The first column gives 1953 union membership and the second shows the percentage increase this was over 1939 membership. The third column reports the percentage of nonagricultural employment organized into unions in 1953, and the last column shows the percentage of the voting-age population belonging to unions in 1953. The third and fourth columns afford some idea of the present and potential electoral strength of union membership. Persons of voting age who were members of *union families* naturally exceeded the 17 per cent represented by union members in the country as a whole. Not all members of union families voted—nor were all union members of voting age—but in 1948 and 1952 they seemed to do so at a slightly higher rate than the rest of the population.[14]

Sixty-seven per cent of union members were concentrated in 10 states. Another 10 per cent were located in seven additional states, thus placing approximately three-fourths of union members in approximately

11. In 1959, Teamster President James R. Hoffa announced plans to set up a national political organization within his union to campaign against unfriendly lawmakers in 1960. Teamster leaders were said to believe they could raise $9,000,000 for the purpose.—*Wall Street Journal,* July 21, 1959.

12. The higher level of political activity in the CIO is indicated, for example, by the finding that among comparable groups of CIO and AFL men, 25 per cent of the former and 15 per cent of the latter met a definition of active political participant.—William H. Riker, "The CIO in Politics, 1936-1946" (Ph.D. dissertation, Harvard University, 1948), pp. 158-59.

13. For many years it was impossible to get usable estimates of union membership by states, but information has now been compiled for 1939 and 1953. See the valuable study by Leo Troy, *Distribution of Union Membership among the States 1939 and 1953* (New York: National Bureau of Economic Research, Inc., 1957), Occasional Paper 56, 32 pp. As the author observes, "statistics of union membership have never met exacting standards."

14. In 1948, 23 per cent, and in 1952, 26 per cent, of respondents in studies by the Survey Research Center came from families headed by a labor union member. In 1948, 73 per cent of these voted, as compared with 62 per cent of others; in 1952 the respective percentages were 77 and 73.—Angus Campbell, Gerald Gurin, and Warren E. Miller, *The Voter Decides* (Evanston: Row, Peterson and Company, 1954), p. 75.

Table 20

LABOR UNION MEMBERSHIP, GROWTH, AND PERCENTAGE OF VOTING POPULATION: BY STATES, 1953[a]

State	Union Membership (in thousands)	Percentage Increase 1939-1953	Per Cent of Nonagricultural Employment Organized	Union Membership as Percentage of Population of Voting Age
Alabama	168.3	163	25	10
Arizona	55.7	257	28	12
Arkansas	67.9	172	22	6
California	1,392.5	228	36	18
Colorado	114.2	184	28	14
Connecticut	232.1	267	27	17
Delaware	25.8	345	18	12
Florida	135.9	212	16	7
Georgia	135.8	280	15	6
Idaho	29.1	153	22	9
Illinois	1,358.7	130	40	23
Indiana	569.6	222	40	22
Iowa	159.2	115	25	9
Kansas	130.8	233	24	11
Kentucky	155.1	83	25	9
Louisiana	135.8	259	20	8
Maine	58.9	288	21	11
Maryland	203.6	248	25	13
Massachusetts	546.1	161	30	18
Michigan	1,062.0	295	43	25
Minnesota	327.6	145	38	17
Mississippi	50.0	285	15	4
Missouri	510.5	184	40	19
Montana	72.5	82	47	20
Nebraska	68.6	153	20	8
Nevada	21.8	246	30	19
New Hampshire	43.1	307	25	12
New Jersey	645.4	222	35	19
New Mexico	25.0	184	14	7
New York	2,051.8	114	34	20
North Carolina	83.8	226	8	4
North Dakota	17.3	119	16	5
Ohio	1,162.6	171	38	22
Oklahoma	86.7	157	16	7
Oregon	201.5	160	43	20
Pennsylvania	1,540.7	109	40	22
Rhode Island	82.8	235	27	16
South Carolina	49.7	307	9	4
South Dakota	17.4	185	14	4
Tennessee	187.3	164	23	9
Texas	374.8	239	17	8
Utah	56.9	167	26	14
Vermont	19.6	131	19	8
Virginia	156.1	128	17	8
Washington	393.6	125	53	26
West Virginia	223.9	46	44	19
Wisconsin	418.7	116	38	19
Wyoming	24.2	68	29	14
District of Columbia	107.8	52	21	..
Not distributed by state	458.5	...	..	..
United States	16,217.3	149	33	17

[a] All data except the last column come from Leo Troy, *Distribution of Union Membership Among the States 1939 and 1953* (New York: National Bureau of Economic Research, Inc., 1957), Occasional Paper 56. The last column was computed, using the state estimates of 1952 population of voting age appearing in U.S. Bureau of the Census, *Statistical Abstract of the United States: 1957* (Washington: Government Printing Office, 1957), p. 351.

one-third of the states. These 17 states were the only ones in which the percentage of union members among persons of voting age matched or exceeded the national percentage and in which at the same time the percentage of nonagricultural employees organized equalled 30 or more. The financial resources and voting strength of organized labor were therefore concentrated in these two groups of states:[15]

	Union Members, 1953		
	Number	*% of Voting-Age Population*	*% of Nonagricultural Employees*
New York	2,051,800	20	34
Pennsylvania	1,540,700	22	40
California	1,392,500	18	36
Illinois	1,358,700	23	40
Ohio	1,162,600	22	38
Michigan	1,062,000	25	43
New Jersey	645,400	19	35
Indiana	569,600	22	40
Massachusetts	546,100	18	30
Missouri	510,500	19	40
Total (10)	10,839,900	—	—
Wisconsin	418,700	19	38
Washington	393,600	26	53
Minnesota	327,600	17	38
West Virginia	223,900	19	44
Oregon	201,500	20	43
Montana	72,500	20	47
Nevada	21,800	19	30
Total (7)	1,659,600	—	—

The composition of union membership within individual states varied considerably, with consequent political implications. For example, the United Automobile Workers embraced 55 per cent of union membership in Michigan and the United Mine Workers more than 50 per cent in West Virginia. The Auto Workers and the United Steelworkers combined held 35 per cent of union membership in Indiana and 30 per cent in Ohio. In Pennsylvania, the Steelworkers, Mine Workers, and the Teamsters together came to around 40 per cent of state membership, and in California something over a third were centered in the Teamsters, Machinists,

15. The first group contains the 10 states with the largest number of union members. The second group consists of the seven remaining states in which the percentage of voting-age population who were union members equalled 17 or more *and* the percentage of nonagricultural employees who were union members equalled 30 or more.

and Carpenters.[16] Elsewhere, union membership was usually more widely diffused among separate, and sometimes competing, union organizations.

Varieties of political action.—Labor political action displays many forms and degrees of intensity. In parts of southern California, New York, and Chicago, for example, it has resembled that of a political party, with many campaign functions performed under the aegis of organized labor on behalf of a defaulting Democratic party. In Michigan, political factions within the labor movement have fought for control of the Democratic party and through it have achieved a measure of political dominance in the state.[17] In other locations, labor campaign efforts have been supplementary to those of party structures. In some places, little electioneering of any kind has been undertaken, and labor efforts have been confined to conventional lobbying.[18]

What has been attempted and accomplished has depended among other things on the personalities and attitudes of labor leaders and on the diverse traditions, objectives, and circumstances of individual trade unions. The American labor movement is a highly complex social phenomenon with myriads of dissimilar features at lower levels. These diversities are multiplied in the alliances and organizational arrangements improvised for political purposes within organized labor and between labor organizations and other political groups.[19]

The main outlines of organized labor's financial role in politics can be laid down, but within the general patterns are many variations.

Generally, three types of labor-union organizations may be active in politics, and they may be found at three political levels.

First are the trade unions themselves. They are organized as locals. The locals are customarily linked together as a national or international union, with those within a limited geographical area frequently being joined in an intermediate-level organization. The affiliated units that make up an international union are generally autonomous, although the degree varies much from one union to another, and in recent years has tended to decline in most. In the building trades, for example,

16. Troy, *op. cit.*, pp. 14-15.

17. For the narrative of internal dissensions within both parties in Michigan, see Stephen B. and Vera H. Sarasohn, *Political Party Patterns in Michigan* (Detroit: Wayne State University Press, 1957), 76 pp. An increasing closeness between the CIO-Political Action Committee in the Detroit area and the Democratic party and the effects of this on the Republicans are discussed in N. A. Masters, "The Politics of Union Endorsement of Candidates in the Detroit Area," *Midwest Journal of Political Science,* 2 (1957), 136-50.

18. Fay Calkins presents five interesting case studies of different types of labor political activity in *The CIO and the Democratic Party* (Chicago: University of Chicago Press, 1952), 162 pp.

19. For the detailed description of affairs in one state, see Joseph LeVow Steinberg, "Labor in Massachusetts Politics—The Internal Organization of the CIO and AFL for Political Action, 1948-1955," (Senior honors thesis, Harvard University, 1956).

the locals enjoy great autonomy. Among the coal miners, on the other hand, who work in an industry operated on a national basis, the top leadership exerts substantial control over the locals, particularly in such matters as strike calls and the making of agreements.[20]

Second, many unions are associated in a relatively loose federation, the AFL-CIO, which provides the major organizational framework for the American labor movement. In addition to the international unions, a sizeable number of locals not associated with internationals are affiliated directly with the AFL-CIO. The presence of these separate organizations contributes to diverse political activities. The differing origins of AFL and of CIO unions likewise do so. The antecedent organization of the AFL developed in the 1880's. The AFL has been composed traditionally of horizontally organized unions of individuals skilled in the same craft, like carpentry. The antecedent of the Congress of Industrial Organizations developed in the 1930's, its archetype being a union organized vertically throughout an entire industry, like steel. While all international unions within the AFL-CIO display considerable independence, the CIO historically has tended to exert more authority over its affiliated unions than the AFL. At state and local levels there are "central" bodies in which AFL-CIO unions at those levels may be associated.

The third relevant type of labor organization is the political league or political action committee. These are separately organized but originate and operate under the aegis of groups of the two previous types.

In each of these three types of organization, units may be active at local levels (in Congressional districts, in cities, and in more restricted areas), at the state level, and at the nationwide, or federal, level.

Thus, the basic unit of the labor movement is the union local. Many of these are joined in international unions. Many locals and internationals are affiliated with the AFL-CIO at local, state, and national levels. Attached to many of these union organizations at all levels is an array of political committees. In all of the politically relevant relationships, variety rather than uniformity marks the patterns of political action.

Varieties of labor political money.—Four types of labor money that flow through these organizational patterns have significance in the nomination and election of public officials. (1) The so-called *free funds* come from voluntary contributions by union members and others. These monies may be donated to candidates and spent without regard to legal restrictions on the use of funds derived from dues. (2) *Nonfederal contributions,* that is, contributions from union treasuries (dues money) on behalf of candidates for nonfederal offices, are permitted in

20. George Kozmetsky, *Financial Reports of Labor Unions* (Boston: Graduate School of Business Administration, Harvard University, 1950), pp. 16-18.

most states.[21] (3) Unions themselves use dues money for what their leaders call *educational expenditures.* In their external purposes at least, these are intended (a) to inform union members about the candidates and issues on which they may vote,[22] and (b) to encourage them to register and vote. Many of these union-financed activities are indistinguishable from get-out-the-vote drives, for example, of nonpartisan organizations; others are indistinguishable from the campaign activities of party organizations, though no gifts to candidates or their campaign committees are included. (4) Finally, expenditures are made from union dues for what are sometimes called *public service* activities, such as radio news programs, which may have, like other such programs, a partisan slant in their net impact.

2. THE STRUCTURE OF LABOR POLITICAL ACTIVITY

Unlike their counterparts in Great Britain and many other nations, American trade unions have not organized a separate political party of their own. Even the Liberal party in New York, the only one of its kind, functions more like a pressure group than a full-fledged independent party.[23] There are obstacles to the formation of any new party, but additional factors such as the diversity and social mobility of the labor force have historically led most labor organizations to seek political goals through the established parties.[24]

The political invigoration of labor occurred during the New Deal in the form of active collaboration with the Democratic party. Working alliances developed at the national level and in many states and localities, and labor's financial and other campaign resources helped to reduce the imbalance between Republicans and Democrats. Some labor leaders acquired an influential role inside the Democratic party. The intimacy of the liaison varied from state to state and union to union, and everywhere labor's spokesmen held to a cardinal dictum: labor's interest in all candidates and parties is solely utilitarian. Can they help in achieving labor's social, economic, and political goals?[25]

21. In all but four in 1959, the year in which Wisconsin's Catlin law banning union political donations was repealed.

22. The United Auto Workers claim, further, the right to inform not just union members, but the public as well.

23. Gus Tyler, *A New Philosophy for Labor* (New York: The Fund for the Republic, 1959), p. 7. By naming to its own ticket candidates nominated by the Democratic and Republican parties, the Liberal party provides a means by which the preferred candidates from the other parties can be voted for on a straight ticket.

Off and on throughout their history, unions have made donations to political parties. Even during the period of AFL political aloofness individual unions gave modest sums to such as the Socialist and Farmer-Labor parties.—Louise Overacker, "Labor Rides the Political Waves," *Current History,* 7 (1944), p. 468.

24. For a discussion of factors discouraging the formation of a labor party, see Avery Leiserson, "Organized Labor as a Pressure Group," *The Annals,* 274 (1951), 108-17.

25. The following was said of the 1956 elections: "In dozens of states and districts

Other organized interests adopt similar attitudes, but the political activities of labor tend to be more conspicuous. True, few large campaign gifts are made in the names of individual labor leaders.[26] But special political committees are formed, and union organizations themselves possess considerable campaign potential. In explicitness of purpose and openness of action, the operations of these groups are often more visible than the political exertions of other social interests that proceed covertly, or through individuals working conventionally within party organizations. To raise meaningful sums by solicitation of voluntary contributions itself entails publicity. Given the political predilections of many editors, any systematic political activity by labor organizations is not likely to go unnoticed.

Most of the free funds raised by solicitation from union members is spent, especially at state and national levels, through the special political committees. Some dues money, however, is also transferred to these political action organizations, though more is spent directly by unions themselves. Estimates of the volume of free money raised are offered later, and the numerous types of campaign-connected expenditures made directly from union treasuries are explored. The full financial involvement of labor organizations and their members in nomination and election campaigns—which manifestly must be counted in millions of dollars each election year—cannot be fixed precisely, which is true also for corporate and other groups. To do so literally would require a dollar value for every type of influence and energy that bears on the choice of candidates and elected officials. It is possible, nevertheless, to identify some of the outlines of labor's special campaign organizations and of the money spent through them and otherwise. In doing so, the complex and varied character of labor's financial involvement in politics becomes evident.

The national level.—The gross receipts and disbursements of national labor political committees that submitted reports to the Clerk of the United States House of Representatives are shown in Table 21 for 1952, 1954, 1956, and 1958. These are the committees that were associated with the headquarters of international unions and the AFL and

---

local union leaders felt there was no significant difference between candidates and declined to give either nominee an endorsement or active support."—*AFL-CIO News,* November 10, 1956, quoted in Labor Research Association, *Labor Fact Book* (New York: International Publishers), 13 (1957), p. 146.

26. The names of over 2,000 officials of national and international unions, national political action and education committees, and state labor councils, federations of labor, and industrial union councils were checked against the file of 8,100 persons known to have made gifts of $500 or larger in 1956. Eighteen were found; all reported as giving to Democrats ($17,750) and two also to Republicans ($2,500). —Derived from Gore Committee *Report,* Exs. 13 and 26. The officials were transmitting agents, and in no instances were the contributions personal ones.—Letter to author from Henry Zon, Director of Research, COPE, dated August 5, 1959.

Table 21

CONTINUING LABOR POLITICAL COMMITTEES, NATIONAL LEVEL: GROSS RECEIPTS AND DISBURSEMENTS, 1952, 1954, 1956, AND 1958[a]

Committee	1952		1954		1956		1958	
	Receipts	Disbursements	Receipts	Disbursements	Receipts	Disbursements	Receipts	Disbursements
(1) AFL—Labor's League for Political Education	$ 252,003	$ 249,258	$ 389,573	$ 485,082	$ 35,699	$ 148,080	(b)	(b)
(2) CIO-Political Action Committee—Individual Contributions Account	418,789	505,722	351,887	415,042	6,020	23,220	(b)	(b)
(3) —Educational Account	354,731	433,259	329,124	339,992	6,361	8,134	(b)	(b)
(4) AFL-CIO—Committee on Political Education—Individual Contributions Fund	(b)	(b)	(b)	(b)	708,937	670,985	589,225	709,813
(5) Amalgamated Political Action Committee (of Amalgamated Clothing Workers)	46,414	43,125	28,687	18,143	69,653	64,608	39,708	44,715
(6) Hat, Cap, and Millinery Workers Campaign Committee	14,893	13,767	4,309	4,000	9,575	5,454	(c)	(c)
(7) International Ladies' Garment Workers' Campaign Committee[d]	395,289	265,345	179,039	44,827	273,174	149,521	267,402	107,716
(8) Machinists Non-Partisan Political League—Educational Fund	23,755	20,762	43,912	37,133	76,507	55,152	74,647	70,459
(9) — General Fund	(c)	(c)	50,877	43,445	(c)	(c)	50,202	79,727

(10) Railway Labor's Political League	95,388	88,644	86,003	82,940	102,527	104,470	77,271	78,801
(11) Textile Workers Union of America Political Education Fund	7,969	14,480	5,869	6,039	30,533	21,000	26,636	35,063
(12) Trainmen's Political Education League	14,700	13,698	14,211	12,833	13,236	9,701	14,463	14,305
(13) United Automobile Workers CIO-PAC	170,027	135,013	200,827	255,175	161,499	245,137	199,131[e]	243,790[e]
(14) United Brotherhood of Carpenters Nonpartisan Committee	50,014[f]	34,549[f]						
(15) United Steelworkers of America Political Action Fund—Individual Contributions Account	(c)	(c)	128,863	185,004	130,088	184,835	169,584	192,136
Gross Totals[g]	1,843,972[g]	1,817,622[g]	1,813,181[g]	1,929,655[g]	1,623,809[g]	1,690,297[g]	1,508,269[g]	1,576,525[g]

[a] From reports filed with the Clerk of the U.S. House of Representatives. Generally, receipts include cash on hand at beginning of year. Deficits are made up by between-elections income. 1954, 1956, and 1958 data were taken from *Congressional Quarterly*, 13 (1955), 378; 15 (1957), 513; 17 (1959), 511. ILGWU 1954 figures were supplied by the Union.

One or two national-level committees that reported tiny sums in one year only are not included. Four organizations not included in the table submitted reports to the Gore Committee covering September 1—November 30, 1956, showing receipts and total disbursements, respectively, as follows: United Rubber, Cork, Linoleum and Plastic Workers of America (AFL-CIO), $4,133, $4,133; Oil, Chemical and Atomic Workers International Union (AFL-CIO), $2,135, $2,117; Railway Engine Service Employees' Educational Political League, $314, $313; and the International Union of Electrical, Radio and Machine Workers (AFL-CIO). $28,506, $29,720. Four organizations not included in the table reported 1958 receipts and total disbursements, respectively, as follows: International Brotherhood of Electrical Workers COPE, $42,597, $40,874; International Union of Electrical, Radio and Machine Workers COPE, $5,953, $4,658; Oil, Chemical and Atomic Workers International Union (Denver), $66,011, $57,026; and the Political Committee of the International Typographers Union (Indianapolis), $14,845, $12,967.

Various discrepancies between these figures and those in the Gore Committee *Report*, pp. 43-44, are explained by different periods of time covered and the inclusion in the Gore Committee figures of some "educational" money not reported to the Clerk. COPE does not report to the Clerk the cost of its political education activities.

[b] Organization not in existence. COPE superseded CIO-PAC and LLPE on February 1, 1956.

[c] No report.

[d] A new ILGWU Campaign Committee was created for each election. For the accumulated surplus, see footnote 61 on page 193, below.

[e] UAW CIO-PAC account was closed September, 15, 1958. Its funds were transferred to UAW-COPE (which reported receipts of $81,505, disbursements of $76,074) and to the Committee for Good Government (which reported receipts of $71,454, disbursements of $56,201), both of Detroit. Figures in table are net for these three organizations.—*Congressional Quarterly*, 17 (1959) 509.

[f] For period January 1, 1948—January 1, 1953. $6,000 more was reported spent through January 2, 1957.—*Congressional Quarterly Almanac*, 13 (1957), 247.

[g] These totals may count some money twice. For example, in 1952 a total of at least $65,388 was transferred from one group to another among those shown; in 1956 the figure was at least $297,333.

CIO. Generally, the reports indicate that a net total of between $1,500,000 and $1,750,000 was raised and spent in each of the four election years.[27] In addition to these sums, other substantial amounts of politically relevant money were handled by national-level labor groups, both unions and political committees. They were not reported because in the confusion that exists concerning legal definitions they were declared by the groups involved to be nonpolitical or educational in character or for some other reason not covered by federal reporting requirements.

The AFL-CIO's COPE in 1956, for example, reported to the Clerk only its funds derived from individual contributions (around $671,000 spent).[28] Testimony before the McClellan Lobby Committee revealed two additional sums: an educational fund of $290,000 and about $435,000 for the cost of operating COPE, which came out of the general funds of the AFL-CIO. Total COPE disbursements were thus more than twice the reported sum spent from voluntary gifts.[29] While the unions most conspicuously active in campaigns are represented in the reports,[30] there is no way of knowing how many have taken the position held by the United Mine Workers. The Mine Workers, long headed by John L. Lewis, has campaigned through its own special committee, Labor's Non-Partisan League. The League in 1956 operated entirely with union funds, making no contributions and limiting its expenditures to what was called political education. Yet its director was quoted as saying its main activity was to distribute voting records and urge UMW members "to work and support endorsed candidates."[31] The Mine Workers and the Teamsters in 1958 said that all of their campaign expenditures were made at state and local levels and were therefore not reportable to the Clerk of the House,[32] although other national-level groups have chosen to report what appear to be comparable outlays.

State and local activities.—Even less information from formal reports is usually available at lower levels. The information collected by the

27. As indicated in footnote (g) of the table, the gross totals count some money more than once. William H. Riker made computations for 1944 based on data collected in reports and hearings of Senate and House committees. There was knowledge of money collected and spent by unions or under labor control at *several* governmental levels, receipts totalling about $2,286,000 and expenditures about $2,226,000.—*Op. cit.,* pp. 130-31.

28. *Congressional Quarterly,* 15 (1957), 513.

29. *Hearings,* p. 907.

30. For example, the Labor Research Association listed six unions as most actively pro-Democratic in 1956, all of which had political committees that reported to the Clerk of the House of Representatives (the United Automobile Workers, Machinists, International Ladies' Garment Workers, Textile Workers, Clothing Workers, and the Steelworkers).—*Op. cit.,* p. 145.

31. *Congressional Quarterly,* 14 (1956), 1158.

32. *Ibid.,* 17 (1959), 509. Harold J. Gibbons, a Teamster vice president and executive assistant to President James R. Hoffa, said that in 1958 Teamster locals in six states where right-to-work measures were on the ballot raised $400,000 to fight them—a sum matched by funds from the international union. He thought that final totals might reach $1,000,000.—*New York Times,* November 14, 1958.

Gore Committee on state and local labor groups in 1956, however, surpasses any previously compiled. As shown in Table 22, about $520,000 was available to state AFL-CIO groups during the campaign period, September 1–November 30.[33] About $128,000 was reported available to other state groups, and some $346,000 was so reported by 112 local labor political organizations located in the 100 largest counties.

Table 22

LABOR POLITICAL COMMITTEES, STATE AND LOCAL: FUNDS AVAILABLE AND TOTAL DISBURSEMENTS, SEPTEMBER 1–NOVEMBER 30, 1956[a]

No.[b]	Type of Committee	Funds Available[c]	Total Disbursement
	State		
20	Committees on Political Education (COPE)—Affiliated with State Labor Councils[d]	$159,922	$137,538
23	Labor's Leagues for Political Education (LLPE)—Affiliated with State Federations of Labor[d]	133,535	105,702
27	CIO-Political Action Committees (PAC)—Affiliated with State Industrial Union Councils[d]	226,464	196,351
	Totals for 70 AFL-CIO State Political Committees	*519,921*	*439,591*
27	Machinist's Non-Partisan Leagues	58,373	52,002
8	Miscellaneous	70,076	42,107
	Local		
112	All types—Located in the 100 largest counties	346,134	296,644

[a] Gore Committee, *Report*, pp. 32-36; 47; Ex. 29, pp. 18-22. The Gore Committee's questionnaires called for information on all receipts and disbursements of a political committee if any portion of them was used in an attempt to influence a Federal election.
[b] Including committees reporting no receipts and disbursements.
[c] These include cash on hand September 1, plus receipts during the subsequent three months.
[d] At the time of the 1956 campaign, state AFL and CIO groups had merged in some states and not in others. In a few instances, the reporting organization was the labor organization itself (e.g., a state industrial union council) rather than its political committee. In some states, both CIO-PAC's and COPE's were active. In those cases, the COPE's are reported with the LLPE's as affiliated with the AFL.

The reasons for the incompleteness of these figures help illuminate the structure of labor political activity as well as certain operating attitudes toward their political activities adopted by labor leaders. There are no directories of state and local labor political committees. The Gore Committee tried, nevertheless, to learn what state and district political committees were associated with the important unions. The enthusiasm of labor officials for the enterprise was somewhat short of overwhelming. An examination of reports filed with state authorities in 1952 had turned up an Amalgamated Clothing Workers political committee in Massachusetts, a Steelworkers CIO-PAC and a Rail Labor

33. The total for the full year would run larger. A comparison in 21 cases of funds available during the full year 1952 with those for the campaign period 1956 revealed that in some of them (mostly committees with small receipts) sums for the limited 1956 period were higher than for the full year 1952.

Committee in Pennsylvania, a Textile Union Political Fund Committee in New York, as well as many groups associated with union locals, joint boards, city industrial union councils, and the like.[34] When queried by the Gore Committee staff, the international headquarters of unions and their affiliated political committees generally professed to have no information about these state and local groups that could be used for canvassing them systematically by questionnaire. Nor was help forthcoming from district and regional offices. Questionnaires were sent to 42 Teamsters' joint councils (answer: they are not affiliated with any state political action or education committee); to 28 district offices of the United Mine Workers (answer from 27: they had no receipts and expenditures and were not affiliated with any state political action or education committee); and to 16 regional offices of the United Automobile Workers (answer: all expenditures on behalf of federal candidates were made through the national UAW-CIO political action committee).[35]

Although the figures in Table 22 do not cover all state and local labor political organizations,[36] conversations with labor leaders about the over-all structure of labor political action confirm inferences from the imperfect data. The backbone of the political committee system is the COPE organization at all levels (formerly the AFL's Labor's League for Political Education and the CIO-Political Action Committee). Of lesser importance, but similar in type, is Railway Labor's Political League, with which a number of railway unions (including some in the AFL-CIO) are associated. As previously indicated, a few international unions have national political-action organizations of their own, some of which work within COPE and some of which do not. Some of these have units at state and local levels, particularly the Machinists. Actually, all politically active unions customarily have state and local political

34. National labor political committees report contributions from state and local groups, indicating something of their number and variety. For data on national labor campaign funds in 1952 see Gore Committee *Hearings,* part 2, pp. 533-40.

Guidance manuals handed down from national political committees often expose comprehensive ambitions. A set of suggestions for organizational structure circulating in Connecticut in the early 1950's had emanated from the national CIO-PAC. One of the objectives listed for the state CIO-PAC was: "To establish active congressional and county PACs; to assist congressional and county PACs in developing permanent local union PACs, city, ward, precinct and neighborhood PAC units and other activities, and to coordinate activities among PAC units for state senatorial and other PAC activities involving more than one county."

35. Gore Committee *Report,* p. 46.

36. The local coverage is particularly unsatisfactory. In the 100 largest counties only 112 groups responded to questionnaires, and only 62 of those said they had receipts or disbursements. At the state level, not all committees active in previous years reported in 1956, such as certain state affiliates of railroad unions. Reports filed for the full year 1952 with state authorities by 28 state labor political organizations showed total disbursements of $407,407, and total direct expenditures of $288,269. Twenty-six local groups in Pennsylvania reported total disbursements of $100,879 and total direct expenditures of $54,090.

action committees in those areas where they enjoy numerical strength, sometimes organized jointly with other labor groups.

The character and extent of political action, and of cooperative political action, fluctuate widely at the lower levels. Basically, the political arrangements established depend on the structure of organization and power within the unions themselves. The geographical spread of membership and the organizational patterns of unions differ from one to another. Moreover, there is little congruity between electoral boundaries and the distribution of union membership, a fact that produces further variety in labor political activities. Unity of political action is by no means assured and labor organizations sometimes back

Table 23

TRANSFERS OF FUNDS BY SPECIFIED LABOR POLITICAL COMMITTEES: DESTINATIONS, 1952 AND 1956[a]

Funds transferred to	Funds transferred by committees					
	14 national level—1/1-12/31/52		17 national level—1/1-11/30/56		155 state and local levels—9/1-11/30/56	
	$	%	$	%	$	%
National level						
Total	*216,577*	*26*	*406,433*	*25*	*37,199*	*9*
Labor campaign committees	65,388	8	297,333	18	34,075	8
Democratic party committees	97,889	12	109,000	7	3,124	1
Other	53,300[c]	6	100	(b)	—	—
State and local levels						
Total	*616,341*	*74*	*1,209,560*	*75*	*392,609*	*91*
Labor campaign committees	268,409	32	235,586	15	94,584	22
Democratic party committees	67,150	8	41,818	2	23,765	6
Democratic candidates or their committees for:						
U.S. House of Representatives	79,990	10	333,855	21	136,268	31
U.S. Senate	100,072	12	326,045	20	42,863	10
State and local candidates or their committees	—	—	—	—	68,432	16
Other	100,720[d]	12	272,256[e]	17	26,697[f]	6
Grand total all levels	832,918	100	1,615,993	100	429,808	100

[a] 1952 basic data appear in Gore Committee, *Hearings*, part 2, pp. 533-34, derived from reports filed with the Clerk of the U.S. House of Representatives; those for 1956 come from that Committee's *Report*, pp. 45-48.

[b] Less than 1 per cent.

[c] $51,300 of this to Americans for Democratic Action.

[d] $60,200 of this to the Liberal party; $5,450 to Republican candidates; the rest to Democratic or labor groups.

[e] $140,815 of this went in refunds to unspecified labor locals; $10,000 to the Liberal party; $1,300 to Republican candidates; $34,665 to recipients not fully identified; the rest to Democratic or labor groups.

[f] $2,625 of this went to Republican candidates; $11,191 to recipients not fully identified; the rest to Democratic or labor groups.

Table 24

LABOR DONATIONS TO CANDIDATES FOR FEDERAL OFFICE AND TO THEIR CAMPAIGN COMMITTEES, 1956[a]

Given	By 17 national labor groups—1/1-11/30, 1956	By 155 state and local labor groups—9/1-11/30, 1956
To political committees:		
National level	$109,000	$ 3,124
State and local level (federal)	61,500	7,678
On behalf of specific candidates for:		
U.S. House of Representatives	335,155	138,893
U.S. Senate	326,045	42,863
Total	831,700	192,558
		831,700
Combined total		$1,024,258

[a] Computed from Gore Committee, *Report*, pp. 45-48. This table includes donations benefitting both Republican and Democratic candidates.

rival candidates. The extent to which political committees are significant at any level depends ultimately on the unions supporting them. This is of special importance to COPE, the political committee of a federation that is itself a collection of largely autonomous union organizations.

The specter of an efficient, monolithic campaign structure often conjured up by labor's political foes is a far cry from reality. Within individual unions and political committees, nevertheless, initiative and leadership are more likely to flow downward than upward. The degree of central control in handling funds and in decision-making is far from uniform from one organization and state to another. But organized political action normally does not sprout at the grass roots without cultivation from above,[37] and in certain tightly controlled unions a determined leadership can mobilize both men and money for political action.

Independent, but Democrats preferred.—Most labor money, whatever its source and however spent, went during the 1950's to aid Democratic candidates. The evidence is summarized in Tables 23 and 24. Table 23 concerns the funds transferred by certain important categories of labor political committees to candidates and other political committees in 1952 and 1956. Most of the money went either to other labor committees or to Democratic candidates. Democratic party committees received relatively little cash.[38] Table 24 abstracts the 1956 information

37. Interesting details of CIO-PAC financing in Massachusetts appear in Steinberg, *op. cit.*, pp. 101-3, 106-7, 125-27.

38. The sort of thing that led one Democratic state chairman in 1959 to cry aloud that he wished labor would operate within the party so that candidates would feel responsible to the party instead of to labor.

from Table 23 that pertains to candidates for federal offices and committees backing them. All of it went to aid Democratic candidates except $3,925 which was split among eight Republican aspirants to the House. All of the more than $1,000,000 involved presumably originated as voluntary contributions (only such money may be used on behalf of federal candidates), which constituted about one-half of labor's funds from this source during 1956. It is hardly disputable that the mass of remaining labor political money also benefited Democrats.[39]

But organized labor considers itself an independent political force pursuing a policy of "nonpartisan endorsement"—usually supporting Democrats, to be sure, but unwilling to turn its resources willy-nilly over to Democratic party leaders. The Gore Committee found that in 1956 gifts from national labor committees went to Democratic *party* committees in only 14 states, and the only ones of consequence (above $1,625) were in states with Senate races. By contrast, national labor money went to back Democratic Senatorial *candidates* in 22 of the 33 states from which senators were elected, the remaining 11 consisting of seven southern and two northern one-party states plus Arizona and Kansas.[40] One or more Democratic candidates for the House of Representatives received national labor gifts in every state but six, all of the latter being one-party states except New Mexico. Even donations from state and local labor committees were made to Democratic organizations in only 14 states, whereas Democratic Senatorial candidates in 16 and House candidates in 22 were favored with such gifts, as were candidates for state and local offices in 20.[41]

Building on strength.—Greatest labor financial support is likely to flow to states with large numbers of union voters and strong pro-labor

39. Labor contributions in 1958 reported to the Clerk of the House were directed to 34 candidates for the United States Senate, 31 of whom were Democrats, 2 Republican, and 1 independent; 199 House candidates were down for labor contributions, including 191 Democrats, 2 Liberals, and 6 Republicans.—*Congressional Quarterly,* 17 (1959), 509.

An analysis of funds transferred by 15 national labor groups for the calendar year 1952 showed: to national political committees, $149,189; on behalf of candidates for Senate, $101,572; for House, $83,940; to state and local party committees, $67,150. All beneficiaries were Democratic except one candidate for the Senate and five for the House, who were Republicans and together received $5,450. An amount of $60,200 also went to the Liberal party in New York, which supported the Democratic presidential candidate. For details, see Gore Committee *Hearings,* part 2, pp. 533-35.

40. The reports from which the information was drawn did not cover nominations.

41. Of 29 candidates for the United States Senate backed by AFL-CIO local political groups in 1956, 12 won; of 288 backed for the House, 159 were elected; of 24 gubernatorial candidates, 16 were successful.—Labor Research Association, *op. cit.,* p. 146, citing *COPE Report,* January, 1957. In 1954, winners among candidates endorsed by CIO groups were, for the Senate, 16 of 26; for the House, 126 of 256. Among candidates endorsed by AFL-LLPE's, winners were, 18 of 30 for the Senate and 154 out of an unspecified number for the House.—*Ibid.,* 12 (1955), p. 126.

candidates, two not wholly unconnected characteristics. Despite subventions to other areas,[42] the general impact of transfers of labor money is to enhance campaign activities in areas where labor already possesses its greatest political strength. The six states to which the largest amounts of national labor money were transferred in 1956—Pennsylvania, Oregon, New York, Indiana, California, and Illinois—were all among the 17 states listed on page 175 in which organized labor has the greatest voting potential. In fact, four of them were the four states with the largest numbers of union members, and five were among the first ten. (In the exceptional state, Oregon, labor's great and faithful champion, Wayne Morse, was a Senatorial candidate.) To each of these states went more than $53,000 in transfers—to labor campaign committees, candidates, and other political groups. There were six additional states to which sums in excess of $35,000 were sent, four of them appearing on the list of 17—Michigan, New Jersey, Wisconsin and Washington—and the remaining two, Maryland and Connecticut, both were states with large union memberships.[43]

The policy orientation of labor political finance is indicated by the candidates supported. Candidates favored almost invariably have a record of "right" voting on social and economic issues of concern to labor leadership or are opposing candidates who do not.[44] Not all such candidates, however, necessarily receive labor's financial backing. Labor money in some cases supplies a large percentage of a candidate's campaign needs,[45] but some evidence suggests that pro-labor candidates with other financial resources are not as likely to receive labor contributions as less well-financed pro-labor candidates. Also, labor money

42. Labor money, like other political money, is more likely to follow than to create political opportunity. Maine is a state of modest labor membership that formerly attracted little labor money. The Democratic revolution led by Edmund S. Muskie has changed things. Of slightly over $96,000 reported spent on behalf of Democratic candidates in 1958, $35,500 came from labor groups, much of it from outside the state. Another $17,500 was transferred in from national-level Democratic committees.—Alfred Schretter, "Campaign Finances: Maine, 1958," (Bowdoin, Maine: Bowdoin Citizenship Clearing House, 1959) (mimeographed), pp. 6, 9.

43. Gore Committee *Report,* pp. 45-48, lists the sums sent to each state. A similar situation seems to have obtained in 1958—*Congressional Quarterly,* 17 (1959), 510; in 1954—*Newsweek,* March 2, 1956, p. 31; and in 1952—Gore Committee *Hearings,* part 2, p. 534.

44. The Congressional voting records of 17 candidates for the House and 6 for the Senate in 1952, from 12 selected states, were studied. Contributions by CIO-PAC were made to one candidate in each of the 23 races. When incumbents were supported, they had usually voted "right"—by CIO-PAC definition—on all the issues examined. When incumbents were opposed, they had usually voted "wrong" on the overwhelming majority of them.—Bradbury Seasholes, "Labor Union Financial Participation in the 1952 Election" (Master's thesis, University of North Carolina, 1958), p. 105.

45. Around one-seventh of the direct expenses of national-level pro-Democratic committees in 1952 and in 1956 were met with labor money.

seems to be attracted to the closer contests,[46] which should comfort those observers who view skeptically the motives of contributors who bet on sure winners.

The fund-raising function.—Analysis of receipts and disbursements reported by labor political committees shows the committees to be more important as fund-raising and distributing agencies than as campaign organizations. A larger share of labor-committee disbursements in 1952 and 1956 went out as transfers of funds to other groups than was spent directly by the committees themselves. (See Table 25.) Much of this money went to other labor committees, but even the receiving committees were largely transmitting rather than spending organizations. The notable exception is found at the local level, where labor committees spent most of their money themselves.[47] The data in Table 26 show that in 1956 a large share of the money available to labor committees came in the form of transfers.[48]

Table 25

DISBURSEMENTS BY LABOR POLITICAL COMMITTEES: PERCENTAGE TRANSFERRED TO OTHER GROUPS AND SPENT DIRECTLY, 1952 AND 1956[a]

Period	Type and No. of Committees[b]	Total Disbursements	Percentage	
			Transferred	Spent Directly
1/1-12/31/52	14 national level	$1,818,789	46[c]	44[c]
1/1-11/30/56	17 national level	2,156,728	75	25
9/1-11/30/56	155 state and local levels:	*830,344*	*52*	*48*
	19 COPE, state level	137,538	83	17
	19 LLPE, state level	105,702	71	29
	24 CIO-PAC, state level	196,351	54	46
	19 Machinists NPL, state level	52,002	79	21
	66 local level	296,644	19	81
	8 miscellaneous	42,107	85	15

[a] 1952 basic data appear in Gore Committee, *Hearings*, part 2, p. 533, derived from reports filed with the Clerk of the U.S. House of Representatives; those for 1956 come from that committee's *Report*, pp. 45-47.
[b] Number refers only to committees that had receipts or made disbursements.
[c] It was not clear from the reports filed with the Clerk of the U.S. House of Representatives, from which this information was drawn, how 10 per cent of the money had been used. Some of it was doubtless held as surplus.

46. *Ibid.*, pp. 111-16. With very few cases to examine, Seasholes found only a faint tendency to favor pro-labor candidates with working-class backgrounds over other pro-labor candidates who might have been supported and were not. The same was true with respect to candidates with Congressional committee assignments important to labor.—Pp. 106-11.

47. For a breakdown of the purposes for which direct expenditures were made, see page 398, below.

48. Information on receipts of state and local committees was confined to the period September 1–November 30. The large proportion of funds on hand September 1 suggests that income from voluntary contributions may have come in earlier in the year.

Table 26

LABOR POLITICAL COMMITTEES: SOURCES OF FUNDS, 1956[a]

No. and Type of Committees	Total		Cash on hand 9/1/56		Recieved from							
					Individuals		Sale of tickets to dinners, etc.		Other organizations		Other sources	
	$	%	$	%	$	%	$	%	$	%	$	%
17 National level 1/1-11/30...	1,912,990	100	....	..	1,395,076	73	619	..	464,270	24	53,025	3
155 State and local levels 9/1-11/30												
Total.......	*994,504*	100	*329,313*	*33*	*160,042*	*16*	*34,248*	*3*	*420,175*	*43*	*50,726*	*5*
19 State COPE...	159,922	100	58,552	37	8,251	5	5,000	3	79,925	50	8,194	5
19 State LLPE....	133,535	100	78,392	59	13,075	10	115	..	26,609	20	15,344	11
24 State CIO-PAC	226,464	100	65,220	29	33,082	14	1,410	1	119,156	53	7,596	3
19 State MNPL...	58,373	100	28,706	49	23,548	40	......	..	6,119	11	......	
66 Local.....	346,134	100	69,496	20	50,224	15	27,723	8	184,544	53	14,147	4
8 Miscellaneous...	70,076	100	28,947	41	31,862	46	......	..	3,822	5	5,445	8

[a] Computed from Gore Committee, *Report*, pp. 41, 47. The totals are gross, with no adjustments made for transfers of funds among committees included in the tabulation.

3. FREE, BUT NOT EASY

About 30 per cent of all persons who made campaign contributions for the 1956 elections came from labor-union families. Roughly one of every eight union members made a political gift, or around 2,200,000 such people.[49] These individual contributions did not constitute the largest phase of labor's financial part in the elections, but they were an important aspect of it.

The legal context.—Before 1944, most labor campaign money came from dues paid by members into union treasuries. The unfamiliar surge of political action that began in 1936 alarmed labor's opponents and produced demands for legislation curtailing it. Concern was also expressed for union members who disagreed with their union's political stand. They found it desirable or necessary to belong to a union, yet a portion of their dues could be used on behalf of candidates they opposed.

The Smith-Connally War Labor Disputes Act passed by Congress in 1943 prohibited labor *unions* from making *contributions* in connection with *elections* for *federal* office.[50] Labor's political committees were

49. Derived from responses in a nationwide study by the Survey Research Center, University of Michigan. As used here, a "union family" is one in which the person interviewed or the head of his household was a member of a trade union.

50. The British had wrestled with the same problem at the beginning of the century when the Labor party, supported by trade-union funds, became a clear

not covered, and the Act was to expire six months after the end of the war. The CIO-Political Action Committee chose to interpret the legislation as precluding it from using union funds in connection with federal elections, which it declared to begin with the naming of the major party nominees. It inaugurated an "A Buck for Roosevelt" program to raise by voluntary subscriptions a fund that could be spent free of the Smith-Connally bans. In 1947, the Taft-Hartley Labor Management Relations Act extended the prohibition to include *expenditures* as well as contributions, made the restrictions applicable to *nominations* as well as general elections, and put the legislation on a permanent basis.[51] After 1943, labor organizations began soliciting members and friends for money that could be used freely in federal elections and could be given to federal candidates.[52] Knowledge of the volume of these individual contributions is by no means perfect, but enough is known to reveal the order of magnitude of labor spending from this source.

One in eight.—On February 1, 1956, the newly merged AFL-CIO launched its Committee on Political Education. The monies handled by COPE coming from individual contributions are accounted for separately in official reports, provide clues to the total volume of money given individually by union members, and confirm other estimates of the

---

threat to the established parties. The result was a statute of 1913 that legalized union political gifts but provided that union members who did not wish their money used for such purposes would be protected by filing a written petition to that effect. This arrangement for contracting out, as it is called, prevailed until 1927, when a Conservative government changed it to one for contracting in. Union members were required to take affirmative action to participate in the political fund of the union, a requirement that was reversed again when the Labor government came to power following World War II.—See Louise Overacker, *Presidential Campaign Funds* (Boston: Boston University Press, 1946), pp. 51-55.

Whether or not unions in the United States may compel their members to pay dues to finance lobbying and other political activities was the subject of litigation during 1959. On February 25, in the Allen case, the North Carolina Supreme Court held, in effect, that they could, a decision running contrary to an earlier ruling by the Georgia Supreme Court in the Looper case. The suits were almost identical, both arising under the Railway Labor Act and both involving employees of the Southern Railway. The employees sought to prevent enforcement of the union-shop contract on the grounds that dues they would be forced to pay would be used "in substantial part for purposes not germaine to collective bargaining but to support ideological and political doctrines and candidates they are not willing to support." Presumably the United States Supreme Court would eventually rule on the question. See *Congressional Quarterly—Review of Politics and the Issues,* 15 (April 1959), 59-60.

51. Overacker, *Presidential Campaign Funds,* pp. 57-61. See the testimony of Sidney Hillman, Green Committee *Hearings,* part 1, 58 pp. For a review of federal statutes and relevant cases, see Joseph Tanenhaus, "Organized Labor's Political Spending: The Law and Its Consequences," *Journal of Politics,* 16 (1954), 441-71.

52. One estimate puts voluntary contributions of union members in 1936 at less than 5 per cent of the amount spent for campaign purposes out of union treasuries. —Riker, *op. cit.,* pp. 139-40.

number of persons who make such gifts.[53] During 1956, COPE reported $708,937 available to it from individual gifts.[54] Under COPE accounting procedures, this represented about 50 cents of every dollar collected by union organizations cooperating with COPE, and the average gift per contributor was thought to be about one dollar.[55] On this basis, around 1,400,000 different persons gave funds available to COPE during 1956, a period in which the membership of unions participating in COPE totalled around 11,250,000.[56] Thus about 12.5 per cent, or one out of eight members, made voluntary gifts.[57]

53. COPE replaced the AFL's Labor's League for Political Education and the CIO's Political Action Committee, which had been created in 1947 and 1943 respectively. Some $193,000 was transferred from the older groups to the new one in 1956 and their former directors became co-directors of the new special political arm.—Gore Committee *Hearings,* part 1, p. 60.

54. From report to the Clerk of the U.S. House of Representatives.— *Congressional Quarterly,* 15 (1957), 513. Approximately $582,503 was contributed during the calendar year, a sum computed from total receipts less individual contributions that were on hand with LLPE and CIO-PAC on December 31, 1955. The latter equals the amount transferred February 1 minus collections during January 1956.—Gore Committee *Hearings,* part 1, p. 60.

55. McClellan Lobby Committee, *Hearings,* p. 904. Under the former LLPE procedure, the full contribution of an individual was forwarded to LLPE, then half refunded to the collecting organization. Under the former CIO-PAC procedure, only its share, half of that collected, was normally forwarded to the national office. These procedures were continued in 1956, but the sums here reported by COPE are the net after refunds were made. Hence, under both procedures, total collections came to double the sum available to COPE. In computing the percentage of a local's membership deemed to have made a voluntary contribution, James McDevitt and Jack Kroll, COPE's co-directors, consider one dollar to be the average individual contribution, though readily conceding there are doubtless cases in which individuals give more and less.—McClellan Lobby Committee, *Hearings,* p. 901. After 1956, COPE's periodical "Political Memo" listed hundreds of locals receiving honor awards "for having contributed the equivalent of $1 from each of their members." Voluntary gifts collected by the Machinists Non-Partisan Political League were estimated to average 90 cents.—*Ibid.,* p. 865. In 1952, 39,304 members of four ILGWU locals affiliated with the New York Dress Joint Board gave contributions averaging $2.57 each.—International Ladies' Garment Workers' Union, General Executive Board, *Report to the 28th Convention* (New York: ABCO Press, 1953), p. 98.

56. This included unions representing about 70 to 75 per cent of AFL-CIO membership. The Carpenters and the Teamsters, with a combined membership of over 2,000,000 did not, for example, participate in COPE, although some locals of nonparticipating internationals did.—McClellan Lobby Committee, *Hearings,* pp. 900-1.

57. About one out of eight Machinists made a voluntary gift in 1956.—McClellan Lobby Committee, *Hearings,* pp. 864-65. Auto Workers officials have claimed that one of four members of their locals give, though the estimate appears high.—Kornhauser, Sheppard, and Mayer, *op. cit.,* p. 125. Only 9 per cent of members of UAW families in a Detroit sample said they gave in 1956. The percentage for members of other union families was slightly less.—Data provided by Samuel J. Eldersveld and Daniel Katz from their Detroit Area Study, 1956. The politically energetic ILGWU claimed that voluntary contributions to its campaign committee in 1952 were made by about half the membership, a claim within reason.—ILGWU, *op. cit.,* p. 39. Both the Auto Workers and the ILGWU carry on unusually vigorous

There were an additional 6,000,000 or so union members resident in the United States. If they participated at the same rate as members connected with COPE, the total number of individuals in the United States giving to labor political funds would equal about 2,150,000. This is not far from the estimate of 2,200,000 union givers based on the study of the Survey Research Center. It is doubtful, however, that as large a proportion of union members not connected with COPE gave as of those who were. Although the data are hardly precise enough for the difference to cause concern, it seems explainable. Some union givers gave to political activities not connected with COPE, especially to local Democratic party groups[58] and to supplementary fund-raising campaigns conducted by unions that cooperated with COPE but had additional fund-raising efforts of their own, like the Auto Workers[59] and the Steelworkers.[60] Crude though they are, these estimates from independent data are sufficiently consistent to fix the probable outer limit of labor's voluntary contributions for the 1956 elections at about $2,200,000.[61] This appears to be higher than in previous years, although comparisons are difficult,[62] and to be in line with the findings of

---

solicitation programs. In 1945, 32 per cent of all British trade union members contracted in, and the percentage was much higher in some of them.—Riker, *op. cit.*, p. 141.

58. Programs to solicit party funds among union members have often been resisted by union leadership.

59. Gore Committee *Hearings*, part 2, p. 332.

60. McClellan Lobby Committee, *Hearings*, pp. 988-89, 1006.

61. Included in the above computations were $126,000 of individual contributions made to LLPE and CIO-PAC before 1956. In its question on contributing, the Survey Research Center did not specify the time period covered except to refer to the "campaign." With the mounting emphasis on year-around political giving, it is possible that some respondents conceived of gifts made before 1956 as aiding a party or candidate in the 1956 campaign.

Voluntary contributions have not in general been so abundant as to permit carry-overs from year to year. The ILGWU Campaign Committees, however, have accumulated surpluses which would presumably come in handy should fund-raising become difficult some year as a result of unemployment or other cause. The accumulated balance at the end of 1958 totaled $511,797.—International Ladies' Garment Workers' Union, *Thirtieth Convention, Report and Record* (New York: Pitel Press, 1959), "Financial and Statistical Report," p. 10.

62. Joseph Tanenhaus constructed from standard sources the following table of political *expenditures* reported as financed by voluntary contributions:

	CIO-PAC	*LLPE*
1944	$470,852	—
1946	151,693	—
1948	515,003	$312,196
1950	511,386	556,252
1952	505,721	249,257

—*Op. cit.*, 462. The LLPE drive in 1950 was for two-dollar gifts. The figures for other years represent the proceeds from one-dollar drives, although correspondence with union officials indicates that in some cases the entire dollar was reported as a receipt and in others only fifty cents. The Survey Research Center's 1952 study suggests substantially fewer contributors in union families than indicated by the CIO-PAC and LLPE financial reports.

one private survey in 1958.[63]

How voluntary?—The fact that in 1956 one out of eight union members said they made a contribution (or bought a ticket or something to help a candidate or party)—compared with about one of 11 among other respondents—reveals what labor leaders themselves have long known: to raise campaign funds from union members by voluntary contributions is an excruciatingly difficult task. Appeals of labor leaders for funds, often distorted in the headlines, sometimes mislead opponents as well as friends as to the true results of solicitations for voluntary funds.[64]

The available reports do not tell in detail the unions from whose members the voluntary funds come. The backbone of support seems to come from the aggressive, politically conscious unions like the ILGWU, the Auto Workers, the Steelworkers, and the Machinists. These are just the ones, in fact, that have political action committees of their own which usually handle the supply of free money that is passed on to COPE.[65] The procedures by which the voluntary funds are solicited vary in detail from one organization to another. In 1956, COPE distributed "dollar voluntary books" containing receipts to its participating organizations. A copy of each receipt was supposed to find its way with the gift back to the COPE office in Washington.[66] In New York's Garment Workers locals, where most of the money is raised by shop stewards, printed contribution sheets listing all members have been used, the names being checked off when contributions are made. The solicitations are carried out variously by the officials of union locals or of local political action groups, who are often the same. As in other types of fund-raising, the energy and persistence of solicitors, and the philosophy and scheme of the soliciting plan, vary. A casual comment at the end of a local's business meeting is less likely to raise money than tough and repeated talks from the leadership. Union officials readily confess that a great range exists in the intensity of interest and activity among locals, even within highly politicized unions.[67] There are oc-

63. Which found 7 per cent of skilled and semi-skilled laborers saying they made a Democratic donation, and 4 per cent saying they gave to the Republicans.

64. For example, before the 1956 campaign, the press reported Walter Reuther as calling for contributions equalling 25 cents for each AFL-CIO member, a story that might lead some to think that $4,000,000 of campaign money from this source alone would lie at the disposal of labor leaders.

65. On the UAW-CIO-PAC, see Gore Committee *Hearings,* part 2, p. 332; on the Steelworkers' PAC, which was formed in 1955, see McClellan Lobby Committee, *Hearings,* pp. 988-89; on the Machinists Non-Partisan Political League, see *ibid.,* pp. 844ff.

66. McClellan Lobby Committee, *Hearings,* pp. 900, 902.

67. Only about 60 or 70 per cent of ILGWU locals engage actively in political fund-raising. A 1951 study of District 9, International Association of Machinists, showed wide disagreement among a sample of stewards and officers when asked whether members *actually* are asked for voluntary contributions to finance political

casional charges of coercion,[68] but generally the energetic solicitations seem to confine themselves to the characteristic device of all effective fund-raising: creating a climate of social pressure that induces generosity. Some locals report 100 per cent participation by their members, but these are usually small groups of 50 or less.[69] Leaders note that raffles, entertainments of various kinds, and other standard fund-raising devices are employed[70] to raise free funds, the proceeds often coming from union members or their families.

---

activities: 37 per cent said always or usually, 25 per cent said sometimes, 26 per cent said seldom or never, and 12 per cent said they did not know. They also disagreed in response to other questions about political action practices, though not so markedly.—Hjalmar Rosen and R. A. Hudson Rosen, *The Union Member Speaks* (New York: Prentice-Hall, Inc., 1955), pp. 52-53, 132.

68. It was shown that during Senator Robert A. Taft's 1950 campaign in Ohio a check-off system was employed in some plants to raise voluntary PAC contributions. Union officials claimed this had been done at the request of members desiring to contribute. Only half of the 5,000 members of the locals involved gave anything, and they were given an opportunity to withdraw their one-dollar contributions, which three of them did.—U.S. Senate Subcommittee on Privileges and Elections, *Hearings* (Washington: Government Printing Office, 1952), p. 240. In the same year, according to a report from Connecticut, one international employed a check-off assessment coupled with the offer of a refund to those desiring it. Applications for refunds were heavy in some locals, and under similar circumstances two years later it was said that in one area 400 refunds were requested.

69. John T. O'Brien, coordinator of the Machinists' Non-Partisan Political League, reported that in 1956 perhaps 100 of the 1,900 locals in his union contributed 100 per cent. These were usually groups of 20 or so members.—McClellan Lobby Committee *Hearings,* p. 865. James L. McDevitt, co-director of COPE, knew of one local with over 500 members that reported unanimous participation but noted that such groups generally had no more than 50 or 60 members.—*Ibid.,* p. 901.

The range of attitudes that may be found among members of the same local is indicated by a survey made in 1949 of a selected portion of the membership of Teamsters Local 688, St. Louis. The following question was asked: "During an election year, how much money would you be willing to give in order to help candidates friendly to labor?" Some 23 per cent said they would give nothing, 17 per cent said they did not know, and 11 per cent gave no answer, these constituting more than half the sample. Another 24 per cent said they would give something, without specifying the amount; 11 per cent would give over two dollars and the approximately 14 per cent remaining would give up to that amount. From a different question, it was concluded that a majority could be found who professed willingness to give one dollar voluntarily (a conclusion not inconsistent with these responses).—Arnold M. Rose, *Union Solidarity—The Internal Cohesion of a Labor Union* (Minneapolis: The University of Minnesota Press, 1952), p. 81.

70. For example, the Toy and Novelty Workers of America, Local 223, had a separate organization during 1952 called "the Liberal Group." "Each year the members of the Union hold an annual dance under the auspices of the Liberal Group. The Liberal Group obtained its resources from advertisements of employers and friends in an annual catalogue printed and distributed by the Liberal Group. The advertisements were the usual 'Compliments of' and the advertisements cost from $5.00 to $100.00, depending upon the fraction of the page used in the annual catalogue." Part of the proceeds was used to buy $100 worth of tickets to a dinner given by the Liberal party in New York, and $1,000 went for an ad in the Liberal party's *Digest.* For another example, the Pottstown, Pennsylvania, CIO-PAC in 1952 reported receiving $1,076 from the sale of Adlai buttons.

Perspective.—The two million dollars or so of free funds that 17 million union members gave in 1956 about equalled the reported voluntary contributions of $500 and over made by 742 officials of the nation's 225 largest business concerns.[71] The sum came to about three-tenths of 1 per cent of annual union dues. It is fair to suppose that individually union members gave many times as much to philanthropic causes.[72] It is certain that through union dues and assessments they gave much more to political campaigns. The free funds are nevertheless of special significance. They provide a legal way for labor interests to engage in certain types of federal campaigning and they release other funds for other political uses.

4. DUES MONEY IN POLITICS

Labor groups occasionally receive campaign money from sources outside the labor movement. In general, however, all their campaign funds not supplied voluntarily by union members come ultimately from union dues. Some of this money can be traced; it shows up in the reports of political committees specified as originating in union treasuries. Most of it, however, is spent directly in campaign-connected activities and does not pass through labor's separately organized political arms.[73]

Tactics of definition.—The discussion of this phase of labor politics ordinarily proceeds in a thunderhead of emotion. In the competitive political climate that prevails, labor leaders understandably emphasize a narrow conception of what is to be called partisan, or political, or campaign, activity. Contrariwise, those intent on demonstrating deep union financial involvement in such activities employ broad definitions. There is no line in nature that divides the political from the nonpolitical, the partisan from the nonpartisan. Men must create their own definitions.

The only purpose here is to identify union financial activities connected with political campaigning. To do so argues neither that they should be limited by statute nor that they should be extolled as rights

71. See pages 115-16, above.

72. In 1950, persons with incomes under $5,000 gave more than two billion dollars in philanthropic contributions, half the national total.—John Price Jones, *The American Giver—A Review of American Generosity* (New York: The Inter-River Press, 1954), p. 40.

73. The McClellan Labor-Management Committee developed information showing corruption within certain labor unions and about relationships between certain labor leaders and figures in the underworld. As this is being written, however, very little has appeared about campaign contributions, a phase of the Committee's inquiry that was delayed until after other investigations were made. Charges that political donations were made from "flower funds" to which members or locals contributed—ostensibly to pay for such things as the funeral expenses of departed brethren—were bandied about, but public testimony had not been developed. A "Report on the McClellan Committee Hearings," bearing an endorsement by the Chairman on the jacket, is Sylvester Petro's *Power Unlimited—The Corruption of Union Leadership* (New York: The Ronald Press Company, 1959).

of citizenship. It is necessary to identify them, however, to understand this aspect of organized labor's political behavior, as an effort has been made to understand that of business groups.

There is no central source of information about union finances open to the public.[74] The financial reports made to union members differ greatly in form, detail, and accessibility,[75] as do the categories under which campaign-connected expenditures may appear. After examining a large number of financial statements rendered by treasurers of the largest *international* unions, and reading them in connection with officers' reports, it becomes possible, nevertheless, to spot the kinds of union expenditures that, in different unions, relate to political campaigning. It is usually impossible to put a dollar value on the politically significant portion of these activities. Even when this can be done, the practices of one union cannot be taken as representative of others. Also, much campaign-connected activity is financed by union *locals* and not accounted for in the reports of their international headquarters. Despite these limitations, an exploration of union financial reports discloses something of the range of union campaign-connected activities and frames an agenda for further inquiry.[76]

Campaign-connected expenditures from union treasuries may be made under at least 13 different headings.[77] The list that follows can-

74. The Taft-Hartley Act requires unions to deposit copies of their financial reports with the Department of Labor. Efforts made during 1956 and 1957 through private and Congressional channels to get access to these reports were unavailing. George Kozmetsky apparently had better luck in the 1940's.—*Op. cit.*, p. 13. The McClellan Labor-Management Committee condemned the fact that no attempt is made to determine whether these reports are accurate. There was even sentiment to make them public.—*Interim Report* (Washington: Government Printing Office, 1958) (Senate Report No. 1417, 85th Congress, 2nd Session), pp. 451, 462.

75. Some appear in union periodicals, others in convention proceedings, others in officers' reports, others are merely said to have been distributed to convention delegates or sent directly to locals. Some are brief and general; others are detailed. The McClellan Labor-Management Committee observed: "Financial reports to rank-and-file members have often been false, sketchy, and even in these forms largely unavailable for perusal by the membership."—*Ibid.*, p. 5. Presumably this characterization applies especially to the reports and records of local and district organizations whose leaders are out to fleece the membership or who are engaged in other illegal operations.

76. In recent years, none of the interrogation of labor officials by Congressional committees studying campaign finance appears to have been grounded in a thorough knowledge of the reports made by union officers to their membership. A detailed probing of their meaning would do more to illuminate labor's political involvement than a month of fractious querying along the customary lines.

77. The breadth of one union's conception of political action was expounded in a resolution adopted at the 1956 convention of the Amalgamated Clothing Workers of America, the union of the late Sidney Hillman, first chairman of CIO-PAC, and of Jack Kroll, co-director of COPE:

"RESOLVED, that the 20th Biennial Convention of the Amalgamated Clothing Workers of America:

"1. Urges every local union and joint board to bend every effort to the job of political action. We must pursue the job of voluntary contributions; we must

not be exhaustive, for accounting practices and political goals vary radically among unions. Illustrations from one union cannot be projected as typical of all organized labor. Outlays related to political campaigns may, as in the case of corporation accounts, lie hidden under many labels.[78] Nevertheless, it is useful to suggest the principal places to look for such expenses. The 13 categories are: (1) donations, (2) political department, (3) citizenship program, (4) education and information, (5) communications, (6) public service activities, (7) public relations, (8) research, (9) legislative activities, (10) legal department, (11) expense accounts, (12) general administrative costs, and (13) salaries.

Donations.—In many countries, subsidies from dues money in union treasuries sustain labor-oriented political parties and profoundly affect the party system of the nation.[79] American union leaders, as a general proposition, would rather spend the money themselves than turn it over to party politicians.[80] Where outright donations are made to campaigns, they prefer giving to political committees they already dominate, which

---

cooperate with other organizations to build ward and precinct organizations; we must intensify the campaign for registration and voting; we must publicize the records of all candidates on the basic issues; and we must work with other unions and enlightened farm, civic, and other groups for an intensive election campaign in local communities.

"2. Calls every member to make sure that he, his family, his friends, and his neighbors fulfill their duty as citizens by registering and voting. It is particularly important that the wives and husbands of Amalgamated members take an equal interest in our political action job.

"3. Pledges its full and continuing support to the Committee on Political Education, AFL-CIO."

—Amalgamated Clothing Workers of America, Twentieth Biennial Convention—*GEB Report and Proceedings* (1956), p. 331.

78. Some unions, for example, have accumulated large surpluses invested in business enterprises. Any money finding its way into campaign channels from these businesses might be viewed as properly belonging to union members.

79. A fact related to Maurice Duverger's observation that "the greatest sums for propaganda are today no longer expended by the Conservative parties who are backed by the 'financial powers,' but by the mass parties which are backed by a crowd of members whose subscriptions provide a very large working capital."—*Political Parties—Their Organization and Activity in The Modern State* (translated by Barbara and Robert North) (New York: John Wiley & Sons, 1954), p. 366.

Union financial support of labor parties is especially significant in Commonwealth countries, and is made more so where compulsory unionism prevails and contracting out is not permitted. Note Henry W. Ehrmann (ed.), *Interest Groups on Four Continents* (Pittsburgh: University of Pittsburgh Press, 1958), p. 21, on Australia, and Louise Overacker, "The New Zealand Labor Party," *American Political Science Review,* 49 (1955), 717-18.

80. In 1950 George Kozmetsky noted: "On the whole, donations by internationals for political or charitable causes have not been very large. In the reports examined it was noted that very few internationals made donations for political purposes, and in most cases the amounts contributed were negligible. . . . Donations to public causes such as Red Cross and Community Chest were not large in comparison with total expenditures."—*Op. cit.,* p. 31.

may include party committees, or to candidates whose loyalty they trust. Under the law, only free funds may go to federal candidates and to committees backing them. Donations from union treasuries may go for other campaign purposes, though they generally do not show up in the public reports of the international unions.

The ILGWU, a union of about 450,000 members, is explicit, however, about its donations to all sorts of causes, which totalled $1,275,487 during the three-year period ending March 31, 1956. Of this amount, $28,000 went to units of the Liberal party, $12,000 to the Americans for Democratic Action, and $10,500 to New York state and city campaign groups. (An additional $36,000 went to ADA, listed elsewhere as "Dues and Per Capita to Other Organizations.") During the previous three years, out of a slightly larger volume of total donations, $78,425 went to corresponding groups (in addition to per capita payments of $36,000 to ADA and $35,000 to LLPE).[81] Many labor political action committees show donations to their educational accounts from local, state, and international labor groups (although this does not say whether the sums were also treated as "donations" on union books). In 1952, for example, the CIO-PAC Educational Account reported receiving $341,942 from unions in sums of $500 or more. Eight district and local Steelworkers organizations gave sums ranging up to $25,000, and the national organization gave $61,500. Fifteen other labor organizations (most of them not included in the 12 largest unions), made gifts, among them $100,000 from the CIO itself (which was supported by union funds) and $75,000 from the Auto Workers.[82]

Political committee reports at state and local levels frequently do not discriminate between money received from voluntary funds and that received from dues,[83] and further confusion results from the irregular use of such phrases as "per capita payments from locals." (The latter was found on occasion to refer explicitly to voluntary contributions only, on other occasions to refer to donations from union funds, and more often to go unexplained.) Nevertheless, labor leaders and politicians in the field testify that both locals and international unions make donations to labor political committees, to party committees, and to candidates.[84] Where close liaison exists between political and labor

81. International Ladies' Garment Workers' Union, "Financial and Statistical Report" (1956), pp. 14, 27-30; "Financial and Statistical Report" (1953), pp. 12, 25-28.

82. Details given in Gore Committee *Hearings,* part 2, p. 538.

83. A fact that may result from lax accounting habits or intent to obfuscate, in either case one likely to be noted by antagonists, such as the Republican Policy Committee of the Senate.—"The Labor Bosses—America's Third Party," *Congressional Record,* 85th Congress, 2nd Session, June 16, 1958, vol. 104, no. 98, p. 10216.

84. State and local labor organizations reported to the Gore Committee that between September 1 and November 30, 1956, they gave some $68,000 to state and local candidates or their committees, a large share of which (if not all) may be assumed to have been dues money.—*Report,* pp. 47-48. Eighteen labor leaders

leaders, as in Michigan, union subsidies may assume considerable importance.[85] Because the donations can be made or guaranteed early in a campaign before other fund-raising reaches its peak, they may possess unusual tactical importance. Union donations, even those technically made on behalf of candidates for nonfederal offices, can in effect assist federal candidates. One labor-favored member of Congress pointed out that union donations made to local party committees, where it became mingled with income from other sources, was used directly in Congressional campaigns and also transferred to Congressional campaign committees. At the least, union money employed in state and local races releases party money for other purposes.

Political department.—Unlike most unions, the ILGWU has focused its political activities in a department bearing the name. Its Political Department, headed by Gus Tyler, was established in 1947. In the three years before April 1, 1953, $67,866 was spent through it, and in the subsequent three years, $101,375.[86] The function assigned to this department reveals the broad conception of political action adopted by politically aggressive unions: "to prepare union members and their families for fuller participation in the political life of the community, state and nation," this purpose to be sought through "a variety of channels: educational, organizational, legislative action, research, voluntary fund contributions." And it is stipulated that the educational phase of this work is a year-around job.[87] The Auto Workers have a Political Action Department headed by Roy Reuther with the same comprehensive goals as those of the ILGWU.[88]

Citizenship.—The Auto Workers pursue their political action goals in part through a special Citizenship Fund. The international union puts five cents of each member's monthly dues into a Citizenship Fund, and local unions do the same. Pursuant to the UAW Constitution, the money is to be used "for the purpose of strengthening democracy by encouraging members, and citizens generally, to register and vote in

---

have already been noted as having had contributions recorded in their names in amounts of $500 or more in 1956. Such donations are often organization gifts transmitted by the official in whose name they are reported. Roy Reuther, head of the Political Action Department of the UAW, was reported as giving $5,000 to Senator Alben Barkley's campaign in Kentucky in 1954 and $1,000 to the Democratic national committee. Both sums were declared by Walter Reuther to have come from UAW voluntary contributions.—Gore Committee *Hearings,* part 2, pp. 313-14.

85. Michigan CIO unions gave $200,000 to Democratic candidates for statewide office in that state in 1950, according to the Democratic state chairman.—Calkins, *op. cit.,* p. 131.

86. "Financial and Statistical Report" (1953), p. 11; (1956), p. 13. The amount for the 33 months ending December 31, 1958, was $137,135—(1959), p. 13.

87. *Twenty-Ninth Convention Report and Record,* p. 210.

88. United Automobile, Aircraft and Agricultural Implement Workers of America (UAW), *Report of Walter P. Reuther, President, to the 16th Constitutional Convention,* 1957, p. 122-D.

community, state, and national elections and to carry on organizational and educational programs directed toward the achievement of an ever higher understanding of citizenship responsibility and the need for active participation in the affairs of a free and democratic society."[89] During the seven years 1952-58 the income of the international's Citizenship Fund averaged over $775,000 per year, and expenditures from it averaged over $790,000 per year. Expenditures from these funds by the Political Action Department, later changed to the Citizenship Department, ran well over $300,000 annually for the years 1954-58.[90]

The politically prominent unions are not alone in emphasizing the relationship between citizenship activities and the achievement of labor's political goals through the election of public officials. At the 1954 convention of the Carpenters, the Committee on Political Education exhibited the same viewpoint. To repeal or prevent restrictive legislation, it argued, the union must educate working people to elect legislators who believe in better standards of living for all people. To do this, the committee recommended programs for voter registration, voluntary contributions, and political discussion in union locals.[91] After endorsing Stevenson and Kefauver at their 1956 convention, the International Union of Electrical, Radio and Machine Workers (AFL-CIO) passed a resolution highly partisan in tone that called, among other things, for a registration and voting drive and the distribution of educational materials.[92] Similar conceptions of the political significance of citizenship activities are evidenced in many union documents.[93]

Education and information.—Education and information are seldom neutral phenomena. In the training classes and institutes that many unions sponsor, discussions of political action are a fixed part. The 1956 report of the Education Department of the Machinists noted this and observed that the fate of anti-labor legislation depends on "how well the membership of trade unions understand the need for united political action in the same way as they understand united effort at the wage negotiation table or on a picket line."[94] Education "should be closely integrated with *all* functions and departments of the union."[95]

89. *Ibid.*, p. 183.

90. For details, see Table 27 on page 207. The financial information comes from the reports of the Board of International Trustees and International Secretary-Treasurer, Emil Mazey, published each six months.

91. United Brotherhood of Carpenters and Joiners of America, *Proceedings of the Twenty-Seventh General Convention* (1954), p. 376.

92. *Proceedings, Seventh Constitutional Convention* (1956), p. 122.

93. For another example, see the report of the President and General Secretary-Treasurer of the United Hatters, Cap and Millinery Workers International Union, *Report and Proceedings, Eighth Convention* (1953), p. 112.

94. International Association of Machinists, *Proceedings of the 24th Grand Lodge Convention* (1956), p. 56.

95. *Ibid.*, p. 60. Unions not usually identified in the public view with political action programs may, nevertheless, emphasize political education. The President of the Hotel and Restaurant Employees opened the 1953 convention of his union

Labor organizations are not the only ones who conceive of education and information programs as a means to political ends. Business and other groups also spend huge sums in partisan activities under the same rubrics.[96] The partisan bias of labor-educational activities is evident enough, but it is easy to overrate the effectiveness and to underrate the obstacles faced by such activities. The report of a Democratic leader after a vigorous campaign in one industrial state indicates the situation with which all labor partisan activities must deal, including the educatonal and information programs:

> It is suggested that the problem of convincing union members in political matters has not yet reached the stage that they can be successfully reached any easier than any other typical group of citizens. They do not seem to take for granted the political wisdom of their leadership or even their colleagues who take part in the most democratic forms of political endorsement. The case must be made on its merits—patiently, thoroughly and objectively. In my state, at least, there remain thousands of dues-paying union members who do not identify themsleves as "labor" prototypes.

Communications and public service activities.—Union newspapers and other periodicals, as well as radio and television facilities financed by unions, carry campaign material. It ranges from reports of union endorsements, of legislative votes, and of other news items, through editorial opinion and political exhortation. There were about 800 labor papers and magazines in the United States in 1956—including weeklies, bimonthlies, monthlies, and one daily—reaching between 20 and 30 million readers.[97] All newspapers in the nation totalled around 9,000,

by declaring: "Political Education must be a major concern of our International Union, as well as of every local, joint board, and state council. . . ."—Matthew Josephson, *Union House Union Bar—The History of the Hotel and Restaurant Employees and Bartenders International Union AFL-CIO* (New York: Random House, 1956), pp. 339-40, citing 1953 convention proceedings, pp. 78-79.

96. The Natural Gas and Oil Resources Committee spent $1,753,000 between October, 1954, and March, 1956, in a "long range public information program, national in scope, to inform the public concerning the business of exploring for and producing natural gas, the harmful effects of Federal regulation, and the benefits of an unregulated industry. . . ." Most of the money went to or through Hill & Knowlton, a public relations firm, and most of it was claimed for tax purposes as regular operating expenses of the firms that contributed to the committee. The committee did not register under the lobbying act on the grounds it was engaged solely in an education and information program.—McClellan Lobby Committee, *Report,* pp. 11-17; *Hearings,* pp. 114-15. The battle over California's Proposition 4 in 1956, in which several million dollars of expenditures were reported, was preceded by "educational campaigns" costing approximately $2,000,000 before the Proposition was even drawn up.—Leonard Carl Rowe, "Political Campaign Funds in California" (Ph.D. dissertation, University of California, 1957), p. 91. The American Farm Bureau Federation has taken to rating United States senators on their voting records, on one occasion saying, "We hope that state and county farm bureaus will draw their own conclusions."—*New York Times,* October 19, 1958.

97. These periodicals fell into four groups: general national publications such as put out by the CIO-AFL; national organs of the international unions (of 199

with some 3,400 other periodicals in addition.[98] As in all publishing and broadcasting, the presentation of news and editorial opinion may reflect a political viewpoint. In the experience of these union undertakings, they frequently have. At election time, in some localities, union periodicals and broadcasting become, in effect, campaign vehicles, though the assignment of a monetary value to the campaign effort is difficult.[99]

Public relations and research.—Many corporate political expenditures are headed public relations. The term is less used in labor circles, but there is keen awareness of the function and some activities bearing the name show up. Research is a concept of longer heritage in the unions. As one reads the descriptions of research and public relations activities, it becomes clear that some of them contribute directly to political campaigns. The Auto Workers tend to be more explicit about such things than most unions, and the report of its Research and Engineering Department for 1956 notes that the Department serves as the informational arm for all union activities including legislative activity and political action.[100] The report on the Machinists' public relations program emphasized the importance of the union's publications to the achievement of its political goals.[101]

Miscellaneous categories and salaries.—Among the remaining budget categories through which campaign-connected activities may be financed, salaries are by far the most important. The work of union legal departments and of those concerned with legislative matters spills over from time to time into campaign affairs. It is also clear that a delicate cost accounting system would apportion to campaign work some of the costs absorbed under general headings like expense accounts and ad-

unions in 1954, 166 issued a total of 175 publications); papers published by state AFL and CIO organizations (of 95 such organizations in 1954, 49 issued 52 publications, figures presumably affected by the subsequent merger); and local papers of general labor interest that may or may not be issued by union groups.—U.S. Department of Labor, *The American Workers' Fact Book—1956,* pp. 326-27. Over 1,700 labor union periodicals that have been published in the United States and Canada are listed in Bernard G. Naas and Carmelita S. Sakr, *American Labor Union Periodicals—A Guide to Their Location* (Ithaca: Cornell University, 1956), p. vii. Union periodicals, like union educational programs, are of political significance in many nations, apparently including Communist Yugoslavia.—Ehrmann, *op. cit.,* p. 219.

98. U.S. Bureau of the Census, *Statistical Abstract of the United States: 1957* (Washington: Government Printing Office, 1957), p. 522.

99. There are random illustrations, however. The California Machinists Non-Partisan Political League submitted reports to the Clerk of the United States House of Representatives during 1952, pursuant to the Corrupt Practices Act regulating federal elections. Receipts of $99,618 were shown. Contributions from 44 local Machinists lodges totalled $96,114. The following statement appeared above the list of contributions: "The contributions of this committee were specifically contributed towards sustaining a public service Television Program sponsored under the auspices of the California Machinists Non-Partisan Political League."

100. *Op. cit.,* p. 136-D.

101. *Op. cit.,* pp. 50-51.

ministration. But salaries—the value of campaign services rendered by persons paid out of union funds—is the most important of these items.

Many union leaders publicly and explicitly urge that union officials and employees devote time during elections to campaign activities. Regardless of whether these energies are expended in programs to get out the vote, or to encourage an intelligent vote, they will obviously benefit some candidates more than others. When UAW locals take on additional personnel during a political campaign, they are, according to Walter Reuther, paid out of the citizenship funds mentioned above.[102] But Mr. Reuther emphasizes that all union officials are urged to participate in registration drives and related activities,[103] and persons who have worked for the UAW, the CIO, and other dues-supported organizations report that a high percentage of staff time during elections is spent on partisan campaigning.[104] The ILGWU reports, with more than a trace of pride, that members of its Political Department staff have "served directly in political campaigns of key interest and importance to the union: doing research, running meetings, directing campaigns, preparing speeches."[105] Reports of ILGWU locals reflect the same enthusiasm, a result in part at least, it may be assumed, of staff efforts. In one of several cases, campaign activities were reported with "union officers and many shop chairmen cooperating with Volunteers for Stevenson and similar organizations."[106] The Amalgamated Clothing Workers claimed that officers and members of its Chicago Joint Board

102. Senator Barry Goldwater suggested in 1956 that union funds set aside for payments to members during layoffs may be used to pay for election work. Messrs. McDevitt and Kroll, co-directors of COPE, denied that COPE has access to such funds but declined to discuss union practices with regard to them. Senator Goldwater asked the Gore Committee to inquire whether expenditures from such funds rose during the campaign period. He also desired to know the number of individuals engaged in election work "in COPE."—Gore Committee *Hearings,* part 2, pp. 313-16. The latter would probably be impossible to learn, given the multiplicity of state and local COPE organizations and their tenuous administrative relationship to the national COPE. The former question, like all serious efforts to probe the variety of guises under which corporate and union funds find their way into campaigns, poses extraordinarily difficult problems of investigation. The Gore Committee staff devoted great time to the construction of questionnaires to provide information on these matters, but the enterprise had not been completed when the life of the special staff expired.

103. Gore Committee *Hearings,* part 2, pp. 326-30, 370-71, 382.

104. The secretary-treasurer of one state Industrial Union Council estimated that, over-all, 20 per cent of his organization's activities concerned political campaigning. Steinberg found in Massachusetts that full-time PAC workers were sometimes carried on the payroll of international unions, sometimes were lent by the internationals part-time, and sometimes were lent but paid by PAC.—*Op. cit.,* pp. 105-06.

105. General Executive Board, *Report to the 29th Convention* (New York: ABCO Press, 1956), p. 210.

106. *Twenty-Eighth Convention, Report and Record,* p. 113; see also pp. 104, 111, 198.

participated energetically in the election campaigns of two federal candidates, Senator Paul Douglas and Representative Sidney Yates.[107]

Labor unions are often admirably equipped to conduct effective registration and get-out-the-vote drives. Internal dissensions may pose difficulties, as once in Connecticut when several AFL locals declined to release their membership rolls to permit a check on the members' eligibility to vote. The ability to organize such drives successfully, however, is one of labor's greatest political assets,[108] and the costs of doing so are frequently met out of dues. Some 1,549 UAW temporary election workers in the Detroit area in 1956 were hired with dues money paid to locals.[109] A high labor official in California stated that, in the last week or two of the 1952 campaign, labor forces furnished about 1,000 full-time election workers in that state, whether paid or not left unsaid. The effects of this brand of political action can be crucial in the outcome of elections, and the cost of it may be reported in many places, including union salaries.[110]

Price tags.—Most of the illustrations offered have been drawn from the politically energetic unions. They have been cited solely to make one point: that union financial participation in elections takes many forms. Not all variations have been mentioned, but enough has been said to indicate some of the ways one of the great organized interests of the nation—union labor—has sought social and economic goals through election politics. It is just as difficult to measure in financial terms the campaign involvement of labor leaders, individual unions, and of organized labor as a whole as to measure that of businessmen and business groups. In neither case can skill, energy, influence, and leadership be satisfactorily translated into financial terms. Limited types of campaign

107. *Op. cit.*, p. 62.

108. The defeat of the right-to-work amendments in several states in 1958 was apparently due in important measure to organized labor's efforts to increase the registration and turnout of its own membership. In specific areas voter registration surveys have revealed startlingly low registration among union members, and the rewarding effects of attempts to raise it.—E.g., Connecticut CIO Council, "Voter Registration Survey—1954." COPE's "Political Memo" is full of notices of registration (and poll tax) drives. The issue for January 13, 1958, reported that the Working Agreement of Local 1179 of the Amalgamated Association of Street & Electric Railway Employees in Jamaica, New York, provided that election day is a paid holiday for all employees who show proof they are registered to vote. Local 1179 received COPE's Citation for Meritorious Service, as do all locals achieving substantially complete registration.

109. McClellan Lobby Committee, *Report*, pp. 160-61.

110. The Survey Research Center's 1956 study found that among respondents who had voted for Stevenson, 5 per cent of members of union families said they had done campaign work for a party or candidate (beyond merely talking to people, making a contribution, or going to meetings), whereas only 3 per cent of nonunion respondents said they had done so. Among Eisenhower voters the relationship was reversed, the percentages being, respectively, 4 and 5. Among all union respondents, 21 per cent said they wore a campaign button or put a sticker on their car, while 13.5 per cent of nonunion respondents said they did so.

involvement can be so measured, like the contributions of businessmen and the expenditures of labor political action groups, although the full measure of these is not always known. By far the most important political impact of both business and labor forces is felt not through their financial part in politics, but through the web of personal and institutional influences by which they are linked to large numbers of people in relationships of dependence and respect. And here a point is reached beyond which the effort to put a dollar value on political participation and political influence becomes meaningless.

Nevertheless, attempts are continuously made in public discussion to reckon organized labor's financial role in politics. Some labor leaders protest vehemently against any effort to put a price tag on total union political action. Yet, without making some attempt there is no way to assess their contention that organized labor operates at an over-all financial disadvantage in politics. Such calculations as can be made do, in fact, support their claim. It is possible to get a sense of relative magnitudes by examining the financial statements of one union. In political affairs, the United Automobile Workers is one of the nation's two or three most vigorous unions. It has never been coy about its political activities and it makes public a more detailed accounting of its receipts and disbursements than do most of the country's unions (and corporations). Table 27 presents seven categories of expenditures that are in some part, often small part, directly connected with political campaigning. These are shown for six-month periods covering the six years ending December 31, 1958; and they are intended to embrace all of the important categories of disbursements that may have direct relevance to campaigning.[111] The UAW is far from typical of American trade unions in its political activities; its experience does not permit conclusions applicable to all organized labor, except to indicate outer limits of political involvement within which organized labor as a whole would fall.

The international union receives 60 cents per year from each member for its Citizenship Fund. UAW locals collect a corresponding sum for their Citizenship Funds, which means that each UAW member contributes $1.20 per year for this purpose. These funds are spent toward the general goal of a large and informed electorate, and manifestly in their net effect they aid candidates and points of view approved by union leadership.[112] The table shows that more of these funds is spent in election years than in others, and more is spent in the second half of

111. Though probably not all. For example, "donations" appear at various places in the reports and it is not always certain what kinds of donations are involved.

112. About this empirical fact there can be little real dispute. It is a matter of choice whether one wishes to dub what goes on as partisan, political campaigning, or to call it the education of voters to the issues and interests involved in the election. The nature of existing statutes induces labor's antagonists to do the former, and labor leaders to do the latter. No neat line separates the two types of phenomena, they in actuality being intimately intertwined and often identical.

Table 27

SELECTED DISBURSEMENTS BY THE UNITED AUTOMOBILE WORKERS, INTERNATIONAL UNION, 1953-1958[a]
(in dollars)

Time Period	Total	General Fund			Educational Fund	Citizenship Fund			Organizing and Office Salaries for Full Year
		Editorial	Radio	Research and Engineering		Regular	PAC Dept.	Total	
Jan. 1-June 30, 1953	12,300,836	293,064		76,437	230,847	178,111	134,233	312,344	
July 1-Dec. 31, 1953	11,616,912	298,539	43,813[b]	85,747	236,867	81,693	143,687	225,380	4,794,251
Jan. 1-June 30, 1954	8,955,570	290,968	(c)	79,495	328,477	322,847	167,245	490,092	
July 1-Dec. 31, 1954	12,332,688	299,635	23,614	80,896	350,406	451,199	217,198	668,397	5,090,778
Jan. 1-June 30, 1955	13,131,279	288,644	196,944	86,119	249,903	108,278	158,817	267,095	
July 1-Dec. 31, 1955	18,018,257	312,446	341,269	99,436	222,779	147,174	161,143	308,317	5,585,098
Jan. 1-June 30, 1956	17,395,409	435,747	311,203	86,013	302,371	113,586	190,899	304,485	
July 1-Dec. 31, 1956	11,126,016	367,124	329,744	87,808	273,224	437,846	176,213	614,059	3,060,748
Jan. 1-June 30, 1957	13,075,231	375,331[d]	440,153	98,435	260,561	108,798	201,985[e]	310,783	
July 1-Dec. 31, 1957	13,460,833	336,526[d]	321,277	110,366	214,923	86,216	162,672[e]	248,888	7,541,922
Jan. 1-June 30, 1958	12,785,511	682,665[d]	409,789	90,982	189,360	76,630	182,086[e]	258,716	
July 1-Dec. 31, 1958	32,830,610[f]	429,463[d]	207,000	97,081	187,689	321,311	150,550[e]	471,861	(g)

[a] Taken from the reports of the Board of International Trustees and International Secretary-Treasurer, Emil Mazey.
[b] News broadcasting, full year.
[c] No expenditures shown.
[d] Entry under "Publications."
[e] Entry under "Citizenship Department."
[f] Total disbursements fluctuate with expenditures from Strike Fund, which totalled $2,959,199 in 1957 and $22,127,403 in 1958.
[g] Not given.

those years than in the first. A good deal has been said about the use of union employees in campaigns. The total for organizing and office salaries paid by the international union amounted to about $3,000,000 in 1956. If half the full staff had devoted an average of two full weeks of office time to campaign work in 1956, the salary cost would have been only about $58,000. Most of the editorial cost each year went to support the UAW newspaper. It provided an outlet for editorial opinion and for the presentation of news, including political news, as did the costs of radio programs and of operating the UAW's station at Windsor, Canada. As already noted, some research activities and some of the programs paid out of the Educational Fund bear on political campaigns.[113] If 25 per cent of the UAW international's editorial, radio, research, and educational activities, and all of its citizenship activities, are arbitrarily declared to have been campaign-connected in 1956, the total UAW international's campaign-connected expenditures in 1956 would have come to less than $1,500,000. If an equal amount was spent by UAW locals—also nothing but a guess—the total for this union would have been about $3,000,000, or less than $2.50 per member. This represents an outside figure for one of the most aggressive of all unions; for the 17,385,000 members of the labor movement resident in the United States, the per capita average would be a small fraction of it.

Crude though all of this is, the conclusion seems inescapable that labor money in politics from all sources pays a much smaller share of the nation's campaign-connected costs than union members constitute of the population of voting age. The voting-age population was estimated to be 102,743,000 in 1956. Union members made up around 17 per cent of it. Total cash campaign expenditures were estimated as $155,000,000, with at least 5 per cent additional in contributions in kind.[114] Other campaign-connected expenditures, comparable to those included in the UAW tabulation (e.g., editorial and voter-registration costs), would push the total to many tens of millions of dollars more. Seventeen per cent of whatever total might be reached would far exceed any reasonable guess at the total of labor money in politics.

5. MINORITY RIGHTS AND GROUP POLITICS

Senator Barry Goldwater, Republican of Arizona, has been the most perceptive and persistent recent critic of labor's financial activities in politics. (Much of the useful testimony given by labor leaders before Congressional committees has come in response to his queries.) Senator Goldwater's basic concern in the whole field, as he puts it, "is the fact that political liberties of some American workers are jeopardized when

113. The May, 1954, issue of *UAW-CIO Ammunition,* "Official publication of the Education Department," labeled itself on page one as "PACKED FOR POLITICAL ACTION, this issue of AMMUNITION contains articles, suggested leaflets and much other material about the relationship between workers and politics."

114. See above, pages 7-8, and below pages 372, 380.

the union takes dues money and spends it for political purposes." The problem to him is not a legal one, but a moral one. Between 40 and 50 per cent of union members favored the Republican presidential candidate in 1952 and 1956. Yet virtually all money spent in the presidential race through organized labor channels went on behalf of his Democratic opponent. Is it *right* for union leaders to spend money collected as compulsory dues for political causes with which a member paying the dues disagrees?[115]

In reply, labor's leaders argue three things. First, political action is a proper activity of unions, essential for the achievement of the economic and social goals for which they are organized, and expenditures out of union funds are a form of that activity.[116] Other interests in society, both organized and unorganized, engage in effective political action and, to maintain its competitive position in the group politics of America, organized labor must do likewise. Second, labor organizations are run by majority rule, and dues money must inevitably be spent for many purposes to which minorities are opposed. Third, many forms of financially important political action undertaken with dues money are guaranteed civil liberties under the Constitution that should not be interfered with.[117]

Federal legislation seeks to protect individual union members by making it unlawful for any labor organization to make a contribution or expenditure "in connection with" an election for federal office, or in connection with a primary election, political convention, or caucus held to choose candidates for Federal office.[118] Since many traditional rights and obligations of citizenship must be exercised in connection with the whole election system if it is to function, many problems of definition and enforcement arise. The discussion of the subject usually takes a futile turn at this point, with a wrangle over what is educational and what is political, the criteria shifting with each protagonist. Many activities are in truth educational, civic, political, and partisan—as the terms are normally used—all at the same time. Regardless of legal

115. McClellan Lobby Committee, *Hearings*, pp. 995-96.

116. There is some evidence, aside from the proceedings of union meetings, that many members agree. A 1949 survey among a selected group of members of Teamsters Local 688 in St. Louis were asked: "How much time and money should your union put into getting candidates elected to public office who are friendly to labor?" The percentages responding as follows were: A great deal, 30.6; some, 48.7; very little, 7.9; none at all, 7.1; do not know, no answer, 5.7.—Rose, *op. cit.*, p. 80. A 1951 study among the membership of District 9 of the International Association of Machinists—a union with its own set of nonpartisan leagues—led to this conclusion: ". . . the rank and file is split right down the middle about whether the union should be active in politics at all. Half the union members say yes, while the other half are dubious."—Rosen and Rosen, *op. cit.*, p. 37.

117. The hearings of the Gore and McClellan Lobby Committees report several apologias by labor leaders along these lines.

118. *U.S. Code*, Title 18, sec. 610.

definitions, and regardless of constitutional rights, the empirical fact remains that a great deal of union dues money is spent on activities that are intended to affect the outcome of federal and other elections, and presumably do. The same is true of many expenditures from the treasuries of corporations, trade associations, and other organized sectors of the economy and the society.

In all of these expenditures by all of these groups there is a measure of compulsion, and some sacrifice of minority preferences. It is perhaps correct that a stockholder is free to sell his stock if he dislikes the politics of the corporate management. But he may do so at a loss, or at great inconvenience, or at the peril of other economic disadvantages. Given the cloud of obscurity in which campaign-connected expenditures are made, he may never be entirely sure just how extensively corporate funds are involved. A union member can, it could be argued, change his skill or his job. But this is hardly a course that in reality is open to him; the freedom of stockholders to withdraw from corporations, of corporations to withdraw from trade associations, and of professional men to withdraw from their professional societies may in fact be similarly restricted. The fact would seem to be that membership in any organized group possessed of political interests commits an individual to indirect involvement in the political process. The character of this involvement will be determined by those who dominate the group. There is no escape from politics for the individual. When he spends his money at a local store, part of the price he pays may wind up as a campaign donation, and unwittingly he thus favors one candidate over another by shopping one place instead of another.

Any organized or unorganized group in society possesses an inherent political potential. Ministers of the cloth have swayed their parishioners. Country doctors have been revered as political seers. Chambers of commerce and farm bureaus have behaved as partisan political structures. Compulsions to conformity can be active in any group. Doubtless some of the voluntary dollars given by union members are so prompted, but campaign solicitations among other economic groups are solicited under similar conditions. Republican finance committees are merely the political action committees of business, raising money, though more of it, by the same intrinsic means as do the political action committees of labor.

Groups with political interests at stake mobilize their political potential with varying degrees of intensity and efficiency. Certain segments of organized labor and certain segments of organized business have displayed great energy in doing so. To expect them not to in the American political system is like expecting water not to run down hill. Perhaps one limit was reached in those Detroit Congressional districts where the regular Democratic organization was replaced by the CIO-

PAC,[119] or in other districts where the endorsement of one candidate by leaders of a business hierarchy effectively cuts off financial support to any potential opponents.

Much of the concern over organized labor in politics stems from its novelty. Business interests long dominated the politics of the nation—which is not to say the intent or the results were either bad or good—and more recently a new type of organized interest has entered the arena. Detached concern among some persons for the functioning of a political system brings forth proposals for its regulation, but the great energies behind reform and revision originate in groups whose interests are more directly affected. The attempts to regulate the role of corporations and labor organizations in politics come largely from their antagonists. Labor's opponents want its participation shackled. Labor leaders advocate limits on the sums individuals may give to campaigns—and few union members could afford the sums to be limited.

It is more realistic to view the debate over labor's political finances as a struggle for the control of government than as a legal or moral issue. The debate may be waged in moral terms, and its result may be expressed in legal ones, but the origins and the stakes of the debate are the social and economic advantages that accompany political power.

119. Samuel J. Eldersveld, *Political Affiliation in Metropolitan Detroit* (Ann Arbor: Bureau of Government Research, University of Michigan, 1957), p. 87.

8

RAISING THE MONEY—OLD PROS AND NEW

In 1937, John D. M. Hamilton set about rebuilding a badly shattered Republican party. He was chairman of the Republican national committee and the road back from the Landon debacle of the previous year seemed a long one. One of his first steps was to ask the help of a little-known, dedicated Republican businessman from Pittsburgh named Carlton G. Ketchum. Two decades later Mr. Ketchum was only slightly better known outside the financial circles of his own party, but in the interval a fundamental reconstruction of Republican-party fund-raising had been achieved, and he was its chief advocate and architect.

Mr. Ketchum was a professional, and he was in politics, but he was not a professional politician. He was a professional fund-raiser. His role in Republican affairs symbolizes graphically the increasing specialization and reliance on *expertise* that characterize campaign activities in both parties. In the loose language of the trade, he is called a financial politician, as opposed to a political politician. The distinction between the two concepts—roughly of those who marshal the resources and of those who spend them—is an important one in understanding basic differences between the financial management of the major parties and in examining certain internal dissensions that rack them both.

Very little money wells up spontaneously from the body politic. American parties customarily lack the "extreme devices" for coercing campaign contributions that an observer of Latin American politics noted. Most of the year-around costs of political parties and most campaign war chests in the United States must be raised by *persuading* solid citizens to part with their solid dollars. The tactics and techniques by which this feat is achieved have displayed increasing variety since the first election of Franklin Roosevelt.

1. THE CHANGING SHAPE OF SOLICITING

The year 1936 was a turning point in the history of political party fund-raising. The policies and methods of Franklin Roosevelt's first term produced political alignments more along economic-class lines than any since the McKinley-Bryan era. The shifts in large campaign gifts between 1932 and 1936 reflected changed attitudes toward the New Deal. The shifts themselves affected fund-raising problems and opportunities facing each party. But other things happened too, during the New Deal and in the years that followed, to produce a steady evolution in the procedures of fund-raising and in the financial organization of the parties.

Congress in 1907 had prohibited contributions by corporations, and during the early part of the twentieth century most states followed suit.[1] A heavy campaign burden consequently fell on wealthy individuals. Beginning in the 1930's, the enactment of steep progressive income taxes, gift taxes, and inheritance taxes shrank the number of patrons willing and able to make political donations in five and six figures.[2] The Hatch Act of 1940 forbade gifts by individuals to certain classes of political committees of over $5,000 per person per year, making it inconvenient for large contributors to give as freely as they once had. These developments affected both parties, and the task of Democratic managers was further complicated by restrictions on labor union political activities commencing with the Smith-Connally Anti-Strike Act in 1943.[3]

With the New Deal, war, and the war-in-peace economy that followed, enormous numbers of persons came into new relationships with government. In 1956 federal expenditures equalled about one-sixth of the gross national product. Of great importance to political solicitors was the dependence on government of the economy in general and of myriads of individual businesses. More persons were touched more directly by government than ever before and became more susceptible to being touched by political fund-raisers than ever before.

Political campaigning used to be confined largely to the few months preceding an election. During the 1930's the involvement of politically attentive publics so increased in intensity that demands were made to wage continuous war against, or for, the New Deal.[4] Moreover, the

1. For a summary of early legislation and the circumstances leading to its adoption, see Louise Overacker, *Money in Elections* (New York: The Macmillan Company, 1932), pp. 228-48, 289-320. Corporate gifts rose in significance as assessments of government employees fell, becoming notably visible in the presidential election of 1888.—Matthew Josephson, *The Politicos—1865-1896* (New York: Harcourt, Brace and Company, 1938), pp. 423ff.

2. One Pennsylvania Republican fund-raiser kept a list of party stalwarts as they died, dolefully recording by the name of each the annual cost of his demise to the party.

3. For a summary and history of the adoption of this later legislation, see Louise Overacker, *Presidential Campaign Funds* (Boston: Boston University Press, 1946), pp. 25-71.

4. Note the political awakening of Joseph N. Pew, Jr., that brought forth funds for the Republican national committee, as described in Charles W. Van Devander, *The Big Bosses* (New York: Howell, Soskin, Publishers, 1944), pp. 152-53.

optimum use of radio and television, especially the latter, requires advance planning and highly technical skills. Financial understandings must be made well before a campaign officially opens, and those who design the tactical use of the media need to know what resources they can count on. The need for party funds in off-years as well as in campaign years, and early in the year as well as late, grew.

Money-raising techniques used for nonpolitical causes had developed markedly during the 1920's and 1930's. Their refinement and application following World War II reflected the technological specialization and prosperity that typified the whole economy. Spectacular importance was claimed for the whipping boys of the new culture, the gentlemen with advertising and public relations addresses on Madison Avenue who claimed an ability to manipulate the public's tastes and opinions. Spectacular results were clearly achieved by their close cousins, the professional fund-raising counsels. It would have been extraordinary had their impact not been felt in the ways politicians raise money, as well as in the ways they spend it.

The confluence of these varied influences led to the trend personified by Mr. Ketchum's efforts to bring professional fund-raising skills to the service of Republican soliciting. It contributed also to the large-scale political use of fund-raising dinners, inaugurated before the 1936 election by the Democratic party. And along with the dinners came an increasing number of devices to attract large numbers of small contributions. These three developments gave political money-raising in the 1950's an entirely different shape, if not an altogether different substance, from any it had had before.

2. THE REPUBLICAN MODEL AND ITS VARIANTS

The central financial organ of the Republican party since 1936 has been its national finance committee. This body was created to coordinate financial planning and fund-raising for the Republican national committee, the Republican Senatorial campaign committee, and the Republican Congressional campaign committee. Its chairmen give it tone. In 1952 Sinclair Weeks of Massachusetts, wealthy industrialist and banker who subsequently became Secretary of Commerce, headed the committee. In 1954 an important Minneapolis grain dealer, F. Peavey Heffelfinger, held the job, and in 1956 it fell to John Clifford Folger of Washington, D.C., an investment banker. Spencer T. Olin, of Illinois and the giant Olin Mathieson Chemical Corporation, served in 1958. The committee has customarily been comprised of a finance chairman in each state and territory, along with 25 or so members-at-large, to some extent geographically representative, some of the latter so decorated because they give heavily to the party, some because they are adept at getting others to do so. Representatives of the committee meet with representatives of the three national-level campaign committees (national, Senatorial, Congressional) to agree upon a budget for each and to fix a sum the finance committee will seek to raise.[5] The national finance committee in turn assigns a quota to each state. State committees customarily accept the quotas assigned, only rarely seeking to negotiate a lower one.[6]

Mr. Ketchum was attached to the national finance committee as finance director off and on after 1937, and from that position worked with others to introduce professional fund-raising skills at state and local levels.[7] As early as 1932 he had tried to convince Republican

5. Chapter 11, below, discusses intercommittee, intraparty transfers of funds and their organizational significance.

6. Members-at-large of the national finance committee do not solicit directly within a state without approval of the state organization, and what they raise is credited to the state's quota. In working out a state's quota, six factors are normally employed: the state's electoral votes, population, number of Republican voters in the last presidential election, number of occupied dwelling units, personal income-tax collections, and purchasing power. Philip S. Wilder, Jr., reports: "Each state and territory's percentage of the national total of each of these items is determined, and the average of these six figures is the percentage of the national budget which is assigned as a quota for each state or territory."—"The National Committee of the Party in Power, 1953-1958" (mimeographed, a paper delivered at the annual meeting of the American Political Science Association, 1958), p. 17. On occasion other factors also have a bearing. In 1952 the national finance committee asked Texas Republicans for considerably more than the formula would have provided.

The national committee does not make public the quotas it assigns, but state leaders discuss them freely. They have been $1,000 or lower in some of the southern states and territories. Georgia's in 1953 was $15,000 and in 1954, $30,000. In the latter year others were: Idaho, $22,000; Minnesota, $94,000; Texas, $130,000; Illinois, $310,000; California, $400,000. New York usually runs around 15 per cent of the national total. Drew Pearson published in 1955 what appeared to be the quotas for that year. The lowest shown was the Virgin Islands at $950 (with Alaska and Puerto Rico the only other areas less than $5,000) and the highest was New York at $271,719 (followed by California at $191,273 and Pennsylvania at $165,300). North Carolina's $20,453 was the median figure.—*The News and Observer* (Raleigh, N.C.), March 2, 1955.

The national finance committee seldom meets its goal, as the following comparisons of the sums sought and raised, respectively, for the years 1944-53 indicate: 1944, $4,000,000-$3,709,615; 1945, $750,000-$674,041; 1946, $1,925,000-$1,631,313; 1947, $900,000-$826,228; 1948, $4,000,000-$3,607,065; 1949, $900,000-$294,479; 1950, $1,952,000-$1,407,582; 1951, $1,200,000-$1,050,666; 1952, $4,800,000-$5,466,534; 1953, $1,900,000-$1,793,658.

Wilder, *loc. cit.,* shows the number of states and territories meeting various percentages of their quotas as follows during 1955-57:

	1955	*1956*	*1957*
Met or exceeded quota	41	40	7
Raised 80-100 per cent	0	0	2
50-80 per cent	2	7	11
20-50 per cent	5	4	11
0-20 per cent	5	2	22

7. Under the leadership of Will Hays, chairman of the Republican national committee, experienced "money-drive" men were employed on salary to raise money for the Republican campaign of 1920. Avowedly seeking to reach a large number of contributors, and to profit from recent experience with fund-raising for war purposes, Hays and associates set up a system of national, state, and local "ways

leaders of the potentialities that lay in improved soliciting procedures—an effort that would lead his firm during the next 26 years to manage more than 90 Republican fund-raising campaigns in at least 16 states.[8] His services had been employed in Connecticut in 1932 and in 1934, and it was during this period that he first organized Republican fund-raising in his home county, Allegheny County, Pennsylvania, one of the most important financially to the GOP in the nation. In 1936, Republican leaders in Ohio, Missouri, and Pennsylvania had used his services, but the nationwide development did not commence until 1937.[9]

The model.—No political practices are precisely uniform in all states, but efforts to create an efficient nationwide money-raising organization have produced similarities among GOP procedures in many of them. Republican politicians and their financial backers at state and local levels have received with varying degrees of enthusiasm the organizational admonitions reaching them from the national finance committee in Washington. Nevertheless, the extent to which most of the financially important states have adopted the recommendations made to them, or have developed similar procedures on their own, is impressive. The best way to understand the varieties that have developed is to look first at the ideal model.

The cardinal features are five in number.[10]

First, all Republican solicitations are made in a ***unified campaign***—like a United Fund Drive—carried out at each political level, in each jurisdiction. All Republican fund-raising in a county, for example, would be undertaken ideally by that county's finance committee, which

---

and means" committees that displayed in incipient form some of the features later pressed for by Mr. Ketchum. Operating costs ran high, the results were not thought outstanding, and the plan was not revived for use in 1924.—James K. Pollock, *Party Campaign Funds* (Alfred A. Knopf, Inc., 1926), pp. 71-77. Mr. Hays comments on the scheme in *The Memoirs of Will H. Hays* (Garden City: Doubleday & Company, Inc., 1955), pp. 274-75.

8. Ketchum, Inc., of Pittsburgh, works for a flat fee (rather than for a percentage of funds raised), billing political clients on the same basis as other clients. Campaign-finance reports showed some of its 1952 fees to be as follows: $27,900 from the Indiana Republican State Central Committee (receipts: $324,786); $18,530 from the New York United Republican Finance Committee (receipts: $1,517,409); and $27,563 from the Allegheny County, Pennsylvania, Republican Finance Committee (receipts: $664,032). In 1956, eight of the firm's approximately 80 professional personnel were employed on political accounts. In October of 1956, Mr. Ketchum estimated his firm's fees for political work so far that year to be around $150,000. See his testimony before the Gore Committee *Hearings,* part 2, pp. 445-55.

9. Mr. Ketchum gave an early report on the effort in "Political Financing, 1937 Model," *Public Opinion Quarterly,* 2 (1938), 135-40.

10. Freely discussed by most acquainted with them and set forth, or implicit, in such publications as "Republican Fund-Raising—Some of the 'Hows'" (printed), 29 pp., and "Fund Raising Manual" (mimeographed), 24 pp., both issued by the Republican national finance committee.

assumes responsibility for supplying the needs of all Republican activities and candidates in the area, as well as quotas to other committees.

Second, fund-raising activities are *centralized in a state finance committee* with which county committees enter contractual agreements.[11] The counties undertake to raise specified quotas, all funds collected in a county being sent to the state committee, which issues receipts, makes records, and refunds an agreed-upon portion to the county. The state finance committee fills the national quotas and serves as the financial control center for the party in the state.

Third, fund-raising is *separately organized from the "political" activities* of the party. The theory is that most regular politicians do not make good fund-raisers, and persons who make good fund-raisers usually do not make good politicians. Finance committees review the budgets submitted to them by operating units of the party (the corresponding county or state regular committee, for example), much as a government budget bureau would do, reaching through negotiation the amount of money the finance committee will undertake to provide. Except at this stage, and for turning over the funds collected, the finance committees are supposed to operate independently of the party's regular committees.

Fourth, the finance committees are intended to provide *continuous, year-around programming* of the party's fund-raising. Only by institutionalizing the solicitation program, with continuing professional staff and systematic records, can maximum success be achieved.

Finally, through these single-purpose, continuing finance committees the *technical skills of professional fund-raising,* so successful in other spheres, are brought to the service of party finance.

Over-all, it is argued that conflicting solicitations will be eliminated, fraudulant solicitations by outsiders will be reduced, efficient party management will be encouraged, the confidence of contributors will be won, more money will be raised more cheaply, and the regular politicians can devote their undivided energies to active campaigning.[12]

Departures from the model.—The extent to which Republican fund-raising approaches this organizational ideal differs from state to state.

11. The national finance committee circulates a "sample contract" in its mimeographed manual, "Republican Fundraising Data Sheets."

12. The British Conservative party has taken steps to broaden its financial base, especially in the formation of its Central Board of Finance, a body that seems to be responsible for the solicitation of middle-sized gifts in the Provincial Areas for use by the central party organization. If more were known about its inner workings, certain limited similarities to the Republican finance system might become apparent. See R. T. McKenzie, *British Political Parties* (London: Heinemann Limited, 1955), pp. 209-12. In their purpose to establish order and responsibility in the management of business's money in politics, and hence to create confidence that the money is used more or less as intended, the German sponsors' associations perform certain of the functions sought through the Republican finance committees. See Arnold J. Heidenhimer, "German Party Finance: The CDU," *American Political Science Review,* 51 (1957), 376-78.

In some states it differs from year to year. Even where a system has been effective for many years, the competence and enthusiasm of the current finance chairman may affect profoundly its operation.[13] Where procedures are newly established, or the principle of a unified, centralized finance campaign are not accepted wholeheartedly by party leaders, a finance chairman through his energy and skill can influence importantly the allegiance shown to the finance committee's program, and in fact the amount of money raised.

In the late 1950's, roughly two-thirds of the states and territories, including all of the populous, industrially important states, had a centrally organized Republican finance system generally compatible with the model outlined above. The remaining areas fell into two groups. In one, fund-raising was to some extent centralized, but was carried out largely on a "personal basis." One or a small group of key figures raised the state money, but they inclined less toward county quotas, wide coverage, and medium-size gifts than toward appeals based on friendship to tried and true party benefactors who would make king-size donations. In the other group of states, confusion reigned, with factional splits within the party often combining with other difficulties to produce various types of incoherent and unsystematic solicitation practices.[14]

13. The organization of power within a state party may bear directly on the organization of fund-raising. One student relates the development of the centralized finance system in Connecticut to the concentration of party control at the state level under the leadership of J. Henry Roraback, 1912-37.—John Robert Owens, "Party Campaign Funds in Connecticut, 1950-1954" (Ph.D. dissertation, Syracuse University, 1956), pp. 301-3.

14. The situation prevailing in some of the 53 states and territories changes from year to year. In 1954, the 53 areas could be classified as follows:

(1a) Thirty areas in which organized fund-raising generally like the national finance committee's model was found. Among these were 14 in which salaried, full-time, year-around fund-raising personnel were employed: California, Colorado, Connecticut, Illinois, Indiana, Iowa, Michigan, Minnesota, New Jersey, New York, Ohio, Pennsylvania, Washington, and Wisconsin. In Utah a part-time person was so employed. The remaining 15 areas were: Arkansas, Delaware, Florida, Idaho, Kansas, Maine, Massachusetts, Nebraska, Nevada, North Dakota, Oregon, South Dakota, Wyoming, District of Columbia, and Hawaii.

(1b) Six areas in which systematic, organized fund-raising resembled the model somewhat less, but in which a fairly highly developed system of county quotas and unified fund-raising activity was usually found. One of the states in this group, Kentucky, had full-time, paid personnel. The others were Montana, New Hampshire, Oklahoma, Tennessee, and West Virginia.

(2) Ten areas in which some type of unified solicitation program was found but without county quotas and with activities largely of a personal kind, usually organized around an individual or small group who depended upon personal appeals to a coterie of the wealthy faithful: Alabama, Georgia, Mississippi, New Mexico, North Carolina, Texas, Vermont, Alaska, Puerto Rico, and the Virgin Islands.

(3) Seven areas in which fund-raising was badly divided among more than one group, or in which there was little organization at all or some other source of confusion: Arizona, Louisiana, Maryland, Missouri, Rhode Island, South Carolina, and Virginia.

The big industrial states are cited by Republican party financiers as having the best money-raising programs. The state finance committees in Illinois, Massachusetts, New York, Ohio, and Pennsylvania together raised more than $6,500,000 during 1952, and more than $4,500,000 between September 1 and November 30, 1956.[15] Ohio commands greatest prestige among the technicians. It has operated continuously on a professional basis since 1936. When Minnesotans set up a state finance operation in 1953, they sent the man who would run it to Columbus for a week of observation and instruction. In Ohio, as sometimes elsewhere, procedures are mechanized, with IBM equipment used. In a campaign year, three or four professionals have usually been employed in addition to the salaried finance director, one probably assigned to each of the major metropolitan areas of the state. The clerical staff is considerably larger.[16] Counties outside the metropolitan areas have customarily been organized into districts with a finance chairman in charge of each, and with a finance chairman and finance committee in each county. The state finance committee has been able as a rule to reach agreements with over 60 of the state's 88 counties, including all of the large ones, and the county organizations have in fact sent in their solicitations, the state office thereafter rebating the county's agreed-on share.[17] Ohio, like

---

When queried in 1958, 42 of the 48 Republican state chairmen reported that a separately organized finance committee had operated in their state during 1956. Of those, 18 stated the committee had kept open a separate office with its own personnel throughout 1956 and 1957, all but two of them being states included in categories (1a) and (1b) above. Missouri and Rhode Island were the additions. (Both these states were in category (3) in 1954. So was Arizona, whose chairman reported that a finance committee office was opened in 1957.) All of the 42 save three (Alabama, Indiana, and Kansas) said the state committee normally depends on the finance committee for a "large part" of its income.

15. Of 259 persons known by the Gore Committee to have given an aggregate of $5,000 or more to politics in 1956, 33 per cent gave New York State as their permanent address (two-thirds of those in New York City). The percentages for other states were Pennsylvania, 11; California, 10; Connecticut, 7; Delaware, Illinois, and Texas, 6 each.

16. The number of employees reported by several finance committees (on the last payroll of each month) during 1952 tells something of the scope and ascending tempo of their operations. The numbers in parenthesis indicate the employees receiving $500 or more during the month.

	Jan.	*Feb.*	*Mar.*	*Apr.*	*May*	*June*	*July*	*Aug.*	*Sep.*	*Oct.*	*Nov.*	*Dec.*
Pa.	9(2)	9(2)	10(2)	11(2)	14(2)	16(2)	19(2)	20(2)	28(3)	28(3)	33(4)	24(2)
N.Y.	9	9	13	20	25	29(2)	32(2)	34(1)	46(1)	54(1)	14	11
Neb.	1	1	1	1	3	2	2	2	2	1	2	
Allegheny Co.,Pa.	2(1)		2	2	5	7	6	6	6	6	6	6

17. A person who worked during the summer of 1952 on the staff of the Clark County, Ohio, Republican finance committee reports the organization and procedures in that county to have followed closely the ideal form. In fact, an employee of Ketchum, Inc., hired by the state finance committee, spent about six weeks working with the county committee. In a county of 112,000 people, $50,503 was raised, all of it transmitted to the state committee, which rebated $24,039.—John A. Corry, "Party Finance in the Eisenhower Campaign and the Problem of Legislative Control" (Senior thesis, Princeton University, 1953), pp. 35-40.

other states, has "mendicant counties"—those wishing to keep for local purposes monies collected in the county and doubting the plea that through cooperative effort they will benefit more in the long run.

Arrangements among state and local finance committees vary with conditions in each state. In Pennsylvania, as the result of a dust up during the 1940's, Allegheny County, in which Pittsburgh is located, handles its funds independently (in excess of $650,000 in both 1952 and 1956). It sends an allotment to the state finance committee. Most of the other counties forward their total collections under a rebate arrangement with the state finance committee. An alert finance director, here as elsewhere, may advance a rebate on assurances the county's transmission is in the mails. In New York, the United Republican Finance Committee functions in the eight metropolitan counties. Its agreement with the counties allows them to retain contributions of $25.00 or less. The rest of New York's 54 counties have operated more independently, for the most part holding the funds they raise except for small quotas handed on to an upstate finance committee of minor significance. In Illinois, where the counties around Chicago (Cook, Lake, and Du Page) have long dominated the financial picture, many downstate counties in the past frankly saw to their own needs first before transmitting funds to the state level. In 1956 a degree of organization was finally achieved outside the Chicago area and a full-time director employed to manage a separate finance operation. In California, only 20 of the 58 counties had finance committees in August before the 1954 elections. The county allocations that year, made on the basis of Republican registration, were not intended to meet all campaign requirements but to provide for the national quota ($400,000) and for state organizational needs ($113,955).[18]

Businessman's avocation: fund-raising.—A visitor to the headquarters of a well-organized Republican finance committee senses the same atmosphere that pervades a giant philanthropic drive. Here are the same banks of files classifying thousands of prospects—some by size of contribution, some by place of business, some by place of residence.[19] Here are the same packets of instructions for solicitors, pledge cards, transmittal slips, progress records, and other paraphernalia found in any professionally run Community Chest or United Fund drive in a large

18. The organization of Republican fund-raising in California is described in Leonard Carl Rowe, "Political Campaign Funds in California" (Ph.D. dissertation, University of California, 1957), pp. 115-31.

19. Business organizations are useful in political as well as charitable fund-raising. In 1954 the Ford Motor Company employed 108,000 persons in the Detroit area, at least 864 of whom made contributions to the Wayne County Republican finance committee. The gifts, most of them in sums of two digits beginning at $25.00, ranged from $5.00 to $1,000, averaged $67.82, and totalled $58,594.93. Virtually all were made between the middle of September and the end of October.

city.[20] Here also are many of the same men and women. Energetic members of the business community whose positions and inclinations lead them into charitable fund-raising are, for the same qualities, likely to be pulled into political fund-raising as well. John S. Ames, Jr., for example, elected chairman of the Massachusetts Republican state finance committee in 1957, had served previously as general chairman of a Red Cross Drive and as industrial chairman for USO campaigns. Edward L. Ryerson, chairman of the Republican Citizens Finance Committee of Illinois in 1952 and 1954, had a long history of participation in civic fund-raising enterprises, including the presidency for several years of Community Chests and Councils, Incorporated. Among the 202 individuals who served during the election years 1952-58 as state finance chairmen and members-at-large of the Republican national finance committee, information from standard reference sources could be obtained on about half (97). Of those, 92 per cent reported a history of non-political community service of one kind or another, averaging five civic activities each. The percentage reporting specific experience in non-political fund-raising was 31. The true percentage was unquestionably

20. A person accustomed to the haphazard, informal jumble that has traditionally characterized political activities in the United States is easily impressed by the bales of work forms, pep letters, organization charts, and statistical summaries with which the staffs of many of the finance committees are happy to load him. There is a temptation to reproduce them all and to describe in detail the variations from one state to another in the concepts of organization and procedure employed.

Invariably there is a separate division to handle special gifts (or "advance gifts" as they are sometimes called). The New York United Republican Finance Committee used 56 solicitors in its special gifts division in 1952, each working 15 to 50 names, divided into an "A" list (those who gave $3,000 or more in the previous year, or previous comparable election year), and a "B" list (those who gave less). Almost as often there is a women's division (with at least one state finance director operating on the assumption that 75 per cent of American wealth is controlled by the ladies). In less populous places solicitations tend to be organized around residential areas. The business section of a town may even be broken up on a geographical basis.

In the huge metropolitan centers, however, whence come the bulk of the funds, organization along "industry" lines is common. The president of a bank in Philadelphia calls a meeting of the presidents of other banks, asking each to see that his organization is canvassed. The solicitors' organization chart in another state—and the progress report forms—reveal the whole program to be split into three main industry divisions, each with sections and subsections, and ultimately 59 occupational groups: accountants, advertising, alcoholic beverages, amusements, architects and engineers, attorneys, auto dealers, auto manufacturers, etc. In another place, shippers have been divided according to nationality, so that a suitable solicitor could be put in charge of each group.

Opinions differ on how exclusively solicitations should be organized along industry lines. In some localities the size of the fish to be hooked is the first consideration. The president of a railroad summoned a luncheon meeting, not of other railroad people, but of heads of business enterprises of comparable importance to his own. Prospective contributors are often rated according to what they are expected to give, and persons with similar capacity assigned to solicit them. Amid all the technical variations, however, the distinguishing feature is a businesslike approach by businessmen to the task at hand.

higher, perhaps approaching 100, for many solicitation assignments are inappropriate for inclusion in *Who's Who* entries.

The productiveness of a unified Republican fund-raising program depends basically on ability to appeal successfully to businessmen for soliciting as well as contributing.[21] It is no accident that the states in which Republicans have failed to adopt an effective, modern soliciting system are for the most part states where Republicans make the poorest electoral showing. Where Democrats dominate state and local affairs, the difficulties of launching a unified fund-raising program are considerable. Politically active businessmen sympathetic toward the Republican party nationally may nevertheless wish to maintain a Democratic state government, or at least maintain rapport with the Democratic state government. Their participation in Democratic politics often takes the form of campaign donations. They are happier sending their funds to the national sphere through the United States mails or via a like-minded intermediary.[22]

Imperfections in practice.—Even in states with strong Republican followings and organized finance programs, however, all may not go well. Some difficulties arise out of substantive issues of politics. The estrangement of President Eisenhower and Senator McCarthy after 1953 provoked forthright declarations hostile to Ike and national fund-raising by both solicitors and contributors in the Midwest. The Illinois finance committee's 1954 receipts were only 90 per cent of those in 1950, whereas its income in 1952 had been 130 per cent of that in 1948.

Other difficulties are related to the initiative and quality of finance committee personnel. Following the 1952 election more than half the state finance chairmen (53 per cent) withdrew and had to be replaced. It was claimed the shift adversely affected the subsequent campaign. If so, the difficulties were progressive, for an even larger number resigned after 1954 (62 per cent) and in 1958 only about one-fourth (26 per cent) of the state finance chairmen had held the same post in 1956. Only five persons served continuously through all four elections between 1952 and 1958.[23] The changes in the national finance chairmanship—four shifts in six years—combined with the turnover in the states to produce a deterioration of the Republican fund-raising organization in many areas.

21. Rowe found that 31 types of business were represented in 1956 on the membership of the United San Francisco Republican Finance Committee and that 22 of 24 members of its executive committee were officials of large corporations.—*Op. cit.*, pp. 122-23.

22. For comments on the contributing behavior of "presidential Republicans," see Alexander Heard, *A Two-Party South?* (Chapel Hill: University of North Carolina Press, 1952), pp. 116, 143.

23. The rate of turnover among the members-at-large of the national finance committee was almost identical to the rate among the state finance chairmen (within one percentage point) in each of the three years.

One of the frequent failings, in the eyes of the experts, is a delay in starting solicitations until the beginning of the election campaign. The theory of the system calls for year-around fund-raising in all years. The habit of delay has existed in many states, but to some New York is a chief offender. The late nomination of candidates in that state provides a plausible reason for waiting until contributors know who the candidates are. Some critics from other states, however, stoutly hold that this is no excuse and what the big-city boys need to do is get on the ball.

A late start by a united effort does little to inspire confidence among candidates aching for victory. It therefore contributes to the difficulties of maintaining a *unified* fund drive. Other more fundamental causes, however, are involved. In all areas, candidates use independent campaign funds of varying degrees of importance. One top Republican charged with heat that two "sitting United States senators" regularly violate their word and engage in private fund-raising campaigns, outside the circle of their family and intimate friends, campaigns that sabotage the party's attempts at a united effort. More basic, however, are inevitable contributors with special ties to individual candidates. They do not want to throw their funds into the common pot.

In addition to the personal campaign funds of candidates, there are volunteer committees that raise money in competition with the regular finance committees. These are sometimes composed simply of adherents of a particular candidate, bound together by common personal loyalty to him. More often, such groups are formed to attract funds and votes from independent voters, or special occupational groups, or citizens with common leanings in policy who wish to be selective in whom they support.

The most important of these groups financially in the Eisenhower years was the Citizens for Eisenhower-Nixon (the name was adjusted slightly in off-years). To the regular Republican finance people the Citizens, with state and local committees in many states, were in every year a plain headache. By definition they challenge the cardinal principle that more money can be raised from affluent prospects through a single, well-planned appeal than from multiple solicitations.[24] The decisions to use the Citizens have been made at the highest political level, and various steps were taken to coordinate their work with that of the regular party organization. There was a good deal of conferring and splitting of prospect lists in some places.[25] By the standards of political

24. Fund-raisers loyal to the principle of single solicitation even oppose the "blitz" campaigns carried out late in a campaign by the regular finance people. This is a standard device used off and on in various forms by both parties. Republicans often put a team of solicitors on the phone appealing to a selected list for $1,000 each, over and above what has been given before.

25. Finance-committee solicitors frequently accept several checks from the same contributor, fanning them out to desired destinations, which sometimes include volunteer as well as regular committees.

campaigning, the gestures toward cooperation were, by and large, remarkably effective, though not enough so to mollify all the regulars. The fact remains, nevertheless, that the Citizens organization became part of the continuing fund-raising structure of the Republican party during the Eisenhower regime.

Finance committee members frankly confess they are tolerated by political Republicans only because of belief in their ability to rustle funds for the party from sources that would not otherwise give so much. The regulars do not want rivals for power within the party. Nor do they want their own special supplies of money siphoned away from them. In theory there will be more for all through a united effort. The unity does not generally extend, however, to ward and precinct organizations in the metropolitan areas. In Cook County, Illinois, for example, the Republican ward organizations run their own finances with traditional independence. There is no suggestion that they forward their revenue up the line and subsist on a rebate fixed by negotiated agreement. The political Republicans also raise funds at higher levels. They work among their "friends," as one state finance chairman put it, "whom they have done business with, persons who want to be friendly with political and government leaders." These are as a rule small businessmen, but "there are some big ones too." Some of such money finds its way to the finance committees, but some is distributed through other channels.

3. DEMOCRATIC FRENZY

The oft-proclaimed similarity between the major American political parties does not extend to their financial organization and procedures. The similarities between the national committees and conventions, the elements of national consensus expressed in party platforms, and the aspects of party organization prescribed by state laws clothe the parties with the same external appearance. Rarely is the necessary field work possible to ascertain for a series of states the detailed operations that expose the character of parties as administrative organizations, as instruments of competitive politics, and as institutions of democratic government.

Out of many conversations with financial and political functionaries in all parts of the country,[26] however, there emerge two distinctly different profiles of party fund-raising. Democratic efforts to meet the costs of politics can most easily be understood if contrasted with the Republican activities just described.

Despite substantial efforts made at national headquarters beginning in 1958, no comparable machinery of solicitation is visible among Democrats. Democratic fund-raising has traditionally been typified by informality and confusion. There have been no grand strategies over the

26. In the course of the present study, interviews were held in over half the states (with intensive explorations in a dozen of them) and with individuals of nationwide experience.

years laid out in sober memoranda for the party chieftains, no multi-colored booklets for state and local guidance—or at least none that one can come by.[27] What generally goes on, it eventually becomes apparent, resembles in many ways what the Republicans do in the one-fourth to one-third of the states where their fund-raising is described as "not organized." When George Killion was treasurer of the Democratic national committee, in the 1940's, he tried to hire Carlton Ketchum's services. But that gentleman is a Republican with his heart as well as his head, and while willing to sell to his own side he would not sell to the enemy. Neither at the national level nor elsewhere has the Democratic party made use of professional fund-raisers on anything like the scale Republicans have done.[28]

Except in some of the small-sum campaigns, Democrats have not combined soliciting for the national committees with soliciting to meet state and local needs. They have not tried consistently to develop a separate corps of financial Democrats, in contrast to political Democrats. Nor have they tried systematically to coordinate the financial operations of committees and candidates who in the same locality burn up the party's scarce resources. They have in general not exhibited the concern for planned, diligent fund-raising that their financial disadvantage in most quarters would seem to impel.

National level.—The Democratic national committee has confined its concern over the years largely to its own war chest, and to the Democratic Senatorial and Congressional campaign committees. Traditionally, the "normal" pattern has required the national committeeman from each state to see that his state's contribution to the national committee is made.[29] Myron Blalock, the Texas member from 1940 until

27. Since 1956 the national committee has emphasized solicitations of small contributions, with a consequent stepping up in the distribution of instructional and hortatory materials.

28. The American Association of Fund-Raising Counsel was in 1959 composed of 31 professional fund-raising organizations. Only two or three firms among them, other than Ketchum, Inc., were known to have engaged in political fund-raising on any significant scale. There were some 400 other fund-raising firms in 1959 not members of this association, most of them small, among which perhaps ten or a dozen were known to have had any consecutive experience in political soliciting. The general impression seems to be that outside of Ketchum, Inc., professional fund-raisers have usually had limited or unhappy experience in political work. On occasion, of course, technicians skilled in money-raising are made available by their employers to help in political campaigns.

As to public relations firms and political fund-raising, see pages 418-19, below.

29. The national committee early in 1953 "inaugurated" a quota system. The basis for assigning the quotas was vague, "ability to pay based on previous experience" combined with population being the closest thing to a formula that could be found.

The Democratic national committee has not, however, been so skittish as its Republican counterpart about making the quotas public. The report made by Chairman Stephen A. Mitchell and Treasurer Stanley Woodward to the committee in New Orleans on December 4, 1954, and given to the press, listed minimum quotas for the two-year period 1953-54 for each state and territory. The lowest

1948, is sometimes cited as the acme of the fund-raising national committeeman. He concentrated on monies for national purposes. He is remembered as moving grandly from one plush hotel to another across Texas, summoning a few chosen chieftains at each stand. They in turn invited prospective donors to enjoy Mr. Blalock's open hospitality. In the resulting joy, Mr. Blalock put the bite. The trouble has been, however, that often a national committeeman possesses neither the personality, position, nor personal resources to make him an effective solicitor. A committeeman who is also governor of his state may be well situated to assume responsibility for the national quota. But more often than not a committeeman is chosen because he is acceptable to a range of factional interests within his state, a criterion not necessarily related to skill in raising money.

As a consequence, national leaders have frequently asked that someone else assume the burden. Some national committeemen are happy to be rid of it and have eagerly helped saddle a United States senator, another state political leader, or a businessman with the task. Other committeemen, personally resentful or caught in a factional squeeze, have resisted. At times national leaders have gone into states without their assistance to get help from persons of their own choice.

Responsibility at the top has generally rested with the treasurer of the national committee. He has shared it irregularly with a national finance chairman[30] and regularly with the chairman of the national committee, whose show is at stake and who devotes a major share of his attention to problems of money.[31] Coordination with the Senatorial and Congressional campaign committees has been sought through consultation with the staff and chairmen of those committees, with due deference to the party leadership in each body. A large share of the Senatorial committee's income has usually come from contributions made directly to it, while the Congressional committee has largely depended on funds staked it by the national committee. If a single person can be said to coordinate these top-level continuing committees, he is the chairman of

was $1,000 for the Virgin Islands (next were 8 states at $5,000) and the highest was $160,000 for New York (Texas followed at $140,000 and Pennsylvania at $125,000). The 1956 quotas, set August 18, 1956, represented for most of the states and territories an increase of about 60 per cent over the 1953-54 quotas. The Virgin Islands again was assigned the lowest, $2,000, with Maine following at $5,000 and eight other areas with quotas of $8,000. New York drew the highest, $275,000, Texas came next with $200,000, Pennsylvania with $175,000, and Illinois with $165,000. The median figure was Wisconsin's $42,000. Quotas are lowered in nonelection years. The three-year total of quotas for 1956-59 seemed, in fact, to be only slightly higher for most states than those for 1956 alone.—*New York Times,* November 8, 1959.

30. During the period 1928-58, no national finance chairman was designated in about half the years, including a good many years of Congressional elections.

31. For a brief discussion of the financial and other functions of national committee chairmen, see Cabell Phillips, "Party Chairman: Study in Feuds and Funds," *The New York Times Magazine,* July 1, 1956, pp. 10ff.

the national committee, whose word on occasion has been final. Coordination with the volunteer national-level committees is something else. Dwight R. G. Palmer, Democratic national treasurer in 1952, had substantial influence, though not direct control, over the financial affairs of Stevenson's Springfield headquarters and the Stevenson-Sparkman Forum committee in New York (set up by a friend at his request). But the Volunteers for Stevenson, who guarded jealously whatever they collected, were something else. By the lights of many who were involved, the lack of coordination was a nightmare in both Stevenson campaigns, the separate headquarters maintained by the candidate, even though located in Washington in 1956, contributing to the problem.[32]

A loose kind of Democratic national finance committee of 75 to 100 donors and solicitors has usually existed on paper, though, when queried, some of the listed members have not been sure whether they were on the committee or not, and what they were supposed to do if they were. The membership has customarily been difficult to ascertain, the Democrats being consistently less formal and public about their fund-raising machinery than the Republicans. One Democratic national treasurer, in fact, refused point blank to make known the membership of his national finance committee.[33]

Always of crucial importance to Democratic national fund-raising is the circle of active solicitors on whom the current treasurer or finance chairman depends to pull in the bulk of the needed funds. These are individuals who can raise anywhere from $10,000 or $20,000 to over $100,000. Persons long experienced in Democratic fund-raising say that 10 or 20 such people may be active in a campaign, and apparently about three-fourths of those busy in one year are likely to be helpful

32. There are naturally different perspectives on the matter. Hugh A. Bone reports that the national committee under Paul Butler "retained centralized control over the collection and disbursement of major campaign funds, the allocation of network time, and responsibility for major publicity."—*Party Committees and National Politics* (Seattle: University of Washington Press, 1958), pp. 59-60. Democratic potentates privately describe something less than an amiable relationship, and Jack Redding stated bluntly that James Finnegan, head of Stevenson's personal campaign headquarters, "was the chairman in all but name and Butler was given little opportunity to influence the campaign."—*Inside the Democratic Party* (New York: The Bobbs-Merrill Company, Inc., 1958), p. 308.

See Chapter 11, below, for a discussion of transfers of funds among party committees.

33. Word of a national finance committee occasionally gets into print, and persons in the states discuss it freely, though attaching little importance to it. In the spring of 1953 the Democratic national chairman announced that a 300-member "advisory council" had been created to help raise $750,000 a year for the party's national operations.—UP dispatch, April 1, 1953. On August 6, 1954, a much publicized meeting was held in Kansas City to make plans for financing the upcoming elections.—*Kansas City Times,* August 7, 1954. Those invited were expected to make pledges which they would honor, or would get others to honor. About 60 persons attended, one of whom styled the proceedings as "a terrible bore, poorly managed, pointless."

again four years later. This group, the *real* Democratic finance committee, has been far more important in its actual functioning than the corresponding members-at-large of the Republican national finance committee. In the absence of a system that can assure adequate income from the state quotas, the national campaign effort is vitally dependent on them.[34]

The organization of national Democratic fund-raising changes as those in charge of it change. During some of the successful periods, a system of regional directors has been employed. When Edwin W. Pauley was national treasurer, for example, the country was divided into six areas, each with a finance director whose job included raising money personally and keeping after the finance chairmen in the states within his region. Great emphasis was placed on getting help in each state from skilled fund-raisers regardless of whether they held party position. Each regional director was expected to make daily reports to Washington. If he could not put one of his state chairmen in motion, he was given assistance from Washington in doing so, or in effecting a replacement. Such replacements were generally made only after consultation with leading Democrats in the state. In late August, 1956, it was announced that under the new national finance chairman the nation was to be divided into eight regions of six states each for the purpose of fund-raising drives.[35] But these organizational arrangements are not marked by a high degree of order or consistency. A snapshot taken one year is soon out of date.

State and local levels.—What is true of one state, moreover, may not be true elsewhere. One national treasurer argued stoutly that a different pattern is to be found in every state.

Two general uniformities nevertheless prevail: (1) Just as soliciting for national purposes is normally separated from soliciting for state purposes, over most of the country state and local financial operations have been conducted independently of each other. (2) At any given level, several competing solicitations usually go on simultaneously.

From time to time exceptions show up. The Democratic state committee of Kansas in 1952 led an effort to centralize all fund-raising above the county level in one office, an office which would make a single solicitation on behalf of all national, state, and Congressional candidates. In 1956 the financial management of the two Kentucky United States Senatorial campaigns was largely concentrated in one office. In some Minnesota counties it has been usual for one county committee to solicit funds for all Democratic-Farmer Labor candidates in the county. In 1959 there was evidence of increased efforts toward state and local coordination in several states, e.g., Colorado, Iowa, and Wisconsin. But nowhere can be found the sort of sustained, integrated program to

34. The informal character of what Redding called the "finance committee" in 1948 is indicated by his description of an early meeting, *op. cit.,* pp. 167-70.

35. *New York Times,* August 22, 1956.

which Republicans aspire. As a consequence, many of the party faithful are solicited several times,[36] and the practices followed usually leave much to be desired.[37]

Causes.—Neither natural perversity nor an aversion to large sums of money accounts for Democratic failure to develop an orderly fund-raising system. No one familiar with the practices of the two parties can long avoid the conclusion that Democratic resources would be augmented if they did. Paul M. Butler himself, speaking in 1956 as chairman of the Democratic national committee, proclaimed his aim to develop an integrated finance plan for all segments of the Democratic party, from the precincts up.[38] But in 1956, as before, there were few if any Democratic finance committees conducting integrated solicitation programs in the states.[39] In 1958, Butler appointed Kenneth Birkhead as finance director of the national committee. Mr. Birkhead was a knowledgeable individual with experience on the staff of the Senatorial campaign committee. Not unacquainted with the usual methods, he was nevertheless charged with broadening the base of Democratic financial

36. A condition about which opinions differ. One gentleman from Texas, with collections of many tens of thousands to his credit, lamented the "dribble system" whereby cagy contributors parcel out their funds a little at a time accompanying each gift with bits of tactical advice. An old hand in the District of Columbia, however, gaily applauded the system: "You should hit a guy from all directions!"

37. As in the case of Republican operations, the temptation to elaborate on the variety of state and local activities must be resisted. Democratic fund-raising in California is described by Rowe, who sat in on some finance-committee sessions, *op. cit.*, pp. 131-39. Owens reports on Democratic practices in Connecticut and particularly notes that large contributors tend to identify with candidates rather than with the party, a telling comment on the state of party financial organization. —*Op. cit.*, p. 307. Clifton H. Scott seems to have accomplished wonders in Arkansas in 1936 with mass appeals for funds, an experience he was still enthusiastic about 16 years later.—U.S. House of Representatives Special Committee to Investigate Campaign Expenditures, 1952, *Hearings* (Washington: Government Printing Office, 1952), pp. 121-28.

38. Gore Committee *Hearings*, part 2, p. 403.

39. There have been many Democratic state finance committees organized to handle the proceeds of fund-raising dinners. See pages 237 and 309-11, below. A canvass of the 48 Democratic state chairmen in 1958 found 25 saying that a separately organized state finance committee had operated in their state in 1956. The evidence, however, indicated that a Democratic finance committee, even though separately organized in the eyes of the state chairman, was quite a different thing from a conventionally organized Republican finance committee. Only 14 of the 25 chairmen said that the state committee normally depends on the finance committee for a "large share" of its income, and only 8 said the committee kept a separate office with its own personnel open throughout 1956 and 1957. (Compare with Republican experience above, page 219.)

In 1958, the Democratic party in 19 or 20 states employed at least one "permanent," full-time professional staff worker, some of whom engaged in fund-raising.—Francis M. Carney, "Toward More Responsible Parties: Some Notes on the Staff Organization of the Democratic National Committee" (mimeographed, a paper delivered at the annual meeting of the American Political Science Association, 1958), p. 15.

support by attracting masses of small gifts.[40] Why, observers would speculate, is not an effort made to emulate the eminently successful Republican procedures?

The root of the matter can be found in the nature of the financial constituencies of the Democratic party. The Republican system functions most successfully in a sympathetic business community. In presidential elections generally, and in states of vigorous party competition especially, businessmen offer infinitely better hunting for Republican than Democratic solicitors. This is so much the case in many places that it has seemed pointless, or impossible, for Democrats to organize a systematic canvass of business and financial enterprises.[41] They have fallen back, instead, on individuals who know the politically unorthodox businessmen and the companies and industries where Democratic sympathizers may be found. These are identified and solicited by a network of personal acquaintanceships in contrast to a blanket solicitation throughout the business district. An occasional Democratic committee, like the state committee in New York, maintains lists of contributors that guide soliciting from one year to the next.[42] In New York, the textile industry and the entertainment world are canvassed rather thoroughly by Democrats, where they find much support, but comparable wealthy constituencies are hard to locate in most other states. Generally, such records as are kept are maintained by candidates and other individuals for personal or factional use. One specialist in Louisville had his private file which he used in numerous philanthropic as well as political campaigns. (Like their Republican peers, Democratic solicitors tend to be active in nonpolitical civic affairs.[43]) Where sustained drives to cultivate small contributions have been made, contributor files are likely to be encountered.

40. See pages 255-58, below. Mr. Birkhead left the committee in 1959.

41. The Republican enthusiasms of key business leaders can have a depressing effect on such Democratic sympathies as may exist among their associates. Columnist Thomas L. Stokes reported that during the Bender-Burke Senate race in Ohio in 1954 the activities of Secretary of the Treasury George M. Humphrey, Ohio industrial and financial leader (and appropriately enough formerly president of the M. A. Hanna Company of Cleveland), had the effect of discouraging contributions to Democrat Burke. It was claimed that a manufacturer friendly to Burke planned a fund-raising luncheon, but after word got around the luncheon was cancelled. It was thought relevant that the manufacturer sold to one of the Hanna enterprises.—*The News and Observer* (Raleigh, N.C.), October 16, 1954.

42. Bennett Cerf tells that Elliot Paul, who wrote "The Last Time I Saw Paris," was once hired by Massachusetts Democrats to prepare a list of taxpayers with incomes exceeding $5,000. The list, intended to help with solicitations, brought forth such an effusive letter of appreciation that Mr. Paul took a copy of his work around to the Republicans and sold it to them for twice what he had charged the Democrats.—*This Week,* October 25, 1953.

43. Of 47 persons known to have rendered important fund-raising service to the Democratic national committee, information from standard reference sources was obtained on 35. Of the 35, 86 per cent reported experience in civic activities of various kinds, averaging four each. Twenty per cent reported nonpolitical soliciting experience. Compare with Republican data on page 221.

Democratic fund-raising procedures are affected by the nature of the financial constituencies to whom they must look for support. Funds from organized labor and government employees have already been discussed, and several specific soliciting devices used by both parties are treated in the following chapter. In order to raise large-size donations, Democratic politicians cannot rely on *generalized* support from the business community, but are forced to look to individuals and groups with fairly immediate stakes in government, similar to the "friends" of Chicago Republican politicians referred to earlier. These solicitations are made by political Democrats rather than by financial Democrats in ways considerably less visible than those of the Republican finance committees. The personal knowledge of experienced solicitors takes on high value. Political fund-raising and the administration of government are brought closer together. Almost everywhere one encounters individuals of both parties whose special role is periodically to dun some special group of contractors. There are related practices, like the rebates to party coffers on premiums paid for insurance on state properties, a procedure long useful to both sides in Connecticut, and familiar in Georgia, Pennsylvania, and elsewhere.

The preference of the business community for the Republican party has effects beyond the financial advantage immediately accruing to Republican candidates in particular elections. Democratic managers seldom have the working capital between campaigns necessary to initiate well-planned, well-staffed, technically proficient fund-raising organizations, the full dividends from which would be forthcoming two or three elections hence. Moreover, poverty-stricken precinct, county, and state leaders view with skepticism any proposal that would send their hard-dug cash to some central pool, even though promised a portion would be returned. They also view with understandable reserve the proposition that if they give up some of their cash now they will in a few years get back more than they can raise going it alone.[44] Republican state and local chieftains who enjoy more of a financial cushion can better enter such cooperative schemes, especially when urged to do so by their local benefactors among businessmen, to whom such schemes make sense.

Unification in soliciting is harder for Democrats to achieve, too. A general commitment to Republican victory at state and national levels is not difficult for businessmen who do Republican soliciting and giving. Most of them are at least one step removed from the factional frictions of daily party politics. They do not mind chipping in to a common pot.

44. Hoary party veterans are likely to answer talk about streamlined fund-raising with recollections of critical shortages from earlier campaigns and how they were met. Some exasperating episodes are described in Redding, *op. cit.*, pp. 235-37, as is the famous occasion in 1948 when President Truman's train was stranded in Oklahoma for want of funds. "But this couldn't happen to Harry S. Truman, not in Oklahoma. Governor Turner and W. Elmer Harber of Shawnee, Oklahoma, held a collection party in the President's car and raised enough cash to finance the rest of the current trip and, also, another cross-country trip."—P. 273.

Much Democratic money is perforce solicited by active politicians embroiled in the strife of nominating, electing, and governing. Democratic fund-raising is consequently factionally sensitive; harmonious and common action is difficult to achieve. Beyond these factors, however, is another that issues from the party's financial instability. Being and feeling at a financial disadvantage and lacking such backlog as might result from more effective advance work, Democratic managers during a campaign are almost invariably thrown into a frenzy of financial activity, at times approaching panic. Frenzy breeds boners and both breed themselves, so that most Democratic fund-raising during the heat of a campaign becomes a morass of confusion.[45]

In this confusion lies a beam of hope for Democrats. They cannot do much about the predilections of wealthy persons who support the opposition, but their party can lift itself by its own bootstraps through improving the primary efficiency of its soliciting, and by adapting to its own needs what is appropriate from the experience of Republicans and nonpolitical fund-raisers.[46]

45. Which may account for the fact that several days after the election in 1954 a Democrat received an urgent appeal for funds over the facsimile signature of Adlai Stevenson. The letter commenced: "Once more we are in the middle of another great campaign. . . ."

46. By mid-1959, the Democratic national committee's "750 Club" had raised in large gifts almost half of its announced goal of $750,000 to repay debts left after the 1956 campaign. An intention to organize a 750 Club in each state was announced at the outset.—*Democratic Digest,* January-February, 1959, p. 20. The over-all effort was described from inside the committee as probably the best co-ordinated fund-raising attempt since a series of fund-raising dinners organized during Stephen Mitchell's tenure as chairman in 1953-54.

The climate of Democratic operations during Mitchell's term as chairman was suggested by the report of Stanley Woodward to the national committee when he withdrew as its treasurer in December, 1954. The report recommended that soliciting of large contributions should be placed on a year-around basis and asserted that the treasurer's office had a card index of substantial contributions received at the national committee since (but apparently not including) 1948. It was also suggested that a small advisory group might be useful in reaching large contributors regularly and advising on fund-raising.

One wonders why a party in search of funds had not long before created all of the advisory committees it needed and organized an orderly, annual solicitation of its wealthy supporters. An outsider would think, too, that a card file of contributors might run back more than one presidential election. (Public reports went back much further.) It was incredible if, as someone claimed, one of the national chairmen destroyed part of the old records in indignation at some of the party's previous financial supporters. But how else to explain it—unless the discontinuity and highly personal nature of the party's fund-raising were actually as great as they seemed.

9

RAISING THE MONEY—BY PANHANDLING AND PROFITS

On October 29, 1884, at Delmonico's Restaurant, Jay Gould and Russell Sage played host at a banquet that came to be called Belshazzar's Feast. James G. Blaine, eloquent orator and Republican candidate for president, addressed 200 of New York's wealthiest men. He claimed for the state of New York an increased wealth of four and one-half billion dollars during the previous twenty years, and he claimed for the Republican party "the credit of organizing and maintaining the industrial system . . . which enabled you to make this marvellous progress." His conclusion was followed by an emergency appeal for party funds.

This was not the first fund-raising dinner, nor the most successful,[1] but it foretold a happy turn for campaign managers half a century later. Of all the new contrivances devised since the First New Deal to meet the costs of politics, the fund-raising dinner is the most important. The proceeds nowadays are assured in advance by the sale of tickets, and so successfully that the procedure has been mimicked by a host of other revenue-yielding entertainments. Teas for TV, bean feeds, golf days, cocktail parties, bridge nights, luncheons, breakfasts, and abundant other profit-making events have become standard political operations. Trinkets of all kinds, including the silver sole with the hole, are hawked on the streets and in the clubs of America, all for the greater solvency of candidates and parties.[2] And along with the accelerated

1. Matthew Josephson, *The Politicos—1865-1896* (New York: Harcourt, Brace and Company, 1938), pp. 369-72. Funds were solicited in the 1860's and 1870's at intimate meetings, including a Washington dinner mentioned in Ellis Parson Oberholzer, *Jay Cooke—Financier of the Civil War* (Philadelphia: George W. Jacobs and Co., 1907), vol. 2, p. 252.

2. Presumably not for party profit, however, were the 18k gold elephants "with ruby eyes . . . handmade to our order" offered in 1956 by Black, Starr and Gorham through an advertisement in *The New Yorker,* for $82.50. In the illustration partisanship, or business acumen, showed through: two elephants were displayed, no donkey.

vending of gimmicks for political profit have come renewed efforts to attract large numbers of small campaign contributions. These practices, supplementing the solicitation of moderate and large contributions discussed in the previous chapter, have become integral aspects of political fund-raising in America.

1. DINNERS AND DOLLARS

The fund-raising dinners are not significant because they have changed the sources of political revenues, nor because they have increased the number of persons who give to politics. They are noteworthy as a procedural invention by which under modern conditions money can be raised successfully from customary sources. They are an adaptation to new conditions of personal and corporate taxation and to the latest statutes regulating campaign finance. The dinners provide a device by which public employees, persons of wealth, corporations, and others with a stake in politics can be induced to make political gifts. Beyond this, under skilled management they become a means of attracting funds from persons only marginally involved in political finance and thus produce greater income than might otherwise be obtained. The dinners have proved especially effective in raising money between campaigns when partisan temperatures are low. They are an illustration of the mounting consequence of technical innovation in the management of American political parties.

Fiscal importance.—By the 1950's, proceeds from political dinners probably accounted for one-third of the total income of state party committees[3] through the four-year election cycle. In off-years they provided a substantially larger proportion of party income. It seems likely that in a majority of the states in every year the dinners provided more than half the funds used by the state organizations of both parties to meet the routine costs of year-around operations and to supply donations to the national committees. Democrats raise fewer dollars by this means than Republicans, but the dollars probably constitute a greater share of their financial resources.

Dinners are regularly given by national-level political committees themselves, and in many metropolitan areas both parties use them, along with other forms of profit-making entertainment. Some ward, district, and county organizations employed such devices before the dinners came into general use throughout the nation.[4] Special political groups at all levels stage fund-raising meals, in connection with nomination as well as election campaigns. All in all, fund-raising meals netted around $10,000,000 for political purposes during 1956. The total may have

3. Meaning, in this context, state central committees, state finance committees, and state volunteer committees bearing the name of the President or presidential candidates.

4. Roy V. Peel, *The Political Clubs of New York* (New York: G. P. Putnam's Sons, 1935), pp. 71-86; Edward J. Flynn, *You're the Boss* (New York: The Viking Press, 1947), pp. 113-14.

reached $5,000,000 in 1955, and in the mid-term year 1954 probably fell between these amounts.

Adaptability.—The dinners are successful and useful for several reasons. Each is a sharply focused event that can be timed carefully and completed, with profits available, by a date specified in advance. Every dinner affords a sounding board for party publicity and a rallying ground for party faithful, both especially welcome when campaigning is out of season. More importantly, the dinners provide an excuse for special solicitations among persons inclined to give only during election years in connection with specific candidacies. An inducement is offered, sometimes something the contributor actually wants, like the right to attend a closed-circuit telecast. And being flexible affairs, the dinners are readily adaptable to the requirements of individual occasions and localities.

Tickets to the most publicized dinners cost $100 per plate, although politicians speak darkly of more select $2,500 affairs, and often the price falls to $50 or $25 for functions primarily of state interest. There have been profitable occasions when tickets cost only $5 or $10. Dinners can be arranged with felicity at any political level from precinct up.[5] Their size, moreover, can be adapted with ease to anticipated attendance, some occasions achieving their purpose with fewer than a hundred persons present while others attract thousands. And the dinners can be timed to capitalize on developments of special political interest, such as Senator Walter George's retirement from the Senate in 1956, or to meet specific financial needs, such as Senator McCarthy's Chicago broadcast in 1952, or to maintain a steady flow of income between elections, which is part of the grand design of Republican finance.

The maximum sale of dinner tickets inevitably depends on creating an environment of social pressure around prospective purchasers. The "visual recognition"—as one set of instructions for staging the dinners phrased it—that results from attendance leads many persons, or their wives, to want to attend, or at least to want not to be absent. Political figures of significance usually decorate the proceedings, and few of the boys will risk not being one of the boys on such an occasion. Besides, the dinners offer the kind of back-thumping fellowship on which political personalities thrive.[6]

5. The *Democratic Digest* for April, 1959 (p. 8), listed 23 party dinners scheduled during that month from coast to coast, four sponsored by Congressional district organizations, eight by statewide groups, and 11 by county organizations.

6. Tammany leader Carmine G. DeSapio is said for years to have reviewed personally the seating arrangements for the annual New York County Democratic dinner. "With upward of 2,000 guests to be seated, this is an all-day task. He usually performs it on the Sunday before the dinner, locking himself in a hotel room with two or three knowledgeable assistants. When it is over he knows where every guest of political importance will be sitting and why."—Leo Egan, "The How and Why of De Sapio," *New York Times Magazine,* September 14, 1958, p. 25.

Machinery for marketing the tickets can be fitted easily to many types of financial constituencies.[7] Most of the tickets to the annual Jefferson-Jackson Day dinner in North Carolina are sold through quotas allocated to the 100 Democratic county committees. In many counties the quotas are met by passing the hat among the affluent party faithful, the same who supply funds on other occasions. The sale of dinner tickets in Kentucky has often been handled through a quota system too, the responsibility being placed on the "patronage chairman" who is in charge of distributing public jobs in each county.[8] In metropolitan areas, especially among Republicans, all tickets may be taken the day they go on sale. One state finance chairman recalled a $100-per-plate dinner addressed by Vice President Nixon. "I called forty men together right here in this room and assigned them twenty-five tickets each. Some of them paid for the tickets themselves; others sold them in retail fashion for $100 each; but we made each of the forty persons responsible for the $2500." In another city, a finance committee of 300 was invited to lunch to plan a dinner at which Secretary of Defense Wilson would speak. One hundred persons showed up and before it was over 67½ tables of ten $100-places each had been sold, "and we knew we could have the dinner." In all, 165 tables were eventually sold through a canvass similar to that conducted in a regular solicitation for campaign funds. When there is no handy machinery for marketing tickets in large blocs, they have been sold successfully by volunteers one at a time. At a $25.00 dinner in Texas for Alben Barkley, one customer obliged by paying $5,000 for a single ticket. Two nephews did the same.[9]

A further flexible feature of the dinners is useful in soliciting. Nobody seems sure to what extent federal and state statutes require political organizations receiving profits from the dinners to report the names of those who bought tickets.[10] Practices vary substantially, even within the same jurisdiction. Some committees list purchasers of dinner tickets

7. Many organizations use subscription dinners. The Americans for Democratic Action reported that its Roosevelt Day dinners yielded a "substantial part" of its annual budget in 1949 and 1950.—Buchanan Committee *Hearings* (Washington: Government Printing Office, 1950), part 6, p. 109. The McClellan Labor-Management Committee found that a testimonial dinner for a labor official could become a means of extorting funds from employers with whom the union dealt.—*Interim Report,* pp. 110-13.

8. Although federal legislation makes it unlawful for certain federal and state employees to be concerned "directly or indirectly" in the sale of dinner tickets of a political organization, apparently these employees can legally purchase tickets themselves. And if the practical politicians are to be believed, they do. See the pamphlet issued periodically by the Civil Service Commission called "Political Activity of Federal Officers and Employees."

9. A New York party official estimated that in his experience 60 per cent of all tickets sold are for entire tables.—*New York Times,* April 23, 1955.

10. A leading member of Congress sent his check for a dinner held in the spring of 1959 made out for $100.01. He wanted to be sure his purchase was reported and said he did not know whether contributions of $100, or only those *over* $100, were covered by existing law.

in their official reports, as often as not mixed indiscriminately with other contributors. Sometimes the proceeds are reported by the organizational units through which tickets were sold ("1st district, $2,300; 2nd district, $4,110," etc.). More commonly, *ad hoc* dinner committees are set up, and party committees merely report the net income, such as "$95,000 from banquet."[11]

Techniques for launching the affairs have become well standardized. Often fancy tickets are printed, maybe showing how the profits will be distributed,[12] a special letterhead is made up, and the usual paraphernalia of a major fund drive come into evidence. The labor required, in fact, is one obstacle to frequent use of the dinners. The people who sell as well as those who buy the tickets have limits to their enthusiasm. (It takes some doing just to get into one room 40 men who can pledge $2,500 each.)

Because buying a dinner ticket is both a purchase of food and a political contribution, a felicitous ambiguity about the act has grown up. Democrats and Republicans acting in other capacities every day buy their way into sports events, night clubs, and stage shows, and charge them to expense accounts. Expense accounts are used widely to entertain customers, creditors, employees and others, or in a day of high income taxes simply to supplement the income of those authorized to use them. The accounting required has frequently been loose. To charge tickets for political dinners to such expense accounts does not require extravagant ingenuity. One hears, in fact, of tickets bought directly on company public relations and advertising accounts, although where illegal the risks would seem to hold the practice to a minimum.[13] One learns in confidence of trade associations that purchase blocks of tickets and pass on the cost as assessments on their member companies. Indeed, representatives of the Association of American Railroads told a Senate committee that their Association during 1955 and 1956 had bought nine $100-a-seat places at a dinner honoring Speaker Sam Rayburn and ten $50.00 places for a meal sponsored by a District of

11. Democratic dinners are more likely to be managed by *ad hoc* committees; the Republican affairs are more often the handiwork of a standing party committee, usually a finance committee.

12. A red, white, and blue pasteboard was printed for the "Crusade to Victory" dinner sponsored by the Utah Republican Finance Committee on May 22, 1952, and addressed by Senator Everett M. Dirksen of Illinois. The outlines of a fierce eagle in flight, with talons ready for the pounce, covered the central portion. The dinner was held at the Rainbow Randevu and the disposition of the $100 was shown as $7.00 for cost of the dinner, $2.00 for all other expenses, and $91.00 for the finance committee.

13. The treasurer of one power company in a southern state regularly has tickets to the local Democratic party dinner available for employees and others connected with the company. Whatever the source of the tickets, it appears to be close to the company's purse. One Congressman confided that an airline official in at least one instance offered him and other members of the House tickets to a Jefferson Day dinner. Some accepted.

Columbia Republican Women's group.[14] The importance of business organizations can be inferred from this admonition in a Republican memorandum: "The *Business and Industry* chairman must enlist a ticket sales force of men who promote ticket sales throughout the major industries in the community. The job of this division is one of contacting the most likely corporations in an effort to interest them in buying an entire table or group of tables for their executives, associates or customers. Banks, large industries, hotels, department stores, substantial automobile dealers, etc., are often among the most promising prospects in this category."

Financial efficiency.—Fund-raising devices are evaluated not only by the sums they raise but by the expense of doing so. Close check can be kept on the out-of-pocket costs of fund-raising dinners, and in most circumstances on the proceeds. The cost of a $100-per-plate dinner can usually be held to between 7 and 10 per cent of gross, but as the price declines, the proportionate expenses rise. The costs of a $50.00 affair may run to 15 or 20 per cent, of a $25.00 meal to 20 or 25 per cent.[15] As in all things, profits vary with the rigor of the management.[16]

14. McClellan Lobby Committee *Hearings,* p. 720.

15. A Democratic $25.00 dinner in Texas that grossed $119,000 cost only $9,000, or less than 8 per cent.

Higher in cost was a Democratic dinner at the Murat Temple in Indianapolis on April 19, 1952, for which tickets also sold at $25.00. Of the gross of $38,705, 32 per cent, or $12,527 went for expenses.

The Democratic dinner held in Raleigh, North Carolina, February 25, 1956, grossed about $34,000 with expenses about 15 per cent.—*The News and Observer* (Raleigh, N.C.), February 26, 1956.

A Republican dinner in Atlanta on November 6, 1953, grossed $38,297.50 from the sale of 1530 tickets at $25.00 each, plus a few dollars in gifts. Expenses, which ran under 20 per cent, included $6,877.50 paid to the hotel for the dinner, plus $693.29 for miscellaneous costs, $360 of which was postage. "Cost of printing the invitations in two colors, stationery, tickets, etc., was donated."—*The Georgia Republican* (Atlanta), June 1, 1954.

At a dinner on September 23, 1954, also in Atlanta, costs came to about 25 per cent, with 750 tickets sold at $25.00 for a gross of $18,750 and with expenses around $4,700.—*Ibid.,* September 30, 1954.

The 1956 "Eisenhower Birthday Dinner Committee" in Maryland reported that it took in $66,250, with expenses of $5,260, or 8 per cent.

Presumably this was a $100 dinner, as was the one put on in 1956 in Minnesota by the Republicans. Cash receipts from ticket sales and contributions there totalled $137,082. Expenses came to 12 per cent, as follows: advertising $1,600; attorney fees, $350; brochures, $376; decorating and flowers, $848; entertainment, $755; equipment rental, $10; food, $10,041; mailing service, $321; menus, $166; pictures, $104; postage, $379; tickets, $184; and telecast costs, $1,128, for a total of $16,262.

A different sort of meal was offered in the Minneapolis auditorium in September, 1954, when Adlai Stevenson appeared at a "bean feed." Tickets cost only one dollar, but a net profit of $19,000 was realized on a gross income of $27,000. The remarkably low cost for such a low-priced affair (only 30 per cent of the gross) was possible because all the food was donated, including 1½ tons of wieners, 900 gallons of beans, 18,000 slices of bread, and 10,000 cartons of milk ("no coffee, because of the dairy farmers").

16. One newly appointed Democratic national treasurer some years ago was

Special precautions are taken in many solicitations to avoid the hidden cost that would result if stalwart contributors of large sums were permitted to buy, for the small price of a ticket or a table, an immunity against further solicitation. In some areas, profits are increased by the sale of space in a printed program. Less used throughout the country generally than in New York, the advertising in these books provides labor unions, corporations, and others an indirect means of making political donations out of their organizational accounts.[17]

Sums raised.—The ways dinner receipts and expenditures are reported, or not reported, complicate the task of estimating how much income is netted by the dinners, and what proportion it constitutes of total political receipts. Aware of the deficiencies in existing information, the Gore Committee asked political organizations to report their income during the 1956 general elections under four headings, one of which was "sale of tickets to dinners, luncheons, and similar fund-raising events (net proceeds)." Detailed examination of the responses indicated, however, that income was usually reported under this heading only when the reporting organization had itself conducted the fund-raising enterprise; and then the figure tended to be gross rather than net income, with expenses reported elsewhere. In some instances, such income appeared under "contributions by individuals," another of the four headings. When a special committee had arranged the dinner, the proceeds were frequently shown as received from "other committees, associations, and organizations" or "other sources"—the remaining two categories.

After adjustments had been made in the reports submitted to the Gore Committee, Table 28 was constructed to summarize what they showed about the relative importance of dinner proceeds to the political revenues of the country *during the campaign*—September 1 to November 30, 1956.

The grand total shown by this compilation as coming from dinners during the campaign period is impressive: $2,260,000, or almost 6 per

---

aghast to discover the cavalier expenditures made in connection with the dinners. Staff members arrived at New York's Waldorf Astoria Hotel a couple of days in advance of one dinner and charged the high living to the national committee. The treasurer learned, too, that lots of tickets were not claimed by their purchasers and that "about forty of the girls from Washington" were coming up to use them, instead of letting the full $100 go for profit. He discovered something about the frills that attach to such affairs—white orchids ("I mean plural, not singular") for the ladyfolk of the dignitaries. He put a stop to the foolishness, in the latter case by having the $820 bill transferred to his personal account. Neither the foolishness, nor this way of meeting it, appears to be typical of practices in either party. Moreover, at least one volunteer laborer in the Democratic vineyard considered a couple of free tickets hardly more than his due.

17. Of the Liberal party's dinner held in the Commodore Hotel in New York on April 25, 1955, the *New York Times* wrote: "The diners paid $10 a plate, but most of the estimated $125,000 profit came from a thick souvenir journal."—April 26, 1955. The "Liberal Digest" at times runs three-fourths of an inch thick.

Table 28

NET RECEIPTS FROM FUND-RAISING DINNERS,[a] SEPTEMBER 1–NOVEMBER 30, 1956
(in thousands of dollars)

Committees Reporting to Gore Committee		Rep.				Dem.				Grand
		Regular	Finance	Volunteer	Total	Regular	Volunteer	Total	Labor	Total
National	Value	3	...	....	3	36	....	36	1	40
	% national receipts	0.1	...	....	0.1	1.2	....	1.0	0.1	0.5
State	Value	203	248	197	648	370	332	702	7	1357
	% state receipts	3.7	3.3	10.3	4.3	14.1	23.5	17.3	1.7	7.0
Local	Value	250	191	10	451	355	12	367	28	846
	% local receipts	7.4	8.1	1.6	7.0	14.3	10.3	14.1	10.0	9.1
Senatorial	Value	0			0	17		17		17
	% Senatorial receipts	0.0			0.0	1.3		1.3		0.8
Total reporting	Value	456	439	207	1102	778	344	1122	36	2260
	% total receipts	3.9	4.4	5.4	4.3	8.3	15.9	9.7	2.2	5.8

[a] Derived from Gore Committee *Report*, pp. 40-41, on basis of data from all national-level campaign committees and approximately 95 per cent of state-level committees active on behalf of candidates for federal office. Local reports were limited to party committees in the 100 largest counties and the New York metropolitan area. In some instances gross rather than net receipts were reported.

cent of the income of the committees reporting. The relative importance of this source of income is better understood, however, when the figures for state-level and local-level committees are examined separately. Table 28 shows more than 17 per cent of the funds of Democratic regular and volunteer state-level committees originating with dinners during the campaign period. Democratic leaders in state after state asserted, however, that the dinners were of greatest importance in financing the year-around activities of the party, including donations to the Democratic national committee, and that the dinners were generally held between rather than during campaigns.[18] When the reports of state committees available in various places contain the necessary details, they confirm the oral testimony. Four illustrations, covering differing periods of time, are presented in Table 29.

Table 29

RELATIVE IMPORTANCE OF DEMOCRATIC STATE-LEVEL FUND-RAISING DINNERS: FOUR CASES
(rounded to thousands)

Dem. State Central Committee in	Period of Time	Total Disbursements	Income from Contributions[a]	Approximate Net Income from Dinner Proceeds
Indiana	1/ 1/52-11/15/52	$313,000	$240,000	$26,000
Iowa	11/25/50-11/25/52	163,000	86,000	69,000
Virginia	9/30/48- 2/28/53	52,000	4,000	48,000[b]
Wisconsin[c]	7/ 1/51- 6/30/52	76,000	26,000	28,000

[a] Not including loans, transfers of funds from other organizations, nor dinner proceeds.
[b] After contributions to Democratic national committee out of dinner proceeds had been made. There were five dinners during the period, net proceeds (after national committee payments) ranging from $2,700 in 1949 to $13,000 in 1952.—*Public Affairs in Virginia* (Bedford), May 1953.
[c] The Democratic Organizing Committee of Wisconsin.

The situation with state-level Republican committees is not basically different from that among Democrats. Table 28 shows that between 4 and 5 per cent of the income of state committees during the campaign came from dinners. Although this is to be compared with a corresponding Democratic percentage of over 17, the Republican money actually raised was only slightly less. The amount was dwarfed by the much greater Republican revenues from other sources. The general effectiveness of Republican fund-raising gives that party a better chance

18. For example, interviews on this point were held in California, Connecticut, Illinois, Kentucky, Minnesota, New Jersey, New York, North Carolina, and Texas. And from other sources information was available about Indiana, Iowa, Massachusetts, Nebraska, Pennsylvania, Tennessee, Virginia, and Wisconsin. A dinner held in Harrisburg, Pennsylvania, in 1957, addressed by Harry Truman, attracted over 4,000 persons, and was said to have reaped a profit in excess of $500,000.—Edward F. Cooke and G. Edward Janosik, *Guide to Pennsylvania Politics* (New York: Henry Holt and Company, 1957), p. 89.

to respect the maxim for dinners laid down in italics in one of the party's manuals: "This is an excellent device in *odd-numbered years.*"[19] Democratic managers often fall back on the dinners after a campaign has begun because of an urgent need to get money from somewhere, anywhere. Republican information from individual states accents the importance of the dinners in financing routine party operations.[20] Table 30 presents four illustrations of Republican experience.

Table 30

RELATIVE IMPORTANCE OF REPUBLICAN STATE-LEVEL FUND-RAISING DINNERS: FOUR CASES
(rounded to thousands)

Rep. Committee	Period of Time	Total Disburse-ments	Income from Contribu-tions[a]	Approximate Net Income from Dinner Proceeds
Georgia state central	8/52–11/25/52	$ 76,000	$ 77,000	$ 40,000[b]
A midwestern state finance	1/1/53–12/31/53	306,000	85,000	166,000
A midwestern state finance	1/1/54–12/31/54	622,000	330,000[c]	158,000[c]
North Carolina state executive	1/1/52–11/22/52	40,000	16,000	14,000
Utah state finance	2/52–10/29/52	94,000	5,000	92,000

[a] Not including loans, transfers of funds from other organizations, nor dinner proceeds.
[b] Accounted for separately and not involved in the total disbursements shown.
[c] Not including income of women's division, which was, however, involved in total disbursements.

The testimony of state leaders and such financial reports as are relevant lead to the plausible conclusion that somewhere around one-third of the aggregate income of state party committees—regular, finance, and volunteer—during the course of the four-year political cycle comes from fund-raising dinners. It is also reasonable to infer that in both parties, in more than half the states, a majority of the funds needed to meet the costs of running the party between elections and to meet the national quotas is raised through the dinners.[21]

19. A Republican official stated: "The 'best organized' states for Republican fund-raising generally depend less on dinners and more on direct solicitations by volunteer workers for their income than do the 'less successful' states."

20. For example, interviews on this point were held in California, Georgia, Illinois, New York, Pennsylvania, and Texas, and from other sources information was available about Maryland, North Carolina, and Utah. Herbert E. Alexander found that the Democratic and Republican regular state committees in New York derive from 50 to 90 per cent of their income from their annual $100-per-plate dinners, even in election years. The Republican state committee functions primarily with dinner funds, individual contributions being raised by the finance committee.—"The Role of the Volunteer Political Fund Raiser: A Case Study in New York in 1952" (Ph.D. dissertation, Yale University, 1958), pp. 18, 160.

21. In 1958, each of the 96 state chairmen was asked the following question: "Does a large part of your committee's income normally come from fund-raising dinners (sponsored by your committee or some other group)?" In each party 34 chairmen (71 per cent) answered yes.

To sense the full importance of the dinners requires a look at their use at local and national levels as well. The 100 counties from which the Gore Committee sought data in 1956 were the most populous in the nation. The Democratic responses showed that over 14 per cent of total income of the committees reporting were provided by dinner proceeds, and the corresponding Republican figure was 7 per cent. In these counties the dinners are more widely used for local fund-raising than in smaller and more rural counties. In 1955, Leo Egan, after consulting party leaders in New York State, reported that in that nonelection year around 120 "big dinners" would be held. He was told that the dinner season ordinarily ran from the end of Lent until the end of July. Some local groups might start in February, but the earlier dates were usually reserved for fund-raising events sponsored by the national committees. The dinners in New York State in 1955 ranged from $100-per-plate metropolitan affairs given by the state committees, with 2,000 or 3,000 in attendance, to $10-a-plate dinners in rural counties, with 125 present. The $25.00 dinners sponsored by some of the district organizations in New York City drew as many as 500 and 1,000 persons.[22]

Table 28 may convey the impression that national-level committees did not benefit significantly from money-raising dinners during the 1956 campaign. On the contrary, many state quotas are filled by dinner proceeds, and some dinners are sponsored directly by the national committees. The state money often finds its way aloft as a transfer of funds without identification as to the way it was collected.[23] Perhaps the most famous of the nationally sponsored dinners was the "Salute to Eisenhower" series held on January 20, 1956, which netted between $4,000,000 and $5,000,000. Half of this remained with the various state finance and state central committees and half was divided among the national, Senatorial, and Congressional campaign committees. A program featuring talks by top party leaders was piped over closed-circuit television to 53 banquets held in 37 states and territories, with tickets priced $100

22. *New York Times,* April 23, 1955. In the three months following the adjournment of the New York legislature on April 2, 1955, Governor Harriman addressed nine fund-raising dinners, seven arranged by Democrats, one by the Liberal party, and one by the Citizens Union.—*Ibid.,* July 5, 1955. New York is not the only metropolitan area where dinners are important. Chicago political leaders emphasize the dependence of ward organizations on dinners and related fund-raising devices. The Republican central committee of Philadelphia County reported for the period from January 3, 1951, to January 4, 1952, an income from this source of $94,000. Income from contributions (not including loans, transfer of funds from other organizations, and dinner proceeds) was $96,000. Total disbursements were $457,000.

23. Even so, identifiable transfers of funds from state-level Jefferson-Jackson Day Dinner committees to the Democratic national committee averaged $417,000 annually during the years 1945-50, amounting to 31 per cent of the national committee's total receipts during the period. Joan Combs Grace discusses these data, and fluctuations in the volume of money raised by dinners, in "The Impact of Campaign Funds on Party and Factional Structures" (Master's thesis, University of North Carolina, 1958), pp. 50-63.

and down.[24] Later in the year, on October 2, a series of 30 dinners was held under Democratic auspices, linked by closed-circuit television. This event partly accounts for the dinner income reported to the Gore Committee by Democratic state committees.

When the $4,000,000 or $5,000,000 raised by Republicans in January, 1956, is added to more than $2,250,000 reported to the Gore Committee as raised during the campaign, known dinner proceeds during 1956 approximate $7,000,000. From what has been indicated about practices throughout the country, it seems likely that at least another $3,000,000 was collected during the year, or a total of $10,000,000 in 1956.[25] Collections from this source in 1955 were probably about half of this. Egan reported that at least $1,100,000 would be collected in New York State that year. Press reports of eight Republican dinners around the country in 1955 indicated net proceeds of more than $1,000,000.[26] In April of that year 3,400 persons were reported to have attended a $100-per-plate dinner honoring Speaker Rayburn in Washington.

The popularity of the dinners with the financial managers of both parties rose steadily following 1950.[27] Their increasing use was ac-

24. Seemingly dependable reports published after the banquet referred to a net of $5,000,000 derived from 63 banquets, the figures used in the author's *Money and Politics* (New York: Public Affairs Pamphlet No. 242, 1956), p. 22. Edward L. Bacher, executive secretary of the Republican national finance committee, kindly provided the more precise information. As so often the case in both parties, Mr. Bacher pointed out: "It was not possible to accurately figure the net proceeds of these dinners. . . ." On January 20, 1958, banquets were held in 38 cities in 27 states and the District of Columbia, rendering a profit somewhere over $1,000,000.—*New York Times,* January 21, 1958; *Wall Street Journal,* July 10, 1958.

25. In addition to fund-raising meals arranged by party committees, there are those organized to aid individual candidates, such as the $50.00 luncheon for Wayne Morse held in July, 1956, and the $100 dinner held in New York in April of that year to raise money for Adlai Stevenson's nomination campaign. The Stevenson dinner was reported to have attracted 1800 persons. The financial report of the Stevenson Campaign Fund showed income of $38,350 "From Special Dinner Fund."

26. At an additional dinner, an unusual post-election banquet to help pay the campaign deficit of the defeated Republican candidate for mayor of Chicago, Robert E. Merriam, 800 persons paid $50 each.—Robert E. Merriam and Rachel M. Goetz, *Going Into Politics* (New York: Harper and Brothers, 1957), p. 40.

27. Under the chairmanship of Stephen A. Mitchell, the Democratic national committee sponsored a series of nine $100-per-plate regional dinners during 1953 and 1954. At eight of them Adlai Stevenson spoke. (Mr. Stevenson also addressed more than two dozen other fund-raising events arranged locally across the country during 1953 and 1954.) Around $725,000 was grossed and the dinners were given large credit for helping overcome the deficit remaining after 1952.—Report of Stanley Woodward, treasurer of the Democratic national committee, December 4, 1954.

Under Paul M. Butler, who succeeded Mitchell in 1955, the national committee continued to stimulate or arrange regional and national dinners to supply funds for itself and the Democratic Senatorial and Congressional campaign committees. The Rayburn dinner was given in 1955. One honoring the one-hundredth anniversary of the birth of Woodrow Wilson was given in April, 1956. Another was

companied by the increasing use of other devices to entice the money of old and new supporters into political channels. None of the others rivalled the dinners in fiscal power, but all gave evidence of the burgeoning concern with soliciting techniques among practical politicians.

2. TEA AND TRINKETS

Within the British Labor party, football pools and social events have grown so popular as ways of raising funds that the party's traditional reliance on trade-union money is threatened. In many Conservative party constituency organizations, more income is derived from whist tournaments and similar social gatherings than from the gifts of businessmen, the party's traditional financial props.[28]

Urban political organizations in the United States have long depended on numerous types of social events for a significant portion of their income. The use of social occasions, to which admission is charged or at which appeals for donations are made, has spread up the political ladder in recent years, now reaching presidential candidates themselves. At heart, many of the occasions differ little from the dinners, except that more modest sums are raised. Accompanying the teas, cocktail parties, and card parties has been a trend toward the sale of commodities at inflated profits for the benefit of political causes. Through such appeals numerous persons become political contributors, helping to explain the sharp rise in the number of Americans who give to politics.

Events social.—The financially successful occasions are tailored to the clientele. This is as much true of the established practices in metropolitan areas as of later adaptations. The Chicago ward organizations of both parties rely on a variety of fund-raising events in addition to dinners to finance their operations. Golf days have been popular, on which an organization rents a golf club and through admission charges and other sales reaps profits for its treasury. Some organizations have little trouble netting upwards of $5,000 by this means. Tickets to picnics, prize fights, and other attractions are retailed for political profit. They can be assigned in sizeable blocks to precinct captains who are held responsible for raising their full value. Among the willing customers are persons desiring to ingratiate themselves with the organization: e.g., public employees, aspiring politicians, persons touched by

arranged in July of that year to honor retiring Senator Walter George, the proceeds to help finance Democratic Senatorial candidates. In 1957, 1958, and 1959, dinners were held in Washington at $100 per plate, attendance in the latter two years being reported in the press as 3,000 and 2,400, respectively. A series of special birthday celebrations honoring Harry Truman's seventy-fifth birthday on May 8, 1959, was also billed as a fund-raising function.

28. Frank C. Newman, "Money and Elections Law in Britain—Guide for America?" *Western Political Quarterly,* 10 (1957), 595-98.

codes and inspections, "a fellow who wants to get a curb lowered."[29] In Cleveland a well-run political club raises $2,000 to $3,000 annually through card parties and similar entertainments. The women's auxiliaries of county organizations in Pennsylvania undertake bazaars, boat excursions, barbecues, and dances.[30] Often the burden of patronizing as well as arranging these affairs falls on the party faithful, a circumstance that led Edward J. Flynn, on becoming boss of the Bronx in 1922, to induce assembly district leaders to suspend the profitable district clambakes and picnics in favor of an annual dinner and journal to be supported by the party's more affluent friends.[31]

The political distance between clambakes and cocktail parties is short. Fund-raising cocktail parties have become a standard feature in some urban and suburban settings. Their use in New York's "silk stocking" Congressional district on the upper east side has attracted particular attention, where Democratic candidate Tony Akers especially has benefited by their use.[32] They rely on the candidate or another important political figure to be present, on a person to make the pitch (often after the principal has left), on two or three lead-off contributions (often arranged in advance), and on a host who will foot the bill for the party (a contribution that will not show up in the records). When given at a prestige address, the parties ("those terrible things," as they were called by one of New York's wealthiest women, constantly entreated to give them in her home) attract guests who would not otherwise be invited, as well as guests who, because they *would* otherwise be invited, feel an obligation to go, and to pay. Hundreds of dollars are taken in at some of the smaller gatherings, many thousands at larger ones

29. The late Mayor Kelly of Chicago succeeded in making into a community project the raising of funds for his annual Christmas benefit program by which precinct captains of the Kelly-Nash organization played Santa Claus to poor children in their districts. An all-city championship football game and a "Night of Stars" in the Chicago Stadium were staged, the latter enjoying the best that Hollywood and night-club entertainment could provide. Around $400,000 a year came from these sources, in 1941 the Christmas fund reaching $470,000.—Charles W. Van Devander, *The Big Bosses* (New York: Howell, Soskin, Publishers, 1944), pp. 277-78. The "Mayor's Field Day" in Boston, by which $60,000 for the Mayor's charities was raised from 18,000 people in Fenway Park in 1957, was founded by James Michael Curley.—*The Boston Daily Globe,* June 11, 1957.

30. Cooke and Janosik, *op. cit.,* p. 91.

31. Flynn argued that those who did the party's work at elections should not also be asked to support the party financially. No profits were intended from the early $10.00 dinners, but advertisements in the journal yielded $45,000 to $50,000 a year. Right after the war a $100 dinner was given, with no journal, 800 persons attending for a profit of about $60,000. Flynn noted that "those asked to subscribe to the dinners were persons who were very little affected by their contributions," in contrast to those who supported the clambakes.—*Op. cit.,* pp. 113-14. A search of the best-known books on municipal government and politics published since 1900 yielded few references to the techniques of urban political fund-raising. There are occasional allusions to ward picnics and to the incentives that prompt contributions.

32. *New York Times,* May 30, 1956.

attended by a presidential candidate on tour. One Connecticut Democrat who makes substantial political donations holds that cocktail parties have proved in his experience the best way to raise campaign funds. Teas and coffee hours are operated in much the same way, generally with lower yields.[33] Under Paul M. Butler's leadership the Democratic national committee has promoted a Democratic Party Night each spring. All sorts of low-priced fund-raising social affairs are billed, reportedly reaching into 44 states in 1957, including a 10-cent supper in drought-hit Bent County, Colorado.[34] The proceeds are expected to be divided among local, state, and national committees, but usable estimates of over-all revenues cannot be made.

Gadgets for profit.—Trinkets by the carload have entered the commerce of politics. Campaign souvenirs have long been used, certainly since the second quarter of the nineteenth century. Now they are peddled to earn income as well as to spread evidence of popular support. In 1956, the Allen Adler Company of Los Angeles sold 200,000 of the Stevenson-shoe lapel pins to Democratic groups. The wholesale cost came to $97,736,[35] and the shoes were generally retailed at $1.00 or more, possibly netting a profit of as much as $100,000.[36] The New York State Citizens for Eisenhower reported income from jewelry sales in 1956 amounting to $136,956, and five New York Citizens' county committees reported $16,225 more. Michigan's Democratic state central committee showed $39,828 received from the sale of novelties in the same year. Auto stickers, mailing seals, pens, pencils, mirrors, bracelets, tie clips, badges, buttons, and other ornaments of the person are sold in state and local as well as national campaigns.[37] But the New York and

33. Occasionally schemes are proposed for use throughout the entire party organization. Mrs. Katie Louchheim, Democratic women's director, in 1955 outlined a program of "Teas for TV." One woman in each county was to invite ten others to tea, at one dollar a cup, each of these to invite ten others, and so on, leading to a goal in each county of $11,110. (If carried out in the over 3,000 counties of the United States, the teas would yield a happy $34,000,000.) Mrs. Louchheim doubtless thought the idea might be adapted successfully in scattered locations, as indeed it was.—AP dispatch, April 15, 1955.

34. *New York Times,* May 22, 1957.

35. Gore Committee *Report,* p. 64. The Committee had information on six wholesalers whose gross sales of political specialty items in 1956 came to $677,988. What proportion of the items was intended for resale was not known.

36. Though not necessarily. The National Stevenson for President Committee's financial statement in connection with the nomination campaign records $7,590.73 received from sales of silver shoe pins, with Silver Shoe Committee expenses totalling $5,396.57, of which $4,212 was for pins, and the rest for advertising and administrative costs.

37. To aid Texas Senatorial candidate Ralph W. Yarborough in 1957, Mark Adams and Creekmore Fath put out a skillfully written "political profile" called "Yarborough—Portrait of a Steadfast Candidate." With 80 photographs in its 64 pages and priced at 25 cents, more than 93,000 copies were sold before the election. Presumably free, however, were the little cakes of soap circulated during the New York mayoralty campaign in 1953 bearing on the wrapper an injunction to wash the city clean with Wagner.

Michigan illustrations are not typical,[38] and the profits meet only a tiny share, however measured, of the costs of American politics.[39] The marketing of the gadgets requires great labor,[40] and so far would seem to find its greatest meaning in the sense of commitment aroused in those who buy and sell them. Shrewd political managers, sensing this, sometimes force upon contributors, especially of small sums, buttons, literature, even campaign kits, as a way of stimulating campaign activity. Years ago in Alabama a casehardened politician engineered a popular subscription to buy Governor Bibb Graves a Cadillac. No one was permitted to give more than one dollar. Only ex-service men were allowed to give at all. The gesture bred great enthusiasm, men travelling halfway across the state to see the car that was part theirs, and the man to whom they had given it.

The sale of advertising space in menus and souvenir books has been alluded to in connection with fund-raising dinners. The device is an old one. The late Boss Ed Crump is said to have shaken down the liquor

---

Be it acknowledged that lotteries and raffles have a place in American politics, though not a large one. In 1949, the CIO-PAC raised $48,000 in Ohio by raffling off a car and other hardware at 25 cents per ticket.—U.S. Senate Subcommittee on Privileges and Elections, *Hearings* (Washington: Government Printing Office, 1952), pp. 168-69.

38. They were derived from reports submitted to the Gore Committee covering the period September 1–November 30, 1956. At least 25 state-level and 21 local-level committees mentioned income from sales of buttons, badges, stickers, souvenirs, and other campaign materials. There were more Republican than Democratic committees in the group, many were volunteer committees, and in most cases the returns were small.

39. Of larger significance for the immediate beneficiaries have been some of the political auctions. An auction of paintings in New York was said to have produced some $30,000 for Mr. Stevenson's campaign in 1952.

In 1955, the women's division of the Rockland County, New York, Democratic county committee attracted 5,000 bidders at its annual auction, which it was hoped would yield $20,000. The offerings included colored drawings by many well-known artists and cartoonists (e.g., Democrat Bill Mauldin) along with a brace of horses and mementos contributed by prominent political figures.—*New York Times,* May 31, 1955.

One gets the impression that political personalities would be well advised to keep an auction cupboard from which to supply the needs of public sales. The Women's National Democratic Club in Washington, D.C., in the same year, put on the bloc, among other things, a wool blanket from Governor Harriman of New York, a pair of gold cuff links from Governor Clement of Tennessee, a "set of fine old China" from Senator and Mrs. Alben Barkley, a "battered old China doll" roughed up by Tallulah Bankhead in more callow days, a coon-skin cap from Senator Estes Kefauver, and a monogrammed handkerchief of FDR. A gold-headed cane that belonged to Woodrow Wilson was bid for spiritedly, finally going for $625. The representative of a group desiring to give it to former President Truman was outbid by a house guest of Mr. and Mrs. Leslie Biffle, who gave it to his hostess. —AP dispatch, April 25, 1955; Drew Pearson in *The News and Observer* (Raleigh, N.C.), May 15, 1955.

40. The Republican national finance committee warns against selling articles to raise money, calling the procedure inefficient.—"Fund Raising Manual" (mimeographed), p. 13.

dealers of Shelby County, Tennessee, by sending men around to solicit ads for a little paper put out by a political club under his control. A more permissive approach is found in Minnesota where candidates for statewide office on occasion have sent a canned advertisement on behalf of themselves to all the county papers in the state. If the local editor can find someone to pay for it, he runs the ad. In Connecticut, the listing a contributor gets on a dinner program may depend on the amount given. To be called a sponsor cost $100 in one instance. Party directories and handbooks in many states rely on advertising revenues to help pay their cost, or to make a profit. The most publicized of all such arrangements was the *Book of the Democratic Convention of 1936.* Advertising in it worth $380,000 was sold, which with income from sales of the book itself brought in gross revenues of about $860,000, and a net of more than $250,000 to the Democratic national committee.[41] The venture also brought a prohibition, adopted as part of the Hatch Act four years later, against the purchase of any goods, commondities, advertising, or articles, the proceeds of which would inure directly or indirectly to the benefit of a candidate for federal office or a committee supporting his candidacy. The violations would seem to be legion.[42] The Gore Committee and both national party chairmen have called for clarification and remedial legislation.[43]

3. BIG MONEY IN LITTLE SUMS

Once anxieties over campaign finance became acute early in the present century, advocates of reform proposed that the number of con-

41. See U.S. Senate Special Committee to Investigate Campaign Expenditures of Presidential, Vice-Presidential, and Senatorial Candidates in 1936 (cited hereafter as the Lonergan Committee), *Report* (Washington: Government Printing Office, 1937) (Senate Report No. 151, 75th Congress, 1st Session), pp. 18-19; and Louise Overacker, "Campaign Funds in the Presidential Election of 1936," *American Political Science Review,* 31 (1937), 479-80.

42. *U.S. Code,* Title 18, sec. 608(b).

When the Democratic national committee launched the pocket-sized *Democratic Digest* in 1953, Republican officials muttered that its sale violated this prohibition. Deciding to sell no ads, the national committee apparently proceeded on the assumption that any statute preventing it from publishing its views would in a court showdown be held contrary to the First Amendment to the Constitution, which states that Congress shall make no law abridging freedom of speech or of the press. Skeptics offered the sardonic opinion that the law was not applicable anyway, since there were no profits and there were not likely to be any, as proved to be the case.

43. Gore Committee *Report,* p. 19; U.S. House of Representatives Special Committee to Investigate Campaign Expenditures, 1956, *Hearings* (Washington: Government Printing Office, 1957), pp. 3, 75. The national chairmen were especially interested in gaining the unqualified right to distribute campaign materials at cost to state and local campaign committees. The Hatch legislation prevented the Democratic national committee from carrying through its plans to publish a 1940 convention book, but not until after $340,000 in advertising had been sold on a commission basis for a net of $170,000.—Louise Overacker, "Campaign Finance in the Presidential Election of 1940," *American Political Science Review,* 35 (1941), 704.

tributors be increased and that greater reliance be placed upon small donations. Lincoln Steffens seems to have been among the first. In 1904 he urged, without avail, that Theodore Roosevelt's frenzied toadying to Harriman, Frick, and other moneybags would be unnecessary if the President would appeal to the "little people" for contributions of one to five dollars.[44] The suggestion immediately pleases those who believe in a one-man-one-vote concept of democratic government, and in the years that followed efforts to broaden the financial base were made in both parties.[45]

William D. Jamieson, finance director of the Democratic national committee in Woodrow Wilson's administration, devised a mail solicitation plan using a national file of 400,000 names. Expensive to administer, it reportedly stimulated contributions by about 300,000 persons from 1916 to 1920. In 1924, through a Contributors Committee and a series of subcommittees, 90,000 persons were said to have given to the Republican national committee. These and related attempts to spread the costs of campaigning won differing amounts of applause. None demonstrated sufficient success, however, to become an established part of either party's campaign apparatus.[46] But the ambition persisted.

Attempts to attract mass financial support have been made largely through four types of appeal: (1) the sale of certificates or other forms of panhandling and (2) solicitations by mail, these two types involving direct appeals to specific individuals; and broadside requests (3) over the air or (4) through printed advertisements. Experience with each type has been limited, only infrequently with sufficient records surviving to make an evaluation possible. As a consequence, members of the same political team disagree deeply over the feasibility of various schemes and over the lessons to be learned from experiments with them. Two general conclusions, nevertheless, are justified. First, experience with certain mass solicitations has clearly been successful within the limits set by their sponsors. Second, under existing legal conditions even if such appeals were successfully employed on a national basis, candidates and parties would still look for some of their support to medium and large contributions.

Lessons from the Ruml Plan.—From time to time in American politics significant sums have been collected in small change. If those who

44. Matthew Josephson, *The President Makers* (New York: Harcourt, Brace and Company, 1940), p. 162. Large numbers of little people who were public employees had contributed for decades, but they were deemed undesirable on other scores. See pages 145-46, above.

45. See James K. Pollock, *Party Campaign Funds* (New York: Alfred A. Knopf, Inc., 1926), pp. 67-83; and Louise Overacker, *Money in Elections* (New York: The Macmillan Company, 1932), pp. 113-18.

46. Several Republican attempts were made in the more populous states during the 1920's and 1930's to raise money in one dollar sums. The conclusion: "We found out the hard way that even a vigorously fought battle for dollar contributions winds up with an average cost never less than 35 per cent of what is produced, and sometimes far higher."

were there can be believed, the suds bucket collections of Governor Kissin' Jim Folsom of Alabama and the offerings dropped into the miniature flour barrels of Texas' Senator Pappy O'Daniel were no mean pickings, nor was the quarter of a million dollars raised at rallies for Henry Wallace ("by an artist in sob appeal") in 200 cities during his 1948 presidential race.[47]

In 1952, Beardsley Ruml, a novice to political finance, was named finance chairman for the Democratic national committee. Mr. Ruml sought to exploit the latent giving power in the general population by setting up a widespread, responsible system for the solicitation of small contributions. He wanted to reach masses of people who had never given before and probably did not even know how to go about it. Mr. Ruml was struck that he himself had never been asked to make a political contribution.

What is known about the results of Ruml's Five-Dollar Certificate Plan is largely due to the work of John Van Doren. Mr. Van Doren consulted widely among those who participated in the effort and studied with meticulous care such records as could be located after two and three years had gone by.[48] The basic elements of the Plan were simple. It was one-half of a two-part program to get the money needed for the Democratic presidential campaign. Mr. Ruml had no aversion to large contributions as such, with which the other part was concerned, but he was unable or unwilling to raise them in quantity and others took over the task. Five-dollar receipts, somewhat larger than United States paper currency, were printed in New York, bound with stubs and duplicates in booklets of five, and shipped from a New York office of the Democratic national committee to each state, where they were to be distributed to smaller areas. It was expected that 60 per cent of the proceeds would be forwarded to the national committee and the re-

47. Colorful southerners and third party candidates do not always fare so well. Passing the hat along with prayer and song became standard features of Populist rallies in Texas in the nineties. Though better than nothing, little money was forthcoming in those parlous times.—Roscoe C. Martin, *The People's Party in Texas* (Austin: University of Texas Press, 1933), pp. 172-74. The Social Credit party in Canada, some of whose leaders have been fundamentalist evangelists, has relied on evangelical techniques for raising much of its money.—Ernest Eugene Harrill, "The Structure of Organization and Power in Canadian Political Parties: A Study in Party Financing" (Ph.D. dissertation, University of North Carolina, 1958), pp. 249-50, 254.

48. *Big Money in Little Sums* (Chapel Hill: Institute for Research in Social Science, University of North Carolina, 1956), 82 pp., a study of small contributions in political party fund-raising prepared for the Louis H. Harris Memorial Fund. In addition to describing procedures and assessing results, with analysis of factors affecting performance in various localities, the monograph publishes two interesting tables. One shows the distribution by states of five-dollar booklets (for each state: the number printed, number shipped, number destroyed by the printer after the campaign, and the number unaccounted for). The other table summarizes what is known from several sources of the sales in each state.

mainder kept in the states where collected to meet the costs of the solicitation and to help finance state and local campaign activities.

In all, it appears that 800,000 booklets were printed, about 500,000 had been shipped by October 14 (2,500,000 certificates with a potential value of $12,500,000), and about 300,000 were destroyed by the printer after the election. As best can be determined, the national committee received $218,000 from the operation, and total sales reached around $600,000 (120,000 certificates). Ruml had spoken at first of selling 1,000,000 certificates but had subsequently confined his speculations on the possibilities to several hundred thousand contributions. This goal was not reached, nor was an important share of the national committee's needs supplied (less than 10 per cent of 1952 receipts). The Plan required the expenditure of some money by the committee and of considerable energy by Ruml and numerous staff members, all of which might have been put to other use. The Plan was, therefore, in 1952, a failure.[49]

The roots of the trouble are instructive. They were not peculiar to 1952, but neither did they preclude a more successful similar operation in the future. The difficulties trace back to two traditional characteristics of American political parties. The Democratic party lacked the stable and technically equipped staff necessary to launch and administer such a far-flung activity. The heterogeneity of party interests in different localities and at different political levels, moreover, produced a notable lack of agreement on the desirability of this kind of fund-raising and on who should get the money resulting from it.

The failure of the Plan is often attributed to the lateness with which it was started and to the chaos that attended its execution. It was obvious, however, that Mr. Ruml and his associates achieved something of a minor miracle in the speed with which they organized. The idea seems to have come to Ruml on August 19, the day after accepting appointment as finance chairman, and to have been accepted by Stevenson four days later. The first announcement was made on September 11. The drive was scheduled to begin October 8 and to last one week, though of course it went on longer. The fault in scheduling did not lie with individuals, but with a party administrative structure unequipped to plan and execute such a demanding scheme.

In addition, there was always considerable skepticism among some Democrats around the national committee and on the White House staff as to the practicality of the Plan. Some experienced hands thought it inherently too costly, citing limited efforts said to have been made in

49. Compare with the results of the "dollar drives" and other appeals for small donations in Woodrow Wilson's 1912 campaign. Gifts of less than $100, totalling $318,910 from 88,229 persons, supplied 29 per cent of the national campaign fund. The corresponding percentage in 1952 was 13.—Arthur S. Link, *Wilson—The Road to the White House* (Princeton: Princeton University Press, 1947), pp. 484-85.

previous years that cost almost as much to operate as the money taken in. Counting losses in the form of contributions by people who supposedly gave less than they would otherwise have done, some old hands argued that the Ruml Plan actually cost the party money. In any event, it became clear early in the operation of the Plan, though late by any other measure, that cooperation from the regular party organizations would not be automatic. Important state and local leaders disliked the rigid way they were expected to account for the books. More important, they did not want their own sources of revenue undercut by direct solicitations for the national committee. Nor did they want a new political structure established for fund-raising purposes that might rival or upset existing relationships. Such pockets of success as the Plan enjoyed were usually the work of volunteers,[50] and the cooperation shown them by regular party people was something less than enthusiastic. In no state except Kentucky did the Democratic state organization really put itself behind the Plan.

The importance of technique.—The experience of the Ruml Plan suggests that successful mass solicitation is to a significant extent a matter of tehcnique, a matter of system, continuity, and skill in designing appeals for specific audiences—all of which require competent and cooperative staffing. In Texas, $55,000-worth of certificates were sold on short notice because Creekmore Fath had the records and the knowledge necessary to get certificates quickly into the hands of people likely to buy them and likely to sell them. The following year, Fath and his associates were able to sell several thousand subscriptions to the *Democratic Digest* (at an inflated price, the profit being divided between county and state headquarters) because they had a mailing file of the likely market. In the District of Columbia, a group of women in 1952 raised $52,518 from the sale of certificates (plus $3,500 or so in street collections), an undertaking distinguished, for this type of activity, by meticulous organization.[51] After Eisenhower's first election,

50. An observation documented by Van Doren, but also made elsewhere. In Chapel Hill, North Carolina, volunteers turned to with enthusiasm, but the party organization of Orange County, where it is located, devoted its energies to other ends. Later interviews with a sample of adults in Orange and adjoining Person County showed the effects of the volunteer activity in the urban sections of Orange:

		Orange	*Person*
Rural areas:	number of persons interviewed	110	179
	number who said they had contributed, 1952	8	6
Urban areas:	number of persons interviewed	119	94
	number who said they had contributed, 1952	16	2

The interviews were conducted in connection with studies of North Carolina county politics by Frederick H. Harris, Jr., and Edwin H. Rhyne.

51. Common-sense procedures have paid off in other places in other years. In the 18 months or so following the general election of 1948, the Democratic State Club of Missouri raised $45,000 or $50,000 in $5.00 sums by using a records system operated by a paid staff.—Kefauver Crime Committee *Hearings*, part 4, p. 167; part 4-A, pp. 313-14.

Republicans in Georgia, under the leadership of finance chairman Robert Snodgrass, initiated a series of professionally designed "direct-by-mail" solicitations to a carefully maintained file of prospects. Although precise results were not disclosed, gratifying successes were claimed.[52] Since the days of Mark Hanna everybody has known that organization and system pay off in soliciting large gifts. They also pay off in the search for small gifts.

The cost of money.—The cost of raising money in small amounts naturally runs higher than the cost of raising it in large amounts—whether costs be measured in dollars or energy. Numerous pin points of experience with financial overtures made through advertisements and on the air demonstrate the existence of an exploitable public, but they also demonstrate the high cost of appealing to it successfully. Some advertising appeals do not even pay for themselves, although presumably worth something as advertisements.[53] More successful have been solicitations by the Committee for a More Effective Congress. It sponsored the Clean Politics Appeal of 1956, on behalf of five candidates for the United States Senate, an operation that yielded $71,621 from 8,007 contributions.[54] Ten advertisements ran in various magazines and the *New York Times,* and reprints were mailed to selected lists. The total cost was $15,735, or 22 per cent of the proceeds. By contrast, the costs of the Republican national finance committee are usually cited as between 3 and 5 per cent of total receipts (although this computation does not take state and county operations into account). On its own motion, the *New York Post* ran a coupon advertisement during the last four weeks of the 1952 campaign asking contributions for the New York Volunteers for Stevenson. The names of those who contributed were printed. Of almost 18,000 responses to the ad, more than half were in amounts of one dollar. In all, $110,616 came in, apparently at no cost to the beneficiaries. During 1952 there were other newspaper and radio appeals in the *New York Times* and over WQXR. The Ruml Plan office for New York took in more than $128,000, the more important part coming in response to ads and not from the sale of

52. Advocates of mail solicitation sometimes claim preference for it on the ground that solicitors can thus be avoided who might "lose" some of their collections before turning them in, or who might claim political influence for themselves in return for their labors.

53. For example, William Ayres, Republican candidate for the U.S. House of Representatives from Ohio, headed one ad with the plea, "BILL AYRES NEEDS YOUR HELP." There followed three pictures of the candidate at various stages of his life, and the ad closed with an invitation to readers to send dollar bills to his campaign. In one paper alone the advertisement cost $200. Total contributions attributed to the ad were $51.—Stephen K. Bailey and Howard D. Samuel, *Congress at Work* (New York: Henry Holt and Company, 1952), pp. 42-43.

54. Mimeographed report to contributors.

certificates. But the cost ran to $68,000.[55] Dramatic political appearances on the air have produced large numbers of gifts. Following his defeat in 1928, Al Smith made a radio appeal that attracted $126,000 from approximately 25,000 contributors.[56] Richard Nixon's famous Checkers television speech in September, 1952, provoked an enormous public response which included many thousand donations, including enough to pay the cost of the broadcast,[57] which had another purpose.

Financial efficiency manifestly is affected by the volume of funds raised, the size of contributions, and the techniques of solicitation. The efficiency of mass solicitation programs especially mounts, however, as stability and professionalization of staff increase. The whole Republican united fund-raising program is in fact directed toward the development of stable policies, perfected procedures, and skilled staff. Only thus can the continuity and technical expertness essential for maximum results be maintained. "Political" Republicans at state and local levels go along with the united finance committees because they are persuaded that in the long run the party will get more money, meaning ultimately more money for themselves. Similarly, only if effective results are achieved can a Democratic program, the Ruml Plan or any other, enlist the optimum support of state and local leaders.

Staff development is an essential (though not sufficient) prerequisite for effective mass solicitation by any political party. Stability in fund-raising procedures and in party management generally is likely to result when the same individuals or faction control party machinery over a long period of time. The prototype urban political machines exhibited some of the advantages of this type of stability. But most American party organizations undergo frequent changes of control. In such a context the only way administrative stability and technical proficiency can be achieved is through the development of a proficient party bureaucracy.

A trend.—The experience of 1952 did not discourage Democrats from further efforts to popularize political finance. In subsequent years the country saw a wide variety of efforts to stimulate small campaign contributions. During 1954 a group of Democrats reportedly collected over $4,000 from an estimated 15,000 people in one eight-hour stint of panhandling in Washington, D.C. In several localities that same year, the ladies of the Democracy campaigned with the slogan, "Drop a dollar

55. Van Doren, *op. cit.*, pp. 39-40. Persons near the 1950 Impellitteri campaign for mayor of New York claim that newspaper ads proclaiming "beat the bosses with a buck" produced a lot of money.

56. Louise Overacker, *Money in Elections,* p. 118.

57. Earl Mazo, *Richard Nixon—A Political and Personal Portrait* (New York: Harper & Brothers Publishers, 1959), p. 135. One source says the speech drew 2,000,000 letters and $65,000 in campaign gifts.—Herbert R. Craig, "Distinctive Features of Radio-TV in the 1952 Presidential Campaign" (Master's thesis, University of Iowa, 1954), pp. 88-89. *U.S. News and World Report,* December 19, 1952, asserted that the broadcast brought in 25,000 contributions.

in the hat, help elect a Democrat."[58] The next year in Radnor Township, a Republican stronghold outside of Philadelphia, Democrats started their fourth annual "People's Fund," an effort to collect from every registered Democrat.[59] Candidates made personal gestures in tune with the times. To aid Senator Kefauver's 1954 campaign for renomination, a "Dollars for Democracy" campaign was announced for the sale of one-dollar certificates throughout Tennessee. Orville Freeman, successful Democratic-Farmer Labor candidate for governor in Minnesota the same year, was assisted by a buck-a-month contributing scheme. In Austin, Texas, loyalist Democrats maintained a file on 6,000 followers to whom mail solicitations were sent. During Senator Humphrey's campaign for reelection to the Senate from Minnesota, it was claimed that $34,000 was raised from the sales of Humphrey campaign buttons at one dollar each; and that a letter appeal sent at a cost of $4,000 to 90,000 persons on the Senator's mailing list brought in $21,000. From Ohio it was reported that Democratic Senatorial candidate Thomas A. Burke asked supporters willing to contribute to his campaign to leave their porch lights burning so his helpers could come around to collect—a plan reportedly thwarted by an alert criminal element that got there first.

Republican money-raising in 1954 and 1956 displayed less novelty, with only occasional attention to unconventional gimmicks.[60] The finance committees continued to do the job. The Democrats, however, persevered with their experiments. Fund-raising certificates similar to those designed for the Ruml Plan, except in more than one denomination, appeared during the Stevenson campaign for the nomination.[61] They were designed to be usable in the general election campaign, and in some places were. During the election campaign, certificates were distributed from Washington by the Stevenson-Kefauver Campaign Committee. The returns, however, came in, not only to this group, but also

58. *New York Times,* July 22, October 12, 1954.

59. Only 700, however, against 8,000 Republicans. The county chairman was frank enough, proclaiming that in Radnor Township "there's never been a Democrat elected—unless he was an Indian."—*New York Times,* October 3, 1955.

60. Mrs. Leonard K. Firestone of the tire manufacturing family was given credit for the Republican "fund-raising project" by which participants in the plan, instead of sending the usual Christmas gifts in 1956, would mail a check to the united Republican fund. The persons this deprived of their Yule offerings were to receive instead a greeting reading: "Merry Christmas. Thank you for sharing your Christmas with Ike."—*New York Times,* October 9, 1956.

Another scheme of the chain-letter variety, advanced by toymaker Louis Marx, presumably profited the party more. A man puts up $150, gets 150 friends to put up $15, each of those gets 150 to put up $1.50. If 150 of these chains were run out completely, $5,422,500 would be raised and 3,360,150 individuals would be involved. A good many people were reported to have contributed a good many hundred dollars under this plan, which is true however of most Republican plans. —*Ibid.,* September 1, 1956.

61. On Stevenson's popular appeals for help in financing his nomination campaign, see pages 342-43, below.

to the national committee and to the Washington headquarters of the Volunteers for Stevenson-Kefauver. In the heat of the campaign, on October 16, 1956, a nationwide, door-to-door "Dollars for Democrats" fund-raising drive was urged by the national leadership. As in 1952, nobody knew just what the results of these efforts were, although in some places important sums were apparently raised, most notably in California where an amount variously estimated at between $160,000 and $185,000 was collected.[62] There were interesting demonstrations of initiative in various places, such as Linn County, Iowa, and Lancaster County, Pennsylvania,[63] and while the Democratic program as a whole was still cast in its conventional mold, it showed signs of continued change. A mail solicitation from the national committee, for example, sent out in 1956 prompted 20,000 contributions worth about $220,000. Chairman Paul M. Butler claimed the number of gifts to his committee shot up dramatically in 1956 and gave credit to his party's widespread financial appeals.[64]

In the summer of 1957, Mr. Butler initiated a Sustaining Membership Plan by which he hoped to provide the national committee with a steady income.[65] During that year, 12,616 persons pledged or gave

62. The take in Los Angeles County alone was put at $75,000.—Totton J. Anderson, "The 1956 Election in California," *Western Political Quarterly,* 10 (1957), 114. The resistance of local leaders was again felt in some places, and in Pennsylvania "many political workers chose to contribute $10 or $15 from their own funds rather than solicit party members."—Cooke and Janosik, *op. cit.,* p. 93.

63. In Linn County, Republican dominated, a personal solicitation campaign, originally designed by Gene A. Ford for the whole state, yielded $2,700, more than double the usual Democratic campaign fund. In Lancaster County, letters were sent to about 23,000 registered Democrats asking for a five-dollar contribution spread over five months. In all, gross receipts equalled $6,324, with total expenses $2,783, for a net yield of $3,541. Richard F. Schier describes the Lancaster County experience in "Political Fund Raising and the Small Contributor: A Case Study," *Western Political Quarterly,* 11 (1958), 104-12. Total Democratic party receipts in the county during the campaign, exclusive of the "dues," came to $42,000. Sidney Wise and Mr. Schier kindly provided additional information about Lancaster County.

64. Mr. Butler stated that in the four weeks following the national convention the number of contributions received by the national committee in 1948, 1952, and 1956 were, respectively, 139, 614, and 13,117. He also testified that the total contributions to his committee in 1948 numbered 9,470; in 1952, 26,202; and through October 9 in 1956, 39,951.—Gore Committee *Hearings,* part 2, pp. 396-98. There are many perils in comparisons between years. See pages 46-47, above.

65. A similar dues system established by the Republican national committee in 1937 brought in slightly over $220,000 annually for the three years it operated. The system was abandoned because some feared it would reduce large contributions from some donors.

Formal party dues are a significant source of income for many political parties abroad. Dues have never been important in the major American parties because of the nature of the parties and of party membership, both deeply rooted in the political system. The distinction made by Maurice Duverger between "cadre" and "mass" parties rests in important part on how much of a party's financial requirements is supplied by a regular subscription among its members.—*Political*

$185,008.[66] By the fall of 1959, over 35,000 persons had become sustaining members.

In 1958, a full-time finance director was appointed. Full-time fund-raisers were also at work in a few states. In that year both parties sought to take advantage of the nonpartisan nationwide appeal for political contributions conducted by the American Heritage Foundation and the Advertising Council.[67] Perhaps $90,000 to $100,000 (one-fifth of it from California), or around 10 per cent of the Democratic national committee's receipts during the year, could be attributed to the Dollars-for-Democrats drive. The best informed guess seemed to be that the take for all levels across the nation might have been $450,000 or $500,000.

Parties—Their Organization and Activity in the Modern State (New York: John Wiley & Sons, Inc., 1954), especially pp. 1-3, 58-67, 72-76. See also Philip Williams, *Politics in Post-War France—Parties and the Constitution in the Fourth Republic* (London: Longmans, Green & Company, 1954), pp. 51, 63, 90, 94, 363-65. One of the key attributes of "parties of integration" as conceived of by Sigmund Neumann is a permanent dues-paying membership.—*Modern Political Parties—Approaches to Comparative Politics* (Chicago: University of Chicago Press, 1956), p. 404.

Minor American parties have been financed by various means, including dues from members. See, for example, Nathan Fine, *Labor and Farmer Labor Parties in the United States, 1828-1928* (New York: Rand School of Social Science, 1928). A few major-party political organizations, especially in urban areas, collect dues regularly. For a discussion of Republican and Democratic dues-paying memberships in one state, see Leon D. Epstein, *Politics in Wisconsin* (Madison: University of Wisconsin Press, 1958), pp. 79-82.

66. Francis M. Carney, "Toward More Responsible Parties: Some Notes on the Staff Organization of the Democratic National Committee" (mimeographed, a paper delivered at the annual meeting of the American Political Science Association, 1958), p. 11.

67. For a discussion of this and related attempts by legislation and otherwise to alter the basic character of political fund-raising in the United States, see pages 429-71, below. On the rise in the number of contributors generally, see pages 41-47, above.

10

THE SOLICITORS—MIDDLEMEN IN INFLUENCE

WHO BUYS WHOM is what most people want to know about campaign finance. The buying of influence has been the dramatic focal point of most attention to political contributions. That nothing specific is delivered in return for most contributions, and nothing at all for many, only heightens the significance of those channels to special influence that do exist.

Much of the $100,000,000 or more that on the average is spent annually for campaign purposes requires intricate processes of solicitation to attract it into the political stream. True, some money snakes up from sinister sources, threatening the virtue of public men tempted to accept it. But in most campaigns, the truly burdensome chore is raising money. Those who do it occupy positions of singular importance in the political entourage. There are functional as well as legal reasons why candidates and party managers may depend more directly on solicitors than on contributors.[1] This becomes especially so the more distant a candidate stands from his constituents—that is, the larger his constituency and the more complex his campaign operations.

Solicitors serve as middlemen between contributors and the candidates or the party they benefit.[2] Just as a solicitor understands and explains the politician's need for money, he is aware of the political

1. Candidates often keep themselves deliberately ignorant of many facts of campaign finance to avoid the necessity for mentioning them on personal reports. There are also tactical reasons for insulating candidates from politically disreputable sources of money, like the underworld.

2. Not a phenomenon confined to the United States. Of business monies channeled into Japanese political life before World War I, for example: "Frequently the funds were handled through intermediaries, with party members playing key roles and often being chosen because of their access to funds."—Robert A. Scalapino, "Japan: Between Traditionalism and Democracy," in Sigmund Neumann (ed.), *Modern Political Parties* (Chicago: The University of Chicago Press, 1956), p. 324.

interests of those who provide it. American government is representative government. The processes by which representation is achieved are both direct and indirect, and the middlemen-solicitors constitute one of the many linkages between citizens and the decision points of their government.[3] In the course of recruiting funds, solicitors create a type of informal organization among contributors who share common interests. Moreover, the network of solicitors that grows up around candidates, especially for high office, in some circumstances rivals in influence the more visible party organization. And in the pre-nomination processes of candidate selection that take place outside the public view and before formal procedures begin to operate, key fund-raisers often have a decisive voice.[4]

The process of soliciting political money, with the liaison functions that often accompany it, is customarily focused around loyalty to either (1) a candidate, (2) a party, (3) a policy, or (4) a contributor. Some solicitors are attached to a particular candidate, as observable in direct primaries in states where the party organization takes little part. Others work from a formal or informal position within a party such as the finance chairmen of the national committees. Certain solicitors do not attach themselves primarily to candidates or parties but work with any party or candidate who will advance the policies they deem important. Some fund-raisers operate chiefly as trusted advisers to contributors.

These concerns and relationships may be thought of as four postures from which solicitors work. Individual solicitors may move from one of these postures to another, at times may occupy more than one. A few solicitors fall neatly and consistently into one category, but most do not. The sort of objectives solicitors have in mind is not the basis for the classification. All, for example, are likely to be vitally interested in public policies, and one can hardly seek victory for a party and not its candidates. Neither are personal qualities the basis. Solicitors of all types must know, or come to know, the people to whom to appeal for money and how to win their confidence. The significant feature is the proximity of the solicitor to political power. Solicitors attached to successful candidates are closest to the processes of governmental decision-making. Those operating from party posts are next. Those attached to contributors are most remote. The political leverage a solicitor can exert depends on which one or more of these postures he operates from and how well he does it.[5]

3. Note Oliver Garceau, "Research in the Political Process," *American Political Science Review,* 45 (1951), pp. 69-85.

4. On the solicitor in nominations, see pages 318-43, below.

5. The only study of types and functions of political solicitors is that made of elite fund-raisers in New York by Herbert E. Alexander. The subject is much neglected. Mr. Alexander examined seven leading textbooks on American government, and seven leading textbooks on American political parties, and found that only one of the 14 mentioned fund-raisers.—"The Role of the Volunteer Political

1. PARTY SOLICITORS AND THE CHARACTER OF AN ADMINISTRATION

A person with extensive White House experience concludes that the character of a president's administration is set by the persons who raise large blocks of money for the party. When matters that interest them are up for decision, around they come. A chance to state their case is guaranteed, which is all many of them need. The chief rustler of funds for the other party in an important state described with conviction how his fund-raising had brought him influence in party nominations from mayor to president. Moreover, he selected carefully which demands of his contributors were referred to Washington. No passive pipeline, he conveyed the messages he wanted received and let the others lie.

What kinds of people hold such power?

Republicans.—The members of the Republican national finance committee are almost invariably successful businessmen, financiers, or their lawyers. So are the members of the state finance committees, though usually less prominent. At all levels, leading Republican fund-raisers characteristically possess impressive records of community service, including experience in nonpolitical fund-raising.[6] The same type of individual customarily leads Republican volunteer committees.

Any New York committee headed in 1952 by the board chairman of the Chase National Bank constituted, by definition, a powerful engine for raising money. Winthrop W. Aldrich, Chase's chairman, was also chairman of the United Republican Finance Committee of New York. By his heritage (his father was Nelson P. Aldrich, Rhode Island's famed "dictator" of the United States Senate), by his family connections (among others, his brother-in-law is John D. Rockefeller, Jr.), by his schooling (Harvard College and Law School), by his directorships in America's leading corporations, and by his long and faithful support of religious, charitable, and educational enterprises (he held more than half a dozen honorary degrees), Mr. Aldrich was equipped by name alone to extract both energy and money from the financial and business world of metropolitan New York. In that same year the national Citizens for Eisenhower-Nixon operated nearby. Two of its principal leaders were Sidney Weinberg, widely experienced and widely known partner in Goldman, Sachs, & Company, investment bankers, and John Hay Whit-

---

Fund Raiser: A Case Study in New York in 1952" (Ph.D. dissertation, Yale University, 1958), 302 pp. See especially Chapter 5, "Access and the Roles of the Fund Raiser," and Chapter 6, "Classifications of Fund Raisers."

6. See pages 220-22, above. The list of national finance committee members is always available from its Washington headquarters. In 1959, *Fortune* received questionnaires from 1700 "men bossing the 500 biggest industrial enterprises plus the fifty biggest companies in the fields of life insurance, commercial banking, transportation, utilities, merchandising, and some eighty miscellaneous enterprises." Almost 80 per cent were Republicans. Sixty per cent said they take no part in raising party funds, presumably meaning that 40 per cent, or almost 700, do.—60 (December, 1959), 139, 208.

ney, financier, whose personal and financial connections were on the order of those of Mr. Aldrich. Mr. Whitney, in fact, succeeded to Mr. Aldrich's job as New York finance chairman in 1956. In Delaware, the Republican finance chairman has been Lammot du Pont Copeland. In Illinois, it was for a time Edward L. Ryerson, whose positions included the board chairmanship of Inland Steel as well as a host of business and civic directorships. Across most of the nation, to a greater or lesser extent, such has been the leadership of Republican fund-raising. In the context of subtle pressures that pervades any hierarchy of business relationships, men such as these can rally the assistance of countless others in a canvass for political donations. As one of them put it, any alert fellow will see an opportunity in the chore of soliciting to meet new people and to show his talents.

Democrats.—A large proportion of Democratic fund-raisers are also successful businessmen, and typically they also have a record of civic activity including nonpolitical money-raising.[7] Lacking a formal finance-committee system from which to operate, however, Democratic solicitors are more dependent than Republicans on their own knowledge of prospects and on personal skill in solicitation. With occasional exceptions, there are no ready-made lists to be handed Democratic solicitors to check the names they wish to approach. They have to provide their own lists. Moreover, the Democratic solicitor is usually on his own. He lacks formal organizational status that authenticates him as a party representative. Many a Democratic solicitor has been rebuffed by persons preferring to give via someone better known in party councils. A solicitor whose station in life gives him the knowledge and confidence of persons who will make healthy Democratic donations is a valuable party property.

A Republican solicitor speaks of raising $60,000 or $70,000 from his list of prospects; the chairman of a finance committee is given credit for a million and a quarter, meaning the receipts of his committee. Personal qualities always affect results, but on the Republican side it is the system that is essentially responsible for the results. To apportion a dollar-credit among individuals who took part at some level or other is impossible. Among Democratic solicitors, however, there is more exact identification between the sums raised and the persons responsible for them. In a way, Abraham Feinberg is the archetype of the Democratic fund-raiser. Mr. Feinberg's personal solicitations since the early 1940's have been measured in the hundreds of thousands of dollars. Like many political fund-raisers, he has remained relatively obscure, seldom mentioned in the press and rarely hailed outside close party circles for his vital role. Yet any discussion of Democratic fund-raising among those close to it during Mr. Feinberg's active period ultimately leads to mention of his importance.

7. See page 230, above.

Mr. Feinberg is a garment manufacturer who lives in New York, but those facts are of secondary importance to his role as a political fund-raiser. What *is* important is that he is a dedicated Zionist with long and successful experience in raising funds for Jewish causes including Israel.[8] His undeviating devotion to Israel and its future has created trust in him among others of similar concern. When he asks for contributions, and for others to help him get them, his voice is heard with respect, and the response has been great. When such a man is in circulation, the word gets around; Mr. Feinberg has received requests for funds on behalf of candidates at all levels of government in all parts of the United States.

Not all important Democratic solicitors enjoy Mr. Feinberg's stable clientele with its stable interest in public policy. But each works a constituency of some kind, usually associated with his business or professional activities. The Democratic national committee does not publicize its key money-raisers, nor does any other unit of the party, but there seems to be agreement on the significant role played by a good many individuals at one time or another.[9] Who is active in any given year

8. Mr. Feinberg, chairman of the board of Julius Kayser & Company, lingerie manufacturers, and president of Hamilton Mills, in 1954 was elected chairman of the board of trustees of Brandeis University. Later that year he was chosen president of the Development Corporation of Israel, sole underwriter of internal improvement bonds for Israel, with a goal to float bonds worth $350,000,000.

9. For the record, the treasurers and finance chairmen of the Democratic national committee for the years 1928-58 are here listed. The list was compiled from published sources with great help from the memory of a former employee of the committee. The national committee itself, however, does not have the records necessary to check the list for accuracy. A finance chairman was not appointed in all years, and on several occasions the post of treasurer was apparently occupied by an individual for only a few days or weeks, or by an employee of the committee serving as acting treasurer. These persons are not included on the list. When two persons served a portion of the same year, the later appointee is listed for that year.

Year	*Treasurer*	*Finance Chairman*
1928	James W. Gerard	Jesse H. Jones
1929	James W. Gerard	—
1930	James W. Gerard	—
1931	James W. Gerard	—
1932	Frank C. Walker	James W. Gerard
1933	Frank C. Walker	—
1934	Walter J. Cummings	James W. Gerard
1935	Walter J. Cummings	—
1936	W. Forbes Morgan	Frank C. Walker
1937	W. Forbes Morgan	Wayne Johnson
1938	Oliver Quayle	Wayne Johnson
1939	Oliver Quayle	Wayne Johnson
1940	Oliver Quayle	Wayne Johnson
1941	R. J. Reynolds	—
1942	Edwin W. Pauley	—
1943	Edwin W. Pauley	—
1944	Edwin W. Pauley	James W. Gerard

depends on many variables including the leadership of the national committee, the presidential candidate if one is running, issues that are current, disappointments and rewards recently received, and factors affecting the personal availability of the individual—all, it may be noted, considerations that also produce changes in the corps of Republican solicitors from year to year. Whoever the solicitors may be, however, the process is the same. A large segment of the Democratic national committee's funds has traditionally come via persons who have solicited them from individuals who share economic or political interests:[10] e.g., the fishing

1945	George Killion	—
1946	George Killion	—
1947	George Killion	—
1948	Joseph L. Blythe	Louis A. Johnson
1949	Sidney Salomon	Nathan Lichtblau
1950	Sidney Salomon	Nathan Lichtblau
1951	Sidney Salomon	Nathan Lichtblau
1952	Dwight R. G. Palmer	Beardsley Ruml
1953	Stanley Woodward	—
1954	Stanley Woodward	—
1955	Matthew McCloskey	—
1956	Matthew McCloskey	Roger L. Stevens
1957	Matthew McCloskey	—
1958	Matthew McCloskey	—

Persons who become treasurer or finance chairman of the Democratic national committee have usually, though not always, already won a reputation for effective soliciting. Within each state there are individuals on whom Democratic candidates depend but whose activities are oriented toward state and local, rather than national, concerns. Listed here are *some* of the persons who at one time or another in the 20 years before 1957 were deemed by top Democratic officials to have been important fund-raisers: Francis Adams, N.Y.; Charles U. Bay, N.Y.; Nick Bez, Washington State; Jacob Blaustein, Md.; Edgar W. Brown, S.C.; James Bruce, N.Y.; Travis Bryan, Texas; S. A. Carraway; Oscar L. Chapman, Col., D.C.; Carroll Cone, Ark., N.Y.; F. Joseph (Jiggs) Donohue, D.C.; William Feazle, La.; Albert M. Greenfield, Pa.; Stephen H. Harrington, Minn.; Louis H. Harris, N.Y.; Edward H. Heller, Cal.; Joe Higgins; Melvin Hildreth, D.C.; Lyndon B. Johnson, Texas; William G. Johnston, Cal.; Frank E. Karelson, N.Y.; Edward Kelly, Ill.; Robert S. Kerr, Okla.; Dan A. Kimball, Cal.; William H. Kittrell, Texas; Milton Kronheim, D.C.; Dick Mazy; Maury Maverick, Texas; Perle Mesta, D.C.; Tom Miller, Texas; Wiley Moore, Ga.; Thomas A. Morgan, N.Y.; deLesseps Morrison, La.; Francis Myers, Pa.; James McCahey; Frank E. McKinney, Ind.; J. R. Parten, Texas; Richard C. Patterson, Jr., N.Y.; Stuyvesant Peabody, Ill.; Sam Rayburn, Texas; Lawrence Wood Robert, Ga.; James Shepard; Paul Slip; Joe Shane, Cal.; Laurence Steinhardt, N.Y.; Walter Surrey, D.C.; Roy Turner, Okla.; Louis Wehle, N.Y.; Francis Whitehair, Fla.

10. Just how large is difficult to estimate, given the diverse manners in which funds are handled. One important solicitor customarily asks that checks be sent by the donor to him for forwarding. Others ask that checks be sent direct to the recipient. When a person gives to more than one recipient, the solicitor may suggest how the contributions should be divided. From what several Democratic leaders have said, it appears that in many past years, if the personal efforts of the treasurer and finance chairman themselves are included, most of the income of the national committee, and of the Senatorial and Congressional campaign groups, has resulted from the activities of two dozen or fewer key solicitors.

industry in the northwest, a section of the oil industry in the southwest, insurance in the midwest, assorted liberals in the east, the Cook County Democratic organization in Illinois, and the nation's clothing industry. Like the Republican party, the Democratic party could not survive under present conditions without blocks of funds like these.[11]

Rewards for service.—Fund-raisers, like others who render partisan services, may wind up in important public positions. And many do not. Mr. Aldrich was followed as Ambassador in London, just as he was followed as finance chairman in New York, by Mr. Whitney. There were a dozen reasons aside from his fund-raising, a fellow New Yorker argued, why Mr. Aldrich's appointment was appropriate, and the same could be said of Mr. Whitney. Perhaps it could be said with equal truth of other important Republican solicitors who were appointed to high posts in the Eisenhower Administration, such as Sinclair Weeks (Secretary of Commerce), Harold E. Talbott (Secretary of the Air Force), R. Douglas Stuart (Ambassador to Canada), and Charles S. Thomas (Secretary of the Navy). But no one could argue that their financial services to the party had not fortified their eligibility for political appointment. The same has been true of important fund-raisers in Democratic administrations: for example, Dan A. Kimball (Secretary of the Navy), Charles U. Bay (Ambassador to Norway), James W. Gerard (Ambassador to Germany), Jesse H. Jones (Chairman of the Reconstruction Finance Corporation), and Richard C. Patterson, Jr. (a series of diplomatic assignments). But in both parties illustrations abound of faithful servants who have held no partisan political appointment.[12]

The rapport established between solicitors and persons in their own party who wield government power inevitably opens opportunities to influence public decisions. Individuals who have been on the receiving end of pressures, others who have themselves brought pressure to bear,

11. It should not be inferred that individuals in given segments of the economy are solicited solely by one fund-raiser, nor that they unanimously support the same party. The personal trail of solicitors can often be detected in the reports of receipts made by political committees. The reports frequently show gifts received from several persons at the same business address on the same day. In 1952, 13 officials of Burlington Industries—the nation's fifty-seventh largest industrial corporation in 1956, with headquarters in Greensboro, North Carolina—showed up on the records of various committees as making political gifts of $500 or more. The Democratic national committee recorded contributions from seven of them as received on October 28 and 29. The North Carolina Citizens for Eisenhower-Nixon recorded gifts from six others, all dated November 12, and all giving the contributor's address as care of J. E. Broyhill of Lenoir. Mr. Broyhill has long been the most conspicuous Republican fund-raiser in the state and has served as his party's national committeeman.

12. Alexander studied intensively the personal histories of 30 important fund-raisers (both parties) in New York. Nine had never accepted any form of government appointment. The remaining 21 had occupied a total of 51 different positions, many of them part-time and honorary, many of them significant. Of these, 34 were federal jobs, eight state, and nine local.—*Op. cit.*, pp. 100-7.

and party people who have watched the exercise of influence at close range, all agree that solicitors in both parties often become channels of access to the decision-points of government. On jobs, clearance through regular party channels is customary and conflicts sometimes occur between finance people, desiring to reward generous donors, and others needing competent help to get a job done. On matters of party or government policy, fund-raisers may assert themselves independently. When a man who has raised $100,000 calls up, said one aide to a Democratic president, and asks that a friend be given a hearing, there is no way to say no, especially if the friend is a contributor, or may become one. A Republican with an overview of his party's affairs observed that the united finance committees constitute a source of power within the party separate from the hierarchy of regular political committees. State finance chairmen may go straight to Washington, straight to the White House. Since many state parties are deeply divided internally on policy questions, the views of individual fund-raisers may depart sharply from those of the party's political officers. One Republican state chairman remarked ruefully that at the national conclaves of his party the state finance chairmen were shown greater deference by national leaders than the heads of the regular state committees.[13]

Edwin W. Pauley, independent California oilman and treasurer of the Democratic national committee from 1942 to 1945, is cited as his party's most successful money-raiser by many persons deeply experienced in Democratic finance. Mr. Pauley was systematic as well as hard working, which cannot be said of all who have held his job. A man of means himself, he was able to deal with other men of means. His reputation led his peers to trust their political contributions with him. He knew, and knew how to find out, who around the country could be productive solicitors, and he was willing to use them. No one charged with the Democratic party's national financing can succeed without this last quality, which is the real reason, it is universally repeated, Beardsley Ruml failed as national finance chairman in 1952.[14] But Mr. Pauley's

13. According to their proponents, the separate Republican finance committees help to insulate the party's fund-raisers from supplicants for special favors. "All that is handled by the state committee and the other regular party committees," a veteran of the finance committee in New York said impatiently. An official of the finance committee in Pennsylvania noted that contractors and purveyors to the state were more likely to contribute to the regular state and county committees than to the finance committees.

The extent to which Republican solicitors communicate requests from persons whom they have solicited appears to vary. A senior bank official who had collected for about eight years claimed that none of those who had given through him had ever asked him for a favor. Many other solicitors who were interviewed, however, recounted instances in which they had been consulted by candidates or party leaders, or in which they had acted in response to a contributor's plea.

14. Some old hands complained contemptuously that Mr. Ruml not only did not know the key solicitors, but he set out to eliminate some he had heard about. There seems to be no question that Mr. Stevenson and Mr. Ruml both looked

real key to success was something additional. He looked about to find out who had benefited from the Democratic administration[15] and then asked them for funds. In addition to being shrewd and diligent, Mr. Pauley is tough. Money was the result. The procedure assumes that for the *quid* there will be a *quo*.

The diaries of James Forrestal reveal his intense anxieties over American policy toward Palestine. He reported conversations during 1947 with Postmaster General Robert E. Hannegan, for some years previous the chairman of the Democratic national committee. It was evident that at least one group of large contributors could count on having its concerns remembered: what the President did, warned Mr. Hannegan in the cabinet, "would have a very great influence and great effect on the raising of funds for the Democratic National Committee."[16] The Palestine question involved such crucial matters of foreign policy and so much domestic political dynamite that the President informed national committee officials he would handle the matter in the White House. He added, and it must have been wistfully, the thing would be handled outside the field of political pressures.[17] Zionists are not the only group of financial supporters whose interests have been discussed in the cabinet and handled in the White House, nor were party gifts the sole source of their influence (the appealing nature of their cause and the location of their voters being two others).[18] Their experience

upon the Democratic soliciting corps, or what they knew of it, as a "varied lot," and that the former instructed the latter to keep his skirts clear of certain persons who it was thought would abuse the access that service to the party would give them.

15. Including five broad categories during this war period: the relatives of European refugees, those touched most deeply by the persecutions of Jews, those in the construction and contracting business who favored large spending and construction programs, those who held important appointive posts, and labor.

16. Walter Millis, with the collaboration of E. S. Duffield (eds.), *The Forrestal Diaries* (New York: The Viking Press, 1951), p. 309. Note also the observation made by Senator Howard McGrath of Rhode Island (who followed Hannegan as national chairman) in a conversation with Forrestal: "In the first place, Jewish sources were responsible for a substantial part of the contributions to the Democratic National Committee, and many of these contributions were made 'with a distinct idea on the part of the givers that they will have an opportunity to express their views and have them seriously considered on such questions as the present Palestine question.' "—P. 345.

17. Jack Redding, *Inside the Democratic Party* (New York: The Bobbs-Merrill Company, Inc., 1958), p. 149.

18. This illustration is used for the convenience of the published references. Former President Truman has expounded his views fully on the whole set of Palestine-Israel issues, and traces his attitude to the days before he occupied the White House. "When I was in the Senate, I had told my colleagues, Senator Wagner of New York and Senator Taft of Ohio, that I would go along on a resolution putting the Senate on record in favor of the speedy achievement of the Jewish homeland."—*Memoirs by Harry S. Truman—Years of Trial and Hope* (Garden City: Doubleday and Company, Inc., 1956), vol. 2, pp. 133-34; see also pp. 132-69. The President's attitude at various specific junctures was not always certain in advance to those involved, however. Samuel Lubell cites "Truman's

illustrates the fact, however, as many Democratic politicians have acknowledged, that those who solicit funds from any financial constituency may become a political agent of that constituency.

Party differences.—Discussions with experienced financial operators in both parties led to the recognition of certain factors that help determine the amount of influence solicitors exercise in party councils. The importance of an individual solicitor, and therefore his potential influence, seems to vary with at least four factors: (1) how large the sums he collects are compared with the other income of the party; (2) how far short the party is of its essential requirements; (3) how personal the apparatus of solicitation is, as compared with an institutionalized set of fund-raising procedures and relationships;[19] and (4) the ability of the solicitor to obtain funds with assurance and speed. When a party's candidate is desperately short of funds, lacking an adequate fund-raising organization, the man who can produce large sums of money fast becomes a crucial—though not necessarily visible—political figure. When he provides it from his own resources he stands in the same relationship to his beneficiaries as when he raises it from others. But the day when one or two giant contributors could finance an entire campaign is largely past; the role of the solicitor is steadily enhanced.

Republicans generally enjoy larger and readier financial resources than Democrats. They have a widespread, well-formed hierarchy of continuing fund-raising committees to exploit these resources, a facility lacking throughout most of the Democratic party. Democratic lore brims with tales of financial crisis. Dwight R. G. Palmer, as treasurer in Mr. Stevenson's first presidential race, like others before and since, found it necessary to give personal guarantees before arrangements for certain broadcasts could be completed. Republican financial troubles are neither so frequent nor so acute, and as a consequence Republican dependence on individuals with special, quick access to funds is less than that of Democrats. This is not to say that the viewpoints of their financial supporters in general are less well reflected in Republican actions and policies. But ironically, because theirs is the party of fewer funds, Democrats are often more dependent on particular sources of funds and therefore are potentially more vulnerable to pressures from those who provide them.

---

shilly-shallying on Palestine" as one cause of the large Jewish protest vote that went to Wallace in 1948.—*The Future of American Politics* (New York: Harper & Brothers, 1952), pp. 207-8. For a discussion of the origins and extent of Democratic solidarity among Jewish voters, see Lawrence H. Fuchs, *The Political Behavior of American Jews* (Glencoe, Illinois: The Free Press, 1956).

19. Certainly experience in military (and other administrative) organizations indicates that when formality breaks down, and relationships between individuals become increasingly personal and decreasingly official, favoritism in administration, especially in matters affecting personnel, rises. Democratic fund-raising is clearly a more clubby, individual affair than that of the Republican finance committees.

2. OTHER TYPES OF SOLICITORS

Party solicitation accounts for only a portion of the campaign money raised in the United States. Persons concerned chiefly with public policies without special attachment to any party also raise money. Candidates have their financial managers, too. Finally, there are confidential advisers to political patrons who perform a money-raising function.

Policy-oriented solicitors.—The National Committee for an Effective Congress is a formally organized group which submits reports required by law of "political committees" to the Clerk of the United States House of Representatives. Its momentum and purposes derive chiefly from two persons, George E. Agree and Maurice Rosenblatt. Its activities illustrate an important type of political operation which usually proceeds on a much less formal basis and in considerably greater obscurity. The NCEC is interested in public policy, and one way it expresses this interest is by contributing to Congressional candidates whose views, regardless of party, fit its liberal orientation. Between November 7, 1953, and December 31, 1954, for example, the NCEC collected $98,422 and disbursed $93,277. The receipts (from several sections of the country, but chiefly from New York and California) included around 200 sums of $100 or more, plus many smaller ones. The disbursements included 52 donations totalling $30,611 to the campaign funds of 19 candidates for the House or Senate. These candidates were located in 18 states, and, while most were Democrats, they included three Republican Senatorial candidates. The NCEC has, in addition, sponsored special financial drives on behalf of selected candidates, such as the Civil Liberties Appeal in 1952 and the Clean Politics Appeal in 1956.[20]

About a dozen campaign groups operating more or less like the NCEC, submitting campaign reports, and not identified by name or organizational connection with either party, are normally found engaged in national-level fund-raising. They took in something over $600,000 in both 1952 and 1956, of which 15 to 20 per cent was passed on for use by others, the rest being spent by the collecting group.[21] The organizations reporting the largest sums in both years were the Americans for Democratic Action and The Christian Nationalist Crusade.

20. From May through November 7, 1952, NCEC collected for itself $31,068; from January 1 through November 20, 1956, it collected for itself about $75,400. The 1952 Civil Liberties Appeal raised $15,107 during the period October 8 through November 18, and the 1956 Clean Politics Appeal took in altogether $71,726. In 1954, there was also a Citizens' Fund for Case and Cooper and a 1954 Campaign Appeal, for Case, Cooper, Paul Douglas, and Richard Neuberger, both of less significance.

21. In 1952, 14 such groups disbursed $622,822, transferring 18 per cent of that amount to other organizations or candidate committees; through November 30, 1956, 11 such groups disbursed $677,075, 14 per cent by transfer. For 1956, see the Gore Committee *Report,* pp. 41-44; the activities of the 1952 groups are discussed in Joan Combs Grace, "The Impact of Campaign Funds on Party and Factional Structures" (Master's thesis, University of North Carolina, 1958), pp. 113-18.

These groups bring persons who share common political sympathies into common linkage with the political process. In addition to the dozen or so activities referred to, which operate in the open, there are many less visible but more important policy-oriented, fund-raising operations. Many policy-oriented solicitors make their collections quietly, and simply hand the proceeds to candidates or party committees without spending any themselves. Of this shade are the political vice presidents of large corporations and the officials of labor unions who comb their special constituencies for donations on behalf of candidates or party groups who, in the context of the moment, look like the best risks available. Such a solicitor operates not from a formal or informal party position, like the member of a finance committee, but from outside the party structure. He does not necessarily lack access to the inside, indeed to gain it is part of his goal, and sometimes his starting point. But he is primarily interested in specific policies, and to advance these policy interests he raises money for candidates who are sympathetic to them. As a wholesaler of campaign funds he attracts some money that would not otherwise have been contributed or would not have reached the same destinations.

Policy-oriented solicitors function in many different ways. There is a publicity-shy, seldom mentioned political solicitor in one of the eastern cities[22] whose concern is foreign policy, and only foreign policy. Domestic issues leave him "cold as a dog's nose." A Republican himself, he solicits from a wide assortment of persons in both parties for various committees through which he works. He also carries on what he calls "personal" fund-raising for candidates. Over the years he has raised in all many tens of thousands of dollars. He argues that he and his "fronts," as he calls the committees with which he works, perform a vital function by giving persons who cannot afford to be identified publicly with a partisan political group or a "propaganda movement" an opportunity to assert themselves politically.

The policy-oriented solicitor does not always aid candidates of both parties. The multiplicity of factional divisions along lines of issue within each major party offers ample opportunity to push almost any viewpoint one possesses. Solicitors do this by participation in nominating contests and also by selective assistance to candidates of their own party—collecting funds, however, without regard to the party preferences of the donors. A Republican cabinet officer has been heard to say that previously his only form of political activity was to spot candidates who would, by his lights, make good public servants, and then raise money for them. One prominent Democrat who opened law offices in Washington after Mr. Eisenhower became president operates in a similar way. On one occasion he wrote 25 acquaintances asking for contributions to a Democratic candidate running in California. All

22. He agreed to talk about his widespread activities only after assurances that neither his name nor that of any of the groups through which he has worked would appear in print.

but one responded with a gift. In another election he drew donations from his clients, many of them Republicans who could not afford to give openly to Democrats, and funnelled them to six or eight candidates for the United States Senate. Not only can a solicitor of this type encourage prospective candidates to seek or accept a nomination, but as a close associate observed, one can talk an entirely different language to a senator when he has "given" the Senator $4,000 or $5,000 for his campaign than when he has not. Conspicuous success may land a policy-oriented solicitor on a formal or informal party finance committee. This, in fact, is the story of many a finance chairman.[23]

Candidate-oriented solicitors.—An important slice of all political fund-raising is candidate-oriented. Even within Republican ranks, with the all-party finance committees, significant supplemental solicitation takes place. In direct primaries in competitive party states, the promise of funds held forth by candidate-oriented solicitors can be crucial in vying for the endorsement of the party organization. In direct primaries in one-party states, candidate-solicitation becomes all-important.[24] In any contest in which party competition becomes confused or dim, fund-raising tends to become organized around individual candidates.[25]

Candidate-oriented solicitors are readily observable in the entourage of any politician who aspires to a presidential nomination. James A. Farley tells of the critical fund-raising undertaken in 1931 and 1932 on behalf of Franklin Roosevelt by Frank C. Walker, Eddie Dowling, Henry Morgenthau, Sr., and James W. Gerard.[26] Numerous persons

23. Successful solicitation may be a boost to "political" party office too, or so Mr. F. Joseph (Jiggs) Donohue, an important Democratic fund-raiser in the District of Columbia, who served as a Commissioner of the District, seemed to think. In 1954, Mr. Donohue offered himself as a compromise candidate for the chairmanship of the Democratic national committee. "He told a meeting of Mid-west and Western State representatives yesterday he would be in position to raise adequate funds for the National Committee so that it could begin the 1956 campaign without delay."—Gould Lincoln in *The Evening Star* (Washington, D.C.), December 4, 1954.

24. For a discussion of sources of southern campaign funds, from which ready inferences about the processes of solicitation can be made, see V. O. Key, Jr., *Southern Politics in State and Nation* (New York: Alfred A. Knopf, Inc., 1949), pp. 470-80. The candidate is usually the focal point of political activity, including financial activity. In the highly structured factional politics of Virginia, however, a kind of party-oriented soliciting, which is really soliciting on behalf of the Byrd organization, has been frequent.

25. In the chaotic politics of California, with its crucial party primaries, a campaign manager who can collect funds and sponsors is said to be a must.—Don M. Muchmore, "Parties and Candidates in California," in David Farrelly and Ivan Hinderaker, *The Politics of California—A Book of Readings* (New York: Ronald Press Company, 1951), p. 95. Where established fund-raising machinery, whether of party or faction, cannot be relied upon, the candidate is most dependent on rallying *ad hoc* solicitors.

26. *Behind the Ballots—The Personal History of a Politician* (New York: Harcourt, Brace and Company, 1938), pp. 72-73. "I hate to think what would have happened if the men just mentioned had not been around to pull us over

who had a hand in raising money for General Eisenhower both before and after the 1952 convention have cited their respect and affection for him personally as the explanation of their activity. The wave of enthusiasm for Ike that swept the business community, carrying along many young men who had never before taken part in politics, released much fund-raising energy that was clearly candidate-oriented.[27]

Contributor-oriented solicitors.—The three types of solicitation sketched so far assume initiative on the part of the solicitor. There is another kind of solicitor who is generally more passive and whose usefulness stems from the confidence in which he is held by potential contributors. He is an adviser to persons of wealth, and while his political views may be deeply held and well known, he operates primarily neither from attachment to a party, nor to candidates, nor to special brands of public policy. He is called upon by his principals to investigate requests made to them for funds. Reciprocally, he may relay to them appeals that come to him because of his identification with them. Some of these persons are employees, such as the private secretary to a brewery head who claimed to exercise great freedom in distributing his boss's political donations. Another such person is a sophisticated court jester to some of the Texas oil kings, trusted because he gives wise counsel and knows the limits of his relationship. His alertness has been especially appreciated in getting his principals in on the ground floor of certain candidacies and party operations. That some of these contributor-oriented go-betweens take the initiative in proferring contributions became evident in 1956 when John Neff offered his famous contribution of $2,500 to the campaign fund of Senator Francis Case of South Dakota. The money was given to Mr. Neff by Elmer Patman, who got it originally from Howard B. Keck, president of Superior Oil Company, for which Mr. Patman was a full-time employee. One of Mr. Patman's duties, it came out in the investigation that followed, was to "expedite" Mr. Keck's campaign contributions, a function of a contributor-oriented solicitor.[28]

---

the financial dry spots." Edward J. Flynn records a longer list of who donated $2,000 or more each to get the campaign launched.—*You're the Boss* (New York: The Viking Press, 1947), pp. 84-85.

27. The same individual may raise money for a candidate and, separately or subsequently, for a party. Candidate solicitors often display the same personal qualities mentioned earlier in connection with party solicitors, e.g. a record of nonpolitical money-raising. Robert Cutler, who served as special assistant to President Eisenhower for National Security Affairs, was a community-chest solicitor in the thirties, helped raise money for Columbia University's American Assembly when Ike was president of that institution, and long before the 1952 nomination was at work rallying funds for the General. See Anthony Leviero, "Untouchable, Unreachable and Unquotable," *New York Times Magazine,* January 30, 1955, p. 68.

28. U.S. Senate Select Committee for Contribution Investigation, *Report* (Washington: Government Printing Office, 1956) (Senate Report No. 1724, 84th Congress, 2nd Session), pp. 3-5.

People who have money are likely to use it. Those who choose to use some of it in politics, whatever the incentive, have to set up ways to do so. They can give to the obvious committees, but eventually others will also ask them for gifts. Unless knowledgeable themselves, prudent persons turn for advice to people they trust who are. They in turn may consult others. An intricate chain of personal relationships often develops, linked together by successive mutual confidences. The end product, respected advice for the prospective donor, may be transmitted from an informed person via five or six intermediaries. Through such communication patterns do persons of like mind establish a common front of action.[29] American politics is knit together by a series of such underground railroads of information. Persons in one place get to know persons in other places with whom they share points of view. They turn to each other when they want the word on developments in the other's locality. Especially valued is information about candidates for the Senate and House of Representatives. Though elected by state and local constituencies, their actions affect the whole nation. Contributors inclined to vote with their money away from home need advice about remote situations. They often want to be told about worthy brethren in need.[30]

In travelling around the United States one soon learns, for example, the confidence in which Jonathan Daniels, North Carolina author and editor, is held by many liberal Democrats outside his own section. His word on the politics of his state has carried weight with solicitors and contributors elsewhere in the country. Mr. Daniels is a reliable local correspondent. His counterparts are found in all states. Politically attentive people, sharing other slants toward public questions, have

29. The phenomenon of course characterizes many human relationships, and the history of political money-raising is replete with examples. Harold L. Ickes described his experiences in raising a kitty for Charles E. Merriam's nomination and election campaigns of 1911 to become mayor of Chicago. Ickes, acting for Merriam, appealed to his friend Walter S. Rogers, confidential secretary to Charles R. Crane. Through Rogers he appealed to Crane himself, and ultimately in combination with others to Julius Rosenwald, who, "delightfully naive" about politics, told his friend Crane to put as much money in the campaign as he wanted to and he, Rosenwald, would give him a check for half of it on his return from Europe.—*Autobiography of a Curmudgeon* (New York: Reynal Hitchcock, 1943), pp. 122-24.

30. Solicitors often bridge social as well as geographic distances. The social gap between upper-class financial supporters and more rough-cut political types may be especially evident in local politics. This is not simply a matter of what makes a good solicitor, although it is because of this gap that some men become solicitors while others do not. The solicitors serve as intermediaries through whom disparate elements of a community become hooked together in political alliance. Note the discussion of class connections and campaign funds in W. Lloyd Warner, *Democracy in Jonesville—A Study in Quality and Inequality* (New York: Harper & Brothers, 1949): "The class connections and the social skills of the lower-class individuals who serve as wheel horses simply do not qualify them for establishing successful relations either outside the county or with financially important groups within the county."—Pp. 230-31.

their own trusted local contacts, too. These advisory types are usually less known to the public than other sorts of solicitors whose more aggressive tactics are necessarily more conspicuous. Many lawyers and public relations men engage regularly in confidential political advising. As one of the latter put it, when the big guys find you do well by them in the advice you give, they keep asking for it. Lawyers perform a general intermediary function in society in representing the interests of clients in strange surroundings. Advice on political donations is one aspect of the function. Some lawyers are asked to give it often, and their proximity to politics equips them well to do so.[31]

The gigantic task of fueling the American electoral machine is largely achieved by the four types of solicitation that have been outlined. The activities of solicitors introduce a rationalizing and organizing element into political finance, joining together contributors of common purpose in pursuit of their shared goals.

3. COMPETING POLITICAL STRUCTURES

Aside from its importance as a path to access or specific privileges, political fund-raising may find importance as a basis for political organization. When a solicitor circulates on behalf of a common cause among politically interested people, he may create a structure of loyalties to himself personally. When he represents a fund-raising organization, institutional loyalties may develop. Not all solicitors seize the opportunities open to them. Others have with telling effect; as they have moved about among contributors and party officials, receiving and giving courtesies, certain solicitors have knitted together cliques or factions that have played a potent part in intraparty struggles. Such elements of factional and party organization have been influential in nomination contests, in marshalling the support of voters and of those who lead them, in the organization and functioning of legislatures, in fact wherever the haul and pull of politics go on. It is not surprising that party politicians often shy away from fund-raising schemes that might create a political organization to rival their own.[32]

Multiple nonparty structures.—The American party system is comprised of a large number of diverse and frequently overlapping structures of personal relationships. The most obvious of these are the hierarchies of party officers and committee members. Hardly less central, where

31. "'What about this man Cleveland?' wrote James J. Hill, the Western railroad-builder, to Tilden. 'He is all right,' replied the corporation lawyer. Hill thereupon sent Manning $10,000—and telegraphed his associates in the West 'to get busy' for Mr. Cleveland."—Matthew Josephson, *The Politicos—1865-1896* (New York: Harcourt, Brace & Company, 1938), p. 362.

32. Control over the supplies of money received from officeholders, among others, was one source of power of the old urban bosses in the United States. Earlier in British politics the parliamentary party whips played the key role in party finance, one appropriate to their responsibilities as whips. Unless substitute sources of discipline are found, dispersion of control over fund-raising necessarily results in a fractionalization of party power.

they are different, are the configurations of key supporters of candidates through whom election campaigns are organized. A campaign manager may be prized for his skills in propagandizing and in pasting together a headquarters organization, but his crucial contribution will depend more on the network of friendships he can bring to the support of his candidate.[33] Structures of personal relationships that have political significance are not all political on the surface. The political influence enjoyed by utility companies and railroads in many states (more so formerly than recently) derived in part from the personal and professional loyalties that developed around their widespread system of offices, managers, customers, and local retainers. More is involved than obvious mutual interests. Personal rapport and knowledge of personalities and situations enable an individual to realize on the political potential inherent in most large, strategically located groups of people.

C. Hamilton Moses, long president of the Arkansas Power and Light Company, knew the political life of his state well before he came to that position. Yet his reputation as a political force mounted after he assumed it. If his contemporaries in Arkansas are to be believed, the two things were closely related. Among numerous other activities, Mr. Moses has been a director of the Committee for Economic Development and a leader of its activities in his state as president of the Arkansas State Chamber of Commerce (the Arkansas Economic Council, 1945-47). One of his admirers, close to the CED, concluded that all Mr. Moses had to do when the chips were down in a political campaign was to energize the people with whom he had worked so successfully at the end of World War II in CED's community self-appraisal program. In California the Chambers of Commerce constitute in their political orientation an informal organization that at times has functioned largely within the Republican party. The networks of labor locals in industrialized states offer another set of relationships capable of exploitation for political purposes.[34] Joseph T. Meek, long-time executive secretary of the Illinois Federation of Retail Associations, was highly successful for many years in stimulating his retail connections to political action within the Republican party. His potency was evident in 1954 when he sought the GOP Senatorial nomination against several opponents. Every Republican state senator supported him save one, and that one had a law partner in the race. Many a war hero blessed with a

33. This is to some extent true even where a virile party organization wields real power. Where it does not, the importance of individuals who command some kind of organization of their own skyrockets. A campaign manager who has friends and can rally sponsors for his candidate is of enormous value in California's jumbled party politics. Among the southern states, the premium on such people seems highest in Georgia where the county-unit system requires intimate knowledge and close acquaintanceships in each of the state's 159 counties.

34. Note Stephen B. and Vera H. Sarasohn, *Political Party Patterns in Michigan* (Detroit: Wayne State University Press, 1957), pp. 45-68.

regiment from his own state has found in the comradeship of the trenches a starting point for a personal political following.

Financial structures.—There are many types of supplemental political structures, of which these illustrations are a few. It is no surprise that in an activity as close to the heart of politics as fund-raising there exists similar high potential for organizing political power. The ability of fund-raisers to pinch off the flow of cash, or part of it, enhances this potential.[35] Whether the potential is invariably exploited, or whether the resulting political structure invariably dominates, is not here the point. The point is that both sometimes occur. The ways money is raised create sets of political loyalties within each of the parties, and even across party lines, that weaken the regular organizational hierarchies in representing the diverse and competing interests that make up American society.

The activities of any type of solicitor may lay the basis for a structure of personal influence. In internal party affairs, party-oriented solicitors are most likely to develop significant factional leadership. It was obvious in Georgia following 1952, for example, that behind the financial activities of the state finance chairman, Robert Snodgrass, lay the assumption that the expansion and invigoration of the Republican party could best be achieved through the development of a faithful corps of contributors and lower-level finance chairmen. The latter were for the most part different individuals from the regular party officers. In California, steps toward Democratic unity for years foundered on fears of rival organizational developments, the latter frequently rooted in fund-raising aspirations, as witness the conflict between the Dime-a-Day-for-Democracy movement and the Democratic Clubs.[36] In at least one state, proposals to employ a full-time party executive to organize local party units for fund-raising and program-planning were rejected. Party leaders feared he would build organizational strength around himself.[37] Henry Wallace seems to feel that Edwin W. Pauley commanded considerable influence as treasurer of the Democratic national committee. Wallace quotes George Allen on Pauley: "For more than a year before the 1944 Convention he toured the country raising money for the party and, incidentally, mobilizing opposition to Wallace's nomination. As he went from city to city on party business he primed local leaders to men-

35. This condition is found wherever parties must raise their own funds. In some of the provinces of Australia, for example, the policies of the United Australia party have allegedly been controlled by a consultative council (and subsequently by another body) that raised and controlled party funds.—Louise Overacker, *The Australian Party System* (New Haven: Yale University Press, 1952), pp. 216-18.

36. See Francis Carney, *The Rise of the Democratic Clubs in California* (New York: Henry Holt and Company, 1958), esp. p. 11.

37. Most of the time the hired hands in the central office of a party organization remain just that. A person who can engender cooperation among local politicos throughout his state may, in contrast, develop political standing of his own.

tion to Roosevelt, when the opportunities presented themselves, that the Democratic ticket would suffer seriously from the presence of Wallace on it in the 1944 campaign."[38] A presidential candidate who had been a governor was queried about the part of solicitors in his experience. Do they warrant the importance suggested by episodes like these? "Oh my God, yes," he exploded, therewith to dwell on the troubles they had caused him.[39]

The significance of fund-raising practices to the organizational characteristics of political parties is manifest in various settings. Not many members of the United States Senate or House of Representatives can control the destiny of more money than needed for their own campaigning. Occasionally one of them can, however, like the late Senator Robert A. Taft. The Senior Senator from Ohio commanded great confidence in certain circles of wealth. Campaign money found its way easily to colleagues in the Senate, and perhaps candidates elsewhere, whom he blessed. Regardless of how explicit Senator Taft was or was not in discussions of funds, his factional ties within and outside the Senate were unquestionably strengthened by the financial benefits that flowed to politicians with whom he kept political company. Senator Joseph R. McCarthy's influence with wealthy contributors accounted for donations made by them to other candidates, like Senator John Marshall Butler of Maryland. James F. Byrnes, influential senator from South Carolina during the New Deal, was able to direct financial aid to colleagues, some of it the money of his friend Bernard Baruch, who liked to collect southern "old masters" by backing them in southern Senatorial primaries.[40] There seems little doubt that the Democratic party's chief pipeline for

38. Text of an address by Henry A. Wallace for delivery to the Harvard Law School Forum, in *U.S. News and World Report,* April 6, 1956. The Allen quotation is from *Presidents Who Have Known Me* (New York: Simon and Schuster, 1950), p. 123. Allen devotes a chapter to Wallace's dumping called "The Conspiracy of the Pure in Heart."

39. One order of difficulty solicitors eager to build their own importance are wont to cause candidates was experienced by Culbert Olson when he was elected governor of California. He had 150 jobs to fill that would pay well, no more than 500 that paid anything at all. Although he had promised very few himself, "persons who admit they call him Culbert must have promised 100,000 jobs in the process of raising maybe $1,500,000 in campaign funds and wangling all those votes."—Robert E. Burke, *Olson's New Deal for California* (Berkeley and Los Angeles: University of California Press, 1953), p. 37, quoting the *San Francisco News,* November 10, 1938.

Mayor O'Dwyer of New York, as well as many others, was said to have been compromised by injudicious fund-raisers acting without the full knowledge of their principal. Keeping check on solicitors who are overly solicitous of the aspirations of prospective contributors is a worrisome chore about which campaign treasurers as well as candidates complain.

40. James F. Byrnes, *All In One Lifetime* (New York: Harper & Brothers, 1958), p. 101. Mr. Baruch does not mention his role as supplier of campaign money in his autobiography, *My Own Story* (New York: Henry Holt, 1957), but one of his contemporaries does in *The Secret Diary of Harold L. Ickes—The Inside Struggle, 1936-1939* (New York: Simon and Schuster, 1954), pp. 164, 328.

funds out of Texas long has been Sam Rayburn. Mr. Sam may off and on be Speaker of the United States House of Representatives, but his role, and that of his Texas colleague at the other end of the Capitol, Senate Majority Leader Lyndon B. Johnson, is also that of collector and distributor of Texas money. Both men fortify their other formidable talents for legislative and factional leadership with the ability to summon aid for friends in distress, a convenient resource in the logrolling, back-scratching reciprocity of United States politics.[41]

The Republican trend toward segregating and identifying publicly the money-raising organization of the party has been noted. Perhaps the process had its beginning when the great American shopkeeper, John Wanamaker, made his price for service to Harrison's cause in 1888 the "creation of an advisory board of businessmen alone, with its own treasurer and unrestricted power to raise money and decide upon its expenditure."[42] The finance committees did not then and do not now monopolize Republican money-raising,[43] but they are becoming increasingly well set as party institutions and as formal avenues to party service. They are largely manned by persons without other political experience.[44] They constitute distinctive political structures, and at

41. Messrs. Rayburn and Johnson are strategically situated for Texas oil interests, whose foremost concern is to preserve the 27.5 per cent depletion allowance, a matter that rests initially with Congress. This is one reason a weathered Democratic solicitor in Texas says he does less message-carrying for his contributors than is probably true "in the East." "Oh, things come up occasionally, but often the Congressional delegation is able to be more helpful." Drew Pearson has written that when Lyndon Johnson "was a young congressman from Texas in 1938 . . . he hired a room in the rear of Washington's Munsey Building and passed out $110,000 in cash to fellow Democrats who needed election help. It was not his money, of course. It was oil-gas money from Texas."—*The News and Observer* (Raleigh, N.C.), February 8, 1956.

A person close to the fuss between the Taft and Ike people following the 1952 Republican nomination observed that until the Morningside Agreement, Taft's supporters not only refused to work for the party but also to raise money from the established sources.

42. Josephson, *op. cit.*, p. 423.

43. *The Memoirs of Will H. Hays* (Garden City: Doubleday & Company, Inc., 1955), pp. 155-59, has interesting passages on Mr. Hays's contact as Republican national chairman in 1918 and 1920 with leading financial supporters of the party.

44. Of 97 persons who served on the Republican national finance committee during the years 1952-58, on whom information could be obtained, 30 per cent had held nonfinancial positions in the party. The percentage was somewhat higher among the state finance chairmen on the committee than among the at-large members (35 per cent to 21 per cent). The impression is easily gained that Democratic fund-raisers are more likely to be active also in other kinds of political work. Nevertheless, among 35 persons who had raised important sums of money for the Democratic national committee, only 20 per cent were found to have held nonfinancial party posts. Many solicitors would probably not engage in any political activity if this avenue were not open to them.

The Republican finance chairman of one of Ohio's most populous counties told how he got into the game. A successful businessman, but relative newcomer, he wanted "to become part of the community." After a few years he went to a

times rival other political structures when particular decisions are to be made.[45] Within the Democratic party the relationships are more confused, but divisive tendencies are present. What do these add up to in the broad scheme of American government?

4. FUNCTIONAL REPRESENTATION

The Ecuadoran Constitution of 1946 provided that 12 of the 45 members of the Ecuadoran Senate be chosen as "functional senators." It provided that two each should come from agriculture, commerce, labor, and industry (each pair divided between the two main geographical sections), and one each from public education, private education, the armed forces, and journalism and the scientific and literary societies. To be eligible for selection, an individual must have been affiliated for at least a year with the economic, professional, or occupational group he would represent, these groups being variously organized into twelve electoral colleges to name the senators. George I. Blanksten, surveying the operations of the functional-senator system after a few years, concluded that it operated in accordance with the realities of Ecuadoran politics: "With the exception of the two functional senators for labor—this group is small, undeveloped, and essentially unorganized in Ecuador—the system has in general given realistic recognition to the major instruments of power which underlie the political system as it actually operates, and little dissatisfaction has been expressed with functional representation as provided for in the latest constitution. This situation contrasts markedly with Ecuadoran experience under the Constitution of 1945, which gave unrealistically heavy representation to labor."[46]

Regardless of whether one approves, a degree of functional representation is achieved in the United States through the activities of the middlemen who solicit campaign funds. Contrary to that of Ecuador, the American government does not accord formal recognition in its legislatures to the "instruments of power" that undergird the nation's

---

politically active friend to ask how he could become active too. The friend advised that with his age and other characteristics the only way for him to get into politics was via fund-raising, so he volunteered for the county finance committee and eventually became its chairman.

45. Philip S. Wilder, Jr., has reported that apparently on no occasion since the national finance committee was created have its leaders made a serious attempt to control party policy through their control over the purse.—"The National Committee of the Party in Power, 1953-1958" (mimeographed, a paper delivered at the annual meeting of the American Political Science Association, 1958), p. 18. In the absence of a frontal attack, the party's fund-raisers can nevertheless bring important pressures to bear through the multiple points of access open to them, and many seem to have done so. The national finance chairman is appointed by the chairman of the national committee, and state finance chairmen are chosen by the national finance chairman after consultation with local party leaders and others. As in most matters political, the practices are not always neatly defined and consistent.

46. *Ecuador: Constitutions and Caudillos* (Berkeley and Los Angeles: University of California Press, 1951), pp. 106-7.

social, economic, and political life. Yet no popular government in history has yet survived that did not in some way permit such interests to exercise effective means of petition. The American federal and state governments have set up many procedures to facilitate consultation with interests directly touched by public policy (legislative committee hearings and executive commissions being only two of them). Hosts of less formal modes of consultation inexorably emerge whenever affected interests feel the need.

Solicitors have a special role in giving organized expression to the interests represented in campaign contributions. The variety of incentives and situations that lead persons to make political gifts has been discussed. Definite expectations accompany some contributions; none at all accompany others. Contributors, even of sums as large as $500, are too numerous and diverse for their voices to be heard effectively if each spoke individually. Certain solicitors serve as contributors' agents —relaying, explaining, screening, mediating, anticipating, in many subtle and varied ways conveying their expectations. At the same time, they interpret to contributors the problems, limitations, and conflicting demands faced by public officials. In sum, they supply a two-way communications system between important financial constituencies and government.

Some policy-oriented solicitors speak for interests that bridge party lines, for what might be called inter-party factions.[47] Others build political followings, and therefore political influence, on the basis of contributions that individually would have no special significance. The concerns of contributors and solicitors do not invariably coincide, but many factors that make for effective solicitation reflect a basic harmony between asker and giver. Thus, whether operating as largely independent individuals (frequently the case among Democrats), or largely in a close system with others (frequently the case among Republicans), solicitors are in a position, when they choose, to speak on behalf of an important set of participants in the political process. Whether these interests should be denied this opportunity, and whether other channels of political representation should be constructed for them, are separate questions. But the roles solicitors play as representatives of functional interests—irregular and confused though the process may be—are directly relevant to the capacities of democratic government to maintain the flexibility and responsiveness necessary for governing a vast and heterogeneous nation. In one form or another functional representation has

47. The activities of fund-raisers often expose more rational political alignments than do party lines. The chairman of the Republican finance committee in Texas, for example, W. H. Francis, Jr., was an energetic fund-raiser in Governor Allan Shivers' 1954 campaign for renomination in the Democratic primary. The key money-raiser for Eisenhower in Louisiana at one time was Mr. Harry Latter, who steadfastly refused to call himself a Republican. In both instances, these men solicited funds for Ike without regard to party labels but with high regard for deeper running political sympathies.

always been a fact of complex democratic governments. In the nineteenth century, senators of the United States did indeed, as often charged, represent something more than a state. They crassly represented particular crops, types of business, even individual corporations. The functional representation of interests in the House of Commons is to this day a fundamental characteristic of the greatly respected British government.[48] The question is ever not whether special interests shall be represented in a democratic government, but how.

48. See Samuel H. Beer, "The Representation of Interests in British Government: Historical Background," *American Political Science Review,* 51 (1957), 613-50, and R. T. McKenzie, "Parties, Pressure Groups, and the British Political Process," *Political Quarterly,* 29 (1958), 5-16.

11

FUND-RAISING AND PARTY COHESION

THE STUDY OF public administration has ignored American political parties. Not, it may be assumed, because they are not in an important sense public. Rather, because they are rarely viewed as administrative organizations. They are not bracketed with the military, the corporations, the civil government, as a type of bureaucracy worthy of study. Yet they administer tens of millions of dollars annually through permanent and transient organizations. The administrative aspects of some European parties have been analyzed. There, greater formality and greater simplicity of structure make the task somewhat manageable. The internal operations of the American parties are so diverse and obscure as to render them almost impossible of systematic examination. Uniform data on political parties in the American states are largely confined to election results and to brief categories of formal and legal information. Little that is detailed and dependable is available concerning internal administrative operations, including financial operations.

Transfers of funds among political committees and candidates have not been comprehensively studied. A large amount of money is handed around, however, among political committees at the same political level and between different levels, and among party and nonparty political organizations. Observing the movements of funds from one political unit to another offers an opportunity to glimpse the parties in action along one plane of their operations. Knowledge of transfers is not complete, and at best the indicators of party processes that can be constructed from them are crude and tentative. If, however, the influence of contributors and solicitors accompanies money as it moves from the outside world into political life, the influence of politicians may accompany it as it is transmitted among committees and candidates within a party.

In this chapter, a body of data on transfers of funds is summarized in a series of tables. The data do not lead to startling discoveries, but they elaborate and deepen our understanding of several familiar features of political-party life. (1) The dependence of national-level operations in both parties on fund-raising by state and local units lights up some of the stern realities of the much discussed decentralization of power in American political parties. (2) The part played in campaigns by volunteer committees, finance committees, and other types of political committees becomes clearer as their role in raising money for themselves and others is examined. (3) Finally, differences among the activities of individual committees and among the organizational relationships existing within political parties are brought sharply to light. Not only are differences evident between the major parties, but also between state organizations of the same party.

Because data of this kind have not been pulled together before, it seems desirable to lay them out in some detail. They may have significance not detected here. A word of warning, however, is in order. Financial transactions are often purely formal, and their significance can easily be misinterpreted. The fund-raising practices discussed in the previous chapters ought especially to be kept in mind. The nature of the Republican finance-committee system, for example, makes it inevitable that more money will be channeled around among Republican than Democratic committees. While this is an important distinction between the parties, its full meaning is not apparent from financial information alone.

1. PARTY INTRADEPENDENCE

American political parties are composed of many separate units that function in substantial independence of each other. Normally the national-level committees do not participate in the nominating activities of state organizations; state and local organizations may at times refuse to support effectively the nominees of the national convention. Within states, candidates on the same party ticket often campaign separately from each other. Each party is an aggregation of committees and clubs interconnected in many different and changing ways. The extent of party cohesion, however measured, differs from one sector of a party's structure to another.

Within these loose and diffuse structures, nevertheless, a great deal of money flows from one organizational unit to another. The reliance of some of them on others for financial support suggests a dimension of interconnectedness within each party that otherwise may not be apparent. Control of the purse strings is traditionally thought to be decisive in the functioning of an organization. While the life blood of politics is votes and not money, the need of some party units to lean on others for money inevitably makes them attentive to those through whom it is supplied.

Volume of transfers.—Seldom is it realized how important transfers of funds can be as a source of income for particular organizations. Most political money starts out as some kind of individual contribution, but a high percentage of both the receipts and disbursements of most political committees takes the form of organizational transfers.[1]

About one-third of the combined receipts of the Democratic national committee and its allied Senatorial and Congressional campaign committees came from other organizations during the years 1944-56. Among the corresponding Republican committees, the proportion was well over half. Moreover, as Table 31 shows, the percentage of receipts in the form of transfers during this period rose for both parties in presidential election years and in mid-term election years.[2] Other national-level

Table 31

PERCENTAGE OF THE COMBINED TOTAL RECEIPTS OF THE THREE REGULAR NATIONAL-LEVEL COMMITTEES OF BOTH PARTIES RECEIVED AS TRANSFERS OF FUNDS, BY YEARS, 1944-56[a]

Year	Rep.			Dem.		
	Presidential Years	Mid-term Years	Off-Years	Presidential Years	Mid-term Years	Off-Years
1944	41			11		
1945			66			52
1946		25			36	
1947			9			35
1948	41			27		
1949			56			43
1950		53			40	
1951			74			12
1952	56			20		
1953			78			36
1954		54			41	
1955			68			36
1956	63			48		
Annual Averages (in thousands of dollars)						
(i) Transfers	$2,696	$ 921	$ 691	$ 725	$ 559	$ 379
(ii) Total Receipts	$5,048	$1,853	$1,089	$2,535	$1,414	$1,087
% i/ii	53	50	63	29	40	35

[a] The Republican national committee, Senatorial campaign committee, and Congressional campaign committee are taken as one group; the Democratic national committee, Senatorial campaign committee and the two Congressional campaign committees are taken as the other. Movements of funds among the committees within each group were excluded from the tabulation, hence the percentages will differ from other computations in which this was not done. Because of ambiguities in the reports from which the table was constructed, the totals and percentages may in a few cases be inflated by classifying as transfers various miscellaneous receipts, i.e., income other than individual contributions. In rare cases, too, one committee may in fact have been a subcommittee of another committee, and movements of funds between the two classed as transfers.

1. Joan Combs Grace analyzes organizational transfers, principally during 1952, in "The Impact of Campaign Funds on Party and Factional Structures" (Master's thesis, University of North Carolina, 1958), 211 pp.

2. The committees of each party for which data are presented in Table 31 are treated as though they were a single organization to avoid counting any money that was shifted among themselves. On the operating relationships among these

Table 32

TRANSFERS OF FUNDS, NATIONAL-LEVEL POLITICAL COMMITTEES, BY PARTY, 1952 AND 1956

Committees	% of Total Receipts and Volume (in thousands) of Receipts by Transfer[a]				% of Total Disbursements and Volume (in thousands) of Disbursements by Transfer[a]			
	1952		1956		1952		1956	
	$	%	$	%	$	%	$	%
Republican								
National	$1,394	46	$1,390	47	$ 1	0	$ 113	4
Senatorial	491	60	1,018	67	336	44	376	25
Congressional	1,368	73	2,385	83	340	20	526	19
Citizens for Eisenhower	337	19	554	33	39	3	194	13
Miscellaneous[b]	76	14	74	30	90	17	9	3
All	$3,666	46	$5,421	59	$806	11	$1,218	14
Democratic								
National	$ 498	21	$1,286	50	$176	6	$ 211	8
Senatorial	0	0	152	53	81	96	247	93
Congressional[c]	58	41	114	49	19	28	189	83
Headquarters[d]	52	21	652	53	3	1	0	0
Volunteers for Stevenson	75	10	301	52	0	0	10	2
Stevenson-Sparkman Forum	273	34	—	—	36	5	—	—
Miscellaneous[e]	15	21	2	2	2	2	21	20
All	$ 971	22	$2,507	51	$317	7	$ 678	14

[a] Because of ambiguities in the reports from which the table was constructed, the totals and percentages may in a few cases be inflated by classifying as transfers various miscellaneous receipts, i.e., income other than individual contributions. In rare cases, too, one committee may in fact have been a subcommittee of another committee, and movements of funds between the two classed as transfers. Included in this table are all transfers of funds, whether involving another *party* political committee or some other type of political committee (e.g., labor).

[b] Fourteen committees in 1952, seven in 1956.

[c] Democratic Congressional Campaign Committee and Democratic National Congressional Committee combined.

[d] For 1952, the 1952 Campaign Headquarters and Travel Committee, Springfield, Illinois; for 1956, the Stevenson-Kefauver Campaign Committee.

[e] Eight committees in 1952, five in 1956.

campaign groups, like the Citizens for Eisenhower and the Volunteers for Stevenson in 1952 and 1956, also depended on cooperating organizations for a substantial percentage of their financial resources. Table 32 indicates that when all national-level Republican committees are taken together (18 in 1952 and 11 in 1956), the percentage of total receipts coming from other groups was 46 in 1952 and 59 in 1956. The corresponding Democratic percentages (15 committees in 1952 and 11 in 1956) were 22 and 51.[3] These top operating committees bore the brunt

top-level committees of each party, see Hugh A. Bone, *Party Committees and National Politics* (Seattle: University of Washington Press, 1958), pp. x, xiii, 126-65. On the campaign activities of the Senate policy committees, see pp. 166-81.

3. As to one reason for the jump, see footnote 29, page 225, above.

of national-level campaigning. Yet they in turn passed on to other groups an average of 9 per cent in 1952 and 14 per cent in 1956 of the funds they received, and the practice was not confined to the aid that would naturally be given by the Senatorial and Congressional campaign committees to candidates.

Large transfers of funds also characterize political finance at state and local levels. During the active campaign period in 1956, September 1–November 30, Republican state and local committees for which information was available received more than one-third of their income by transfer and disbursed an even larger proportion by this method. Republican efforts to maintain a unified finance-committee system insure a greater volume of transfers among its committees at all levels. Yet the Democratic percentages, although less in each instance, as shown by Table 33, were still significant.

Grass-roots financing.—In discussing factors that explain party

Table 33

TRANSFERS OF FUNDS, STATE AND LOCAL POLITICAL COMMITTEES: BY TYPES OF COMMITTEE AND PARTY, SEPTEMBER 1–NOVEMBER 30, 1956[a]

Type of Committee	Received by Transfer[b]				Disbursed as Transfers[b]			
	Rep.		Dem.		Rep.		Dem.	
	$ (in thousands)	% of Total Receipts	$ (in thousands)	% of Total Receipts	$ (in thousands)	% of Total Disbursements	$ (in thousands)	% of Total Disbursements
State								
Regular	$3,786	66	$ 613	23	$1,643	27	$ 670	23
Finance[c]	1,246	17	—	—	6,155	82	—	—
Volunteer	364	19	174	12	517	28	350	26
Senatorial[d]	430	37	618	47	118	10	116	8
Total State	$5,826	36	$1,405	26	$8,433	51	$1,136	20
Local								
Regular	$1,767	53	$ 495	20	$ 748	22	$ 315	12
Finance	188	8	—	—	1,917	74	—	—
Volunteer	211	35	18	16	83	14	67	43
Total Local	$2,166	34	$ 513	20	$2,748	42	$ 382	14

[a] These include all committees reporting to the Gore Committee whose reports were usable: approximately 345 at the state level and 347 at the local level. Included are transfers among party committees and between party committees and labor or other nonparty groups. This table summarizes more detailed information appearing in Tables 36-39, pages 300-7, below.

[b] Because of ambiguities in the reports from which the table was constructed, the totals and percentages may in a few cases be inflated by classifying as transfers various miscellaneous receipts, i.e., income other than individual contributions. In rare cases, too, one committee may in fact have been a subcommittee of another committee, and movements of funds between the two classed as transfers.

[c] There was no regular system of Democratic finance committees in operation; a few committees bearing the name were classified as regular committees.

[d] Includes some local-level Senatorial campaign committees.

centralization and decentralization in certain countries, Maurice Duverger points out:

> The method of financing is also very important. In middle-class parties, where election expenses are for the most part defrayed by the candidates or their local backers, the caucuses at the base are richer than the centre and therefore independent. On the other hand, if the financial backers have acquired the habit of directly subsidizing the centre, it can exercise greater pressure upon the local groups. In parties financed by large and regular subscriptions . . . it is most important to know what is the distribution of resources between the centre and the local branches.[4]

Duverger attributes the conspicuous centralization of British parties in part to the "distribution of electoral funds from the centre." The importance of this condition was emphasized in an earlier time by James Bryce. With an eye on foreign experience, the Committee on Political Parties of the American Political Science Association recommended the repeal of United States statutory limitations on the size of contributions and expenditures that "work toward a scattering of responsibility for the collecting of funds among a large number of independent party and non-party committees."[5] Anything, moreover, that broadened the base of a party's financial support, the Committee urged, would check the irresponsible influence of large financial supporters and hence contribute to more responsible control of political funds through the party leadership. The national leadership of the American parties could thus be strengthened, thereby increasing their internal cohesion and capacity to govern.[6]

The origins and destinations of the money transferred within each American party explain the Committee's concern. When the movement of funds is tracked, the dependence of national-level party organizations on fund-raising organized at state and local levels becomes evident. At the same time, there is no corresponding reliance by party candidates at lower levels on subventions from above. Table 34 shows the sources of Republican and Democratic national campaign funds for the full year 1956 that came from *party* political committees. In both parties, national-level committees relied heavily upon funds allocated to them from a large number of state and local groups. The Republican national committee, for example, received over $1,000,000, 37 per cent of its total receipts, as transfers from state-level committees in 44 states, and over

4. *Political Parties—Their Organization and Activity in the Modern State* (translated by Barbara and Robert North) (New York: John Wiley & Sons, Inc., 1954), p. 59. Philip Williams offers information on this point.—*Politics in Post-War France—Parties and the Constitution in the Fourth Republic* (London: Longmans, Green & Co., 1954), e.g. p. 63.

5. "Toward a More Responsible Two-Party System," *American Political Science Review*, 44 (1950), Supplement, p. 75.

6. The point of view is still very much alive. See Stephen K. Bailey, *The Condition of Our National Political Parties* (New York: The Fund for the Republic, 1959), pp. 10-13.

$250,000 more in transfers from local Republican organizations in 24 states. The financial activities of the Republican Senatorial and Congressional campaign committees are closely coordinated with those of the national committee, and with them the dependence on funds transferred from below was even greater. Two-thirds of the Senatorial committee's receipts, or almost $1,000,000, and four-fifths of the Congressional committee's income, or more than $2,250,000, were received as transfers from a large number of state and local groups. On the Democratic side, the sums and the percentages were both smaller, but about two-fifths

Table 34

SOURCES OF FUNDS TRANSFERRED TO NATIONAL-LEVEL PARTY POLITICAL COMMITTEES FROM OTHER *PARTY* POLITICAL COMMITTEES,[a] 1956

Committees	% of Total Receipts and Volume (in thousands) of Receipts by Transfer from Committees at these levels								
	National[b]			State			Local		
	$	No. of Committees	% of Total Receipts	$	No. of States[c]	% of Total Receipts	$	No of States[c]	% of Total Receipts
Republican									
National	$ 0	0	0	$1,088	44	37	$258	24	9
Senatorial	0	0	0	954	26	63	39	5	3
Congressional	3	1	(d)	2,044	40	71	268	8	9
Citizens for Eisenhower	12	4	1	479	26	29	53	7	3
7 Miscellaneous[e]	8	4	3	20[f]	27[f]	8	2	2	1
Total[b]	$ 23		(d)	$4,585		50	$620		7
Democratic									
National	$ 62[g]	11[h]	2	$1,009	45	39	$138	40	5
Senatorial	135[i]	1[i]	47	15	2	5	2	2	1
Congressional[j]	107	1	46	6	2	2	0	0	0
Headquarters	51[k]	2	4	421	25	34	53	21	4
Volunteers for Stevenson	1	3	(d)	220	35	38	59	31	10
5 Miscellaneous	0	0	0	0	0	0	0	0	0
Total[b]	$356		7	$1,671		34	$252		5

[a] Included are regular, finance, and volunteer campaign groups affiliated with the parties or created for campaign purposes. Labor political committees and other nonparty continuing groups are not. The latter are included in the tabulations for Tables 33 and 36-39, hence an entry in those tables may exceed the corresponding entry here even though this table covers a longer period of time, the full calendar year.

[b] Included in the national column are transfers from one national-level committee to another.

[c] Number of states in which the committees sending money to the national level were located.

[d] Less than 0.5 per cent.

[e] The dollar amounts are the totals arrived at by adding the transfers of the several committees together; the number of committees and states is the number of *different* committees or states involved.

[f] One committee, the National Federation of Republican Women, accounted for $16,000, received from 27 states.

[g] $49,000 of this came from the Stevenson-Kefauver Campaign Dinner Committee.

[h] This includes a number of minute, unimportant groups not included among the national-level committees usually treated.

[i] $135,000 received from the Walter F. George Testimonial Dinner Committee.

[j] Democratic Congressional Campaign Committee and Democratic National Congressional Committee combined.

[k] From the Stevenson-Kefauver Campaign Dinner Committee and Nation-wide TV Dinner Committee.

of all receipts of the national groups came from a sizeable number of state and local organizations spread widely throughout the country.

National leadership, limited.—The financial dependence of the national units of party organization on units at other levels is symptomatic of the general distribution of power and activity throughout the parties. Not even in the Republican party, with its finance-committee system sponsored from the top, does the national leadership have an independent source of funds sufficient for its purposes. Although the initiative comes largely from above, whether a finance-committee system is adopted in a state depends ultimately on whether a sufficient segment of local Republican leadership wants it. Prospective finance-committee leaders are often identified and in effect designated by the national finance chairman, but the designation requires the tolerance of local party leadership. Ideally, the principle of united fund-raising guarantees each phase of Republican party activity, including the national level, a predetermined share of what money comes in. To some extent, then, the national organization has a dependable source of income. The whole finance-committee system could not operate successfully, however, without support from state and local leaders. The national organization is ultimately dependent upon their cooperation.

The experience of the Democratic national committee has been different, but with the same effect. It has frequently been expected that the national committeeman would solicit in his state for the national committee. The Jefferson-Jackson Day dinners have often been organized by state organizations to supply their quotas to the national committee. In some states, "volunteers" have raised funds for a presidential candidate in the face of hostility from those in control of the party organization. But in this, as in all other instances, the national organization must depend chiefly on persons who habitually function at state and local levels, and whose primary loyalties lie there. They are also persons with views to express and sometimes with demands to make.

We are told that in 1896 Mark Hanna set up complete machinery for the Republican presidential campaign and provided an extraordinary degree of central direction. He "infused all its men, from top to bottom, with his confidence and resolution,"[7] and, it seems evident, with dollars raised along Wall and other streets. The newly tapped reservoirs of corporate money fed the national campaign headquarters, giving it a source of independent propulsion not enjoyed in later years. The national organization of neither American party in the mid-twentieth century possessed a sufficient financial constituency of its own so organized as to free it from financial dependence on the state and local leadership.[8] The national leadership has on occasion rejected the demands of

7. Matthew Josephson, *The Politicos, 1865-1896* (New York: Harcourt, Brace and Company, 1938), p. 695.

8. Some contributors insist on giving directly to the national level and refuse to give for state and local purposes (others insist on the reverse). But this

important state and local leaders, but the paucity of its independent financial resources, along with other factors, circumscribes its freedom and denies it a potential source of stability. The cumulative effect pushes the center of political gravity further down in the party structure than it need otherwise be.

In times of internal party dissensions, disaffected leaders in the states have threatened to withhold funds. Early in the Dixiecratic crisis of 1948, leaders in some southern states warned they would withhold the customary donations made by their state organizations to the Democratic national committee.[9] In fact, the loss of southern revenues undoubtedly helped account for the parlous condition of the Democratic national treasury that year. During the McCarthy years, that Senator's followers often brought pressure on Republican fund-raising committees to backslide on their national quotas if the Eisenhower leadership did not change its attitude toward McCarthy. If state organizations remained impervious to this pressure, it was because the state fund-raising apparatus was in the hands of people who took a different view of the Senator, and of the President, and not because of loyalty to the national organization per se.

In nations with parties called well disciplined, an oft-cited source of central-party leadership is control over campaign funds.[10] In nominations and in other matters, constituency organizations are respectful of the views of a central organization that can supply or withhold endorsement and money needed to wage the election campaign. In labor parties, particularly, does central control over campaign funds appear to be an important element in the complex of restraints which national party organizations impose on local branches and on members who seek and reach public office. In the same nations, local units of parties that draw heavily on wealthy local contributors, or that offer candidates who are

---

nationally-oriented financial constituency is not large enough to give the national organization financial independence.

9. Marquis Childs, "Dixie Rights Revolt Threat to Party Funds," *Atlanta Journal,* February 12, 1948.

10. In analyzing the lack of central domination by the Revolutionary party in Mexico, L. Vincent Padgett finds the key to be party finance. There has been no directly affiliated dues-paying membership significant in numbers or discipline, no national party treasury to supply the needs of state and local candidates. At all levels, party committees are dependent on donations from various functional (economic and vocational) organizations and the government.—"Mexico's One-Party System: A Re-Evaluation," *American Political Science Review,* 51 (1957), 995-96.

Many factors affect the centralization of party power. The spread of civil service reform, competitive bidding, and social services at government expense along with other conditions have led Avery Leiserson to conclude that "the constituency organizations in the United States are perhaps the most autonomous, decentralized, locally oriented levels of party organization in the world."—*Parties and Politics* (New York: Alfred A. Knopf, 1958), p. 194.

able to foot some of their own campaign bills, enjoy greater independence than their labor counterparts.[11]

Rare is the official of a national committee in the United States who dabbles in the nominating activities of his party at state or local levels. Intervention from on high invariably provokes an adverse reaction. The outsiders are condemned for interfering in what is declared to be the exclusive concern of the party in the constituency. In 1954, Stephen Mitchell, chairman of the Democratic national committee, kicked up a fuss with an unusual public declaration that aid from the national committee would be withheld from two Democrats in California who were seeking nomination to Congress. The questions that had been raised when Representative Robert Condon was denied a certain security clearance, and James Roosevelt's marital difficulties, both widely publicized, should not in Mr. Mitchell's view have become the burdens of the Democratic party. The "general welfare of the party" required the national committee to withhold its approval and financial assistance, when asked for them.[12] But such episodes are unusual, and their greatest significance is symbolic. A national committee has neither money nor influence sufficient to veto the preferences of local party organizations, nor to direct the outcome of conventions or primaries.[13]

Aid to federal candidates.—The national leadership sends some campaign money to selected party nominees. (Note Table 35.) The sums provided are usually small, they usually supply only a small proportion of the candidate's requirements, and much of the money came in the first place from the lower levels of party organization. Almost every candidate for the United States Senate who must fight for election receives some donation from his party's Senatorial campaign committee. In 1956, of 32 states in which senators were chosen, Republican candidates received aid in 26 and Democratic candidates in 23. The Republican subventions from this source were greatest to Oregon, $58,670, where erstwhile Republican Wayne Morse was running on the Democratic ticket. Most of the money went to the regular Republican state committee. The donations from the Republican Senatorial committee averaged $13,200 for all states receiving aid. The Democratic Senatorial campaign committee forwarded its largest sums to Kentucky, where two senators were being elected, a total of $62,000. (One of the Democratic candidates in Kentucky was the Democratic whip of the Senate, who had also been the chairman of the Democratic Senatorial

11. Leslie Lipson, *The Politics of Equality—New Zealand's Adventures in Democracy* (Chicago: University of Chicago Press, 1948), pp. 249-50.

12. The text of Mr. Mitchell's letter on this subject to the national committeeman from California appeared in the *New York Times,* April 5, 1954. California's cross-filing system, in which members of both parties could compete for both party nominations, gave the party organization a special interest in the primaries.

13. It appears that a group called the Democrats of Texas received financial and organizational aid from the Democratic national committee in the late 1950's to help it in the factional rivalries within Texas' deeply divided Democratic party.

Table 35

DESTINATIONS OF FUNDS TRANSFERRED FROM NATIONAL-LEVEL PARTY POLITICAL COMMITTEES TO OTHER *PARTY* POLITICAL COMMITTEES[a], 1956

Committees	% of Total Disbursements and Volume (in thousands) of Disbursements by Transfer to Committees at these levels								
	National[b]			State			Local		
	$	No. of Commit-tees	% of Total Dis-burse-ments	$	No. of States[c]	% of Total Dis-burse-ments	$	No. of States[c]	% of Total Dis-burse-ments
Republican									
National	$ 0	0	(d)	$ 103	12	4	$10	1	(d)
Senatorial	0	0	0	344[e]	26[f]	23	3	1	(d)
Congressional	0	0	0	518[g]	46[f]	19	8	3	(d)
Citizens for Eisenhower	11	3	1	165	22	11	17	4	1
7 Miscellaneous	1	3	(d)	8[h]	25[h]	3	0	0	0
Total[b]	$ 12		(d)	$1,138		13	$38		(d)
Democratic									
National	$124[i]	7	5	$ 62[j]	7[j]	2	$25	1	1
Senatorial	0	0	0	247[e]	23[f]	93	0	0	0
Congressional[k]	5	1	2	177[g]	43[f]	72	7	2	3
Headquarters	0	0	0	0	0	0	0	0	0
Volunteers for Stevenson	0	0	0	10	3	2	0	0	0
5 Miscellaneous	21	2	20	0	0	0	0	0	0
Total[b]	$150		3	$ 496		10	$32		(d)

[a] Included are regular, finance, and volunteer campaign groups affiliated with the parties or created for campaign purposes. Labor political committees and other nonparty continuing groups are not. The latter are included in the tabulations for Tables 33 and 36-39, hence an entry in those tables may exceed the corresponding entry here even though this table covers a longer period of time, the full calendar year.

[b] Included in the national column are transfers from one national committee to another.

[c] Number of states in which committees receiving money from the national level were located.

[d] Less than 0.5 per cent.

[e] Including transfers to candidates for U.S. Senate or committees backing them.

[f] Number of states represented by candidates receiving transfers.

[g] Including transfers to candidates for U.S. House of Representatives or committees backing them.

[h] One committee, the Young Republican National Campaign Committee, accounted for $1,561 sent to 25 states.

[i] $100,425 to the *Democratic Digest* was not classed as a transfer.

[j] Includes two states in which sum transferred was $5.

[k] Democratic Congressional Campaign Committee and Democratic National Congressional Committee combined.

campaign committee, Senator Earle C. Clements.) The average for all recipient states was $10,700.

A smaller proportion of the candidates running for the lower house of Congress in 1956 was favored by help from the national Congressional campaign committees, but the selection was based on need and not on degree of loyalty to any party program.[14] Some 245 Republican and

14. The late Victor Hunt Harding emphasized that the Democratic Congressional campaign committee kept no record whatsoever of Democratic Congressional voting records. In 1944, he did intervene in a Wisconsin race by withholding his committee's financial support from a nominee who, though chosen in a Democratic primary, was thought to be a Communist. The committee has been operated,

186 Democratic candidates were given direct aid, with state committees and other party groups receiving additional sums. No Republican candidate seems to have received more than $4,000 directly from this source, and the average was around $2,000. The Democratic figures were about $2,000 and $900 respectively.[15]

Individual candidates are helped in less direct ways by the national party leadership.[16] An important though unascertainable amount of money is routed to candidates and committees below the national level by finance officials in both parties, money that does not appear on the books of any national-level committee.[17] The word is spread, in some instances by the White House staff, of favored candidates in need. As a result, they receive money direct from contributors and fund-raisers that otherwise would not have reached them. This indirect financial help to a candidate may well strengthen his ties with the party leadership. But the assistance is usually a product of mutual respect and

---

however, as a service agency to all Democrats. On the way the committee distributes its funds, see the description by one who has served as its treasurer, Jack Redding, *Inside the Democratic Party* (New York: The Bobbs-Merrill Company, Inc., 1958), pp. 302-5.

15. Here the analysis has been confined to sums sent by the Senatorial and Congressional campaign committees to Senate and House candidates. In presidential years, money on occasion goes from other national-level committees to such candidates, but the sums are not generally important. See Tables 37 and 39 on pages 302 and 306, below. It was claimed in 1954 that an Eisenhower endorsement of a Republican candidate would entitle the anointed to a healthy gift from the Citizens for Eisenhower organization, which had been reactivated to help elect an Eisenhower Congress.—Drew Pearson in *The News and Observer* (Raleigh, N.C.), June 20, 1954. In 1952, 26 Republican and 20 Democratic Senatorial candidates received national aid. Among candidates for the House, the figures were 243 and 55 respectively.

16. Guy B. Hathorn studied the financial transactions of the Senatorial and Congressional campaign committees. He described "exchange" funds as amounts collected in various states in fulfillment of quotas and transmitted upward with the understanding that they would be returned to the state organization. "Directed" funds are gifts made under agreement that the money will go to a specified candidate's campaign. He reported that Republican "exchange" funds never leave the states and do not show up on committee reports made to the United States House of Representatives. This is true of only some Democratic "exchange" money. Both parties are said to use "directed" monies, but there is difficulty in identifying them on the reports.—"Congressional and Senatorial Campaign Committees in the Mid-term Election Year 1954," *Southwestern Social Science Quarterly,* 37 (1956), 211-12.

17. Persons who examine campaign reports filed in various parts of the country quickly begin to recognize the names of individuals who give in more than one jurisdiction. Interviews with contributors and fund-raisers reveal that many such donations are routed by or at the suggestion of solicitors. For data suggestive of the relative importance of out-of-state gifts in Senatorial campaign expenditures, see the Gore Committee *Report,* pp. 48-53. Joseph L. Bernd reports that when Senator Walter F. George of Georgia was running in 1950 his managers returned nearly $100,000 of out-of-state money not needed in the campaign.—*The Role of Campaign Funds in Georgia Primary Elections, 1936-1958* (Macon: The Georgia Journal, Inc., 1958), p. 3.

mutual interests already existing, and not of an effort to build party solidarity.

Money and party development.—National leaders of the parties have rarely conceived of financial management as a way to develop party unity and to build a stable organizational structure. There has been a trend toward year-around fund-raising in recent times, but generally money has arrived during the heat of a campaign. It has been devoted to current needs and the sort of aid to federal candidates that has been described. In occasional instances, national leaders have seen special significance in particular elections for state or local offices. The gubernatorial election in Maine, when it came in September, has attracted funds from top Democratic managers hoping to capture a psychological advantage for the November contests. In this case, however, and generally, both parties have concentrated on meeting current requirements and have felt unable to raise their sights beyond the pending campaign. Democrats may argue they have no funds to do otherwise. But even the more affluent Republicans drain funds away from the struggling Republican organizations in the South. They might, instead, make grants to encourage aggressive local leadership to build and sustain the organizational machinery necessary to capitalize on such popular potential as the party has in that region.[18]

There has been much talk of new ways to finance the parties. Any changes that freed national party committees of financial dependence on state organizations could affect importantly the loci of party power. If a national committee were able to channel funds selectively to lower levels, its role would be radically changed. Even if, as in some proposals for federal subsidy, formulae were provided for automatically allocating sums to state organizations or to candidates, important changes would occur. The basic federal structure of the American parties is rooted in the federal structure of the American government. Financial manipulation could never overcome that basic condition. But alterations in the ways the parties are financed could affect substantially the capacity of each party to develop within itself a more cohesive operational structure.[19]

18. At all levels the volume of campaign expenditures follows electoral strength, with little tendency toward missionary investments in weak areas. The amount of campaign expenditures reported by Republican county organizations in North Carolina counties in 1956 (when Eisenhower received 49.3 per cent of the state's total popular vote) followed closely the size of the Republican vote in the county. The same was true in 1958.—Anne Baldwin Norford, "A Study of Money, Its Sources and Expenditure, in the Republican Party of North Carolina" (term paper, University of North Carolina, 1959), 21 pp.

19. The fact that federal and state elections are held simultaneously in most states would appear to handicap the development of independent fund-raising by the national parties. If federal and state elections came at different times, as they do in Canada, the ability of the national party organization to develop separate sources of income would no doubt be enhanced.

2. OPERATIONAL UNITY

By the usual standards of management analysis, American political parties have traditionally been inefficient entities. Their internal administrative practices have presented an appalling spectacle to the expert in organization and procedure. Despite an increasing professionalization of fund-raising and of campaign management, most political organizations are still inefficient and wasteful, whether raising or spending money.

The effectiveness of a political party rests on more, however, than competence in office administration. Aside from political judgment and popular appeal that underlie all party fortunes, over-all effectiveness depends also on unity of purpose and on implementing common purposes through unified or coordinated operations. Neither kind of unity prevails extensively throughout either of the major American parties. The lack of operational unity among party committees at the same and different levels during political campaigns is especially conspicuous to students of party organization. The fragmentation of effort cannot be discerned from financial transactions alone, but financial transactions reveal certain functional relationships and lines of communication among cooperating political organizations. These relationships cannot normally be changed at will, for political parties function in an environment of prodigious pressures that render them more the servant than the master of their own fate. To trace the broad outlines of the relationships, however, exposes certain of the operating conditions and suggests some of the limitations under which American politicians work.

Career politicians are inclined to view with marked disfavor the creation of special campaign committees that threaten their own interests. They often express this discontent in complaints over the difficulties of coordinating campaigns that are conducted through several more or less independent organizations. In truth, varying degrees of chaos inevitably result. Yet the functional purposes behind the separate campaign arms reflect realities of politics. The "volunteer" committees, especially, are often created to do a job beyond the capacity of the regular party machinery.

Presidential contests.—The major volunteer committees in a presidential election serve in both parties to solicit support and funds from persons who do not find the regular party organizations appealing. Independent voters, and disaffected followers of the opposing party, find in the volunteer groups an acceptable place to spend their energies or send their checks. Such groups have long been a fixture of presidential campaigning. The importance they have reached is indicated by the probability that in 1952 volunteer committees at all levels spent on behalf of the presidential candidates at least $15,000,000.

Many volunteer committees are hardly "voluntary" at all, being creatures of regular party organizations. They may be subsidized from party treasuries and serve as fronts to make special appeals to special constituencies.[20] Under such circumstances, relative coordination in campaign direction can be achieved. When volunteer groups are truly voluntary, however, arising on their own motion and often manned by amateurs, conflict is inevitable. Such was the Citizens for Eisenhower, created originally in 1952 in pursuit of the presidential nomination. It was converted to the Citizens for Eisenhower-Nixon in the subsequent general election campaign. Most such organizations dissolve following each election, as did the Citizens, but the latter was revived in each of the next three national-election years as a supplementary Republican campaign organization. In each year procedures for consultation among representatives of the Citizens and the regular party committees at the national level were set up, and a measure of coordination was ac-

20. Many illustrations of this practice were encountered in studying the financial reports of state-level volunteer committees active in 1952. For example, the Ohio Farmers for Stevenson reported that virtually all of its $3,010 came from the Democratic state central committee. The same occurs in elections for other offices than president. In 1952, an organization called the Labor League for Taft Committee for the Reelection of John Bricker was supplied $8,000 by the Ohio Republican state committee and lesser sums by the John W. Bricker Campaign Fund. Mr. Bricker was a candidate for the United States Senate. In 1954, in Oregon, it appeared that the Democrats for Cordon Committee was actually financed by the Cordon for United States Senate Committee, a Republican campaign organization.

There is nothing new in all this. In 1932, Harold L. Ickes headed up a Western Independent Republican Committee for Roosevelt. "We did our job on an appropriation of $10,000 made to us by the Democratic National Committee."—*Autobiography of a Curmudgeon* (New York: Reynal & Hitchcock, 1943), p. 262. In 1928, the Smith Independent Organizations Committee received an allocation of $500,000 from the Democratic national committee, about half of which was parcelled out to some dozen groups like the North Dakota Agriculture Relief League Committee and the Minnesota All Parties, Smith-Robinson Club.—U.S. Senate Special Committee Investigating Presidential Campaign Expenditures, *Report* (Senate Report No. 2024, 70th Congress, 2nd Session), pp. 26-27.

In the South, Negro campaign committees are often financed covertly by the main campaign organization of the candidates they support. In some states, e.g. Wisconsin and Minnesota, legal limitations on regular party organizations have forced the parties to conduct many of their activities through auxiliary groups. On the relationships between party organizations and volunteer groups in California, see Dean R. Cresap, *Party Politics in the Golden State* (Los Angeles: The Haynes Foundation, 1954), pp. 26-29.

It should be recorded that there is some history of special political committees organized with intent to defraud. Several of these have shown up around Chicago. Commenting on investigations in New Jersey of the State Republican League and the Republican Citizens Committee, a Senate committee observed in 1945: "The revelations there pointed strongly to a condition in which ostensible political organizations were in reality organizations for private profit, suggestive of the high-pressure fake charity campaigns so frequently exposed."—Green Committee *Report*, p. 5.

complished.[21] Nevertheless, there was grumbling at the independent manner in which the Citizens operated.[22]

That they constituted a parallel and largely self-contained campaign structure is revealed by the financial activities of the organization during the 1956 campaign. Tables 36 and 37 record the movement of funds among Republican political committees between September 1 and November 30, 1956. (Tables 36, 37, 38, and 39 present the details of information summarized in Table 33.[23]) They show that most of the

21. For example, a two-page memorandum dated May 21, 1954, "to clarify the objectives and operating methods of National CITIZENS FOR EISENHOWER Congressional Committee," was sent in the name of the Republican national finance chairman to state finance chairmen and members of the national finance committee. It set forth, in particular, the relationships to obtain between the Citizens at all levels and the regular Republican organization: e.g., "NCECC will make it clear to any Republican contributors that contributions to CITIZENS are in addition to and not in lieu of contributions to the regular Republican Party." Comments on the arrangements for coordinating the Citizens organization with the regular party national-level committees in 1952 appear in Stanley Kelley, Jr., *Professional Public Relations and Political Power* (Baltimore: The Johns Hopkins Press, 1956), pp. 147-51.

22. A high leader in the Citizens for Eisenhower in 1952 recalled that there were a few days near the beginning of the campaign when the top leaders of the Citizens and of the party seemed unable to get together. The Citizens leaders, "with tongue in cheek," then threatened to strike out on their own campaign, a gesture that was thought to have led to a more flexible attitude among party leaders and to a scheme for cooperative campaigning. A Republican chief in Oregon blamed his party's 1954 reverses in that state on the Citizens organization, which he said behaved like "a party within a party." He declared that fund-raising by state and county Republican committees was hampered and actually failed because of the multiplicity of campaign headquarters, each with its own fund drive.—*New York Times*, November 12, 1954. The laments of party officials go far back. See *The Memoirs of Will H. Hays* (Garden City: Doubleday & Company, Inc., 1955), p. 274.

23. For the first time, students have something resembling comprehensive information about transfers of money among political committees. Data reported to the Gore Committee by national, state, and local political committees have been summarized in Tables 36 through 39. Even though most political expenditures are made during this concentrated campaign period (September 1–November 30), transfers of funds occurring earlier constitute an integral aspect of campaign finance. For example, national-level Republican committees during the calendar year 1956 showed total receipts by transfer of slightly more than $5,400,000, whereas less than one-third of this sum (slightly more than $1,700,000) came in between September 1 and November 30. The Democratic figure for the full year was approximately $2,500,000, about two-thirds (again some $1,700,000) within the shorter period.

Data were not available from all the committees operating at each level in each party. Hence the transactions represented in each of the four tables do not represent transfers within a "closed" system that will be found to balance against each other. In Table 36, for example, $783,000 is shown as received by the Republican Congressional campaign committee from committees at the state level. Yet in Table 37 state-level committees are shown as sending only $365,000 to this committee. The larger figure is that reported by the Congressional committee as received by it from all state-level groups, not all of whom, however, made reports

money received by the Citizens for Eisenhower-Nixon at national, state, and local levels was spent by that organization itself on campaign operations. Of the reported funds at the disposal of the national and local groups, only 14 per cent were passed on to other organizations, and among the state-level organizations the percentage was only 28 (Table 37). Moreover, the bulk of the transfers went to other units of the Citizens organization, most importantly from Citizens state committees to the national Citizens organization. The Citizens thus did not serve as a fund-raising mechanism to finance general party activities. They sent some money to the regular Republican committees and to the finance committees, but the volunteer groups reported receiving almost three

---

used in computing the second figure. This situation obtains for both parties.

Further inconsistencies among the tables are accounted for by the sums appearing in the "unallocated" columns, at the extreme right hand of each table. These are funds specified by a committee as being transferred, but without the other participant in the action being named.

Other characteristics of campaign financing account for seeming inconsistencies. The Republican national finance committee acts as a receiving and disbursing agent, yet it does not make reports, the funds it handles being accounted for by other committees. When reports showed transfers to the national finance committee, and there was no evidence of the committee to which the money was passed by the national finance committee, the Republican national committee was taken to be the destination, although the money may have gone elsewhere. Thus, in Table 37, total transfers sent by state finance committees to the national committee are shown as $121,000, whereas in Table 36 the total shown as received by the national committee from these sources appears as $19,000. This wrinkle, and another one, are well illustrated by the Americans for Eisenhower, the main Ike organization in Louisiana, which reported sending $45,000 in all to the Republican national finance committee and receiving $5,000 from it, for a net of $40,000. At the other end, these transactions showed up as $10,000 received by the Republican national committee, and $30,000 by the Republican Congressional campaign committee, with the other $5,000 not recorded as either a receipt or a disbursement.

At state and local levels, too, the origin or destination of funds may not be clear from the reports, or the funds may be relayed by the first destination without being run through its books, rendering impossible a neat dovetailing of reported transactions. The Democratic Senatorial campaign committee reported transferring $168,000 to state-level committees (Table 39), $23,000 of it to regular committees and $145,000 to campaign committees for individual senators. State-level committees reported receiving the same total sum (Table 38), but $62,000 of it by regular committees and $106,000 by Senatorial groups.

The general sloppiness that characterizes much campaign reporting breeds difficulties. Committee transfers were often reported as the personal contribution of the committee treasurer or other member who happened to transmit the sum. Committee reports did not always balance internally, indicating errors or omissions. Moreover, some transfers were in transit on the beginning and ending dates of the reporting period, one end of the transaction therefore being reportable while the other was not. Some committees were more meticulous in observing the beginning and ending dates than others, this sometimes being clear from the reports themselves, at other times becoming apparent after an individual inquiry about a transaction, and at still other times remaining cloudy. Minor discrepancies, usually of $1,000, stemmed from the practice of rounding off totals in tabulating.

times as much from the regular and finance committees as they sent to them. These receipts by the Citizens were relatively small in the total context of their operations, however, and their independence was not compromised by them.

In contrast, the Volunteers for Stevenson-Kefauver raised funds for the regular Democratic campaign, especially at the national level. As Tables 38 and 39 show, they acted on a small scale like the Republican finance committees. Negligible money went to Volunteer groups from the regular committees, whereas the national committee and its functional adjunct, the Stevenson-Kefauver Campaign Committee, received respectable sums from them. In both parties the volunteer organizations bore important campaign expenses that would otherwise have fallen on regular committees. But the reliance of the regular Democratic effort on direct subsidies from these *ad hoc* groups reflects the absence of a robust, continuing, national fund-raising scheme.[24] Whether affluent or poor, the parties seek direct or indirect financial help from auxiliary campaign groups and pay whatever price may be entailed by the operational complexities thus created.

State and local candidates.—Much is said about the location of political power in the United States at state and local levels. The impression is sometimes conveyed that political party organizations at these levels possess more tight-fisted power and greater organizational unity than is actually the case. Throughout the United States, special campaign committees on behalf of candidates for state and local offices spring up much as they do for presidential candidates. Control over American political activity is not just decentralized. In most states it is also fragmented at each political level. If full campaign responsibility were lodged in a nominee's party organization, as is true in many foreign settings, such *ad hoc* candidate committees would not be found.

The heterogeneity of political interests that develops around the long ballot accounts in part for the fragmentation of many party activities. Even in states of strong party competition, and in races for important offices such as United States senator, separate candidate committees displaying high degrees of autonomy are found in operation. These conditions are reflected in their financial activities, as study of Tables 36 through 39 will indicate. The committees active on behalf of Senatorial candidates[25] performed important fund-raising functions, even in the Republican party with its principle of united fund-raising. More than 50 per cent of Democratic money and more than 60 per cent of Republi-

24. Democratic volunteer groups have at times worked closely with the national committee during presidential campaigns, as the Truman-Barkley Clubs did in 1948.—Redding, *op. cit.*, 215-16. At local levels volunteers have often taken over the conduct of campaigning. Also they have raised important sums of money: in 1952 the New York County Volunteers for Stevenson collected $426,000.

25. The Gore Committee, which collected the data used in constructing the tables, did not concern itself with gubernatorial and other nonfederal campaign activities.

Table 36

TRANSFERS OF FUNDS AMONG POLITICAL COMMITTEES: *RECEIPTS* REPORTED BY *REPUBLICAN* COMMITTEES, SEPTEMBER 1–NOVEMBER 30, 1956[a]
(in thousands of dollars)

Committees Reporting Funds Received by Transfer	Total Rec'd by Transfer	% of Total Rec's	Received from Following Types of Committees[b]																								
			At National Level						At State Level										At Local Level									
			RNC	SCC	CCC	CE	Misc	Tot[d]	Reg	Fin	Vol	USS	USHR	Din	Cand	Club	Misc	Tot[d]	Reg	Fin	Vol	Din	Cand	Club	Misc	Tot[d]	Misc	Unallocated[c]
National Level																												
Rep. National Comm.	$ 174	15							89	19	11						8	127	14	25				7		46		1
Senatorial Camp. Comm.	223	39							34	164							7	204	1	14					5	19		
Congressional Camp. Comm.	859[a]	68					2	2	182	555	32					1	13	783	9	56	5				3	73		
Citizens for Eisenhower	451	37							88	14	280			10		3		395		7	44			1		51	3	2
7 Miscellaneous	12	9				6		6	3			1					2	6										1
Total[d]	$1719	39				6	2	8	395	752	323	1		10		4	30	1515	23	102	49			8	8	189	3	4

State Level																												
Regular	$3786	66	30	96	44	3	2	174	6	2479	12	48	2	45	4	11	103	2709	386	362				25	17	789		112
Finance	1246	17	7	15				22	27			2	1	5	9		3	47	837	237				16	20	1110	38	30
Volunteer	364	19	50	30	30	103	1	214	19	33	3	1					2	58	20	45	5					70	2	22
U.S. Senate	430	37	3	48		2		52	177	39		38				1	10	266	25	56	1			6		89		23
Total[d]	$5826	36	90	188	74	107	3	461	229	2551	15	89	2	50	14	12	119	3080	1267	701	5			48	37	2058	40	186
Local Level																												
Regular	$1767	53			1			1	215	533	4	3	1		8	4	11	779	64	547	1			11	11	635	4	349
Finance	188	8		6	6			11	2	13			6		1	1	55	78	14	20				26	23	84	3	12
Volunteer	211	35				7		7	1	145	28							175	9		3			1		12		17
Total[d]	$2166	34		6	6	7		19	218	691	33	3	7		9	5	66	1031	87	567	4			38	33	731	7	379
Grand Totals[d]	$9711	36	90	194	80	121	5	488	842	3994	371	92	9	60	22	21	214	5626	1378	1370	59			93	78	2979	50	569

[a] The committees listed down the left margin reported receiving the money indicated from the committees listed across the top. Derived from reports made to the Gore Committee covering the limited period, September 1–November 30, 1956. Information for the Congressional Campaign committees was derived from reports made to the Clerk of the U.S. House of Representatives.

[b] The national-level committees are the same as those listed down the left margin. The abbreviations for the state-level committees are: Reg, regular; Fin, finance; Vol, Citizens for Eisenhower or equivalent; USS, candidates for U.S. Senate and their committees; USHR, candidates for U.S. House of Representatives and their committees; Din, special dinner committees; Cand, candidates for other statewide offices and their committees; Club, women's clubs and similar groups; Misc, state committees not otherwise classified. Abbreviations for county-level are the same. The national, state, and local committees are all either units of the party organization or are aligned as partisan backers of the party's candidates. Transactions with nonparty groups appear in the general Miscellaneous column. Included in USS are a few county-level committees on behalf of Senatorial candidates.

[c] Money reported as received from other organizations without specifying organization. The questionnaires did not ask committees to itemize transfers of funds of less than $500 each that were received from other organizations, which explains some of the amount unaccounted for.

[d] All figures in this table have been rounded to the nearest $1,000. Entries of less than $500 are not shown. The totals were added before rounding, which explains any discrepancies between the totals and the sum of the rounded components that make up the totals.

Table 37

TRANSFERS OF FUNDS AMONG POLITICAL COMMITTEES: *DISBURSEMENTS* REPORTED BY *REPUBLICAN* COMMITTEES, SEPTEMBER 1–NOVEMBER 30, 1956[a]
(in thousands of dollars)

Committees Reporting Funds Disbursed by Transfer	Total Dis-bur'd by Trans-fer	% of Total Dis-b'ts	Disbursed to the Following Types of Committees[b]																									
			At National Level						At State Level										At Local Level								
			RNC	SCC	CCC	CE	Misc	Tot[d]	Reg	Fin	Vol	USS	USHR	Din	Cand	Club	Misc	Tot[d]	Reg	Fin	Vol	Cand	Club	Misc	Tot[d]	Misc	Unallo-cated[c]
National Level																											
Rep. National Comm.	$ 97	7							*33*	*7*	*45*		*2*					87						*10*	10		
Senatorial Camp. Comm.	182	16							*100*	*5*		*69*					*5*	179	*3*					*1*	4		
Congressional Camp. Comm.	330[a]	21[e]							*58*	*17*	*30*		*223*					328		*3*					3		
Citizens for Eisenhower	160	14									*75*						*5*	80			*2*				2		78
7 Miscellaneous	9	6																								7	2
Total[d]	$ 779	15							191	29	150	69	225				10	674	3	3	2			11	18	7	80

State Level																											
Regular	$ 1643	27	165	18	79	60	3	325	37	11	65	216	66		227	3	12	638	361	19	16	9	7	1	412	3	266
Finance	6155	82	121	139	286	6		551	2918	50	169	34	256		137		59	3622	1181	680		5	1	2	1869	49	64
Volunteer	517	28	45			275	2	321	10	87	15	3	9	1			1	124	1	18	45				65	1	5
U.S. Senate	118	10							51		1	47						99	4	2					6	1	12
Total[d]	$ 8433	51	331	156	365	341	5	1197	3015	148	250	299	331	1	363	3	72	4483	1546	720	61	14	9	3	2353	53	347
Local Level																											
Regular	$ 748	22	26	12				37	158		1	22	46		1			229	337	3	8	31	1	4	385		97
Finance	1917	74	17	12	2			31	251	167	170	84	86		6		15	780	732	5		58			795		311
Volunteer	83	14			5	36		41	3	10	7					1		21	6		14			1	21		
Total[d]	$ 2748	42	43	24	7	36		109	412	177	178	106	132		7	1	15	1029	1075	8	23	89	1	4	1200		408
Grand Totals[d]	$11960	41	373	180	372	377	5	1307	3618	354	579	474	689	1	371	4	98	6187	2624	730	86	102	10	18	3571	60	836

[a] The committees listed down the left margin reported sending the sums indicated to the committees listed across the top. Derived from reports made to the Gore Committee for the limited period, September 1–November 30, 1956. Information for the Congressional Campaign committees was derived from reports made to the Clerk of the U.S. House of Representatives.

[b] See note (b) Table 36.

[c] Money reported as sent to other organizations without specifying the organizations.

[d] See note (d) Table 36.

[e] This percentage computed from data for the period September 1–December 31, 1956.

Table 38

TRANSFERS OF FUNDS AMONG POLITICAL COMMITTEES: *RECEIPTS* REPORTED BY *DEMOCRATIC* COMMITTEES, SEPTEMBER 1–NOVEMBER 30, 1956[a]
(in thousands of dollars)

Committees Reporting Funds Received by Transfer	Total Rec'd by Transfer	% of Total Rec's	Received from Following Types of Committees[b]																											
			At National Level								At State Level										At Local Level									
			DNC	SKCC	SCC	CCC	VS	Din	Misc	Tot	Reg	Fin	Vol	USS	USHR	Din	Cand	Club	Misc	Tot	Reg	Vol	Din	Cand	Club	Misc	Tot	Lab	Misc	Unallocated[c]
National Level																														
Dem. National Comm.	$ 823	50						49	8	57	236	148	210			31			9	635	26	4	39		3	5	77	14	4	36
Stevenson-Kefauver Camp. Comm.	489	41						51	5	56	100	36	156			8			61	361	23	12	3		1	3	41	21	1	8
Senatorial Camp. Comm.	16	9									15									15					1		1			
Congressional Camp. Comm.	51[a]	32	46							46	5									5										
Volunteers for Stevenson	294	55						1		1	5		195						4	205	1	21					23	21		45
Total[d]	$1673	46[e]	46					101	13	160	361	184	562			38			75	1220	50	38	42		5	8	142	56	5	89

State Level																														
Regular	$ 613	23	*5*		*62*	*1*				68	*17*	*2*	*28*	*13*		*32*	*30*	*2*	*16*	139	*162*				*3*	*5*	170	40	3	192
Volunteer	174	12					*6*			6	*9*		*11*					*1*	*4*	25	*1*	*16*			*18*		34	36	1	73
U.S. Senate	618	47			*106*			*26*		132	*39*		*10*	*19*					*9*	77	*4*	*2*			*4*		10	295	42	61
Total[d]	$1405	26	5		168	1	6	26		206	65	2	48	32		32	30	2	29	241	167	18			25	5	214	371	46	326
Local Level																														
Regular	$ 495	20		*3*						3	*79*	*8*	*1*	*2*	*5*		*16*		*4*	114	*18*		*8*	*6*	*36*	*72*	139	15	6	219
Volunteer	18	16									*1*		*8*							9						*1*	1	5		4
Total[d]	$ 513	20		3						3	80	8	9	2	5		16		4	124	18		8	6	36	72	139	20	6	223
Grand Totals[d]	$3591	31	51	3	168	1	6	127	13	368	506	194	620	34	6	70	46	3	108	1586	234	56	49	6	65	85	496	446	57	638

[a] See note (a) Table 36. The Democratic Congressional Campaign Committee and the Democratic National Congressional Committee were treated as one.

[b] The national-level committees are the same as those listed down the left margin. The abbreviations for the state-level committees are: Reg, regular; Fin, finance; Vol, Volunteers for Stevenson or equivalent; USS, candidates for U.S. Senate and their committees; USHR, candidates for U.S. House of Representatives and their committees; Din, special dinner committees; Cand, candidates for other statewide offices and their committees; Club, women's clubs and similar groups; Misc, state committees not otherwise classified. Abbreviations for county-level are the same. The national, state, and local committees are all either units of the party organization or are aligned as partisan backers of the party's candidates. Transactions with nonparty groups appear in the general Miscellaneous column. Included in USS are a few county-level committees on behalf of Senatorial candidates. Lab refers to labor organizations, both political committees and unions.

[c] Money reported as received from other organizations without specifying the organizations. The questionnaires did not ask committees to itemize transfers of funds of less than $500 each that were received from other organizations, which explains some of the amount unaccounted for.

[d] See note (d) Table 36.

[e] None of the national-level miscellaneous committees reported receipts by transfer during the period in question. Their total receipts were included in the computation of this percentage

Table 39

TRANSFERS OF FUNDS AMONG POLITICAL COMMITTEES: *DISBURSEMENTS* REPORTED BY *DEMOCRATIC* COMMITTEES, SEPTEMBER 1–NOVEMBER 30, 1956[a]
(in thousands of dollars)

Committees Reporting Funds Disbursed by Transfer	Total Disbur'd by Transfer	% of Total Dis-b'ts	Disbursed to the Following Types of Committees[b]: At National Level							At State Level									At Local Level							
			DNC	SKCC	SCC	CCC	VS	Misc	Tot[d]	Reg	Fin	Vol	USS	USHR	Din	Cand	Misc	Tot[d]	Reg	Vol	Din	Cand	Club	Misc	Tot[d]	Unallocated[c]
National Level																										
Dem. National Comm.	$ 74	4				*46*	*1*	*24*	71		*2*							3								
Stev.-Kefauver Camp. Comm.	0	0																								
Senatorial Camp. Comm.	168	91								*23*			*145*					168								
Congressional Camp. Comm.	182	93[e]	*5*						5					*172*				172	*5*						5	
Volunteers for Stevenson	10	2										*10*						10								
4 Miscellaneous	21	20	*9*	*13*					21																	
Total[d]	$ 455	13	14	13		46	1	24	97	24	2	10	145	172				353	5						5	

State Level																									
Regular	$ 670	23	*133*	*40*	*5*			178	*6*		*24*	*16*	*31*	*1*	*10*	*6*	93	*274*	*1*		*21*			295	103
Volunteer	350	26	*133*	*46*		*84*		263	*8*	*1*	*6*					*3*	17	*2*	*43*			*1*		46	23
U.S. Senate	116	8							*80*			*19*	*7*		*2*		108	*3*						3	6
Total[d]	$1136	20	267	85	5	84		441	94	1	29	35	37	1	11	9	218	278	44		21	*1*		345	132
Local Level																									
Regular	$ 315	12	*6*	*5*				11	*51*	*2*	*3*	*3*	*8*			*6*	74	*61*	*2*	*2*	*48*	*1*	*1*	114	116
Volunteer	67	43		*13*		7		20			*37*						37	*4*	*4*					9	2
Total[d]	$ 382	14	6	18		7		31	51	2	40	3	8			6	110	65	6	2	48	1	1	123	118
Grand Totals[d]	$1973	17	287	115	51	92	24	569	169	5	79	183	218	1	11	15	681	349	50	2	69	2	1	473	251

[a] See note (a) Table 37. The Democratic Congressional Campaign Committee and the Democratic National Congressional Committee were treated as one.

[b] The national-level committees are the same as those listed down the left margin. The abbreviations for the state-level committees are: Reg, regular, Fin, finance; Vol, volunteers for Stevenson or equivalent; USS, candidates for U.S. Senate and their committees; USHR, candidates for U.S. House of Representatives and their committees; Din, special dinner committees; Cand, candidates for other statewide offices and their committees; Misc, state committees not otherwise classified. Abbreviations for county-level are the same; Club, refers to women's clubs and similar groups. The national, state, and local committees are all either units of the party organization or are aligned as partisan backers of the party's candidates. Transactions with nonparty groups appear in the general Miscellaneous column. Included in USS are a few county-level committees on behalf of Senatorial candidates.

[c] Money reported as sent to other organizations without specifying the organizations, or without adequate identification for classifying.

[d] See note (d) Table 36.

[e] This percentage computed from data for the period September 1–December 31, 1956.

can money reported received by Senatorial campaign committees at state and local levels came from contributions by individuals to those committees. These committees held on to most of such money, as well as to most of the funds coming to them from other sources: in both parties the Senatorial committees spent more than 90 per cent of their disbursements themselves. The rest they generally gave to other organizations working on behalf of Senatorial candidates. While these financial transactions do not measure the full range and significance of campaign activity, they point to the limited organizational cohesion of the parties even at the state level.[26]

From time to time conclusions are drawn concerning the effect on party responsibility of the diverse sources of funds that support candidates for the houses of Congress. Whether the effect is as divisive as usually supposed is hard to say, but it seems clear that Democratic candidates are more dependent for financial support on groups outside the formal party structure than are Republicans. Most funds reported as transferred to Republican Senatorial committees originated with the party's regular or finance committees at local, state, and national levels. In contrast, almost one-half such Democratic money came from separately organized labor sources and another substantial share came from "miscellaneous" groups.[27] These and other features of campaign operations do not reflect the unfettered preferences of party managers. They are, more often, the product of pressing needs and the opportunities to meet those needs that lie at hand.

That much can be done to improve the economy of campaign administration and the effectiveness of fund-raising within both parties there is no doubt. The nature of the parties, however, and the interests they

26. Not a conclusion that can be drawn from bookkeeping data alone. Doubtless some individual contributions were directed to Senatorial campaign committees by party fund-raisers, and some Senatorial committees worked more closely with the regular party organization than others. One gets the impression in Michigan, for example, that despite a variety of seemingly independent volunteer and candidate committees the Democratic state chairman has been able to keep a hand on things. As one visits many states with campaigns in progress, however, he is not impressed by a high degree of synchronization of campaign activities, and those busiest in the campaigns are not either.

27. As has been discussed earlier, special-interest money finds its way into politics as contributions to campaign committees. The relatively small amount of money received in both parties directly from nonparty organizations is indicated by the sums in the Miscellaneous columns in Tables 36 and 38.

Campaign work by nonparty groups in some sectors is highly important to the parties. Labor groups have even entered agreements with party committees to assume responsibility for the campaign in specified precincts. In Chicago, the Independent Voters of Illinois, a local affiliate of the Americans for Democratic Action, has on occasion campaigned actively on behalf of Republicans and Democrats in the same election, engaging in door-bell pushing and the other usual exercises of the canvass.

embrace, preclude building the kind of party organizations that would be technically most efficient and operationally most cohesive.[28]

3. A NOTE ON ORGANIZATIONAL DIFFERENCES

In contrast to the organization of business interests, political parties display widely dissimilar characteristics from nation to nation.[29] The features that distinguish parties from each other are less their programs and supporters than the nature of their organization.[30] In comparisons of differences, the broad organizational features that set the major American parties apart from those elsewhere overshadow differences between the American parties and among the numerous state and local units that make them up. Yet the study of party finance exposes the notable division of labor and specialization of function that characterize political committees in the United States. Differences in the ways money is raised and spent highlight differences in organization, procedure, and purpose. They provide clues to the range of differences that exist within the American parties and their constituent units.

Campaign activity within both parties is largely divided among four types of political committees. (1) There are regular party committees, usually prescribed by law at state and local levels and culminating in the national committee of each party with its allied Senatorial and Congressional campaign committees. (2) The finance committees of the Republican party at all levels are not duplicated among Democrats, al-

28. When the origins and destinations of the individual transfers of funds summarized in Tables 36 through 39 are examined, it becomes evident that very few are made between committees in different states. Only the District of Columbia "state" committees are likely to send funds away from home. Aspiring politicians generously donate their time to public appearances in states where at the moment they have no constituents. They even donate money when hoping for the favor of national convention delegations, but party committees look up and down more than sideways.

The Gore Committee sought information on loans made during the 1956 campaign among political committees. Very few in amounts of $500 or more were reported, perhaps because such advances may have been made and/or repaid outside of the reporting period, September 1–November 30. The national Citizens for Eisenhower-Nixon advanced money to some of its state groups. More than half the $105,000 in reported Republican loans went from the national to the New York State Citizens organization; and among $64,000 in loans reported repaid during the period, the largest was $16,500 that the California Citizens sent back to the national. Democratic groups reported receiving $210,000 in loans, of which $183,000 went to the Democratic national committee from the regular state committee in Pennsylvania, the home of Matthew McCloskey, the national treasurer, and the site of a whopping fund-raising dinner early in the campaign. Democratic loan repayments were reported as only $9,000.

29. "One of the most striking conclusions of Dr. Brady's book concerns the similarity in type and function of the organization of business interests from nation to nation, despite seemingly widely dissimilar national backgrounds."—Robert S. Lynd in Foreword to Robert A. Brady, *Business as a System of Power* (New York: Columbia University Press, 1943), p. xi.

30. See Duverger, *op. cit.*, pp. xv-xvi. "One of the most marked features of party structure is its heterogeneity."—*Ibid.*, p. 1.

though special Democratic dinner committees often exist solely (during their limited lives) for fund-raising purposes, and hence may be called a type of finance committee. (3) Volunteer committees, so-called, inevitably arise on behalf of presidential candidates and function with varying degrees of liaison alongside the regular party organizations. (4) Finally, in most areas candidate committees are set up to campaign for particular individuals who seek state or local offices. These differ in function from the presidential volunteer committees when they carry the principal burden of the candidate's campaign, which is often. Political clubs of numerous kinds are active, often through one or more of the above kinds of committee, but they are not a type of political organization found generally throughout the states.

There are differences from one state to another, both between the parties and within the same party, in the volume and kind of activity each of these committees undertakes. There are differences also in the resulting web of relationships among the committees within a state that constitutes a party's total campaign structure. To create a typology of state party organizations—something different from a typology of state party systems—would require more dependable indicators of difference than existing financial information provides. It may be useful, nonetheless, to point to certain similarities and dissimilarities in party operations that are evident from what is known about party funds.

Traffic in transfers.—The Republican finance-committee system seeks a higher degree of financial integration than is attempted throughout the Democratic party. The resulting greater traffic in transfers among Republican than among Democratic committees is evident from Tables 31 through 39. Republican receipts from transfers at all levels vastly exceed those of Democrats both in dollars and in the proportion those dollars constitute of total receipts. To handle and direct this flow of funds within party channels requires a degree of financial coordination that is generally lacking among Democrats.

One measure of difference between the four main types of campaign committees within each party at state and local levels can be found in their financial interdependence with other committees. The distinctive fund-raising role of the Republican state finance committees is revealed clearly, for example, in Table 33 on page 286. Taken as a group, they received a comparatively small share of their income as transfers from other committees, less than one-fifth, while disbursing most of it, over four-fifths, as transfers to other groups. The Republican state regular committees, the operating organizations, were, by contrast, in the reverse position. They received two-thirds of their funds as transfers and transmitted only slightly more than one-fourth of their disbursements in that form. The Republican state volunteer committees as a group, it will be recalled, raised and spent most of their own money, while the Senatorial campaign groups looked to others for more than a third of their receipts and spent almost all of their receipts themselves.

The differences between Democratic and Republican fund-raising procedures are also evident. The Democratic Senatorial campaign groups, like their Republican counterparts, received a substantial proportion of their income from other committees and spent most of it themselves. Democratic as well as Republican state volunteer committees largely raised and spent their own money. But in the absence of a regular system of Democratic finance committees,[31] the state regular committees had to raise most of their own war chest, less than one-fourth of their total income taking the form of transfers.

At the local level, the regular and finance committees included in the tabulation displayed characteristics similar to state committees of the same type. The Democratic volunteer committees, however, as already noted, engaged in a measure of fund-raising to assist other groups, while the Republican local volunteers were more dependent on others than were the state volunteers.

Variations within types.—These summary statements concerning the four types of state and local committees suggest general similarities and differences among them as types. The summaries obscure differences that exist, however, among committees of the same type in different states. Tables 40 and 41 demonstrate that wide variation obtains from state to state in the financial activities of committees that are classified alike. Not all regular state committees with the same party, for example, get and dispose of their money in the same ways.

These two tables make a formidable appearance, but when understood can be read quite easily. In Table 40, to illustrate, look at the first narrow column headed "R," with the number 15 immediately below the "R." The whole table pertains to state-level Republican committees, and the "R" at the head of a column refers to regular Republican state committees. (The "F" refers to finance committees, the "V" to volunteer, *ad hoc* committees supporting the party's presidential candidate, and the "S" to *ad hoc* committees supporting the party's Senatorial candidates.) The 15 means that there were 15 regular Republican state committees that received between 0 and 10 per cent (the percentage category in the extreme left-hand column) of their total receipts in the form of transfers from other political committees (the general heading under which this "R" column appears). Reading down this column it is seen, furthermore, that there were also four Republican state committees that received between 61 and 70 per cent of their total receipts by transfer from other political committees; 10 received between 91 and 100 per cent in this way. The total at the foot of the column indicates that 41 regular committees are accounted for in this column, the number for which usable information was available.

31. Some of the state-level Democratic committees submitting information used in constructing Tables 38 and 39 were classified as finance committees. Virtually all of the money (Table 38) came from three committees, and the bulk of it in one transaction from one committee in Pennsylvania.

Table 40

DIVERSITY AMONG SELECTED *REPUBLICAN* STATE POLITICAL COMMITTEES IN SOURCES AND USES OF FUNDS, SEPTEMBER 1–NOVEMBER 30, 1956[a]

%	No. of Committees of Type Indicated Falling in Each Percentage Range																																			
	Transfers with Other Political Committees												% of Direct Expenditures Going for Following Purposes[b]																							
	% of Total Receipts from Others				% of Total Disbursements to Others				% of Total Disbursements Spent Directly				Radio				Television				Advertising				Literature				Billboards				Others			
	R[c]	F[c]	V[c]	S[c]	R	F	V	S	R	F	V	S	R	F	V	S	R	F	V	S	R	F	V	S	R	F	V	S	R	F	V	S	R	F	V	S
0-10.......	15	18	38	12	16	–	27	19	1	18	–	1	23	23	38	19	13	21	38	14	17	23	30	13	13	21	17	9	28	23	45	24	2	5	5	4
11-20.......	1	2	–	2	3	–	6	2	–	3	3	–	7	–	5	3	10	1	6	7	11	–	4	4	10	2	16	5	2	1	2	1	2	2	3	4
21-30.......	2	3	2	2	5	1	3	3	2	–	1	–	2	–	2	1	4	–	4	2	3	1	8	3	4	1	7	5	1	–	1	–	9	–	6	2
31-40.......	1	1	2	5	4	1	4	–	6	2	2	1	–	1	1	–	2	1	–	1	–	–	2	2	3	–	3	3	–	–	–	–	4	1	5	7

41-50	1	–	1	1	3	3	2	–	–	–	–	1	–	–	–	1	1	–	–	1	1	–	3	–	–	–	1	1	1	–	–	–	5	–	8	2
51-60	2	1	4	–	–	–	–	1	3	3	2	–	–	–	1	–	1	–	–	–	–	–	–	1	2	–	1	2	–	–	–	–	3	1	2	2
61-70	4	–	–	2	6	2	2	1	4	1	4	–	–	–	–	1	1	1	–	–	–	–	–	–	–	–	1	–	–	–	–	–	3	1	3	1
71-80	2	1	–	2	2	–	1	–	5	1	3	3	–	–	–	–	–	–	–	–	–	–	1	1	–	–	1	–	–	–	–	–	1	–	7	1
81-90	3	1	1	1	–	3	3	–	3	–	6	2	–	–	–	–	–	–	–	–	–	–	–	1	–	–	1	–	–	–	–	–	2	1	5	2
91-100	10	1	–	–	1	18	–	1	16	–	27	19	–	–	1	–	–	–	–	–	–	–	–	–	–	–	–	–	–	–	–	–	1	13	4	–
Total	41	28	48	27	40	28	48	27	40	28	48	27	32	24	48	25	32	24	48	25	32	24	48	25	32	24	48	25	32	24	48	25	32	24	48	25

[a] Derived from Gore Committee information. Generally, no more than one committee of each type from each state was included in the tabulation, although in a few instances there was more than one volunteer committee or more than one Senatorial committee from a single state. The District of Columbia and U.S. territories and possessions were treated as states. The reports of a few committees were complete in certain particulars and not complete in others. A report might show, for example, what portion of a committee's total receipts came from transfers, but not show what portion of its total disbursements took the form of transfers. Even if the latter were shown, the report might not itemize the disbursements other than transfers, that is, the direct expenditures. Consequently, the number of committees of the same type that are accounted for in each of the columns may not always be the same. In the case of each committee, transfers to other organizations plus direct expenditures equal total disbursements.

[b] Radio and television expenditures include charges for time on air and other costs in connection with broadcasts. Advertising refers to that in newspapers and periodicals. Literature includes costs of printing, purchase, and distribution. Billboards are those outdoor. Other includes all other purposes of expenditures, such as overhead, salaries, and travel.

[c] "R" refers to regular Republican state committees; "F" to that party's state finance committees; "V" to volunteer, *ad hoc* groups supporting Eisenhower and Nixon; "S" to *ad hoc* committees supporting Republican Senatorial candidates.

Table 41

DIVERSITY AMONG SELECTED *DEMOCRATIC* STATE POLITICAL COMMITTEES IN SOURCES AND USES OF FUNDS, SEPTEMBER 1–NOVEMBER 30, 1956[a]

%	No. of Committees of Type Indicated Falling in Each Percentage Range																										
	Transfers with Other Political Committees									% of Direct Expenditures Going for Following Purposes[b]																	
	% of Total Receipts from Others			% of Total Disbursements to Others			% of Total Disbursements Spent Directly			Radio			Television			Advertising			Literature			Billboards			Others		
	R[c]	V[c]	S[c]	R	V	S	R	V	S	R	V	S	R	V	S	R	V	S	R	V	S	R	V	S	R	V	S
0-10...	18	21	12	22	13	25	–	1	2	40	30	25	29	26	20	31	25	16	18	6	15	45	36	32	3	2	6
11-20...	10	7	2	6	4	4	1	–	1	6	3	3	9	2	5	12	6	7	9	11	4	3	–	1	3	2	7
21-30...	5	4	1	3	5	–	1	5	1	2	1	5	2	5	4	4	4	3	10	8	6	–	–	1	3	–	7
31-40...	1	–	1	8	2	–	4	–	–	–	1	1	5	–	2	–	1	2	6	5	5	–	–	–	6	8	4
41-50...	5	2	2	1	3	2	2	4	–	–	1	–	1	2	2	1	–	–	3	2	3	–	–	–	7	8	4
51-60...	4	–	2	2	4	–	1	3	2	–	–	–	–	1	–	–	–	2	1	1	1	–	–	–	6	4	2
61-70...	4	1	5	4	–	–	8	2	–	–	–	–	1	–	–	–	–	1	1	–	–	–	–	–	9	8	1
71-80...	1	–	2	1	5	1	3	5	–	–	–	–	–	–	–	–	–	–	–	–	–	–	–	–	4	2	1
81-90...	1	1	3	1	–	1	6	4	4	–	–	–	–	–	1	–	–	1	–	2	–	–	–	–	2	–	–
91-100..	–	2	4	–	1	2	22	13	25	–	–	–	1	–	–	–	–	2	–	1	–	–	–	–	5	2	2
Total...	49	38	34	48	37	35	48	37	35	48	36	34	48	36	34	48	36	34	48	36	34	48	36	34	48	36	34

[a] See note (a) Table 40.
[b] See note (b) Table 40.

Moving to the right, the next "R" column falls under the general heading, "% of Total Disbursements to Others," meaning the percentage of total disbursements that took the form of transfers. From this column it can be seen that 16 regular committees transferred only between 0 and 10 per cent of their disbursements to other committees. This means necessarily that they spent between 91 and 100 per cent directly—that is, spent the money themselves—a fact indicated by the bottom entry in the "R" column (opposite 91-100) under the next general heading to the right, "% of Total Disbursements Spent Directly."

Close scrutiny of the information on transfers of funds reported in the two tables shows the general tendencies described above for each type of committee, e.g., the regular committees are more likely than the finance committees to receive a large share of their income by transfer, and less likely to disburse a large share of it by transfer. But in some states the regular committee departs from the norm, as do committees of the other types, and some of the variations between states among committees of the same kind—and which might be expected to conduct their affairs more or less alike—are considerable.

The purposes for which direct expenditures were made by state-level committees also show a lack of uniformity from state to state in the functions undertaken by the committees. For illustration, look under the television heading in Table 41. One regular Democratic committee (all of Table 41 pertains to Democratic committees) spent between 91 and 100 per cent of its total direct expenditures for television. Another one spent between 61 and 70 per cent of its direct expenditures for that purpose; the number of committees for which the percentage was 0 to 10, however, was 29, well over half of the 48 regular committees included in the tabulation. A committee that makes 90 per cent or more of its direct expenditures for television necessarily will spend 10 per cent or less for the other purposes listed in the table: radio, advertising, etc. Because the total direct expenditures of a committee are often divided among several purposes, most committees devote no more than 30 per cent of their direct expenditures to any single type of expenditure. A fair number of exceptions can be noted, however, in both Tables 40 and 41.

The purposes for which campaign money is needed vary to some extent with the communications and organizational requirements of an area. More significantly, however, the variations from state to state and from one type of committee to another point to a division of political labor among political committees within the same state, a condition observable on the ground in many state campaign activities. Most of all, they suggest that in disposing of money as well as in raising it different kinds of interrelationships and degrees of cohesion may be found among the American state parties.[32]

32. Only the active campaign period is covered by Tables 40 and 41. Data for

An illustration.—Students who search for uniform categories of information on the internal operations of state parties find themselves in a vacuum. Unhappily, financial data do not satisfactorily fill the vacuum. The 1956 information collected by the Gore Committee, for example, did not include reports on campaign activities directed solely at state and local offices. It consequently does not afford a comprehensive picture of campaign activity within individual states. More inclusive information was obtained for a few states, however, in 1952, and one kind of analysis possible can be illustrated.

The two parties in Massachusetts presented the sharpest comparisons.[33] The Democratic state committee spent directly all of the more than $440,000 disbursed from its treasury, sending nothing to other groups. It operated independently, as measured by these terms, of numerous campaign committees active on behalf of Democratic Senatorial candidate John F. Kennedy, which together received and spent about $350,000. The party's candidate for governor, Paul Dever, also had a special campaign committee that raised about $140,000 of its own money. No sums were reported sent by the state committee to committees backing other candidates, of which there were many, nor to any local campaign group throughout the state. Volunteer committees on behalf of presidential candidate Stevenson sprang up at local and state levels and, along with labor and other independent groups, carried an important share of the campaign burden. The Democratic campaign organization was thus conducted by a large number of financially autonomous units at all levels within the state.[34]

---

the full year, or a full election cycle, might reveal different results, though it seems improbable that uniform practices among committees would be found.

Data from local-level political committees indicate that the specialized activities in which they engage also vary widely. Among 32 regular Republican local committees, for example, the following number spent the indicated percentages of their total disbursements themselves: 21, 91-100 per cent; 3, 81-90 per cent; 1, 51-60 per cent; 1, 41-50 per cent; 1, 31-40 per cent; 1, 21-30 per cent; 3, 11-20 per cent; 1, 0-10 per cent. Among 25 regular Democratic local committees, for another illustration, the following number spent the indicated percentages of their total expenditures for newspaper and periodical advertising: 1, 91-100 per cent; 2, 31-40 per cent; 1, 21-30 per cent; 3, 11-20 per cent; 18, 0-10 per cent.

33. The flow of funds among political committees during 1952 was studied by Joan Combs Grace for the general elections in Massachusetts, Maryland, and North Carolina, and for the Democratic primaries in the latter two states.—*Op. cit.*, pp. 125-72. "Political Campaign Financing: Massachusetts in 1952," also treating the subject, was a paper by Hugh Douglas Price (typescript, Cambridge, Massachusetts, 1954). Portions of the paper were summarized by Mr. Price in "Campaign Finance in Massachusetts in 1952," *Public Policy*, 6 (1955), 25-46. Detailed scrutiny of contributor lists in Massachusetts and other states usually reveals that different candidates and different types of committees enjoy support from different kinds of contributors, a factor that reflects as well as conduces to the atomization of political life.

34. The role of the state committee was altered in 1956, when the sums it handled during the campaign totalled only about $13,000. The state chairman ex-

The relationships among Republican campaign organizations were quite different. The state committee channelled a quarter of its approximately $1,050,000 in disbursements to other groups. Local Republican campaign committees relied almost exclusively on subventions from the state committee, and funds were sent to an abundance of other committees, including special committees backing the party's candidate for president and other offices. Most of the Republican Senatorial campaign, moreover, was conducted through the state committee. The Republican campaign possessed a degree of financial integration unknown to the Democratic effort.

There are other states where this kind of organizational analysis is possible from the kinds of financial information presently available in public reports. Connecticut, New York, and Pennsylvania are three of them.[35] If studied over a series of elections, changes in the financial organization of the parties and differences between the parties could be interpreted significantly and related to other aspects of party structure and function. This dimension of organizational difference is relevant to proposals for increased party discipline and to many recommendations for changing the sources and methods of raising campaign money.

---

plained that the important campaigning in the latter year was conducted entirely through committees completely independent of the state committee.

35. Party differences in Connecticut resemble those in Massachusetts.—Duane Lockard, *New England State Politics* (Princeton: Princeton University Press, 1959), pp. 252-53, 258.

12

FUND-RAISING AND NOMINATIONS

NOMINATING CANDIDATES for public office is the distinctive business of political parties in the United States. Despite this, none of the processes through which Americans govern themselves is more obscure than those by which candidates for a party's nomination are proposed and winnowed. In these hidden proceedings, money probably has a more important impact than in any other phase of politics. Inescapable financial requirements attach to almost every candidacy. Unless an aspirant can meet these himself, assurance of assistance from contributors and solicitors is essential. Whether help is granted or withheld often determines who enters the political lists. Yet other considerations are involved, too, and they limit the king-making power of the financiers.

1. MONEY: NECESSARY BUT NOT SUFFICIENT

Key financial decisions in politics are taken privately. They are taken beyond the view of most politicians whose labors constitute organized campaign activity. The secrecy cloaking such decisions produces exaggerated notions of the freedom with which they are made. In deciding whether to encourage or discourage a prospective candidate, financial politicians remember, or soon learn, that campaign money may be essential for success, but it does not vest those who supply it with dictatorial power.

Availability.—The number of potential candidates whom financial backers may realistically choose among is confined to the small number deemed to be "available." Availability embraces all the factors that make for a good risk at the polls, including the endorsement of essential factional and party leaders. Suppliers of cash on occasion decide the fate of individual aspirants, but their influence is circumscribed by the demands of an electoral system in which success rests ultimately on some form of popular appeal. The requirements for success in any jurisdiction are so restrictive they usually disqualify most of the populace from consideration as serious candidates.[1] The reverse of this coin is that the power of a politician's appeal may, on rare occasions, free him altogether from the normal financial necessities. Especially so of established vote-getters, this can be true also of relative newcomers. Adlai Stevenson was nominated for the presidency in 1952 with, by normal standards, no expenditures.[2]

Political appeal and access to campaign money are only two of the many factors that affect the selection of candidates. Lord Bryce long ago found the greatest weakness of American democracy in the quality of persons who direct its public affairs. Lacking a dedicated leisure class, and lacking a tradition that would condone its control of government if one existed, the United States has looked elsewhere for its political leadership. The financial demands and compensation of public offices consequently affect crucially the kinds of people who are willing to seek a nomination and the conditions under which they do so. If the remuneration is small, as it usually has been,[3] some men shy away, and

1. Sidney Hyman figured that the "natural aristocracy" from which United States presidents are chosen probably amounts at any one time to no more than 100 men in the whole population. He concluded that southerners, females, colored peoples, residents of small states, and some 11 other categories are in fact excluded from candidacy by the requirements of the system by which the president is chosen.—*The American President* (New York: Harper & Brothers, 1954), pp. 231-32. He later formulated "Nine Tests for the Presidential Hopeful," *New York Times Magazine,* January 4, 1959, pp. 11ff.

2. Walter Johnson, *How We Drafted Adlai Stevenson* (New York: Alfred A. Knopf, 1955), pp. 33-35, 43-44. Self-propelled candidates sometimes come along determined to seek candidacy regardless of help or hindrance from others. Customarily their campaign activities are meager and they attract a tiny fraction of the votes. Occasionally such an individual behaves like a major contender, as did a Texan named Dudley T. Dougherty, who ran against Senator Lyndon B. Johnson in the 1954 Democratic primary. He was not taken seriously by those in the know. But he was wealthy and the $94,330 he reported spending through his headquarters alone would seem like a serious sum, at least to anyone but a Texan.

3. The level of Congressional salaries in 1954 led a special public commission to the conclusion that they tended "to confine those positions to persons of independent wealth or outside earnings."—The Commission on Judicial and Congressional Salaries, *Report* (Washington: Government Printing Office, 1954) (House Document No. 300, 83rd Congress, 2nd Session), p. 19. One state senator concluded that "you have to be rich, retired, or crooked not to suffer financially in most state legislatures." He calculated that roughly half the 6,000 state legislators who would take office in 1956 would be serving for the first time. His own income in Connecticut was $300 per year for several months of work.—Duane Lockard, "The Tribulations of a State Senator," *The Reporter,* May 17, 1956, p. 24.

As a reminder that the picture is not all one-sided, it should be recorded that Glen Taylor of Idaho, who suffered many privations in earlier years, was accustomed to say unabashedly that he "had never had it so good" as while enjoying the income and perquisites of a United States senator. Some local government posts, especially those paid on a fee basis, afford gratifying income. A bizarre illustration was the tax collector of Franklin Borough near Johnstown, Pennsylvania. In 1953 one Joseph Tomaskovich, an $85-a-week steelworker, was elected to the post, one duty of which was to deposit annually the tax check of the Bethlehem Steel Corporation, an item of $400,000 in total collections of $500,000,

others are tempted into dubious practices.[4] Low salaries and periodic improprieties have reduced the prestige of public service.[5] All these things limit the pool of talent from which candidates for public office can be drawn. None is as important, however, as the difficulty of harmonizing a political career with most American livelihoods. No prudent person runs for office who cannot afford to lose. There are few lines of work that provide the freedom of schedule, and the assurance of future income, necessary to sustain a career in elective politics.

Occupational eligibility to run the risks of politics is the most important selective factor in the recruitment of candidates for elective office. The overwhelming importance of lawyers in American politics can be attributed primarily to the compatibility of political and legal careers.[6] Businessmen as a rule rank next to lawyers in numerical importance in elective positions, with persons in mass communications, agriculture,

for which act the collector, paid on a percentage basis, stood to collect $10,000 per year.—*Life,* November 16, 1953.

4. The late Governor Harold Hoffman of New Jersey, a genial and ebullient politician who made off with $300,000 in state funds in the 1930's and was able to cover up for almost twenty years, gave his simple conclusion in a private letter to his daughter: "No poor man should ever get into the field of elective politics." Mr. Hoffman reported that he first got into difficulties when he made withdrawals from inactive accounts in a bank with which he was associated in order to cover his campaign deficit when he first ran for Congress. He overspent himself in Washington, leading to further misappropriations. "Then during the Gubernatorial primary and general election, I suffered further disappointments at the hands of friends who promised to pay election expenses, but, it subsequently developed, only at the price of state favors which I considered impossible to grant."—Harold H. Martin, "The Mystery of Harold Hoffman," *Saturday Evening Post,* October 23, 1954, pp. 116-17.

5. It is a fair conclusion that the standards of morality in public office in the United States are substantially more exacting than in private business or private life. For a discussion of the reasons, see Paul H. Appleby, *Morality and Administration in Democratic Government* (Baton Rouge: Louisiana State University Press, 1952), esp. pp. 44-50. Moreover, the prestige value of public employment in general seems on the rise.—Morris Janowitz and Deil Wright, "The Prestige of Public Employment: 1929 and 1954," *Public Administration Review,* 16 (1956), 15-21. Nevertheless, public opinion polls show a high proportion of parents who would not wish their children to seek careers in politics, attitudes that necessarily condition the outlook of the children when they later become adults.

6. Skills of mediation and persuasion rewarding in both careers doubtless account in part for the attractiveness of political life to many lawyers. It may be normal, likewise, that those who apply the law would feel called to the processes by which it is made. See Robert E. Agger, "Lawyers in Politics: The Starting Point for a New Research Program," *Temple Law Quarterly,* 29 (1956), 434-52. Data on the frequency of lawyers in political positions appear in numerous places. See especially Albert P. Blaustein and Charles O. Porter, *The American Lawyer—A Summary of the Survey of the Legal Profession* (Chicago: University of Chicago Press, 1954), p. 97, and Joseph A. Schlesinger, "The Emergence of Political Leadership—A Case Study of American Governors" (Ph.D. dissertation, Yale University, 1954), pp. 244-45. Also see Schlesinger's *How They Became Governor* (East Lansing: Governmental Research Bureau, Michigan State University, 1957), 103 pp.

and other professions following behind.[7] Trade union officials have begun to make an appearance in recent years. *Which* lawyers, businessmen, publishers, farmers, union officials, or others are available depends on many variables of personal incentive and political effectiveness. Within these many limits, solicitors and contributors of campaign funds wield great power in the nomination of candidates.

Money needed.—In states where *general election* costs are burdensome, persons regularly concerned with supplying party money carry weight in the deliberations that precede nominations. So it has been, for example, with many members of Republican finance committees. When the party lacks established fund-raising machinery, the nominee and his factional supporters must assume a major responsibility for financing the general-election campaign. In these circumstances, backers who will undertake to do so become a respected asset in the contest for the nomination.

The ability to raise money for *nomination* campaigns, however, is more crucial. Here, political careers are launched or thwarted. Here, persons with access to money find their greatest opportunity to influence the selection of public officials, and therefore the conduct of the public's business.[8] Party labels automatically attract dollars as well as votes. An aspiring politician is more exposed to the influence of political financiers before he gets on the ticket than after.

The amount of money needed to pursue a nomination varies greatly. Most states now require the major parties to nominate by direct primary for important posts. Originally, primaries were adopted partly as a move against the influence exerted by wealthy groups in nominating conventions. While the bribery of delegates has been eliminated, it is hardly provable that a lesser representation of wealthy interests in the nominating process has resulted. Given the kinds of campaigning that have evolved, it seems likely that use of the primary has, on balance,

7. An occupational analysis of 52 Indiana county party chairmen of both parties, 1952-54, and of 418 members of the Indiana House of Representatives, 1937-53, revealed that political leadership in that state is exercised principally by persons in "promotional occupations," businesses depending on meeting and interesting other people where political contacts can be put to immediate profit.—Frank James Munger, "Two-Party Politics in the State of Indiana" (Ph.D. dissertation, Harvard University, 1955), pp. 254-61.

Differences between states and between parties within the same state, and changes over time, indicate that the selection of candidates is a function of the occupational composition of the population, the policy orientation of the parties, the political determination of organized labor, and other factors, including the occupational eligibility of potential candidates. See V. O. Key, Jr., *American State Politics: An Introduction* (New York: Alfred A. Knopf, 1956), pp. 254-65.

8. In pre-nomination maneuvering, concern for general-election financing is naturally greatest in states of vigorous party competition; the importance of financing primary campaigns is greatest in states of lopsided party strength.

increased the costs of politics.[9] Primary expenses easily rival those of general elections and, where party competition is tepid, exceed them. What the specific amounts are in particular settings varies. Factors that affect the level of general-election costs also affect those of primaries,[10] and therefore affect the minimum-essential sums candidates for a nomination must be able to count on to run a meaningful race. There are common features, however, in the processes by which candidates hope to provide these sums.

2. THE WINNOWING OF CANDIDATES

The Senate of the United States was once called a millionaires' club, and even in more recent years millionaires have occupied some of its

9. Nominating processes were long regarded as the private affairs of voluntary associations. As such they have not been subject to the same scrutiny by investigative groups nor to the same public-reporting requirements as general elections. The difficulties of learning campaign costs under convention systems are especially great. Any judgment as to the relative expensiveness to candidates of the two means of nomination is necessarily impressionistic. The best informed students of the subject in the 1920's were not persuaded that campaigning in a direct primary was more costly than campaigning for a convention nomination.—Charles E. Merriam and Louise Overacker, *Primary Elections* (Chicago: University of Chicago Press, 1928), pp. 247-53.

Campaigning for a convention nomination in the 1950's could be expensive, too, as the evident outlays on behalf of Nelson A. Rockefeller's successful try for New York's Republican gubernatorial nomination in 1958 were a reminder. Official reports told little of the New York story, but in some states measurable sums are accounted for. Three aspirants for one of the Republican nominations for United States senator made by convention in Connecticut in 1952 reported expenditures totalling around $41,000, and other expenditures may have been made. In Indiana in the same year one committee backing George N. Craig for the gubernatorial nomination in the Republican convention reported spending some $18,500 and a committee on behalf of Senator William E. Jenner's renomination in the same convention reported expenditures of about $45,000.

Such reports show that expenditures generally go for organizational purposes such as travel, subventions to agents, meetings, salaries, and headquarters overhead. Expenditures for publicity, printing, broadcast time, and the like consume a smaller proportion of the budget than in campaigns that must appeal primarily to masses of individual voters. (On the contrary, Merriam and Overacker observed in 1928: "The expense of maintaining an organization, the outlays for workers and for advertising are as great for selecting delegates as for selecting candidates."—*Ibid.*, p. 251.)

Competitors for a convention nomination often withdraw before final votes are taken and sometimes before their names are placed before the convention. Candidates in primaries find it more awkward to stop campaigning, and therefore to stop spending, even in a race that has become obviously hopeless.

Campaigning for a nomination may be conducted as preparation for the general election to follow, hence nominating expenditures may in reality be general-election expenditures. Senator Jenner, who was unopposed at the Indiana Republican convention in 1952, must have had his eye on the general election during his preconvention activities. In any event, more than $63,000 in contributions was reported received before the convention by his committee, which sum exceeded the nomination expenses of that committee by more than $18,000.

10. See pages 380-87, below.

seats. Whenever a rich man succeeds in politics, his wealth is assigned substantial credit. The credit is often well placed, for an individual's personal resources can profoundly influence the conditions under which he enters political life, and whether he enters it at all. The ability to finance a period of political apprenticeship greatly enhances a politician's availability. A determined candidate for a nomination who can pay his own way cannot be stopped from competing.[11]

The nationwide activities on behalf of Senator John F. Kennedy's presidential hopes before the 1960 Democratic convention could not have been conveniently financed, if at all, without the aid of personal and family funds.[12] Certainly the public careers of Nelson Rockefeller and Averell Harriman were built on their private fortunes.[13] In almost every state, local politicos can point to a rich man, or a rich man's son, or a rich woman's husband, who by reason of his money has made him-

11. Novelist John O'Hara has given a vivid portrayal of a campaign of personal build-up that a man of wealth and political ambition may indulge in. The Honorable Joseph Benjamin Chapin of Gibbsville, Pennsylvania—and of *Ten North Frederick* (New York: Random House, 1955)—found, however, that neither years of tactful self-promotion nor his large donations to the party treasury were sufficient to gain the needed endorsement of the party professionals.

12. Without invidious comparison, an instance of family financial help designed for wider popular appeal may be reported. It was announced in the heat of Senator Estes Kefauver's 1954 renomination race that his daughter, Linda, had given $30 to his campaign, the accumulation of a year's savings.—*The Tennessean* (Nashville), July 25, 1954.

13. Manifestly, other considerations equal, a man with money is better off in politics than one without it. He is especially favored if, like Mr. Rockefeller, he has developed socially approved ways of using it, or, like Mr. Harriman, he has used his freedom to develop a useful set of personal and social skills. The considerable political assets of both men have all in one way or another derived from their financial assets. This is not to say that others would have capitalized on them as well—many have not—nor that they themselves would not have taken advantage of whatever circumstances they found themselves in.

The advantages of financial leeway in any line of endeavor are too obvious to require special emphasis. The tales of Rockefeller's search for a pre-convention press secretary in the spring of 1957 revealed the advantage of being able not only to pay extraordinary salaries but to guarantee tenure in a family enterprise, win or lose. The advantages of affluence extend to the lowest as well as the highest reaches of politics. Many a precinct chairman has been compelled to give money as well as time to his party, and in all the political roles from precinct to presidency personal financial resources prove a convenience, and sometimes a necessity. Raymond Moley has reported on the heavy financial burden carried by himself and others of FDR's brain-trusters before and after the 1932 election. Presumably there were compensations, eventually some of them even financial, in serving the great master.—*After Seven Years* (New York: Harper & Brothers, 1939), pp. 19, 180, 283-84.

The cost of travelling to a far city for the national nominating conventions can be a limiting factor in the selection of delegates. Efforts to meet these difficulties are usually inadequate. In 1952, Republican state headquarters in Wisconsin offered each delegate $100 to help defray his expenses; in North Dakota the state itself gave each delegate $200 toward this end.—Paul T. David, Malcolm Moos, and Ralph M. Goldman, *Presidential Nominating Politics in 1952* (Baltimore: The Johns Hopkins Press, 1954), vol. 4, pp. 140, 245.

self a conspicuous participant in the state's politics. But rich men, it so happens, are no more assured of winning elections than are poor men. Wealth of political talent is more important in the end than wealth of dollars, which is perhaps why great personal wealth, especially inherited wealth, is not a common characteristic of American politicians. Most men who aspire to elective office must turn to others for the financial support they need.[14]

This necessity opens an opportunity for formal and informal groups to advance candidates of their own choice. The private deliberations of little groups with access to money take on the qualities of nominating conventions.[15] They decide whether to put up the money needed by an applicant for their help, or whether to look around for someone else among those who are politically available. A highly varied interplay goes on between available aspirants and likely backers, the initiative differing in individual cases with the political strength of the potential candidates and with the potential veto power of the financial groups. Financial backers are sometimes forced to "buy in" to a candidate whose electoral strength frees him from total dependence on their help;[16] at other times their word can be sufficient to snuff out the hopes of one who lacks major popular appeal and has no alternative sources of funds.

The party organization.—In many states with stiff party competition, the party organization itself actively participates in the naming of nominees. Organization leaders, including party fund-raisers, become a nominating group that endorses a slate of candidates for the party ticket.[17] The financial resources of an aspirant may add conclusively

14. Even rich men are said to face certain technical difficulties in making their assets liquid in inconspicuous ways so that funds will be available at the time needed. Gradual withdrawals of modest sums over a period of two years, to be held in cash in the wall safe, was recommended by the old pros to one wealthy novice who had political aspirations. The candidate of great personal wealth is also under a handicap in fund-raising. Averell Harriman, in particular, at least before he became Governor of New York, suffered from the disinclination of supporters to contribute to his political activities. As one of them put it: "I've got three million. Harriman's got forty. Let him use his own."

15. A few years ago an important officeholder in California called a meeting of key political associates to advise him on whether to seek his party's nomination for an even higher post. Four of the six were significant as fund-raisers, and a fifth was the party chairman. (The prospective candidate decided against an attempt at that time, in a later year ran and won.) Solicitors and contributors frequently report, in confidence, sums they have put up to enable a prospect to "get around the state to speak and meet people" in order to learn whether he can generate a popular pull.

16. Alert candidates are wary of unsolicited financial backing, especially early in the game when a little money goes a long way. One candidate for governor of New Jersey was reportedly offered $100,000 by "the race track people" while still seeking his party's nomination. He declined it, went on to win the nomination and election.

17. For example, with regard to New York County, the New York State Crime Commission concluded from the testimony of political leaders that "the control over the selection of candidates for elective county-wide positions resides

to his attractiveness to party leaders. Franklin Roosevelt's entry into politics was facilitated, if not effected, by the belief he could be pried loose from "a serviceable wad of money" to assist the cause of Democrats in Dutchess County.[18] At a later date he was urged for the New York gubernatorial nomination by an organization man with the argument, one of four advanced, that he was worth several million dollars and could finance his own campaign if necessary.[19] More usual, however, is the organization's interest in the financial supporters who can provide funds if their man receives endorsement by the organization. A party chairman in Cook County, Illinois, said they put it bluntly to a candidate: "Can you raise the money necessary for an effective campaign?"[20] The separate campaign headquarters maintained by candidates frequently stem from their obligation to raise this money.

It is generally thought improper for organization leaders to spend party funds in nomination contests. To do so cools the enthusiasm of other factions in the party who are asked to contribute to the party coffers. Their money might be used against their own candidates when nominations are next made. Nonetheless, the practice is encountered in many localities. Republican county committees in Pennsylvania have caused concern to state finance officials on this account. In Maryland, in 1952, official reports indicated that some local party committees made expenditures on behalf of Senator Taft's ambitions for the Republican presidential nomination. In the crossfiling system formerly used in California, candidates of both parties customarily entered the primaries of both parties. The primary thereby became a contest between parties as well as among candidates, and party organizations were known to put

ultimately in the county leaders of the respective parties. It was further established that the candidates to be elected from areas smaller than a county are named by the district leaders from such areas."—*Second Report* (Legislative Document No. 40, 1953), p. 15. A veteran observer of Chicago politics emphasized that the principal purpose for which influence is used within both the Republican and Democratic organizations in that city is to affect the choice of nominees. Practices differ widely in different electoral settings, and even between the parties in the same setting.

18. Frank Freidel, *Franklin D. Roosevelt—The Apprenticeship* (Boston: Little, Brown and Company, 1952), pp. 87-88.

19. *Ibid.*, pp. 146-47.

20. Among the persons seeking organization endorsement for the Republican nomination for mayor of Chicago in 1954 was Samuel L. Workman, a wealthy business machine manufacturer. The press reported that Mr. Workman assured the organization slatemakers—they hold formal hearings—that he and his friends could raise the $500,000 needed for his primary and general election expenses.—*Chicago Sun-Times,* December 10, 1954. Robert E. Merriam, who became the Republican nominee, recalled the "vexsome problem of financing. When I was first asked to consider being a candidate for mayor this was one of the questions to which I gave early serious consideration. Those in the know said that it would cost $500,000 to wage a good campaign in the city of Chicago. Where was such a sum to come from?"—Robert E. Merriam and Rachel M. Goetz, *Going Into Politics* (New York: Harper and Brothers, 1957), p. 38.

party money behind favored candidates. At times, even national Democratic and Republican leaders have been charged with using funds of their committees in factional controversies over party nominations.[21] In New York, certain Assembly District leaders have employed party funds to finance primary contests in violation of state law. One such leader, asked if he knew he had been engaged in illegal activity, replied that he did not, and from his length of time in politics he presumed that all political clubs did the same thing.[22]

The use of party funds can considerably enhance the freedom of the organization in choosing whom it will endorse for a nomination. A candidate seeking organization support may or may not thus be relieved from giving certain financial guarantees, but if he is an affluent type, his wealth may become less a source of persuasion that it would otherwise have been. On the other hand, the decline of patronage and other sources of party power has loosened the organizational grip on the nominating process, thus opening the way for greater influence in nominations by sources of money outside the control of the organization. When factions war for control of the party, candidates for nomination to crucial posts are likely to receive generous financial aid from their respective factional supporters, including those whose control of the party organization is threatened. When a general-election victory is in the air, party managers are more inclined than otherwise to allocate their scarce resources to the support of particular candidates.[23] Despite

21. Hugh A. Bone reports, of the 1954 California primary, that Democratic candidates in 13 districts were aided by grants from Washington.—*Party Committees and National Politics* (Seattle: University of Washington Press, 1958), p. 143. The realities are not easy to determine. Fund-raisers often support individual politicians as well as the party itself. Money that might have gone to a party committee can often be diverted to a nomination campaign without passing through anybody's books. There is a custom, sometimes honored, that the deficit of an unsuccessful aspirant for the presidential nomination is taken over by those charged with financing the ensuing election campaign. The practice, when followed, seems to soothe the nerves of the disappointed loser and increase his enthusiasm for the party ticket.

22. New York State Crime commission, *op. cit.,* pp. 11-12. In 1955, a suit was brought by a Democratic Assembly District leader to bar the use of political club funds in financing primary election campaigns, which was described as "the usual method of financing such campaigns."—*New York Times,* August 26, 1955.

23. It is ancient practice to assess candidates for the privilege of running on the party's ticket—a financial requirement, where it exists, that must be added to the others facing those who seek public office and their backers. In the last century, party bosses frequently exacted payments from candidates for the party organization. A candidate for judge might be assessed $15,000, one for Congress $4,000, one for the state legislature, $1,500.—Frederick W. Whitridge, "Political Assessments," in John J. Lalor (ed.), *Cyclopedia of Political Science* (Chicago: Rand, McNally & Co., 1882), vol. 1, pp. 152-55.

When control over nominations is tight in areas of likely party victory, there is a special temptation to charge candidates for the privilege of representing the party. Candidate assessments or contributions show up on reports in many states,

these practices, however, party organizations generally expect prospective candidates, or their friends, to raise all the money needed for a nomination campaign, and to provide substantial assistance in meeting the costs of the general election.[24]

Interest groups.—Outside the party organization, other groups, both organized and informal, recognize their stake in nominations. Some know well that their greatest political victories are won in battles that never get fought. If enough men whom they consider "good men" get nominated and elected, the legislative and administrative battles take care of themselves.[25] It is in this spirit that Joseph T. Meek has for

---

but the amounts and the flexibility of the requirement vary greatly from place to place.

There is some history of the practice in New York City.—New York State Crime Commission, *op. cit.,* p. 11. In Illinois, Democratic general-election candidates have at times been expected to contribute the equivalent of one month's salary of the job sought to the Cook County organization, and Republican candidates have also been subject to regular assessments. Reports of both Republican and Democratic state central committees in Indiana show elective officials among the givers, with "candidate assessments to the Republican state convention" running over $26,000 in one year. The Republican candidate for United States Senate reported paying a $2,000 party assessment in 1952. In most Indiana counties, candidates for county office are expected to give a fixed percentage of their anticipated salary to the campaign fund. Each candidate in the Democratic primary of one Kansas county chipped in 1 per cent of the first year's income of the post he was seeking to help pay the party's costs of holding the primary.

Until the late 1940's, Democratic members of the United States House of Representatives paid modest "voluntary assessments" to help support their Congressional campaign committee. Political assessment of public officials is familiar in some European parties.

24. The burden is likely to fall most heavily on the candidate when his party's chances of success are dim. Henry V. Poor discovered that he personally had to raise virtually all of the $15,000 needed to run, as a sure loser, on the Republican ticket for Congress against Franklin D. Roosevelt, Jr., in 1950, a role he accepted at the behest of the Republican chairman of New York County.—"What It Costs to Run for Office," *Harper's,* May, 1954, pp. 46-52. One Democratic nominee for Congress from Connecticut found to his dismay he could expect little or no help from party sources. The measure of his plight was revealed when he appealed to the person he had just narrowly defeated for the nomination to pay the costs of his campaign.

25. Much the same sentiment has prompted groups of contributors to furnish officeholders with money between elections. Good men are more likely to get nominated and elected again if they can keep their fences mended between elections. In 1955, it became known that a number of supporters had provided Senator Prescott Bush of Connecticut with a fund of $25,000 or more to help finance his interelection campaigning.—Drew Pearson, *The News and Observer* (Raleigh, N.C.), June 14, 1955. The Bush Fund resembled the Nixon Fund which became an issue in the 1952 presidential campaign. Some 76 of Mr. Nixon's supporters gave at least $18,000 to help him send Christmas cards and otherwise bear the costs of serving and remaining, in one capacity or another, in the United States Senate. (The history of the fund and the controversy it produced are described in Earl Mazo, *Richard Nixon—A Political and Personal Portrait* (New York: Harper & Brothers Publishers, 1959), pp. 101-37.)

It is difficult to discern a basic difference between such funds and more con-years urged businessmen to encourage sound candidates to run for public office. Mr. Meek, long the executive secretary of the Illinois Federation of Retail Associations and the unsuccessful Republican candidate for United States Senator against Paul H. Douglas in 1954, has called it an investment. Make an investment in the individual, before he is elected. "You buy life insurance, you buy fire insurance, you buy health insurance, why shouldn't you buy insurance for good legislative performance?" Mr. Meek has advocated—and he has been judged by some as the most effective legislative lobbyist in the history of Illinois—that his clientele seek out men who will make good candidates and give them personal and financial support.[26] It is a type of political action that interest groups of many kinds would like to emulate and that some, including labor unions, actually do.[27]

As is true in many other nations, organized groups in the United States play many different and important parts in the nominating

ventional campaign donations. When one election is over, politicians begin campaigning for the next. If campaign gifts and expenditures are to be sanctioned during the year of an election, it would seem they are equally appropriate the year before or the year after. The politicians usually deny themselves the right to this position by failing to report interelection campaign funds in the same manner they report election-year funds.

The revelation of the Nixon Fund in 1952 led many of that Senator's defenders to point out the existence of similar kinds of arrangements entered into by other elected officials. Senator George D. Aiken of Vermont claimed that "many" senators supplement their income from outside sources, mentioning specifically that some state party committees augment the expense accounts of senators.—*New York Times,* September 21, 1952.

A privately subscribed fund in Illinois out of which the salaries of certain state officials were supplemented while Adlai Stevenson was governor was also made an issue in the same campaign. The purpose of the Illinois fund was to make state salaries high enough to enable men of the quality desired by Mr. Stevenson to accept them. During the ruckus it was recalled that the salary of Woodrow Wilson's Ambassador to the Court of St. James, Walter Hines Page, was supplemented by $25,000 per year, reportedly the gift of Cleveland H. Dodge. Incoming governors and presidents have frequently found it awkward to finance the semi-official activities of themselves and their aides between election and inauguration, sometimes leading to an appeal for private contributions.

26. Mr. Meek has expressed himself in many places. The quotation is from a lecture on state and local legislative activities before the Northwestern School of Commerce, January 24, 1947.

27. The political representatives of special interest groups cruise around many states contacting prospective legislative candidates, urging some of them to run, and arranging to back with money those who do. Democratic-Farmer Labor politicians in Minnesota have complained that candidates for the nonpartisan legislature of their state are particularly susceptible to such blandishments. Lacking the steadying influence of a party label, some legislative candidates "straddle, pollyfox and even wobble" in the face of pressures and inducements emanating from fund-raisers. The similar activities of Arthur H. Samish, for many years the political representative of beer, liquor, and sundry other interests in California, were explored in some detail by the Kefauver Crime Committee.—*Hearings,* part 10, pp. 1161-1228.

process.[28] One group may endorse an individual publicly by formal action. Another may offer covert encouragement through members who speak for the sentiment in their group. The clincher in discussions with a prospective candidate is often some assurance of financial help, and this is more valuable and potentially more influential when it comes early in a prospect's deliberations.[29] Willingness to supply money becomes the outward and tangible sign of a group's interest in an aspirant. Refusal to do so has created many a disappointed office seeker. In jurisdictions with politically active labor organizations, contests for places on the Democratic ticket (and sometimes the Republican ticket) have been decisively affected by the ability of labor leaders to grant or withhold financial support. Other groups with explicit political objectives and a program of open political action have played similar roles. The most influential activity in prenomination politics, however, is not formal action by interest groups. Far more important are the machinations of persons who belong to such groups, or who have access to them, and who sit in councils where candidates are proposed and sifted. There they sometimes serve as an authorized spokesman, sometimes as an informed judge of how far the group's members will go in supporting whom.[30]

Solicitors.—The influence exercised in these processes by formal organizations and their spokesmen is less than the influence of more broadly oriented political fund-raisers. Such fund-raisers often know, or can persuade others that they know, which candidates their financial constituents will and will not support. Such political financiers, if they choose to work at it, can develop considerable weight in party and

28. In Japan, pressure groups even nominate and support their own candidates for the House of Councillors. See Henry Ehrmann (ed.), *Interest Groups on Four Continents* (Pittsburgh: University of Pittsburgh Press, 1958), pp. 152, 265-67. The role in nominations of the German sponsors' associations is discussed in Arnold J. Heidenheimer, "German Party Finance: The CDU," *American Political Science Review,* 51 (1957), 378-79.

29. Writing of nominating politics in Georgia's one-party system, Joseph L. Bernd has observed: "The value of money to the candidate who receives it depends not only upon the amount but also upon the timing of the donation. Five or ten thousand dollars may be vital during the pre-campaign maneuvering, while the same amount, contributed after the bandwagon has begun to roll, may be of negligible importance."—*The Role of Campaign Funds in Georgia Primary Elections, 1936-1958* (Macon: The Georgia Journal, Inc., 1958), p. 4.

30. Former Governor Johnston Murray of Oklahoma reports that he was notified that if he would oppose Senator Robert S. Kerr for the United States Senate in 1954, a war chest of $300,000 would be at his disposal.—"Oklahoma Is in a Mess," *Saturday Evening Post,* April 30, 1955, p. 96. Everybody seems agreed that in Texas the big money people take an "affirmative hand"—as one fund-raiser phrased it—in pre-primary nominating matters, especially for statewide offices. The involvement of such groups allegedly reached the point in California whereby "reactionaries" gave heavily to the gubernatorial nominating campaign of liberal Culbert Olson in 1938 on the theory that he was the Democrat they could beat in the ensuing election.—Robert E. Burke, *Olson's New Deal for California* (Berkeley and Los Angeles: University of California Press, 1953), p. 18.

factional councils where candidacies are debated and frequently decided. Edward H. Heller of San Francisco has long been the most conspicuous Democratic contributor and solicitor in California. An important businessman, he has not sought office but has displayed a continuing interest in the "ideological" goals of his party. In the language of the precincts, "he's not out for himself." All he wants, a close associate observed, is a little something to say about who the candidates are. Mr. Heller has in fact taken a very influential part in the intricate and indirect processes by which California Democratic candidates are chosen,[31] doubtless the most significant aspect of his role as a contributor and solicitor of large funds.[32] His counterparts are discovered in all states and most smaller jurisdictions and form a characteristic part of the top echelon of factional and party hierarchies.

The relationships between those who would like to become nominees and those who command political funds are of many kinds. At one extreme, total initiative lies with the financiers who induce a likely prospect to make a race; at the other, financial politicians feel lucky to get on the bandwagon of a popular tyro who cannot be stopped.[33] Following World War II many seasoned politicos had their eyes opened by the success of brash young veterans who ran for office without the customary advance consultations. In such circumstances, the financial politicians as well as others are likely to settle on the most acceptable alternative before them. As for the candidates themselves, when the harsh necessities of campaigning begin to press, they usually welcome the aid such sources can provide. Financial backers, as a matter of fact, are frequently frustrated by the difficulties of locating good candidates who by their lights would make good officeholders. In one large city the names of

31. Graphically described as they then were by Dean R. Cresap, *Party Politics in the Golden State* (Los Angeles: The Haynes Foundation, 1954), pp. 77-89; and by Don M. Muchmore, "Party and Candidate in California," in David Farrelly and Ivan Hinderaker, *The Politics of California—A Book of Readings* (New York: Ronald Press Company, 1951), esp. pp. 91-93.

32. Peter H. Odegard's inability to discuss with Mr. Heller, then finance chairman of the Democratic State Central Committee, his candidacy for the United States Senatorial nomination seems to have contributed to his decision not to seek the endorsement of the California Democratic Council convention in 1954.—Francis Carney, *The Rise of the Democratic Clubs in California* (New York: Henry Holt and Company, 1958), pp. 14-15.

33. Perhaps as representative as any was the experience of a group of some thirty men with financial resources who looked around Tennessee in 1954 to find someone to whip Senator Estes Kefauver. They got in touch with a former senator, but he was not interested. Before they could produce a likely prospect of their own, the campaign talk of United States Representative Pat Sutton came to their attention. Sutton's war record troubled the group, one of its members reported. "A man who got as many medals as Sutton did must be either reckless or foolish." They grilled him for three hours, nevertheless, the report goes, and found only one or two of his ideas "wrong." So they adopted him and started raising money. They were doomed to disappointment, however, in both the candidate and the outcome.

unappealing prospects for mayor were paraded before a group of important businessmen interested in the governmental reform and commercial revitalization of their area. Finally, a young man appeared with the requisite political sex appeal and the right ideas. "We grabbed him," one of those who put up the money recalled with relief. At first the young man was reluctant. Once "persuaded," he turned to and won. Later, when the Mayor was itching for higher office, his needs again came up for discussion. If the $300,000 necessary for nomination and election could be found, he would make a try. If not, he would not. He tried and, this time, lost.

Financial leeway is of great convenience to those in search of a candidate. Democratic leadership, state and national, concluded in 1928 that Franklin Roosevelt would make the strongest candidate who could be nominated for governor of New York. Moreover, he would improve Governor Smith's chances of carrying New York for the presidency. Roosevelt protested. He had a financial commitment to aid in expanding the facilities at Warm Springs for treating victims of infantile paralysis. In a counter move, John J. Raskob promised to give $50,000 himself and to raise three times that much from others.[34] Not infrequently, candidates have been promised help in meeting old debts and other obligations, as well as in meeting the costs of a campaign, if they will seek nomination for an office.[35] To make and meet commitments of this kind requires that contributors be organized to act in concert. The organization is usually quite informal, and is achieved in the person of the principal fund-raisers who know the interests of those from whom they solicit.[36]

Fund-raisers, and the contributors behind them, can be effective also in discouraging persons from becoming candidates for a nomination. In 1948, a liberal Democrat spent several months campaigning around his district in California in hopes of becoming the Democratic nominee for Congress. He eventually abandoned the effort. It became apparent that the only source of the needed campaign funds, said to have been $2,000, was a labor organization, and the leaders in control of the money preferred another man. The decision in 1956 of the late Walter F. George to retire after 34 years in the United States Senate illustrated vividly the power of financial backers over nominations. Senator George had announced he would seek nomination in the Georgia Democratic primary, as he had six times before. But the nomination was also desired by for-

34. Bernard Bellush, *Franklin D. Roosevelt as Governor of New York* (New York: Columbia University Press, 1955), pp. 8-9.

35. One incident that reached public notice was the guarantee that Lieutenant Governor Joe R. Hanley of New York said he received if he would agree to run for United States senator, instead of for governor of that state, in 1950. He would be enabled to pay off some personal debts whether he won or lost.—*New York Times*, February 20, 1955.

36. See the discussion of the fund-raiser as a political middleman, pages 259-81, above.

mer Governor Herman Talmadge. The Governor was younger and more vigorous and had a political life expectancy of about 40 years longer. In this context, the advice of financial advisers that the sources of funds were against him and that he should withdraw was sufficient for the Senator.[37] The sequence of events is not always so neat, and candidates forced to withdraw from a lost cause find the absence of financial backing a somewhat more palatable reason to give publicly than the absence of popular support.[38] But the proportion of potential candidacies pinched off by the negative attitude of political financiers is far greater than ever reaches public notice. Sometimes candidates anticipate the financial reactions. It is extraordinarily difficult to get men of achievement to run for public office on the Republican ticket throughout most of the South. Progressive Republicans thought they had such a businessman lined up to make the race for governor of Louisiana in 1956. A few days before President Eisenhower vetoed the natural gas bill, the prospective candidate told party leaders that a veto would make it impossible for him to run. His associates in the oil and gas companies would not put up the money for him to campaign on the same ticket with a president who had vetoed the act.

Key fund-raisers are likely to be active in all phases of political finance, giving the contributors and interests they represent a voice in nominations that often is crucial.[39] Solicitors temporarily dragooned

37. The George-Talmadge relationship in a rapidly changing Georgia was described by George McMillan in ". . . So Goes the South," *Collier's,* June 8, 1956, pp. 42-47. It was stated that in California, in 1958, Governor Goodwin J. Knight agreed to refrain from running for governor that year only after being told by Republican fund-raisers they would not finance his campaign if he did.

38. Among those whose withdrawal in recent years has been attributed by themselves or their supporters to lack of funds are New York's famed Judge Samuel S. Leibowitz, designated by the city Fusion party in 1953 as its candidate for mayor (*New York Times,* July 2, 1953) ; Governor Roy J. Turner of Oklahoma, who dropped out of the 1954 race for the Democratic nomination for United States senator against incumbent Robert S. Kerr (*ibid.,* July 14, 1954) ; Clendenin J. Ryan, independent candidate for governor of New Jersey in 1953 (*ibid.,* September 1, 1953) ; Robert Whitehead, aspirant for the Democratic nomination for governor of Virginia in 1953 (*Richmond Times-Dispatch,* February 26, 1953) ; and Addison Hewlett, who abandoned his ambitions for North Carolina's Democratic gubernatorial nomination in 1960 (*The News and Observer* [Raleigh, N.C.], January 22, 1960).

The illustrations are not confined to the United States. When Carlos P. Romulo withdrew his candidacy for president of the Philippines in 1953, he declared his party's treasury bankrupt and observers reported a switch in the financial interests that had hitherto backed him.—*Evening Star* (Washington, D.C.), August 21, 1953.

39. The paucity of financial information concerning nominations precludes a systematic comparison of contributors to nomination and election campaigns. Some important contributors obviously confine their donations to the general election. These are likely to be persons who give to the party more or less regularly out of habit and who are not deeply involved politically. There are others, especially in states of lopsided party strength, who give only to nomination campaigns.

Among *large* givers, however, the overlap seems to be considerable between

into money-raising out of party or personal loyalty are not likely to be active in nomination finances. Nor are the novices most important who appear in almost every campaign attached to individual candidates, even though some render important financial services for a short period. The fund-raisers who stay with it continuously are the ones who show up in the private councils where candidates for nomination are decided upon, and where the character of political life is molded.

3. PRESIDENTIAL NOMINATIONS: A SPECIAL CASE

The opaque mists that enshroud nominating finances in general also envelope presidential nominations. Occasional breaks in the haze make it possible, nevertheless, to discern many of the same basic features that characterize nominations for lesser posts. As at lower levels, non-financial factors influence presidential nominations, only more so. As in contests for other offices, the factional followings of candidates differ sharply from each other. The problems and opportunities before individuals who would seek the presidency are determined by many conditions, often personal, lending great individuality to presidential nominating campaigns and to their finances.[40] When the candidacy is sought through active campaigning, especially in primaries, funds become necessary. For candidates who cannot provide their own, financial backers are essential.

By comparison with general-election campaigns, few financial records are kept in the pre-convention period. Those that are kept are destroyed or disappear into files that quickly become locked or lost. The absence of any federal reporting requirement makes campaign treasurers reluctant

---

those who support nomination and general-election activities. The significance of the choice of candidates is not lost on those who give the largest sums to general elections. Among 259 persons who gave $5,000 or more in general-election campaign contributions in 1956, 73 (28 per cent) said they also gave to the war chests of persons seeking party nominations. Some persons among the 259 declined to provide information regarding their gifts to nomination campaigns, and the list of 259 was selected at the outset from general election contributors, so the true overlap is unquestionably higher.

As a group, the 73 who gave to nomination as well as election activities were highly involved politically. Thirty-one gave to aspirants to the presidential nomination, as well as to other candidates for nomination. All but six of the 73 made contributions at two or more levels of government, and about three-fifths of them made donations at three or more levels, and most of them gave to a large number of different recipients.

40. One factor that affects the level and character of presidential nominating costs is the nature of the competition for the nomination. A president desiring to succeed himself faces only minor pre-convention campaign problems (e.g. Ike in 1956) compared to the leader of an insurgent faction that must win in a contest with the previous leadership (e.g. F.D.R. in 1932). Although not designed for our purposes, the classification of presidential nominations made by Paul T. David and Ralph M. Goldman is of interest. They found three types which have operated to confirm existing party leadership and seven in which succession in party leadership comes about.—"Presidential Nominating Patterns," *Western Political Quarterly,* 8 (1955), 865-80.

to let outsiders see their records. What they interpret as a public policy on general-election finances often induces treasurers to make more information available concerning general elections that they are technically required to do by law. If contributors object to such disclosures, campaign accountants can reply that most of the information is supposedly made public anyway. In the absence of this protection, and in the presence of the highly personal quality of many pre-convention activities, candidates and their managers are generally silent to requests for financial information.

The cost of a nomination.—In 1957, a strategy conference assembled by one aspiring politician produced a presidential nomination budget of $2,600,000. The proposed timetable called for considerable build-up activity and culminated in expenditures during 1960 of something over $1,000,000. Based on past experience, how realistic was the estimate?

The sums needed always depend on what is done. The only organized campaign committee backing the reluctant Stevenson in 1952 spent slightly less than $20,000 between February and the end of the convention in July.[41] The Governor and his personal associates only spent around $1,350, most of it during Democratic convention week and much of that on "liquor for newsmen." At the same time, however, Senator Kefauver's open candidacy for the Democratic nomination required at least $356,387. The Senator claimed that while he had been supported by a good many small committees that were somewhat spontaneous and unorganized—he entered presidential primaries in 13 states—the campaign was financed almost entirely through one national committee, and this figure therefore gave a substantially true picture of the costs of his campaign.[42]

The principal national campaign group seeking the Republican presidential nomination for Dwight D. Eisenhower in 1952, the Citizens for Eisenhower, handled around $1,200,000, between $500,000 and $600,000 of the sum reportedly expended in states where presidential primaries were held.[43] Additional substantial amounts were raised and spent by other groups throughout the country. One such, with headquarters in Memphis, between November, 1951, and the nomination raised $220,000 from contributors around the South. Some $60,000 was left over and used in the subsequent general election. Fifty state and local committees in South Dakota reported spending around $45,000 for Ike's nomination.[44] While at least $16,000 of this came officially from the

41. Johnson, *op. cit.*, p. 118.

42. One report filed in Florida showed expenditures between April 4 and June 2, 1952, of $7,538, of which $5,101 came from Kefauver's offices in Washington.

43. Testimony of Walter Williams, a principal leader.—U.S. House of Representatives Special Committee to Investigate Campaign Expenditures, 1952 *Hearings*, p. 111. Hugh A. Bone cites a total of $1,500,000, apparently based on a later interview with Mr. Williams.—*Op. cit.*, p. 29.

44. It was said of the contest for delegates: "It is probably safe to say that the campaign ranked as the most costly primary ever waged in South Dakota."—David, Moos, and Goldman, *op. cit.*, vol. 4, p. 266.

national-level committee, most of the rest apparently came from elsewhere. Estimates of amounts spent in several states are available, but the proportion coming from local sources is not clear. Eisenhower expenditures in New Jersey were put at $75,000, in New Hampshire at $65,000, in the third Congressional District of Maine at $4,000, and in Oregon at around $43,000 through a state-level committee, plus additional sums raised and spent through county committees.[45] Guesses in Texas ran into the millions, though later interviews with persons active in the campaign made them seem exaggerated.[46]

One Eisenhower adviser, during the discussions before Ike agreed to run in 1952, is said to have estimated that $4,000,000 would be needed to create the climate of opinion and do the other things necessary to get him into the race and nominated. It would seem that organized pre-convention efforts at all levels totalled at least $2,500,000, which is probably as good an estimate as any of the total thus involved. Time, goods, and services contributed without reimbursement by individuals and organizations to the Eisenhower nomination effort clearly had a dollar value running into additional millions.[47] Taft expenditures on behalf of the 1952 nomination appeared to run above those of Eisenhower, in part because the Taft candidacy was launched much earlier.[48]

45. *Ibid.*, vol. 2, pp. 197, 37, 13; vol. 5, p. 200.

46. The most accurate statement on "the large sums of money which were undoubtedly spent in Texas" came from O. Douglas Weeks: "no trustworthy estimate can be made of the receipts and expenditures connected with the pre-convention campaigns in behalf of the various delegations."—*Texas Presidential Politics in 1952* (Austin: Institute of Public Affairs, University of Texas, 1953) (Public Affairs Series No. 16), p. 95.

47. It is never possible to estimate with confidence the aggregate value of such contributions in kind. One person who kept some kind of tally thought that one corporation alone, an automobile manufacturer, had in this way indirectly aided Ike's pre-convention activities to the value of about $1,250,000. Some measure of the involvement of business leaders is suggested by the fact that, on a single day in 1952, the headquarters of the Michigan delegation to the Republican national convention was visited by six top officials of the motor industry: Henry Ford II, Ernest R. Breech, and John S. Bugas of the Ford Motor Company; Charles E. Wilson, Harlow Curtice, and Harry Anderson of the General Motors Corporation. —David, Moos, and Goldman, *op. cit.*, vol. 4, p. 53. Business and banking pressures rather than political pressures are said to have been responsible for the shift of some delegate support from Taft to Ike.

The political activities of business leaders were always important in Senator Taft's attempts to win the nomination and were a central factor in Wendell Willkie's 1940 nomination.—Donald Bruce Johnson, "Wendell Willkie and the Republican Party" (Ph.D. dissertation, University of Illinois, 1952), pp. 54-115. Company activities take many forms. It was reported that in anticipation of the 1960 Democratic convention Governor Robert B. Meyner of New Jersey went on a speaking tour in 1958, using an airplane placed at his disposal by Engelhard Industries of New Jersey.—*New York Times,* August 5, 1958.

48. When queries were put to Benjamin E. Tate, long Taft's finance chief, he said he had neither the files nor the time to answer, but he volunteered two generalizations: "No. 1. The amount of money spent in politics is completely indecent. No. 2. One half of the money is wasted but you do not know which

The less important candidates in 1952, and their backers, are no more informative on the subject of the sums spent in pre-convention campaigning. Senator Richard B. Russell entered the primary only in Florida. A report filed in that state showed expenditures of $27,800, of which $6,000 was noted as coming from Russell's Atlanta headquarters. One Texan thought he knew where $75,000 for Russell's effort came from. Judging from external appearances, this amount may have been enough to finance all the limited activities of the Senator's central headquarters. Some $200,000 was said to have been put by another contributor into various activities on behalf of General MacArthur. The Kerr and Harriman gestures toward the Democratic nomination and the Stassen try for the Republican position together ran into hundreds of thousands of dollars.[49] In all, in 1952, probably around $5,000,000 was handled through headquarters at the *national* level on behalf of all candidates for the presidential nomination. Perhaps one-fourth or one-third of this was passed on to state and local groups for use within their localities, so that expenditures actually made at the *national* level may have run around $3,500,000. Total costs at all levels ran to at least twice this figure, with goods and services contributed in kind also being counted in millions.[50]

In the absence of an open contest for the Republican nomination, total presidential nominating costs in 1956 fell. Democrats Stevenson and Kefauver nevertheless went at it hammer and tongs in a series of grueling and costly presidential primaries, and others, notably Governor Harriman, carried on a campaign for the nomination. Reports on Kefauver's central expenditures are not available, but he was said to have wound up with a deficit of $40,000 or more and with total costs through *national* headquarters comparable to those of 1952.[51] Republicans

half." Estimates of Taft expenditures ran to $250,000 in New Jersey, $50,000 in New Hampshire, at least $58,000 in Ohio.—David, Moos, and Goldman, *op. cit.*, vol. 2, pp. 197, 37; vol. 4, p. 18. About 40 Taft committees in South Dakota reported spending slightly more than $40,000.

49. Senator Brien McMahon of Connecticut lay dying of cancer during the Democratic convention. He was honored by having his name placed in nomination. The McMahon for President Club reported disbursing $5,950 of which $323 was turned over to the Damon Runyan Memorial Fund.

50. In populous California, Democratic pre-primary campaigning was estimated at a maximum of $100,000. On the Republican side, Governor Warren's campaigning was estimated at between $50,000 and $100,000 (with highest guesses reaching $150,000), and the anti-Warren forces were said to have spent around $500,000, with some claims running to twice that sum.—David, Moos, and Goldman, *op. cit.*, vol. 5, pp. 227-28.

51. The deficit figure was widely quoted in the press. On May 23, 1956, Bascom N. Timmons quoted the Kefauver headquarters as saying that up to that time $125,000 had been collected and spent for the Senator.—*The News and Observer* (Raleigh, N.C.), May 23, 1956. The corresponding Stevenson figure was "at least" $375,000, which was slightly less than half of what proved to be the expenditures of the two chief Stevenson national-level groups for the whole campaign.

charged during the later general-election campaign that Harriman had spent some $2,000,000 seeking the Democratic nomination, which he denied.[52] Two national-level committees were active on behalf of Steven-

Table 42

DISBURSEMENTS BY TWO NATIONAL-LEVEL PRESIDENTIAL NOMINATION CAMPAIGN COMMITTEES FOR STEVENSON, 1956

	National Stevenson for President Committee 11/22/55-4/20/58	Stevenson Campaign Committee to 8/31/57	Total
Total disbursements	$297,447	$ 565,580	$ 863,027
Transferred from NSPC to SCC	−79,175	....	− 79,175
Net disbursements	218,272	565,580	783,852
Transferred to state groups	−39,741	−115,530	−155,271
Direct expenditures	$178,531	$450,050	$628,581

son, the National Stevenson for President Committee and the Stevenson Campaign Committee. As indicated in Table 42, the combined net disbursements of these two *national-level* groups alone came to $783,852, of which $628,581 were direct expenditures.[53]

There is little opportunity to compare presidential nominating expenses in 1952 or 1956 with those of earlier years. Congressional inquiries into campaigns as far back as 1912 have exposed minimum expenditures on behalf of single candidates running into hundreds of thousands of dollars. Sums adding up to $1,773,303 were spent on behalf of Leonard Wood for the 1920 Republican presidential nomination, when each dollar was worth considerably more than in 1956, and the total did not include activities of many state and local groups.[54] Even when gross totals of this sort have been known, there has been little information on ways the money was used. It seems evident that the presidential primaries have increased presidential nominating costs. Indeed, increased costs are frequently a product of increased popularization of politics. In the struggles for delegates under the old state-convention systems of the nineteenth century, funds were used notoriously.

52. *New York Times,* December 11 and 15, 1956. After Governor Harriman's defeat in the New York gubernatorial election of 1958, an effort was made to learn something about the financial aspects of his past presidential nominating activities. A close associate reported his impression that it would be several years, at least, before Harriman would give out any information. "Harriman is as close-mouthed about his personal affairs as anyone I've ever known."

53. One got the impression that Stevenson's state-level expenditures outran Kefauver's in several areas. In Minnesota, Stevenson's backers were said to have spent at least $100,000 and Kefauver about one-fifth that sum.—Drew Pearson in *The News and Observer* (Raleigh, N.C.), March 24, 1956.

54. Louise Overacker, *The Presidential Primary* (New York: The Macmillan Company, 1926), pp. 149-58; also her *Money in Elections* (New York: The Macmillan Company, 1932), pp. 69-70.

In many instances delegates were bribed outright. Convention politics can be expensive, even in the absence of corruption, but primary campaigning costs more.[55] The number of states providing for presidential primaries reached a peak in 1916, with several states abandoning them after that date. In 1956, there were 19 states that provided for one type of presidential primary or another, and in three other areas delegates to the national conventions could be selected at primaries with no direct vote being cast for president or vice president.[56] Inevitably, candidates who enter the presidential primaries must be prepared to meet the financial requirements of popular election campaigning.

The nature of nominating costs.—The costs of campaigning within individual states comprise one broad category of presidential nominating expense. Where presidential primaries are held, the level and character of expenditures are subject to many variables that affect the costs of state campaigns generally.[57] In all states, however, political leaders and convention delegates are sensitive to the mood of the electorate. Even where delegates are not chosen by primary, an appealing popular image of the candidate is important. Moreover, if a nomination is to be pursued, the favor of state and local factions must be curried. A great deal of travel, writing, and talking go into this last endeavor, with free meals and entertainment along the way.[58] Even passive candidates have trusted friends or paid specialists on the road sounding the local sentiment. As the delegates are chosen, elaborate efforts are undertaken to learn their leanings and to bombard them with appeals.[59]

55. See the discussion in David, Moos, and Goldman, *op. cit.,* vol. 1, pp. 206-7. Cf. footnote 9, page 322, above, for Merriam and Overacker's contrary conclusion.

56. Richard D. Hupman and Samuel H. Still, Jr., *Manner of Selecting Delegates to National Political Conventions and the Nomination and Election of Presidential Electors* (Washington: Government Printing Office, 1955), p. 5. Minnesota and Missouri did away with their presidential primaries in 1959.

57. See pages 380-87, below. In some states, candidates for delegate make personal expenditures, but the written and verbal reports of their outlays indicate that generally they are modest, a condition that seems to have existed from the beginning.—Louise Overacker, *The Presidential Primary,* pp. 150-52. Assessments and other expenses of delegates are discussed in David, Moos, and Goldman, *op. cit.,* vol. 2, p. 199; vol. 4, pp. 82-83, 90, 209, and in the forthcoming volume under Mr. David's senior authorship, *The Politics of National Party Conventions.* In 1952, 4.3 per cent of the delegates to the Democratic national convention and 6.2 per cent of those to the Republican national convention were known to have made at least one campaign contribution of $500 or more to some candidate or political committee.

58. Expenditures of many kinds are required. Averell Harriman, who avoided the presidential-primary route in 1956, announced the appointment in July of that year of a series of regional chairmen and staff personnel to spur his candidacy, some of whom presumably had to be paid.—*New York Times,* July 2, 1956. It was later alleged that Harriman forces offered to pay the back bills of the Kefauver primary campaign if the latter would switch his delegate support to the former.—Marquis Childs, "Harriman Evangelism," *The News and Observer* (Raleigh, N.C.), August 6, 1956.

59. Each major campaign headquarters in 1952 maintained as complete a

The direct expenditures by the two national-level committees behind Adlai Stevenson's 1956 nomination drive are summarized in Table 43.

Table 43

DIRECT EXPENDITURES BY TWO NATIONAL-LEVEL PRESIDENTIAL NOMINATION CAMPAIGN COMMITTEES FOR STEVENSON, 1956

	National Stevenson for President Committee 11/22/55-4/20/58	Stevenson Campaign Committee to 8/31/57	Total	
			$	%
Salaries	*$ 43,825*	*$152,018*	*$195,843*	*31*
Travel	*13,536*	*99,041*	*112,577*	*18*
Publicity and promotion	*71,630*	*82,097*	*153,727*	*24*
Radio and Television	10,133	584	10,717	2
Recordings, pictures, films		23,494	23,494	4
Printing, mailing, postage, press releases	22,516	43,585	66,101	11
Buttons, stickers, etc.	653	3,708	4,361	(a)
Advertising in publications	2,460		2,460	(a)
Meetings, meals, visitors, conferences, etc.	11,645	3,679	15,324	2
Public relations services	13,848		13,848	2
Public opinion surveys, etc.	10,375	7,047	17,422	3
Office expenses	*37,828*	*78,816*	*116,644*	*19*
Equipment and fixtures, purchase and rent, net	4,356	8,722	13,078	2
Telephone and telegraph	12,879	33,473	46,352	7
Rent and light	10,025	13,638	23,663	4
Stationery and supplies	5,054	11,002	16,056	3
Miscellaneous	5,514	11,981	17,495	3
National convention expenses	*315*	*38,078*	*38,393*	*6*
Fund-raising services	*6,000*		*6,000*	*1*
Silver Shoe Committee	*5,397*		*5,397*	*1*
Total direct expenditures	178,531	450,050	628,581	100

[a] Less than 1 per cent.

dossier as possible on every delegate.—David, Moos, and Goldman, *op. cit.*, vol. 1, pp. 189-90. Of the preliminaries to the 1928 Democratic convention, James W. Gerard, a supporter of Al Smith, recalled: ". . . as soon as the delegates were chosen we arranged for private investigators to give us reports on each of them—such things as their business affiliations, religion, and so on."—*My First Eighty-Three Years in America—The Memoirs of James W. Gerard* (Garden City, New York: Doubleday & Company, 1951), pp. 313-14. Mr. Gerard also reported shelling out at the 1932 convention, where he favored Franklin Roosevelt, "eight hundred dollars on the floor of the convention to a western delegate to help him entertain his delegates and keep them happy and loyal."—*Ibid.*, pp. 322-23.

They give some idea of the expenditures that can be made through a central headquarters. Most of the money went in one way or another for publicity and communications. The breakdown available of Estes Kefauver's 1952 central headquarters expenses, in so far as it goes, shows a pattern not greatly at variance with that of Stevenson four years later:

Salaries	$ 85,572	24%
Radio	8,520	2
Television	5,307	2
Printing	46,702	13
Advertising	55,054	16
Rent of quarters	25,673	7
Other	129,559	36
Total	$356,387	100%

How much of the "other" Kefauver expenses took the form of subsidies to states and localities is not known.

Money, in addition to that associated directly with the primaries, is raised and spent through local channels on the initiative of local followers.[60] But the leadership of a presidential nominating campaign must be focused at the top, and the funds needed for a headquarters operation must be raised by those closely associated with the candidate.

The full role of a central organization is not reflected, however, in reports of headquarters expenditures. A substantial share of the money spent in the states is solicited by fund-raisers associated with the central organization. These sums may never go through the books of the headquarters. This seems especially the case with candidates who attract large financing. The 1952 South Dakota Republican primary illustrates the point. About $45,000 was spent through a large number of committees on behalf of Ike's nomination. While $16,000 of this came formally from the national-level committee backing Ike, another $15,000 came from prominent persons like John Hay Whitney of New York and M. Robert Guggenheim of Washington whose gifts were obviously channeled into the state as part of the over-all campaign effort. Mr. Guggenheim's two $3,000 gifts were sent to two of the small Eisenhower committees and, in one case, then transferred to the principal state committee. The same procedure appeared on the Taft side. Slightly more than $40,000 was reported spent, of which $14,000 came in the name of

60. Publicity efforts, for example, are not confined to the national level. The leader of one regional group active for Ike in 1952 reported hiring a retired major general. They gave him a five-minute news broadcast five days a week over 228 radio stations from November, 1951, until the nomination. The broadcasts were nonpolitical to the extent they did not plug Eisenhower's candidacy, but they were otherwise designed to play up the "objectionable" items in the news and to create a demand to change the crowd in Washington. The same group distributed free a filmed television series, as well as conventional campaign material, overtly publicizing the Eisenhower candidacy.

Taft's principal national fund-raiser, Benjamin E. Tate, and at least $11,000 more in the name of non-residents of South Dakota like Charles S. Payson, who incidentally was Mr. Whitney's brother-in-law.

A perspective is gained from analyzing certain Stevenson pre-convention contributions in 1956. There were 259 persons who reported to the Senate Subcommittee on Privileges and Elections political gifts totalling $5,000 or more during 1956. Among these were 28 who said they gave to the Stevenson nomination campaign. Their total contributions for this purpose came to slightly over $129,000, of which $21,500 went to the Stevenson Campaign Committee and $38,500 to the National Stevenson for President Committee, the headquarters groups. Some $69,000, however, or 53 per cent, were directed to committees in eight different states, and the directing was not left entirely to chance. Some of the money may have found its way back to the national groups, but much, perhaps all of it, seemed intended to finance local activities.[61] So much money, in fact, was handled in the Stevenson pre-convention campaign outside the headquarters accounting that Roger L. Stevens, in charge of Mr. Stevenson's finances, declared the headquarters reports meaningless. Mr. Stevens refused to elaborate, but it seems probable from the information in the reports and from other sources that the total Stevenson outlays for the 1956 nomination ran to at least $1,500,000, plus other hundreds of thousands of dollars in gifts of goods and services.[62]

Raising the money.—Expenditures of this size are not always necessary, but no person can actively seek a presidential nomination without a good deal more money at his disposal than most politicians can command.[63] In the earliest stages, when the bug begins to bite hard, an intimate corps of campaign bankers usually goes to work. They are more visible in the history books than at the time. Sixteen months before the Democratic convention of 1912 nominated Woodrow Wilson, "a little group of friends" persuaded him to let them undertake a publicity campaign. The object was "the creation of such a strong public opinion in favor of his candidacy that the pressure could not be resisted by the party leaders." The three friends among themselves raised an initial

61. Two of the Stevenson contributors also gave to Kefauver ($8,500) and two others to Harriman ($2,000). Among the 259 contributors in the analysis, only two others showed gifts to Kefauver ($8,500) and one other to Harriman ($2,500).

62. The salary of one of Stevenson's chief staff members was carried for several months by a member of a prominent publishing family. The value of Roger L. Stevens' time alone, which might be put at $300,000 or $400,000 a year in his other pursuits, would be considerable. (Mr. Stevens has boasted that he raised more money for Stevenson in 1956 than had ever been raised before for a presidential candidate, though how he could know is not clear.)

63. The activities of a rich man during the build-up period are described by Cabell Phillips in "How to Be a Presidential Candidate," *New York Times Magazine,* July 13, 1958.

fund of $3,000 to launch the enterprise.[64] In March of 1931, four of Franklin Roosevelt's friends brought together $16,000 as a nucleus with which to start his campaign for the 1932 nomination.[65] This kind of ground-floor support is always necessary, and may be desirable on behalf of those who seek the vice-presidency as well. About $15,000 was collected by a friend of Henry A. Wallace, and used over a period of years before the 1940 Democratic convention to help nominate him for that post. And as a special case, it should be noted that the abortive attempt in 1956 to dump Vice President Nixon required money. One contributor reported giving Harold Stassen $4,000 in August for a political poll in connection with Mr. Stassen's attempt to substitute Christian A. Herter for Mr. Nixon as the vice presidential nominee. E. L. Cord, a Stevenson supporter in Nevada, contributed a total of $55,000 to an *ad hoc* "Maryland Committee," which was standing by to push the candidacy of former Governor Dan Thornton of Colorado should Mr. Nixon hit a snag. A movement that came to naught favoring Mr. Herter for president or vice president had, in fact, been initiated the year before by Arthur J. Goldsmith, a liberal Republican of New York fond of promoting his favorite politicians for high office and of raising money for them.[66]

An available candidate who is clearly presidential timber will by definition attract financial support. Nonetheless, collecting the amount of money spent by several candidates during the 1950's requires enormous work by persons possessing influence and skill in fund-raising. The personal role of the finance chairman and his fund-raisers becomes even more crucial than in normal party campaigning. There, at least to some extent, established machinery of solicitation and a corps of faithful followers are to be found. In contrast, the candidate for nomination is on his own, and political opportunists are not unmindful of his plight.[67]

Attempts have been made to raise important sums by mass appeals. Senator Kefauver was said to have collected $7,000 or $8,000 in dimes

64. They were Walter Hines Page, Walter L. McCorkle, and William F. McCombs.—Frank Parker Stockbridge, "How Woodrow Wilson Won His Nomination," *The Current History Magazine,* 20 (1924), 561.

65. According to James A. Farley: Frank C. Walker, $5,000; Henry Morgenthau, Sr., $5,000; William H. Woodin, $5,000; and William A. Julian, $1,000.—*Behind the Ballots—The Personal History of a Politician* (New York: Harcourt, Brace and Company, 1938), p. 72. Edward J. Flynn reports that a group of 15, including three of the above, each donated $2,000 at an early stage to forward F.D.R.'s candidacy.—*You're the Boss* (New York: The Viking Press, 1947), pp. 84-85.

66. Mazo, *op. cit.,* p. 162.

67. Lansdell K. Christie cut a wide swath through the Stevenson camp in 1956, both before and after his nomination. Mr. Christie had contributed to General Eisenhower's campaign in 1952, but according to the gossip he did not find the new administration hospitable and in 1956 went looking elsewhere. He not only underwrote various of the nomination activities, and contributed heavily to the general-election campaign, but went around picking up luncheon checks and otherwise ingratiating himself in Democratic quarters.

and dollars by passing the hat in Minnesota in 1956.[68] Table 44 shows the reported income from various mailings and other solicitations of the two main Stevenson committees that year.[69] As can be inferred from the table, however, in this case as in most others important reliance must be placed on hard money from large gifts.

Table 44

RECEIPTS BY TWO NATIONAL-LEVEL PRESIDENTIAL NOMINATION CAMPAIGN COMMITTEES FOR STEVENSON, 1956

	National Stevenson for President Committee 11/22/55-4/20/58	Stevenson Campaign Committee to 8/31/57	Total
Contributions	*$192,295*	*$421,851*	*$614,146*
Through:			
November, 1955, letter	83,251		
Radio Appeal (Box 1111)	1,663		
Letter to "Springfield" list	19,747		
The 23,000 mailing	19,243		
March, 1956, mailing	16,406		
March, 1956, telegrams	19,785		
"Let's Talk Sense" Fund raising	21,020		
May, 1956, mailing	7,478		
June, 1956, mailing	3,702		
Otherwise obtained	*97,529*		*97,529*
Special dinner fund		*38,350*	*38,350*
Sales of silver shoe pins	*7,591*		*7,591*
Interest on telephone deposit	*32*		*32*
Transferred from NSPC		*105,379*	*105,379*
Received by NSPC for account SCC		25,379	
From receipts of NSPC		80,000[a]	
Total	*$297,447*	*$565,580*	*$863,027*

[a] Shown as a disbursement of $79,175 by NSPC.

Many of the features familiar in general-election financing are therefore found. The frequent absence of the kinds of regulations that apply to general elections, however, permits greater freedom in financing nominations. Individuals may give larger sums with less likelihood of publicity and less concern for the law. But they need not give unless they want to, and effective solicitors are essential to success. As at other political levels, contributors and solicitors who constitute a party's or a faction's financial constituencies comprise opinion groups to be reckoned with. They are consciously and unconsciously deferred to by others, and while not all-powerful, exercise a veto capable of stifling many a budding candidacy.

68. Drew Pearson in *The News and Observer* (Raleigh, N.C.), March 24, 1956.

69. Fund-raising efforts went on at local levels in various places to attract money and support to Stevenson. In St. Louis, for example, on one Sunday about 400 volunteer workers pulled in between $5,000 and $6,000. The solicitation was organized by a public relations firm at no cost.

13

ANOTHER AMERICAN DILEMMA

King Canute could not stay the tides with a royal decree, nor have Americans reduced the financial needs of campaigns by passing laws. No other nation has attempted so much, nor accomplished so much, in the regulation of campaign finance,[1] yet the over-all result is regularly declared by politicians and observers alike to be failure. The extraordinary ambition of state and federal statutes is the chief reason. This ambition is partly a product of the moral absolutism and limitless optimism with which Americans have approached many public problems.[2] That much of the highly varied body of legislation has been unenforced or unenforceable evidences a public dilemma. Statutes privately approved and publicly endorsed are found incompatible with the operating requirements of the political system. The consequence has been dismay and lethargy, and little energy for change not sparked by narrow partisan incentives.

No aspect of campaign finance has commanded more attention than its legal regulation. The imperfections of statutes and the constitutional issues they raise are regularly aired in the press and in the law reviews. Many state and federal efforts are, as described by one observer, dead timber, yet others have had important consequences for the conduct of elections. The general impressions of failure that prevail obscure many detailed recesses of the subject. There is wide variation from state to state in the goals sought, the means employed, and the results achieved by legislative action. The conventions of politics and the details of draftsmanship differ from setting to setting, altering the impact of statutory controls that are identical in appearance or intent.

No purpose would be served by cataloging the minutiae of attempts and failures, but the broad aspects of existing regulations must be under-

1. Elaborate controls are found in some countries, particularly the Philippines and Japan. But effectiveness there is uneven, too, and the problem is simpler than in the multi-level United States political system.

2. Denis W. Brogan, *The American Character* (2nd ed.; New York: Vintage Books, 1956), p. 63.

stood before alternative proposals for control can be weighed.[3] Past legislation has almost invariably been negative in character, restricting the sources or amounts of contributions, restricting the uses or amounts of expenditures. Even requirements for public reporting have been passive, with provision seldom made for enforcement or for the meaningful use of any information the reports might contain. State legislatures have tinkered continuously with the details of existing statutes, sometimes making general revisions or abolishing them altogether. A hint of a new, positive approach has emerged in recent years, but with rare exceptions basic change has been imperceptible.[4] The federal Congress, despite excited charges of ill-doing, has displayed (through 1959) a consistent reluctance to convert bills into acts. The inertia results from a complex of habits and adaptations to existing statutes that vest successful politicians with an interest in the *status quo*. It is encouraged, moveover, by the realization that the traditional expectations of campaign regulation collide with the necessities of campaign conduct.

1. RESTRICTIONS ON SOURCES

Some of the restrictions on sources of campaign money have already been discussed in connection with campaign contributions. In some instances, the purposes of the statutes have been substantially accomplished, as is true of the limitations on soliciting federal employees.[5] In others, legal prohibitions are ignored with impunity. Numerous ways

3. Variations in detailed regulations are so numerous from state to state they defy easy classification and summary. Useful compilations of state and federal legislation, nevertheless, have appeared in Congressional documents, especially U.S. Senate Subcommittee on Privileges and Elections, *Election Law Guidebook 1956* (Washington: Government Printing Office, 1956) (Senate Document No. 116, 84th Congress, 2nd Session), 150 pp., and McClellan Lobby Committee, *Final Report,* pp. 238-340. See also Pamela Ford, *Regulation of Campaign Finance* (Berkeley: Bureau of Public Administration, University of California, 1955), 49 pp.; John S. Bottomly, "Corrupt Practices in Political Campaigns," *Boston University Law Review,* 30 (1950), 331-81; S. Sydney Minualt, *Corrupt Practices Legislation in the 48 States* (Chicago: The Council of State Governments, 1942) (mimeographed) 39 pp.; Louise Overacker, *Money in Elections* (New York: The Macmillan Company, 1932), pp. 203-373; Earl R. Sikes, *State and Federal Corrupt-Practices Legislation* (Durham: Duke University Press, 1928), 321 pp.; James K. Pollock, *Party Campaign Funds* (New York: Alfred A. Knopf, 1926), pp. 7-22. A compact review of the history and study of the public regulation of campaign finance appears in Jo Desha Lucas, "The Strength of Ten: Three-Quarters of a Century of Purity in Election Finance," *Northwestern University Law Review,* 51 (1957), 675-92.

4. Between 1951 and 1957, three-fourths of the states amended their statutes in some way, and one-fourth of them undertook either extensive changes or a general revision. Among the latter, the Florida action initiated in 1951 seemed most significant. See the discussion of its early trial in Elston E. Roady, "Florida's New Campaign Expense Law and the 1952 Democratic Gubernatorial Primaries," *American Political Science Review,* 48 (1954), 465-76. On the Minnesota action in 1955 and the California action two years later granting certain tax concessions for political outlays, see pages 445-48, below.

5. See pages 146-50, above.

around the prohibitions against donations from corporate and labor-union treasuries have been illustrated.[6] The federal prohibition against buying goods, commodities, advertising, or articles of any kind for the benefit of federal candidates is manifestly violated right and left.[7] A provision making it unlawful for "whoever" enters into a contract with the United States government to make a political contribution goes ignored.[8] There is, moreover, an apparent federal interdiction against loans by national banks in connection with nomination and election campaigns. It, also, is disregarded.[9]

6. See pages 129-35 and 196-208, above.

7. See pages 247-49, above.

8. See pages 143-45, above.

9. Sec. 610 of Title 18, *U.S. Code,* prohibits national banks from making contributions or expenditures in connection with any nomination or election. Sec. 591 defines both contributions and expenditures to include loans. Yet, political committees often report receiving bank loans. The Gore Committee *Report* noted 19 such cases in 1956, 15 of which were over $5,000 in amount (pp. 64-65).

When queried, bank officials have taken one of three positions: (1) They have pled ignorance of the apparent prohibition. (2) They have claimed that the loans were personal loans negotiated by private individuals. Although the funds thus obtained were sometimes deposited to the credit of a political committee, and the interest and repayments came out of committee funds, bankers have held the loans to be personal ones. (Under secs. 591 and 608 (a), a personal loan to an interstate committee would presumably be subject to the $5,000 limit on individual contributions. Perhaps it is significant that no loans of more than $5,000 to national-level committees were noted.) (3) Bank officials have also held that the loans were made in the regular course of business under standard conditions and were not contrary to sec. 610. The Gore Committee *Report* concluded that neither of these latter views "appears to be supported by the language of the Corrupt Practices Act, nor by its legislative history" (p. 16). Sec. 271 of the Internal Revenue Code of 1954, however, might be thought to give sanction to the third position. It states that no deduction shall be allowed a taxpayer *other than a bank* "by reason of the worthlessness of any debt owed by a political party."

Sec. 271 grew out of rulings of the Commissioner of Internal Revenue that individuals who made unrepaid loans to political organizations might report them as nonbusiness bad debts that could be offset against capital gains. Large sums were frequently lent by individuals. Between 1940 and 1948, for example, R. J. Reynolds was reported to have lent $310,000 to the New York Democratic state committee; Marshall Field, $50,000; and David A. Schulte, $50,000.—*Congressional Quarterly Almanac,* 8 (1952), 350. The 1952 reports examined showed loans from individuals in both parties, e.g., $30,000 from A. D. Welsh to the Missouri Republican finance committee and $25,000 from W. A. Harriman to the Pennsylvania Fund for Stevenson-Sparkman.

Politicians in both parties look upon bank loans as regular procedure. In New York, one Republican finance committee official was also an officer of an important bank. Secure in his knowledge of Republican resources, he was said by an associate to guarantee up to $50,000 any time without collateral. A check of a committee report revealed that, indeed, a loan of $50,000 had been made by his bank in 1952. One Democratic officer described an informal type of borrowing he engaged in. Faced by a deadline for advance payments for broadcasts, he gave a "bad" check and then induced broadcasting officials to accept it on his guarantee that he would make up any shortage found at the time the check was cashed. A business house that carries the bills of a political committee would seem, in effect, to be lending it money, but nobody, least of all the politicians, has raised questions about the practice.

One important limitation on sources of campaign gifts that requires special examination has not so far been treated: prohibitions against contributing more than a specified sum to a candidate or committee. The prohibition is not wholly effective, but it has influenced importantly the means by which political campaigns are financed.

Size of contributions.—Ironically, the legal regulation most meticulously respected is the one most often denounced as farcical: the limit on the size of individual contributions. The Hatch Act makes it illegal to contribute "directly or indirectly" an aggregate in excess of $5,000 during a calendar year: (1) to or on behalf of a candidate for nomination or election to a federal office; or (2) to or on behalf of any organization engaged in furthering, advancing, or advocating the nomination or election of such a candidate, or the success of any national political party. The statute excludes, however, "contributions made to or by a State or local committee or other State or local organization or to similar committees or organizations in the District of Columbia or in any Territory or Possession of the United States."[10] In recent years, four states—Florida, Massachusetts, Nebraska, and West Virginia—have also had some kind of limit on individual contributions, ranging from $1,000 to $5,000.

The politicians adapted readily to the federal statute (and to the state statutes, too). Contributors who wish to may give openly up to $5,000 to each of any number of national-level committees active during general elections. They may also give to candidates and their supporting committees in states and localities. The total gifts of an individual on behalf of one or more federal campaigns thus often far exceeds $5,000 per year. Moreover, the absence of state limitations makes it possible to give more than $5,000 at a time in most states, and the sums thus given can be transferred by the committees receiving the money to other groups at any level.

These practices are perpetually held up to shame. Sometimes they are denounced as evasions of the obvious intent, or what should have been the obvious intent, of the Hatch Act limitation. More often, they are cited as loopholes that render suspect the motives of the legislators who made the law. Legislative intent is, indeed, an elusive commodity. The only intent evident from the legislative history of this provision was the desire, by southern opponents of other provisions of the bill, to kill the whole proposal by tacking on the limit of $5,000 on individual gifts.[11] The limitation was sponsored by Senator John Bankhead of Alabama, who at first suggested $1,000, proclaiming, "We know that

10. *U.S. Code,* Title 18, sec. 608(a).

11. The interpretation of Louise Overacker in *Presidential Campaign Funds* (Boston: Boston University Press, 1946), pp. 26-27. The book has an approving introduction by Senator Theodore Francis Green, the chairman of the Subcommittee on Privileges and Elections, the Senate committee most concerned with this legislation.

money is the chief source of corruption." Senator Hatch voted against the Bankhead amendment as "not pertinent" to his measure; there was no debate on the limitation in either the Senate or the House, which is a fair index of Congressional interest in the matter over the years. Contributors who give the maximum permissible to several different committees may discomfort their political opponents, but they are hardly evadng the law. Some individuals, however, give over $5,000 to the *same* committee by giving under more than one name, a clear violation of the statute.[12]

Three effects of the federal limitation are to some extent important. First, standing alone, it would seem to encourage an increase in the number of political organizations through which gifts are received and campaigns are carried on.[13] A multiplicity of campaign groups contributes to diffusion of control, hence to inefficiency and irresponsibility. Contributors come into contact with a larger number of candidates (or their representatives) than when their donations are funneled to one main committee. Second, the limitation has made it less convenient than formerly to give large sums to federal campaigns. It has no doubt reduced the size of contributions that might have been made by certain affluent individuals. Finally, political committees doubtless feel less dependent on individual donors of $5,000 than on a benefactor who, as in former days, could put up larger amounts, even enough to underwrite the essential costs of a campaign with one check. Such a contributor commanded respect, and it is doubtful that even the solicitor of huge funds has quite the direct impact of one man, one check.

Gift taxes.—In any event, other factors are probably more important in limiting the size of political contributions than the Hatch Act and the corresponding state statutes.[14] Of enormous significance in limiting the size of political gifts is the gift tax. A gift of more than $3,000 to one recipient within a calendar year may become subject to a special gift tax. (Donations to certain charitable, educational, etc., institutions are exempt, and gifts made by one spouse to a third person may be considered as being made half by each spouse.) The amount taxable in a given year is the amount by which each taxable gift exceeds $3,000, added to the amounts by which other taxable gifts do the same. Thus, the taxable amount is cumulative from gift to gift within each year. It

12. See pages 359-62, below. Such gifts, it would appear, might properly become subject to gift taxes when they exceed an aggregate of $3,000 for each recipient. This wrinkle apparently had not occurred to the Internal Revenue Service, nor to many others, until the matter was raised in connection with the gifts, made in several different names, by Mr. Cyrus Eaton, Sr., to Labor's Nonpartisan League, a committee opposing Senator Robert Taft's reelection in Ohio in 1950.—U.S. Senate Subcommittee on Privileges and Elections, *Hearings* (Washington: Government Printing Office, 1952), p. 540.

13. So runs the theory, one to be examined more critically when ceilings on total expenditures are discussed. See pages 353-55, below.

14. See pages 212-14, above.

is also cumulative from year to year.[15] The rate of the tax is progressive, the schedule going into effect in 1942 beginning at 2¼ per cent for taxable amounts up to $5,000 and reaching a maximum of 57¾ per cent at $10,000,000.

The effect of these provisions is evident from the frequency with which $3,000 gifts are made in comparison with those above and below that sum. Table 45 presents a tabulation of the amounts in which a random sample of contributors made gifts of $500 and over during 1952 and 1956. The clustering at $3,000 is noticeable in both years. (It is

Table 45

FREQUENCY OF CONTRIBUTIONS OF SPECIFIED SIZES, $500 AND OVER, MADE BY A SAMPLE OF CONTRIBUTORS, 1952 AND 1956[a]

Amount of Each Contribution	Percentage of Total *No.* of Contribuions Made in Each Amount	
	1952	1956
$ 500	44.9	41.9
1,000	29.6	28.1
1,500	2.4	3.4
2,000	4.3	4.8
2,500	2.7	3.2
3,000	5.1[b]	8.0
5,000	0.8	1.2
Other amounts between $500-$5,000	10.2	9.4
Total	100.0	100.0
Number of Contributors in Sample	800	776
Approximate Number of Contributors from which Sample was Drawn	9,500	8,100

[a] Examined were the contributions made by a random sample of all contributors who were known to have given at least one sum of $500 or more during the year in question.
[b] The percentage for each party was: Democratic, 2.5; Republican, 6.7.
[c] The percentage for each party was: Democratic, 5.6; Republican, 8.7.

15. The first gift tax applied to part of 1924 and to 1925. No gift tax was levied again until June 6, 1932, since which date one has been in effect. The exemption on aggregate gifts to one donee, within one calendar year, was at first $5,000, was lowered to $4,000 for the years 1939-42, and to $3,000 beginning with 1943. The rates were revised upward on three occasions. The year-to-year cumulative effect is achieved in this way. A tax is figured at current rates on the aggregate net gifts after June 6, 1932, but not including the gifts of the latest year, the year for which a tax is being computed. A tax is also figured at current rates on total aggregate net gifts after June 6, 1932. The tax to be paid is the difference between the two amounts. A lump-sum exemption of $30,000 is granted on gifts made after the 1932 date. This may be taken only once. (This exemption was $50,000 through 1935, and $40,000 for the years 1936-42.)—Internal Revenue Service, U.S. Treasury Department, *Statistics of Income for 1950* (Washington: Government Printing Office, 1954), part 1, pp. 341-43; *Statistics of Income for 1953* (Washington: Government Printing Office, 1957), part 1, pp. 88, 103.

likely, moreover, that some gifts over $3,000 could be split between husband and wife and hence would not be taxable.) The contributing records of 38 individuals who gave $20,000 or more to political causes in 1956 reveals a similar respect for the $3,000 maximum. These individuals (or couples) made 729 different gifts, 161 of which (22 per cent) were for $3,000 and only 29 of which (4 per cent) were in excess of that sum.[16] The effects of this tax provision on contributing habits reduces enormously the significance of the Hatch Act limitation of $5,000. Moreover, it suggests the potency of the taxing power for other purposes in regulating political giving.

2. CEILINGS ON EXPENDITURES

Prohibitions against bribery were the earliest legal restraints imposed on the use of money in politics. It was a crime in English common law, and wherever modern voting systems have been installed bribery has been outlawed. Some states also forbid expenditures for other specified purposes,[17] but it is difficult to perceive that these prohibitions have significantly affected electoral practices. Only rarely does the responsibility for enforcing them weigh heavily on public officials, and when it does, partisan motives may, with some reason, be suspected. Of greater import is the attempt to purify politics by limiting the amounts of money that may legally be spent in elections.

State gestures.—Like the limits on individual gifts, the ceilings on campaign expenditures are ridiculed. Ceilings first appeared in the statutes of California and Missouri in 1893, and later many states adopted and some abandoned them. In 1956, there were 33 states in which ceilings of some kind applied.[18] The ceilings were presumably enacted to reduce the influence of expenditures on the outcome of elec-

16. For example, in 1956 Lansdell K. Christie reported 32 separate Democratic gifts, 17 of which were for $3,000, and Mrs. Joan W. Payson reported 29 separate Republican gifts, 19 of which were for $3,000. (The total of contributions to one recipient is deemed to be one gift.)

17. Proscribed in some states, for example, are the payment of poll taxes, payment for withdrawal of a candidate, payment toward establishing or maintaining voting residence, and payment for such things as transporting voters, furnishing liquor on election day, and entertaining to promote an election. Some statutes attempt to protect candidates by making it illegal for organizations and individuals to solicit them during a campaign for sundry worthy and unworthy causes.

Closely related to these restrictions are requirements in federal law and in most of the states for the identification on campaign literature of those responsible for printing and distributing it. Expenditures declared to be *lawful* for campaign purposes are enumerated in more than thirty states. The enumerations have usually not kept pace with technological developments in communications and changes in campaign practices.

18. In all but six cases, where primaries alone were covered, ceilings applied to nomination and general-election campaigns. The 15 states with no ceilings were: California, Delaware, Florida, Illinois, Louisiana, Maine, Nebraska, Nevada, North Carolina, Pennsylvania, Rhode Island, South Carolina, Texas, Vermont, and Washington. In 1957, Georgia repealed its ceilings.

tions and to curb the political influence of wealth. They have failed to do either. It would be hard, in fact, to prove that legislators really thought they could. The statutes are all drawn so that, as interpreted, it is legally possible to exceed whatever limit is set. Even so, politicians often choose to ignore the law rather than to take advantage of the available loopholes.

In most states, the limits apply only to expenditures by a candidate, leaving the campaign committees supporting him free of any restriction. In some, the limit extends to expenditures by a candidate plus those made on his behalf with his "knowledge and consent." The latter flexible concept is usually interpreted to leave the candidate judicially ignorant of most campaign activities on his behalf. In a few states, limits apply also to committees, but not so as to bring all of a candidate's committees effectively under one ceiling. Even where statutes appear to concentrate responsibility for receipts and expenditures on a candidate or some designated agent, and to make the limits apply to all expenditures on behalf of a candidate, technical features of the law usually provide ways around the requirements.[19] The height of the ceilings varies greatly from state to state, always expressed in dollars and never in the the things dollars buy.[20]

Under prevailing circumstances, the state limits seem purposeless. In the face of manifestly unsatisfactory results, a movement to abandon them has developed. Seven states abolished ceilings between 1942 and 1956.[21] Legislators are often cornered, however, by elements of public opinion favoring "effective" ceilings. Effective ceilings are difficult if not impossible to design, and the result of urging legislators to enact them has frequently been inaction, or merely a raising of existing ceilings, which occurred in eleven states during the same period.[22] No one could claim seriously that the presence, absence, or level of ceilings would make any real difference in what was spent.[23]

19. Almost half the states have exempted expenditures of greater or lesser importance; in West Virginia the exemptions seem to embrace most that a candidate or his managers would want to do. In New Jersey, candidates and managers could disavow expenditures made without their authority, thus thwarting the effort to centralize responsibility implicit in requirements for the designation of depositories and appointment of agents. In Utah, provisions directed at limiting expenditures did not apply to those made by persons residing within a county where the expenditure was incurred.

20. The ceilings depend to some extent on the size of the jurisdiction. For governor and United States senator, they run from $5,000 and under in such states as Ohio, Oklahoma, New Hampshire, and Utah, up to $50,000, the highest limit, in Alabama and New Jersey. Some limitations are expressed as a percentage of the annual salary of the office sought, ranging from 10 per cent to 100, and occasionally as so many cents per vote cast in a previous election.

21. California, Florida, Louisiana, Nebraska, Nevada, North Carolina, and Texas.

22. Alabama, Indiana, Massachusetts, Mississippi, Missouri, New Hampshire, New York, Oklahoma, Virginia, Wisconsin, and Wyoming.

23. Legal limits on total expenditures have proved ineffective also in other nations, e.g., Japan.—Nobutaka Ike, *Japanese Politics* (New York: Alfred A. Knopf, 1957), p. 200.

Federal limits.—Under the Corrupt Practices Act of 1925, any candidate for United States senator may spend up to $10,000 and any candidate for United States representative up to $2,500, unless state law prescribes a lower figure. These limits may be raised to a maximum of $25,000 and $5,000, respectively, depending on the number of votes cast in the last election,[24] and important categories of expenditures are specifically excluded from the limits.[25]

The federal limitation of $3,000,000 on the amount that an interstate political committee may receive or spend during a calendar year was enacted under the same circumstances as the limit of $5,000 on individual gifts. The committee ceiling was inserted by the House Judiciary Committee into the Hatch Act of 1940 and adopted without debate at either end of the Capitol.[26] The limit was drastic. On occasion in previous years both the Democratic and Republican national committees had spent well over $3,000,000. Moreover, the dollar costs of campaigning were inevitably rising. And there was nothing in the experience of the states from which the honorable members came to suggest that a flat ceiling could be maintained. Moreover, notions of propriety concerning campaign expenditures could have disciplinary effects even in the absence of formal limitations. In the inconstant chemistry of politics, cries have been raised off and on against candidates whose campaigns were known to have cost large sums, and Frank L. Smith and William S. Vare had even been denied seats in the United States Senate partly because of the volume of money used on their behalf. There was nothing in the manner in which the federal ceiling on committee funds came about to suggest careful purpose or a weighing of the probable effects.[27]

24. The limit, within the maximums named, becomes "An amount equal to the amount obtained by multiplying three cents by the total number of votes cast at the last general election for all candidates for the office which the candidate seeks. . ." —Sec. 309(b)(1). Federal ceilings were first imposed in 1911, when the aggregate amount that might be spent for nomination and election was limited to $10,000 for Senate candidates and to $5,000 for House candidates.

25. See page 358, below.

26. Overacker, *Presidential Campaign Funds,* pp. 26-27.

27. The measure, in *U.S. Code,* Title 18, sec. 609, provides:

1. No political committee shall receive contributions or make expenditures aggregating more than $3,000,000 during any calendar year.

2. The applicable definition of committee (given in sec. 591) includes "any committee, association, or organization which accepts contributions or makes expenditures for the purpose of influencing or attempting to influence the election of candidates or presidential and vice presidential electors (1) in two or more States, or (2) whether or not in more than one State, if such committee, association, or organization (other than a duly organized State or local committee or a political party) is a branch or subsidiary of a national committee, association, or organization."

3. Any contributions received or expenditures made "on behalf of any political committee with the knowledge and consent of the chairman or treasurer of such

Ceilings and campaign organization.—Both politicians and students have maintained that the chief effect of legal ceilings on expenditures has been a decentralization of campaign management.[28] This has produced, it is thought, greater diffusion of party power and responsibility than would otherwise have existed. The use of multiple committees without doubt makes it possible for aggregate expenditures to exceed the expressed limit.[29] (It also enables a contributor to back a candidate with as many donations of maximum legal size—or gift-tax size—as there are committees to receive them.) What effect ceilings have actually had on the number of committees created is more difficult to discern. Long before there were federal ceilings, presidential campaigns were regularly conducted through a variety of campaign organizations. Professor Pollock noted that nearly $1,000,000 was spent in 1916 on behalf of the presidential candidates through nonparty committees, only some of which had any connection with the regular party structure.[30] Professor Overacker observed in 1932 that each national campaign found an increasing number of nonparty organizations submitting financial reports.[31] Many of these were fronts for the national committees, but apparently many were not.

Numerous campaign committees active following the Hatch Act were created for essentially the same reasons they were created before it: to appeal for the votes and funds of special constituencies. After its study of the 1940 presidential campaign, the Gillette Committee concluded that "innumerable" independent committees had been created as a result of the limitations on contributions and expenditures in the Hatch Act adopted that year.[32] But the Lonergan Committee, four years earlier, had called attention to the "innumerable" emergency committees and

committee shall be deemed to be received or made by such committee."

4. Violations by the committee are deemed to be violations by the chairman and treasurer and any other person responsible for the violation.

28. For an analysis of the effects on party organization in one state of the statutory regulation of campaign finance and other party matters, see G. Theodore Mitau, "The Status of Political Party Organization in Minnesota Law: Selected Aspects of Party Statutes and Political Dynamics," *Minnesota Law Review,* 40 (1956), 561-79.

29. There was a great to-do immediately after approval of the second Hatch Act on July 19, 1940. Senator Hatch maintained that Congress intended the limit of $3,000,000 to apply to the aggregate collections and expenditures of all national-level committees supporting one candidate, rather than to each of them. Candidate Willkie agreed and announced the limit would be kept, which it was not. In practice, the limit has applied to the sums run through the books of any one committee.

30. ". . . considerable sums are raised and disbursed by collateral or subsidiary or non-party committees. There are also many personal and other unofficial committees which come into existence during a campaign, and spend money. In some cases these organizations are supported and directed by the official party committees; in others they have no connections with them."—Pollock, *op. cit.,* pp. 55-56. Nonparty groups were also active at state and local levels, irrespective of ceilings.

31. *Money in Elections,* p. 267.

32. *Report,* p. 8.

organizations created across state boundaries and within individual states during "every national campaign."[33]

While it seems true that ceilings have not significantly increased the number of committees in action during a campaign, they have had a decentralizing effect by making some of them very important. It seems evident that more money is spent or held at the state level, especially on the Republican side, because of the $3,000,000 limitation, than would otherwise be the case.[34] Also, the national committee of each party is induced to enter a more intimate partnership with its party's Senatorial and Congressional campaign committees than would otherwise be necessary. And the important voluntary committee systems of the parties (e.g., the Citizens and the Volunteers)[35] doubtless operate with greater independence, though their *raison d'être* is found elsewhere.

Without the federal ceilings on expenditures, campaign funds running through the books of the national committees would unquestionably be larger than they were in 1952 and 1956.[36] Campaign accounting would be more orderly, and presumably more informative, unless present arrangements were maintained for that very reason. How profound a

33. *Report,* p. 25. The available data on the number of *ad hoc* groups and their sources of funds do not permit the desired comparative analysis of experience before and since 1940. In 1952 and 1956, however, the number of significant national-level campaign groups was not large. (See pages 396-97, below.) Nor was there anything to indicate that special committees had been organized within individual states to handle funds that would have gone to national-level committees in the absence of the Hatch Act.

Experience at the state level may be instructive. In Illinois, a state without ceilings or campaign reports, special candidate committees regularly spring up as auxiliaries to the party machinery. Other special-constituency groups, like the Independent Voters of Illinois, have also been active in campaigns. These campaign groups tell something about the organization of interests and the nature of party structure in the area. In Illinois, at least, they are not the product of statutory ceilings on expenditures.

34. At the beginning of 1940, the Republican national committee had a number of joint fund-raising agreements by which monies collected by the national committee were remitted to state committees. There was also a series of fund-raising subcommittees of the national committee, by which the money was collected. To accommodate to the new law, the joint fund-raising agreements between the national and state committees were cancelled, the subcommittees were abolished, and a series of state finance committees appeared in their stead.—Louise Overacker, "Campaign Finance in the Presidential Election of 1940," *American Political Science Review,* 35 (1941), 704-5.

35. Financially active in other years as well as in presidential-election years: in 1957 the National Citizens for Eisenhower reported receipts of $362,143, expenditures of $501,436, and in 1958, respectively, of $762,601 and $767,297. (The Stevenson-Kefauver Campaign Committee in 1957 showed receipts of $79,064 and expenses of $131,752. There was no report for 1958.)—*Congressional Quarterly,* 16 (1958), 183; 17 (1959), 650.

36. Total expenditures (including unpaid bills as well as transfers) of the Democratic national committee exceeded $5,340,000 in 1928 and $5,190,000 in 1936, and the corresponding Republican figures were $6,250,000 and $8,890,000.—Overacker, "Campaign Finance in the Presidential Election of 1940." p. 705.

nationalizing effect abolition of the federal ceiling would have, however, is problematical. Although ceilings have to some extent encouraged dispersion in the financial management of campaigns, the distribution of power within the parties both before and after the Hatch Act is rooted in deeper soil.[37]

A state case.—In 1951, the General Assembly of North Carolina abolished the low ceilings that had applied for some years to expenditures by candidates for party nominations. Three years later, nine of the state's most active and experienced politicians were asked a series of questions regarding the effects of the change. All had been candidates for important office, or had been active as campaign managers or fund-raisers, or had held important positions in the Democratic party. When asked whether the change had affected in any way the manner in which money was raised and spent, all said "no." Had it affected the ways campaigns are organized and conducted? All said "no." Had the change made candidates any better informed concerning the identity of the contributors to their campaigns? Five said "no"; four said "yes." Had greater coordination in the handling of campaign finances by state headquarters resulted? Four said "yes" and five "no."

Most state and local politicians doubt the importance of campaign ceilings and are largely uninterested in them.[38] It may well be that their most significant consequence has been to handicap efforts to learn how much money is spent in areas where ceilings are in effect.[39]

3. PUBLICITY

After considerable public discussion, a Swedish government investigating committee concluded in 1952 that to compel the disclosure of political contributors would place free government in jeopardy. Despite special concern over contributions of foreign origin, the committee held that "a filing of the names of contributors would actually conflict with the principle of secrecy of the ballot."[40] The Norwegian government,

37. See the discussion of fund-raising and party cohesion above, pages 282-317.

38. In another connection, questions were asked of a number of North Carolina citizens to determine their familiarity with the laws affecting campaign finance. One of the respondents had been governor of the state when the ceilings were repealed. He was not sure whether there were any ceilings or not.

39. Instances of attempted enforcement are rare. A candidate for chairman of the commissioners of DeKalb County, Georgia, astonished his part of the world in 1956 by reporting expenditures of $27,443, $2,443 over the legal limit. Unknowingly he had exceeded the limit, he said, and conscience compelled him to report it. There was grave talk of impeachment, and at least one defeated opponent (who, like the other defeated opponents, had filed no report of his own expenses) called with a straight face for the miscreant to resign. It was gratefully found that penalties applied only in case the law were "willfully and wrongfully" violated, which manifestly it had not been, and editors wrote on the theme: "When the Law Becomes a Joke—Change It"—which is what was done.—*Atlanta Constitution,* October 7, 1956.

40. *The Commercial and Financial Chronicle,* January 24, 1952. The practical obstacles to enforcing effective disclosure were said to have been crucial in the deliberations.

through legislative committees and a Royal Commission, also undertook an extended consideration of compulsory publication of the financial accounts of political parties. Any disclosures should be voluntary, it was concluded; "desirable as it might be to compel public disclosure, it would not be feasible to devise effective legislation without encroaching on democratic ideas and principles. And the price would be out of proportion to the gain."[41]

Indeed, most nations have declined to seek disclosure of political finances. The executive secretary of a major Canadian party observed that the Catholic Church releases no financial information; why should a political party? In Great Britain, of special interest, compulsory disclosure is attempted for only a slender sector of campaign operations.[42] Yet, in the United States, for half a century compulsory publicity of political accounts has been the cornerstone of legal regulation. Publicity is advocated as an automatic regulator, inducing self-discipline among political contenders and arming the electorate with important information. It is a controversial goal—although the climate of politics discourages dissent from it. And it is an incredibly ambitious goal.

American experience has been extensive. Federal, state, and local reporting requirements often differ, but experience at these levels displays many common characteristics. The most manageable way to review this experience is to examine the results of federal regulation, followed by reference to special characteristics of reporting at lower levels. It is essential to appraise existing practices carefully if more effective publicity systems are to be devised. Moreover, much of what is known about campaign finance has been derived from official reports. To study the general subject of money in politics requires an appreciation of their values and limitations. The reports reveal a great deal about certain segments of political finance; they make possible reasonable projections of other phases; and they help very little with much else. Not to know all the contours of the Indian Ocean, however, does not render useless the charts of Long Island Sound. The challenge to the student is to know what he has.

United States law.—In mid-1959, 43 states had some kind of publicity system. The other five included, in addition to Illinois and Rhode Island, three states in which reporting requirements had been repealed within recent years: Delaware, Louisiana, and Nevada. The character of state

41. *News of Norway* (Issued by the Norwegian Information Service, Washington, D.C.), March 24, 1955, p. 46. On campaign finance in Norway, see Jasper B. Shannon, *Money and Politics* (New York: Random House, 1959), pp. 64-82.

42. Conservative party officials have opposed disclosure of party accounts on the ground that basic differences in the make-up and operations of different party organizations, and their relationships to nonparty groups, make the publication of comparative figures misleading. In other words, the financial strength of the Labor party would not be so fully revealed as that of the Conservative party by the publication of party accounts.—R. T. McKenzie, *British Political Parties* (London: William Heinemann Limited, 1955), pp. 595-96.

legislation varied greatly as did the results obtained from it.[43] New York was the first state, in 1890, to adopt a publicity statute, and several others quickly followed. After the elections of 1904, a move for federal legislation took shape in the National Publicity Law Association under the leadership of Perry Belmont. The organization enjoyed bipartisan support, but the first measure was passed in 1910 largely through Democratic efforts.[44] The law was modified in 1911, and again in 1925 when the Corrupt Practices Act was adopted.

With the adjournment of Congress in 1959, the publicity provisions of the 1925 measure were still in effect. They apply to three types of committees or persons active in general elections.

FIRST, certain "political committees" are required to make reports. The term is defined to include a committee, association, or organization that accepts contributions or makes expenditures for the purpose of trying to influence the election of candidates for Federal office—provided that it does this in two or more states, *or,* regardless of whether it does so, if it is a branch or subsidiary of a national committee, association, or organization, *other than* a duly organized state or local committee of a political party.[45]

Every political committee must have a chairman and a treasurer. The treasurer must keep a detailed and exact account of: (a) all contributions made to or for such a committee; (b) the name and address of every person making any such contribution, and the date; (c) all expenditures made by or on behalf of such committee; and (d) the name and address of every person to whom such expenditure is made, and the date. The treasurer must also keep a receipted bill, giving particulars, for every expenditure over $10. He must keep the bills and accounts for at least two years from the date of filing the statement referring to them.[46]

43. According to Ford, *op. cit.,* pp. 38-42: In 10 states, candidates but not parties or committees had to report (Arkansas, Georgia (1955), Idaho, Mississippi, North Dakota, South Carolina, Texas, Vermont, Virginia, and Washington—most of them one-party states); elsewhere the requirements covered political committees as well; in 14 states either individuals who made expenditures or campaign depositories (e.g., banks) had reporting obligations. Information on disbursements only was called for in 6 states (Arkansas, South Carolina, Utah, Vermont, Virginia, and Washington), whereas elsewhere receipts were also covered. The requirements applied only to primaries in six states (Arizona, Arkansas, Idaho, Mississippi, Vermont, and Washington), but to primaries and general elections in the others. The majority of the states required reports after the voting, but 17 provided for reports both before and after (Alabama, Arizona, Florida, Georgia, Kentucky, Mississippi, Nebraska, New Hampshire, New Jersey, New York, North Carolina, South Carolina, Tennessee, Texas, Utah, West Virginia, and Wisconsin).

44. For Mr. Belmont's story of the movement, see *An American Democrat* (New York: Columbia University Press, 1940), pp. 472-98, and his *The Abolition of the Secrecy of Party Funds—The Origin of the Movement, Its Purpose and Effect* (Washington: Government Printing Office, 1912) (Senate Document No. 495, 62nd Congress, 2nd Session), 88 pp.

45. Sec. 302(c).

46. Sec. 303. Sec. 304 requires every person who receives a contribution for a political committee to report it, with the name and address of the giver, and the date, to the treasurer within five days of its receipt, or earlier if requested by the treasurer.

The treasurer must make reports to the Clerk of the United States House of Representatives. These are at least four every year: between the 1st and 10th of March, June, and September, and on the 1st of January. In years of a general election (when candidates are to be elected on the same date in two or more states), two additional reports are required: between the 15th and 10th days prior to the election, and on the 5th day prior to it. Each report must be cumulative, covering the period from the first of the year to the day preceding the filing of the report, and the one submitted on January 1 must cover the preceding calendar year.[47]

The treasurers report must include: (a) the name and address of every person who has made an aggregate contribution of $100 or more within the calendar year, along with the amount and date; (b) the total of all other contributions within the calendar year; (c) the total of all contributions within the calendar year; (d) the name and address of every person to whom an aggregate expenditure of $10 or more has been made during the calendar year, along with the amount, date, and purpose; (e) the total of all other expenditures during the calendar year; (f) the total of all expenditures within the calendar year.[48]

SECOND, every person other than a political committee who spends an aggregate of $50 or more in a calendar year (other than by contribution to a political committee) to influence elections to either house of Congress in two or more states must file with the Clerk of the House a statement of expenditures like that called for above.[49]

THIRD, candidates for both houses of Congress must submit certain reports. Senatorial candidates submit them to the Secretary of the Senate, House candidates to the Clerk of the House. Two reports are called for: one, not less than 10 nor more than 15 days before the election; the other, within thirty days after it; in each case the report must be cumulative and complete through the day preceding the filing of the report.[50]

The candidate is required to report contributions and expenditures handled by him personally, or by someone else "for him with his knowledge and consent" in aid or support of his candidacy.

The report must show each contribution and the name of the person making it; and it must show each expenditure and the name of the person to whom made, except that expenditures for certain specified purposes need not be itemized. Only the total of these exempt expenditures need be given.[51] Money spent for the following uses is exempt: assessments, fees or charges levied by the laws of the state where the candidate resides; necessary personal traveling or subsistence; stationery, postage, writing or printing—other than for use in billboards or in newspapers; distribution of letters, circulars, or posters; and telephone and telegraph service.[52]

47. When there has been no change in an entry reported on a previous statement, the amount only need be carried forward and the other information need not be repeated.

48. Sec. 305.

49. Sec. 306.

50. As with committee reports, when an entry remains the same, the total only need be carried forward, and the supporting details need not be repeated.

51. Sec. 307.

52. Sec. 309(c).

All of the three types of reports required by Federal law must be verified by oath or affirmation and must be kept by the Clerk or the Secretary for two years from the date of filing. They are considered part of the public records and are to be open to public inspection.[53]

No responsibility is placed on any public official to compel submission of the reports, to examine them, or to report seeming violations to the Attorney General.

Dummy contributors.—J. P. Morgan once growled that he would even vote the Democratic ticket to get Theodore Roosevelt out of the White House. "If he had his way we'd all do business with glass pockets."[54] Other citizens, including politicians, likewise hold that a measure of secrecy facilitates financial business. The result is a degree of inaccuracy and incompleteness in most important campaign reports.

There are many reasons for making secret donations, and many ways to do so. On occasion, contributors wish to avoid the $5,000 federal limit on individual gifts to one organization. The classic illustration is provided by Welburn Mayock, self-styled "furtive little lawyer" who served as counsel of the Democratic national committee in 1948, a year of notable penury. During the presidential campaign, Mr. Mayock took a contribution of $30,000 to the Democratic national finance chairman, Louis A. Johnson. That officer, overjoyed we are plausibly told, quickly noted that 30 is more than five and returned the funds to Mr. Mayock, who proceeded to funnel the money to the national committee in the form of gifts from individuals and "institutions" around the country. ". . . I and the individuals strutted as great contributors, and I got rid of the $30,000 and got the money where it was supposed to go."

Two persons sent in $5,000 checks as a routine action at the request of the chairman of the Democratic county committee in San Francisco. "I had no knowledge of the source, knew nothing of the background and never heard of Mr. Mayock," said one attorney. Another recalled that the attorney handling contributions in his part of California asked him and several others if he could use their names. "I asked him whether or not using my name would carry any financial, moral or legal responsibility. He said no. He said it was just a way of getting around a law that neither party paid any attention to." Testifying before a Congressional committee, Mr. Mayock stated that the institution he had in mind was a state or local political committee and that the sum transmitted through it exceeded $5,000. He conceded the transactions were illegal, but not unusual. He had handled other contributions in the same way from individuals who did not want their names on the Democratic books, such as Republicans in favor of President Truman's reelection.[55]

53. Sec. 308.

54. John K. Winkler, *Morgan the Magnificent—The Life of J. Pierpont Morgan (1837-1913)* (New York: The Vanguard Press, 1930), p. 223.

55. The $30,000 was part of a $65,000 fee paid to Mayock by William S. Lasdon

The climate of politics in the United States exposes contributors to harrassment by the press and exploitation by the opposition. Even persons with no need or intent to evade the law are led to give under false names. Cyrus Eaton, Sr., explained why he gave $30,000 to a local Ohio organization in 1950 through intermediaries. "It is a long established custom in Ohio to do it that way and in this instance it seemed to me desirable to have the contributions made in the name of others rather than do it directly in my own name."[56] Solicitors report that persons whom they approach for contributions often say, in effect, "If you won't get my name in the papers and have a lot of reporters calling me up in the middle of the night, I will give you something." After being interviewed by a federal investigator in 1956, the donor of a legitimate, publicly reported campaign gift declared he would give no more if doing so were going to provoke investigations. His party's fund-raisers, it may be surmised, would be sympathetic and find ways to protect him in the future.

Many individuals fear reprisals if their political preferences become known. Donors to both sides of a contest fear the public prejudice against this practice. Many contributors protest that to give publicly precludes their having normal business relationships with government and normal personal relations with politicians. Sensationalists in the press, and among opposition politicians, manufacture charges of cause-and-effect relationships that, while untrue, are impossible to refute. Candidates themselves express reluctance to record gifts from minority groups (and the underworld) for fear of reactions among voters. "Texas oil money" has become a negative symbol of such potency that candidates have refused gifts that could be identified as such—not because they disliked the money, or the source, but because they wanted to avoid the gaff of publicity that might follow. Donors with other special stakes in politics realize that if their gifts became known, they, and the recipients, would be harpooned by all and sundry.

Those who advocate full disclosure argue that any gift unable to stand the light of day should not be made. Or, at least, persons making it should pay the penalty of public reaction. However this may be, in addition to the rascals, there are many citizens who feel that contributing

---

for representing a chemical company in getting a favorable tax ruling from the Treasury Department. Republicans charged mischief; Democratic Treasury officials denied it. Mr. Mayock's full testimony affords a vivid vignette of a political lawyer in action and a fund-raiser's techniques for obscuring the source of money. See U.S. House of Representatives Subcommittee on Administration of the Internal Revenue Laws of the Committee on Ways and Means, *Hearings* (Washington: Government Printing Office, 1953), part D, pp. 1411-58, esp. pp. 1438-48. Mr. Mayock was acquitted in a tax case involving this episode.—*New York Times,* July 28, 1959.

The Kefauver Crime Committee heard testimony on the use of fictitious names in Missouri.—*Hearings,* part 4, pp. 164-65.

56. U.S. Senate Subcommittee on Privileges and Elections, *Hearings* (Washington: Government Printing Office, 1952), p. 536.

is like voting, a personal matter and nobody else's business. Their attitudes obstruct the working of publicity laws.[57]

What proportion of the names listed as contributors on federal reports are dummies is difficult to say. Practices fluctuate somewhat with changes in party personnel. Because of the exposed position of committees at the national level, and because the regular national party groups have permanent staffs, the reports submitted by them often possess a high degree of technical accuracy. The reports appear to include all contributions that go through committee books and to be listed in the names in which the receipts are issued. (The Republican national committee submits a copy of all receipts as part of its report, and several other Republican groups at national and state levels do the same.) But solicitors point out that Mr. Mayock is not the only contributor whose benefactions have arrived under false colors. One former national treasurer observed that "the real money" goes unreported, by which he meant not the majority of the money, but the sensitive money. Many unlikely names appear on the reports. Every politician has allies willing to have their names stuck to campaign gifts.[58] Campaign errand boys, especially in state races, are put down for more than most of them could earn in a month, or six.[59] One Colorado Senatorial candidate readily revealed that the gift reported in his name had not been his money. A state chairman in Kansas rejected $2,500 proffered by a brewery association and observed the money arriving later via individual gifts. Secretaries, lawyers, public relations advisers, confidential friends, and relatives of prominent persons show up as handsome givers.[60]

Nevertheless, despite these sources of inaccuracy, at the national level probably more than 80 per cent of the persons listed for gifts of $100 and above are actual contributors of the amounts shown.[61] Practices

57. Typical of many contributors with whom interviews were sought was the opening remark of one: "I'm just old-fashioned enough to think that there are some things which are still private, so I think we'd better say no as far as this interview is concerned." This person eventually granted the interview; some did not. A southern state chairman righteously refused access to his copy of the party's official report, required by law. He insisted it was not a "public record."

58. Some are not so willing, such as the giver of $10.00 who without his knowledge was reported for $500—an untimely action in light of the contributor's current embarrassment at the local bank.

59. When a list of 1952 contributors of $10,000 and over was made public in 1956, newspaper correspondents tracked down several of the names. One of them involved a minor government employee whose annual salary in 1952 was less than 40 per cent of the amount of the gifts attributed to him.

60. The public relations adviser to one of America's wealthiest families wanted it clear that any gifts reported in his name were not made with his money. Himself a Democrat, he could give to Democratic candidates, whereas a Democratic gift with the name of one of his employers attached would create a commotion. As a matter of public relations, also, his employers disliked to give directly to individual candidates and did so through lieutenants who could be reimbursed.

61. There are many marginal cases, like that of the Washington attorney in a high tax bracket who took a small fee and asked his client to send a contribution to a designated candidate. Whose money was it?

differ from one group to another, and campaign officials themselves do not agree on the extent to which dummy names are used.[62] Committees with ample funds from respectable sources presumably receive fewer cloaked gifts than committees whose poverty forces them to take what they can get where they can get it. For some committees, the percentage of true reportings is undoubtedly higher.[63] After all, gifts too hot to handle can be routed to state or local committees, if necessary in localities where no reports are required. The traffic in transfers among committees offers ample opportunity to get the money back.

Completeness.—Aside from the accuracy of official reports is the matter of completeness. Unreported cash is handled in all political campaigns. A national finance chairman called the amount "significant." While the quantity is less at the national than at state levels,[64] situations arise in presidential campaigns in which money must be spent immediately and discreetly, and cash is better for both purposes.[65] Managers of candidates on tour have quietly received funds and paid current expenses without drawing a check. Especially at lower levels, contributors may "take on a project" as a Texas campaign manager, who is also a public

62. Data on the point are hardly abundant. One slant on the general reliability of committee reports can be obtained, nevertheless, by comparing the contributions they report with those reported by individual contributors.

In 1956, 259 persons submitted itemized lists of their contributions to the Gore Committee. These persons were shown by political-committee reports in the committee's possession to have contributed an aggregate of $5,000 or more during that year. The lists submitted by the contributors themselves included 1,073 gifts of such size, date, and destination that they should have been included on the political-committee reports submitted to the Gore Committee. After tracing for each of the 1,073 gifts, it was concluded that 90 per cent of them showed up where they were supposed to on the committee reports. The committees reported 17 gifts as being made by some of the 259 individuals but which did not appear on the lists submitted by those individuals.

63. The desire to avoid publicity is nevertheless evident even where reports are apparently accurate. Among 97 donors of from $50.00 to under $100 to the Citizens for Eisenhower-Nixon of Shelby County, Tennessee, in 1952, there were 84 who gave in amounts of $99 or more, including 57 who gave $99.99. If the committee had been required to report under existing federal statutes, the contributors below $100 need not have been named. As it was, a Senate subcommittee lowered the limit in making a special call for information.

64. Arthur H. Samish testified that 95 per cent of the voluminous campaign contributions he handled for his business clients in California were made in cash. The recipients therefore had some choice in how they did or did not account for them.—Kefauver Crime Committee, *Hearings,* part 10, pp. 1190-91. Abe Allenberg's tale of collections received and spent by him personally in a Florida gubernatorial primary is illustrative of practice in many places.—*Ibid.,* part 1, pp. 484-85.

65. A politico tells of secrecy surrounding cash operations in 1952. He was instructed to proceed to a specified hotel room in Chicago, where he was given a paper sack and told to deliver it to a specified hotel room in another city. The sack contained bills of large denomination. The carrier knew not how much, whence they came, or where they were going, but doubted they would show up in a report.

relations counselor, put it, and pay the bills direct.[66] There is a limit to the costs associated with presidential candidates that can be handled *sub rosa,* but in more obscure political sectors the risks are less, or by the terms of applicable statutes, nonexistent.[67]

Reports of expenditures pursuant to federal statute are more accurate than reports of contributors. Some sums paid out as advances, expense accounts, and the like, go for purposes that can only be surmised. But funds unaccounted for generally constitute a small percentage of total outlays.[68] The significant deficiency in statements of expenditures generally lies in their incomplete coverage, rather than in inaccuracies.[69]

Technical deficiencies.—The financial accounts political groups keep are conditioned by the kinds of public reports they are required to file. The task of preparing the reports required by the Federal Corrupt Practices Act, and by some state statutes, is considerable, and they vary greatly in form and in quality. Republican reports are generally in better technical shape, largely because their committees are better staffed. But the reports of virtually every national-level committee that reported to the Clerk of the House in 1952 had some kind of major or minor inconsistency. Itemizations frequently did not add up to the totals they were supposed to represent. Reports for the new year might not show the deficit or surplus appearing at the close of the old year. The reports are supposed to be cumulative from the first of the year, with contributors and expenditures itemized each time for previous as well as the current reporting period (unless no business was done during the current period). Few committees attempt to meet this onerous requirement. The stipulation that federal reports should cover activities through the day preceding that on which they are submitted puts the accounting officers who try to meet it in a periodic swirl. Especially disruptive is the requirement that a report be submitted on New Year's day covering the full previous year. To meet the deadline, the Republican na-

66. Personnel in a New Hampshire office-supply firm refused to make contributions but took over a mailing operation free. In the same state a taxi firm customarily provides a number of cars free on election day. Jack Redding provides good illustrations of contributions in kind to the 1948 presidential campaign made by persons in the film industry, printing, and the press.—*Inside the Democratic Party* (New York: The Bobbs-Merrill Company, Inc., 1958), pp. 249-50, 258-59, 261.

67. One legislative candidate in North Carolina asked that an important gift be held until after he had submitted his finance report. The dodges are legion. The practice of "palming" money to a candidate in a few locations would seem to be another.

68. See pages 387-99, below.

69. The opportunities for concealment are numerous, and illustrations are encountered particularly in connection with state and local reports. A Minnesota legislative candidate reported all his expenditures, except such personal ones as telephone bills, gas and oil costs, contributions at church meetings—which came to 45 per cent of the amount reported. A Connecticut speech-writer was always paid in cash, and he figured he knew why. A candidate for mayor kept a tab at a local bar, and the bill would not come in until after the campaign.

tional committee, for one, has closed out its activities several days before the end of the year.

The fact is, reports called for by both federal and state statutes take little cognizance of the operating problems of those who must submit or use them. No standard form is furnished to federal political committees, and those provided to candidates for senator and representative are hopelessly inadequate. In less than half the states forms are provided or stipulated by statute. The reports submitted pursuant to state laws are irregular in form and often do not provide the information called for.[70] Where they do, the condition of the reports usually precludes their easy use.

Some Republican committees habitually submit copies of all receipts they issue (from a penny up) as their report of contributions. In the case of the national committee, these take the form of a bale of oversized, tissue accounting sheets, sixth carbon, too dim for easy reading, always easily torn. The report of the Republican finance committee of Pennsylvania in 1952 was accompanied by 3700 transmittal slips listing contributions of all sizes. The 1952 committee reports to the Clerk of the House ran to well over 10,000 pages, accounting for upward of $20,000,000 in receipts. The volume of paper is enormous in state depositories too: 1442 committee reports were made to the New York Secretary of State in 1952 (others went to the New York City Board of Elections); approximately 1,000 were filed with his Connecticut counterpart two years later; and in Massachusetts the number regularly exceeds 2,000. Because of the latitude in federal reporting dates, reports from different committees may not cover the same periods of time, hence are not precisely comparable. The summary figures called for on the face of the reports sometimes conform to the specifications of the statute. Those that do can reasonably be compared with others that do. Many committees, however, send along whatever summaries their bookkeeping system happens to make available. To sort and sift the data for the kinds of compilations and comparisons attempted in this book required the exertions of several meticulous persons over a period of many months. The reports contain raw data, uncategorized in any substantial way for fast use or comparative analysis.[71] The daily press is necessarily

70. Deficiencies vary from state to state. They include such things as failure to show the full name or address of contributors, failure to provide dates of contributions or expenditures, failure to identify the purpose of expenditures, using categories that mask the sources of funds ("anonymous gifts") or their uses ("for services"), failure to identify clearly the organization submitting the report and its responsible officers, and the submission of reports that are internally inconsistent or that overlap reports submitted by subsidiary or cooperating groups or the candidates they support.

71. Especially in state reports are expenditures identified in such diverse and ambiguous ways that it becomes almost impossible to determine the actual purpose of financial outlays. The lack of standard categories calls for extremes of tedious labor even to summarize individual reports and makes comparisons with other reports, or from year to year, almost hopeless.

confined to the sort of exercise a pair of newspapermen from a state newspaper were observed in. They took a report of contributors, one running down the left-hand margin for newsworthy local names and the other fingering the right-hand column for dramatic sums.

The conditions under which campaign reports are available to the public often handicap their intelligent use. The personnel of the House File Clerk's office where federal committee reports are kept are personally cooperative. But the reports can be examined only during regular working hours. When Congress is in session, this is a normal workday. During the rest of the year, it has been customary to admit visitors only between 10:00 A.M. and 3:00 P.M., five days a week.[72] Table space is available for one or two people. Notes may be made in pen or pencil. The instructions given visitors vary from time to time, but on one occasion it was announced that the reports were for inspection only, not for verbatim copying. In practice, however, the reports can be abstracted in detail, or, indeed, copied, if by hand. The use of mechanical copying equipment is prohibited.[73]

The circumstances of the employees having custody of the reports affect the reception they give to visitors. They are all political appointees, dependent on the intricate network of personal esteem and service that connects them to the Clerk, or the Speaker, or the Minority Leader, or some other source of political favor. One week the visitor is permitted to copy the log that lists all committees filing reports. Another week he is informed that word has been received that the log cannot be shown, and no report is to be made available unless asked for by the name of the committee submitting it. If a novice shows up in an off week, he has no way of learning the names of the committees reporting and therefore no way to ask to see their reports. On one occasion the log was made available on condition it would not be "published in a newspaper," a precaution taken "to protect this office"—to protect it from, among other things, a deluge of requests to see the reports. For many years old reports were periodically sent to the National Archives. There they might be examined if permission were first obtained from the File Clerk. (The log, or Register Book, in which the reports are listed with the numbers necessary for finding them in Archives, was kept in the File Clerk's office, and no copy was available near the reports themselves.) In the spring of 1955, with Democratic control of the House reestablished, reports more than two years old in the custody of the File Clerk were removed and apparently burned or sold for scrap. An adequate explanation was not forthcoming through private or official inquiries.

72. Only one state depository was encountered that was open less than 40 hours per week.

73. Generally there is no restriction on copying in the state depositories. In one state, in fact, the Secretary of State simply gave the original reports to the inquiring visitor and told him to keep them.

The only reasonable surmise was that for partisan reasons the new leadership desired the reports destroyed.[74]

Public understanding.—After more than half a century of experience at federal and state levels, it is clear that a sharp distinction separates disclosure from public understanding of what is disclosed. No state or federal reporting system has kept the public systematically informed of the purposes for which money is spent. Dramatic costs are extracted for today's quote, but no evolving picture of how money is spent by the committees reporting has been forthcoming. The task of analyzing information on expenditures has been too demanding for any public or private agency.

Contributions have attracted more attention. More newsworthy, and more significant in the eyes of most, they have been publicized hit-and-miss in the papers, and occasionally on a systematic basis by Congressional committees. The only serious effort to give continuing, impartial, widespread publicity to important political contributors has been made by the *Congressional Quarterly*. It has done an able and useful job by making raw data from political committee reports available to the press and other subscribers. But even this effort, carried out at great expense to the publishers, cannot substitute for the kind of sustained analysis and impartial summarizing essential to achieve the goals claimed for the principle of public disclosure.

Coverage.—Under the present federal statute, some 100 to 150 groups report to the Clerk of the House in the even, election years; in off-years, the number usually falls below 50.[75] About one-third of those reporting in an election year are avowedly active across state lines on behalf of federal candidates. These include the regular and volunteer national-level party committees, various labor and miscellaneous organizations,

74. Research for this study, in the materials that were destroyed, had been completed in early 1955.

The Republican Assistant Attorney General, Warren Olney III, chided Democrats in Congress who had complained that executive departments were withholding documents from Congress. It was reported that the Justice Department wanted Democratic national committee reports for 1949-52 in connection with grand jury investigations of Internal Revenue Service scandals during the Truman administration. The report of the Republican national committee was also said to be desired in connection with a grand jury investigation of lobbying on the natural gas bill.—Anthony Lewis, *New York Times,* June 26, 1956.

In a few states the authorities meticulously lock up the reports as soon as they legally can; in most places, however, they are allowed to accumulate indefinitely. The 1956 reports of several important state and local committees in Pennsylvania (both parties) "somehow disappeared" from the files of the Secretary of the Commonwealth.—James Reichley, *The Art of Government—Reform and Organization Politics in Philadelphia* (New York: The Fund for the Republic, 1959), p. 58.

75. The number of "political committees" reporting to the Clerk of the House of Representatives pursuant to Section 302(c) of the Corrupt Practices Act was as follows in the years indicated: 1949, 46; 1950, 98; 1951, 45; 1952, 156; 1953, 42; 1954, 154; 1955, 47; 1956, 140; 1957, 48; 1958, 96.

and minor political parties. The rest of the organizations reporting are self-selected state and local groups that, on their own initiative, elect to report. Committees on behalf of several candidates for the House of Representatives are usually present. Several local or state labor groups, and one or two individuals, are likely to report.[76] For years the Pennsylvania Republican finance committee regularly submitted its voluminous reports. It stopped after 1954. Few other Republican finance committees ever did so, except that in New York, which continued the practice. In 1956, the Republican state committee in Wyoming and the Kentucky Volunteers for Stevenson-Kefauver favored the Clerk with reports, but their counterparts in other states did not.

When queried as to why some committees chose to report and others did not, committee officers invariably replied they had acted on advice of counsel. Advice of counsel not being uniform, a hodge-podge of financial statements is made available to the public as though it were a coherent body of data. In the resulting mélange, apples get added to oranges to produce bananas. Public understanding of campaign finance will be obstructed as long as the publicity system is conducted with little regard for consistency and for classification of the organizations expected to report.[77]

The federal requirement that individuals who spend $50.00 or over in more than one state, other than by a contribution, on behalf of a candidate for either house of Congress must submit reports has not produced any worth mention. The requirement that candidates for the House and Senate report contributions and expenditures handled by them personally, or by others with their knowledge and consent, has produced reports which, though no doubt technically accurate in most instances, are often meaningless. Funds handled by committees are

76. In 1956, for example, some 47 of the 140 reporting organizations were clearly involved in interstate campaigning in support of federal candidates. In addition, 34 state-level groups reported, including 21 familiar committees associated with the major parties and 10 state labor committees. From the local level, 34 committees sent in reports, 24 of which were labor political committees. Two individual contributors (H. R. Cullen of Houston and Frederick McKee of Pittsburgh) and 23 committees on behalf of Congressional candidates were also present.

77. There are many technical problems, including a need to dovetail with lobbying controls. One interstate group—whose wary chief exacted the promise that it go unnamed before he would discuss its affairs—was advised by its attorney to report both as a lobby organization and as a political committee.

All receipts of the organization from its *members* were to be reported as receipts for general lobbying purposes, regardless of amount, unless the funds were specifically earmarked for campaign purposes. All receipts from persons *not* formally members of the group would be considered as campaign contributions. If funds from members were used for campaign purposes, they would be shown on the lobby report as lump-sum, outgoing transfers, and on the political committee report similarly as incoming transfers from the committee. The political committee report would therefore show as individual contributors only those members who gave gifts subsequent to paying their dues, and any nonmembers.

usually not included in the candidates' statements, and ordinarily these are the bulk of the monies.[78]

Conditions of success.—Much said about deficiencies in the federal reporting system applies also to state efforts, yet state experience has not been uniform. In New Jersey a state campaign treasurer reflected derisively on the "misty amounts" reported over his name. A Minnesota man of experience spoke of pulling a total out of the air to enter on a finance report, and then shaping the breakdown to fit it. From a list of a thousand contributors, you pull off a few "harmless" names to meet the requirements of the law, reported a Kentucky state finance chairman, rendering the reports "totally meaningless." These practices are more prevalent than not, yet in a handful of states the reports display sufficient accuracy and completeness to make them useful sources of information for a tenacious student and potential sources of information for the public.

Many millions of dollars are accurately, and more or less systematically, accounted for each election year by campaign reports in Connecticut, Florida, Maryland, Massachusetts, New York, North Carolina, Ohio, Oregon, and Pennsylvania. In all of these states deficiencies are to be found, but, in all, certain reports are submitted with sufficient regularity, consistency of form, and completeness to be of interest. The tasks of summarizing and analyzing them, and circulating the results, are seldom attempted. But a body of data, important in the context, at least lies waiting.

The nine states listed are those in which field research revealed the 1952 reports to be of unusual value.[79] The state regulatory statutes shared several features in common: (1) There were either no ceilings on the amounts that could be spent, or the ceilings applied only to candidates and not to political committees. It was possible, in other words, to report accurately without breaching some ceiling on receipts or expenditures. (2) Candidates *and* committees were required to report in all these states. (3) The reports were to cover receipts as well as expenditures, (4) nominations as well as general elections. (5) In all the states there was some procedure for inspecting the reports submitted, and/or reporting to an enforcing authority if a required report did not arrive. In a few of the states the latter responsibility was not lodged in a public official. Instead, procedures were set up by which others might, in effect, do the same thing.[80] (6) In all the states except one an official

78. The Gore Committee *Report,* pp. 49-53, compares the expenditures reported by Senatorial candidates in 1956 pursuant to federal statute with expenditures of campaign committees on their behalf. With a few exceptions, committee funds were several times those reported by candidates.

79. The 1952 Oregon reports were destroyed. Those for 1954 were available.

80. The press supplies many stories of receiving officers who return reports for correction because they display on their surface some evidence of illegality, e.g., a gift in the name of a corporation, expenditures that exceed legal limits. Penalties against those who violate the reporting requirements are almost never

report form was prescribed. (7) In all of the states except one a central depository was designated to receive reports from statewide activities, and often local reports as well.[81]

The writing of a statute, of course, is not enough. State officials are notably reluctant to enforce any statutes regulating campaign finance, much less those pertaining to campaign reports.[82] The seriousness with which they view the reports can be decisive in the results obtained. Experience in Connecticut is instructive. Attention to enforcement has fluctuated in that state. Earlier than 1950 the office of the Secretary of State displayed slight interest in the reports submitted, or not submitted, to it. Only a small percentage of the affected candidates and committees reported and there were no prosecutions. Reports were submitted chiefly by important state candidates, the state central committees of the parties, and scattered town committees. A new secretary of state, a Republican, studied her responsibilities under the law, and with the help of the state

---

exacted. Rare is the kind of report that came from Alabama in 1954: both candidates for sheriff in the run-off primary in Chilton County were declared disqualified because they filed their expense accounts late. In Crenshaw County, the day before, two other candidates were similarly knocked out of the run-off.—*Birmingham Age-Herald,* May 29, 1954.

81. It is possible that in a state like Michigan, where reports are made to local depositories, a comprehensive canvass of all counties in the state would show much money accounted for. (After this was written it was learned that John P. White and John R. Owens are preparing an analysis based on a complete set of 1956 reports filed with the county clerks that was assembled in 1957 by the Attorney General of Michigan.) Exploratory forays in three states revealed, however, that reports easily get lost in the county depositories. Individuals disinclined to report also stood a better chance that their derelictions would be overlooked. A canvass was made in Maryland, nevertheless, a state without central reporting, with useful results.

Maine, Montana, New Hampshire, and Wyoming had statutes in 1952 that in general possessed the seven characteristics enumerated in the text. The Maine reports were destroyed about six months after the election, the law requiring that they be kept only that long. Detailed evaluations of the reporting systems in Montana and New Hampshire discovered serious deficiencies in the ways the statutes were administered.

82. For a thorough report on the lack of enforcement of campaign finance regulations in Maryland, with detailed specifications of failures on the part of candidates and others to conform to the law, and of judicial attitudes toward them, see Dwynal B. Pettengill, "Regulation of Campaign Finance—The Maryland Experience," *Maryland Law Review,* 19 (1959), 91-124.

Massachusetts has a procedure by which the Secretary of the Commonwealth refers to the Attorney General reports appearing not to be in conformity with the law. In 1954, he so referred 49 of the 2,856 reports submitted to his office. He also reported to the Attorney General 297 candidates and committees who failed to file at all.—Commonwealth of Massachusetts, *Election Statistics, 1950-54* (Public Document No. 43). Among 81 reports filed in South Dakota in 1952, 29 contained some deviation from the legal requirements.

In other nations requiring campaign reports, enforcement is also often lax. Some sort of record must have been set in the Philippines in 1951. Of 24,000 candidates, only 2,000 filed the required statements on time.—Avelina B. Lim, "Money and Philippine Politics" (typescript), p. 8.

party chairmen initiated an educational campaign. The state committee of both parties sent letters to candidates and local committees, and the Republican state committee sent out copies of the official reporting forms (as did the Secretary). Substantial improvement was achieved in 1952, with all state committees and committees backing candidates for the United States Senate and House reporting, along with 90 per cent of the local volunteer committees for Eisenhower and Stevenson and 76 per cent of the 338 town committees. In 1954, the results were better still, the percentage of complying town committees rising to 90.

Such energetic concern is unusual. Competent, passive fulfillment of their clearly defined legal responsibilities is the best to be hoped for from officials, even in the states with the most useful reports. The more general attitude is reflected by the comments of an attorney general in the West—"All of us are a bunch of liars"—and of an assistant secretary of state in the Midwest—"So far as this office is concerned those reports are an unmitigated damned headache."[83]

83. The ignorance and indifference of state officials seem to have declined somewhat since Pollock's experiences in the 1920's. He reported an amusing and shocking set of episodes revealing that many officials had no knowledge of the laws in their own states.—*Op. cit.,* p. 256. Nevertheless, incidents occur like that in Indiana in 1954. A spokesman in the Secretary of State's office advised a visitor that the state party central committees filed no reports anywhere, whereas by statute they were supposed to and did, though not in the Secretary's office.

14

THE COSTS OF POLITICS

PROBLEMS OF CAMPAIGN finance have cluttered the Congressional calendar for decades. They arise, basically, because it costs money to conduct free elections. That legal ceilings on campaign expenditures have proved ineffective cannot be attributed simply to the machinations of perverse and ingenious men. Politicians spend money because each, in the situation he finds himself in, cannot avoid it. The money spent has a functional utility that makes it essential to the electoral process.

Campaign practices change faster than most other aspects of party or factional life. Many adaptations politicians make to the changing context of their operations can first be seen in the style and methods of campaigns. The ways elections are conducted, the channels of communication and the forms of organization employed, respond sensitively to external, nonpolitical conditions. Some of these quickly affect the purposes for which campaign money is spent and the avenues by which it is routed within the party system. From the nation's beginning, radical innovations have periodically altered campaign procedures. A new time of innovation and of worriment followed World War II. Many people felt deep concern for the health of the country's politics. The sums spent in campaigns rose, and the things they were spent for changed. That the fundamental functions of campaigning were altered, however, was less certain. Form changes more readily than substance. The nature of both, however, affects the possibilities and difficulties of legal regulation.

1. COSTS IN PERSPECTIVE

Public discussion of campaign finance during the 1950's was colored by two basic assumptions: that political campaigning in the United States was costly compared with campaigning elsewhere and that costs were rising. These assumptions produced a conclusion: campaign costs are "too high." The conclusion implied that somebody knew how high they should be, yet nobody, except perhaps the legislators who adopted the arbitrary ceilings, had much to say on that point. And the assumptions themselves were of dubious validity.

The United States bill.—In Chapter 1 the total cash outlay for all campaigning in the United States in 1952 was placed at approximately $140,000,000. The estimate includes out-of-pocket expenditures made by parties, committees, and individuals for nomination and general election campaigning for all offices at all levels during the calendar year.[1] Campaign contributions in the form of goods and services, even not counting part-time voluntary help,[2] came in market value to *at least* another 5 per cent.

1. The estimate was reached in this way. The 48 states were divided on the basis of their electoral votes into three classes: I, 9 states with 15 or more; II, 25 states with 6 to 14; and III, 14 states with 3 to 5. From each class, four states were chosen for which the best campaign finance information was available. An inventory was then made of all nomination and general election contests held in each of the 12 states during 1952. An estimate was made of direct expenditures in connection with each contest (or type of contest, where numerous local offices were involved).

In making each of these estimates, official reports submitted by individuals, parties, candidates, labor and other groups were used when available. They were adjusted to avoid duplication of funds transferred from one group to another. They were adjusted on the basis of information on the completeness of the reports provided by interviews and known from the intended coverage of the reports.

An estimate of total direct expenditures was made for each of the 12 states; the state average for each presidential vote cast in the state was computed; and the mean of the average for each group of four states was computed. The mean cost per presidential vote for each of the three classes of states was then used to compute the total estimated expenditures of all states in each class, and the results added together to give the estimate of all state and local expenditures. The estimate of national-level expenditures was reached by adding all known expenditures and making adjustments (based on interviews) for presidential nominations and other unreported outlays. Then 15 per cent of the total estimate was added to cover the vague realm politicians call under-the-table money.

This is no actuarial table. The difficulties of choosing "sample states" and projecting information about them to embrace the entire Union would in any event be immense. The necessity for capitalizing on data that were adventitiously available further complicated the task. The weakest part of the estimate is that for county, town, and city elections. No data from external sources, however, have been encountered that seem inconsistent with it. If the over-all estimate were 25 per cent over or under, the total cost in 1952 would have been no more than $175,000,000 and no less than $105,000,000, either a small sum in the total sweep of United States government.

The average expenditures per presidential vote cast in the 12 states used were as follows: Class I: California, $2.04; Pennsylvania, $1.75; Massachusetts, $2.12; New York, $1.19—average $1.78; Class II: Colorado, $1.20; Connecticut, $1.57; Maryland, $1.83; North Carolina, $1.22—average $1.45; Class III: Montana, $2.35; New Hampshire, $1.59; Utah, $1.18; Wyoming, $1.32—average $1.61. The figure would be expected to vary from state to state in accordance with numerous factors, including the number and character of nomination and election contests held for other than the presidency. The total estimated expenditures were much higher in some states than others: for example, $10,500,000 in California, $765,000 in Colorado, and $620,000 in Montana.

2. Which can assume enormous proportions: the Montgomery County (Ohio)

In modern America, $140,000,000 is not, *prima facie,* a large sum. The federal, state, and local governments that are manned by elected officials collected taxes in 1952 of some $80,000,000,000 (1957 estimate: $99,000,000,000), from a national income of $292,000,000,000 (1957 estimate: $364,000,000,000). Political campaigns are concerned with communicating to a wide public. In 1952, one advertising agency alone handled billings exceeding the $140,000,000 estimate for all political campaigns. Two others spent almost as much. A stockholders' fight for control of one corporation called forth more than $1,000,000 in campaign expenses.[3] It was said that one contribution to one candidate in one labor union election amounted to $40,000.[4] Nothing about the national income nor the scope of expenditures for public and private activities in the United States suggests automatically that Americans pay more for choosing their elective officials than is reasonable. More may be spent in specific instances than required by specific standards of necessity, but the over-all financial burden is light compared with the nation's resources that are deployed for other ends.[5]

Foreign comparisons.—Also, it is not clear that campaign costs are invariably higher in the United States than in other nations with popular elections. Less is known regarding campaign finance elsewhere, but a few gross comparisons are possible.

According to the 1952 estimate for the United States, a nation of over 150,000,000 people, the cash cost of electioneering for the year was around 90 cents per capita.[6] This estimate covered all nominations and elections throughout the several levels of government. Candidates for many different offices were active, some types of contests requiring very

Citizens for Eisenhower Committee calculated that in pre-convention and election activities in 1952 its volunteer workers contributed 9,145 hours to Ike's cause.

3. Robert R. Young admitted spending about $500,000 in his successful effort to gain control of the New York Central Railroad, and the existing management spent slightly more in its unsuccessful effort to retain it.—*Fortune,* 50 (1954), 87.

4. Allegedly given by Captain William V. Bradley, president of the International Longshoremen's Association (independent), to the election campaign of Ray White for the post of secretary-treasurer of the Seafarers' International Union (AFL).—*Norfolk Virginian-Pilot,* December 31, 1954.

5. Illustrations abound of nonpolitical costs that dwarf those of campaigning, beginning with the $200,000,000 or so of which Californians are relieved each year by slot machines and the almost $500,000,000 in bad checks cashed in 1953. In 1955, the General Motors Corporation spent $62,500,000 on newspaper advertising alone, with Ford putting in $29,600,000, and Chrysler $24,000,000 for the same purposes. In the six years following World War II, mail subsidies to air lines averaged $88,000,000 annually. Al Capone's operations seem to have grossed well over $100,000,000 a year, with the payroll of Chicago officials—all of them, personally or through their superiors, ultimately responsible at the ballot box—taking $2,000,000 of it.

6. For comparisons between nations, per capita expenditures are a more convenient indicator of relative costs than expenditures per eligible voter or per vote cast. They are probably more appropriate, too, given the varieties in settings and institutions from nation to nation.

little money and some much more. Most voters cast ballots to fill at least six different offices, and the average was actually much higher. The mean per capita cost per elective office filled (nomination, often by primary, *and* election) was thus a maximum of 15 cents. If it were assumed that in fact expenditures in a given constituency were made only on behalf of candidates for three offices, e.g., president, governor, and United States representative, then the per capita per office cost would be 30 cents. Clumsy though this index is, it is interesting to compare costs computed in a similar way for elections abroad.

In a British Parliamentary election, voters choose among candidates for one office only. The cost per capita in the year of a Parliamentary election appears conservatively to be at least 16 cents, and if account were taken of the considerable volume of off-year expenditures, the cost per capita per election would be substantially higher.[7] Comparatively more seems to be spent by party organizations between elections in Great Britain than in the United States. The 1957 Bundestag elections in West Germany are said to have involved, at a minimum, the cash expenditure of 50,000,000 marks.[8] This amounts to $12,500,000 in a nation of 50,000,000 people, or 25 cents per capita. The impression given of the Italian Parliamentary elections in the spring of 1958 is that per capita expenditures ran to nearly 50 cents.[9] Elections in Israel in 1955 probably outdid anything ever seen in a large American jurisdiction:

7. The actual costs of British campaigning are not known, but bases exist for estimates. An over-all estimate for the entire year and for the Parliamentary election of 1950 was arrived at as follows: total expenditures during the campaign period reported from the constituencies on behalf of 1,868 candidates for 625 seats, £1,170,124; estimated 1950 income of National Executive of Labor Party, £350,000; estimated 1950 expenditures by local Labor party organizations not in election period, £200,000; estimated direct expenditures by unions and others for Labor party, £50,000; estimated unreported Conservative and Liberal party expenditures, £1,000,000; for a grand total of £2,770,124, or (at $2.80) $7,760,000, which is about 16 cents for each of 50,000,000 people.

The estimate may well be low. Herman Finer puts total constituency organization and headquarters expenses at roughly £3,250,000 per year, *any* year.—*Governments of Greater European Powers* (New York: Henry Holt and Company, 1956), pp. 87-88. It is quite difficult to learn much about expenditures made between elections and by the central offices of the Conservative and Liberal parties, but the reports of the National Executive Committee to the Annual Conference of the Labor party, the financial reports of unions, and the report on trade unions of the Chief Registrar of Friendly Societies provide a good base for Labor party estimates. Large amounts of voluntary labor are contributed to both parties.

8. F. R. Allemann, "German Election Funds," *The New Leader,* August 26, 1957, pp. 5-6. "One of the most conservative published estimates" placed CDU expenditures alone at 10,000,000 marks in the 1953 election. (Costs reportedly mounted sharply in 1957.) Year-round party expenses in Germany are substantial, too. See Arnold J. Heidenheimer, "German Party Finance: The CDU," *American Political Science Review,* 51 (1957), 269-85, especially 283.

9. Ernest O. Hauser, "He Does Things Big," *The Saturday Evening Post,* September 20, 1958, p. 70. The subtitle reads: "Not even the colorful excesses of some of America's most notorious spenders can match the exploits of flamboyant Achille Lauro, Italy's amazing superpolitician."

over $5.00 per capita.[10] Comparisons of this sort are fraught with difficulties,[11] but at least they allay fears that the United States is seized by a unique malady.

Are costs rising?—The widespread impression that campaign costs rose steadily through the 1950's grew from several circumstances. Much campaign energy focused around the new use of television, a medium that reached a wide audience with remarkable ease, but at a high cost for each broadcast, and a cost that had to be met in advance. Moreover, the price of many other campaign items was shown to be dramatically higher than in earlier years. It was reported, for example, that between 1940 and 1955 the average gross cost of a black-and-white page advertisement in certain national magazines rose over 100 per cent; the gross cost of a page advertisement in a large number of morning newspapers rose over 200 per cent; the comparable rise for evening newspapers was over 118 per cent; and the gross time cost for a half hour of radio and television over the full facilities of the National Broadcasting Company in 1955 was more than 500 per cent higher than the corresponding charge for radio in 1940.[12] Candidates themselves, moreover, complained of increased financial burdens bearing on them personally. And political committees reported larger expenditures as the years went by. There could be no doubt that dollar outlays for campaigning were moving upward.

Whether the *real total costs* of campaigning—as measured by the purchasing power of the dollars spent—were rising was another matter. During the period 1940-55 alluded to above, the consumer's price index rose more than 90 per cent, the dollar value of per capita personal income 215 per cent, and the dollar value of the total national income more than 250 per cent. In other words, dollars on the whole brought only slightly more than half in 1955 what they had in 1940, and throughout the nation there were seven dollars where there had been two before. This is not to say that in all circumstances campaigners got only half as much for their dollars during the 1950's as they had in 1940, nor that all campaigners had three or four times as many to spend. But it does mean that in company with most other economic activities in the country, campaign budgets would normally be expected to increase markedly after World War II.

Grand totals of political expenditures for a series of years do not exist, but significant sectors of campaign activity can be compared over time. These show a generally consistent pattern of rising campaign

10. Marver H. Bernstein estimated party expenditures at about $10,000,000—*The Politics of Israel* (Princeton: Princeton University Press, 1957), p. 85.

11. Expenditures by particular candidates in particular campaigns may far exceed the averages indicated here. Presumably, concurrent campaigning on a party ticket *ought* to lower the cost of campaigning for each candidate, but seldom is full-slate joint campaigning actually found in the United States.

12. Testimony of Carroll P. Newton, Vice President of Batten, Barton, Durstine and Osborne, Gore Committee *Hearings*, part 2, p. 440.

costs consonant with the rising price level, the rising national income, and growth of the population and number of voters. The facts that can be marshalled should sober the discussion of campaign finance. Contrary to most belief, campaign costs are not caught by a runaway inflation that threatens with new dangers the good health of American politics. The data for several types of campaign operations will be examined in order.

1. As always, the most dependable data pertain to national-level campaign activities. There are several ways to judge the reality of the increases that have occurred in the amounts of money spent. Professor Overacker compared *direct expenditures* of the two national committees in the presidential years 1912 through 1928—during which period there were no legislative inducements to divide the national campaign effort among several committees. She found that although total direct expenditures (which do not include transfers of funds to other groups) rose from $2,870,000 in 1912 to $7,220,000 in 1928, the cost per presidential vote cast remained virtually the same, between 19 and 20 cents—and this during a period when the price level rose 40 per cent. (The percentage of the national income represented by the two sums remained the same—.008.)[13] By 1952, total direct expenditures by national campaign organizations associated with the parties had risen to $11,140,000, and by 1956 to $12,090,000, but these sums represented only 18 and 19 cents, respectively, for each presidential vote cast. (The percentage of the national income thus consumed fell in both years to .004.)

An examination of national campaign expenditures for 1940, 1944, 1952, and 1956 further reveals that campaign costs follow general trends in the price level. Although information for these four years is not precisely comparable, it is sufficiently so for present purposes. All of the elections in question followed the enactment of the Hatch Acts which affected the financial organization of the parties. The data show that the total combined direct expenditures of national-level political committees, regular and volunteer, of both parties were greater in 1952 than 1940 by 42 per cent, and in 1956 by 54 per cent:[14]

13. Louise Overacker, *Money in Elections* (New York: The Macmillan Company, 1932), pp. 79-81. The 1912 figure includes expenditures by the Roosevelt Progressives as well as by the Republican and Democratic national committees.

14. The 1940 information was derived from the Gillette Committee *Report,* pp. 10-12, 115, 142, utilizing also Louise Overacker, "Campaign Finance in the Presidential Election of 1940," *American Political Science Review,* 35 (1941), 713. Although the report indicates awareness of transfers of funds, and indeed identifies some, it is possible that the figure for direct expenditures presented here includes some money transferred to other committees. It is highly unlikely that any transfers so included would be sufficient to alter this analysis.

The 1944 information was derived from the Green Committee *Report,* pp. 79, 242-44. The elimination of transfers is more certain. Some expenditures by labor groups are included in the 1944 figure, though not in the other years. The only effect of eliminating these labor funds from 1944 would be to drop the total expenses of the two parties even lower than they were in 1940. The 1940 and 1944 totals do not include expenditures by the Congressional campaign committees,

	Total Direct Expenses, National-Level Committees, Both Major Parties Combined	*Percentage Change From 1940*
1940	$ 7,830,000	—
1944	7,660,000	— 2
1952	11,140,000	+42
1956	12,090,000[15]	+54

The increase was not as large as the change in the price level and growth of the nation would lead one to expect.[16]

2. Most campaigning is carried on, however, through state and local activities. If a different proportion of the total campaign burden were borne by state and local campaign groups in the 1950's than in 1940 or 1944, the rate of national-level expenditures would be a false index to the level of total expenditures. Suggestive indicators of change in campaign costs can be found for the lower levels, too. It is possible to compare the volume of activities of certain state and local committees for 1940, 1944, and 1952. They point to the kind of dollar increases that would normally be expected.[17]

Roughly comparable information on *total disbursements*[18] in 1940

whereas the totals for later years do, a fact that tends to exaggerate the increases between the earlier and later years.

15. This figure covers the full calendar year and is slightly more than $300,000 higher than the total generally used elsewhere in this book for the combined direct expenditures of the two parties in 1956. The smaller figure, which covers the first eleven months, is used because it can be itemized by types of expenditure whereas the breakdown is not available for the full calendar year.

16. Although small in the total context of campaign finance, it should be noted that off-year activities of the national-level party committees have tended to increase at a more rapid rate than election-year exertions. A similar tendency seems to exist at the state level.

The combined *total disbursements* of the two regular national committees were as follows: in years following a presidential election—1937, $2,090,000; 1953, $2,130,000; 1957, $1,950,000; in years following a mid-term election—1939, $1,470,-000; 1955, $2,170,000. The combined *total receipts* of the national, Senatorial, and Congressional campaign committees of both parties were as follows: in the years following a presidential election—1945, $1,570,000; 1953, $2,660,000; 1957, $2,150,-000; in the years following a mid-term election—1947, $1,540,000; 1955, $3,060,000.

17. The areas for comparison were chosen on the basis of availability of comparable information. The 1956 information collected by the Gore Committee from state and local committees is not used. It covered only the period September 1–November 30, and consequently is not wholly comparable with the data for earlier calendar years. The 1940 data used here come from the Gillette Committee *Report*, pp. 106-29, and from Overacker, "Campaign Finance in the Presidential Election of 1940," p. 708. Information for 1944 about most of these groups is also at hand in the Green Committee *Report*, pp. 102-21, and on county committees, pp. 241-42. A generally consistent drop occurred in 1944, similar to that of the national-level committees.

18. Data on direct expenses, the preferred index since they include no transfers of funds to other groups, were not available for the earlier years. Total disburse-

and 1952 was usable for 41 regular party state committees (21 Democratic, 20 Republican). Any committee whose function within the total party operations of its state[19] was known to have changed between the two years was eliminated from the comparison. The total disbursements of the 41 groups rose from $4,490,000 in 1940 to $6,150,000 in 1952, an increase of 37 per cent. In addition, comparable *total receipts* for nine Republican state finance committees—a more significant criterion for them than expenditures—were examined. They were found to have risen from $5,490,000 to $8,030,000, an increase of 46 per cent.

3. Information on the *total disbursements* of local campaign groups was available only for county committees in Pennsylvania, and a comparison of 1944, rather than 1940, with 1952 was necessary. Political expenditures at the national and state levels were generally lower in 1944 than in 1940, no doubt because of the war, and presumably they were lower at local levels also. In any event, the disbursements of 93 regular party county committees in Pennsylvania (45 Democratic and 48 Republican) showed a boost from $1,180,000 in 1944 to $1,890,000 in 1952, or an increase of 59 per cent.[20]

Dollar outlays by these regular state and local party groups rose—as was true of the national-level groups—less than the 90 per cent increase between 1940 and 1952 in the consumer's price index. But may not new campaign groups other than the regular party committees have come into operation after 1940 to absorb an increased financial burden? The number of volunteer committees spurted upward in 1940, but there is no evidence that their importance increased thereafter.[21]

4. The growth in over-all national-level *direct expenditures* between 1940 and 1956 was accounted for by a rise in the outlays of the regular, not the volunteer, organizations. The Associated Willkie Clubs of

---

ments nevertheless serve satisfactorily for our purpose: namely, comparing the volume of money flowing through a regular party committee at two different times. There is a better chance that the same committee's practices regarding transfers of funds will remain constant over a period of time than that the practices of two different committees will be found comparable at any given time. Total disbursements are not satisfactory, for example, for comparing the relative financial resources of competing parties, as discussed on pages 19-20, above. In some states, Republican finance committees for fund-raising purposes developed between 1940 and 1952. Any such cases not eliminated from the computations would tend to lower erroneously the observed relative increase in 1952, though not enough to upset the use of the data for this analysis.

19. See pages 309-17, above.

20. In these computations differences in the magnitude of change between individual state and local committees were in frequent evidence. Some even showed a decline, as did the Republican state committee in Indiana, one home of the 1940 Republican presidential nominee. Individual fluctuations are explainable by many factors, including the energies of leaders in a given campaign year. The increases for the bulk of the committees, however, tended to hover around the group averages.

21. See pages 353-55, above.

America, the Democrats for Willkie, and the Citizens' Information Committee, all national groups, in 1940 spent a total of $1,950,000, more than all Republican national volunteer and Republican national miscellaneous campaign committees combined in 1956. The Democratic direct expenditures for national *ad hoc* groups showed an increase between the two years from something over $470,000 to about $660,000.[22]

5. What went on among volunteer committees at state and local levels is more difficult to determine, yet their importance does not seem to have increased significantly.

The Gillette Committee in 1940 collected information on about 150 *ad hoc* groups at all levels that were organized to further the campaign of either Mr. Willkie or Mr. Roosevelt. With some difficulty the state-level *ad hoc* groups were sorted out from these. They accounted for around 11 per cent of the expenditures reported for all state-level committees for which information was obtained by the Committee. No reports were listed from a great many states, and it is to be presumed that the Committee's coverage of the regular state committees was more complete than that of the volunteer committees formed to support the presidential candidates. In 1956, the Gore Committee assembled information from a much larger number of *ad hoc* presidential campaign groups. The coverage was more complete for the state level, and the volunteer organizations were found to have made 23 per cent of state-level campaign expenditures. They made 9 per cent of those reported at the local level.[23]

While coverage at these levels in 1956 was doubtless not complete, the 1940 data for *ad hoc* groups was less so. It cannot be concluded, therefore, that a significantly more important share of the presidential campaign effort in 1956 was conducted through the volunteer groups than in 1940. Even if this were true, however, in 1956 the volunteer presidential committees did not play so important a role in state and local campaign activities as to render unsuitable the expenditures of regular party committees as indexes to trends in the levels of state and local spending.

6. One may ask, of course, whether *ad hoc* committees on behalf of candidates for offices other than the presidency increased in importance after 1940. There is no evidence that this was the case, and the impressionistic evidence is largely negative. In 1936, the Lonergan Committee referred to the innumerable independent state political committees

22. The Stevenson-Kefauver Campaign Committee, which spent directly slightly over $1,000,000 in 1956, is not considered a volunteer organization, but rather, like the 1952 Headquarters and Travel Committee, Springfield, as an adjunct of the regular party campaign machinery.

23. Derived from the Gillette Committee *Report,* pp. 39-40. Volunteer committees are generally active only during the campaign, so the 1956 data for the period September 1–November 30 are comparable to the 1940 calendar-year material in this respect. There was no significant advance in the volume of expenditures by minor parties and miscellaneous campaign groups.

then in existence as "tremendous in scope and financial import."[24] For many years candidate committees have operated across the whole country, and there is no reason to believe that these activities were greater in 1956 than in 1940.

7. Finally, there is the possibility that the invisible portion of the campaign iceberg has increased more rapidly than the visible portion. Individuals have always paid for advertising and made other expenditures out of their own or somebody else's funds without going through accountable committees. Proportionately, a larger share of total campaign costs may well have been handled thus in *earlier* days. More lenient tax laws made it easier, at least under some circumstances, for wealthy individuals to accumulate and use large sums of cash for political purposes. The increased emphasis on systematic party solicitations in the later period, moreover, would seem to draw more of the available funds into formal channels. These are merely hunches, but in the absence of contrary evidence they appear plausible.

With allowance for a wide margin of error—even if the above computations underestimate the climb of campaign costs by 50 per cent—the costs of campaigning rose between 1940 and 1956 no faster than the cost of living.[25] Whether they will rise in the future at a faster rate remains to be seen. Direct expenditures at the national level in 1956 were between 8 and 9 per cent above 1952. This sharp rise could largely be attributed to the increased use of television.[26] Television consumes a much smaller share of the state and local campaign bill, however. There is no basis for comparing expenditures at state and local levels in 1952 and 1956, but any increase that occurred was doubtless under that at the national level.

The point has been to temper the discussion of campaign finance. There are many qualifications to the customary sweeping assumptions that American campaigning is unusually costly and that its costs are ever rising. Why campaign expenditures rise or fall depends on many things, to which we now turn.

2. VARIABLES THAT INFLUENCE CAMPAIGN COSTS

The concept of cost.—Most interest in campaign costs focuses on individual campaigns. The difficulties of determining the cost of any single campaign, however, are formidable. Despite glib assertions of what it costs to get elected governor, or how much a congressman spent last time, no consistent definition of campaign cost is applied in the usual discussions. Many different components can be embraced by the con-

24. *Report*, p. 25.

25. An unusual rise in the costs of nominating campaigns or of nonpartisan elections would not be detected by the above analysis of general-election finances. Evidence is hard to find, however, to support the hypothesis that the sums spent for these activities have risen relatively so much more than the sums spent in general elections that they affect materially the conclusions of this analysis.

26. See pages 403-5, below.

cept. Often persons who speak with most assurance concerning total figures are least sure of what they cover. Numerous elements may properly be included, but there are obstacles to finding out what value should be assigned to each.

Expenditures are made through party and other political committees for the benefit of candidates. When a committee supports more than one candidate, frequently the case, what share of the committee's expenditures should be assigned to the campaign bill of each candidate? Occasionally a party organization—like the United Republican Finance Committee of Los Angeles County in 1956—submits a report that allocates specific expenditures to a specific candidate—in this case, Senator Thomas H. Kuchel.[27] But generally the records do not do this. Even if they did, sums are spent through party committees for advertising and organizational work on behalf of several candidates at once. It is doubtful that any cost accounting procedure could satisfactorily apportion such expenditures among all the candidates on the slate in a way that would reflect the relative importance to each of the monies spent.

Campaign activity for any single national, state, or district office is often carried on at all three of those levels. A candidate for United States senator benefits from nationwide exertions on behalf of his party, and from precinct expenditures by his local aides, as well as from the undertakings of himself and his state manager. These splits in campaign organization make an accurate tally of campaign costs virtually impossible. In addition to monies raised and disbursed through a candidate's headquarters, local groups frequently raise and spend funds of which no accounting is made to any central organization. Generally, no one *can* know how much money was used. A meticulous canvass of all campaign operations can yield a plausible estimate, but this exercise is considered to be of little use by practicing politicians and is too laborious for most others.

Sometimes the campaign costs of a candidate are thought of simply as the funds for which the candidate himself, with his managers, is responsible. These may take the form of a quota to be contributed to the party's budget. More often, and perhaps in addition, they may be the dollars necessary to run the candidate's personal headquarters and to meet the expenses on tour of himself and his entourage. Even such identifiable costs, however, are often necessarily vague. Supporters may pay directly for services and supplies or make them available at less than normal cost. Even if such obstacles to an accurate accounting of campaign expenditures did not exist, the kinds of books kept by many *ad hoc* campaign groups (and some others as well) do not record accurately the costs of the frantic crash operations most of them are engaged in.

In the study of campaign costs, where the financial burdens fall and how they are met are more important in the selection of candidates and

27. Gore Committee *Report,* p. 49.

their backers than the total sums spent. In a campaign involving a million dollars, much of it may be raised and spent through established party machinery. The requirements on a candidate are entirely different when, even though only a tenth as much is needed, he is responsible for raising all of it himself or through his personal followers.

Variables.—Every influence that conditions the shape of American life sooner or later bears on the style and conduct of American politics. There are several specific kinds of factors, however, that affect directly the volume of political expenditures. Each of these is of a different order from the others. Some help to explain differences between the United States and other nations; some expose changes that have taken place within the United States; others relate to differences between one jurisdiction and another, or between one election and another in the same jurisdiction. Four types are especially important.

(1) *The nature of the electorate,* its social organization and the suffrage requirements, has a profound effect on the type of campaigning that exists. (2) Characteristics of the *election-and-party system,* some of legal origin and others not, account for differences. (3) Within the institutional setting fixed by these two sets of influences are *situational factors* peculiar to individual campaigns that lead to radical fluctuations in campaign outlays. (4) Finally, more general *societal characteristics,* including the state of prosperity and technology, form the milieux of political campaigns and fix specific aspects of them.

Implied in the discerned effects of these four sets of variables is a general proposition: as popular involvement in the selection of public officials increases, so do the costs of campaigning. To reduce the costs and not alter unintentionally the conditions of popular government therefore requires knowledge of why the money is spent.

The electorate.—In a hereditary monarchy, the cost of changing rulers is confined to the expense of a royal funeral and a coronation. Where there is no election, there are no election expenses. The degree and character of popular participation in elections has a formidable effect on the requirements and costs of campaigning. Like England, the United States has experienced a steady broadening of the popular base of politics as property and other qualifications for voting and holding office have been lowered.

The early presidential elections, when electors from many states were chosen by state legislatures, posed entirely different problems for the canvass from those which emerged as the practice of naming electors by popular vote grew. The changes were not simply in the number of persons who had to be addressed.[28] Changes occurred

28. One student of Swedish elections concluded that between 1915 and 1950 the cost of an electoral struggle seemed "to be doubled 20 times" [*sic*]. He relates this development to the sharp increase in electoral participation and the accompanying rise in party propaganda and organizational activities.—Elis Hastad (translated by Richard Kanost), "Swedish Party Organization" (Stockholm: The Swedish Institute, 1951) (mimeographed), pp. 31-34.

in the social organization and political followerships that accompanied the ever widening suffrage and growing population. A landed gentleman could not command his seat in the English Parliament as a matter of course, as once many had. The gentlemen of Virginia and Massachusetts who served the United States as its first presidents possessed few of the qualities later found essential for success before a diversified and ambitious electorate. Campaigns designed to whoop it up for the common man began to appear and with them an increasing need for a "war chest."[29] Somebody had to pay for the bands, badges, banners, and barbecues that appeared in 1840; and for the "log-cabin headquarters at every crossroads, with the latch string out and hard cider always on tap."[30]

The popularization of politics increases its costs. Campaigning for statewide office in Virginia in the second quarter of the twentieth century without question cost less than in other southern states of comparable population. The explanation lay in the astonishingly low turnout of voters and in the "well-knit organization" guided by Senator Byrd—as a top Byrd leader was proud to point out.[31] In the early days of industrial labor it cost little for plant owners to pass the political word among their employees. The growth of politically conscious unions has hiked the cost of competing for these votes.

Elections and the party system.—The characteristics of the electoral system and of the parties that compete within it are closely connected with each other. They both affect directly the level of political costs. Some of these features are legal in character and others are found in patterned behavior without legal roots.

The extraordinarily long ballot in much of the United States is importantly responsible for the level of total campaign costs, as is the use of nominating procedures involving large-scale popular participation (usual-

29. A term, we are told, that gained coinage with other analogies between political and military warfare during the nineteenth century. "Campaign fund" was apparently not used until after the Civil War.—Eugene H. Roseboom, *A History of Presidential Elections* (New York: The Macmillan Company, 1957), p. 25. Explicit, systematic information about early campaign costs does not seem to exist, although inferences of gross relative costs can be made.

30. Roseboom, *op. cit.*, p. 121. The use of band music and songs is described by one author as the most remarkable innovation.—George Stimpson, *A Book About American Politics* (New York: Harper and Brothers Publishers, 1952), p. 126.

31. See V. O. Key, Jr., *Southern Politics in State and Nation* (New York: Alfred A. Knopf, 1949), pp. 19-35, 463-70.

Richards S. Childs has for half a century pointed to the consequences of "unwieldy constituencies"—constituencies so large a candidate cannot conduct a canvass by personal exertions and private financial means. He argues that campaign costs necessarily rise with increases in the size of constituencies. See his *Civic Victories—The Story of an Unfinished Revolution* (New York: Harper and Brothers Publishers, 1952), pp. 48-56, and successive drafts of the National Municipal League's "Model State Campaign Contributions and Expenditures Law" (the third draft, mimeographed, dated November, 1959), pp. 5-6.

ly primaries, but conventions as well). The larger the number of elections, and the more complex the party structures organized to compete in them, the more they cost. Moreover, the more reluctant government is to carry the cost of operating the election system, the greater the burden on politicians and their financial supporters. American practice still leaves in private hands most of the responsibility for getting voters registered and to the polls, a costly phase of electioneering that in some countries is a public charge.

Campaign styles, too, influence costs. Joint campaigning by candidates presumably lowers the cost to each of public speeches and their broadcasting.[32] The coffee hours in California provide candidates with an inexpensive campaign forum suitable to the social structure and living habits of constituents. The length of campaigns, often inherited from times when campaign conditions were radically different, affects the financial burden. Taboos on campaign practices do too. In France, posters may be hung only in designated places where appear the posters of all parties. In Britain, radio and television broadcasting is severely limited, and such political time as is allowed is provided free. Many detailed features of custom and regulation influence the characteristics and hence the costs of electioneering.

The intensity and extent of competition within and between the parties also affect costs. Factional contests waged in primary elections for control of nominations and party posts can exceed the costs of a general election. Wide use of presidential primaries, for a prime example, under modern conditions spirals the costs of presidential politics sharply upward. The spread of competition between the parties, moreover, brings with it an increase in campaigning. Constituencies content to return officials to office without opposition help keep the costs of politics low. The nationalization of political issues observed in the United States in recent years has, however, decreased the areas of one-party dominance. It may be true also that competition has intensified as the controversial subjects debated in a campaign have increased in number and complexity. The impact of many specific issues formerly of concern to limited sectors of the electorate is now felt more widely, although whether the result is confusion and apathy or increased involvement is sometimes difficult to tell. Activating voters in the United States has always seemed to require more effort then in many other nations. Intense interest in election issues has contributed to a high turnout of voters in European elections and to much volunteer campaign labor,[33] the latter a factor that would persumably help keep costs down. The heat of competition, however, in systems where many

32. An observer in Norway thought the emphasis on the national party, as opposed to individual candidates, helped keep Norwegian election expenditures down.

33. Harold F. Gosnell, *Why Europe Votes* (Chicago: University of Chicago Press, 1930), p. 211.

highly doctrinaire parties compete against each other can run up the campaign bill, as apparently has happened in Israel.[34]

Situational factors.—Much discussion of costs implies an unreal degree of stability in campaign processes. Amounts spent, however defined, fluctuate widely, even within a setting fixed by a constant electorate and electoral system. In contests for the same office in the same state, expenditures may go up and down sharply from year to year.[35] An issue or a personality can convert one year's placid canvass into a torrid rivalry the next. Expenditures vary likewise with the duties and opportunities of office. Races for sheriff are likely to attract more money than races for other county posts. Moreover, the campaign procedures appropriate to the locale, the candidate, and the office differ from one jurisdiction to another. A congressman with half a state to cover has a different task from one whose constituents are crowded together in mid-Manhattan. A gnarled veteran with a coterie of beholden precinct workers can campaign for less than a newcomer who must build a following. A party backed by a partisan newspaper is relieved of certain advertising costs that fall on parties that buy their space. (The presence of a large number of sharply partisan papers in some nations is said to reduce the campaign burden on the parties.) The skill of candidates and managers in their use of funds affects how much they spend, and the financial resources of candidates may have a determinative effect on the sums raised and spent. Candidates tend to attract funds in rough proportion to their electoral appeal, but a wealthy adventurer—or a subsidized political party, familiar abroad—can bid up the cost of a campaign merely by the use of a private purse.[36]

Societal characteristics.—The preceding discussion illustrates certain types of variables that cause campaign expenditures to vary. Aside from immediate situational factors, many of those mentioned are institutional in character and could, technically speaking, be altered by statute. There are more basic characteristics of society, however, that bear on the conduct and costs of campaigns.

The level of prosperity is one. The United States has been a society of abundance from its beginning. This abundance, distributed as a high

34. Bernstein, *op. cit.*, pp. 54-56, 84-85. The costs of between-campaign operations are naturally higher among "parties of integration" that seek to influence all aspects of its members' lives.

35. Detailed discussions with candidates and campaign managers in 11 southern states revealed that in virtually every state certain winning candidates had "spent" between two and five times as much as certain other winning candidates during a 15-year period. This was true even when those who campaigned with little or no funds were eliminated from consideration. In some states the range was even greater. Unstructured aspects of southern Democratic primaries may make such variations more likely than in general elections between continuing party organizations, though dramatic shifts in total outlays are found in two-party areas too.

36. The success of new political fund-raising techniques is, in the opinion of some, making unaccustomed amounts of money available and hence is pushing up the amounts spent.

standard of living for most of its people, has been essential for the kind of democratic system the country has enjoyed.[37] The abundance has contributed also to the flamboyance of campaigning, to the sums of money at the disposal of politicians, and to the ability of the country to finance a large number of simultaneous campaigns for different offices. To be spent, money must be available, and in the United States, as in other nations where per capita campaign costs per office may be higher, the level of campaign expenditures, like the level of recreational and educational expenditures, depends in part on national prosperity. Transitory fluctuations in the business cycle affect campaign contributions, as Boss Flynn noted in connection with Al Smith's campaign in the lush year 1928.[38] In a deeper sense, the volume of economic activity and opportunity automatically generates a continuing concern for public policy on the part of just the people best able to invest money in a political system. Perhaps it is the nature of all political systems that those with the greatest stakes possess favored means of influencing government. In the history of the United States, economic exploitation and development has often depended on the policies of government—sometimes the positive assistance of government, sometimes the passive tolerance of government. Those standing to benefit, or fearing to suffer, could seek their aims through the electoral system. Frequently doing so, they fought with their handiest weapon, money, ballooning the sums spent as the importance of election contests to economic activity mounted.

Economic abundance has given birth to personal characteristics relevant to the style of electioneering. In the United States, for example, Americans are said to possess a whole-hog kind of enthusiasm that is infused with optimism and energy. "The American is ready to tackle any problem with the expectation that he can bring it to a swift conclusion."[39] He therefore bulls his way into political campaigning in a hell-and-thunder mood that cracks many restraints of propriety and normally spends all the dollars at hand. Not sparing the horses in other races, Americans do not do so in politics. In politics their horses are dollars. They sell candidates and hawk slogans as they sell investments and root for the Dodgers, by force of habit.

Technological achievement and economic abundance usually travel hand in hand. Together they have produced a stream of innovations in transportation and communications that bear directly on campaign

37. See David M. Potter, *People of Plenty—Economic Abundance and the American Character* (Chicago: University of Chicago Press, 1954), p. 126 and *passim;* and Seymour Martin Lipset, "Some Social Requisites of Democracy: Economic Democracy and Political Legitimacy," *American Political Science Review,* 53 (1959), 75-85.

38. Edward J. Flynn, *You're the Boss* (New York: The Viking Press, 1947), p. 70.

39. Gabriel A. Almond, discussing the work of Margaret Mead.—*The American People and Foreign Policy* (New York: Harcourt, Brace and Company, 1950), p. 43.

costs;[40] they have also created highly complex societies that impose multiple demands on the loyalty and attention-span of individuals and groups. In the United States, citizens have clustered in vast urban concentrations, remote from the front stoop where country politicos formerly lingered. An intense competition for their attention has developed.[41] Political appeals must compete, not only against other political appeals, but also against throngs of nonpolitical attractions as well. In 1840 "ten acres of people" would attend a political jamboree at Dayton, Ohio,[42] because, quite literally, they had nothing better to do. They did have something better to do in the 1950's, or so they thought, and politicians claiming their attention had to work and pay for it.

Political competitors in modern industrial nations have more avenues of communication on which to spend their money than do politicians in simpler societies. With the growth of organized groups and the multiplication of political interests, numerous nonparty organizations as well as political parties undertake campaign activities. And energetic competitors seek to exploit all channels to the individual. They subject him to a bombardment of personal and mass communications that is discussed contemporaneously under the heading of cross-pressure analysis. To launch most of these communications requires money.

The range and number of factors that affect the level at which campaigns are financed have seldom been referred to in legislative discussions of statutory ceilings in the United States, but they warrant consideration by anyone who would fashion controls that will actually limit the sums needed for campaigning. Unless the pressures behind campaign expenditures are understood, efforts to cap them will inevitably prove futile. Statutory lids will be blown off like the lids on liquor sales during prohibition, and with similar consequences.

3. THE USES OF CAMPAIGN FUNDS

An official of the Democratic national committee was asked what aspect of campaign finance perplexed him most. He replied readily that most of all he wanted to know how the Republicans spend their money. After two national campaigns, he still could not understand what they did with so much of it.

The curiosity was well-founded. No comprehensive information has been available on how campaign money is used at different political levels. Occasionally the budget of a single candidate or committee has been published. But the task of classifying and tabulating expenditures made by the large number of committees that in most places make up the main campaign effort has been so burdensome that until after 1952

40. As to radio and television, see pages 403-5, below.

41. See Potter, *op. cit.*, pp. 172-73; and C. Wright Mills on the competitive diversion offered by modern "synthetic celebrities."—*The Power Elite* (New York: Oxford University Press, 1956), p. 250.

42. Roseboom, *op. cit.*, p. 121.

students did not undertake it. Investigating committees of Congress before 1956 did not do so either.[43]

The uses of campaign funds are endlessly varied. They reflect the state of technology, of social and political organization, of manners, tastes, and morals. An elderly Georgia lady beamed whenever she met the local judge on the bus. He was an elected judge and always paid her fare. A Democratic committee employed the Pinkerton National Detective Agency in one state, and a different private eye claims the Republican national committee among his oldest clients.[44] Lissome models charged $15.00 to appear at an Ike rally in Connecticut, and a New Jersey Democratic Senatorial candidate was touched $25.00 for the Annual Kids Day in Metuchen. Radio and television broadcasting eat up millions of dollars. Thousands go to pay for rent, electricity, telephone, telegraph, auto hire, airplanes, airplane tickets, registration drives, hill-billy bands, public relations counsel, the social security tax on payrolls. Money pays for writers and for printing what they write, for advertising in many blatant forms, and for boodle in many subtle guises. All these expenditures are interlarded with outlays for the hire of donkeys and elephants, for comic books, poll taxes, and sample ballots, for gifts to the United Negro College Fund and the Police Relief Association, for a $5.25 traffic ticket in Maryland and $66.30 worth of "convention liquor' in St. Louis; for a $15.00 corsage for Margaret Truman in New Hampshire and a $30.00 one for Mamie in Connecticut. But the odd minutiae[45] and the impressive sums obstruct the vision as well as aid it. Expenses must be categorized and summarized if comparisons are to be made between the parties and between different types of campaigns. Unless base points for comparison are developed, efforts to chart trends in expenditures for specific purposes—essential for effective regulation—prove futile.

The importance of television and radio.—Relatively dependable data are available for a large slice of campaign activity in 1952 and 1956.[46]

43. Throughout the hearings held by committees over the decades there are frequent references to specific expenditures, but no tracing of consistent categories of expenses even for the national campaign organizations. Politicians do not take to this sort of thing. The pace of campaigns is so hectic, the turnover of personnel so frequent, and politicians are such extroverts that little self-study takes place in any but the plushest campaign organizations.

An aspect of party finance about which reports are not made, and which is almost always ignored, is the financing of the national conventions. A projected study by Herbert E. Alexander for the Citizens' Research Foundation will be the first examination of the subject.

44. William S. Fairfield and Charles Clift, "The Private Eyes," *The Reporter*, February 10, 1955, p. 25.

45. Lest it be thought that campaign curiosa are confined to the United States, recall the Italian candidate who dispensed shoes to his followers: but only one foot of each pair, the other to be claimed after voting on election day.

46. The reports from which the information was drawn do not pretend to cover all campaign operations. Nor are all campaign reports equally reliable, as the discussion on pages 359-64 indicates. The validity of using such reports at all

Table 46 shows the percentage of direct expenditures made by political committees at several government levels that went for selected purposes during the general election of 1956.[47] Over two-fifths of all money spent by national campaign groups and about one fourth spent by state groups went for radio and television. These proportions have enormous significance for the legal regulation of campaign finance and particularly for efforts to curtail total election costs. It has proved impossible to enforce restrictions on expenditures for most campaign

---

rests on three assumptions: that it is possible to evaluate the relative accuracy and completeness of individual reports by field inquiries, and by other means, and to discard those that are fictitious; that the organizations submitting reports thought to be dependable are moderately representative of other campaign operations similar in type—therefore the usable reports serve as an index to the activities of other groups; and that it is useful to know how specific, well defined campaign groups use their money even though there may be other activities for which information is lacking.

The coverage of the reports, on the rare occasions when they can be checked by independent means, is often surprisingly good. Political committees questioned by the Gore Committee reported radio and television expenditures between September 1 and November 30, 1956, of $6,916,000. The Committee did not question many state and local groups that made campaign expenditures. It did, however, ask radio and television stations and networks to report expenditures for political broadcasts of all kinds during the same period. The total reported by them came to $9,907,000. The political-committee reports, in other words, accounted for 70 per cent of *all* radio and television expenditures that were made during the period and therefore clearly a very high percentage of such expenditures that were made by themselves.

Joan Sacknitz Carver has described more fully than possible here several aspects of political spending in 1952.—"A Study of Campaign Expenditures by Selected Committees in 1952," (Master's Thesis, University of North Carolina, 1957), 242 pp.

47. For present purposes, the data for organizations at the national level can be considered complete.

At the state level, substantially all regular party committees and volunteer groups active in the presidential race are represented. The state-level data do not include information from committees set up especially to support candidates for statewide offices, although the adjacent column reports relatively complete data for candidate committees active in United States Senate races. Some of these committees operated over only a portion of a state, but generally the information comes from statewide candidate committees and is a usable indicator of the purposes for which money is spent through such groups.

The local-level data pertain exclusively to the 100 most populous counties in the nation; expenditures by some labor and miscellaneous groups are included, but most of them were made by regular party groups and volunteer committees active in the presidential race. The local-level information consequently is not representative of local-level expenditures in the nation as a whole. This is a principal reason why the total column does not reflect accurately the way the nation's entire election bill was divided.

The table includes no expenditures in connection with nominations and no expenditures made before September 1 or after November 30. Most general-election expenses are incurred between those dates, however, and what is known of expenditures in primaries indicates that money is used in roughly the same ways as in general elections. Attempts to compare systematically the uses of funds in primaries and general elections in the same or similar settings proved futile because of the scarcity of usable data on primary campaigns.

purposes. There are no central control points. Newspaper and periodical advertising can be placed by thousands of different individuals in thousands of different publications. Most other kinds of campaign expenditures are similarly difficult to control.[48] Television and radio are exceptions. The unique characteristics of broadcasting make feasible its detailed control by federal authority. Through licensing and regulatory procedures it is possible to limit expenditures for broadcasts, either by limiting the time that may be sold or by making it available at reduced prices. Neither of these things can be accomplished for any other important item of campaign expense.

Table 46

PERCENTAGE OF DIRECT EXPENDITURES MADE BY POLITICAL COMMITTEES FOR SELECTED PURPOSES: GENERAL ELECTION CAMPAIGN, SEPTEMBER 1–NOVEMBER 30, 1956[a]

Purpose	Type of Committee[b]				
	National Level	State Level	U.S. Senatorial	Local Level	Total[c]
Millions of dollars spent....	$7.3	$10.3	$2.3	$6.5	$26.4
Radio[d]........	4	8	8	3	6
Television[d]........	39	16	20	7	21
Newspaper and periodical advertising........	2	10	16	9	8
Printing, purchase and distribution of literature....	15	15	19	21	17
Outdoor billboards........	(e)	3	5	3	2
Other........	40	48	32	57	46
Total........	100%	100%	100%	100%	100%

[a] Derived from the Gore Committee *Report*, pp. 39-40.
[b] Included are regular, finance, and volunteer committees affiliated with each party, plus labor and miscellaneous minor party and nonparty groups. These embrace: the 35 significant committees at the national level, excluding the national-level Congressional campaign committees (their expenditures for the calendar year appear on page 397); 267 committees at the state level; 78 state and local-level committees on behalf of U.S. Senatorial candidates; and 350 committees at the local level in the 100 most populous counties.
[c] Not to be taken as fully representative of total campaign expenditures in the nation. See footnote 47, page 389.
[d] Includes charges for time on air and other costs in connection with the broadcasts.
[e] Less than 0.5 per cent.

48. Senate investigators in 1948 sought to learn the particulars of billboard advertising on behalf of a candidate for the Senatorial nomination in Oklahoma. Apparently about $17,000 was spent on this form of advertising. Within a few weeks after the primary, investigators interviewed approximately 60 per cent of the billboard organizations involved, plus others. They concluded that five firms did not handle any of the advertising in question. Two that did so did not know who had contracted or paid for it. Five others could give no evidence of the actual source of the funds paid them. One firm said the account in question was paid by unidentified local people. Apparently instructions were given that stickers be attached to billboards indicating that they had been paid for by a particular committee backing the Senatorial candidate, without regard to who actually did pay the cost.

At each political level, money goes into the activities most appropriate in meeting the problems of communication and organization faced at that level. The large amounts of money reported in the "other" category obscures some of the detailed differences.[49] Certain contrasts, nevertheless, are apparent. State campaign groups make relatively larger use of newspaper and periodical advertising than do national-level committees[50] and go in for billboards in addition. At the local level, broadcasting costs dropped in the 100 largest counties to one-tenth of the total of all costs, and the costs of literature ate up a larger share of total outlays than at the higher levels.

Party similarities.—In Table 47, the information appearing in Table 46 is shown separately for each of the major parties. Despite the fact the parties have different total amounts at their disposal, at all levels

Table 47

THE PARTIES SPENT THEIR MONEY IN THE SAME WAYS: PERCENTAGE OF DIRECT EXPENDITURES USED FOR SELECTED PURPOSES BY PARTY COMMITTEES, SEPTEMBER 1–NOVEMBER 30, 2 1956[a]

Purpose	Type of Committee[b]									
	National Level		State Level		U.S. Senatorial		Local Level		Total[c]	
	Rep.	Dem.	Rep.	Dem.	Rep.	Dem.	Rep.	Dem.	Rep.	Dem.
Millions of Dollars Spent	$3.4	$3.3	$7.0	$3.1	$1.0	$1.3	$3.8	$2.4	$15.2	$10.1
Radio[d]	2	7	9	6	8	8	3	2	6	5
Television	40	43	18	14	15	24	7	7	20	23
Newspaper and periodical advertising	2	1	11	8	16	17	10	8	9	7
Printing, purchase and distribution of literature	10	19	12	19	18	19	22	18	14	19
Outdoor billboards	0	0	3	2	5	5	3	3	3	2
Other	46	30	47	51	38	27	55	62	48	44
Total	100%	100%	100%	100%	100%	100%	100%	100%	100%	100%

[a] Derived from the Gore Committee *Report,* pp. 39-40.

[b] These are regular, finance, and volunteer committees affiliated with each party, not including labor, miscellaneous minor party, and other nonparty groups, and not including the Congressional campaign committees.

[c] Not to be taken as fully representative of total campaign expenditures in the nation. See footnote 47, page 389.

[d] Includes charges for time on air and other costs in connection with the broadcasts.

49. The Gore Committee limited its requested breakdown of expenditures to certain types deemed of greatest relevance to problems of legislative regulation. An itemization of all expenditures was not sought.

50. Historically, it has been characteristic of both parties that an important share of the small amount of newspaper advertising placed from national headquarters goes to papers serving minority ethnic groups. C. W. Smith, Jr., showed that practically all expenditures by the Democratic national committee for newspaper advertising in 1944 went to papers of racial groups, especially the Negro press.—"Campaign Communications Media," *The Annals,* 259 (1948), 90-97. See also James K. Pollock, *Party Campaign Funds* (New York: Alfred A. Knopf, 1926), p. 150.

they generally spend their monies in about the same proportions for the same purposes. Even when Republican organizations tend to spend a larger proportion for a specific purpose at one level than their Democratic counterparts, and less at another, the percentages of total expenditures end up remarkably close to each other. For this reason the total column is the most significant one in Table 47. There the similarity between the parties is marked.

These two tables cover only the campaign period. Table 48 presents similar information for 1952 that covers the full calendar year. With all expenses incurred during the year included, the similarity between the parties at the national level is extremely close. Data are offered on statewide expenditures in three states and on local expenditures in three states.[51] General consistencies between the parties within each state and between the states can also be observed.

Be it noted, moreover, that even in 1952, when many fewer television stations were operating than in 1956, the proportion of funds going for broadcasts was substantial.[52] Insofar as comparisons between the years are possible, other similarities appear. The items in the 1956 table for periodical and newspaper advertising, printing, and billboards are embraced in the 1952 table under other publicity and propaganda. Included in the latter category were also the costs of making campaign films and the cost of buttons and similar novelties, plus some minor items. The categories (and local committees) are not precisely alike, and the time periods covered are different, but the proportion of expenses going for "other publicity and propaganda" in both years shows up roughly similar for the national and local levels—the only two levels where they can be compared.[53]

51. The 1956 data were computed from information submitted to the Gore Committee on uniform questionnaires.

The 1952 national-level percentages were computed from reports filed with the Clerk of the United States House of Representatives. The 1952 state and local material was compiled from reports in state and local depositories, submitted on a variety of forms pursuant to different statutes. Only the most diligent labor by the persons collecting and classifying the material made it possible to arrive at party summaries that could be compared. The data varied in adequacy too much from state to state to permit a nationwide summary of the state and local information. The states presented here were those for which the best comparative information for both parties was available.

52. Because the 1952 data pertain to the whole year, the radio and television percentages for that year would be expected to be lower. Political committees in 1956 were asked to report charges for time on the air and other costs in connection with broadcasts. It is probable that in tabulating the 1952 material some costs that were actually incurred in connection with broadcasts were not identifiable as such and were classified as other publicity and propaganda, thus to a slight extent depressing artificially the 1952 radio-television percentage.

53. The percentages are as follows:

	1952		*1956*	
	Rep.	*Dem.*	*Rep.*	*Dem.*
National level	16	18	12	20
Local level (mean)	32	27	35	29

Table 48

THE PARTIES SPENT THEIR MONEY IN THE SAME WAYS: PERCENTAGE OF DIRECT EXPENDITURES USED FOR SELECTED PURPOSES BY PARTY COMMITTEES, JANUARY 1–DECEMBER 31, 1952

Purpose	Type of Committee													
	National Level		State Level						Local Level					
	All		Connecticut[a]		Maryland		Ohio		Connecticut[a]		Maryland		Pennsylavania	
	Rep.	Dem.	Rep.	Dem.	Rep.	Dem.	Rep.	Dem.	Rep.	Dem.	Rep.	Dem.	Rep.	Dem.
Number of Committees	18	15	10	10	9	5	9	8	198	136	36	31	98	77
Millions of Dollars Spent	$6.6	$4.5	$.46	$.28	$.14	$.11	$.65	$.15	$.33	$.21	$.19	$.14	$1.7	$.80
Radio and Television[b]	31	34	65[c]	85[c]	62[c]	77[c]	56[c]	66[c]	6	8	5	4	8	5
Other Publicity and Propaganda[b]	16	18							30	30	35	28	32	21
Salaries and Expense Accounts	19	20	14	5	7	6	13	9	9	6	2	4	8	4
Overhead	15	15	13	8	18	11	22	17	23	21	16	17	9	14
Field Activities	15	9	5	2	7	5	6	4	12	10	5	4	10	7
Special Expenditures	4	4	3	0	4	0	2	4	0	2	4	3	6	4
Election Day	0	0	0	0	2	1	1	0	20	23	33	40	27	45
Total	100%	100%	100%	100%	100%	100%	100%	100%	100%	100%	100%	100%	100%	100%

[a] Connecticut data for state and local levels combined appear in the Gore Committee *Hearings*, part 2, p. 246.
[b] A distinction between these two categories could not always be maintained, especially when lump sum payments were made to advertising or public relations firms that did not segregate broadcast charges from others. Hence expenditures for radio-television and for other publicity are combined for the state-level committees. It was not possible to separate radio from television costs because of the frequency with which committees made single payments covering charges for both.
[c] The figures given for state-level committees combine radio, television, and other publicity and propoganda.

Functional specialization.—The 1952 information exposes several types of expenditure that could not be separately identified for 1956. Salaries and expense accounts consume a diminishing share of campaign resources at each lower level. Field activities—meetings, speakers, brass bands, sound trucks, etc.—show no such consistency, one explanation lying in differences in campaign practices between states.

One of the most important of all campaign costs is election-day expenses, the sums spent to get voters to the polls and to apply last-minute persuasion. No expenditures for this purpose are made directly by the national-level committees, and only rarely does a state-level committee do so.[54] Election-day activities are necessarily financed through local committees. Among the three states in the table, from one-fifth to almost one-half of local-level expenses went for election-day operations. In large urban settings, the money is often passed to ward and precinct leaders who pay poll workers, hire transportation, and energize the faithful. In other locales, the money may be spent directly by the county or city organization. It is probable that election-day expenses of all types account for as much as one-eighth of the total election bill in the United States. These expenditures, perhaps around $18,000,000 in 1952 and 1956, are of enormous importance to the outcome of elections, but less so than formerly.[55] Bribery has declined generally, volunteer labor is frequently mobilized on a large scale, and other means of appealing to voters have been developed.[56]

54. One notable exception was the Democratic state committee of Pennsylvania which reported 36 per cent of its direct (and total) expenditures going for election-day work. A Kentucky manager says that in his state it is sometimes necessary to send election-day money from state headquarters into two-thirds of the counties.

55. After this estimate was made, it was found that Dayton D. McKean had made an earlier one of "$17,500,000 for a national election, plus an amount for which a fair estimate cannot be made for primaries, local, and special elections." Professor McKean figured $50.00 each for 70,000 precincts where one party dominates, and $200 each for 70,000 others.—*Party and Pressure Politics* (Boston: Houghton-Mifflin Company, 1949), p. 342.

56. Campaign reports often record in detail the sums parceled out to precinct captains and to election-day workers for specific services. The bulk of election-day outlays are made through regular party committees. Among the 1952 local-level reports for the three states included in Table 48, 77 per cent of the regular party committees and 15 per cent of the volunteer groups reported making election-day expenditures.

The Gore Committee asked for 1956 election-day information from only a portion of the local committees to which it sent questionnaires, all of them in the 100 most populous counties. The information obtained, however, showed that 42 per cent of the total disbursements of 51 regular Democratic groups located in 23 states went for election-day expenses, as compared with 2 per cent of the disbursements of 22 volunteer groups in 9 states; among Republicans, 33 was the percentage for 55 regular committees located in 24 states, as compared with 1 per cent of the disbursements of 42 volunteer committees in 15 states.

At one time, election-day money was synonymous with corruption. The more spent, the greater the corruption, was the view, contributing substantially to the development of public attitudes hostile to all money in politics. In a modern

By combining the expenditures of all committees supporting each party, as done in Tables 47 and 48, it is possible to analyze a party's total campaign effort in a way not permitted when committees are examined individually. Interrelationships among party groups have been examined in Chapter 11, where the transfers of funds revealed something of the dependence of campaign committees on each other and of the cooperative action found in campaigns. As indicated there,[57] committees display a marked functional specialization in the way they spend their money. The nature of the specialization among national-level committees can be seen in Tables 49 and 50. The former categorizes expenditures made by each of the important groups in both parties in 1952, and the latter does the same for 1956. In 1952, the most noticeable differences between committees were on the Democratic side. The second most important committee, the Stevenson-Sparkman Forum, made 94 per cent of its direct expenditures for radio and television broadcasts. The percentage for the Democratic national committee, the only one to handle more funds, was 14. The Springfield headquarters committee put 2 per cent of its direct expenses into broadcasts while the Volunteers for Stevenson devoted 56 per cent of theirs to this purpose. The Headquarters group put 96 per cent of the funds they spent themselves into personnel, overhead and field activities, whereas the corresponding percentage for the Forum was 1 and for the national committee, 58. The diversity of the activities of Republican groups in 1952 can be read from the same table, and for both parties in 1956 from Table 50. The same sort of functional specialization was found at state and local levels in 1952, as Table 51 illustrates, and as did Tables 40 and 41 on pages 312-14. That different types of labor political organizations also used radically different percentages of their funds for specified purposes is clear from Table 52.

The specialization of function found among important campaign groups has severely handicapped past efforts to compare party expenditures and to detect changes in spending practices over time. Often it has been necessary to infer the relative financial resources of parties and

---

metropolitan precinct, $20.00 or $50.00 or $200 can be disposed of easily without necessarily violating law or propriety. Many subventions, however, blend a concern over needed costs with recognition of local leaders whose aid is essential in their areas. One bonus system worked out in a southern city accorded Negro leaders election-day expenses at so much for each vote cast above an agreed upon minimum. Northward, in a voting district called Whiskey Point, $50.00 the night before an election paid to the proper storekeeper has produced a welter of activity the next day, and also a lopsided vote. Ability to make election-day expenditures is often taken as evidence of the virility of a political organization. The ritual must be satisfied, one observer points out, and when it is, it automatically stimulates additional uncompensated enthusiasm. The outlays have a multiplying effect, producing $100 worth of work for $10.00.

Election-day activities costing money are crucial in many countries, including Great Britain.—Finer, *op. cit.*, pp. 79-80.

57. See pages 309-17, above.

Table 49

HOW THE NATIONAL-LEVEL POLITICAL COMMITTEES USED THEIR MONEY: PERCENTAGE OF DIRECT EXPENDITURES GOING FOR SPECIFIED PURPOSES, JANUARY 1–DECEMBER 31, 1952

Purpose	Committee													
	Republican						Democratic							
	National	Senatorial	Congressional	Citizens[a]	14 Miscellaneous[b]	Total	National	Senatorial	Congressional[c]	Volunteers[d]	Headquarters[e]	Forum[f]	8 Miscellaneous[g]	Total
Total Disbursements (in thousands $)[h]	3,000	772	1,666	1,415	521	$7,374	2,812	84	68	757	315	779	75	$4,890
Direct Expenditures (in thousands $)[h]	2,999	434	1,323	1,396	437	$6,589	2,636	4	49	757	274	742	71	$4,533
Radio and Television	21	58	30	42	36	31	14	0	1	56	2	94	33	34
Other Publicity and Propaganda	10	8	21	23	31	16	23	3	1	24	2	5	15	18
Salaries and Expense Accounts	28	8	20	8	4	19	28	36	63	6	32	0	23	20
Overhead	18	5	10	18	9	15	19	59	21	9	31	1	18	15
Field Activities	20	18	11	6	13	15	11	2	3	2	33	0	9	9
Special Expenditures	3	3	8	3	7	4	5	0	11	3	0	0	2	4
Total	100%	100%	100%	100%	100%	100%	100%	100%	100%	100%	100%	100%	100%	100%

[a] Citizens for Eisenhower-Nixon.

[b] With total disbursements (in thousands $), these were: National Professional Committee for Eisenhower-Nixon, 122; McCarthy Broadcast Dinner Committee, 97; Hoover Broadcast Fund, 54; Wedemeyer Broadcast Fund, 51; Spots for Eisenhower, 50; Eisenhower Bandwagon Committee, 38; Campaign Committee of the Women's National Republican Clubs, 28; Dana C. Smith ("Nixon Fund"), 25; National Federation of Republican Women, 23; Volunteers for Taft (showed expenditures during general election period), 14; Grass Roots Boy Radio Committee, 7; Labor-Business Crusaders for Eisenhower, 6; Young Industry for Eisenhower, 3; National Committee of Columbia University Alumni for Eisenhower, 3.

[c] Democratic Congressional Campaign Committee and Democratic National Congressional Committee combined.

[d] National Volunteers for Stevenson.

[e] 1952 Campaign Headquarters and Travel Committee, Springfield, Illinois.

[f] Stevenson-Sparkman Forum Committee.

[g] With total disbursements (in thousands $), these were: Labor's Committee for Election of Stevenson and Sparkman, 24; Sparkman Campaign Committee, 20; Young Democratic Clubs of America, 14; Independent Businessmen to Elect Stevenson and Sparkman, 10; Democratic Women for India Edwards for Vice-President (showed expenditures during general election period), 4; Republicans for Stevenson Committee, 2; Committee for the Circulation of Stevenson's Papers, less than 1; Students for Stevenson, less than 1.

[h] Discrepancies of minor importance were discovered in the reports of many committees when the total of itemized disbursements listed in a report was computed and compared with the summary total shown on the face of the report. In figuring the percentages, the computed totals were used and are shown here. Other adjustments were necessary to take account of disburse-

Table 50

HOW THE NATIONAL-LEVEL POLITICAL COMMITTEES USED THEIR MONEY: PERCENTAGE OF DIRECT EXPENDITURES GOING FOR SPECIFIED PURPOSES, JANUARY 1–NOBEMBER 30, 1956[a]

Purpose	Committee												
	Republican						Democratic						
	National	Senatorial	Congressional	Citizens[b]	7 Miscellaneous[c]	Total	National	Senatorial	Congressional[d]	Volunteers[e]	Headquarters[f]	4 Miscellaneous[g]	Total
Total Disbursements (in thousands $)[h]	2,769	1,470	2,778	1,510	263	$8,790	2,619	269	230	493	1,092	102	$4,805
Direct Expenditures (in thousands $)[h]	2,656	1,161	2,271	1,323	255	$7,666	2,388	18	41	484	1,092	83	$4,106
Radio	1	2	7	1	0	3	5	0	0	9	5	11	5
Television	8	62	24	37	50	27	34	0	0	30	46	24	36
Radio-Television, unseparated	4	3	17	0	0	7	0	0	0	0	0	0	0
Newspaper and periodical advertising	2	0	5	0	6	2	1	0	0	1	0	16	1
Printing, purchase and distribution of literature	16	6	6	9	10	10	16	0	0	20	14	41	16
Other	69	27	41	53	34	51	44	100	100	40	35	8	42
Total	100%	100%	100%	100%	100%	100%	100%	100%	100%	100%	100%	100%	100%

[a] Derived from the Gore Committee *Report*, pp. 41-43. The information generally originated in reports filed with the Clerk of the U.S. House of Representatives for the period January 1–August 31, and in reports filed with the Gore Committee for the period September 1–November 30. All the Congressional committee information, which covers the full year, came from reports filed with the Clerk.

[b] Citizens for Eisenhower-Nixon.

[c] With total disbursements (in thousands $) these were: Salute Dinner Television Committee, Eastern Division, 105; National Federation of Republican Women, 38; Independent Democrats for Eisenhower (Sept. 1–Nov. 30), 34; National Ike Day Committee, 33; Women's National Republican Club (Sept. 1–Nov. 30), 30; Committee of the Arts and Sciences for Eisenhower, 18; Young Republican National Campaign Committee, 5.

[d] Democratic Congressional Campaign Committee and Democratic National Congressional Committee combined.

[e] Volunteers for Stevenson.

[f] Stevenson-Kefauver Campaign Committee.

[g] With total disbursements (in thousands $), these were (all for Sept. 1–Nov. 30): Businessmen for Stevenson-Kefauver, 62; National Business Council for Stevenson, 35; Conservationists for Stevenson-Kefauver, 5; Committee of Independents for Stevenson-Kefauver, less than 1. The breakdown of the direct expenditures of one minor miscellaneous committee was not known, and it is not here included.

[h] Minor discrepancies were sometimes found when the total of itemized disbursements listed in a report was computed and compared with the summary total shown on the face of the report. Efforts to reconcile the differences were made, along with other minor adjustments to take account of overlapping reporting dates and the like, accounting for certain implied inconsistencies between these figures and figures used elsewhere, especially in Table 32, p. 285, which, however, pertains to the full calendar year.

Table 51

FUNCTIONAL SPECIALIZATION OF SELECTED STATE AND LOCAL COMMITTEES: PERCENTAGE OF DIRECT EXPENDITURES GOING FOR SPECIFIED PURPOSES, 1952[a]

Purpose	Committees							
	Connecticut				Maryland		Pennsylvania	
	Rep. State Central	Eisenhower for Pres.	Dem. State Central	Reelection of Sen. Benton (Dem.)	Dem. County	U.S. Repre-sentative (Dem.)	Rep. County	Eisenhower Local
Thousands of Dollars Spent..	$293	$ 63	$ 28	$141	$ 65	$ 59	$1,364	$248
Radio and Television........	66	35	53[b]	91[b]	2	6	4	34
Other Publicity and Propaganda............	12	18			26	34	28	42
Salaries and Expense Accounts	13	14	11	4	4	12	7	5
Overhead................	7	24	26	4	15	23	17[c]	11
Field Activities............	2	9	10	1	4	5	11	7
Election Day..............	0	0	0	0	49	20	33	1
Total.....................	100%	100%	100%	100%	100%	100%	100%	100%

[a] Generally for the calendar year.
[b] The combined figure for radio, television, and other publicity and propaganda.
[c] Includes 8 per cent special expenditures.

Table 52

FUNCTIONAL SPECIALIZATION AMONG TYPES OF LABOR POLITICAL COMMITTEES: PERCENTAGE OF DIRECT EXPENDITURES GOING FOR SPECIFIED PURPOSES, 1952 AND 1956[a]

	Type of Committees			Detail for 155 State and Local Committees, 9/1-11/30/56					
	14 National 1/1-12/31/52	17 National 1/1-11/30/56	155 State and Local 9/1-11/30/56	19 State COPE	19 State LLPE	24 State CIO-PAC	19 State MNPL	66 Local	8 Misc.
Dollars spent...........	797,544	540,735	400,536	22,907	30,463	91,114	10,779	238,980	6,293
Radio.................	0	5	3	(b)	8	1	1	3	34
Television.............	0	10	9	0	0	30	0	4	0
Radio-Television when not separable........	25	0	2	4	0	0	0	3	0
Newspaper and periodical advertising..........	0	4	9	9	3	10	46	[b]	5
Printing, purchase, distribution of literature.	40	30	35	53	57	26	27	35	22
Outdoor billboards.......	0	2	3	0	(b)	3	0	4	0
Election-day expenses....	0	0	16	10	(b)	5	6	23	33
Other.................	35[c]	49	23	24	32	25	20	21	6
Total................	100%	100%	100%	100%	100%	100%	100%	100%	100%

[a] 1952 data appear in Gore Committee *Hearings*, part 2, pp. 533-35, derived from reports filed with the Clerk of the U.S. House of Representatives; 1956 computations based on Gore Committee *Report*, pp. 41, 47.
[b] Less than 1 per cent.
[c] Salaries and expense accounts, 19; overhead, 10; field activities, 5; special expenditures, 1.

candidates by studying the two national committees alone, or those plus a limited number of others. The tabulations made here, imperfect though they be, suggest the kinds of information that could regularly be accumulated and classified by official reporting systems. The use of standard categories over a period of elections would reveal why political campaigns cost what they do and whether the uses of money were changing. Those inclined to assess their social or political utility would have a stable basis for doing so. Those inclined to impose ceilings on total costs would have an improved chance of knowing where and how cuts might effectively be made.[58]

58. Comparative information on expenses in other election systems is seldom assembled. J. F. S. Ross has analyzed constituency expenditures in two British Parliamentary elections, 1950 and 1951.—*Elections and Electors* (London: Eyre & Spottiswoode, 1955), pp. 269-91. An official Swedish document reports figures of interest for 1948 and 1949.—*Om Offentlig Redovisning av den Politiska Propagandans Finansiering—Partifinansieringssakkunnigas Betänkande* (Lund: Berlingska Boktryckeriet, 1951), pp. 68-83.

15

THE ORGANIZATION AND FUNCTIONS OF CAMPAIGNS

ALTHOUGH ENTIRELY unlike in external appearance, election campaigns may serve identical political functions. In their consequences, the torch-lit, whooped-up speakings of 1860 may not differ from the klieg-lit, souped-up broadcasts of 1960. Boisterous campaigning at a crossroads tavern in one century may be equivalent to a televised carnival in another. The requirements for an effective television personality have been lampooned; but it has not been shown that these, while different, are more deleterious to political debate than the bull-horn voice and chautauqua talents that prospered in another era. One gathers that Mr. Lincoln's anecdotes, not all of which presumably were original with him, illuminated some issues and obscured some. Mr. Eisenhower's capsule simplifications of public problems, not all of which presumably are original with others, achieve the same ends.

If political campaigns are functional, their functions may well be accomplished by different means under different conditions. Processes of communications and organization may change without altering significantly the functions themselves. To see the meaning of trends in campaign expenditures is harder than to detect the trends.

1. CAMPAIGN TRENDS

A change in American campaign habits always arouses foreboding. In the election of 1836 William Henry Harrison made the first public appeal by a presidential candidate that resembled a modern campaign speech. During the next four years the novel practice grew, and Representative John Quincy Adams, himself once a president, recorded his exasperation:

> Here is a revolution in the habits and manners of the people. Where will it end? . . .
>
> Electioneering for the Presidency has spread its contagion to the President himself, to his now only competitor, to his immediate predecessor. . . .

> One of the most remarkable peculiarities of the present time is that the principal leaders of the political parties are travelling about the country from State to State, and holding forth, like Methodist preachers, hour after hour, to assembled multitudes, under the broad canopy of heaven.[1]

Nearly a century later, speaking through the president of the Southern Publishers Association, newspapers protested the growing use of radio broadcasting by the major parties.[2] The arrival of television and the campaign airplane stimulated a fresh splash of commentary, some of it hopeful, but most of it apprehensive. Ability to gauge the consequences of changed campaign practices is severely limited. It is difficult enough to discern the effects on voters of particular campaign appeals. It is even more difficult to understand the import for the political system of altered ways of making the appeals.

The evolution of campaigns.—American national campaigning has evolved through five broad periods, as measured by the things for which money has been spent.

Limited public campaigning characterized the Republic's first third century. Before the time of Jackson and Harrison, the presidential contest was a relatively staid procedure in both tempo and scope. The visible exertions of the candidates were slight, although organizational work was often of prime importance. Most of the canvassing, as it was called, took the form of preachments by supporters from stump and pulpit, of debate in the highly partisan press, of private correspondence, and of persuasive activities on election day. There was no lack of raucous contention for lesser offices, with due attention to the frailties of voters,[3] but the suffrage was limited and the focus of presidential politics was as often on legislatures as on the people.

The torchlight era commenced with Jackson's election, symbolic of a shift in political power from the leadership of the eastern patriciate. The controversies surrounding Old Hickory deepened political competition. The United States Bank spent heavily in the campaign of 1832, but Jackson appealed directly to the masses against the "Money Monster." They understood and showed it in torchlight processions and hickory-pole raisings.[4] The hard-cider campaign of 1840 demonstrated in full

1. *Memoirs of John Quincy Adams* (Philadelphia: J. B. Lippincott & Company, 1876), pp. 352, 355-56. See George Stimpson, *A Book About American Politics* (New York: Harper & Brothers Publishers, 1952), p. 399.

2. Roy V. Peel and Thomas C. Donnelly, *The 1932 Campaign—An Analysis* (New York: Farrar & Rinehart, Inc., 1935), pp. 116-17.

3. It is written that in 1777 James Madison was defeated for reelection to the legislature in Virginia because he refused to distribute free whiskey to the voters—the custom, if not the whiskey, having been imported from England. A privileges-and-election committee reviewing the case declined to construe gifts of liquor and other presents to voters as bribery and corruption.—Stimpson, *op. cit.*, p. 395.

4. Eugene H. Roseboom, *A History of Presidential Elections* (New York: The Macmillan Company, 1957), p. 104.

swing a new style of canvassing that would last until the end of the century.

The presidential stump speech grew in importance. After its first use by Harrison, other candidates occasionally took to the hustings, notably Douglas, Bell, and Breckenridge in 1860—but not Lincoln. Garfield spoke 70 times during the 1880 campaign, the most active stumper since Harrison and the only one aside from Tippecanoe to get elected. Not until 1928 did speeches by candidates on tour become a fixture of presidential campaigning.[5]

Campaigning has always been concerned with two basic processes: communications and organization. Public attitudes are sensed and assessed in various ways, but chiefly through these processes are efforts made to mobilize popular support. In the flamboyant campaigning of the torchlight period, the emphasis lay on organization. Financial demands mounted and both parties began to draw on wealthy backers for funds. The municipal machine became the hallmark of American politics. These organizations sold their influence, and individuals sold their votes, on a massive scale. Appeals to the electorate were made through newspapers, broadsides, processions, public speaking, but field activities consumed the giant share of national and state campaign budgets, and election-day expenses consumed the largest share of local budgets. Traveling organizers arranged the support of local leaders, plotted ways to corral votes, negotiated the tactics of personalities and issues. It was said that in 1896 the Republican national committee hired 1,400 organizers and sent them wherever they were most needed.[6]

The era of campaign literature began in 1880. Handbills and other printed materials had been campaign fixtures for decades, but a mounting number of printing presses and a fall in the price of paper produced an unprecedented torrent of printed words. In 1896, the Republican national committee alone was said to have distributed from its headquarters 300,000,000 pieces, weighing, somebody calculated, 2,000 tons.[7] The torches literally went out that year, the year that marked "the first use of modern political campaigning methods. . . . The printed word came to supplement the fiery orator. . . ."[8] The new century brought sharply mounting expenditures for communications, i.e., campaign publicity. Pollock reported in 1926 that the combined costs of advertising candidates, and printing and distributing their speeches and other tracts, constituted the most important item of campaign expense at national, state, and local levels.[9] During the years 1912-24, something like

5. For a tracing of certain presidential campaign practices, see *ibid.*, pp. 394-406.

6. Louise Overacker, *Money in Elections* (New York: The Macmillan Company, 1932), pp. 22-23.

7. Luther B. Little, "The Printing Press in Politics," *Munsey's Magazine*, 23 (1900), 741.

8. Scott M. Cutlip and Allen H. Center, *Effective Public Relations* (New York: Prentice-Hall, Inc., 1952), p. 44.

9. James K. Pollock, *Party Campaign Funds* (New York: Alfred A. Knopf, 1926), pp. 146-47.

40 per cent of total expenditures went for newspaper and periodical advertising, news bureau services, outdoor billboards, lithographs, and the printing and sending of campaign literature. The profession of advertising grew, along with mass mailings and other techniques facilitating access to large publics. Politics followed business in making use of them.[10]

Radio campaigning produced a sudden decline in 1928 of expenditures for newspaper advertising by the two national committees. Radio had been used but slightly in 1924, and at small cost to the parties. Four years later it emerged as a major campaign innovation,[11] to remain until 1952 the distinctive medium of communications characterizing those years.

Television campaigning, after a limited initiation in 1948, began its dominance of campaign communications in 1952.

The displacement principle.—Throughout the history of campaigning, a process of displacement has gone on. As new forms of campaigning develop, they displace older ones. It has already been suggested that the cost of national-level campaigning did not increase between the 1920's and 1950's, if allowances are made for changes in the price level and in the size of the electorate.[12] Moreover, at the end of that period, publicity as a whole consumed no larger share of national campaign-committee expenditures than it had at the beginning.[13] Yet in 1952, two-thirds of communications costs were attributable to radio and television, whereas in 1920 there had been no significant charges for these items. Expenditures were made for other kinds of communications. Even in 1928, in fact, radio accounted for only 18 and 10 per cent, respectively, of the expenses of the Democratic and Republican national committees. In other words, by 1952 broadcasting had significantly *displaced* other publicity devices in the campaign budgets of the national campaign organizations.

Between 1952 and 1956, however, the story was different. Radio and television broadcasting by *national-level* campaign groups not only further displaced other media of publicity but had the additional effect of increasing total costs. The percentages of total direct expenditures and the dollar amounts were as follows:

10. Pollock, *op. cit.,* pp. 146-52; Overacker, *op. cit.,* pp. 24-28.

11. Overacker, *op. cit.,* pp. 24-25, 28-29.

12. See pages 375-80, above.

13. Pollock placed the costs of publicity in the early 1920's at over 40 per cent of the direct expenditures of national campaign committees, and Overacker estimated them at 50 per cent for the late 1920's. In 1952, the corresponding figure was 49. See *ibid.,* p. 23. Pollock's percentage derived from *op. cit.,* p. 146. Another estimate, made in 1924, and available to Pollock, placed the cost of his publicity items at 40 per cent of the total for all parties.—"Where the Campaign Money Goes," *Commerce and Finance,* 13 (1924), 1688.

	1952				1956			
	Rep.	*Dem.*	*Other*[14]	*Total*	*Rep.*	*Dem.*	*Other*[14]	*Total*
Radio and TV:	31%	34%	16%	30%	37%	41%	11%	36%
(in millions)	$2.0	$1.5	$0.2	$3.7	$2.8	$1.7	$0.1	$4.6
Other publicity:	16%	18%	33%	19%	12%	17%	37%	16%
(in millions)	$1.1	$0.8	$0.5	$2.4	$1.0	$0.7	$0.4	$2.1
Other expenditures:	53%	48%	51%	51%	51%	42%	52%	48%
(in millions)	$3.5	$2.2	$0.7	$6.4	$3.8	$1.7	$0.6	$6.1
Total:	100%	100%	100%	100%	100%	100%	100%	100%
(in millions)	$6.6	$4.5	$1.4	$12.5	$7.6	$4.1	$1.1	$12.8

For both parties, the percentage and the dollars spent for broadcasting went up, and the percentage and the dollars spent for other types of publicity went down. The percentage also went down in both cases for the remaining campaign costs, although only in the case of the Democrats did the dollar outlays decline. The fall in these categories was never-the-less not sufficient to offset the broadcasting increases.

Separate radio and television data for 1952 and 1956 are not available for these or other groups of campaign committees. It is nonetheless clear from other information that the increase in 1956 can be attributed to television and that expenditures for radio declined as those for television rose. Total expenditures made at *all political levels* for federal candidates were reported separately by stations and networks for these media in both years. The percentage of combined radio-television expenditures going for television rose from 49 in 1952 to 72 four years later:[15]

	1952			1956		
	Rep.	*Dem.*	*Total*	*Rep.*	*Dem.*	*Total*
Radio:	52%	49%	51%	27%	29%	28%
(in millions)	$1.8	$1.3	$3.1	$1.0	$0.9	$1.9
Television:	48%	51%	49%	73%	71%	72%
(in millions)	$1.6	$1.3	$2.9	$3.0	$2.1	$5.1
Total:	100%	100%	100%	100%	100%	100%
(in millions)	$3.4	$2.6	$6.0	$4.0	$3.0	$7.0

While a degree of displacement had occurred,[16] expenditures for

14. Includes labor, minor parties, and miscellaneous nonparty groups.

15. In 1952, the period covered ran from August 1 through the election. In 1956, it began September 1. In general, for what was attempted, the coverage was probably more complete in 1956, and the reporting more accurate, because of the kinds of questionnaires used and the way the information was tabulated. Data for 1956 came from the Gore Committee *Report,* Ex. 24, pp. 1-3, and for 1952 from U.S. Senate Subcommittee on Privileges and Election, *Report* (Washington: Government Printing Office, 1953) (Subcommittee Print) p. 2. The "other" party data for the two years did not seem comparable. The 1952 figure for radio was $38,000, and for television, $3,500; in 1956 they were $164,000 and $152,000, respectively.

16. Observable in campaign budgets at local levels, too. One faction in a Georgia county spent nothing for television in 1950 and $664 in 1954. Radio and

radio broadcasting did not decline as much as those for television rose. Total broadcasting costs increased from $6,000,000 to $7,000,000 between the two elections. These are the costs of federal campaigns only, however. When all radio and television party broadcasts are taken into account, the jump was about 20 per cent, or from $8,000,000 in 1952 to $9,600,000 in 1956.[17] How much of this was offset by reductions in campaign expenditures for other than broadcasting cannot be said. A portion of it doubtless was offset, and even if it were not, $1,600,000 is only a tiny fraction of the total United States general-election bill. The data suggest, incidentally, that the jump in campaign costs after 1952 was probably not as sharp as is usually supposed.[18]

2. MASS COMMUNICATIONS CAMPAIGNING

Politicians campaign at all governmental levels and for many offices. The changes that take place in campaign practices, however, do not occur equally in all kinds of elections. Many local candidates have been left relatively untouched by the shift from printed publicity to radio and television. For them, personal canvassing continues the chief requisite for success.

Campaigns are more likely to be altered by new media of communications in large constituencies. In large constituencies, also, changes in population and in social patterns are more likely to require new modes of campaign organization. Presidential campaigns seem to register most readily the innovations that periodically occur. The significance of such changes is more difficult to discern than the changes themselves, but what is true of presidential politics will often be true to varying extents of lesser offices.

Television: new medium, old process?—In 1960, the United States found itself deep in an era of mass communications campaigning. The era had commenced at the end of the previous century, and its most notable current manifestation was television. What the coming of television means to American politics and American society has been the subject of much foreboding and much optimism. The impact on the structure of American values and on the ability of the United States to understand its problems and meet them with consensus might well prove

---

press expenditures, however, declined by $899.—Joseph L. Bernd, *The Role of Campaign Funds in Georgia Primary Elections, 1936-1958* (Macon: The Georgia Journal, Inc., 1958), p. 9.

17. The 1956 total is derived from the Gore Committee *Report, loc. cit.* The 1952 total is derived by adding to the total of $6,000,000 for Federal campaigns presented in the text an estimate for state and local campaign broadcasts (which were not included in the inquiry from which the 1952 data were computed). This estimate, $2,000,000, was made by Harold E. Fellows, president of the National Association of Radio and Television Broadcasters.—U.S. Senate Subcommittee on Privileges and Elections, *Hearings* (Washington: Government Printing Office, 1955), pp. 97-98. The actual total for such broadcasts in 1956 was $2,495,000, 56 per cent of it for television.

18. See pages 8 and 380, above.

profound. Yet its impact on voting behavior was uncertain,[19] and some of its other presumed consequences might be more apparent than real. Innovations in campaign practice have always prompted grave predictions by those accustomed to the old ways.[20]

A large proportion of the people of the United States unquestionably follow politics over television; a large share of them assign it as the most important source of their campaign information.[21] Not all the consequences claimed for its use might be as portentous, however, as seemed to some at first. It was pointed out, for example, that television enabled candidates to become quickly "known" throughout large constituencies. Adlai Stevenson was declared by many to have benefited accordingly in 1952. Nonetheless, the United States across its history has chosen many successful presidents who were not personally exhibited to a large share of the voters. Moreover, 56 years before, and sans microphones, William Jennings Bryan at the age of 36 had converted himself into a national figure in an equally short period of time.

It has been observed, too, that the speed and coverage of television also served Richard Nixon well in 1952. The vice presidential candidate was able to answer the Nixon Fund charges promptly, personally, and before a large audience. That the medium would reduce the incidence of campaign slander—the meaning some of Mr. Nixon's supporters saw in the episode—was, however, by no means assured. Critics held that the very tactics employed by Mr. Nixon then and on other occasions corrupted political debate. But the one-way feature of mass communications has always tempted ardent campaigners down lines less permissible in face-to-face colloquies.[22] Some individuals clearly prospered before the cameras. That Stevenson and Nixon and others possessed a set of

19. See pages 24-34, above.

20. Disinterested observers have tried a hand, too. In the early days of radio, W. F. Ogburn listed, among 150 consequences for society of the invention of radio, the prospect that political fund-raising would be made easier and that campaign promises might be more binding.—"The Influence of Invention and Discovery," in President's Committee on Social Trends, *Recent Social Trends in the United States* (one-volume ed.; New York: McGraw-Hill Book Company, Inc., 1934), p. 156.

21. One survey in 1952 found that 53 per cent of the respondents said that they paid attention to the campaign on television; 31 per cent gave it as the most important source of their information, with radio following at 27 per cent and newspapers at 22.—Angus Campbell, Gerald Gurin, and Warren E. Miller, "Television and the Election," *Scientific American,* 188 (May, 1953), 47.

Even so, at its peak of interest the Republican national convention earned a Hooper rating of only 36 in New York City compared with one of 62 for "I Love Lucy."—Robert Bendiner, "How Much Has TV Changed Campaigning," *New York Times Magazine,* November 2, 1952, p. 13. Between 1952 and 1956 the number of television sets in use more than doubled, and presumably television's importance as a medium of political communication also rose.

22. One of two major categories of campaign literature described in 1900 was the "roorback" and the reply thereto. "To issue and distribute this requires quick work. It is made to influence the thoughtless and the ignorant."—Little, *op. cit.,* p. 741.

personal skills denied other men less suited to the contemporary medium did not seem significant. The same was true in other days, in the days of Franklin Roosevelt's radio voice, of Theodore Roosevelt's boisterous phrase-making, of Thomas Jefferson's agile pen. The types of persons equipped for successful political careers alter with the changing requirements of campaigning. It is difficult to see why at any given moment the random distribution of political talents would favor one politically significant group over another. It is difficult to conclude that the poor have fewer spokesmen or the rich are ridden over because the personal qualities that elected the father will hardly help the son.[23]

The subtle and the lasting effects of television campaigning might in the end prove numerous and profound. As many feared, ability to project personality might, through television campaigning, acquire a primacy hitherto unknown. In the meantime, certain characteristics of the mass communications campaigning that had commenced half a century earlier were visibly accentuated by the use of the new medium. At one time, a candidate's organization consisted principally of a small group of personal aids and a set of treaties with other political leaders. As the importance of publicity mounted, the character of the campaign skills required and the ways they were assembled changed. Organization continued crucial as a campaign function,[24] but the decline of old-style political machines and the growth of direct communications between candidates and voters evidenced the ascending significance of communications, especially its financial significance. The changes were, basically, technological in origin. Inventions in transportation and communications affected campaigning directly and underlay most of the profound alterations that occurred in social organization, in the character of the electorate, and in the nature of political issues. These forces combined to revolutionize the machinery of campaigning and its cost and to touch deeply other aspects of party procedure.[25] Certain of these were especially noteworthy.

23. Other claims have been made for television which skeptics view with reserve. William S. Paley, chairman of the board, Columbia Broadcasting System, suggested after 1952 that the quality of elections would be improved by the extraordinary intimacy of television. It gives voters a more uniform and sharper personal impression of the candidate and a deeper understanding of the issues. By staying home to avoid "the contagious emotions generated by a mass audience," Mr. Paley thought the citizen sitting with the privacy of his television screen could make up his mind in a state of relative tranquillity.—"Television and the Presidential Campaign," an address before the Poor Richard Club of Philadelphia, January 17, 1953. The political interest generated by television is one reason advanced for the increase in presidential voting in 1952 and 1956.

24. Some of the Democratic successes in 1956 and 1958 appeared attributable to improved political organization in state and local areas.

25. Professor Leiserson has observed that the agencies of mass communications have challenged "the central function of the political party as the primary agency of political education for the citizen."—Avery Leiserson, *Parties and Politics—An Institutional and Behavioral Approach* (New York: Alfred A. Knopf, 1958), p. 75. In both Great Britain and the United States, the modern means by which candidates can reach the voters have rendered obsolete many machine practices.

More than a Pheidippides needed.—Pheidippides fell dead as he reached the outskirts of Athens. Modern mass communications have converted many presidential campaigns into marathon races, imposing an astonishing personal burden upon presidential candidates. Hard work is no novelty for American politicians,[26] but candidates for high office have important responsibilities to meet, including the maintenance of good health, if they are to serve well the offices to which they are chosen. It was anomalous that as the ease of communicating to the electorate improved, the labor of doing so increased. In the first year of full radio campaigning, 1928, stump speaking by the candidates became a *standard* feature of presidential campaigns. Curiously enough, television further increased the pressure on candidates to travel, and with the airplane, the time saved in the air multiplied the demands upon the candidates instead of reducing them. Not even his immense popularity and severe illnesses excused President Eisenhower from the stump in 1956, but rather they seemed to make his personal appearances necessary. In 1896, William Jennings Bryan, in an unprecedented orgy or oratory, travelled more than 18,000 miles to deliver some 600 speeches to 5,000,000 people in person.[27] In 1956, Adlai Stevenson, who could be seen and heard by many times this number by going before a television camera—and on numerous occasions was—felt compelled to travel twice the distance by plane, train, and car.[28]

The pressures on presidential candidates to hit the hustings stem from several sources. The spread of competition among the states increases the interest local and national leaders feel in their personal appearances.[29] The visits made by Eisenhower and Stevenson to the South in 1952 and 1956 reflected a trend in evidence elsewhere. Candidates running simultaneously for other positions often want the leaders of the party ticket to visit their states—pleas likely to be treated with respect when the candidates might later assist in presidential relations with Congress. The airplane has limited the ability of the presidential aspirant and his managers to say no. They can no longer plead lack

26. At least if their memoirs are to be believed. Arthur F. Mullen tells of travelling 30,000 miles within the state of Nebraska to organize the Bryan Volunteers in 1908. "I might have hesitated if I'd known that for nine months in that year my life was to be a combination of traveling salesman and African dodger."—*Western Democrat* (New York: Wilfred Funk, Inc., 1940), p. 129.

27. Matthew Josephson, *The Politicos, 1865-1896* (New York: Harcourt, Brace and Company, 1938), p. 688.

28. The president was held to 17,000 miles.—*U.S. News and World Report,* November 9, 1956, p. 98. In 1952, Eisenhower made 228 speeches and covered a shade under 50,000 miles; Stevenson spoke 203 times and went 32,500.—James Reston, "Our Campaign Techniques Re-examined," *New York Times Magazine,* November 9, 1952, p. 8.

29. Eisenhower visited 44 states in 1952 and Stevenson 32.—Malcolm Moos, *The Republicans—A History of Their Party* (New York: Random House, 1956), p. 488.

of time.[30] Moreover, to be broadcast, a speech must be made. A hall of howling partisans adds punch. So candidates accept some of the sounding boards offered to them, and to avoid favoritism they race off to others. The mobility resulting from technological developments leads political interests of all types to press claims for the personal attention of candidates. The growth of organized interest groups has both reflected and created increased demands on government. The plight of the presidential candidate is not solely a product of planes and mikes but of a more complex structure of political interests as well.

The result of it all is a cruel, grueling personal experience that exhausts the candidate. The pace of his day and the multiplicity of his decisions exceed the capacities of the best.[31] (They led one candidate to call his party's nominee for Congress by the name of an opponent, and another after a speech in Bethlehem to thank the good people of Allentown.) Decisions taken and commitments made in the heat of a campaign are always difficult enough. In a day when domestic politics and foreign policy are seldom separate, the campaign no longer constitutes a backyard play that can be forgotten as soon as it is over. Like a president, a presidential candidate needs to be informed, to be alert, to make decisions under such conditions that he may reasonably be held responsible for them. The organizational and staffing needs of the White House finally received attention; the corresponding needs of presidential candidates require attention too.

An era of specialists.—Detailed study of the purposes for which modern campaign funds are used reveals a high degree of specialization in campaign operations. Campaign organizations are neither large nor complex by the standards of contemporary administrative structures in government and business, but the thousands of pages of itemized campaign payments reported for each election emphasize the multiplicity of goods and services called into use. The proliferation of skills employed in the political process extends beyond campaign organizations to all reaches of party and candidate activities.

As a result of this division of labor, a politician becomes a difficult person to define—which reveals, incidentally, that the door to political activity is open to a wide variety of persons.[32] The concept of the

30. The airplane tempted candidates to create their own burdens, too. In August, 1956, Stevenson and Kefauver launched a flying trip to all sections of the country "to lay the groundwork for the greatest grass roots campaign of all time. . . . Its objective is to talk first-hand with local and state leaders rather than to make speeches and public appearances."—*The News and Observer* (Raleigh, N.C.), August 22, 1956.

31. For one personal description of Franklin Roosevelt on tour, see Raymond Moley, *After Seven Years* (New York: Harper & Brothers Publishers 1939), pp. 52-53. Adlai Stevenson conveys the flavor of his agonies in *Major Campaign Speeches—1952* (New York: Random House, 1953), pp. xii-xiii.

32. Also as a result of the division of labor, individuals competent in certain political roles prove to be grossly ignorant of others. This was found true at all

politician as a mediator among conflicting interests embraces the broad functions of parties and factions. But not all individuals significantly active in parties and campaigns are engaged directly in mediating roles, nor are they all clothed with the ulitmate attributes of political leadership, power, representativeness, accountability.[33] In common parlance, all candidates, their managers, and party officers are accepted as politicians, although job descriptions of what even they actually do in different settings would expose many variations. In addition, necessary cogs in the wheels of modern politics include diverse types such as jingle writers, stage directors, public opinion pollsters,[34] advance men, statistical researchers, precinct bosses, interest-group leaders, public relations advisers, contributors, solicitors, finance chairmen, career accountants, field representatives, confidential alter egos, advisers on an infinite number of special policy areas, the head of a women's division, and the head of a Negro division. These just begin the list that makes the campaign organization of the mid-twentieth century a wholly different phenomenon from that which sought Mr. Buchanan's election in 1856 or Judge Parker's in 1904.

Campaign effectiveness and party bureaucracy.—Waste of money has been acute in political campaigns as far back as the record runs. It is not simply that money may stick to the fingers through which it passes (or rather, through which it does not pass). Men of experience have at one time or another estimated that a fourth, a half, even a larger proportion of campaign expenditures went down a useless drain. Administrative inefficiencies have been gross.[35] Political inefficiencies, more important to the effectiveness of the election process, have taken the

---

political levels.

Legislative investigations have also discovered that in the chaos of improvised campaign organizations, operating at white heat, the right hand often does not know what the left is doing. One of the "major sensations" of the investigation of the Illinois Republican Senatorial primary in 1926 by a Senate committee was the "startling ignorance of some of the witnesses who professed their entire willingness to cooperate with Senator Reed in his inquiries." It seemed, among other examples, that the secretary of the Republican national committee did not know the name of the treasurer of his own state party organization.—Carroll Hill Wooddy, *The Case of Frank L. Smith—A Study in Representative Government* (Chicago: The University of Chicago Press, 1931), pp. 37-38.

33. Cf. Leiserson, *op. cit.*, pp. 14-15.

34. For example, one informed guess put expenditures in 1956 and 1958 combined at $1,000,000 for private surveys done for candidates and political parties. The corresponding estimate for 1946 and 1948 was no more than $75,000.—Louis Harris, "Is the Old Survey Order Passing?" *PROD,* 2 (March, 1959), 8-9.

35. Symbolized by the carloads of Republican literature found on a siding in 1896, and the million copies of a document directed at about the same time to organized labor in New York that were printed without a union label, only to be junked and printed again. Politicians readily confess more recent blunders. In 1952, 5,000 "Ike for President" license plates were bought for New Jersey's Mercer County Republicans, but none was ever distributed.—Truman S. Casner, "Money in Politics: New Jersey" (Senior thesis, Princeton University, 1955), p. 7.

form of poor judgments, piqued feelings, unneeded commitments, wretched failures to capitalize on opportunities to build public support. Most campaign headquarters are welters of confusion, a state of affairs inherent in modern conditions of campaigning.

The probabilities and penalties of campaign inefficiency have reached new peaks with the arrival of television. There is a new premium on campaign planning and efficient management. The large costs of network television, to be met in advance, alone require a new kind of timing in the planning and launching of campaigns. Failure to anticipate television needs apparently cost Republicans $300,000 to $400,000 in 1952. Preemption and other charges could have been avoided by advance arrangements,[36] although it might be argued that the money was well spent if it permitted the Republicans to capture a significant part of the audience of the choice commercial shows whose time was pre-empted. The preparation required by modern campaigns often must commence before candidates are chosen.[37]

Few if any party organizations possess the staff necessary to supply the technical and professional skills called for in modern campaigns. To fill this void, and in some localities to help fill larger voids created by generally weak party organizations,[38] public relations people and others from outside the party structure have often stepped in. They claim to offer a steady set of diverse and expert skills that cannot be developed and sustained by party organizations. The parties are not, however, entirely devoid of stable administrative staffs.

36. *New York Times,* October 30, 1955. Not a new phenomenon. In 1916, the Democratic national committee wasted $250,000 through placing advertising by telegram during the campaign instead of contracting for it in advance.—Overacker, *op. cit.,* pp. 86-87.

37. Thus Arthur E. Summerfield, chairman of the Republican national committee during the 1952 campaign, cautioned against shortening presidential campaigns: "The conduct of a national campaign today is a tremendous undertaking. I point out to you gentlemen that to set up an organization in a period of 60 days, which is about all the time you have following the national convention, under the present law, that will first develop a program for the campaign, employ or enlist by the voluntary method personnel to activate that campaign, prepare literature, and do the innumerable other things that have to be done, in addition to the great mass of detail of planning for presidential train and airplane tours, television and radio programs, is a responsibility that I certainly would not recommend that you place upon anyone's shoulders at the present time, in a lesser time than it was my responsibility to do during the past campaign. I ask you to picture it for yourself. You are elected chairman of the Republican or the Democratic National Committee. There is a small number of personnel. You have to get new personnel. You have to go out and find them and when you start to attempt to do that in the limited time that we have under the present statutes, believe me, you have a major undertaking on your hands."—U.S. House of Representatives Special Committee to Investigate Campaign Expenditures, 1952, *Hearings* (Washington: Government Printing Office, 1952), p. 53.

38. See R. J. Pitchell, "The Influence of Professional Campaign Management Firms in Partisan Elections in California," *Western Political Quarterly,* 11 (1958), 278-300.

In October of the nonelection years 1953, 1955, and 1957, the payrolls of the Republican and Democratic national committees averaged 97 and 64 employees, respectively. Taken as a whole, these were hardly career staffs and could not meet the full requirements of election-year campaigning,[39] but compared with a generation before they were monstrous bureaucracies. The situation in the states is more difficult to assess, but some suggestive answers were supplied to a questionnaire by the chairman of each party in each of 48 states.

There is, first of all, a rapid turnover among the state chairmen themselves. While many who reach the post have served a long apprenticeship in other capacities, few linger long enough to provide much continuity in formal leadership. In 1958, over one-fourth of all state chairmen had been in office less than two years, and in both parties over three-fourths had held office less than five years. Only four Republican and three Democratic state chairmen had served as long as nine years.[40] Virtually all state party organizations take on paid staff during a campaign,[41] yet well over one-fourth of the state chairmen said their committee's offices were not kept open throughout 1956 and 1957.[42] The staffing of the 39 Republican and 29 Democratic state headquarters that *were* kept open is indicated by the number of paid personnel normally employed when no campaign was in progress:

Number of states with	*Rep.*	*Dem.*
Secretarial staff only		
Part-time	2	3
Full-time	9	4

39. See Hugh A. Bone, *Party Committees and National Politics* (Seattle: University of Washington Press, 1958), pp. 37-39, 46-48, 130; Jack Redding, *Inside the Democratic Party* (The Bobbs-Merrill Company, Inc., 1958), pp. 120-22. Both parties have been criticized in recent years for the heavy cost of maintaining between-elections staffs. Many old hands view them as unnecessary frills, believing the money could be better spent in October of an election year.

40.

Number of years in office:	*Under 2*	*2-4*	*5-6*	*7-8*	*9-15*	*Over 15*	*Unk.*	*Total*
Number of chairmen—Republican:	18	20	4	1	2	2	1	*48*
Democratic:	9	28	5	3	1	2	0	*48*

41. *Number of employees of state committee at peak of 1956 campaign:*

	0	*1-5*	*6-10*	*11-20*	*Over 20*	*Unk.*	*Total*
Number of committees—Republican:	3	21	9	8	5	2	*48*
Democratic:	4	23	11	7	3	0	*48*

In some states the main campaign burden is carried by separate campaign committees, which in some cases, at least, further lessens any influence the committee's regular staff has on the conduct of the campaign.

42. So reported nine Republican and 19 Democratic state chairmen, but it was clear that some who answered otherwise to the question had in mind their personal offices and not a separate party quarters. When asked how many *county* party organizations kept offices open during 1956 and 1957, the responses were as follows: 0, 18 Rep., 22 Dem.; 1-5, 20 Rep., 15 Dem.; 6-10, 7 Rep., 4 Dem.; other, 3 Rep., 7 Dem.

Professional-level personnel		
Part-time	2	3
Full-time		
1 person	16	12
2-3 persons	6	4
4-5 persons	2	1
over 5 persons	2	2
	39	29

Each state chairman was asked how long these people had been employed by the state committee at the end of 1957. Counting the senior person only in each state, the results were as follows:

Number of states with	*Rep.*	*Dem.*
Secretarial staff only		
Under 5 years	8	5
5-8 years	1	1
Over 8 years	2	1
Professional-level personnel		
Under 5 years	19	14
5-8 years	5	2
Over 8 years	4	6
	39	29

In some states, committees that employed persons of professional status had secretarial employees with greater longevity than the professional.

These are the hired hands of party organizations. In a few instances, politicians of personal influence get on the party payroll, but the personnel summarized here are mostly technicians. They, like their mentors among the political leaders of their areas, often possess experience and shrewdness in the pull and haul of factional and party competition. Their chief significance, however, lies in the contribution they make in meeting the requirements of contemporary political campaigning. What they do not do, it is fair to suppose, others will try to do.[43]

3. COMMERCIAL POLITICIANS

The public relations man has replaced the political boss as an object of opprobrium. Whether rated good or bad, he has significance, like the boss, because he fills a functional need in political operations. Public relations is a recognized occupation, and for some it is a profession. Those who follow it are on their way to a place among the elite corps

43. Some indication of staff activity is revealed by a canvass of state party publications that were said by the state chairmen in 1958 to appear regularly:

Number of issues per year:	*52*	*26*	*12*	*6*	*4*	*Unk.*	*Total*
Number of states—Republican	1	4	16	2	2	0	25
Democratic	2	1	12	1	2	1	19

of American society.[44] The people engaged in it who trade in the coin of politics are commercial politicians.

Carl Byoir, the late, famed public relations consultant credited with the idea for the Roosevelt birthday balls, concluded that public relations "is whatever the individual practioner thinks it is."[45] For political purposes a public relations man is whoever calls himself one. Public relations has become a label of convenience covering any kind of free wheeling political activity one takes a fancy to. Types who used to be known as lobbyists, campaign managers, press agents, confidential advisors, hangers on, or simply as lawyers with a bent for politics, show up in every state bearing the new label.[46] It gives them a vocational base from which to sell their political services. Many of these are of the facilitating, mediating, intermediary kind that are traditionally associated with lawyers and lobbyists. Many are more technical in character, involving writing skills and knowledge of publicity techniques. And, increasingly it would seem, they include knowledge of personalities, of factional rivalries, of interest groups, and of local political history, necessary ingredients of effective political campaigning.

No census records the number of these commercial politicians, nor how numerous and varied are their skills. In 1957, the Public Relations Society of America, whose qualifications for membership are considered relatively strict,[47] had more than 2,600 individual members. Two-thirds of these were employed in public relations departments of large organizations and one-third in public relations counseling firms, the latter numbering slightly over 500, scattered over 25 states. Many other firms as well as individuals practiced public relations, but PRSA's list of counseling firms constitutes the backbone of organized public relations activity.

The financial dimension.—Since the appearance of mass advertising early in the twentieth century, political parties have made large payments

44. As one type among the "specialists in persuasion." All hands now seem to require help from public relations specialists. Fights for control of corporations are managed by them; the Farm Bureau Federation hires them; communities and states engage their services. Candidates are beginning to come from the public relations ranks, as they have from law and journalism, to wit a candidate for mayor of Philadelphia and a congressman from California.

45. *Fortune*, 52 (November, 1955), 232.

46. Indicative of the trend was the remark of California's "secret boss," Artie Samish, later jailed for his casual regard for the tax laws: "Who, me? I represent industry. I'm a lobbyist, a public relations man."—Lester Velie, "The Secret Boss of California," in David Farrelly and Ivan Hinderaker (eds.), *The Politics of California—A Book of Readings* (New York: Ronald Press, 1951), p. 178.

One political freebooter of mediocre talents who had made his way to an important appointive job in Texas government insisted that his profession was public relations. In an earlier day he would have been called, by others at least, a patronage hog.

47. *Fortune*, 54 (November, 1956), 109. There were some 3,300 advertising agencies in the United States in 1956.—*Ibid.*, 54 (September 1956), 224.

to news and advertising agencies for arranging space.[48] At times these agencies presumably added advice and counsel to their services, though the kind and significance is not apparent from the figures. Many modern public relations firms have advertising departments, and much of the money paid to them as well as to advertising agencies still goes for use of mass communications media. To understand the political roles of public relations firms, therefore, it is necessary to ask what they do, not simply how much political money they handle. Nevertheless, a high proportion of the funds of many campaign committees flows through public relations and advertising firms.

In 1952, at the national level, the three most important Democratic campaign committees reported paying nearly $1,000,000 to the Joseph Katz Company alone, and the three top Republican groups paid the Kudner Agency more than $1,200,000.[49] For state and local levels, a sense of the importance of expenditures to public relations and advertising firms can be gained from Table 53. It lists selected campaign committees of several types active in 1952. As much as 90 per cent of the total disbursements of some committees, and frequently more than 50 per cent, were made through such firms.[50] Thirteen states are represented in the table, and the committees include regular party organizations, *ad hoc* candidate committees, local and state committees, committees of both parties. In many other states, candidates and parties have also enjoyed the services of public relations and advertising experts.

The Republican state chairmen in 18 states, and the Democratic chairmen in 15, said in 1958 that their state committees had employed a *public relations* firm at some time during 1956 or 1957. It seems probable in many states that candidate and volunteer committees are even

48. In 1916, the Democratic national committee received a bill for $238,000 from one advertising agency alone for placing newspaper ads throughout the country.—Pollock, *op. cit.*, pp. 149-50.

49. These payments were readily identified. Additional payments to these companies may have been made. Other public relations firms were also employed. The Katz payments constituted 68, 40, and 6 per cent, respectively, of the direct expenditures of the Stevenson-Sparkman Forum, the Volunteers for Stevenson, and the Democratic national committee. The Kudner payments represented 25, 21, and 16 per cent, respectively, of the direct expenditures of the Citizens for Eisenhower-Nixon, the Republican national committee, and the Republican Senatorial campaign committee.

50. The sums in the table do not necessarily represent all the payments of this kind made by a committee, merely those to a particular agency that were identified, and the committees shown do not usually constitute the full campaign effort of the candidate or party to which they pertain. Some committees, as determined by state statutes and the whimseys of bookkeepers, report their expenditures by payee, some by purpose of payment, some without any identification. Generally it is clear that the money went largely for printed material, advertising, and broadcasting—both time on the air and advisory services. Itemizations reveal costs for taking polls, renting billboards, photography, and so on.

Data corresponding to that of 1952 were not accessible for a large number of committees in 1956. Spot checks, however, revealed many payments to public relations firms and advertising agencies.

Table 53

MINIMUM PAYMENTS TO ADVERTISING AGENCIES AND PUBLIC RELATIONS FIRMS BY SELECTED POLITICAL COMMITTEES, 1952[a]

State	Committee	Agency[b]	Amount[c]	% of Committee's Total Disbursements[d]
Conn.	Rep. State	Edward Graceman & Assoc.	$194,012	63
N.Y.	Dem. State	Joseph Katz Co.	13,633	4
N.Y.	Rep. State	Batten, Barton, Durstine & Osborn	227,665	31
Ohio	Rep. State	Mumm, Mullay & Nichols	93,123	14
Ore.	Rep. State	Hal Short & Co.	13,844	35
Utah	Dem. State	Cooper & Crowe Adv. Agency	13,808	45
Utah	Rep. State	George Baker Adv. Agency	5,003	19
Calif.	Eisen.-Nixon. So.	Elwood J. Robinson Co.	37,889	14
Calif.	Eisen.-Nixon, No.	Dimarca-Von Lowenfeldt Assoc.	19,689	25
Conn.	Vols. Stevenson	Green-Brodie, Inc.	16,660	65
Conn.	Eisenhower for Pres.	Edward Graceman & Assoc.	22,011	19
Md.	Dems. for Eisenhower	Cohn-Miller, Inc.	4,174	94
N.Y.	Fund, Stev.-Spark.	Milton Biow Agy.; Joseph Katz Co.	76,185	50
Okla.	Citz. Eisen.-Nixon	Pate Organization	6,000	17
Wash.	Vols. Stevenson	Williams & Gordon	600	5
Conn.	Comm., Senator Benton	Edward Owen & Co.	92,220	65
N.Y.	Pers., Senator Ives	Batten, Barton, Durstine & Osborn	15,628	58
Ore.	3 comms., Sen. Neuberger	Earl Heims Assoc.	58,782	70
Ore.	2 comms., Sen. Cordon	Shwalter Lynch Adv. Agency	69,479	57
Fla.	McCarty, Sen. prim.	Bevis & Tyler Agency	30,446	12
Fla.	Odham, Sen. prim.	Houck & Co. of Florida	83,033	53
Texas	Daniel, Sen prim.	Gregory-Giezendanner Co.	20,098	15
Wis.	Schmitt, Sen. prim.	Houck & Co.	17,264	72
Pa.	Dem. Comm., Phila.	Beacon Agency	29,302	10
Pa.	Rep. Comm., Allg. Co.	4 firms[e]	79,214	25
N.Y.	Vols. Stev., N.Y. Co.	Joseph Katz Co.	20,302	5
Pa.	Vols. Stev., Pitts'g	Bachman, Kelly & Trautman Adv. Agy.	7,930	90
Pa.	Eisen. Citz., S.E. Pa.	Benjamin Eshleman Co.; Falkner & Co.	104,324	60
Wis.	Vols. Stev., Mil. Co.	Maunter Agency	7,373	65
Wis.	Eisen.-Nixon, Mil. Co.	Dayton, Johnson & Hacker	19,969	62

[a] For Neuberger and Cordon, 1954. Unless otherwise indicated, each entry represents one committee and in no case is intended to cover all activities on behalf of a candidate.

[b] Payees shown on campaign reports for publicity, public relations, advertising, professional services, etc.

[c] Identifiable amounts paid to an agency; the agency might actually be responsible for larger expenditures.

[d] Percentage of total disbursements is used because the percentage of total of direct expenditures, which would usually run somewhat higher, was not always ascertainable.

[e] Ketchum, MacLeod, & Grave; Sykes Advertising, Inc.; Cabbot & Kaufman, Inc.; Cavannaugh Morris.

more likely to employ public relations firms than are the regular party groups. Moreover, public relations services are made available in political campaigns via other channels. The Republican finance chairman in a large and important state volunteered that "the biggest loophole" through the statutes regulating campaign finance is the employment of public relations people by corporations on retainer. They do political-campaign work as part of their responsibility to their employer.

The variety of political campaigns in which public relations firms are active is suggested by Table 54. A questionnaire was circulated to 200 public relations counseling firms represented in the membership of the Public Relations Society of America. These were the firms most prominent in their area and thought to be most interested in political accounts. The responses received numbered 130 and covered activities during the years 1952-57. These firms said they rendered services of some kind in a total of 554 campaigns for nomination and election at all levels of politics.[51] They claimed to have had over-all responsibility for the management of the campaign in 183 instances. While these data are not comprehensive—many politically active public relations people are not members of PRSA[52]—they demonstrate that in many parts of the country public relations firms (as opposed to advertising agencies) are importantly involved in the management of campaigns for elective

Table 54

TYPES OF POLITICAL CAMPAIGNS IN WHICH SERVICES WERE RENDERED BY PUBLIC RELATIONS COUNSELING FIRMS, 1952-1957: RESPONSES FROM 130 FIRMS[a]

Office at Stake	Services Rendered in Campaigns for				No. of Times Over-all Campaign Management Undertaken	
	Nomination		Election			
	No. Firms[b]	No. Camps.[b]	No. Firms[b]	No. Camps.[b]	No. Firms[b]	No. Camps.[b]
U.S. President[c]	22	27	28	43	5	9
U.S. Senator	17	19	17	21	8	9
U.S. Representative	19	31	19	32	10	19
Governor	18	24	15	23	8	10
Other statewide	20	45	22	47	11	23
Mayor	14	24	18	31	10	14
Other local	16	53	23	61	18	38
Other	5	48	9	25	7	61
Total	..	271	..	283	..	183

[a] In 1957, 508 firms providing public relations counseling services were represented in the membership list of the Public Relations Society of America. A questionnaire was sent in December, 1957, by the Director, Information Center, of the Society, to 200 firms selected by him. The firms, selected impressionistically, were those most prominent in their states and most likely to have an interest in political-campaign work. The 130 responses received are summarized in this table.

[b] Some firms handled more than one campaign during the six-year period.

[c] Some of the presidential activities referred to were confined to one state.

51. In addition to the offices specified in the table, public relations firms have actively managed candidates for such posts as lieutenant governor, state attorney general, city and district attorney, member of a local governing board, and delegate to a presidential nominating convention.

52. The firms represented in PRSA membership were found in 29 states, those responding to the questionnaire in 24. Seventy-nine per cent of the firms were concentrated, however, in seven states and the District of Columbia (California, Illinois, Michigan, New York, Ohio, Pennsylvania, and Texas); 70 per cent of those responding and 71 per cent of those saying they had rendered political-campaign services were also in those areas.

office (not simply the management of initiative and referenda campaigns, lobbying, and related kinds of political activity).

Services rendered.—Some notion of what public relations firms do in campaigns for public office is disclosed by Table 55. Sixty per cent of the 130 firms responding to the PRSA questionnaire had rendered some kind of service during the years 1952-57. These services ranged from the conventional advertising-agency function of arranging for advertising space or air time to acceptance of full responsibility for the management of a campaign. Other services included fund-raising, counseling on strategy and tactics, preparation of publicity materials, and speech-writing. The part played by public relations counselors in the 1952 presidential campaign has been described by Stanley Kelley, Jr., in a book opening up the whole subject of *Professional Public Relations and Political Power*. Mr. Kelley reported that the Katz Company's services to the Democrats were more confined to purely technical functions than were those of agencies retained by the Republicans, which had a hand in formulating grand strategy.[53] The number of firms that are able and willing to take full responsibility for campaign management is limited. Forty-one placed themselves in this category in Table 55, and the total number in the country is probably not much larger.[54] The 41 were spread among 15 states, but over half of them were located in California, New York, and Texas. The head of a large Texas public relations organization suggested that his state and California are so large, and their politics so heterogeneous, that really six or seven campaigns must be run at once, and to do this requires professional planning and a large staff.[55] When full management is assumed, the budgets on which the public relations firms operate resemble those of a political committee.[56]

53. (Baltimore: The Johns Hopkins Press, 1956), p. 160.

54. Whitaker & Baxter, the best known, estimated that: "Probably there are not more than thirty or forty professional campaign managers in the United States who work full time in this field, or who direct every aspect of a campaign. California, partly because of our widely used initiative-referendum system, has more professional campaign managers than any other state, and the number here would approximate twelve or fifteen. On the other hand, there are probably one hundred or more men and women in this state who are skilled in some phase of campaign work and who are employed by firms like our own during campaign seasons."—Letter to author, December 13, 1957.

55. He classified Texas public relations firms as follows: (1) the larger ones that give complete campaign management to state-office races but who stay out of district and local races; (2) those which handle a city administration's politics, bond issues, school board elections, and the like, and who will handle primary elections for the state legislature and occasionally for Congress, these firms being limited generally to one per city; and (3) one-man shops willing to take on candidates for the legislature, local judge, and similar offices.

56. Only rarely are detailed breakdowns available, but when they are this is the case. For example, the expenses of one $20,000 account were classified as follows: general overhead (rent, postage, telephone and telegraph, etc.), 14 per cent; salaries, 14 per cent; publicity and advertising, 69 per cent; travel expenses, 2 per

Table 55

POLITICAL-CAMPAIGN SERVICES RENDERED BY PUBLIC RELATIONS COUNSELING FIRMS IN CONNECTION WITH NOMINATION AND ELECTION CAMPAIGNS FOR PUBLIC OFFICE, 1952-1957: RESPONSES FROM 130 FIRMS[a]

Service	Firms Performing Indicated Service (of 130 responding)	
	No.	%[b]
Service of some kind performed	78	60
Type of service performed:		
Arrangement of advertising space or air time	57	44
Preparation of publicity materials, speech writing, etc.	66	51
Counseling on strategy or tactics of campaign issues	70	54
Fund-raising	36	28
Over-all campaign management	41	32
Other	14	11
Rendered service for more than one political party	28	22

[a] See note (a) to Table 54.
[b] The percentages are not representative of all public relations firms. See note (a) to Table 54.

Many of the political tasks undertaken by public relations people have long been the province of free-lance specialists. The new importance of the commercial politicians arose from their assumption of communications and organizational activities and associated processes that had traditionally been provided from within parties and factions. The effects of the trend, however, are easy to overjudge. So far, no wholesale displacement of party functionaries has occurred sufficient to convert political campaigns into contests between advertising firms, although the possibility was worth an amusing novel.[57] And the trend was not uniform among the states. Two lines of change warranted special notice, however, both of them evidence of the penetration of commercial politicians into the political process.

One of these has received considerable attention: the effect of a salesman's philosophy of political campaigning on the definition of issues and the nature of debate. Mr. Kelley's treatment of the broad implications of this aspect of mass communications campaigning is especially interesting. The functions of public relations people in building and maintaining party structures have also been noticed. Both of these developments are compatible with the kind of bureaucracies that characterize American parties. The commercial politicians are hired to do what the parties do not do for themselves. When wide discretion is granted the political

cent; and field activities, 1 per cent. In responding to a questionnaire from the Gore Committee, one important state committee reported that a large share of its total expenditures was made through an agency and it had no way of knowing the breakdown.

57. John G. Schneider, *The Golden Kazoo* (New York: Rinehart and Company, 1956), 246 pp.

mercenaries, it usually reflects the inadequacy of party officials and party staffs to handle modern campaign responsibilities.

Organizational significance.—The lush, chaotic politics of California afforded enormous opportunities for anyone who could provide a sensible and economical way to run a political campaign. The presence of large numbers of referenda created contests in which *ad hoc* alignments shifted from one election to the next. New campaign organizations had to be constructed to wage each fight. The cross-filing system in the primaries confused whatever tendencies existed toward stable factional lines within the parties. And there was not much by way of party organization in the first place, a condition partly attributable to California's nonpartisan municipal elections. Whitaker & Baxter and the others responded to a market opportunity created by the frequent referenda and the technical demands of the communications media. The inability of party and factional structures to prosecute political campaigns even for their own candidates created a vacuum. Public relations firms stepped in to fill the vacuum.

Public relations firms seem to play their most important organizational roles in states of weak party organization. One public relations man of considerable Texas experience divided his firm's campaign activities into three phases: helping decide the "pitch" of the campaign; providing the "ammunition"; and managing the field campaign through county and district organizations. Assistance from public relations firms with the first two of these activities is now a stable feature of presidential campaigning and is found in many state and local contests. The development by commercial politicians of personal structures of acquaintanceship and influence has, however, special significance. Some of these organizations claim such a knowledge of personalities, and such a network of relationships in the areas where they operate, that they are called to assist in assembling a candidate's campaign organization. They get to know who is politically active, what their preferences are, what types of candidate they are likely to support, what kinds of work they may be willing to do. Some of the public relations people bring new individuals into political life, activating them when opportune issues and candidates come along. Two or three wisely chosen persons can be the difference "between a county that produces and one that doesn't," said one public relations campaign manager. This is especially true where party committees at local levels are weak or inoperative. To maximize their ability to marshall field organizations, some public relations firms maintain card files on politically useful personalities. They know who can be employed to "cruise" an area, to watch over local efforts, to report shifts in sentiment. Firms that develop special familiarity with one section of a state may be called in by others, so that two or more may be active for the same candidate.[58]

58. The head of a Texas firm wrote as follows: "In Texas, frequently one public relations firm will be assigned the responsibility for a state campaign, and

Organizing is not so packageable a commodity as script-writing. What kind of campaign organization can be energized depends largely on the candidate and the sources of personal, factional, and party support he begins with. The role a public relations firm plays depends also on the latitude the candidate and his aides are willing to give it. Whitaker & Baxter insist on control of the purse and of central decisions on the strategy of issues.[59] They supervise and coordinate county and volunteer organizational efforts, but tight control of local efforts cannot be achieved. By the nature of their work, public relations firms often have knowledge of structures of influence and how to reach them.[60] A public relations firm that has worked with the state medical association, to improve the community relations of the medical profession, not only increases the political potential of doctors, but also increases the ability of that firm to gain the political cooperation of doctors at later times. In all they do, moreover, public relations firms develop stable news outlets useful for many purposes.

Another aspect of commercial politicians adds to their significance. Most effective public relations experts have a recognizable political orientation. To be sure, some are willing to serve more than one party. Table 55 shows that 28 of the 130 firms stated that they had done so. Yet political sympathies frequently cross party lines. Particular commercial politicians tend to belong to one crowd and to work in the campaigns of that crowd.[61] In Texas, in fact, some of the most prominent got started in the mid-1950's as the result of long and successful identification with the fortunes of particular individuals. Mr. Jake Pickle, a lawyer by training who found his way into a public relations and advertising firm, was clearly a Lyndon Johnson man. Mr. John VanCronkhite, who had followed a miscellaneous political career in several states, fortuitously found himself attached to a winner in the person of Governor Allan Shivers (a profitable connection, but one that

---

will then engage other firms in Dallas, Fort Worth, San Antonio, El Paso, and Houston, to expedite the campaign in those specific sectors of the state. I have worked in that fashion on several occasions, handling North Texas as a farm-out from another firm. On other occasions, we have been in full charge of state campaigns and allocated regional responsibility to other firms."

59. Kelley, *op. cit.*, p. 47.

60. Many public relations firms do not consider political campaigns preferred business. One such firm protested that it would not handle political work at all except for two reasons: when the election of a candidate is highly important, it cannot in good conscience refuse a plea to help; and, said the principal officer, "I am willing to get into races at the level of governor or United States senator or attorney general, simply for the friendships I will make that will be useful to me in my business. I don't mean influence peddling; I simply mean that it is frequently useful and convenient to be on a first-name basis with public officials."

61. The difficulties the Democratic national committee has encountered in hiring the services of an appropriate public relations firm have been described in various places. See especially Redding, *op. cit.*, pp. 171-72, 213-15; also Bone *op. cit.*, pp. 87-88.

suffered its ups and downs as time went on). In California, Harry Lerner and Associates worked almost exclusively for Democrats, in contrast to Mr. Lerner's former employers, Whitaker & Baxter, who work the Republican side. In Georgia an advertising firm was identified with one of the governors. In other states, too, the recurring alliance of particular firms with one of the parties, or with a particular candidate, makes them look like components of a party or factional organization. They resemble mercenaries marching beside the regular army. If a public relations firm becomes a continuing component of a factional or party structure, it necessarily accrues influence.

Parties are already dependent on commercial politicians for the expertise required to use mass media effectively. They are dependent upon them in an increasing number of places for planning, budgeting, and supervising the administration of campaigns. Whitaker & Baxter may advance as much as $100,000 to keep operating expenditures flowing smoothly.[62] Party politicians testify that a campaign run by public relations experts is economically more efficient.[63] The $5,000 to $75,000 fee normally paid to manage a statewide race is well earned,[64] and nobody seems to begrudge the standard 15 per cent commission paid for advertising services.

The salesman's philosophy.—There is a manifest danger in employing professional propaganda specialists in political campaigns. Especially if their connection is a transitory one, their role can become highly irresponsible. They concentrate on the short-run goal of influencing votes in an immediate campaign—not, however, a new phenomenon, nor one confined to the United States.[65] This they can do, or like you to

62. Irwin Ross, "The Supersalesmen of California Politics," *Harpers,* 219 (July, 1959), 57. Thus the timing of expenditures may be designed for effectiveness, not controlled by the momentary luck of fund-raisers in digging up the cash. Whitaker & Baxter reported spending $207,687 for Republican Governor Knight in his successful reelection campaign of 1953.—*San Francisco Call-Bulletin,* November 24, 1954. Richfield Oil Corporation in 1956 reported paying $257,845 to them for handling the campaign in favor of Proposition Four, a California oil conservation measure that was defeated.—*Wall Street Journal,* December 11, 1956.

63. Some of the economies of mass production are in evidence. When a national controversy, such as that surrounding the late Senator McCarthy, cuts across state lines, leaflets, posters, and other paraphernalia or propaganda have shown up in several different places, identical in all respects except for the name of the candidate.

64. One budget for a statewide race called for a fee of $5,000, plus a "bonus in event of election" of $2,500!

65. Bias, distortion, skill, and cunning have long characterized political controversy, certainly since the days Samuel Adams wrote "artful" and "carefully biased" reports of events like the Boston Tea Party and "energetically arranged their dissemination."—J. A. R. Pimlott, *Public Relations and American Democracy* (Princeton: Princeton University Press, 1951), p. 6 and *passim.*

Of nineteenth-century printed matter: "No 'copy' in any printing office, unless it is the Bureau of Engraving and Printing, . . . is scrutinized more closely or edited with greater care than copy intended for campaign literature. . . . Paragraphs, sentences, and words are weighed with reference to their effect on the

think they can do, effectively. "My God, it's horrible," shuddered one practitioner recalling a television film of dubious ethical quality. "You can sell 'em anything, especially the women. You can sell half the women a bucket of kraut." He had done it and he knew.[66] The candidate would benefit in the short run. If any boomerangs came sailing back in future years it would be the candidate and not his public relations counselors who would have to catch them. Commercial politicians commanding structures of influence are tempted to operate in the short run too. Their primary goal, after all, is the fee for the service rendered, or the pride of success, and they are less restrained, if restrained at all, by concern for consistencies in policy and by qualms of private conscience. *Their* concern, as one of them said, is whether they can "get a proposition through, or handle a matter, or get the guy in." If so, the fellows for whom they did it "call on you to help them out again."[67]

Neither the public relations profession nor the political profession has developed an effective code of campaign ethics. Yet, in all campaigns, men are restrained by standards of rectitude or by fear of the wages of sin. The line of restraint is set by community expectations and prevailing tastes as well as by personal habits. It seems inescapable that the prospects for improving party and community standards would be enhanced if the responsibility for political campaigns were clearly focused in a stable party bureaucracy. In the era of mass communications campaigning, the parties have not developed adequate campaign machinery. Nor are they always equipped to hold their own with the specialists hired to fill the void. The frequent result is inefficient spending, campaign bloopers, and confusion inside the parties in the performance of their electoral functions.[68]

---

mind of the reader."—Little, *op. cit.*, p. 742. The carefully coached seconding speeches at the 1956 Republican national convention that so infuriated some members of the party seem little different from the large organized delegations that visited McKinley's front porch in 1896, "like so many trained seals, with their expenses paid in advance."—Josephson, *op. cit.*, p. 696.

Concern has been expressed by Canadian politicians that advertising agencies in their country have become too powerful. German party leaders a few years ago dispatched men to the United States to learn the lore of Madison Avenue, with conspicuous effects on the next campaign.

66. For a discussion of the technique, see Frank H. Jones, "The Art of Political Dynamiting," *The Western Political Quarterly* 10 (1957), 374-91. One is constantly reminded, however, that few things are new under the sun. The political cartoon, great weapon of controversy during the latter part of the nineteenth century, found its strength in an oversimplified, visual presentation of a highly partisan viewpoint. Designed to be understood quickly, even by the illiterate, to get a wide circulation, and to trigger conditioned preferences and prejudices, the cartoon in many ways resembled the spot broadcasts and salesman's slogans of a later day. "The Rise and Fall of the Political Cartoon" is the subject of an article by Henry Ladd Smith, *The Saturday Review,* May 29, 1954, pp. 7ff.

67. William L. Worden reports on California's professional campaign managers in "Tales of the Kingmakers," *Saturday Evening Post,* May 23, 1959, pp. 28ff. One conclusion: "Most of them will work either side of the street."

68. "This kind of situation is made to order for the experienced executive,"

4. WHAT SHOULD CAMPAIGNS COST?

In the present state of the craft, there is no conclusive answer. Despite vigorous criticism of the volume of campaign expenditures, no one has designed a model campaign that fixes optimum levels of expenditure under specified conditions. As a matter of fact, not much is said explicitly about what an election campaign ought to accomplish. Campaign theory goes little beyond the general notion that a well-informed electorate will behave more wisely than an ill-informed one.

Two-bits per vote.—The difficulties of defining and determining total expenditures in particular campaigns have already been emphasized. In most localities, nevertheless, there is a limited sector of total costs that candidates or their backers must "see" a reasonable chance of meeting before a campaign can be undertaken. This is the money that must be assembled for use through one or more central headquarters. In many states, local campaign organizations are expected to raise and spend their own funds. In others, especially in primary campaigns, a state headquarters may help finance local campaign operations. The headquarters money must be raised by the candidate or his group of immediate supporters. In most campaigns, once they are underway, modest funds flow automatically to all significant candidates. But to launch a campaign and to keep its central organs functioning require a basic amount of money, and this is the money that must be seen at the outset.

Types of expenditures and levels of costs vary with the office sought, the locale, the candidate, the character of the competition, local financing habits, and other factors alluded to earlier. Yet headquarters' expenditures for statewide races in most of the country run between 10 and 25 cents for every vote cast. Table 56 displays the sums required for *central campaign purposes* (only one item of total campaign expenditures) by candidates for governor or United States senator in a number of states during the 1950's. Other candidates have spent both more and less than the sums in the table, but these are representative under typical conditions. As long as present conditions obtain, sums on this order must be taken into account in legislative proposals for subsidizing or limiting campaign costs. Except for those cases where large-scale local-level financing is required through state headquarters, 25 cents per vote cast is a reasonable working maximum of the money needed—or at least spent.[69] For all national-level campaign committees combined

asserts Robert F. Bradford, former Republican Governor of Massachusetts, in urging businessmen to become personally active in politics.—"Republicans and Sinners," *Harvard Business Review,* 34 (1956), pp. 125-32.

69. Levels of campaign expenditure are often determined in essentially the same manner as some corporate advertising budgets. Asked how his company determined its advertising appropriation, one advertising manager replied: "Why, it's very simple. First I go upstairs to the controller and ask how much they can afford to give us this year. He says a million and a half. Later, the boss comes to me and asks how much we should spend. And I say, 'Oh, about a million and a half.' Then we have an advertising appropriation."—Quoted in Daniel Seligman, "How Much for Advertising," *Fortune,* 54 (December 1956), 123.

in a presidential contest, the corresponding expenditures per party come to about one-half that amount.[70]

Table 56

REPRESENTATIVE CENTRAL CAMPAIGN COSTS, PER VOTE CAST IN ELECTION: SELECTED CONTESTS, 1952-1956[a]

Type of Campaign	Approximate Costs, Central Campaign Responsibility	Approximate No. of Votes Cast	Cents per Vote Cast
Presidential			
1952 Republican National..........	$7,400,000	61,500,000	12
1952 Democratic National.........	6,400,000	61,500,000	10
1956 Republican National..........	9,000,000	62,000,000	14
1956 Democratic National.........	7,300,000	62,000,000	12
Statewide			
California, statewide election.......	300,000-500,000	4,000,000	8-13
Connecticut, statewide election.....	150,000-250,000	950,000	16-26
Illinois, statewide primary.........	100,000-200,000	850,000	12-24
Illinois, statewide election..........	400,000-600,000	3,500,000	11-17
Montana, statewide election........	40,000-60,000	250,000	16-24
New York, statewide election.......	800,000-1,000,000	5,000,000	16-20
Virginia, statewide primary.........	40,000-80,000	350,000	11-22
Oregon, statewide election..........	100,000-150,000	550,000	18-27
Kentucky, statewide primary[b].....	400,000-600,000	500,000	80-120[b]
Kentucky, statewide election[b]......	200,000-400,000	1,000,000	20-40[b]
Tennessee, statewide primary[b].....	150,000-300,000	650,000	23-46[b]
Texas, statewide primary, 1st[b].....	500,000-1,000,000	1,500,000	33-66[b]
Texas, statewide primary, 2nd[b].....	500,000-1,000,000	1,500,000	33-66[b]

[a] These are dependable estimates of the sums passing through central campaign headquarters of significant candidates during particular election campaigns. In some settings, a party committee and several volunteer or candidate committees were involved. Except where indicated, these sums do not generally include large subventions to local campaign groups. Although based on recent campaign experiences, the figures are offered simply to indicate the amount of money that a candidate or his backers must be able to "see" at the outset of a race. In the contests in question some candidates may have spent more and others less than the range presented here.

[b] Includes substantial subventions to local campaign organizations.

70. It is not always true that campaign managers spend all the money they get their hands on. The Citizens for Eisenhower-Nixon in 1952 refunded 16 per cent of each contributor's gift. This was not a course wildly applauded by the party's regular finance officers. Many contributors declined the refund, which the Citizens then sent to help pay for Eisenhower's "transition" headquarters set up at the Commodore Hotel between the election and the inauguration. Citizens officials understood that in 1940 contributors to the Democrats for Willkie had been offered a refund from a surplus existing at the end of that campaign.

Contributors to the 1956 gubernatorial primary campaign of North Carolina's Governor Luther Hodges, who faced little opposition, were returned one-fourth of any gift made to his state headquarters. The Governor, his wife, and immediate members of his staff were not included in the distribution.—*The News and Observer* (Raleigh, N.C.), June 9, 1956.

A defeated candidate for a Wichita municipal office in 1957 turned back to contributors a sum equal to one-fifth of her total expenditures.—Marvin A. Harder, *Nonpartisan Election: A Political Illusion?* (New York: Henry Holt and Company, 1958), p. 12. Sometimes a modest surplus is turned over to a party committee or put into a special fund for future use by the candidate.

Is it worth it?—During the discussion of campaign costs that followed the 1956 elections, a veteran newspaper editor declared that most campaign money is wasted: "Ninety-five per cent . . . would be a low estimate of the waste. The voters could get all the information about issues that would do them any good, all that they could possibly understand, if the two parties would just agree, or be compelled by law, to limit their appeals for votes to a few amply circulated newspaper statements and a few radio and television broadcasts in the five or six weeks before the election."[71] Thus is raised a central query. How useful, how functional, is the money that is spent?

The efforts made by public relations firms to rationalize political campaigning are normally guided by one criterion: the efficient influencing of voters. The energies they and others direct toward influencing voters, however, accomplish other purposes as well. There are latent as well as manifest functions in the use of campaign money.[72] Campaigning is inescapable in a system of popular elections, so that candidates and parties may display themselves, their records, and their views to the scrutiny of the electorate. But the process achieves more than the election of some candidates and the defeat of others.

The socially useful functions of political parties are numerous, and election campaigning contributes substantially to many of them. They are part of what the nation buys with its election money and should be remembered in assessing the social utility of campaign expenditures.

The public and private discussion generated by election campaigns serves to organize agreement and disagreement on public matters. The campaign is a necessary part of the process by which parties and groups reach agreements within themselves and focus the disagreements that separate them.[73] This process in turn is integral to the long-run processes through which public matters are aired, information about them is distributed,[74] and conflicts about them are reconciled or put on the shelf. The political campaign is one of the chief means by which parties achieve the functions claimed for them in American society. An American election campaign is more than a contest between candidates. It is a forum for the representation of interests in which a significant share

71. Louis Graves in the *Chapel Hill Weekly* (N.C.), March 22, 1957.

72. "*Manifest functions* are those objective consequences contributing to the adjustment or adaptation of the system which are intended and recognized by participants in the system; *latent functions,* correlatively, being those which are neither intended nor recognized."—Robert K. Merton, *Social Theory and Social Structure* (Glencoe, Illinois: The Free Press, 1949), p. 51.

73. See Bernard R. Berelson, Paul F. Lazarsfeld, and William N. McPhee, *Voting—A Study of Opinion Formation in a Presidential Campaign* (Chicago: University of Chicago Press, 1954), pp. 147, 231-32.

74. That neither political campaigns nor any other device fully informs the public is well known. Many polls "have shown quite clearly that sizeable portions of the public are grossly ill-informed about important public affairs."—Ralph O. Nafziger, Warren C. Engstrom, and Malcolm S. Maclean, Jr., "The Mass Media and an Informed Public," *Public Opinion Quarterly,* 15 (1951), 105.

of the citizenry feels involved. It is one way the country goes about making up its mind about its common concerns. The sums required to facilitate this discussion and to encourage the myriad of narrower debates that proceed within it exceed those sufficient for candidates and parties to present their programs and personalities.[75]

Large numbers of people relate themselves to their government through the activities of campaigns. They need not ring door bells nor make speeches to become importantly involved in the processes of self-government. The campaign and its surrounding events are, in fact, the one occasion that presses citizens to address themselves to the totality of their government. At other times they are concerned with the property-tax rate, a regulatory commission, a minimum-wage statute, the exercise of public domain, the decision of a revenue officer, the fate of a son overseas. These and other *particular* concerns thrust the citizen at random points into contact with the governments under which he lives. The political campaign asks him to think in larger categories of public concern; it asks him to decide what candidates—usually, which one of two candidates—will, on balance, serve his total interests best. To do this launches a harmonizing, reconciling process within individuals by which consciously or subconsciously they themselves decide what things are most important to them. Faced by the alternative candidates and parties they may perceive the depth or the absence of the choices before them. The processes that go on within individuals are stimulated by the variety and volume of communications that reach them. Some are touched by one medium, others by many; the bombardment of repetitive political messages of a campaign may stimulate *internal* self-governing processes of individuals that otherwise would lie dormant.

The vexed vent their wrongs, can have their say, or hear another say it for them. Their competitive and combative energies find outlet, vicariously and actively, in the conduct and excesses of campaigning. A campaign is sublimated violence and is part of the election process that achieves peaceful transition of authority. As such, those who enter the lists, and some of those whose support they seek and represent, exert or spend themselves to the maximum for victory. The psychological adjustments achieved by campaigns may require greater expenditures than needed for an informed and rational voting decision.

A unity of community, moreover, is bred by common campaign experiences. The bonds woven in politics run to allies. But the bonds even cross battle lines to link opponents with a sense of mutual fate. Old political enemies, like old prizefighters, often stand arm in arm, linked by a private bond more personal than they share with their own lieutenants. Thomas Jefferson and John Adams were even closer after their years of rivalry than before. Despite the raucous charges and

75. In dictatorships that go through the form of popular elections, large amounts of money are often spent. Functionally, however, the elections are not means of choosing public officials but are vehicles for government propagandizing.

frequent bitterness, the typical, eventual result of American elections is a greater sense of unity.[76] Seldom does dispute cut deep enough to vitiate a sense of common process and confidence in it.

It seems likely, too, that the volume and character of communications stimulated by political campaigns contribute to a general sense of community. Sense of community must be fortified periodically if the common tasks of a community are to be met effectively.[77] The mass media lace all hamlets, all cities, all sections of all states together in a common net of information, emotion, dispute. Many feel they are on their way to hell in a hack, but at least for the larger problems everybody is in the same hack. No pretense is offered that electioneering is an unblemished, golden vessel; on the contrary, the confusion of election processes may well contribute to the "reduced sense of responsibility and the absence of effective volition" characterizing many American citizens.[78] The point is that political campaigns serve functions not apparent to the unaided eye and whose value cannot be measured solely in dollars and cents.[79]

76. American political processes contribute to the development of consensus in numerous ways. One study of a Congressional campaign concluded that "the evidence indicates that this campaign did induce a tendency toward consensus on fundamental ideological values; not as a product, but rather as a by-product of its machinations."—William J. Gore and Robert L. Peabody, "The Functions of the Political Campaign: A Case Study," *Western Political Quarterly,* 11 (1958), 68.

77. On the relevance of communications to nationalism, see Karl W. Deutsch, *Nationalism and Social Communication—An Inquiry into the Foundations of Nationality* (New York: John Wiley & Sons, Inc., 1953), especially pp. 46-80, 139-60.

78. Cf. Joseph A. Schumpeter, *Capitalism, Socialism, and Democracy* (New York: Harper & Brothers Publishers, 1942), pp. 261-64.

79. Critics of election costs often compare them with the salary of the office sought. The comparison points up the financial problems faced by candidates, but it may imply, too, that some relationship *ought* to exist between the costs of campaigning and the remuneration of public offices. To the extent that such an implication is intended, it is like complaining that the cost of a scientist's laboratory exceeds his salary. The cost of campaigning is an institutional requirement of the governmental system. It is as inescapable as the cost of staffing, equipping, and constructing the building in which an elected official does his work.

16

POLICIES FOR THE FUTURE

A CHERISHED DEMOCRATIC PRIVILEGE is the right to pour social energy into the endless struggle for governmental reform. That Americans are continuously revising the substance and procedures of their government accounts significantly for the resilience and stamina of the Republic. Sometimes problems get "solved"—as by adoption of the secret ballot. Others prove intractable, like those of campaign finance. After nearly three-quarters of a century of public regulation, the financing of election campaigns is still, in the eyes of many, democracy's greatest unsolved problem.

Many of the alleged abuses are not so much abuses as inevitable accompaniments of democratic government. There can be no representative government without political influence, no popular elections without campaigns of appeal and persuasion. Specific practices, nonetheless, run athwart generally respected concepts of democratic procedure. Demands for reform also stem from concern over the tactical position of particular groups in political conflict.[1] Yet few elected officials trouble themselves with the subject.

Some shun the uncertain risks of tampering with the *status quo;* some are sure that felicitous personal arrangements would be disturbed. Others, although realizing that important power relationships are stabilized in existing practices, doubt that even radical alterations in the ways campaigns are financed could affect the basic social organization and distribution of economic and political power. Some express concern

1. For one example among many, Joseph S. Clark, Jr., then mayor of Philadelphia and subsequently a United States senator, wrote an article in 1953 called "Can the Liberals Rally?" Among three practical problems facing liberals *within* the Democratic party, he listed the necessity "To raise the money necessary to maintain a strong organization and wage a series of political campaigns without selling out to five-percenters and big contributors who use politics for personal gain. . . . Some method, perhaps the Ruml Plan, will have to be adopted for raising large sums of money in relatively small gifts from many people."—*Atlantic Monthly,* July, 1953, p. 29. The other side of the coin: proposals for legislative change often receive a partisan reception.

over the opportunities for partisan enforcement latent in stringent measures and over the invasion of private rights of some proposed controls. Many legislators know the difficulties under which candidates and their managers already campaign and are reluctant to hamstring them further. Many a legislator who in private concedes the significance of campaign finance has concluded that no effective regulation is possible. Maybe it will be possible a thousand years from now, reflected a former governor of Virginia. Perhaps then, he mused, citizens will have developed sufficient responsibility to obey regulations governing campaign finance; as long as you are dealing with the present crowd, there is no way.[2]

Certainly there is no *single* way. The paths to change are several, and not all of them lead through legislative corridors. Political parties themselves and private organizations hold within their hands decisive opportunities to shape the future of political financing. What, if anything, is done will depend on the goals they pursue and the means by which they seek them.[3]

Three goals.—Numerous consequences of the existing system of financing nominations and elections have been observed. These are approved by some participants in politics, lamented by others, depending on their value systems and on their places in the highly competitive political system. Proposed changes similarly find favor or disapproval as their presumed effects are perceived by those with something at stake. The philosophical presuppositions and the operating necessities of American elections nevertheless imply three chief requirements of any system of campaign finance: (1) that sufficient money be available to sustain the great debate that is politics, which means to assure the main con-

2. Considerations like these account for the curious spectacle that followed the famous revelations of Senator Case early in 1956. Legislators responded to the uproar in the press and pushed it along, sensitive to what is newsworthy and ever deferential to the symbols of political virtue. Then 84 senators of the United States joined the majority leader in introducing a bill (S. 3308) to amend the Corrupt Practices Act. But neither that nor any other bill on the subject passed the Senate at that session.

A measure of Senatorial interest in the subject is found in the lack of heated competition for seats on the Senate Committee on Rules and Administration and on its Subcommittee on Privileges and Elections.

3. A panorama of proposals for federal legislation over half a century is conveniently provided by Dorothy Schaffter, "Summary of Recommendations Concerning Campaign Funds, Made by Congressional Committees, 1905-56," and Doris S. Whitney, "Digest of Earlier Committee Recommendations from Published Congressional Reports Relative to the Subject of Campaign Funds and Expenditures, 1905-56," in the McClellan Lobby Committee's *Final Report,* pp. 275-86, 287-317.

The role of the states in the regulation of campaign finance, as in all elections regulation, is potentially more important than that of the federal government. This role is accentuated by Congress' reluctance to regulate the nominating process. Numerous groups, public and private, state and local, have advocated legislative changes. Without examining each individually, it is possible to treat the principles they incorporate in the discussion of the broad trends toward change discussed in this chapter.

testants an opportunity to present themselves and their ideas to the electorate;[4] (2) that the needed sums be obtained in ways that do not inordinately weight the processes of government in favor of special political interests; and (3) that the system command the confidence of the citizenry whose governmental officials are chosen through it.

Four facts.—The measures advocated to achieve these ends are several and controversial. Whatever their merits and whatever success some of them ultimately enjoy, several facts are apparent at the outset: (1) there is no panacea—progress toward any of the three goals must be made piecemeal, along several fronts; (2) Americans (who "tend to see the world in moral terms"[5]) must accept a margin of tolerance in the objectives and success of legal regulations—not all ambitions can be fulfilled; (3) any substantial changes through public or private action must rest ultimately on improved popular understanding of the functional necessity of election expenditures, and on a realization that contemporary abuses are not so much the failings of individual men as of the system itself; and (4) that to achieve the three goals requires positive action by government and organized groups, something more than the negative restrictions of the past.

1. GOVERNMENT SUBSIDIES, DIRECT

Republican Theodore Roosevelt is the hoary prophet of outright government subsidies of political campaigns. He proposed such in 1907; latter-day advocates regularly repair to his standard in search of respectable precedent. In actuality, precedents in practice as well as in proposal abound in many nations including the United States, and more recent supporters of the notion include no less a practical politician than Harry S. Truman.[6]

Complete assumption of campaign costs by the state has not occurred in any modern country,[7] but several nations have provided extensive subsidies of one type or another. Japan, under General MacArthur, by a law of 1947 allowed candidates three free radio addresses, two newspaper advertisements, 20,000 postcards, various transportation privileges, and free proportionate space in an election gazette.[8] Under

4. For many years Peter H. Odegard has advocated the doctrine of "equitable access" to the electorate for all important candidates.

5. A common conclusion of observers at home and abroad throughout United States history.—Robin M. Williams, Jr., *American Society—A Sociological Interpretation* (New York: Alfred A. Knopf, 1952), pp. 396-97.

6. *Memoirs by Harry S. Truman—Years of Trial and Hope* (Garden City, New York: Doubleday & Company, Inc., 1956), vol. 2, pp. 204-5.

7. Robert A. Bicks and Howard I. Friedman, "Regulation of Federal Election Finance: A Case of Misguided Morality," *New York University Law Review,* 28 (1953), 998.

8. The provisions were thought, at first at least, to have had the salubrious effect of enabling a large number of farmers, school teachers, newspapermen, and other impoverished types to run successfully for the Diet. For a brief discussion, see Paul H. Douglas, *Ethics in Government* (Cambridge, Massachusetts: Harvard

the French electoral law of October 5, 1946, certain election expenses were paid by the state, including those for printing, postage, gasoline, and bill-posting.[9] The Costa Rican government reimburses political parties for campaign costs incurred in proportion to the number of votes received by each party.[10] In Uruguay, political parties have been given by the government a sum based on the number of votes received. In 1954, it was four pesos ($1.30) per vote. The Revolutionary party in Mexico has received money at national, state, and local levels from governmental units at each of those levels.[11]

An American precedent.—The principle of government subsidy of party activities is well established in the continental United States. Many general-election costs that once fell on the parties are now taken as the normal responsibility of government, like the printing of ballots. In virtually all states, some of the costs of party primaries, to choose party nominees and in some cases to choose party officers, are paid from public funds. The Commonwealth of Puerto Rico's statute adopted in 1957 providing cash subsidies for *campaign* purposes[12] was the first American attempt of its kind since Colorado's statute of 1909, declared unconstitutional.[13] The Puerto Rican law established an Election Fund.

University Press, 1952), p. 84, and the testimony of Harold F. Gosnell, U.S. House of Representatives Special Committee to Investigate Campaign Expenditures, 1952, *Hearings* (Washington: Government Printing Office, 1952), p. 69.

9. Under the system of proportional representation that prevailed, lists receiving less than 3 per cent of the votes forfeited a deposit of 20,000 francs, a sum deemed small compared with the publicity received. Some of the privileges were restricted to lists receiving 3 per cent (later 5) of the votes. Law No. 46-2151 of October 5, 1946, Arts. 29, 30.—Philip Williams, *Politics in Post-War France—Parties and the Constitution in the Fourth Republic* (London: Longmans, Green & Co., 1954), pp. 344-45.

10. No party receiving less than 10 per cent of the votes is eligible for any reimbursement, however, and the total sum distributed cannot exceed 2 per cent of the government's ordinary budget. In 1958, 7,000,000 colones were distributed among the four largest parties.—Unpublished manuscript of Harry Kantor, referring to Law No. 2036, July 18, 1956. Under earlier practice, going back to the last century, it was apparently the custom for the winning party to reimburse itself for campaign costs out of government revenues without according the same courtesy to its defeated rivals. There was a dust up in 1956 when a controller general disallowed $233,105 of the $1,059,800 that had been reimbursed to the party of President José Figueres. Among the disapproved items were wedding gifts, funeral expenses, liquor bills, and several police fines, all of them campaign costs, judging from the comment, that bore the sanction of considerable precedent. —*New York Times,* June 3, 1956.

11. L. Vincent Padgett, "Mexico's One-Party System: A Re-evaluation," *American Political Science Review,* 51 (1957), 998-99.

12. Law No. 110, approved June 30, 1957, effective July 1, 1957.

13. In Colorado, each party was to be given 25 cents for each vote cast for its nominee for governor at the last preceding election. Half the money was to be kept by the state committee, the rest spread to lower echelons. Gifts by private persons were prohibited, except that the candidate could contribute up to 40 per cent of the yearly salary of the office sought. The State Supreme Court declared the law unconstitutional in 1910 without written opinion.—John S. Bottomly, "Corrupt Practices in Political Campaigns," *Boston University Law Review,* 30 (1950), 380.

Out of it, the Commonwealth Secretary of the Treasury pays, directly to the vendors, orders and vouchers submitted to him by properly accredited party officials covering the party's "maintenance and operation expenses in Puerto Rico."[14] Detailed records must be kept, and reports made periodically.[15] To qualify for the benefits, parties "shall have participated in a general election in all election precincts of Puerto Rico and as a result of which preserved their status of principal parties and gained representation in the Legislature."[16] Each such party may draw annually on the Election Fund for not more than $75,000. In election years as much as $150,000 may be drawn, and unspent balances from previous years may also be used. At the end of the four-year election cycle, however, accumulated balances are covered into the general funds of the Commonwealth. Between August 19, 1957, and December 31, 1958, the Popular Democratic party used $58,529 of the $150,000 available to it for the two calendar years, and the Republican party drew $56,646.[17]

The law prohibits all except certain limited, specifically authorized political contributions. The prohibition extends not only to political parties and candidates but "to any other organization engaged in promoting, fostering, or advocating the election of any candidate or the victory of any political party."[18] A person may contribute voluntarily to the local or central funds of a party, or to both funds, but not more than $200 per year to one of them, nor more than $400 per year to both combined. In election years, the limits are increased to $300 and $600, but the quotas do not carry over from one year to the next. If a donor wishes a local gift to be delivered to a specified candidate, he says so when making it. The treasurer to each party committee is to certify annually that he has not received contributions in excess of the authorized limits, a requirement complied with during the first year and a half by the treasurers of the central committees but not by the local treasurers.[19] The term "contribution" is broadly defined to include private loans,

14. Sec. 5. In the course of preparation and passage of the bill various proposals were made for granting specified free facilities, e.g., free time on the government radio and television stations, free light and power, free advertising space in a newspaper of the Department of Education. The first report on the operation of the statute covered the period August 19, 1957–December 31, 1958. The Popular Democratic party spent $26,741, almost half its total, on radio, television, and movies, whereas the Republican party spent approximately the same sum for periodical advertising.—"Fondo Electoral," Informe de Intervención Núm. DA-59-29 (San Juan: Estado Libre Asociado de Puerto Rico, Oficina del Contralor), Annexo 1.

15. In the early months, both parties were guilty of various procedural deficiencies.—*Ibid.*, pp. 4-6.

16. Sec. 2(b). As noted in the Senate debate on the bill, S. B. 256, this provision tends to benefit existing parties and hence to stabilize political competition, a customary consequence whenever "party" must be defined in connection with extension of a legal privilege.

17. "Fondo Electoral," p. 4.

18. Sec. 7(a).

19. "Fondo Electoral," p. 2.

advances, transfers of valuables other than money, promises to pay, and so on, but it does not include money borrowed directly by authorized officials of a party from recognized banking institutions.[20]

To facilitate the administration of the Act, the Secretary of the Treasury is directed, in consultation with the presidents of the political parties receiving benefits under the Act, to appoint an advisory committee on which all such parties are represented. The committee is charged with advising the Secretary on complaints received from the parties about the administration of the Act.

The Puerto Rican action demonstrates that when political interests dictate, practical politicians can construct administratively feasible ways to accomplish government subsidy. Before the adoption of the Act, Governor Muñoz Marin's party, in the majority, had tried to enforce an internal policy limiting the size of individual gifts it would accept. The party depended heavily on small contributions, including assessments of public employees. The latter were objectionable on several scores, and in some instances they may have been illegal. Moreover, some of Muñoz's political opponents were wealthy and able to pour large sums into political activity. The political bite of the proposal was evident from the opposition to it within both of the parties adverse to Muñoz. In fact, the Independence party declined the payments for which it was eligible on the grounds they were a misuse of public funds.[21]

The Neuberger proposal.—Proposals for direct government subsidy in the United States have in recent years come largely from the left. Numerous individuals within the Democratic party, such as former national treasurer George L. Killion, and within the ranks of labor, such as the California CIO's John A. Despol,[22] have advocated that campaign costs be paid out of public appropriations. The foremost spokesman for the principle in Congress has been Senator Richard L. Neuberger, Democrat of Oregon.

In 1956, Senator Neuberger introduced a bill—joined by Senators Morse, Murray, Douglas, Sparkman, Mansfield, Langer, and Hum-

20. In Senate debate on the bill, it was argued by some that these provisions would not prevent wealthy individuals from contributing indirectly through friends and employees. Proponents pointed to the stiff penalties for violation of the statute as the deterrent: imprisonment in jail for a minimum of six months, a minimum fine of $1,000, disqualification as a candidate for elective office and from holding public office, and disfranchisement.

21. *New York Times,* February 9, 1958.

22. A 1953 bill in the California legislature that enjoyed CIO support would have required the state to pay 25 cents to the state central committee of each political party for each person registered with that party, and a similar sum to each county central committee for those registered and living within the county. Only parties receiving at least 10 per cent of the total primary registrations would be eligible to receive the funds. Democrats, with a heavier registration than Republicans in California, may understandably have been more favorably inclined toward the proposal. In fact, they adopted a plank in their state platform endorsing the principle of financing partisan general-election campaigns from state general funds on an equitable basis. Like many a similar one, the proposal did not pass.

phrey[23]—authorizing payments to the national committee of each party. The sums were intended for use over a two-year period beginning on April 1 following each national election. When a presidential election was due, the amount would be 20 cents per vote for the average number of votes cast for president and delegate in Congress (in certain areas not voting for president) in the last two elections for those offices. In two-year periods not including a presidential election, the sum would be 15 cents per vote for the average number of votes cast for representative and delegate in Congress in the last two elections for those offices. Under the provisions, the amount available from this source to each national committee in 1956 would have been slightly over $11,000,000, and in 1958 about $6,250,000.[24] If total expenditures from private contributions during the two-year period for all a party's federal candidates exceeded the amount received from the subsidy, the subsidy was to be reduced by that amount. In addition, the chairman and treasurer of a national committee would be expected to certify that no individual had contributed more than a total of $100 to the campaign of one or more candidates for federal office of that party. The benefits of the proposed act would be confined to political parties whose candidate for president (or whose candidates for the Houses of Congress) polled at least 10 per cent of the total vote in the next preceding election.

Whatever their merits, proposals like that of Senator Neuberger have not attracted widespread support. Despite provisions for a bipartisan Federal Campaign Contributions Board to handle payments to the parties, various difficulties of administration seemed apparent. The measure would induce greater concentration of party authority at the national level than has traditionally existed in the major American parties. It would seem, at the same time, to encourage the development of two party-systems within what is now each major party, one concerned with candidates for federal office (subsidized) and the other with non-federal candidates (supported by private contributions, unless the states stepped in with subsidies). In many states, nominees already campaign separately from others on the same party slate. Many consider this tendency undesirable. It would be accentuated by the proposed $100 limitation (which would leave much private money available for non-federal campaigns), and by the special opportunity afforded federal candidates to look to the national committees for funds.

23. S. 3242, February 20, 1956, 84th Congress, 2nd Session. Senator Neuberger has expounded his proposal in many forums, including: "Federal Funds for Party Coffers," *The Christian Century,* 73 (January 25, 1956), 105-7, and "Who Should Pay for Political Campaigns?" *The New York Times Magazine,* June 3, 1956, pp. 25ff.

Among others on record as favoring government financing of campaigns are Senator Francis Case (Republican, South Dakota) and Representative John E. Moss (Democrat, California).—Fletcher Knebel, "Must We Always Have a Mess in Washington?" *Look,* September 2, 1958, pp. 18-19.

24. Senator Neuberger's computations in the *Congressional Record,* 84th Congress, 2nd Session, February 20, 1956, vol. 102, p. 2482.

National committee officials would be expected to keep records showing the total sums received in private contributions on behalf of candidates for federal office. This would presumably require that campaign activities for federal candidates be kept separate from those for the party's other candidates. Conceivably, candidates for other offices, and their supporters, would be precluded from doing anything in support of federal candidates if the expenditure of funds were involved. A candidate for governor could not plump for the whole ticket over television—unless some way of allocating the federal candidates' share of the cost could be devised. *Total* expenditures for *all* federal candidates paid for out of private contributions would be limited to the amount of the federal subsidy or the latter would be reduced. It seems ambitious, moreover, to require officials of a party's national committee to certify that no person has made gifts on behalf of all federal candidates totalling in the aggregate more than $100. A revolution in the relationship between the national committees and candidates for president and Congress, and their supporters, would be required before a national committee official could meaningfully certify to such a thing.

The character of the federal system, both governmental and party, complicates attempts to subsidize election costs directly. The Neuberger measure would place in the hands of each national committee the responsibility for distributing the subsidy throughout the states and Congressional districts of the nation. Presumably any prudent committee would develop a formula to relieve its officers of discretion in the distribution of funds. Given the necessity for drafting such a formula, and the possibility it might subsequently be modified, membership on the national committees would take on an importance hitherto unknown—a development, incidentally, that might be desirable on other counts. The right (or obligation) to raise sums from private sources would also have to be allocated to local units if the over-all limit for private gifts were to be respected. Some opponents protest against a new type of federal intervention in an activity that has been traditionally private and largely state and locally oriented. As politicians became aware of the impact of the proposal on the decentralized organization of the parties, and on the existing role of state and local leaders in fund-raising, opposition would seem inescapable.

A modification.—Greater support for an initial attempt at direct federal subsidy would probably be forthcoming if the proposal were simply to make equal grants to the national committee of each major party.[25] The sum might be $9,000,000 in a presidential election year, a third of that in years of mid-term elections and one-sixth of it in off-years, with no special restrictions on the use of the money. Even with no restrictions on private contributions, the persuasiveness of solicitors for national-level campaign activities would be considerably reduced.

25. Provision could be made for minor parties to receive smaller sums if they met specified criteria of size or importance.

The hunting would be happier for those seeking monies for other candidates. This kind of subsidy, by lightening the burden on private sources, might make it possible to limit realistically the total amount an individual could legally contribute during a calendar year to some such sum as $1,000 or $5,000.

Advocates of government subsidies will doubtless find it easier to push less comprehensive and more indirect forms of subsidy than called for in the Neuberger bill. Fortuitous opportunities for pumping public aid into political campaigns exist. The principle of government aid has ample precedent, if logic bears on the situation, which it does not always do. Other types of aid are sufficiently simple, moreover, to be administratively feasible, and some of them might attract political support.[26]

2. COMMUNICATIONS SUBSIDIES

The financial importance of campaign communications long ago led to proposals that government help candidates put their messages before the voters. Free postage, publicly financed campaign pamphlets, and publicly financed advertisements have frequently been advocated to guarantee candidates at least a minimum degree of access to the electorate. More recently, several ways to make radio and television time available on an equitable basis have been suggested. The enormous importance of broadcasting costs in many campaign budgets and the fortuitous feasibility of federal regulation probably make these suggestions the most important being discussed for the revision of campaign finance. The opportunities and problems in making other types of communications subsidies effective, however, are instructive.

Privileges of incumbency.—Elected officials receive many forms of campaign subsidy through the facilities and privileges that inevitably accompany public office.[27] Personnel employed at public expense on the personal staffs of elected officials are inescapably engaged in promoting the political fortunes of their bosses. Incumbents are in demand as speakers and enjoy free air time between elections because of the offices they hold.[28] There seems little way to afford equivalent assistance to the rivals of incumbents, even if it were desirable to do so.

26. Not all types of subsidy are appealing. It is not unknown for government contractors working on cost-plus contracts to charge campaign gifts as a necessary cost, thereby recovering their contributions and turning a profit thereon at the same time. Before federal statutes were changed, it was possible to write off unrepaid "loans" to political organizations as nonbusiness bad debts, the short-term capital losses thus declared being used to offset any gains of the lender. For persons with large incomes the cost of making a political contribution could be substantially reduced by this device.

27. The enterprising wife of an enterprising Louisiana Republican computed the "political money" thus at the disposal of the eight Democratic congressmen in her state—stationary, printing, free postage, salaries of politically active assistants, etc.—at $350,000 in a campaign year.

28. A Texan pointed out that in the fall of 1953 Senator Lyndon Johnson, up

One feasible step in this direction, however, has long been advocated: to extend the postal franking privilege to all candidates for United States senator and representative. Incumbents, already enjoying this form of campaign subsidy, have been reluctant to make the change. Huge quantities of campaign material are distributed yearly under their franks, and some members have even permitted propaganda groups to frank mass mailings that originated in places distant from both Washington and the member's home.[29] The proposal to extend the franking privilege to their campaign opponents has advocates in Congress, but prospects for favorable action are slight. At all levels of politics, incumbents view with reserve steps that might adversely affect advantages they enjoy.

Pamphlets and ads.—Closely related to campaign mailings at public expense are campaign pamphlets and advertisements published under the aegis of state governments, and sometimes at state expense.[30] These forms of subsidy have been extended in referenda on issues as well as in elections of officials.

Seven-eighths of the states require that some sort of publicity be given to issues appearing on the ballot.[31] In two-thirds of the states, state or county officials must inform the public concerning the issues through advertisements in the newspapers. In the other states, and in some of those requiring newspaper advertising, information pamphlets are issued or are optional as an alternative to advertising. There is considerable variety in what is printed in the pamphlets. The full text of ballot measures is not always required. Despite the fact, however, that argumentation of one kind or another is permitted in most of the pamphlets (sometimes at state expense and sometimes at the expense of the advocates), there seems to be little variety in the unappetizing appearance that most of them, as well as most of the newspaper advertisements, make.

State subsidies to publicize candidates have been fewer. Only about one-third of the states issues a publication of any kind listing candidates in primaries, and less than half distribute official lists of general-election candidates. Where sample ballots are printed in newspapers or otherwise distributed at official expense, a useful service is clearly performed.

---

for renomination the next summer, conducted what was in effect a "pre-campaign." He mended fences all over the state, enjoying free air time provided to him as a public service feature because he was an incumbent senator. Another senator has pointed out that such perquisites of incumbency are offset by the necessity for persons in office to vote yes or no on controversial issues which their rivals, out of office, can straddle or avoid.

29. The cost of the Congressional franking privilege was estimated in 1954 at $1,700,000 annually.—*New York Times,* November 29, 1954.

30. A critical and analytical summary of these, drawn on here, is given by O. Charles Press, *Newspaper Advertising and Publicity Pamphlets* (Fargo: North Dakota Institute for Regional Studies, North Dakota Agricultural College, 1955), Social Science Report Number 2, 19 pp.

31. Of the half dozen states with no publicity requirement pertaining to issues. only one uses the initiative and referendum.

Generally, however, the official notices of candidates are unattractive, uncontroversial, and unnoticed. Beginning with Oregon in 1908, eight states have authorized the issuance of official pamphlets to publicize candidates. The most recent was Idaho in 1959.[32] Of the other seven, only five ever actually issued pamphlets, and only North Dakota and Oregon have continued to do so. Ironically, cost is usually the reason for not using them.[33]

On the face of it, state-supported political publicity would appear to offer a feasible, economical, and effective way to implement the principle of equitable access to the electorate. Recent North Dakota and Oregon experience is worth noting. North Dakota, traditionally Republican, issues a single pamphlet in which candidates in the primaries of both parties may appear. Oregon issues a separate pamphlet for each party primary and another for the general election. In both states, charges for advertisements have run from $10.00 to $100 a page, depending on the importance of the office sought. In both states, the pamphlets are mailed at state expense—to those on the county personal-property tax lists in North Dakota, and to all registered voters in Oregon.

In recent general elections, the net cost per voter to the state for the Oregon pamphlets, which pertain to measures as well as candidates, has run between nine and 14 cents per voter:[34]

Year	*Number Printed*	*Net Cost to State*	*Net Cost Per Voter*
1952	851,516	$117,515	13.8¢
1954	819,539	73,588	9.4¢
1956	888,650	104,133	13.9¢
1958	914,400	81,841	13.5¢

Recent net costs to the state of North Dakota have run somewhat lower for primary and general-election pamphlets combined, measures as well as candidates being included:[35]

Year	*Number Printed*[36]	*Net Cost to State*	*Net Cost Per Voter*
1956	190,000	$16,685	3.9¢
1958	192,000	18,696	5.0¢

32. The statute requires printing of pamphlets before primary and general elections. They are to contain pictures of the candidates and statements concerning them, with each candidate paying $150 per page (with a limit of two pages), the state bearing additional printing costs—*State Government,* 32 (1959), 212.

33. Press, *op. cit.*, p. 8.

34. The 1952 pamphlet ran to 108 pages and that of 1954 to 56 pages. In 1956 and 1958, the net cost of pamphlets issued in the primaries came to $79,173 and $51,070, respectively. The pamphlets are issued in many different editions so that voters will receive only material relevant to the votes they must cast.

35. The net cost per voter for pamphlets in the primaries alone (which pertain to measures as well as candidates) amounted to 4.8 cents in 1952 and 3.9 cents in 1954. The 1952 and 1954 figures for both states come from *ibid.*, p. 14; 1956 and 1958 figures were derived from data supplied by the Secretaries of State.

36. This is the number printed for each of the elections; the total for the primary and general election combined would be twice the figure indicated.

Publicity pamphlets came into vogue as part of the progressive reforms of the early twentieth century. In the absence of empirical studies, their effectiveness in achieving intended purposes cannot be confidently judged, which is no less than must be said for most campaign propaganda. Nevertheless, campaign appeals that catch the eye and hold the interest of voters obviously *can* be produced under state auspices. This objective can best be achieved by giving specified space to the contestants, free or for a price, and requiring them to write their own advertisements. Despite the views of some state officials to the contrary,[37] the cost does not seem exorbitant. Mail distribution insures that virtually all voters have an opportunity to see the candidates' statements, and there is no reason a series of publications could not be distributed at state expense. The minimum access to voters thus assured to candidates would appear especially desirable in areas not fully covered by other media of mass communications. By the same token, states with state-owned radio or television stations could make free or cheap time available to contestants as a further step toward facilitating their communication with the voters.[38] Measures such as these are practical. They have repeatedly been advocated by politicians and others, yet within individual states and in the American political community generally there seems little disposition to adopt them.

Television and radio.—Federal regulation of the air waves provides a fortuitous and feasible way of guaranteeing a degree of equitable access to the electorate to candidates for important offices.[39] The access, moreover, can be assured at no cost, or at reduced cost, to the political contestants. Such a step would strike the heart of the entire regulation problem. It would assure candidates an opportunity to reach a large segment of voters, and at the same time would reduce campaign costs. It would accomplish more than state or federal attempts to subsidize other forms of publicity, and could be accomplished more easily. Members of Congress genuinely desiring to alleviate the problems of campaign finance will explore these possibilities.

Some of them have.[40] The broadcasting industry in general and

37. Press, *op. cit.*, pp. 13-15.

38. The problem of determining to whom the privileges of communicating free or cheaply ought to be extended can be solved in most localities by making qualified candidates in primaries or the general election eligible on an equal basis. The requirement of a deposit, to be forfeited should the candidate not receive a specified percentage of the votes cast, would discourage frivolous candidates.

39. The industry itself has taken useful steps to accomplish this purpose by reducing preemption costs, making public service time free, and otherwise. See Gore Committee *Hearings*, part 1, pp. 101, 150.

40. Charles A. H. Thomson provides a detailed discussion of some of the regulatory problems involved in "Television, Politics, and Public Policy," *Public Policy: A Yearbook of the Graduate School of Public Administration*, 8 (1958), 368-406 (issued as Reprint No. 25 by the Brookings Institution). See also his *Television and Presidential Politics—The Experience in 1952 and the Problems Ahead*

almost everyone else agree that Section 315 (a) of the Federal Communications Act, as it stood when Congress adjourned in 1959, ought to be modified. It provided that, when a legally qualified candidate for any public office is permitted to use a broadcasting station, equal opportunities shall be afforded all other such candidates for that office. The requirement restrains any impulses broadcasters may have to grant free time to major and minor candidates, and to arrange special public-service programs featuring them.[41] The classic episode occurred in 1952. One William R. Schneider of Missouri filed for the Republican presidential nomination in Oregon and New Hampshire. He then asked for and received from the Columbia Broadcasting System free radio and television time equal to that granted previously during interviews with General Eisenhower and Senator Taft, also candidates for the Republican presidential nod.[42] Mr. Schneider was by no standard a serious candidate for the presidential nomination, but that did not protect the broadcasters from his demand for free time, possibly very expensive free time from the broadcasters' perspective. A difficulty akin to this also arises when incumbent officeholders who are candidates are called upon to make public statements supporting the united fund and similar community drives. Must all of the other candidates for president—there were 18 or so in 1952 and likewise a goodly number in 1956—be given time equal to that of the President of the United States who has endorsed

(Washington: The Brookings Institution, 1956), 173 pp.

Congressional committees have taken much relevant testimony in recent years from representatives of the industry, the Federal Communications Commission, and others. See the published hearings of the U.S. Senate Subcommittee on Privileges and Elections in 1955 and 1956 and of a Subcommittee of the Committee on Interstate and Foreign Commerce, U.S. House of Representatives, on Miscellaneous Bills to Amend the Communications Act of 1934, held in 1956.

Herbert E. Alexander has prepared a report on the regulation of political broadcasts for the Citizens' Research Foundation. It is scheduled for publication during 1960.

41. About one-third of the network free time given during the 1956 general election campaign went for other than Democratic and Republican broadcasts. Free time between September and the election on November 6 amounted to the following: *radio networks,* 33 hours and 39 minutes (Democratic, 10 hours; Republican, 11 hours, 54 minutes; other, 11 hours, 45 minutes); *television networks,* 32 hours, 26 minutes (Democratic, 9 hours, 55 minutes; Republican, 11 hours, 54 minutes; other, 10 hours, 37 minutes). About 11 per cent of the *radio-station* free time and 14 per cent of *television-station* free time was classified as "other." *Radio-station* free time, which included some of the network time, aggregated over 592 hours, and *television-station* free time, also including some of the network time, aggregated over 186 hours.—Gore Committee *Report,* Ex. 24, pp. 1, 5, 15. The tabulation was made from information provided by all of the networks, from about 90 per cent of the radio stations, and about 97 per cent of the television stations. For an analysis of the television free-time data, see Charles A. H. Thomson, "Television, Politics and Public Policy," pp. 373-76.

42. See testimony of Richard S. Salant, vice president of CBS.—U.S. Senate Subcommittee on Privileges and Elections, *Hearings* (Washington: Government Printing Office, 1955), pp. 174-76.

some worthy cause? Aside from the debatable wisdom of encouraging splinter parties by giving them free broadcasts, there was hardly enough air time to do so. Moreover, if an attempt were made, broadcasters would probably suffer a loss of audience interest, and because of this and other costs involved might find themselves bearing an inordinate financial burden.

The solution to these and related difficulties would seem to lie along the lines of a Senate committee's recommendation made in 1957: require that equal time be accorded a minor party candidate only under certain conditions—e.g., only if his party polled at least 5 per cent of the total vote at the last regular election for the office in question, or, alternatively, if it presented a petition signed by qualified voters amounting to at least 2 per cent of that total vote.[43] This change would enable broadcasters to present major candidates on public-service broadcasts during campaigns, thereby increasing the candidates' opportunities to go before the electorate at no cost to themselves.[44]

The proposal to *require* broadcasters to afford certain candidates (or their spokesmen)[45] specified amounts of equal time for partisan broadcasts offers a more fundamental solution. Some advocates argue that, on principle, the broadcasters should bear the cost of doing so as a

43. McClellan Lobby Committee, *Report,* p. 143. The "handicap" to new and minor parties is apparent, a characteristic, as already noted, of most statutory attempts to define political parties.

44. In 1959, the Federal Communications Commission ruled that all political candidates must be given equal time on radio and television news programs. The decision was made in the case of Lar Daly, an unsuccessful candidate for mayor of Chicago who complained that radio and television stations gave his opponents more time during the campaign than they gave him on their news programs. The ruling precipitated statements from all the major networks that the interpretation could destroy news coverage by broadcasters. In the closing days of the Congressional session in 1959, the Federal Communications Act was amended to exempt bona fide news programs from the equal-time requirements of sec. 315(a). See U.S. House of Representatives Committee on Interstate and Foreign Commerce, *Report* (House Report No. 802, 86th Congress, 1st Session), and the testimony taken by a subcommittee of that Committee, *Hearings* (Washington: Government Printing Office, 1959).

During the years 1950-54, Turkey operated under a law by which each party, depending on its size, was allotted 10 to 20 minutes of radio time per day for several days before an election. In addition, however, speeches by the Prime Minister and other government candidates were broadcast over the government-owned stations as news.

45. Irving Rodgers Merrill analyzed expenditures for television time in the 1952 federal elections and discovered that 40 per cent of the campaign broadcasts were made by spokesmen on behalf of candidates rather than by the candidates themselves. He concluded that existing statutes forced "a greater use of spokesmen than could be attributed to the sheer number of broadcasts required for conduct of a modern television political campaign." He felt that sec. 315 should be extended to cover broadcasts by the "authorizd spokesman" of a candidate.—"Campaign Expenditures and Their Control—A Study of Expenditures for Television Time in the 1952 Federal Election" (Ph.D. dissertation, University of Illinois, 1954), p. v.

condition of the federal license under which they operate. As businessmen intent on staying solvent, the broadcasters object. Some of them also object, however, to the cost being borne by government subsidy. They apparently would oppose any form of subsidy, and in particular they fear this form of government involvement in their own operations.[46] To many persons outside the industry, however, neither objection is persuasive in an industry that already operates entirely by regulation or sufferance of the federal government and in a society in which campaign subsidies are already found in many forms. Moreover, the industry could be protected from undue disruption of normal operations. Advance reservation of political time could be required, and considerable discretion could be vested in the industry for the scheduling of political broadcasts.

How much time ought to be given and to whom are policy and technical questions that affect the feasibility and potential effectiveness of the proposal. During the nine or ten weeks before the 1952 presidential election, Republican radio network broadcasting totalled some 23 hours, and Republican television network broadcasting came to 15 hours. The corresponding Democratic radio time was 23 hours, 15 minutes; the corresponding television time was 19 hours, 50 minutes. The number of stations included in the broadcasts as well as audience attention fluctuated widely.[47] Much of the time, but not all of it, was used personally by the presidential and vice presidential candidates.

Opinion as to the optimum volume of broadcasting for good political health will doubtless differ as long as candidates differ in their campaign talents. With the increase in television stations since 1952, however, something less than the number of network hours consumed that year would seem to be sufficient. Ten well placed hours over radio and television (the same broadcasts), allotted for personal appearances by the presidential and vice presidential candidates, would seem ample. Candidates and their staffs would be partly relieved of the intolerable burdens hitherto imposed by modern mass communications campaigning. It is argued by some, in fact, that a maximum on the amount of live time *permitted* a candidate would be a constructive limitation, with rebroad-

46. See testimony of Harold E. Fellows, president of the National Association of Radio and Television Broadcasters, U.S. Senate Subcommittee on Privileges and Elections, *Hearings* (Washington: Government Printing Office, 1955), pp. 96, 100, and U.S. House of Representatives Special Committee to Investigate Campaign Expenditures, 1956, *Hearings* (Washington: Government Printing Office, 1957), pp. 39-40.

47. Herbert R. Craig, "Distinctive Features of Radio-TV in the 1952 Presidential Campaign" (Master's thesis, State University of Iowa, 1954), pp. 129-39. Compiled from information provided by the networks and from schedule of broadcasts provided by the A. C. Nielson Company.

In addition to the campaign broadcasts, CBS, NBC, and ABC gave an average of 71 network hours to coverage of the Republican national convention and of more than 74 hours to the Democratic national convention, in both cases a substantially longer time than the conventions were in formal session.—Charles A. H. Thomson, *Television and Presidential Politics—The Experience in 1952 and the Problems Ahead,* pp. 38-39.

casting limited or prohibited. If broadcasts were fewer, public interest in them might be heightened. Limitation would also insure an equitable division of time between the major parties. It would certainly reduce the costs, regardless of who bore them. Such limitations have been enforced in other nations—e.g., West Germany, Norway, Canada, Great Britain—some of them as dedicated to free political debate as the United States.[48] There seems to be no reason why such a limitation could not be imposed. After all, broadcasters are under no compulsion to grant political time under existing regulations.

Deciding to whom the privilege of limited, subsidized broadcasts should be extended would present the gravest regulatory problems. The question would be resolved best in terms of administrative feasibility. At the outset, the regulations could be confined to broadcasts by candidates for president and vice president. Network broadcasts beyond the borders of one state could, in fact, be confined to them personally or to their designated representative.[49] Some proposals have advocated the initial inclusion of candidates for all federal offices. At least one broadcaster has recommended that candidates for *all* public offices be afforded limited amounts of desirable free time and that educational-television channels be used as one way of assuring candidates an opportunity to reach the electorate.[50] The difficulties of administration, however, argue

48. Japan has even tried to limit the number of speeches of any kind a candidate can make! This and other severe restrictions have led to enforcement problems.—*New York Times,* February 22, 1955.

49. Presidential candidates eligible for these privileges would have to be defined. One proposal (recommended in connection with sec. 315 of the Communications Act of 1934) would limit privileges to nominees of a political party whose candidate in the preceding presidential election received the support of at least 4 per cent of the popular votes cast, or whose candidacy is supported by petitions filed under state laws signed in the aggregate by persons equalling at least 1 per cent of the popular votes cast in the previous presidential election.—U.S. Senate Committee on Rules and Administration, *Federal Elections Act of 1957* (Washington: Government Printing Office, 1957) (Senate Report No. 792, 85th Congress, 1st Session), pp. 22-23.

50. Nelson Poynter, editor and publisher of the *St. Petersburg Times* (Florida) in an editorial reprinted in a series called *"Who Gave It—Who Got It?"* (n.d.). The costs of television coverage useful to candidates for local and district offices need not be prohibitively high. In 1956, for example, 15 evening minutes on a Maine television station could be bought for $100-$150. Frank Coffin, successful candidate for United States representative, spent less than $1,500 on television during his entire campaign.—John C. Donovan, *Congressional Campaign: Maine Elects a Democrat* (New York: Henry Holt and Company, 1958), p. 10. In 1954, the Democratic candidate for Congress from the sixth district of New Jersey put on three carefully staged fifteen-minute television shows for around $500 each, including production costs.—John Crosby, "TV Achieves Political Wonders," *Pittsburgh Post-Gazette,* December 6, 1954. In 1954, the Federal Communications Commission issued regulations giving effect to a 1952 amendment to the Federal Communications Act designed to prevent broadcasting stations from charging premium rates for political programs.—"Use of Broadcast Facilities by Candidates for Public Office," FCC 54-1155, 9105, Public Notice September 8, 1954.

for a less ambitious beginning. Broadcasters would normally resist any move that cluttered their time, even if paid for, with broadcasts of low appeal. The absence of clear-cut state and local networks, moreover, and the presence of overlapping audience areas create difficulties in allocating or limiting time at local levels that do not arise when only three or four national networks are involved.

Because of the large amounts of campaign money spent for broadcasting, any developments affecting radio or television are of potential political importance. A feasible scheme of pay television, for example, might introduce a new way to raise campaign funds or to pay for political broadcasts.[51] Some developments, including this one, might restrict political debate rather than broaden it. Through the regulation of radio and television broadcasting, however, the nation has a clear opportunity to effect important revisions in its system of campaign finance if it wishes to use it.

3. TAX INCENTIVES[52]

Income-tax incentives were advocated with mounting frequency during the 1950's in part to provide indirect government subsidies for political activities. Tax concessions would dignify political donations by bracketing them in the tax collector's esteem with gifts to educational, eleemosynary, religious, and other worthy causes. Yet the fiscal effect would be to shift to government the burden, or part of the burden, of supporting political campaigns. Two American states did, in fact, acknowledge the propriety of political contributions by authorizing certain deductions in the computation of personal income taxes—Minnesota in 1955 and California in 1957.[53] What the effects of similar action by the federal government and a large number of states would be became a proper subject of inquiry. It was too early to learn from experience, although curiosity was whetted by the failure of a comparable measure in Germany to result, at least in its first year of operation, in any marked increase in direct donations to the parties.[54]

The Minnesota experience.—In 1955, Minnesota adopted a law permitting two types of tax deductions. First, in computing personal in-

51. The Federal Communications Commission has announced conditions under which applications for trial subscription-television operations by television stations would be considered but, in deference to Congressional interest in the matter, decided not to grant any until after the adjournment of the first session of the 86th Congress (1959).—FCC 59-217, 70809, Docket No. 11279, Third Report, adopted March 23, 1959. At the end of July, 1959, no applications had been received under this report.

52. The most exhaustive study made of proposed tax incentives to encourage political contributions is that by Herbert E. Alexander. He analyzes plans that have been advanced, including possible variations in them.—*A Tax Incentive as a Political Instrument* (Princeton: Citizens' Research Foundation, 1959) (mimeographed), 78 pp., scheduled for publication in 1960.

53. The New York State Senate has twice passed a similar measure.

54. Arnold J. Heidenheimer, "German Party Finance: The CDU," *American Political Science Review,* 51 (1957), 381-82.

come taxes, deductions were authorized from gross income for contributions in primaries and general elections to political parties, candidates, and causes. Individual natural persons might deduct up to $100 per year and various party officials other amounts, the highest limit being $1,000 for state chairmen, national committeemen, and national committeewomen.[55] Second, candidates for specified public offices were authorized to deduct unreimbursed campaign expenditures paid by themselves personally. These ranged up to a maximum of $5,000 for candidates for governor and United States senator.[56]

Several proposals for federal and state tax incentives—about two-thirds of the states have personal income taxes—differ radically from the benefits introduced in Minnesota. It is nonetheless useful to examine the experience of Minnesota with political deductions in 1956. The maximum possible benefit under Minnesota's income tax laws was, in any circumstances, small. The maximum rate on taxable net income in 1956 was 10 per cent, so that even the wealthiest taxpayer could recover no more than 10 per cent of a deductible outlay. Most would recover less, or, because of the standard deduction, nothing at all.[57]

In fiscal terms, the impact was slight in 1956, although as taxpayers became acquainted with the notion that political contributions were on a par, at least up to a point, with other tax-favored gifts, it might become greater thereafter. In 1956, 1,422,000 votes were cast in the Minnesota general election for governor. Some 976,370 individual income-tax returns were filed in 1957 covering the previous year. On 45.8 per cent of those, deductions were itemized. In all, as Table 57 shows, an estimated 7,082 persons claimed deductions for political contributions, which amounted to 0.7 per cent of those filing, or a number equivalent to about 0.5 per cent of those voting for governor. (In the United States as a whole, the equivalent of about 13 per cent of the persons voting for

55. Others permitted: Congressional district committeeman or committeewoman, $350; county chairman or chairwoman, $150. These must be officials of political parties, which are defined by statute in a way generally favorable to the existing major parties.—*Minnesota Statutes Annotated,* vol. 19, sec. 290.21 (1958 Supp.).

56. Candidates for other offices were permitted the following maximum deductions: other state office or United States representative, $3,500; state senator, state representative, presidential elector at large, $500; presidential elector from a Congressional district, $100; any other political office, one-fourth the annual salary of the office.—*Ibid.,* sec. 290.09 (1958 Supp.).

57. *Ibid.,* sec. 290.06, shows rates on taxable net income ranging from 1 per cent on the first $1,000 to 10 per cent on over $20,000. The standard deduction is $1,000 on adjusted gross income of $10,000 or more. If such income is less than $10,000, the deduction is 10 per cent thereof.—*Ibid.,* sec. 290.09.

In 1957, California authorized deductions up to $100 for political contributions by individuals in any primary or general election, but the incentive in tax savings thus extended was even less than in Minnesota. Ignoring standard deductions, a married couple with a taxable income of $10,000 or lower would save, because of the tax rates applicable, only $1.00 on a $100 contribution, and a couple with a taxable income of $50,000 or over would save only $6.—*1957 Session Laws,* Chapter 255, p. 908; California *Revenue and Taxation Code,* sec. 17210 (1958 Supp.).

Table 57

MINNESOTA'S EXPERIENCE WITH INCOME-TAX DEDUCTIONS FOR POLITICAL GIFTS, 1956[a]

Gross Income Group $	Contributions												Normal Taxes as Percentage of Gross Income[b] %	Estimated Revenue Loss $
	To Republicans			To Democrats			Unspecified			All				
	No.	Am't $	Average Am't $	No.	Am't $	Average Am't $	No.	Am't $	Average Am't $	No.	Am't $	Average Am't $		
0-4,999	490	13,480	27.51	300	8,740	29.13	540	10,310	19.09	1,330	32,530	24.46	0.16-0.72	152
5,000-9,999	1,419	23,753	16.74	611	15,810	26.31	1,244	29,100	22.39	3,274	68,663	20.97	1.03-2.19	1,082
10,000-14,999	520	10,845	18.48	64	3,574	55.84	224	8,410	37.54	808	22,829	28.25	2.40-3.12	628
15,000-19,999	325	12,350	38.00	32	1,677	52.41	128	5,320	41.56	485	19,347	39.89	3.43	664
20,000-39,999	557	26,510	47.59	38	2,674	70.37	188	10,774	57.31	783	39,958	51.03	4.01-4.35	1,648
40,000-99,999	216	15,748	72.90	11	823	74.82	108	8,690	80.46	335	25,261	75.41	4.39-4.29	1,095
100,000-over	42	3,750	89.29	...	...	...	25	2,350	94.02	67	6,100	91.04	4.13	252
Totals	3,569	106,436	29.82	1,056	33,298	31.53	2,457	74,954	30.51	7,082	214,688	30.31	...	5,521

[a] Information supplied by the Research and Planning Staff, Minnesota Department of Taxation. All personal income-tax returns showing a gross income of $8,000 or more were examined. Information from a 10 per cent sample of other returns provided a basis for estimates in lower income categories.

[b] Rates computed from 1954 and 1955 returns. They were approximately the same for both years with only minor variations. The computation of 1956 rates was not completed at the time the information was supplied. Where two rates are given, they represent rates for subgroups at upper and lower extremes of the gross income group in the table. For example, 0.16 per cent applies to gross income of $0-999 and 0.72 per cent to gross income of $4,000-4,999.

president made a gift in 1956.[58]) Deductions claimed totalled $214,688, clearly a minor percentage of political gifts in Minnesota that year, with an estimated loss of revenue to the state of $5,521. Substantially more Republicans than Democrats appear to have claimed deductions, but the average amount of their claims was lower. The average amount of the claims increased with gross income, but not even at the highest income level was the maximum amount allowable, $100, claimed by all.

Nor did all Minnesota candidates claim tax deductions for unreimbursed campaign expenses in 1956. The number who did so fell considerably below the number of candidates who ran for office. The amounts claimed, however, as indicated in Table 58, may in some instances have approached the candidate's actual expenses, especially for some of the lesser offices. The savings to the candidates, because of the tax rate, were necessarily modest.

Table 58

MINNESOTA'S EXPERIENCE WITH INCOME-TAX DEDUCTIONS FOR UNREIMBURSED CAMPAIGN EXPENSES OF SELECTED TYPES OF CANDIDATES, 1956[a]

Office Sought	No. of Candidates Claiming Deductions	Total Amount Claimed $	Minimum Amount Claimed $	Maximum Amount Claimed $	Average Amount Claimed $
Legislature	49	15,682	20	500[b]	320
Other State Offices	6	4,472	20	3,500	745
City and Village Offices	62	11,634	5	1,943	188
Unspecified	27	3,111	10	500	115

[a] Information supplied by the Research and Planning staff, Minnesota Department of Taxation. Information about some candidates could not be provided because of the ease with which they might have been identified. The number of candidates not claiming deductions is not known, nor is the party designation of those who did. (131 representatives and no senators were elected to the state legislature in 1956.) The number claiming deductions and the value of total deductions claimed are composites of actual and estimated figures derived from the examination procedure. The minimum and maximum amounts claimed are actual figures.

[b] This is the maximum amount allowable. One candidate, however, claimed $1,721.

Federal proposals.—The principle of a federal tax concession of some kind has gained at least formal political support. The Senate Committee on Rules and Administration in 1957 reported favorably a bill allowing taxpayers to claim either a deduction from gross income up to $100 for contributions on behalf of candidates for federal office, or a tax credit of one-half the value of such gifts, to be subtracted from the tax due, up to a maximum credit of $10.00.[59]

58. See pages 41 and 425, above.

59. U.S. Senate Committee on Rules and Administration, *op. cit.*, pp. 24-26. A similar recommendation was not made by the Committee in 1959.—*Federal Elections Act of 1959* (Washington: Government Printing Office, 1959) (Senate Report No. 573, 86th Congress, 1st Session) (not again cited).

The McClellan Lobby Committee asked a group of former United States senators the following question: "Should tax concessions in the form of a tax credit

As the first year of the Minnesota experience suggested, a number of important questions arise aside from objections that may exist on principle to this form of government election subsidy. The immediate effect on government revenue would not itself seem crucial. If the 8,000,000 or so people who gave something to political causes in 1956 each claimed a $10.00 federal tax credit, the loss of revenue would amount to $80,000,000. If tax incentives stimulated an unusually large volume of political gifts, by no means a certainty, concern about overfinancing the electoral process would doubtless precede concern over the loss of revenue. In any event, the rate or amount of the concession could be varied. More serious objections can be raised to any form of concession on the grounds it would lay the basis for other erosions of the tax base.[60] A tax credit, particularly, would surely be sought by worthy causes to which contributions are already tax deductible. A tax credit for political gifts would have to be defended as of unique importance.

A federal tax deduction, as contrasted with a tax credit, would provide persons in the higher income brackets with the greatest incentive to give. Generally, three-fourths or more of the individuals who file federal income tax returns take the standard deduction. They benefit more by doing so than they would by itemizing authorized deductions. (An additional tax deductible gift, one to a political cause, might lead some persons who do not now do so to itemize, but they would be relatively few in number.) A smaller proportion of taxpayers with small incomes itemize, however, and therefore might benefit, than those with larger incomes.[61] Moreover, the progressive character of the federal income tax obviously results in a deductible gift costing the low-income person more than it does the high income person. A person whose income is taxed at 75 per cent[62] pays only $25.00 of a $100 gift. The

---

or of a deduction from gross income be allowed to encourage popular giving to campaigns?" Of the 22 respondents, 10 were favorably disposed, seven were opposed, one was on the fence, and four did not comment.—*Hearings,* pp. 1290-1308.

The details of several stamp and receipt plans by which concessions might be given effect are analyzed by Ellen A. Peters, "Political Campaign Financing: Tax Incentives for Small Contributors," *Louisiana Law Review,* 18 (1958), 414-36; and Stanley S. Surrey, "Tax Benefits for Political Contributions," a memorandum in the McClellan Lobby Committee, *Hearings,* pp. 1257-67.

The line separating (a) political contributions received by an individual from (b) his reportable income sometimes becomes hazy, as does the line separating (c) expenditures that may legitimately be deducted as a business expense, although they have an incidental political usefulness, from (d) forthright campaign expenditures. For a discussion of these and other gray areas, see Arnold Bloom, "Tax Results of Political Contributions," *Taxes—The Tax Magazine,* 34 (1956), pp. 765-76, reprinted from the *Boston University Law Review,* 36 (1956), 170ff.

60. Already a matter of some dimensions. See Joseph A. Pechman, "Erosion of the Individual Income Tax," *National Tax Journal,* 10 (1957), 24-25.

61. U.S. Internal Revenue Service, *Statistics of Income for 1953* (Washington: Government Printing Office, 1957), part 1, pp. 8, 23, 53.

62. Of whom there would be very few. Because of the plethora of modifying, technical, legal provisions, the actual rates paid by persons of large income are

government, or the public, in effect pays the rest. For the individual of lower income who is taxed at 25 per cent, his share of a $100 gift becomes $75.00. A tax deduction would seem to constitute an incentive to a relatively small proportion of the taxpayers, although what the actual effects would be is a matter of debate.[63] Clearly, nevertheless, a deduction would benefit persons of high income most. Candidates who appeal to persons of high income would enjoy a corresponding benefit. For these reasons, some labor leaders and others have actively opposed the deductibility feature and favored the tax credit as an alternative.[64]

The effects that a particular tax incentive would have on the internal structure of the parties, and on the general character of the party system, would depend on the precise nature of the incentive and on how it was administered. Almost any system would place a high premium on effective political organization. Whether a system permitted door-to-door canvassing for potential contributors, or required contributors to go to some central point like a post office to make their contributions, organized effort would appear essential to get large numbers of taxpayers to take advantage of the benefits proffered. The importance of labor and business organizations, as well as of party organizations, in political fund-raising might consequently be increased. The effect under some circumstances would be a broadening of the soliciting corps as well as of the base of contributions. A shifting of the center of gravity in soliciting away from the traditional types of fund-raisers, accustomed to solicit large sums, could be as important a development as an increase in the volume and relative importance of small gifts.

A system that limited tax concessions to gifts made to specified recipients—certain committees or candidates for certain offices—would inevitably affect the relationships among the myriad of formal and in-

usually well below the percentages fixed initially in the statute for the income brackets in question.—Stanley S. Surrey, "The Federal Income Tax Base for Individuals," *Columbia Law Review,* 58 (1958), 816.

63. When the standard deduction went into effect in 1944, fund-raising agencies feared that contributions from small givers would decline. How the rate of giving was actually affected remains debatable.—F. Emerson Andrews, *Philanthropic Giving* (New York: Russell Sage Foundation, 1950), pp. 231-32. It seems probable that making political gifts deductible would in itself encourage some persons to give even though they might not in fact derive a tax benefit.

64. See statement of James McDevitt and Jack Kroll, co-directors of AFL-CIO's COPE, opposing a tax deduction and approving a tax credit.—U.S. House of Representatives Special Committee to Investigate Campaign Expenditures, 1956, *Hearings* (Washington: Government Printing Office, 1957), pp. 27-28. Leonard W. Hall, then chairman of the Republican national committee, opposed the idea of a tax credit.—*Ibid.,* p. 79.

Senator Richard Neuberger has probably advanced the most detailed arguments in opposition to tax deductions. He favors a tax credit. See his observations and computations in the *Congressional Record,* 84th Congress, 2nd Session, March 6, 1956, vol. 102, pp. 3534-36. About one-fifth of those who file income tax returns need pay no tax, hence would not benefit even from a tax credit unless provision were made for a cash refund.

formal groups that campaign in the United States. Such would be true if candidates were given the power to designate official committees to act on their behalf in receiving gifts eligible for the tax benefit. It would be especially true if only certain candidates were given this privilege. Tax benefits confined to candidates for federal offices, for example, would place those candidates and the committees supporting them in a superior position in the world of political finance. A distinction between federal candidates and others might well encourage the development of vertically divided, rival party systems within each of the present major parties, as a system of cash subsidies might do. Or, if federal candidates could use their receipts directly or indirectly on behalf of candidates for other offices, or if they could transfer sums to other individuals or committees that would do so, the favored position of federal candidates would be considerable. Subsidizing one or more sectors of campaign finance through tax benefits would presumably have effects on fund-raising in the unfavored areas. The effect of tax benefits for some candidates on the ability of other candidates to raise funds cannot easily be predicted. The tax-favored areas of politics might well attract larger shares of the available political money and handicap fund-raising in other areas. On the other hand, the total supply of political money available might be increased. Even candidates not directly favored by tax benefits might thus find it easier than formerly to raise money.

The effects and effectiveness of any system of tax benefits would depend directly, though not exclusively, on the detailed features of the system. The administrative desiderata are matters about which there are many opinions. Considerations of secrecy, fraud, administrative cost, feasibility, convenience to the contributors, and so on have produced a variety of proposals. Those for tax deductions generally place political gifts on the same plane as other gifts that may be deducted in computing taxable income. No special requirements were set up in either Minnesota or California for authenticating the political deductions claimed. Proposals for tax credits, on the other hand, have been thought to pose quite different problems. No one has seemed willing to let a taxpayer simply claim the credit on his own word. The approach has been along two general lines, stamp systems and receipt systems.

A political money order plan.—Perhaps the relevant considerations can be illuminated best by describing a system that might achieve most of the goals sought by advocates of tax credits.

An individual desiring (or induced) to make a political contribution would go (or be taken) to a post office. There he would buy a political money order. A political money order would be essentially like other money orders.[65] The order would consist, in addition to the stub, of two parts. (1) On one part the purchaser would sign his name in the

65. Preliminary inquiries have indicated that it would be technically possible to gear a political money order plan to the existing postal money order system and to the machine card system used.

presence of the postal employee.[66] This part would show the amount of the order, but not the name of the recipient, and would be affixed to the income-tax return at the time credit is claimed. It could be affixed in a location that would permit ready comparison of the signature with that on the return itself.[67] (2) The other part of the money order would be given to the purchaser who would fill in the name of the intended recipient and deliver it to him. (Alternatively, the Post Office Department could mail the receipt direct to the recipient.)

Political money orders would be sold in denominations smaller than the amount of the maximum claimable benefit. A contributor could thus make a tax-favored gift to more than one recipient. The recipient would present the money order at *his* home post office to be cashed. Except for presidential candidates, there would be one such post office for each candidate and the committees supporting him. For presidential candidates, there would be one in each state. Each candidate would certify to that post office the recipients he had authorized to handle funds for him. No one else would be permitted to cash the money orders, and they could be cashed at no other post office. At the end of the campaign the total value of cashed money orders in favor of each recipient would be announced. Each candidate accepting tax-favored gifts would be required to file specified reports showing the use of such receipts, as well as the use of other funds received by his designated treasurers.

A carry-over of limited surpluses from one year to the next might be authorized. Presumably, however, part of the purpose of the plan would be defeated if committees or parties were permitted to accumulate large capital accounts over a period of years and then to deluge selected elections with expenditures unmatchable by rivals. If after a period of time it appeared that, in general, more or less money was being raised than was judged desirable, the amount of allowable tax credit could be changed. Funds on hand at the end of an election period, if not carried into the next, could be called in to the federal treasury.[68]

66. By this means it would be hoped to avoid the opportunities for fraud that lie in the stamp plans. The first proposal for a tax credit to gain prominence was made by Professors Charles M. Hardin, Walter Johnson, and Jerome G. Kerwin in a letter to the editor of the *New York Times,* March 3, 1956. They proposed that bona fide political parties be permitted to buy special stamps from the government at the cost of production. The stamps were to be resold to taxpayers at their face value ($5.00), who would attach them to their income tax returns to substantiate claim for a tax credit. There seemed no way, in this preliminary form of the proposal, to prevent wholesale distribution of the stamps at no or low cost, making a neat system of government-subsidized bribery.

67. Some problems would be created in the use of "short" income-tax forms but none that could not be overcome. See Stanley S. Surrey, *op. cit.,* p. 1260.

68. Efforts to reduce surpluses by reducing the future eligibility of recipients for tax-favored gifts until the amount of the surplus was matched by new gifts would probably lead to the creation of new committees rather than to the restraint of old ones. Some of the technical problems would be obviated if no candidates had more than one committee authorized to receive tax-favored gifts.

Under the proposed plan, candidates would be permitted to designate two political committees, each with an authorized treasurer, to receive tax-favored contributions. In the case of a presidential candidate, he would be permitted to designate two national-level committees and two committees within each state. The latter might normally be subdivisions of the former. It might prove prudent at the outset to confine the benefits of an experimental plan to presidential candidates. After experience the plan could be modified or extended, although legislative bodies do not always proceed in as orderly a fashion as this suggestion implies. If the benefits were extended to other than presidential candidates, in either general or primary elections, it would probably prove necessary to fall back on the definitions of candidate found in state statutes. Inevitably, tax benefits might attract frivolous or otherwise undesirable candidates into primary races. On the other hand, a candidate's ability to raise a significant sum in small amounts would in itself indicate his seriousness and popular support. If the benefits were not extended to candidates in primaries, the impact of money on the selection of candidates might become even greater than it already is. The more disinterested donations might be drawn toward the favored arena, the general election.

A tax credit system would appear to be administratively feasible and through the Post Office Department could be carried out at minimum cost. There are ways it could be modified, if desired, to meet various objections. Some observers are concerned that if a large volume of tax-favored gifts (i.e., a large amount of government money) were placed in the hands of politicians, it would be used for other than legitimate campaign purposes. A system of properly administered campaign finance reports could be designed to expose and prevent this. In Puerto Rico the problem has been met by requiring the parties to certify their bills and submit them to a government agency that pays the vendors directly, charging the account of the party. A federal agency such as the Post Office Department would probably look with skepticism on any attempt to graft such an unfamiliar activity to its traditional functions.[69] But the Department has successfully taken on nonpostal responsibilities before, for example, the postal savings system.

Even if bills were paid directly by a government agency a technical opportunity for fraud would always seem to exist. A donor could arrange with a recipient to receive from the recipient a partial refund of the amount of the donation. If the donation were $10.00, the recipient could agree to give the donor $5.00. The recipient would be better off

69. But not all politicians with practical campaign experience: "I think," writes Jack Redding, at one time publicity director of the Democratic national committee, "that the federal government should handle the finances of the major parties, either financing them directly or holding and disbursing all of the money collected by the respective finance committees."—*Inside the Democratic Party* (New York: The Bobbs-Merrill Company, Inc. 1958), p. 104.

by $5.00 and so would the donor. The government would have provided $10.00, only half of which would have gone for the intended purpose. Presumably most candidates or their committees would receive funds in addition to those coming from tax-favored gifts and would therefore have the capital, if not the desire, to engage in this kind of maneuver.

There are various awkward elements of the system. The taxpayer would be required to keep his receipt safe until time to file his income-tax return. Considerably more complex income-tax records must now be accumulated throughout the year by some taxpayers. It would be hoped, however, that such a plan as this would appeal to many persons not accustomed to the clerical burdens of large incomes. Secrecy could be maintained to the extent that it ever can be if one person is to give money to another. Maintenance of reasonable secrecy is an important objective of any system, given the large number of small gifts that the system would hope to attract. The suggested arrangements offer no systematic way in which donors and donees could easily be connected to each other.[70]

The principal doubt concerning this or any other tax-credit plan is the extent to which it would be used. If a donor had to go personally to a post office to make a tax-favored contribution, the number of such contributions would depend, in the short run, on the organized efforts of fund-raisers to get them there and, in the long run, on the development of a socially approved habit of political giving. Provisions might be made by which postal authorities could set up sales points outside the post office. These might even be set up for special occasions, like political rallies, although the necessity for doing so on an impartial basis would be complicating. Treasurers of official party committees might be permitted to purchase as many political money orders as they desired for resale to others.[71] Since no person could claim personally more than a specified maximum tax credit, there would consequently be no special opportunity for fraud.

4. COMMUNITY ACTION

A century and a quarter ago, Alexis de Tocqueville marvelled at the private initiative of Americans. They walked across the street, he reported, formed a committee, and handled the matter, without a by-your-

70. As with money orders and currency, it would be necessary to discourage counterfeiting by use of special paper and by numbering the receipt forms. Probably the number would have to appear on all parts of the form. It would thus be theoretically possible to match the taxpayer's end of the form, submitted to the Internal Revenue district office, with either the stub at the receiving post office or with the recipient's coupon at the paying post office. The prospect seems as unlikely as the exercise would be pointless.

71. Some political contestants would doubtless have access to greater working capital than others. It has been suggested that short-term loans be made available through government guarantee to enable committees to purchase money orders for resale.

leave to any bureaucrat. They are still doing it. Through foundations, institutes, corporations, unions, schools, churches, associations, leagues, movements, drives, and sundry other forms of private cooperative action, Americans meet and deal successfully with a multitude of intrinsically public concerns. Organized philanthropy—private giving to public causes—now ranks in assets among the largest United States industries.

Government itself encourages many forms of private action to do what otherwise government would have to do. The burden of financing American party activities has always fallen chiefly on private persons. In the future as well, the problems of campaign finance can be attacked through private as well as public action. The parties are most immediately involved. They can improve their own ability to raise money, as both of them have, and they can improve public confidence in the ways they spend it.[72]

The respectability of contributing.—What can be done either inside or outside the parties is ultimately limited by popular attitudes toward campaign finance. There appears to be growing understanding of the necessity for campaign expenditures. Yet a Gallup Poll in September, 1956, reported that persons in half of America's families would not contribute $5.00 to the party of their choice if asked to do so, and another 15 per cent were undecided.[73] The fact that 35 per cent said they *would* give, however, has heartened advocates of broader based campaign financing.[74]

The potentialities of any program of solicitation are bounded by the prevailing notions of propriety. Partisan political causes must be thought worthy of support to attract large numbers of contributors. Tax incentives would especially enhance the respectability of political giving. Other forms of government subsidy would do likewise (although heavy subsidies might create doubts of the need for private support). Much can also be done outside of government to give vogue to political giving, but changes in attitudes of this kind require time. Those who would

72. The parties have never kept pace with business in adapting technical and social inventions to their own purposes. The tendency to do so is increased, however, by the development of permanent party staffs. With an eye on mass membership parties in other lands, many participants and observers have advocated a dues system to help American parties meet their need for a stable and adequate source of funds. Some suggestions for imposing a mandatory charge—to participate in a party's nominating process, for example—would have effects similar to that of a poll tax as a prerequisite for voting.

73. *The Washington Post,* September 12, 1956.

74. There are apparently no comparable poll results concerning the expressed willingness of persons to give to other causes. The conclusion drawn from the 1956 Gallup Poll is that about one-third of 48,000,000 families, between 16,000,000 and 17,000,000, would give at least $5.00 if asked. In 1958, another Gallup Poll concluded that 23 per cent of a sample, or approximately 24,000,000 households, would do so.—John C. Cornelius, president, "Annual Report to the Board of Trustees" (New York: The American Heritage Foundation, December 2, 1958) (mimeographed), pp. 1, 6.

work significant reforms must count their time in decades. Many legislative reforms, in fact, must await changes in popular conceptions of what is proper and what is possible.

The American Heritage Foundation tackled a major segment of the challenge in 1958. The Foundation had for several years undertaken campaigns to encourage citizens to vote. Its nonpartisan register-and-vote campaign in 1956 was supported by an estimated $15,000,000 in contributed advertising organized through the Advertising Council, and by the cooperative efforts of a large number of "partner" organizations ranging from the YWCA and AMVETS to the American Farm Bureau Federation and the American Bar Association.[75] The Foundation's decision to include an appeal for political contributions in 1958 was in itself symptomatic of a general trend toward popular approval of this form of political action.[76] With approval of the national chairman of both major parties, the Foundation launched a campaign on the theme: "Want to keep politics clean? Don't pass the buck, but give a buck to the party of your choice." The Foundation and the Advertising Council employed a vast range of carefully planned publicity approaches, and when it was all over they were told by a Gallup Poll that 44 per cent of a sample of American adults reported awareness of the new campaign.[77]

To take advantage of the favorable climate it was hoped would result, the Democratic national committee in May of 1958 announced a "Dollars for Democrats Drive" to be phased over the summer and culminating in a door-to-door solicitation from September 26 to 29.[78] The Republican national committee organized a "United Neighbor Campaign to Broaden the Base of Financial Support" for the period September 14–

75. The American Heritage Foundation, *Progress Report—1956 Non-Partisan "Register, Inform Yourself and Vote" Program* (New York, 1956).

76. Attempts in 1956 to organize a bipartisan advertising campaign to encourage small gifts, to be carried out by the Advertising Council, had failed.—*New York Times,* January 27, 1956.

The whole effort to establish political giving as an approved civic activity received a large boost in 1955 from Philip L. Graham, publisher of *The Washington Post and Times Herald.* In a speech in Chicago on June 1, he urged that a "complete, well-coordinated campaign of public service advertising can create proper citizen support for political campaigns. It can do so quickly. By doing so it can . . . create the most important political reform of the century."

The national finance chairman of one of the major parties was reserved about American Heritage's program: Suppose it proved successful. You turn some of these fellows loose with a lot of money and you cannot tell what they will do with it. It might turn out like the popular election of United States senators, which seemed like a good idea at the beginning but had results nobody looked for.

77. Cornelius, *op. cit.,* p. 6. The campaign included such things as 25,000 local television-station messages, mentions on nearly 100 top television-network shows, editorial or advertising support in virtually all weekly and monthly magazines, over 3,000 three-sheet posters put out by transportation advertising firms, and a large unmber of planted articles in periodicals, including one in the multi-million issue *Reader's Digest,* free reprints of which were sent to 10,000 political leaders. —*Ibid.,* pp. 2-3.

78. Letter from the national chairman to county chairmen dated May 26, 1958.

October 14.[79] Surveys by the Gallup Poll indicated that perhaps as many as 15 per cent of adults were asked by one or the other of the parties to make a contribution—a number equivalent to only one-third of those who knew about the "Contribute to Your Party" campaign. Six per cent said they had made a gift, a number equal to about four of every ten persons solicited.[80]

The idea of encouraging partisan contributions through bipartisan and nonpartisan efforts was picked up by several important corporations. The United States Chamber of Commerce—one of the Foundation's 153 national partner organizations—sent material to 23,000 member firms urging them to participate in the program. Several corporations did, including Standard Oil of New Jersey, Hallmark Cards, General Electric, Ford Motor Company, Consolidated Laundries, Continental Airlines, the Metropolitan Life Insurance Company, and some 20 others cited specifically by the Foundation.[81] The most conspicuous efforts were made by the Aerojet-General Corporation, a subsidiary of the General Tire and Rubber Company located in California. On company initiative, a registration drive was conducted during which some 2,000 "new" voters out of 15,000 employees were registered at the company's two plants. Candidates of both parties were invited to appear at the plants and did so, doubtless a substantial help in creating an atmosphere of political awareness. The solicitations were carried out by volunteer

79. Memorandum to party officials from Julie B. Kirlin, director of the campaign, dated July 30, 1958. An organizational set-up in each state initiated by, but parallel to, the state finance committee system was recommended.—"Organizational Manual for the Neighbor-to-Neighbor Division," (Washington: Republican National Committee) (mimeographed), pp. 5-7.

80. The amount of money raised "as a result of" the campaigns can hardly be estimated with accuracy, although the Foundation's report mentions a guess of between $3,000,000 and $12,000,000 in small gifts. To expect to pinpoint the results of such a campaign is like asking which straw broke the camel's back. A goodly sum would have been raised in small sums whether the Foundation had been active or not. In any event, because of the great decentralization of party financial activities and the absence of comprehensive records and reporting procedures, the parties themselves are not able to make any precise estimates of the sums they raise.

The Republicans concluded that over 1,000 counties participated in their drive, involving more than 200,000 volunteers and contributions from about 900,000 families. On the basis of reports from 105 counties, it was estimated that the total raised in sums of between 10 cents and $200 was around $1,850,000.—Julie Kirlin, "Analysis of the 1958 Republican Neighbor to Neighbor Campaign to Broaden the Base of Financial Support and of the National Advertising Program of the American Heritage Foundation and the Advertising Council In Relation to the Republican Effort" (Washington: Republican National Committee) (mimeographed), p. 3. It is said on reliable authority that Republican door-to-door campaigns in such cities as Detroit, Cleveland, Pittsburgh, and Minneapolis have produced as many as 15,000 "new contributors" in a single effort.

A Democrat, in as good a position as anyone to make a guess, thought that countrywide his party had probably raised no more than $450,000 or $500,000 in the 1958 Dollars for Democrats Drive.

81. Cornelius, *op. cit.*, pp. 4-5.

Republican and Democratic committees at each plant, with 11,500 employees, about three-fourths of the total, giving something over $24,000 divided substantially evenly between the major parties.[82] All activities of these campaigns were carried out after hours except the registration drives which were conducted during lunch periods.[83]

The contributions stimulated by the Aerojet program, slightly over $2.00 per contributor, required a substantial effort. The president of the firm, Dan A. Kimball, was a lifelong Democrat with experience as a fund-raiser and as Secretary of the Navy under Harry Truman. Arthur H. Rude, executive vice president, had long been active in Republican politics. These gentlemen kicked off the program, each giving $500 to his party. Company and union alike gave the stamp of civic grace to political contributing by supporting the program. The Company provided cards with the name of each employee, toward the

82. The contributions were divided about evenly between those made to the parties as such and those earmarked for specific candidates. Most of the latter were directed to the candidates for governor and United States senator. The distribution of funds was as follows:

Sacramento, California, plant:	
Democratic party	$ 4,033.46
Brown, candidate for governor	2,350.53
Engle, candidate for United States senator	1,779.62
Other Democratic	289.00
Total Democratic	8,452.61
Republican party	2,487.01
Knowland, candidate for governor	973.41
Knight, candidate for United States senator	437.59
Other Republican	109.80
Total Republican	4,007.81
Contributed on behalf of referenda, in error	73.00
Campaign drive expenses	673.08
Total Sacramento Plant	$13,206.50
Azusa, California, plant:	
Democratic party	$ 1,996.38
Brown, candidate for governor	1,517.07
Engle, candidate for United States senator	1,100.10
Total Democratic	4,613.55
Republican party	3,306.98
Knowland, candidate for govenror	1,761.93
Knight, candidate for United States senator	650.62
Total Republican	5,719.53
Congressional and local candidates in Azusa area	658.75
Total Azusa Plant	$10,991.83

83. Made possible by California's provision that a deputy registrar of a county may enroll voters living anywhere in his county and may do so at any time and place registrar and prospective voter meet.

goal that all would be solicited, but none more than once. A careful sequence of memoranda to employees and of announcements to the press was released to encourage participation in the program. In all, the results were the product of a sustained commitment by management and of considerable hard work by others.[84]

The labor of soliciting.—The labor required in mass solicitation campaigns can be enormous, and is the principal obstacle to their success. The work is often justified as desirable in itself, regardless of the funds raised, as a way of stimulating political loyalties and of meaningfully involving individuals in the political process. Well that may be, but no one desiring to widen the base of political giving should be deluded by ignoring the volume of planning, organization, and work essential to large-scale soliciting. The enormous effort made in 1958 by the American Heritage Foundation and the Advertising Council to create a climate favorable to political giving has been mentioned. In addition, enormous labor is required to take advantage of a favorable climate.

A successful attempt at bipartisan solicitation undertaken in Alexandria, Minnesota, in May of 1956 is instructive. The local semiweekly newspaper, *The Park Region Echo,* took the lead. It supplied dedicated leadership and sustained publicity over a period of many weeks, in greater quantities than can normally be mustered for a partisan purpose. Mass meetings were held, committees were appointed, articles, advertisements, and editorials were written, and in the end 80 individuals agreed to go from door to door explaining the plan and asking for contributions. Difficulties were encountered in getting suitable endorsements from the parties. The Democrats were agreeable, but the Republican state finance chairman offered strenuous opposition. After a painful delay that nearly proved fatal, Republican Senator Edward Thye joined Democratic Senator Hubert Humphrey in blessing the experiment. To get launched, the enterprise required the personal determination and skill of city editor John Obert (who, among other things, left his paper for a week to bone up on campaign finance), and the ebullient energy of the Honorable Byron G. Allen, commissioner of agriculture of Minnesota, sometime Democratic national committeeman, and without peer in his imaginative and zealous proposals for the reform of political finance.[85]

84. The undertaking is summarized in *The Aerojet-General Plan—How a Corporation Initiated a Good Citizenship Campaign,* published by Aerojet-General Corporation, Azusa, California. George E. Pelletier, director of public relations, supplied additional information.

85. The Alexandria experiment is reported by Mr. Obert in "An Experiment in Campaign Financing," *New Republic,* 134 (June 25, 1956), 7-8, and in "Money, Politics and the Minnesota Story," *Nieman Reports,* 11 (October, 1957), 10-14. See also the testimony of Messrs. Allen and Obert before the McClellan Lobby Committee, *Hearings,* pp. 827-44.

Among Democrat "Barney" Allen's several creations deserving mention is the Minnesota Foundation for Political Education. It is designed to accumulate a trust fund from various sources—e.g., private donations and a percentage of the proceeds of party fund-raising dinners—the income from which in future years

In a town of 6,300 people, 1,000 voters were approached during a three-night period by bipartisan teams of solicitors. Sometimes an independent accompanied the avowed Republicans and Democrats. About 76 per cent of the individuals solicited made a contribution, roughly three times the number of persons who, it was thought, had ever before given during a single campaign. The gifts ranged from eight cents to $100, amounting to $1,200 in all. Those solicited were asked to give to a bipartisan pool—a feature thought important to the drive's success[86]—to be distributed one-third to the national committees, one-third to the state committees, and one-third to the Congressional district committees. The money was divided at each level in the same proportion as the votes cast for the parties at the previous election. A contributor could insist that his contribution go to only one party. Twenty did so. The campaign ran into the resort season, and solicitations were discontinued after three nights. To have gone longer would have required additional exertions that no sponsors could reasonably have been expected to make.

Parallels in philanthropy?—Efforts similar to the Alexandria experiment assume that political contributing can be made appealing like successful educational, charitable, and religious causes. This belief has underlain various partisan attempts to attract mass contributions.[87] It also underlies the belief that successful public subscriptions for a neutral pool of political money are feasible. In Alexandria, the solicitations were made by party representatives, albeit travelling in tandem and collecting for a single fund subsequently to be divided. Conceivably, community-chest or united-fund collections might include political parties among the agencies they support, or a new national organization might be chartered by Congress to raise and disburse political funds.

---

would provide the Democratic-Farmer Labor party with a stable source of funds. See the *Congressional Record,* 83rd Congress, 2nd Session, May 27, 1954, extension of the remarks of Senator Paul H. Douglas, and "Education for Political Action," *Social Progress,* 45 (October, 1954), 18-21.

It was also Mr. Allen's idea to induce party faithful to share in the premiums on a series of 20-pay-life insurance policies on the life (natural, not political) of Senator Hubert Humphrey. If the Senator remained healthy, the party would derive a nest egg from the paid-up policies at the end of 20 years; if not, the funds would provide a modicum of solace in disaster.

86. "The solicitors all agreed that they would be turned down in a very high percentage of calls if they had not made the approach that the American political system needed clean financing. A strictly partisan approach would have brought many refusals."—Letter of Byron G. Allen to William Hard, dated July 24, 1958.

87. Men with experience in political fund-raising offer testimony from time to time of the effects of "educating" people to give financial support to their party. Clifton H. Scott claimed more than ordinary success in soliciting for the Democratic national campaign in Arkansas in 1936, attributing it to his studied efforts to dignify the approach. He is among those who have publicly advocated a program of nonpartisan appeals to encourage citizens to give to the party of their choice.—U.S. House of Representatives Special Committee to Investigate Campaign Expenditures, 1952, *Hearings* (Washington: Government Printing Office, 1952), pp. 121-28.

The Alexandria experiment enjoyed such success as it did partly because of the political atmosphere of Minnesota, and of Alexandria, an atmosphere conditioned by decades of progressive politics and hospitable to political novelties. Radical revisions in the customs of campaign contributing would occur, if at all, at different rates and to different extents in other places.

Proposals for neutral or bipartisan soliciting of political money—through a variety of formulas adaptable to local conditions—are likely to persist. Most practicing politicians remain skeptical. They doubt "the public" will ever accord the respectability to political giving necessary to raise significant sums in this way. Yet, in private conversations, a few of the hard-bitten ones with experience in nonpolitical as well as political fund-raising wonder. They speculate that it might be possible to create the conditions needed to attract large sums through mass appeals and to get them agreeably distributed. Enough might even be so raised, they opine, to reduce significantly the existing dependence of politicians on large individual gifts made directly to them.

The extraordinary growth of philanthropic giving in the United States is a consequence of many factors. The rise in disposable per-capita income, the increase in demand for social services, the professionalization of fund-raising, the tax policies of governments, and developments in the skills of persuasion are among them. About 90 per cent of the six billion or more dollars per year now given to philanthropy in the United States comes from individuals, and another 6 per cent or so comes from corporations (with the balance from foundations and bequests). Professional fund-raisers point out that many times this sum could be claimed by corporate and individual taxpayers, as a group, as deductible philanthropic contributions. From this they conclude that even larger sums can annually be extracted for worthy causes if pursued in the right way.[88] The growth of nonpolitical contributing demonstrates the potentialities, but at the same time it promises competition for newcomers.[89] Reactions have already set in to the manpower demands and the administrative costs of the nation's multiple philanthropic drives.[90] Revelations of abuses of the public's generosity, or gullibility, by fraudu-

88. Arnaud C. Marts, president of Marts & Lundy, Inc., New York, made the point, with figures, in an address in 1954, excerpts from which were subsequently published by his firm in a pamphlet called *The Rising Tide of Philanthropy,* 12 pp.

89. Per-capita philanthropic giving already takes a fair slice of the income even of small donors. In 1946, for example, before the national totals had risen to their later heights, individuals with an average income of between $5,000 and $10,000 on the average gave 3 per cent of their income, or $263. For individuals in the $10,000 to $25,000 bracket, the percentage was 3.3 and the average amount of gifts was $498.—Andrews, *op. cit.,* p. 58.

90. Marion K. Sanders discusses the impatience in "Mutiny of the Bountiful," *Harper's,* December, 1958, pp. 23-31. See also "The Fund-Raising Muddle," *Newsweek,* June 15, 1959, pp, 31-33.

lent appeals have led to demands for stricter legal regulation of all fund-raising,[91] and presumably to a less trusting public.

Two basic facts stand out, nevertheless. The money needed to fuel American political campaigns is comparatively small, perhaps not more than 2 per cent of all philanthropic giving over a four-year period. To raise even this sum, however, requires widespread public approval of the purposes of political expenditures and of this way of meeting them.[92] Acceptance of political contributing as a civic responsibility of individuals depends on many varied factors, local as well as national. The actions taken by government to create confidence in the systems of campaign finance that prevail are among the most important.

5. CREATING CONFIDENCE

Ironically, the extensive efforts made to regulate campaign money have helped breed suspicion of the subject. Defects in regulatory efforts of several types have contributed to a lack of public confidence in the processes of campaign finance—perhaps not always justified, but nonetheless present.

Public disclosure.—Failure to achieve complete disclosure has obscured the fact that citizens in the United States have greater information on political finance than in any other nation. Also, the fact tends to be forgotten that it is entirely possible to design and enforce a system of financial reporting that would command public confidence. Such a system would enhance the ability of government to identify and regulate specific trouble spots of political finance. This, in turn, would help create a climate in which appeals for campaign funds would be received with greater understanding and sympathy.

Politicians are not as devoted to public disclosure as the volume of publicity legislation would indicate. They rarely feel able to oppose the principle—as politicians have done successfully in other nations—but neither do they provide an effective system. It is possible to do so. Once the legislative will is present, the task becomes largely a technical one. The technical complexities are enormous, however, in designing a system of disclosure that can extract significant information from candidates and their treasurers, and make it available in a meaningful way to the public. To remedy the deficiencies of existing systems re-

91. See New York Joint Legislative Committee on Charitable and Philanthropic Agencies and Organizations, *Report* (Albany: Williams Press, Inc., 1954) (Legislative Document No. 26, 1954).

92. With regard to the March of Dimes, for example, see David L. Sills, *The Volunteers—Means and Ends in a National Organization* (Glencoe, Illinois: The Free Press, 1957), pp. 115, 165-72, 175, 179-80. In 1943, 60 per cent of the total value of individual philanthropic contributions came from persons with net incomes of under $3,000, and another 21 per cent from those with net incomes of between $3,000 and $5,000.—Andrews, *op. cit.*, p. 59.

quires that several broad considerations be satisfied, and proposals of various kinds concerning all of them have been advocated.[93]

1. If maximum disclosure is accepted as a goal, existing federal statutes and many state statutes do not attempt the *coverage* necessary. Reporting requirements must extend to nominations by primary and must extend to all important candidates and committees if anything resembling full disclosure is desired. Federal laws did not, at the beginning of 1960, require candidates for nomination to federal office to file reports of any kind; nor, incidentally, did they require reports of presidential and vice presidential candidates in the general election; nor did they in practice require reports from committees active within the borders of a single state on behalf of candidates for federal office.

Efforts to do these things are stoutly resisted. As a rule, the opposition bases its protests on a desire to preserve state and local autonomy.[94] Attempts to effect more satisfactory coverage lead toward the British "law of agency," which also stirs opposition. Students of British politics have attributed the radical improvement in the integrity of British electioneering after the middle of the nineteenth century in part to the requirement that each candidate designate a single election agent to account for the political monies spent on his behalf within his constituency. Conditions in the United States are very different, and the suggestion that candidates designate one responsible treasurer, and one only, strikes many politicians as excessively restrictive. They are accustomed to a variety of campaign committees and the interests they reflect—regular party committees, finance committees, volunteer committees of several kinds, any of which may be separately organized at different political levels and in different geographical areas. Attempts to design an American law of agency usually produces proposals that candidates be permitted, and required, to authorize as many groups as they wish to have campaign on their behalf.[95] Unauthorized groups

93. Herbert E. Alexander has made a thorough study of the factors involved in designing an effective disclosure system and has illustrated the requirements for such a system, in *Proposals for a More Effective Federal Public Reporting System* (Princeton: Citizens' Research Foundation, 1958) (mimeographed) 110 pp., to be published in 1960. See also U.S. Senate Committee on Rules and Administration, *op. cit.*, 32 pp.; and the McClellan Lobby Committee, *Final Report*, pp. 143-55.

94. See the individual views of Senators Herman E. Talmadge and Carl T. Curtis, dissenting from proposals to extend federal regulation to primaries, conventions, and caucuses of political parties, and to include all groups participating in campaign financing that spend $1,000 or more within a calendar year.—U.S. Senate Committee on Rules and Administration, *op. cit.*, pp. 26-32. The McClellan Lobby Committee recommended that reporting requirements be imposed upon groups that in any one year received more than $100 from any one individual or received or spent in the aggregate more than $1,000 in any one year. The eight members divided evenly, however, on whether to recommend extension of coverage to primaries.—*Final Report*, pp. 140, 144.

95. U.S. Senate Committee on Rules and Administration, *op. cit.*, p. 8; McClellan Lobby Committee, *Final Report*, p. 146. Constitutional questions involved in seek-

would not necessarily be prohibited from campaigning. They would be discouraged from doing so, however, by being required to proclaim that they were unauthorized, and, in some proposals, by being denied various privileges, such as the right to receive tax-favored contributions.

2. The *kind of information* called for is crucial to the success of any reporting system. Federal and state reporting forms have, in general, been created without regard for the convenience of those supposed to fill them out[96] and without regard to the use the information might be put to if they were filled out. Given a definition of general purposes, whatever they may be, the task of designing questionnaires becomes chiefly a technical one.

3. Once agreement on broad purposes is reached, constructing ways to *summarize and publicize* the information obtained is also largely a technical task. The importance of the form of the report mounts in geometric progression as the number to be submitted mounts. To handle effectively thousands or tens of thousands of reports submitted periodically to a central depository demands use of the most highly developed techniques for abstracting, summarizing, and processing data. Knowledge of technical procedures must, moreover, be combined with knowledge of the political system about which information is gathered. The varieties of political organizations, of relationships among them, and of the nomenclature by which they are designated, produce an endless host of ambiguities that must be resolved individually if data from the reports are to be treated systematically.

---

ing to concentrate controls in the hands of candidates, and otherwise to limit campaign activities of individuals and groups, are discussed in G. Theodore Mitau, "Selected Aspects of Centralized and Decentralized Control over Campaign Finance: A Commentary on S. 636," *University of Chicago Law Review,* 23 (1956), 620-39.

96. Compare, for example, the questionnaires used by the U.S. Senate Subcommittee on Privileges and Elections in 1952 with those used by it in 1956. The former, distributed by the thousands and running in some instances to seven pages, were printed on thick, oversized, folded paper, virtually impossible to use in a standard typewriter or with normal carbon paper.

Respondents were asked to list contributors alphabetically, within each of several categories of contribution according to size, a chore that by itself would dismay the most diligent treasurer and produce results of only minor utility. (The names would all have had to be copied to cards anyway, if they were to be summarized or publicized in any meaningful way, and then alphabetized with contributors listed on other reports.) The request to list the names of all payees to which expenditures in excess of $10.00 were made would simply lead to further futile agony for those receiving the reports as well as for those filling them out. The compact 1956 questionnaires were designed by the Gore Committee staff with an eye to the convenience of busy campaign treasurers and to the machine processing of the data they would produce. Even so, a high Democratic finance official felt moved to characterize the Gore Committee's work as a "make-life-tough operation." See the forms reproduced in U.S. Senate Subcommittee on Privileges and Elections, *Proposed Amendments to Federal Corrupt Practices Act* (Washington: Government Printing Office, 1953) (Subcommittee print), pp. 15-33 and in the Gore Committee *Report,* Ex. 30.

Moreover, a policy of passive disclosure fails to convey to the public the information available on its political system or about the candidates and parties that ask for its favor. Effective disclosure demands ability to make available in reasonably short time understandable summaries of campaign finance information and of more complete information in such form that those who choose to do so may analyze it.

4. If a reporting system is to be effective, agencies receiving campaign reports must be obligated to require *compliance* with the applicable statutes. They must be able and willing to call effectively upon law enforcement officers to prosecute violations. Enforcement must extend beyond merely requiring submission of required reports.[97] Other legal provisions, pertaining to the content of the reports, must also be enforced.

There is little in federal or state experience to encourage confidence in the ability of existing depositories to meet the requirements outlined for an effective system of disclosure. Possibly a determined state legislature could equip an existing state agency, like the office of the Secretary of State, to administer effective reporting procedures. At the federal level, however, it seems essential for Congress to eschew the inclination to attach to itself responsibility for prying into matters so close to its members. That Congress will be persuaded to do this seems doubtful, unless some startling scandal appears as a catalyst. Nevertheless, a reporting system of maximum usefulness cannot be developed as long as principal responsibility for its administration is vested in the Clerk of the House of Representatives and the Secretary of the Senate.[98] Committees of the House and Senate have produced much of the usable information available on American campaign finance, but neither are they suitable locations to develop an information agency of impartiality and accuracy that will command the respect of the public and the tolerance of politicians.

The only agency of federal or state government that has attempted repeadedly over the years to study problems of campaign money is the

97. This in itself, however, is something. The Senate Subcommittee on Privileges and Elections has in more than one year encountered committees that refused to submit the reports requested. They apparently judged, correctly so far, that the general character of the Subcommittee's activities and the limited tenure of most of its staff favor a quick loss of interest in recalcitrants.

In 1956, the Gore Committee sought to stimulate compliance by releasing to the press a few days before the election a list of committees that had not responded to requests for information. The committees listed were located in 39 states. The principal newspapers in each of those states were checked for the three days following the release. There were virtually no news stories mentioning the delinquents.

Publicity can, however, if employed with skill and determination, serve as an instrument of law enforcement in the regulation of campaign finance as in other spheres. See Francis E. Rourke, "Law Enforcement through Publicity," *University of Chicago Law Review,* 24 (1956-57), 225-55.

98. See pages 365-66, above.

United States Senate Subcommittee on Privileges and Elections (of the Committee on Rules and Administration). The Subcommittee has released reports pertaining to most presidential election years in recent decades, excepting 1948 and 1952.[99] The Subcommittee is, however, also charged with the more newsworthy task of investigating alleged irregularities in the election of senators. This responsibility easily interferes with the more tedious routines of collecting and analyzing information on the sources and uses of campaign money. The regular staff of the Subcommittee has been small and properly confined, for the most part, to lawyers. In presidential election years it has usually been multiplied by temporary additions, a practice necessary to get the manpower to make investigations and to conduct the desired studies of campaign finance, but hardly one conducive to the development of an expert career staff. Moreover, Congressional committees are limited by the closely woven code of reciprocal courtesies that restrain members in their dealings with each other, that even prevent a committee of one house from examining the data on elections to the other.[100] And in the end, whatever a Congressional committee does is open to partisan attack, for most of the time members of the majority party control the programs of work and the staff appointments of committees and subcommittees.[101] To accomplish the goals sought by an optimum

99. The 1952 report was brief and pertained only to broadcasting expenditures.

100. The Senate Subcommittee on Privileges and Elections pointed out that under present law even committees of the Senate had to get special permission of the Speaker of the House in order to have public reports filed with the Clerk of the House photostated.—Committee on Rules and Administration, *op. cit.*, p. 6.

101. A curious spectacle was provoked by the release of the interim report of the Gore Committee just before the election of 1956. The minority member of the three-man Subcommittee, Republican Senator Carl T. Curtis of Nebraska, launched a broadside against the purposes and competence of the report—although it was signed by his own appointee to the staff, the minority counsel.

Some weeks after the final report of the Gore Committee was released, the chairman of the Republican Senatorial campaign committee, Senator Andrew F. Schoeppel of Kansas, made extensive criticisms of the report on the floor of the Senate, to which Senator Gore responded. The controversy was spiced by plausible partisan assertions which, whether or not true, emphasized the suspicions likely to surround any Congressional committee undertaking to report on campaign finances. (Senator Schoeppel's principal statement was circulated by the Republican Senatorial campaign committee, but the Gore rebuttal gained a modest mailing only after former members of the Gore Committee staff chipped in to help bear the cost.)

The Schoeppel critique exposed various minor errors made in the compilation of the data. In fact, the Senator made some of his own in stating his criticisms. These findings confirmed the warnings that at least one consultant to the Gore Committee staff had expressed before the Committee began its studies and on several occasions thereafter: that it was impossible under the conditions of pressure and speed in which the committee worked for anyone, much less persons inexperienced in statistical work, as some of the staff members were, to avoid unintentional errors. Only a well-established staff skilled in the procedures employed and familiar with the kinds of data being processed could avoid

reporting system requires sustained fiscal support and a career staff all of whom are versed in the needed special skills.

These and other considerations have led to the proposal that the Comptroller General of the United States be made the administrator of a federal reporting system. He would be required to receive reports, make them public, compile and release summaries, and submit analyses of receipts and expenditures.[102] The Comptroller General has appeared more frightened than flattered by the prospect.[103] The Census Bureau and the Library of Congress are other nominees. It has also been suggested that a high-level citizens' commission be given the responsibility for continuous scrutiny of campaign finance. One senator has proposed that a major study of the whole area be carried out by a special commission appointed for the purpose by the Chief Justice of the United States.[104] A private individual has proposed that a Registry of Campaign Finance be created. Regardless of what agency might be invented or designated, a stable staff insulated from the harsher political pressures is essential to an effective reporting system. Many agencies of the federal government that periodically release statistics of great importance to partisan politicians and to the economic community are so staffed.

---

such errors, and then only with adequate time for the standard checking considered routine in comparable operations.

The purposeful character of the Schoeppel criticisms was revealed, however, by the Senator's disinclination to acknowledge qualifications on the data expressed in the report. As late as January after the election, the Committee continued to receive reports from campaign committees. Some of these listed contributors of $500 and over. The names of these contributors were put into a master file and were used in compiling various exhibits. As the publication deadline approached, preparation of the more complex exhibits was closed out, and the material sent to the Government Printing Office, on a schedule that would permit the report to be published before the expiration of the Committee's special appropriation on January 31, 1957. The extreme effort to incorporate late reports—some received as late as January 28 were included in the basic tabulations that were printed and bound on January 31—produced discrepancies between exhibits that could have been avoided by ignoring such late reports. In one exhibit, closed out early, Mr. A. might be listed as giving a total of $13,000, whereas in an exhibit closed out a week later his total might read $13,500 because a report received in the interim reported another gift of $500 made by him, theretofore unknown. This procedure, and the necessity for it, were explained in the headnote to each exhibit, but Senator Schoeppel used the discrepancies to try to discredit the report. The basic difficulty arose from the fact that an adequate staff was not assembled far enough in advance of the campaign to permit the kind of planning and preparation necessary to handle the storm of paper inevitable in even a limited inquiry.—See the *Congressional Record,* 85th Congress, 1st Session, March 29, 1957, vol. 103, pp. 4272-95; April 12, 1957, vol. 103, pp. 5003-21; April 29, 1957, vol. 103, pp. 5458-60.

102. Committee on Rules and Administration, *op. cit.,* pp. 10-11; McClellan Lobby Committee, *Final Report,* pp. 149-50.

103. Committee on Rules and Administration, *op. cit.,* pp. 28-30.

104. Senator Richard L. Neuberger, *Congressional Record,* 84th Congress, 2nd Session, April 18, 1956, vol. 102, pp. 57-82.

Effective limitations.—The hoary dispute over campaign ceilings greatly complicates efforts to achieve disclosure. United States senators, among others, differ in their views.[105] For those primarily concerned about disclosure, there can be no doubt that ceilings tend to discourage full reporting. If the ceilings are low, incomplete reporting results, or the number of committees making expenditures increases. Both developments becloud the picture of campaign finance reaching the public. Aside from these considerations, however, politicians in the heat of a campaign are unlikely to refrain from spending money if they feel the need to, and if they have it. Ceilings that in fact or in appearance are broached in every election contribute to the very derogation of the political process that presumably ceilings were originally intended to help prevent.

In contrast, an effective limit on the total sum an individual is permitted to give or spend in politics each year is essential to public confidence in campaign finance. Whether campaign income from any source can effectively be limited depends in part on the adequacy of funds from other sources. If subsidies were adopted, or if the trend toward mass contributing continues, and a larger share of needed campaign money were thus made available, huge donations from single individuals might be forbidden with some possibility of successful enforcement. Effective limitation might be accomplished by a direct prohibition against political gifts aggregating more than a fixed amount each year.[106] A maximum of $20,000 or $10,000 per year per person would probably prove feasible to start with.[107] It should, if possible, apply to all campaign contributions, not merely to those made on behalf of candidates for federal office. A special federal gift tax of confiscatory rate might be imposed on political contributions above a stated maximum. This move would have the incidental effect, probably an advantage, of placing the initiative for enforcement in the Bureau of Internal Revenue. If ceilings

105. Senator Albert Gore of Tennessee has generally favored ceilings on expenditures in all types of races, as indicated by S. 1437, introduced by him in the 85th Congress, 1st Session. Senator Thomas C. Hennings, Jr., of Missouri has been less comprehensive, making no attempt to impose an over-all limit in presidential contests (S. 426). The Committee on Rules and Administration recommended in 1957 a general lifting of ceilings set by federal statute, but not their abolition.—*Op. cit.,* pp. 11-13. Concern over an uninformed public's reaction to the suggestion that limitations on campaign expenditures be repealed seems to color the attitudes of many politicians toward the question.

106. The McClellan Lobby Committee recommended an over-all limit (presumably applicable only to federal elections) of $15,000 per year per individual and a limit of $5,000 on gifts to any one candidate. It also proposed that donors be permitted to give only in their own name and that minors under the age of 18 be permitted to make no contributions in excess of $100.—*Final Report,* p. 142. The Committee on Rules and Administration approved the provision affecting minors but not the limit on aggregate contributions.—*Op. cit.,* p. 12.

107. Labor leaders have urged lower maxima, e.g., Walter Reuther, $20.00 per year, recoverable as a tax credit.—*New York Times,* June 29, 1956. See also the *Proposal of United Automobile Workers for a Five-Dollar Ceiling on Political Contributions* (July 1956), 18 pp.

on aggregate outlays were attempted, some might doubt the desirability of requiring individual contributors to make personal reports of their gifts. Otherwise, persons giving or spending in the aggregate more than a specified sum each year for campaign purposes (such as $5,000) might well be required to file a personal report of their donations and expenditures. To build further public confidence candidates should report their personal contributions and expenditures, regardless of how small.

The need to build public confidence also requires that prohibitions against direct contributions by corporations and labor unions be continued and, if possible, extended. A considerable case can be made for permitting both types of organization to spend and give funds on behalf of candidates for office. The argument is fortified by the difficulties of enforcement.[108] In the nature of things, imperfect enforcement seems likely to persist. Yet the climate of expectations surrounding American politics requires that these restrictions be retained. They impose a limit, albeit an incomplete one, on one form of direct intervention in politics by these highly organized political competitors. Not until stable and socially approved sources of campaign money have been more fully developed can corporate and union gifts be encouraged without damage to the general public's confidence in the electoral system and, indeed, in the corporations and unions themselves.

It is never easy to weigh the political advantages enjoyed by one set of economic interests against those enjoyed by another. Representatives of organized labor assert the political system is loaded against them by the practices of campaign finance. Representatives of organized business claim the same. Only one thing is certain. The balance does not so greatly favor one or the other as to produce a clamor among less directly concerned citizens for a change in the rules.

6. EFFECTIVE DEMOCRACY

In the twentieth century, political institutions in every nation necessarily suffer immense strains. People of relatively stable personal qualities seek through them to live successfully in a world of rapidly altering political requirements. Characteristics of individual mentality and personality change at a glacial pace; the technological and social environment of government changes swiftly and radically. In all societies men attempt to perfect and adapt their political practices to meet the evolving demands imposed upon them.

Essential to the attempt in the United States is a public discourse more mature, serious, and widespread than has recently existed. Equally vital is the need for categories of political allegiance and of personal vision substantially larger than are normally found in American political constituencies and among the public officials chosen to represent them. Many public and private measures can contribute to these ends. Among

108. See pages 129-35 and 196-208, above.

them are policies for financing political campaigns and political debate discussed in this chapter. The immediate objectives are to assure candidates representing important viewpoints an equitable opportunity to express them, to create within public officials a more viable blend of parochial and general loyalties, and to do these things in a fashion that enhances respect for the decisions of government—all to equip governments to reach informed, prompt, and sagacious decisions.

These objectives are as simple and as familiar as the goals of democratic government itself. They remain imperfectly realized. The policies discussed affirmatively in this chapter would contribute, each in its way, to their realization. These are, in brief: cash subsidies to parties and candidates by federal and state governments; government subsidies of campaign communications; government regulation of television and radio broadcasting to reduce costs and make broadcasting opportunities more nearly equal among opponents; tax incentives at all levels to dignify, encourage, and indirectly subsidize political donations; community drives for financial support akin to those conducted on behalf of educational, charitable, and religious causes; statutes designed to achieve effective disclosures of campaign finances; and limitations on an individual's aggregate political gifts, and on the role in campaign finance legally permitted to powerful, highly organized social interests. It is reasonable to expect that in the years ahead an average of $100,000,000 will be spent annually in campaigns to fill elective public offices and that in presidential years expenditures will come nearer to twice that sum. No one of the measures cited is likely by itself to supply this money. Several in combination, however, can reduce the pressures that currently impair public debate, distort the recruitment of political leadership, and obstruct development of greater vision and common sense in the conventions of politics. They can contribute to a sense of enlightened self-interest that is at bottom what Mr. Stimson Bullitt has styled intellectual honesty[109] and to a concept of general welfare that Mr. Walter Lippmann has called the public philosophy.[110]

Perhaps politics can be fair, can be democratic, only in the "breathing spaces of history," as N. S. Rubashov wrote from his political prison in Arthur Koestler's *Darkness at Noon*. A governmental system that on principle seeks to represent a vast diversity of narrow concerns automatically foregoes a degree of cohesion, automatically handicaps itself "at the critical turning points" of history. Americans and democrats are not likely, however, to concede that their conception of popular government has inherently fatal weaknesses. They are more disposed to hope, and even work, for changes that will make their system adequate.

109. *To Be a Politician* (Garden City, New York: Doubleday & Company, Inc., 1959), pp. 140-48.

110. *Essays in the Public Philosophy* (Boston: Little, Brown, and Company, 1955).

The revision of campaign finance requires more than a set of prescriptions for public action. These we have had before, and, while a stint at the barricades invigorates the spirit, something more is needed. The hope in this book has been to illuminate certain general features of representative government as well as the principal causes and characteristics of money in politics. This is, perhaps, in the end, a more audacious ambition than to prescribe a narrow road to salvation. The public habits that comprise campaign practices evolve in response to the total context within which a political system functions.[111] They respond in particular to the expectations of the system held by citizens, expectations that ultimately are rooted in whatever understanding, accurate or inaccurate, there may be of the political system. No fundamental change will be effected in the United States in the processes of campaign finance, by legislation or otherwise, without altered public attitudes and without public recognition of the functions of campaign expenditures, of the propriety of providing them, and of the penalties for not doing so in socially healthy ways.

111. British election financing, for example, is clearly the product of a long evolution. Not legal measures alone, but changing conditions—social and economic, domestic and foreign, material and ideological—have produced present practice, deemed by most Britons as satisfactory. Of interest is W. B. Gwyn's "Financial Aspects of a Parliamentary Career in Aristocratic and Democratic Britain: A Study of the Expense of Membership in the House of Commons with Special Reference to the 19th Century" (Ph.D. dissertation, University of London, 1956).

INDEX